The Man
from
New York

John Quinn riding in Central Park

The Man
from
New York

JOHN QUINN AND HIS FRIENDS

B. L. REID

New York

OXFORD UNIVERSITY PRESS

1968

To Harry Greenwood Grover

He works his work . . .

Preface

MY interest in John Quinn was first aroused by the way in which his name, or his picture, kept cropping up in situations of some cultural significance, his function there only vaguely accounted for. Especially in reading modern literature, I found myself meeting again and again, for no visible good reason, the name or the image of Quinn. When he was identified at all, it was with some such hurried and uninstructive tag as "John Quinn (1870–1924), American lawyer and patron of the arts." I was baffled and curious. Why did he show up in so many different places? one wondered; why was he not back home practicing the law? Why would W. B. Yeats pose so complacently and companionably with this man standing at his shoulder? Why would Yeats write so many letters, such witty, serious, and circumstantial letters, to an American lawyer, addressing him apparently as a cultural equal? What is John Quinn doing posed in a stiff white wing collar in a Paris studio garden with Ezra Pound, Ford Madox Ford, and James Joyce? (Do they know he is there? Did they invite him in?) What was such a man doing in possession of the manuscript of *Ulysses* or *The Waste Land?* Was he the same man who owned Brancusi's *Mlle. Pogany,* Matisse's *Blue Nude,* Picasso's *Three Musicians,* and Rousseau's *Sleeping Gypsy?* One was astonished to discover how many of the capital works of the modern movement in art turned out to have been owned, and owned early, by John Quinn.

Somewhere within the work of almost every major creative impulse in the art and literature of the early century, standing

vii

neither quite at the center nor quite at the edge, Quinn punctually appeared. I began to be attracted by this not quite anonymous, ectoplasmic figure, and to be irritated by his bodilessness. His image in the photographs was interesting, too: he looked like a man of force and intelligence, perhaps of wit. The bare accounts of Quinn in the standard reference sources did little to bring him to life and nothing to explain his ubiquitous presence. I grew convinced that Quinn was entitled to some sort of resurrection, fuller notice than time seemed to have given him; and I promised myself that someday I would do something about it.

Two events warmed and confirmed my impulse: Mrs. Aline Saarinen published an animated account of Quinn as a pioneer collector of modern art in a chapter of *The Proud Possessors* (1958); and Mr. Peter Kavanagh pulled off in 1960 his amusing, queerly impressive feat of printing on a homemade press a little clandestine volume of excerpts from John Quinn's correspondence which he had committed to memory in the Manuscript Room of the New York Public Library. Clearly I was not the only person who found Quinn interesting and deserving of an effort to recover him in the round. When I got the chance I went seriously to work.

I did not know at first what has proved true, that Quinn's immense rich correspondence with many of the most creative spirits of the century has survived almost intact. As will be obvious in my text, this has been my main resource. Some of this material, especially among the letters of W. B. Yeats, Ezra Pound, and James Joyce, has been printed before; but most of it is new, and it seems to me to shed a good deal of fresh light on the modern movement in the arts, and on Irish-American affairs. I tried also to interview, or at least to correspond with, all the persons I could discover (not numerous now, forty-four years after his death) who knew Quinn in life. I was comforted when men like T. S. Eliot and Ezra Pound and Alfred H. Barr, Jr., told me that a biography of Quinn was a thing deserved and needed. When I ran Mr. Pound to earth, after toiling on foot up the mountain behind Rapallo on a hot August day, like a sweaty St. Francis, I found him old and ill and hardly able to speak at all. But when

I asked him if a life of Quinn was a thing worth doing he said: "Certainly."

What was most striking in Quinn's career was the working of his extraordinary efficient energy: the number, the variety, and the importance of the enterprises in which he took part in a useful way during a not very long life. I have concentrated my attention upon the twenty-two years in which Quinn was at work in the great world, and I have tried to show the concurrence of his concurrent lives—as lawyer, Irish-American patriot, patron of writers, patron of artists. My main emphasis rests upon what I feel interested him most in his own life: his work as friend and helper, collector, and general busy hodman of genius. Quinn had an extraordinary affinity for what was excellent in the arts of his day—a union of good instinct, good judgment, good luck, good advice. It was his native powers that collected those factors and kept them moving together, not really gracefully or easily, but persistently and productively.

I have been fascinated with Quinn both as a personality and as a type. He seems to me at once an authentic original, very much himself, self-made, and a representative of a species, perhaps a peculiarly American species: the driving, pragmatical, "successful" man of affairs who finds that not enough, yearns for "culture," finds that not enough, yearns to make "art" but has to content himself with a lesser order of usefulness, with knowing and having rather than making—the artist *manqué*. In telling Quinn's story, however, I have tried not to press this or any other thesis, to let the facts carry both the narrative and the meaning, to offer a minimum of interpretation, to present evidence for the reader's own inductions.

The reader will not wish me to apologize, I think, for being as detailed and circumstantial as the available data permit. Dr. Johnson, who loved "the biographical part of literature" above all other parts, told Boswell that nothing was too little for so little a creature as man. Quinn himself wrote to May Morris, who was editing the writings of her father, William Morris: " . . . to persons who admire a man's work everything personal about him is interesting." Admiring, in the main, Quinn's "work," I have tried to record everything not trivial that I could discover about him. But I have tried to set down what I know, little of what I might surmise. For example, Quinn had a considerable contemporary (and surviving) reputation as a pursuer and conqueror of women: that case would seem to me certainly relevant and certainly interesting, if it could be documented. But I could find little evidence of it (Quinn was a lawyer), and so I have said little about it. I have tried also to avoid overpraise and to give Quinn the shape and the size that the visible facts enjoin.

B. L. REID

South Hadley, Massachusetts
July 1968

Acknowledgments

It is a pleasure to be able at last to name, and to thank publicly, the many persons and the several organizations who have helped me along in the preparation of this book.

My deepest and longest obligation I owe to Mrs. Mary Anderson Conroy and Dr. Thomas F. Conroy. Their help to me has been sustained, detailed, and indispensable, but I think they would prefer not to have it specified. Mrs. Jeanne Robert Foster has given me her blessing and her good will, as well as her warm recollections of John Quinn, the use of her papers, and the benefit of her general good sense in the arts. Mrs. Aline Saarinen generously turned over to me the notes and records she had accumulated in preparing her excellent chapter on Quinn in *The Proud Possessors*.

Mr. Robert W. Hill of the Manuscript Division of the New York Public Library and his assistants not only fulfilled their public duty but reached out to offer me many valuable voluntary services which leave me deeply indebted. I should like also to thank Mr. Harvey Simmonds of the Manuscript Division and the late Dr. John Gordan of the Berg Collection of the New York Public Library. The staff of the Williston Memorial Library of Mount Holyoke College, especially Miss Nancy Devine, have helped me with numerous documentary problems, and always with good humor and dispatch. Mr. William Bond of the Houghton Library at Harvard and Mr. Alf MacLochlainn of the National Library of Ireland have also been particularly helpful in providing access to important papers.

Of the persons aside from Mrs. Conroy and Mrs. Foster who have offered me reminiscences of John Quinn and those associated with him, I wish especially to thank Miss Margaret Anderson, Mr. Alfred H. Barr, Jr., Mr. Horace Brodzky, Mr. Padraic Colum, Mr. Richard

Curle, M. Marcel Duchamp, the late T. S. Eliot, Mr. Barnett Hollander, Mr. Denis Johnston, Mr. Paul Kieffer, Mr. Willard L. King, Mr. Alfred A. Knopf, Sir Shane Leslie, Mr. Ezra Pound, Mrs. Dorothy Pound, Mr. James N. Rosenberg, Mr. Peter Viereck, and Mrs. W. B. Yeats.

I have enjoyed and profited by correspondence and conversation with a number of scholars engaged in studies which were related to mine: Mr. Jackson Bryer on *The Little Review;* Mr. Sidney Geist on Brancusi; Miss Jane Lidderdale on Harriet Shaw Weaver; Mr. William Murphy on John Butler Yeats; Miss Hilary Pyle on James Stephens and Jack B. Yeats; Mr. Geoffrey Sutton on Maud Gonne; Mr. Daniel H. Woodward on T. S. Eliot.

Mr. Richard Ellmann has helped me generously, in person and in print, out of his knowledge of the writers of my period. Mr. Russell Alspach, Mr. C. L. Barber, Mr. John V. Kelleher, Mr. Alan McGee, Mr. Robert O. Preyer, Sister M. Bernetta Quinn, Miss Betty Nye Quinn, and Mr. James F. Spoerri have given me useful scholarly assistance of various kinds. Mr. James McNally and Mr. James Ellis kept keen bibliographical eyes out for me. Mr. Ken Goodwin of the University of Queensland reached out to help from halfway around the world. Mr. Denis Johnston, Mr. Richard Kain, and Mr. Richard Weber gave me the benefit of their experience of things Irish. Mr. Liam Miller of Dublin and Mr. David Clark helped me to use my time in Ireland profitably. Mme. Denise Roché helped me with the French side of things and gave me free access to her husband's papers. Mr. Geoffrey Whatmore and Mr. Harry Cowdell did much to make my time in England both useful and delightful.

In the complicated process of tracing Quinn's correspondents and securing permission to quote from their letters, I have been assisted by many persons. Most generous of all has been Mr. Michael B. Yeats, who not only allowed me to quote from the printed and unprinted letters of five members of the Yeats family but offered many other acts of kindness. Sir Caspar John and Mrs. Dorelia John have been similarly interested and helpful, as has Mr. Edwin John. For special graciousness of this kind I am grateful too to Mrs. Valerie Eliot, Major Richard G. Gregory, Mr. and Mrs. Sean MacBride, Major J. O. Parry, Lady Kathleen Epstein, Mr. H. Montgomery Hyde, Mrs. Lily M. Stephens, Mr. James Laughlin, Mrs. Dorothy Pound, Miss Anne Munro-Kerr of the Society of Authors, and Miss Patricia Butler of A. P. Watt and Son.

I record, with thanks, my indebtedness in the following specific instances for permission to quote from published and unpublished letters:

for letters of Sir Roger Casement, to Major J. O. Parry; for letters of Mr. Padraic Colum, to Mr. Colum; for letters of Joseph Conrad, to Mr. E. C. Brown and J. M. Dent and Sons Ltd.; for letters of T. S. Eliot, to Mrs. Valerie Eliot; for letters of Jacob Epstein, to Lady Kathleen Epstein; for letters of Lady Augusta Gregory, to Major Richard G. Gregory; for letters of Douglas Hyde, to the Royal Bank of Ireland Ltd., Trustee of the Dr. Douglas Hyde Trust; for letters of Augustus John, to Mrs. Dorelia John and Sir Caspar John; for letters of Gwen John, to Mr. Edwin John; for unpublished letters of James Joyce, to the James Joyce Estate and Miss Anne Munro-Kerr for the Society of Authors; for published letters of James Joyce, to Viking Press, Inc., and Faber and Faber Ltd., publishers of *Letters of James Joyce* (edited by Stuart Gilbert and Richard Ellmann, 3 vols., copyright 1966); for letters of Sir Shane Leslie, to Sir Shane Leslie; for letters of Maud Gonne MacBride, to Sean MacBride; for unpublished letters of Mr. Ezra Pound, to Mrs. Dorothy Pound and Mr. James Laughlin for the Committee for Ezra Pound; for published letters of Mr. Ezra Pound, to Harcourt, Brace and World, Inc., publishers of *The Letters of Ezra Pound, 1907–1941* (edited by D. D. Paige, copyright 1950); for letters of Henri-Pierre Roché, to Mme. Denise Roché; for letters of George William Russell, to Mr. Diarmuid Russell; for letters of James Stephens, to Mrs. Iris Wise and the Society of Authors as literary representative of the Estate of James Stephens; for letters of John Millington Synge, to Mrs. Lily M. Stephens and the National City Bank Ltd. of Dublin; for unpublished letters of John Butler Yeats, William Butler Yeats, Jack B. Yeats, Lily Yeats, and Elizabeth C. Yeats, to Mrs. William Butler Yeats, Miss Anne Butler Yeats, and Mr. Michael B. Yeats, and to Miss Patricia Butler for A. P. Watt and Son; for published letters of John Butler Yeats, to Mr. Michael B. Yeats, Miss Patricia Butler for A. P. Watt and Son, and Faber and Faber Ltd., publishers of *J. B. Yeats Letters to His Son W. B. Yeats and Others, 1869–1922* (edited by Joseph Hone, copyright 1944); for published letters of William Butler Yeats, to Miss Anne Yeats, Mr. Michael B. Yeats, Miss Patricia Butler for A. P. Watt and Son, and Rupert Hart-Davis, publishers of *The Letters of W. B. Yeats* (edited by Allan Wade, copyright 1955). Quotations from the letters of John Quinn himself are made with the kind permission of his heirs.

Mrs. Elliott Lyman and Mrs. Helen Canney have given me secretarial services of heroic dimensions.

Mr. Whitney Blake, Mr. John Begg, Mr. Frederick Schneider, Mrs. Manuela Kruger, Mrs. Ivor Lofving, and Miss Vivian Hausch of Oxford University Press in New York and Mr. Jon Stallworthy of Oxford University Press in London have handled my affairs with patience, taste, and wisdom.

My colleague, Mr. Joseph McGrath Bottkol, my former colleague, Mr. Eugene Goodheart, and my wife, Jane Davidson Reid, have read my manuscript with eyes at once skeptical and indulgent and have offered many improvements which I have silently incorporated. To their other services Dr. and Mrs. Conroy added that of a reading of the manuscript which saved me from making certain errors of fact. My wife and my son, Colin Way Reid, have endured and encouraged me and have added to my obligation by cheerfully performing much of the labor on the index to this volume.

Finally, I am grateful for a Fulbright Research Grant to the United Kingdom and for a grant from the American Council of Learned Societies which provided me with the indispensable element, time to work.

B. L. R.

Contents

Contents

Illustrations

*The Man
from
New York*

Beginnings: 1870-1904

TO Irishmen in London and Dublin the John Quinn who descended upon the islands from New York in the summer of 1902 seemed an arresting, improbable, and in some ways amusing figure. He defined himself as a lawyer and showed himself to be an uncommonly knowing amateur of letters. He was a bachelor of thirty-two, of impressive aspect, whose bald crown saved him from being intolerably good looking. He was tall and commanding, an inch over six feet, of slender, strong, well-made figure, of erect bearing, carrying a finely molded head on a longish neck. His features were classically cut and proportioned, the face marked by lively blue eyes and a mobile, risible mouth. When John Butler Yeats showed Quinn to the Dublin portraitist Sarah Purser she " 'looked at him hungrily to paint him.' " [1] But above all Quinn showed himself a doer, and to the loosely ordered Yeatses and to other casual and needy Irishmen, he seemed to wear the imposing and comical air of a secular *deus ex machina*. Quinn bought ten of Jack Yeats's pictures at a cast and commissioned from his father a list of Irish portraits. "John Quinn is the nearest approach to an angel in my experience," John Butler Yeats wrote to his elder son, the poet.[2] Within a month Quinn had done London, Dublin, Galway, and Gort, and had met and affected virtually everybody who was anybody in contemporary Irish letters. Energy so various and good will so efficient had to be tried on and tried out before the Irishmen could tell how to live with it, but all felt the presence of an engaging and potentially useful phenomenon. J. B. Yeats's description of Quinn as a "newly arrived American" could be richly

3

interpreted. Like one of Henry James's classic Americans, Quinn was an "emanation of the great continent," and if James had known him as Quinn knew James's writings he might well have put him in a book.

Both John Quinn's parents were Irish by birth, his father James William Quinn from County Limerick and his mother Mary Quinlan Quinn from County Cork. Mary Quinlan had come to America in 1851 as an orphan of fourteen, had met and married at eighteen the young baker James Quinn of Tiffin, Ohio, the county seat of Seneca County. They produced in all eight children, of whom six survived infancy, two boys and four girls. John was their firstborn. Shortly after his birth the family removed a few miles to Fostoria, Ohio, and that town became their permanent home. James Quinn prospered and was soon directing a staff of bakers. He built the "Quinn Block," a sturdy brick structure with bakery and shop on the ground floor and living apartments above, occupied by the family. From a later more cosmopolitan eminence John Quinn described the town as a "small—flat—uninteresting—Platt-Deutsch —smelly—German—and—thick-skulled-Catholic—diluted with— third-removed-Yankee, community." [3] Fostoria was in fact a representative nineteenth-century midwestern enclave, busy with its own small concerns. Like so many of its kind, it was an ethnic polyglot, with many Germans and a sprinkling of Irish, and one unusual strain, a tribe of Belgians. Down to the time of the First World War three out of four sermons a month in the local Catholic Church were preached in German. The Belgians were glassworkers and conducted the major local industry. A small opera house was visited by traveling musicians and players. Pretty public parks were much frequented by the Germans and Belgians, often observing their own transplanted holidays in their national costumes. The Belgians formed a fine concert band, and Belgian funerals, led by the band and followed by mourners on foot, were a familiar and impressive sight in the streets.

John Quinn grew up here, happy enough but needing wider horizons. His mother was the real force in the family, a person of intellect and ambition, much admired in the town for her self-taught culture and shrewd commonsense. She was a massive influence on her son, and he revered her all his life. By the time of his graduation in the class of 1887 in Fostoria High School, Quinn had already begun to show signs of the bents and the energies which were to direct his later life. As a lad of promising genius he had caught the eye of the principal, Dr. U. H. Squires, a second major influence, who kept Quinn's loyal respect and affection and who was remembered in his pupil's will. Squires pointed Quinn's bookish leaning, and before he left high school he was a reader and collector with a taste astonishing for an Ohio lad in the 1880s. He spent several hundred dollars of his savings, for example, on first editions of Pater, Hardy, Morris, and Meredith, at a time when these were contemporary names. "I became a collector of books," he wrote reminiscently years later, "almost as soon as I ceased to be a collector of marbles, and gave my marbles and bicycle away." [4] He recalled his mother's finding him on his knees on the living-room floor with a heap of new books about him: " 'And how long will those last you?' " with a smile.

His savings suffered from a second of his fascinations, that with politics. When he was eighteen he withdrew five hundred dollars from the bank, bet it on the presidential election, and lost. He said nothing in the family of the episode, but news of it got about the town and ultimately his mother heard the story from the family doctor. She brought her son five hundred-dollar bills. "I don't want you talked about," she said. Quinn went back to the bank and restored the money—with the lie that he had bet the five hundred dollars for a friend who had now returned it. "My father and mother approved of every damned thing I did," he wrote to Ezra Pound much later, "even my follies." [5] Quinn survived such indulgence, but not without acquiring a permanent strain of cockiness. In a more considerable piece of political precocity, he nominated former Governor Charles Foster for Congress while that worthy was yachting on the Atlantic, then ran his campaign for election, all before he was old enough to vote himself.

Young Quinn matriculated at the University of Michigan in the fall of 1888. But at the end of a single year he was carried off to Washington as the private secretary of Governor Foster, who had been named Secretary of the Treasury in the cabinet of President Benjamin Harrison. Governor Foster was a friend of Quinn's mother and valued her counsel, coming regularly to talk with her whenever he was in Fostoria. His handsome daughter Annie was romantically interested in young Quinn, who was unfortunately her junior by several years. Father and daughter had had an eye on him for some time, as a lad of parts, and taking him to Washington in their train was a wise and natural move. Quinn had qualified himself technically for his duties by learning shorthand on his own, with his sister Julia dictating to him, for practice, at progressively faster speeds. He earned his Washington salary of $1,800 a year, and, being John Quinn, found time to study law at Georgetown University. He took a degree there in 1893, and then, with a greater world with its demands and opportunities in view, he went to Harvard where he took a second degree in the law in 1895. Quinn was privileged to sit under Thayer in law, William James in philosophy, and Santayana in art and aesthetics.

Now, at twenty-five, Quinn descended upon New York, where in Algeresque fashion he set out with a clerkship at ten dollars a week in the law offices of General Benjamin F. Tracy. He occupied a single room and took his meals at the West 57th Street boarding house of Mrs. Annie Smith, a Yorkshire widow with an abundantly nubile daughter Ada. Quinn had lived with the Smiths in Washington, in a situation reminiscent of Joyce's story, "The Boarding House," and the Smiths' removal to New York was evidently in part a pursuit of Quinn. But Quinn was of sterner stuff than Joyce's boarder, and it gradually became clear to all hands that he had no intention of marrying Ada Smith. The relationship cooled but continued, and the Smiths drifted into the status of family friends and occasional nuisances. Quinn had resolved to make himself a first-rate lawyer, a specialist in financial law. He had resolved, further, to make himself an educated man and a man of the world. He read and studied incessantly in his free time, and night after night he stayed until the closing of the doors at the great Lenox Library at 70th Street and Fifth Avenue. Aside from the law he was reading primarily the contemporary English masters, particularly Pater, Rossetti, Meredith, Henry James, and Morris, but he read everything, really, the Romantic poets, everything Irish he could find, and a good deal of philosophy and theology. Nietzsche gripped him for years. He read Doellinger, "all of Newman," and supposed himself one of the few men living who had read Harnack's *History of Dogma*, "in seven big volumes, notes and all." [6] But a naturally rational bent of mind was leading him farther and farther away from the devout Catholicism in which he had been reared. The books and pictures which were the characteristic furniture of his life began to accumulate around him. The pictures he bought at this early stage tended to result from his predominantly literary interests: prints, etchings, monochromes, for the most part portraits and generally of his heroes among the writers.

In 1900 Quinn graduated to a junior partnership in the firm of Alexander and Colby, where he remained for six years, until he felt ready to strike out on his own. He was beginning to be known as a rising, useful man, especially to bankers and financiers who needed somebody knowledgeable about the legal paraphernalia of the management and multiplication of money. And he continued as an amateur of politics. He had had three years of direct political life in Washington, he had stood six feet behind Grover Cleveland at Cleveland's second inaugural ceremony in 1893, and in five years with Tracy he had seen a good deal of the workings of the Platt machine from the inside. Now as a Democrat and an Irishman he was being drawn into Tammany circles in New York City.

The year 1902 which took Quinn abroad for the first time was a terrible year for him at home. His father had died in 1897. Now on June 20 he learned by telegram of the grave illness of his mother, to whom he had been far closer. He left New York for Ohio on the first available train, at eight-thirty on the morning of June 21, not knowing that his mother had died a half-hour before his departure. At every point where the train stopped en route, Quinn sent ahead to his mother wires of such affecting sentiment that the telegraph operators began to follow his story and to converse back and forth about it through their instruments. The Fostoria operator called next day to tell the family the story. The Quinns were a passionately close family. The heart of Quinn's sister Annie had been weak, and now, a few days after the death of the mother, it failed, and Annie Quinn died on June 25. John Quinn returned to New York on July 5, deeply shaken.

His first trip to England and Ireland was already planned, and Quinn proceeded with it, sailing from New York on July 15. His only announcement abroad had been an exchange of notes with Jack Yeats in the fall of 1901. Quinn had read in the *Dublin Express* T. W. Rolleston's notice of an exhibition of paintings by J. B. Yeats and Nathaniel Hone; and now his inquiry to Jack brought the news that there were two painting Yeatses whose initials were J. B., and he and his father would both be delighted to show Quinn their pictures, in Dublin or in London. He was already conversant with the prose and verse of Jack's brother, W. B. Yeats. In London Quinn put up at the Carlton and moved eagerly about the city, alone or guided by Jack Yeats. Dining with Sir Charles Dilke he was shocked to hear that Dilke had "after many disappointments, closed . . . the book of new poetry" [7] before ever reaching Yeats. Quinn, in the kind of gesture which was to grow habitual, presented him with four volumes of Yeats's poems and *The Celtic Twilight* and was in due course fervently thanked by Dilke for reopening the book of new poetry. From Jack Yeats, Quinn bought at once nearly a dozen paintings, and from his father he bought a completed portrait of W. B. Yeats and commissioned, at an agreed price of £20 or roughly $100 each, portraits of John O'Leary, Douglas Hyde, and George William Russell ("Æ"). He was setting out to collect images of his heroes in the cultural and political life of Ireland.

From London he proceeded to Dublin, where he reveled in the warm and free flow of Irish talk in the studios, pubs, and homes, finding John Butler Yeats's description of the Irish as "a contentious people" accurate and congenial. "Ireland is most like ancient Athens," J. B. Yeats wrote him in August, "where all were such talkers and disputants. England is like ancient Rome with its legions and cohorts and dull business of conquering the world." [8] In a mere week in Dublin and Gort Quinn found time to meet, to impress and to be impressed by, W. B. Yeats and his sisters Lily and Lollie, Russell, T. W. Rolleston, Douglas Hyde, George Moore, Edward Martyn, and Lady Gregory. At Killeeneen, Craughwell, on the last day of August, Quinn joined in a Gaelic Feis at the new tomb which Lady Gregory had erected of the blind Connacht poet Raftery, and Jack Yeats decorated a program of the day with charming sketches of Quinn, Lady Gregory, Hyde, W. B. Yeats, and himself. At Lady Gregory's great house of Coole Park

Feis program with sketches by Jack Yeats. Clockwise: W. B. Yeats, Douglas Hyde, Quinn, Jack Yeats, Lady Gregory. Courtesy of the Berg Collection, New York Public Library.

Quinn heard Hyde read one of his Gaelic plays; and it must have been at this time that he added his initials to those carved in the bark of her famous signatory beech tree. Years later, remembering the occasion in a letter of July 26, 1913, it seemed to her that she had entertained "an angel unawares." He was bold and efficient enough to attempt, and partly to effect, a reconciliation between W. B. Yeats and George Moore, who had been squabbling over their separate rights to a scenario on which they had ceased to collaborate. Yeats wrote his version as a five-act play, *Where There Is Nothing*, and Quinn supported his right to the material.

Before he sailed for New York on the *Ivernia* on September 2, Quinn had agreed to see to the copyrighting of the play in the United States, and in October he did so by arranging an edition through the firm of John Lane. It was the first of his many such services to Irish writers. Seeing the text of the play, Quinn complimented Yeats upon his work as an affair both of poetry and of action—and sent him several pages of suggested improvements. He had talked much to Yeats of Nietzsche, and he sent him now, in mid-September, his own copy of *Thus Spake Zarathustra* and copies of *The Case of Wagner* and *A Genealogy of Morals*. Thus Yeats owed to Quinn his introduction to the writer he later called "that strong enchanter." Quinn thought Yeats would find Nietzsche's "wonderful epigrammatic style" of use in his own writing, though he admitted that he found "abhorrent" the German's "so-called philosophy . . . of the exaltation of brutality." [9]

On October 23, 1902, John Butler Yeats wrote Quinn the second of the several hundred letters he would send him in the course of the next twenty years. This one from his studio at 43 Harrington Street in Dublin covered eight pages with tiny scrawl. It addressed Quinn as "My dear John Quinn" and explained the salutation in a parenthetical first paragraph:

> (I find every one speaks of you as "John Quinn." This plain forcible unadorned way of appellating you would suggest that there is something of a young Pilgrim Father about you, *as no doubt there is*).

J. B. Yeats thanked Quinn for a check and went on to give news of Dublin after protesting that "nothing has happened since you were here." He admired the calm spirit with which the brothers Fay and their amateur company were setting about offering a repertory of seven plays. They had abandoned their stage in "a Street & Hall into which our Dublin Mrs. Grundy would not show her nose" and moved to larger more respectable quarters "into which Mrs. Grundy might be persuaded to enter." J. B. Yeats had the feeling that the Dublin intellectual pot was simmering and about to come to the boil. The players were a part of that, as were such squabbles as that between George Moore and W. B. Yeats over a literary idea which both valued and both had stolen from George Russell. Moore was turning his own Dublin back parlor into "another storm centre," J. B. Yeats wrote. He looked ahead with relish to the coming show of Irish energies:

> By Jove, we are I fancy in for lots of war & dissention among ourselves—but that is just the atmosphere in which a nation does its best. Dublin will soon be the *most wideawake* city in the world. —You are wideawake over in America, but it is in politics & practical matters—perhaps we shall be wide awake in *ideas literature philosophy drama.*—I hope all sides will stand up & fight their guns well—the church included. *One's best helper is a good opponent.* . . .

J. B. Yeats had finished his portrait of Russell for Quinn and thought it by far the best thing he had ever done. He thanked Quinn for permission to keep the painting on hand for hanging in a Dublin exhibition after Christmas. He had got his old portrait of John O'Leary back from Cork, and was ready to make a copy for Quinn; but he felt O'Leary was such a splendid subject ("He looks very fine—like an old dishevelled Eagle") and felt that his work was in such good train that he yearned to do an entirely new portrait: "I am sure he would like sitting provided I let him smoke." His closing postscript paid a graceful compliment to Quinn: "Dublin seemed to us quite dull after you left."

In November Quinn was delighted to receive the sketch book that John Butler Yeats had been filling for him with pencil drawings of Irish men and women of note, and at once had many of the images framed. J. B. Yeats was fascinated throughout their acquaintance by Quinn as a type, a phenomenon, and he addressed him chaffingly now as "a New World Puritan." Quinn wrote back:

". . . there is nothing of the Puritan in me. . . . They were an un-
loveable and a self-righteous and a bitter lot." [10] But he was wrong
about himself, and Yeats was right: an unrecognized Puritanism
was a deep and durable part of his composition.

Now, five months after the deaths of Quinn's mother and his
sister Annie, his sister Jessie died on December 10, of prolonged
uterine hemorrhages. Quinn was shocked and angry, and felt her
life might easily have been saved by sensible diagnosis and treatment. He had begun to have a morbid horror of death and an active
hatred of disease. Prompt diagnosis and expert medical care became
a kind of obsession, and he became a student of the care of the
body, coming in time to consider himself, with good reason, an
expert lay medical man, diagnosing and prescribing with almost as
much insight as passion. He hated and feared the thought of death
and tried to avoid the sight of death or its accoutrements. Mourning clothes especially made him depressed and angry, and he would
vacate a subway car if a woman in mourning entered it. But none
of this could prevent his family from shrinking around him or make
them invulnerable, and Quinn was moved about this time to cast up
his practical and spiritual account in a set of five admonitions to
himself on a scrap of paper found among his effects after his death:

1) Save as much as possible.
2) Buy few more books as possible—no more expensive sets.
3) Be kind to Jim & Julie & Clara [his remaining brother and
   sisters].
4) Be not rough or rude to or inconsiderate of others who may
   suffer by unthinking speech.
5) Be dignified & keep out of every man's debt. Avoid the brutality of unkind words.

At the end of 1902 John Quinn set about the promotion and
organization of a New York branch of the Irish Literary Society,
on the model of the local societies which Yeats and his friends had
been forming in Ireland. Quinn thought of it as a haven for Irish
letters, a place where New Yorkers of Irish origins and sympathies
could feed their hunger for the culture of their fat! ers. He imagined a library, reading rooms, special rooms, and a hall for lectures,
plays, and music. The project occupied much of his free time for
the next six months. Quinn buttonholed every likely Irishman he

former, and he was needy and willing to go where there might be money. "I hope he will shine forth like the sun for the sake of Ireland and his own too empty pockets," Russell wrote of the scheme on October 29, thereby naming Quinn's own motives: to promote the glory of Ireland and to help a valued friend. By this time Quinn was back in America and was circulating widely photographs and a pamphlet of seductive critical notices of Yeats. He got commitments for more than thirty lectures, mainly in colleges and universities in the east and middle west, and he persuaded Senator Phelan to arrange for lectures at Stanford and Berkeley. Yeats offered, at $75 each, four set subjects having to do with the current Irish cultural "Renaissance," and he was willing and able to speak more briefly and extemporaneously in more casual circumstances.

He landed in New York on the *Oceanic* on November 11 and moved into Quinn's apartment. As in later years he was able to treat the place as his home when in the city, carrying his own latch key, being valeted by Quinn's servant, coming and going at will while Quinn went about his daily law affairs, spending free evenings with Quinn alone or with the guests his host invited in. Quinn felt a profound satisfaction in being the host of genius. He described to Judge Martin J. Keogh, one of his most intimate Irish friends in the law, Yeats's composition of the poem "Never Give All the Heart" while in his company:

> We were discussing questions of high philosophical and social import, and among other things we discussed whether a man should give himself unreservedly or act with a certain reservation in his commerce with fair ladies. A night or two after that as Yeats and I were going out to dinner he was murmuring words over to himself and was greatly delighted at having made a new poem. When we got to the restaurant he wrote it out on a piece of paper substantially as it is now printed in the book. . . .
>
> [*October 14, 1907.*]

In the same letter he summed up his pleasure in their relationship: "Yeats is the one man of absolute genius I have known personally and well." Quinn was in fact a true scholar of Yeats's work, already steeped in it when he wrote at this time to James Gibbons Huneker, the journalist and critic who was to become one of Quinn's closest friends, and who was preparing an article on Yeats for the *New York Sun*. He sent Huneker a copy of *In the Seven Woods*, a new volume of poems published in August, and described the texture of the plays *On Baile's Strand* and the forthcoming *The King's Threshold* as "like marble, as compared with the painting of his earlier poems." [16] "Painting" was a shrewd word to apply to the early poems, and Quinn went on to show a direct insight into the pattern of Yeats's growth:

> . . . every year Yeats has grown more and more critical, more and more careful, more and more self-critical. His earlier poems were not subjected at all to the brooding care of his later ones. The loosening of the verse structure, instead of being a sign of decadence, is with Yeats the result of deliberate artifice and intention, and in this he is but following the best tradition of the last two hundred years.

Such literary prescience in a bustling young New York lawyer must have struck Huneker with some surprise.

Yeats commenced his tour in the east on November 16, appearing at Yale, Harvard, Williams, Amherst, Mount Holyoke, Smith, Vassar, Bryn Mawr, and at several colleges about New York. In Cambridge he met William James, and when he ran low on cash borrowed four dollars from the great Chaucer scholar F. N. Robinson. Quinn beamed upon as many performances as he could reach and took the train with Yeats to Washington for lectures at Catholic University and an audience he had arranged with "the Colonel," as he always called President Theodore Roosevelt. In the middle of December Quinn wrote to Arthur Griffith of the *United Irishman* that Yeats was "incomparably capable and winning"; his lectures were "among the most vital influences that have been felt in this country for many years." [17] Yeats spoke at Carnegie Hall on "The Intellectual Revival in Ireland" with Bourke Cockran, the professional silver-tongue of Irish-American politicians, in the chair. Here as elsewhere the preoccupied bard proved a cool and systematic performer, catching all his trains, never running out of clean shirts, judging his audiences accurately and adjusting his material to suit the local temper and need. Some of Yeats's New York auditors, including jurists and other professional men, regretted that he had not gone into politics and into Parliament. But no, Quinn wrote to Douglas Hyde on January 8, art was Yeats's true call: "Compromise is the soul of politics, and the artist can never compromise." By January, crossing the plains toward California on the Overland Limited, Yeats felt he was coming to understand the feeling of the traveling actor, the homelessness, the weariness, the excitement, the alternate elation and depression, the dangers and comforts of the ego.

He returned east for a brief foray into Canada and a second major speech before the Irish societies of New York, then settled down on March 8 for a few days' rest at Quinn's apartment. Before sailing he presented Quinn with the page proofs of Lady Gregory's *Gods and Fighting Men*. He reported a pleasant passage home: " . . . smoked cigarettes all the time and was quite comfortable." [18] He learned in America that he had lost Maud Gonne, his "woman Homer sung," his "Helen," and his "Pallas Athene," to the "military roisterer" John MacBride, and that would be a permanent sadness. But he was still able to write Quinn in March: "I am facing the world with great hopes and strength and I owe it all to you and I thank you and shall always be grateful." [19] Yeats had liked the Americans, he felt his mind aired and stretched, and for the first time in his life he had some real money in his pocket—$3230.40, to be exact.[20] Quinn knew perfectly well that he had made the practical success of the tour, but the intellectual triumph was Yeats's, and Quinn took pleasure in sending praise after him. To Lady Gregory he wrote that Yeats had impressed Americans as no Irishman had done since the great Parnell. And to George Russell he praised "the fire and the emotion and the power of improvisation of phrase that go to make up a great orator." [21] Russell agreed but felt that Yeats tended too much toward a funereal solemnity. He waited anxiously for Yeats's return that they might renew their long amiably contentious dialogue: " . . . if I hadn't him to fight with it would make a great gap in my life."[22]

When Quinn suggested now that he try his own powers as an orator on an American tour, Russell replied with his customary graceful irony:

> I have been following Yeats' triumphal procession with delight but God forbid I should ever set foot in your country as a lecturer. I feel I am out of tune with electricity and railways and all the inventions and the hurry, and would rather talk simply to an audi-

ence of farmers in Kerry than eloquently to cultivated men. I do
the farmers some good. I would not do the cultivated men any
good. . . .   [*January 20, 1904.*]

Quinn was acting as Russell's agent in negotiations with the American branch of Macmillan's for the printing of *The Divine Vision
and Other Poems,* and for this and other reasons Æ called him "a
good friend," [23] "one of those rare folk whose pleasure is doing
things for others." [24] Russell was a great inward and outward wanderer. He bicycled great distances about the Irish countryside in his
work for the farmers' co-operatives and for the *Irish Homestead*
which was their organ; and always, passionately but patiently, he
was in pursuit of the light within. "I get away from everything
roaming about," he wrote wistfully on September 11, "and I dont
even get to my own soul. . . ." Quinn gave him a virtual *carte
blanche* as regarded his own paintings: " . . . don't give away all
the best ones as you paint them but save five or six for me, and
send them over to me . . . with a memorandum of their amount. I
am very fond of all your pictures that I have and want more of
them when I can get them." [25]

    Quinn's domestic and professional life, aside from his demanding
and satisfying friendships with cultivated Irishmen, was beginning
to find patterns that would be permanent. Whereas he was still a
junior partner in the firm of Alexander and Colby, he was established as an able man of financial law in the eyes of the officers of
the National Bank of Commerce and of such independent men of
money as Thomas Fortune Ryan. He now had the services, as confidential clerk, of the man who would be most nearly indispensable
to his future affairs, the burly Black Irishman Thomas J. Curtin, a
man of Quinn's own age, an expert stenographer, both sensitive and
shrewd in the affairs of the office, and wholly trustworthy in all
relationships. Quinn had left Mrs. Smith's bed and board at last and
occupied his first private apartment at 1 West 87th Street. It was
already a cluttered oasis, packed with books and pictures. A young
Japanese, Sadajiro Kumatani, served him as houseman and valet. His
sister Julia, who was to be the only one of the Quinn siblings to
take a mate, had married on February 24, 1903, a prosperous young
Fostoria druggist, Will Anderson. Quinn ordered a black broad-
cloth suit from Oppenheim and Collins for Julia to wear on her

wedding trip, but it proved to be too big for her "perfect 36 figure," and he had to carry it back to New York in his trunk after the wedding. His remaining sister, Clara, tall, pious, and somewhat managerial, was now a nun and a teacher of music in an Ursuline convent in Tiffin, Ohio. His brother, Jim, remained in Fostoria. The four orphan Quinns were very close, but John Quinn felt at least equally close to his mother's brother, Father Jeremiah Quinlan, parish priest in the prairie town of El Paso, Illinois, near Peoria, a man with much of his own sanguine love of life but of far more serene temperament. Now and as long as he lived Quinn tried to find time at least twice a year for family visits to Ohio and Illinois. Ada Smith, as family friend no longer mistress, had come west for Julia Quinn's marriage. Her more intimate function was now filled by a tall, handsome brunette former schoolteacher named Dorothy Coates. She was to serve for nearly twenty years.

In the winter of 1904 Quinn arranged with Clausen's Gallery for a show of the paintings of Jack Yeats from March 28 to April 16. The painter and his wife, Cottie, accepted Quinn's invitation to use the show as an excuse for a visit to New York and to stay in his apartment. They were there for seven weeks. In her own postscript to a letter of April 2 which W. B. Yeats was dictating to her, Lady Gregory wrote: "My greetings to you & your guests—If you send Jack back as well & in as good heart as you have sent back his brother you will be a wonderful man! WBY is full of happy energy & of bright recollections." Quinn had sold to *McClure's* two stories of Yeats's, "Hanrahan's Vision" and "Hanrahan's Curse," for a hundred dollars each, and he sought to advance Jack's career as well by persuading the editors to employ him to illustrate his brother's stories. In this he succeeded, but the show at Clausen's found harder going. In the long run only twelve pictures were sold for $430, and of those Quinn bought ten himself. After he had seen Jack and his wife off on the *Celtic*, he wrote to W. B. Yeats on May 14 in praise of his brother's personal qualities: "He is one of the most simple and unaffected kind-hearted genuine and sincere men I have ever met and I like him more than I can tell." But of Jack's work in art he had begun to have doubts. He felt that he was too quick and crude, too lazy in much of his work. What he needed was a strong course of the Paris discipline.

W.B. Yeats wrote on May 11 that his income in the two months since returning from his lecture tour had totalled two pounds and thirteen shillings, and he lacked cash to pay his landlady in London. But he had a credit of £400 in America and he asked Quinn's advice on investing it. He told of meeting Queen Alexandra as guest of the Countess of Cromartie at Suffolk House in London. Passing though a corridor to look in upon a party of beautifully dressed children in another room, they had encountered the Queen, and Yeats had been presented. She said that she was an admirer of his poems; he was sufficiently self-possessed not to ask which ones. He wondered whether, as a patriotic Irishman, he should have crossed himself after confrontation with the Queen of England.

George Russell was finding W. B. Yeats and Standish O'Grady the "most alive" people around him. He was afraid that J. B. Yeats would have trouble pinning down O'Grady, who could be "a terror," for Quinn's portrait commission, and recommended that Mr. Yeats simply do a copy of his earlier portrait, which was "really a fine picture of O'Grady at his grimmest and most forbidding. He looked like an old Viking about to massacre a townland, even to the children and women." [26] Mr. Yeats had returned to his old studio on Stephen's Green in Dublin and was busy and happy, but Russell, who found him "the most loveable of all bearing the name," [27] feared that bad drawing and color in his recent work meant that his sight was failing. Æ looked to his own painting as the most spiritual and recreative action of his life, and turned yearningly to it in his free intervals, not long or frequent. He explained to Quinn his difficult mystical ideal:

> What I want to do is to paint landscape as if it had no other existence than as an imagination of the Divine Mind, to paint man as if his life overflowed into that imagination, and to paint the Sidhe [fairies] as mingling with his life; indeed, the unity of God and man and nature in one single being—an almost impossible idea to convey in paint.   [*May 1904.*]

In practice Russell painted with astonishing ease and copiousness, often finishing fifty or sixty canvases in the "spare" time of a single year, and he found an eager market for his work. Like Nathaniel Hone, he hated to let his pictures go from his own hands. After he had reluctantly offered an exhibition during Horse Show week of 1904, he wrote sadly to Quinn, "My exhibition has just opened and my heart is full of woe because I have sold over half of them the first day." He had already sold thirty-seven pictures. With John Quinn, on the other hand, the affection for Russell's dreamy poetic landscapes, of which he continued to buy "five or six" a year, was an early manifestation of a vein of sentiment and rather shapeless spirituality in a nature that preferred to define itself as bluff and empirical.

Quinn had hoped to make his trip abroad, especially to Ireland, an annual affair, a perennial return to the fountain. He managed it for the third successive year in 1904, but not easily. His prosperity was increasing but that meant that he was busier than ever, his duties thickening around him. He was not able to get away until the middle of October, and he had three weeks free which he divided between Dublin and London, with a single day in France. Happily Quinn left a journal of his trip. It is a rather queer document, evidently typed off by a stenographer (in violet ink) from Quinn's scrappy notes, full of impressionistic spelling and of abbreviations, some of which are cryptic. But it is a useful document for it re-creates in some detail what was to be Quinn's last significant visit to Ireland, the one that completed the foundation for his correspondence of the next twenty years with Irish writers and men in public life—a correspondence the persistence and intimacy of which would be inexplicable but for the evidence of friendships amplified and confirmed which this little diary provides, on twenty-six legal-size pages.

There was actually only one French gesture, a visit to Chartres from Paris which occupied Sunday morning, October 23. Quinn gave an hour to inspection of the outside of the cathedral, "the north and south doors of which were very very fine." Of the interior he mentions only the underground crypt, to which he reacted in character: " . . . Bisentine decorations, sickliness—depression left upon me by visit. . . ." He returned to Paris in the afternoon and crossed from Boulogne to Folkestone in the evening: "Crossed the Channel a few hours after the first division of the Russian Fleet had passed the Channel and three hours before they accidently fired on some Fishing Boats off Hull in the North Sea.

Grey misty night." In London Quinn put up at the Carlton and spent Monday on busy bookish errands. He talked at length with the publisher and bookseller Elkin Mathews, notably about Lionel Johnson. Mathews corrected newspaper accounts of the death of Johnson, who had not been picked up in the street as they had announced but had slipped and struck his head on the polished floor of an inn: "After his death two Hospital Nurses came to M's Shop and wanted to buy a copy of J's poems, they said that so delicately organised was he that up to the time of his death the Doctors were unable to locate the fracture." At the Leicester Gallery Quinn looked at works of Charles Conder, William Rothenstein, and Charles Shannon. In the afternoon, after drawing money in the City, he called at half-a-dozen bookshops and galleries, bought a few books and a portfolio of Willam Strahan's etchings after *Don Quixote*. In the evening he took the train to Holyhead and crossed to Ireland in the small hours, angry because, although he had bought first-class and sleeper tickets, he was barred from the state-rooms on the boat and given only an open bunk.

Reaching Dublin at six-thirty in the morning, Quinn checked into the Shelburne Hotel where he found a telegram from George Russell and a letter from one of the Yeats sisters awaiting him. He turned in and slept for two hours. While he was dressing W. B. Yeats came in, "looking very well, full of plans and projects for new Theatre." They walked together to J. B. Yeats's studio at 7 Stephen's Green. Quinn observed portraits of John Redmond, Edward Dowden, Sir Anthony MacDonnell, Lily Yeats, and of the painter himself. There was talk of the sinking of the English fishing smack by the Russian fleet on Sunday: "W. B. Y. said that the English were delighted beyond measure to find themselves for once in the right and were making the most of it— it was such an unexpected emotion for them." Yeats took his father, Quinn, and Padraic Colum to lunch at the Empire Restaurant where the talk was mainly literary. Quinn thought Colum's talk was bright but boyish. They discussed Molière, Turgenev, and Flaubert, and spoke of "objectivity" and "sentimentality" and of the relation of emotions and intellect in writing. Quinn took a stout part in the talk. After lunch Quinn and W. B. Yeats accompanied Colum to the Nassau Hotel, where Colum was to read what purported to be the scenario of a new play:

... but we found that he had no Senario in the proper sense of the word, but merely some vague musings, beginning no where and leading no where. Discussion of the motives of the Play by J.Q. and very temperately and considerately but cautiously by W.B.Y. C. left at about 3 o'clock and promised to re-write the Senario which he had never written.

"At about 4 o'clock Lady G. Came in very fresh and fine," Quinn records. She told of having finished a one-act comedy, *Spreading the News*, and a three-act play, *Kincora*. She also announced that in honor of Quinn's friendship to the theatre company she had invited all the players to meet him at a reception and supper that evening. When they sat down in the evening they were offered chicken, salad, grapes and other fruit, cake, and even flowers, all brought by Lady Gregory from Coole Park at the opposite side of the island. Standish O'Grady sat at the hostess's left and Quinn at her right, followed by Douglas Hyde. Quinn "positively declined" a suggestion that he make a speech. After supper he talked at length of life and letters with O'Grady. Speaking of Quinn's family, O'Grady guessed them to have been Norman in origin. John Butler Yeats made a sketch of the two men as they talked. Mary Walker, one of the principal actresses, chanted W. B. Yeats's "Golden Apples" and Colum's "Over the Hills and Far Away." An actress whose name Quinn had forgotten "also sang in the traditional Irish method." Before the party broke up at one in the morning Mrs. O'Grady promised to see to it that her husband appeared for a sitting next day at J. B. Yeats's studio to advance the work on the portrait being done for Quinn.

Next morning, Wednesday the twenty-sixth, W. B. Yeats again came to Quinn's hotel for breakfast and a two-hour talk. Yeats's squabble with George Moore over their abortive "collaboration" was still unresolved, and Yeats told of being snubbed by George Moore at Arthur Symons's house in London: when Yeats held out his hand "G. M. bolted straight for the door and went home although it was immediately after dinner." Yeats

said that G.M. was a brute saved by intellect, that he had a magnificent mind, that his only emotions were all bad but that his mind when he had a chance to think before he acted saved him. That he had many good qualities and would do many kind things and especially if a thing appealed to his intellect or artistic conscience he was capable of great generosity and kindness which reminded me of Hyde's statement once that the only trace of conscience that M. had about him was his artistic conscience.

At J. B. Yeats's studio talk continued until O'Grady came in at noon and the sitting commenced. O'Grady was wearing a light blue shirt and a blue tie, but J. B. Yeats had already painted in a red tie. Quinn left the studio, bought a white satin tie which O'Grady put on, and Mr. Yeats painted out the red tie and painted in the white one. Mrs. O'Grady came in at one, and the talk turned to ghosts and visions. Quinn promised to send her William James on psychical phenomena. Mrs. O'Grady told of having seen a vision of a ruined Roman temple with a certain long narrow passage which actually came to light only after further excavations five years later than her vision. Standish O'Grady told of taking a copy of his history of Ireland to a Trinity College friend to ask him to notice the book in his newspaper: the friend turned a few pages fastidiously and handed the book back with the comment, " 'The mere names are revolting.' "

At two-fifteen that same day Quinn took the whole party to luncheon at the Shelburne Hotel. O'Grady talked in splendid form, of death and literature and the different ways men have of walking, especially the artists and men of letters who walk as if they loved the earth and were a part of it: " 'Sure, are we not all part of the earth?' " he asked. He and Quinn agreed that they disliked tombs which separated the body from the earth, and O'Grady described the "ghastly" effect of his family vault in which bodies were stacked in coffins on shelves. Quinn and O'Grady joined in approving Walt Whitman as a body in right relation to the earth. When O'Grady mentioned his admiration for Carlyle, J. B. Yeats told of meeting Carlyle walking in Chelsea: "ruddy skinned and glowering." Quinn described the theatrical quality of O'Grady's natural presence: "Not a bit of depression about O. not a bit of pessimism, but a mellow kindliness and great gentleness wonderfully soft voice and his deeper tones as moving as a tragic Actors, a sort of shuddering whisper in his voice."

That evening Quinn took dinner with Lady Gregory and W. B. Yeats at the Nassau Hotel, and then went with them to a rehearsal at the Camden Street Hall, where he also found Douglas Hyde and

John Millington Synge. They saw three acts of Lady Gregory's *Kincora* rehearsed, followed by a performance of Yeats's *The Pot of Broth* in which William Fay added "a great deal of new business" not in the text. Quinn suggested an emendation, Lady Gregory replied, and the whole crowd "marched along together" to the Nassau, where most of them entered and continued the discussion until one in the morning. Quinn felt himself very much a part of things, not a tolerated alien.

On Thursday for the third successive morning Quinn and W. B. Yeats breakfasted together and then adjourned to J. B. Yeats's studio, where they talked the morning away. There ensued another chatty lunch, this one at the University Club, with Land Commissioner W. F. Bailey entertaining Quinn, W. B. Yeats, and "R." (apparently either T. W. Rolleston or, more likely, George Russell). In the afternoon Quinn went shopping and then met Russell at Lady Gregory's for tea. Quinn stayed on for dinner with Lady Gregory and W. B. Yeats, and Russell reappeared just as they were finishing the meal. Quinn and Russell went off to O'Grady's house in Sandymount, where they were joined at nine by Rolleston for a "splendid discussion." Quinn talked of Poe and Swinburne, Rolleston recited his newest poem, and O'Grady talked of the immense prospects of Irish agriculture: "Fecundity of nature—Jerusalem artichokes—2,000% return—no depression—full of hope. . . ." The party broke up at eleven, with Rolleston heading home on his bicycle and Russell and Quinn walking together back into the city. Æ "talked beautifully" on the way, mostly in praise of O'Grady: "a grand simple noble nature—full of personal nobility and dignity, but sometimes of immense gloom, difficult to live with." Russell said that he considered O'Grady the real creator of the Gaelic revival, of the movement for agricultural regeneration, of the Land Conference: when each of his ideas was taken up by others, O'Grady quietly turned to something new. When Quinn and Russell reached the Shelburne after midnight, Russell came in for a bite to eat, and again spoke in praise of O'Grady as "the most conscientious and honorable man in public life in Ireland." Quinn picked up a letter that had come for him from W. B. Yeats and turned in at 2:00 a.m.

On Friday Quinn and W. B. Yeats combined their two morning

rituals by breakfasting at J. B. Yeats's studio. Quinn lunched in
Harcourt Street with Douglas Hyde, and Hyde made a verse for
him in Irish. One of Quinn's chief errands on this trip to Ireland
was to plan a lecture tour for Hyde and the Gaelic League in
America. Quinn was anxious to promote Hyde and his cause, admiring both as native Irish, nonclerical, nonpolitical, and intellectual.
He assured Hyde of nearly certain success and promised to take
care of all the practical details of the tour. But Hyde was doubtful
and finally agreed to take the plunge only after Quinn had personally agreed to guarantee him against any loss. When Quinn returned to J. B. Yeats's studio he found that he had just missed the
famous old Fenian patriot John O'Leary. Mr. Yeats started to work
again on the O'Grady portrait and Quinn stopped him, afraid that
he would ruin it. Again at tea with Lady Gregory, Quinn met the
Hydes, W. B. Yeats, and another of George Moore's sparring
mates, Edward Martyn. After tea Lady Gregory gave Quinn an
account of how his gift of £50 of the preceding summer had been
expended by the players. At dinner at the Shelburne Quinn entertained J. B. Yeats and John O'Leary, and the talk was of politics,
oratory, and women: "The various attractions of French women
English women and Irish women contrasted." The men drank two
quarts of wine with dinner, and Quinn kept a wary eye on
O'Leary, who had a reputation as a heavy tippler. Lady Gregory
told Quinn of purposely omitting whiskey when she had O'Leary
and W. B. Yeats to dinner, and O'Leary's pleading: " 'For the love
of God. . . .' " But when she sent Yeats out for a bottle "the poor
old man only wanted about a spoonful." Over coffee at the Shelburne Quinn and his guests talked of Milton's *Lycidas* and "J. Q.
pointed out the three reasons [unexplained] that he did not think
it could be called a perfect Poem." When J. B. Yeats left for an
appointment at his studio, Quinn and O'Leary boarded a side-car,
and Quinn prepaid O'Leary's fare to Temple Street when he
alighted at the Nassau Hotel, also giving the cabman a sixpence tip.
O'Leary said: " 'For the love of God why do you throw your
money away like that?' " At the Nassau Quinn sat in on a "Tedious
Meeting . . . of the entire Theatrical Company" as they discussed
various practical problems. W. B. Yeats announced that William
Fay was to be put on salary to give his entire time to the Company:

Lady Gregory was to advance £45 and Yeats £30 for the year to guarantee his pay. Again Quinn met Colum, Synge, and Russell, but he went to bed bored just after midnight.

Early the next day, Saturday the twenty-ninth, Quinn went to Russell's house to select paintings for his collection, returned to the city with Russell, then carried the two promised William James volumes to Mrs. O'Grady in Sandymount. After a bit of shopping Quinn took lunch with Rolleston and Russell at the Shelburne, then spent the late afternoon with Russell at George Moore's house, where he admired Moore's two Manets, two Mark Fishers, his Degas drawings, and his David portrait of a woman. Moore scoffed at Yeats's short plays in prose and said that *The Pot of Broth* could have been written by any journalist in three hours. He came back again to his grievance against Yeats for stealing from him Russell's story after agreeing to collaborate in writing it as a play. Walking along with Quinn on his way to Rolleston's house, Moore let it be known that he would like to lecture in America and sounded out Quinn as to how much Yeats had made on his American tour. Before they parted Moore brought himself to admit that Yeats was a great lyric poet. At Rolleston's Quinn met Mrs. Rolleston, kissed their little boy, and approved his own little goddaughter Aideen, "looking like one of Velasquez Infanta." At the Nassau Hotel he joined Lady Gregory, W. B. Yeats, both the Fay brothers, and Stephen Gwynn, "a Trinity College man with a tinge of the Oxford manner," for dinner. After an evening of plays, "unspeakably rotten," he went again in a crowd to Moore's house, where the talk was mainly of novelists and the badness of Irish newspapers. "J. Q. said that Meredith was for him in the novel the one incomparable Artist," and Russell proposed Scott as the greatest English novelist "because he had written out of the man." Moore again walked along with Quinn part way to his hotel, which he reached at two in the morning.

At the studio just after noon on Sunday Quinn found J. B. Yeats trying to work at the hands in his O'Grady portrait from an oversize model. Quinn suggested that Colum pose, but Colum's hands proved too small, and so Quinn ended up posing himself until two-thirty, when he went off to the Nassau Hotel to dinner with Lady Gregory and W. B. Yeats. Yeats talked eloquently of Blake's poetry

and his drawing. Lady Gregory thought the painting of Russell and
J. B. Yeats would be "interesting in 30 years," but that in every
work of theirs there was always "something to forgive." The conversation continued on into the evening at Lady Gregory's house.
Yeats spoke of his greater ease and pleasure in writing criticism than
in writing verse: " . . . when he was at work at Poetry he would
rather be doing anything else, but when he started at criticism had
to be dragged away from it." After Robert, Lady Gregory's son,
had left them, she said to Yeats: " 'Now let us kill ourselves with
work.' " Yeats forthwith dictated to her about 6,000 words for the
1904 *Samhain*, the publication, appearing sporadically, in which he
was promoting the work of the theatre in these years. Yeats then
read over "very beautifully" what he had dictated to Quinn who
was stretched out on a couch. Quinn noted Yeats's manner of per-
fecting his prose for publication: "After dictation writes out entire
thing which is the work of many days in his own hand for the purpose of getting the sound—Every sentence of his first tried as a
specimen sentence and for its sound."

Beyond this stage Quinn's diary notes are jumbled and scrappy,
for the most part undated, and impossible to fix in sequence. At
some point he heard from Russell the story of a wild young poet
named Joyce who, when Yeats asked him to read from his poems
at Russell's house, said to the master: " 'I will to amuse myself but
I warn you in time that I care not a straw what you think or say
about them.' " Quinn appears to have paid two visits to Yeats's
father and sisters in the family home in Dundrum, during one of
which he again met Synge. Lily Yeats showed a drawing by their
father of Willie at the age of three, looking remarkably like his
adult self, with the same long head and lock of black hair over his
forehead. Synge drove with Quinn to Æ's house in Rathgar, where
Quinn met Joyce's future Buck Mulligan, Oliver St. John Gogarty,
"a good looking well dressed young fellow," and a large party that
also included Count and Countess Markievicz, she the former Constance Gore-Booth and an image of beauty in a poem Yeats had
yet to write,[28] and he "a large fine looking chap looking like a
Center in an American Football Team." Before midnight Maud
Gonne came in "looking very charming." Before the evening was
over Russell told the story of Yeats's attending a *séance* with Kath-

arine Tynan, his early poetess friend, and being so efficiently seized that his hands stuck to the table, his head banged against the wall, and he was finally found on his knees reciting the first lines of *Paradise Lost:* "Of Man's first disobedience. . . ."

At Russell's Quinn told the group that for him the most interesting thing in Ireland had been the discovery that "all those who were denounced turned out to be very charming people." He commented several times in his journal on the habitual and brilliant malice in the conversation of Dubliners, and almost the last of his notes runs: "The only three men in Dublin who have not said sharp things about others are R. O. and H. [Russell, O'Grady, and Hyde]."

W. B. Yeats accompanied Quinn back to London in early November for the week that remained of Quinn's vacation, and laid himself out to show something of the city's cultural life. He introduced Quinn at the studio shared by Charles Ricketts and Charles Shannon, both of whom had been active in costuming and setting the plays which were Yeats's ruling passion in this period. Quinn met also the painter Lucien Pissarro, son of the great French impressionist painter Camille Pissarro. Lucien Pissarro and his wife, Esther, were proprietors of the Eragny Press, specializing in fine printing and binding, and Quinn was impressed with their work and much taken with both Lucien and Esther personally. He subscribed for a vellum copy of each of their titles as published, and subsequently saw something of them socially and professionally. He naturally also saw a good deal of Yeats's housemate in Woburn Buildings, the poet, critic, and sybarite Arthur Symons. Quinn found Symons's eclectic intellectuality imposing enough to lead him to describe him to Huneker as "the best critic in England since the death of Pater." [29] Yeats breakfasted with Quinn at the Carlton before driving with him to Waterloo Station to see him off on the boat train for Southampton. At breakfast he inscribed for Julia Quinn, now Mrs. Anderson, a copy of his Fisher Unwin *Poems* of 1904: "To my friend John Quinn's sister."

Quinn was a hardy sailor and he delighted in the "grand storms" which were encountered by the *St. Paul* on its way to New York. He also enjoyed the company of a gay, hard-drinking Polish baron at the captain's table. He wrote back to W. B. Yeats on November

29, to describe the rather heavy-handed fun attending the birth during the voyage of "a Polish Jewish kid" in the steerage. Quinn adopted the position that the child, being Jewish and a wanderer, ought to be "christened" St. Paul after the ship. He collected $62 by carrying about a subscription headed "In honor of St. Paul Dubrow born at sea November 16, 1904, citizen of the world, age one day, and in commemoration of the outcome from the mother of said child. . . ." Quinn and the baron led a procession of first-class passengers down to the hold, where many of the ladies were driven back by the stench. Quinn presented his scroll and his cash, and the baron made a speech to the parents in Polish and explained the symbolism of the name.

1905-1907

IN New York Quinn was soon hard at work in the law again. In his kind of work for banks and corporations the six or eight weeks at the turn of the year were likely to be frantically busy, with the casting up of accounts, stockholders' meetings, the issuance of annual statements, and so on. This year he had returned barely in time to step into the rush. He managed to get off a case of fine rye whiskey as a Christmas present for Jack Yeats. Acknowledging eventual receipt of the gift, Jack reported that because the label on the case had been torn and obscured the package had traveled blindly about the country before finding its way to him. " 'Try Applenoddy,' " somebody had written on the side, and Jack took pleasure in the invention. "That must be some visionary place—like Applepiecoombecrusty—but it has a cheerful, comfortable sound." [1] For many weeks in this winter and spring Quinn was busy every day and nearly every evening in what he called "a legal revolution," the struggle for the control of the great Equitable Life Assurance Society of the United States, of which the father of his partner Alexander was a high officer.

In the forty years before his death in 1899 Henry Baldwin Hyde had brought the Equitable from nothing to one of the three largest insurance companies in the world. When he died he left to his young son, James Hazen Hyde, just out of Harvard, 502 of the mere 1,000 shares of capital stock of the company, a fulcrum which carried absolute control of company policies and of a total of $400,000,000 in assets—but left his son and his fortune in the hands of trustees until he should reach the age of thirty in 1907.

The inexperienced young man and his immense assets, one of the largest bodies of liquid money in the country available for investment at the time, quickly caught the eye of the buccaneering financial dealers of the day, and James Hazen Hyde had soon been made a director of no fewer than forty-six companies, including nineteen banks and trust companies from New York to California.

Members of the Alexander family had been officers of the Equitable from its first days and had profited heavily. The present head of the clan, James W. Alexander, a director and one of young Hyde's trustees, fearing that Hyde and the Equitable assets were about to fall fatally into the hands of an alien and exploitative Wall Street group (including E. H. Harriman, whom Hyde had already invited into the directorate), and moved apparently both by conscience and by self-interest, decided to mount a campaign aimed at keeping control in what he saw as safer hands. In February 1905 he presented Hyde with a demand, signed by virtually every official of the company, that he give up his exclusive control of the Equitable and allow it to be "mutualized," and backed his ultimatum with charges of financial chicanery on the part of Hyde and his new Wall Street associates.

Flurried and hurt by accusations of wrongdoing when he had merely passively followed habits nearly universal in these impressionistic days of laissez-faire capitalism in America, Hyde temporized and retreated and proposed compromises as the big professionals in their Harriman, Hill, or Morgan factions fought each other more and more fiercely for control of the Equitable's tempting cash. In the upshot it was a merely medium-sized wolf, Thomas Fortune Ryan, who finally persuaded Hyde to sell him his 502 shares for only $2,500,000. Hyde retired to Paris, his real love.

The squabble which had begun quietly ended in a noisy scandal of earthquake proportions, shaking open the devious passages of manipulative high finance. Public demand for investigation of the Equitable's affairs, which was bound to involve scrutiny of insurance company financing generally and thereby draw in the country's greatest money men and the largest investment trusts and syndicates, forced Governor Higgins of New York to appoint a legislative investigating committee, the Armstrong Committee. The Committee's examining lawyer, Charles Evans Hughes, by his incisive, scrupulous, and implacable conduct of fifty-seven public hearings in the four months at the end of 1905, established his own reputation, ruined a good many other reputations that needed ruining, and prepared the way for a thorough reformation of insurance practice by legislative action in the first months of the following year.

Whoever else won or lost in such contests, lawyers were sure to profit. As an associate of the Alexanders and as legal adviser to Thomas Fortune Ryan, Quinn was powerfully placed, and his hard, brilliant work in this crisis carried him, at thirty-five, into the first rank of New York financial lawyers. Ever after, Quinn considered the Equitable affair as the decisive event in his legal career. When at last he could breathe more freely, he wrote grandly to W. B. Yeats on June 17, 1905: "The great legal fight I've been in for five months is over now; no more drums or guns or banners but now peace and the hospital and the 'strong smell of chloroform.' "

At the same interval he had been drawn by Yeats into ⹁ very different kind of legal problem, the sordid and difficult business of Maud Gonne's separation and divorce from her husband, John MacBride. Yeats wrote on January 14 to describe "the most painful affair of my life." He spoke in hushed tones of shock of the whole affair, shaken both by the ugliness of the facts and the suffering of the woman still so dear to him. For the sake of Maud, her child, and more or less innocent persons who had become involved with MacBride, and because the prominence of the principals was thought to involve even the good name of Ireland herself, Maud and Yeats and Lady Gregory, who had joined their councils, were resolved to tone down the issues as far as possible. Maud agreed to a quiet separation to keep the political peace, but MacBride, after first concurring, reneged at the terms of separation. It was then resolved to sue for full divorce.

Quinn was asked for his general advice about the conduct of the affair, and asked to do what he could at the American end. John MacBride had spent about three months in the United States in 1904, chiefly in Irish "patriot" circles. Quinn hired detectives to investigate his conduct during the visit and began collecting affidavits that might be of use in the suit against him. He had only fair success, for he met direct opposition from the Clan-na-Gael people, who were anxious to suppress anything scandalous that would soil the name of MacBride, a man so prominent in the "cause," a hero who had led an Irish brigade against England in the Boer War.

In the midst of these crises Quinn's lively transatlantic dialogue with the Irish writers and painters moved on briskly. Jack Yeats wrote of his work dealing with sporting and peasant life. In June he as illustrator and Synge as writer roamed the west of Ireland on commission for the *Manchester Guardian*, and Synge wrote his simple, loving, exquisite sketches of village and peasant life. In the summer Jack illustrated a republication of a volume of 1820, *The Fancy*, by Keats's friend John Hamilton Reynolds. Reynolds's verses in praise of pugilists might be found rather low matter by Edwardian critics, Jack wrote, but Keats himself "would have been prouder of a thick ear than a new sonnet." [2]

Sending Quinn a copy of Synge's *The Well of the Saints* on February 15, W. B. Yeats took time to sum up Synge's role as he saw it in the indigenous Irish theatre's struggle for recognition and respect. He foresaw for Synge's fullblooded art contests such as those that attended the first realistic plays of Ibsen. Synge he viewed as their nearest approach to a true "artistic personality," a genuinely original person, one who had "thought out or felt out a way of looking at the world peculiar to himself." Beside Synge, he said, Tom Moore appeared "merely an incarnate social ambition," and Clarence Mangan "differed merely from the impersonal ballad writers about him in being miserable." The Theatre Society itself was moving away from its old loose democratic organization at this time and, urged on by Russell, submitting itself to oligarchic and presumably more efficient control by Synge, Yeats, and Lady Gregory as a board of directors.

Yeats was constantly revising his three recent verse plays, *The King's Threshold*, *On Baile's Strand*, and *The Shadowy Waters*, after testing them in performance. His intimate friend Florence Farr Emery was to play Dectora in *The Shadowy Waters* for an audience of fifty Theosophists at the Court Theatre in London, and Yeats looked forward to seeing then a device suggested by Charles Ricketts, a glass harp lighted from within by electricity, "so that the harp will seem to burn with supernatural fire." [3] But he was more pleased at the natural fire that he was bringing into the play in rewriting. "It has become a simple passionate play," he wrote on September 16. "I am now correcting the last few lines, and have very joyfully got 'creaking shoes' and 'liquorice root' into what had been a very abstract passage." He went on to confirm his growing faith in "common idiom" and "common passion." That faith would dominate his aesthetics henceforward; it must have been nourished now by Chaucer, whom he was reading in William Morris's magnificent Kelmscott edition, a gift from Quinn and a few other friends.

Quinn now possessed John Butler Yeats's oil portraits of W. B. Yeats, John O'Leary, Standish O'Grady, and George Russell, all of whom he counted as friends, as well as numerous pencil drawings. He had the portraits photographed in New York and sent many prints to Dublin for circulation among the painter's family, friends, and prospective clients. On August 22 he commissioned a portrait of George Moore, but "not large," he cautioned. He was running short of wall space in his apartment and feared he might be driven to seek a house, a prospect uncongenial to his "Arab" feelings. J. B. Yeats's portrait of Douglas Hyde was languishing, and Quinn attributed the delay less to Hyde's reluctance to sit than to the painter's fecklessness and procrastination. Quinn recommended the example of Théophile Gautier's father, who locked his son in his study every day until he had finished an increment of *Mademoiselle de Maupin*. Quinn wanted the picture in advance of Hyde's American lectures, and he promised Mr. Yeats a bonus if he would hand it over in September, when Quinn proposed to visit Ireland. In fact, as Quinn was to learn later to his sorrow, he had had phenomenal luck thus far in extracting pictures from J. B. Yeats, who was a hard and steady worker but pathologically reluctant to declare a work finished and to relinquish his hold. W. B. Yeats described in his memoirs his father's setting out to paint a certain English pond in spring, then pursuing it through the cycle of the seasons till spring came round again, the painter still unsatisfied and the painting unfinished.[4]

Quinn and J. B. Yeats wrote copiously of literature as well as of art. Mr. Yeats had sent over plays of Padraic Colum's with strong praise, but Quinn found the work clever but shallow. He cited the superior example of one of his idols, Meredith, who had "wit, irony, 'the comic spirit' and heart. One must not be so afraid of 'heart' that one casts it out entirely." [5] In fact, he declared, he was generally dissatisfied with the Irish writing he was seeing. Current Irish work was "refined and full of emotion and of yearning and of imagination and of a faint beauty," but it lacked strength and solidity, lacked " 'fundamental brain-stuff,' " in Meredith's phrase. Quinn had been seeking and not finding something grand and epical from Ireland, "a big Irish Tolstoy's 'War and Peace' . . . or an Irish 'Anna Karenin'—something big and full of red blood and real brains." He suggested that George Moore was the man most likely to "become the Irish Balzac in at least one great book." But he thought all the Irish writers needed to steep themselves in such men as Cellini, Cervantes, and Rabelais, "and then turn to Ireland and study and live among the people till they know them. . . ." It is hard to tell in all of these ideas to what extent Quinn is merely seconding principles of W. B. Yeats. The echoic effect is strong.

Quinn was brooding at this time, in jocular terms but in sullen tones, on means of escaping what seemed to him the degrading necessity of paying customs duty on pictures he was importing. If a duty on works of art was itself immoral, as he believed, then to pay it was immoral and thus sinful, and to be avoided in the interest of the moral life. It was the line of reasoning which led, in the last ten years of Quinn's life, to his serial contests with customs and tax legislation affecting art and artists and their patrons. He was fighting with the problem almost till the day he died.

Of his own paintings, which were among those at issue, Æ wrote on July 24: "It is very good of you to want so many." He promised to reserve for Quinn "the best I have" among the pictures in his August exhibition. He spoke of anxiety over money for his family and complained of his own reluctance to work—though he had finished fifty pictures in the past year and a half. But his natural buoyancy and optimism kept showing through: ". . . there is no use in believing in God if one isn't cheerful." He described an idyllic fortnight in company with Padraic Colum in Donegal, he painting, Colum writing: "I used to hesitate between Rosses Point and Dunfanaghy in Donegal, but now I have plumped for Dunfanaghy and will go there when I die and sit on Breaghy Hill or Aughics Head watching the procession of the thoughts of God."

"Come over, please," Russell importuned Quinn at the end of this letter, and Lady Gregory and the Yeatses also urged him warmly. The players were planning a special performance for Quinn in return for his help and general good will, and he was invited to pick the plays he most wanted to see. Until late in the summer Quinn kept hoping to get away, but in September he had to admit it was out of the question this time. He was held close to New York by final details of what he called "the insurance fight" and by new business that was coming his way as a result of his enhanced reputation. "I suppose this is in America the modern counterpart of the tournament of old times, and it must have its own joys," Æ wrote forlornly on September 27. Quinn was trying to pretend to himself, as he could not have done a few years later, that he was not deeply committed to "business," not greatly involved in or troubled by the pressure of affairs. ". . . while I may seem to worry and be intense in business, in fact I'm not," he wrote nonchalantly to John Butler Yeats on August 22; "only I feel that while I am playing the game I might as well play it hard." But Russell, at least, was not fooled by this kind of talk: "I listened with my spine running cold to Jack Yeats's account of the hurry in America. . . . My poor John Quinn, to live in such a hurry." [6]

Quinn was much occupied, as well, with plans for Hyde's tour to commence in the late autumn, and with the interests of his Dublin friends at the Irish Industrial Exhibition held in Madison Square Garden in September. He had persuaded the managers of the show to import the Yeats sisters' Dun Emer products, especially their rugs, tapestries, table covers, and church vestments, and he bullied and persuaded his friends to buy. Something of the size of his young collection of Irish painting is suggested by the fact that he personally lent seventy-eight oils and water colors to the show, chiefly works of John Butler Yeats, Nathaniel Hone, George Russell, and Jack Yeats. On nameplates on the pictures of Jack Yeats, to parallel the "R.H.A." (Royal Hibernian Academy) of the others', Quinn parenthesized the initials "G.I.P."—to stand, as he wrote to Jack on October 13, for "Great Irish Painter."

Deprived of his vacation abroad, Quinn made do with local facilities. Mrs. Annie Smith had given up her Manhattan establishment and bought a big house on Sheepshead Bay, opposite Coney Island. She called her new place "The Calvert," and there Quinn often went for a meal or a weekend, alone or with a guest or two. Sometimes he camped out in a tent on the shore, taking his meals at the big house. At night it was pleasant to watch the lights of the big amusement park, more civilized then than now, across the water. At his apartment he had trained his Japanese boy to serve occasional small dinners; but Quinn liked even more to offer Sunday breakfast to a few good friends, in an easy lounging style followed by wine and cigars and talk of painting and writing. A feature of the summer was the wedding at Judge Martin J. Keogh's "country" place in New Rochelle of the beautiful Irish girl Eleanor Temple Emmet, a direct descendant of the great Robert Emmet. Quinn carried as his present one of Lily Yeats's Dun Emer tapestries and, relaxing his ordinary abstemiousness, drank more champagne than he had drunk in the whole year preceding.

He had made Judge Keogh, an eminent jurist and a cultivated and much-loved man, chairman of Douglas Hyde's American committee. For most of a year preceding and during Hyde's tour Quinn turned his own apartment virtually into an office for Hyde, with a special stenographer, and he gave from two to six hours daily to the cause. Hyde had been the first president of the National Literary Society in Ireland and president of the Gaelic League since its founding in 1893. The Gaelic League was hardly known in America and was regarded with suspicion by the older Irish societies, and Hyde's own name was known chiefly from W. B. Yeats's generous praise of him during his own tour. As a Protestant and an intellectual, Hyde was automatically suspect. But Quinn was resolved on the success of the tour, and he was a nearly irresistible force when so committed. To his close Jesuit friend Father John J. Wynne he wrote of Hyde: "While not a Catholic by birth or training, he understands the Church as well as one of her own sons and is altogether sympathetic and is the best Irishman that I ever knew, Catholic or not." [7] Quinn worked at first with Hyde's advance agent Thomas Concannon, but quickly grew impatient with him and took complete control of the enterprise. He confirmed Hyde's engagements to appear before Irish bodies all over the country, formed a local committee for each address, and worked out with each of them details of organization and publicity. He arranged a supplementary itinerary of college lectures for Hyde's personal benefit, and from thirty-one of these Hyde finally realized more than $3,000. Brushing aside Hyde's more populist notions, Quinn saw to it that the appeal of the lectures was pointed at the class of successful Irish-Americans who had money to give.

Success was not easily realized. Begging Irishmen had formed a long procession in the United States for many years, and Quinn noted to Judge Keogh that Hyde was competing with, among others, a traveling Irish band, a traveling Irish Ladies' Choir, a priest collecting for the Irish National Church at Spiddal, and another priest collecting for the O'Connell Memorial Church.[8] Hyde arrived in New York on November 15 and made his first major speech at Harvard on November 20, then followed W. B. Yeats's tracks to Washington for an audience with Theodore Roosevelt, a veteran Irish enthusiast. Quinn saw the president of the Associated Press to make sure that the interview was noticed nationally. For Hyde's big meeting at Carnegie Hall on Sunday, November 26, boxes had been auctioned for as much as $300 each, $3,250 being realized for the first tier of boxes. But one Finn, who had contracted for a score or more of boxes and 150 single seats, threw them up at the last minute, "apparently with the sinister intention of spoiling the meeting," as Hyde noted in his diary. John Quinn stood at the door and hustled holders of general admission tickets into the boxes to fill them up.

Hyde stumped the country after the smooth and elegant fashion that Quinn had arranged. Quinn wrote and telegraphed ahead to his local committees to make sure that the Hydes would be met, cosseted, and seen off wherever they stopped. Hyde offered a set of lectures expressive of his own special competences: "The Gaelic Revival," "The Last Three Centuries of Irish Literature," "The Poetic Literature of Ireland," and "The Folk Tale in Ireland." He was not a romantic spellbinder, like Yeats, but he made his own strong impression of candor, integrity, and serious scholarship, and contributions came forth at a satisfactory pace. Everywhere the Hydes were warmly entertained by Irish America, and presents including jewelry were pressed upon them to the point that Lucy Hyde began to be rather contemptuously amused at the open-handed Americans. In Boston, according to Hyde's diary entry of December 2: "Lucy was taken out by a committee of ladies, who whizzed her around the city in a motor car, to her intense terror, as she thought every minute would be her last." During intervals in New York the Hydes were entertained at Quinn's apartment, quietly or convivially according to their mood. He put them on board the *Celtic* at last in the middle of June with five big boxes of presents, including bearskins from himself, more than £11,000 "to run the agitation with," and more than £600 for Hyde's personal pocket. On March 9, 1905, when the trip was being planned Hyde had written: "Now, don't be bothering yourself over my trip or putting yourself to any trouble over it." In fact Quinn had given a year's hard work to Hyde and to the Irish language in the midst of a busy career, and Hyde told a fellow passenger on the way home that Quinn had personally spent "thousands of dollars" on them. Not surprisingly, the Hydes remained Quinn's firm friends until he died. Hyde's modest cause had been given a spectacular leg up, and the president of the Gaelic League returned to Ireland with a mantle of international celebrity. Sir Shane Leslie believes that Quinn had in effect, by this early establishment of his stature, "made" Douglas Hyde the eventual first president of Ireland.

Hyde's welcome home was royal. Dublin, Cork, and Kilkenny gave him the freedom of their cities. Hyde described to Quinn his tremendous popular reception in Dublin:

> The whole of O'Connell Street was packed from side to side, and from the Rotunda to below Nelson's Pillar, with one solid mass of people, and they all with one accord cheered for John Quinn, as well they might. I left nobody under any doubt as to whom the American success was due.　　　　[*July 24, 1906.*]

Most of Quinn's Irish friends sent him thanks and praise for his hard work for Hyde and for the cause of Ireland abroad. Standish O'Grady thanked him for "the tremendous great job of work you went through for the language," and complimented him at the same time for the correction of the Irish idea of Americans that Quinn was forcing by his example: ". . . are there many young American men like you?" he asked. Against the example of Quinn he still had to set that of "Boss" Croker, who was spending, by O'Grady's estimate, £7,000 a year on breeding horses in Ireland. "If only I had a seventh of it," he exclaimed, "to breed men and women!" [9] Russell also, typically, felt some philosophical reservations. Hyde, he thought, had achieved enough at home to entitle him to "beg" abroad in the name of Ireland, and he deserved Quinn's hard work and his own success, but he was depressed by the image of a procession of Irishmen crossing the Atlantic hat in hand. The country needed to work for her own salvation at home; it should have been possible to make such successes as Hyde's in Ireland. "A nation ought not to require explaining itself so often as Ireland," he thought sadly.[10] It was a feeling Quinn would soon come to share. Now he accepted Irish gratitude as his due for a task well done. But he saw as well, and wrote to W. B. Yeats to acknowledge, that gratitude needed to move in both directions. The cultural achievement, the eloquence, the warm personal presence of men such as Yeats and Hyde were winning respect in America not only for Ireland but also for the Irish "exiles," the Irish-Americans.[11] And they were bringing to a country that needed it an example of force and capacity grounded in a culture that was not merely Irish but continental.

But Quinn was tiring of the factionalism and the intellectual poverty of what he called "the little Irish" or loosely "the patriots" or "the pathriots," at home and abroad. He sickened of their jealousies, their self-service, their parochial smallmindedness, their windy rhetoric, their unreal visions of the Irish past and the Irish future, their general vulgarity of mind and manners. These qualities he attributed largely to the "medievalism," the repressive intellectual niggardliness of the Irish Catholic Church with its mortmain hold upon the minds of the people. The cultural movement in Ireland and in Irish-America would fail, he felt, until the powers of the Church could be diminished to the point where a free-minded education made possible a fit audience.

In various ways Quinn kept in touch with all the Yeatses throughout 1906. In January he wrote to beg Lily Yeats to nag her father to finish Quinn's portrait of George Moore. Quinn himself had had to maneuver Standish O'Grady into Mr. Yeats's studio, and had seen then and on other occasions what life was like there:

something closer to Plato's Academy than to the workshop of a busy painter meeting deadlines. The other daughter, Elizabeth, or "Lollie," became the third representative of the family to visit the United States and John Quinn, who entertained her for three weeks in the summer. She returned bearing Quinn's gift of cigars, "Delmonico's best," to her father, and he decorated a letter to Quinn in December with a pen sketch of "Clever Protestant curate, nationalist and home ruler, smoking an American cigar." On her train trip home from Queenstown (Cobh) to Kingsbridge, Lollie was pleased to be asked by a schoolboy who had read her name on her traveling bag, " 'Are ye anything to Mr. Jack B. Yeats?' " And later: " 'And there is another Mr. Yeats, isn't there, and he writes poetry?' " [12] Jack Yeats was designing a bookplate for Quinn's library in the form of a "buccaneer guardian" ferocious enough to intimidate borrowers. He promised to "make him look as if he was gnashing his eyeballs till they smoked." [13]

For the second successive summer Quinn was prevented from his trip abroad by exhaustion and the pressure of affairs. His brother, Jim, was sadly ailing in February and March of 1906, and Quinn tried to get to Ohio most weekends to see him, although he was preoccupied with Hyde and with the law. In March Jim Quinn died of tuberculosis, undiagnosed until nearly the end, in Julia Anderson's house in Fostoria. Quinn's family was reduced to his sisters Julia and Clara, the nun, and his uncle Jeremiah Quinlan, the priest. In July he enjoyed a visit in New York from Julia and Father Quinlan. He was staying close to the office for the most part, often working late into the evening and on weekends. He had resolved to strike out for himself, after eleven years in the offices of others, and on the first of August 1906 he did so, though his partners Alexander and Colby begged him to remain with them. He wrote to Florence Farr Emery on December 24: "I cut away in the summer from my former firm and opened up my own shop, and since that time I have been like the captain of a small battleship in action. I have had to be on the bridge almost constantly and have been able to take very little shore leave." Quinn was pleased enough with the figure to use it in most of his reports to his friends of his removal. He tended to get a great deal of mileage from his metaphors. His invaluable clerk and personal friend Thomas J. Curtin accompanied Quinn from the old shop to the new, which was on the thirteenth floor of the National Bank of Commerce Building at 31 Nassau Street, in lower Manhattan in reach of Wall Street. This address he was to occupy, with expanding éclat and prosperity, mounting tension, and a lengthening succession of partners, until the end of his career.

His shore leave in this busy summer was very short, and he took it piecemeal in his tent-camp on Sheepshead Bay. He was tired but happy and optimistic. He wrote to W. B. Yeats on July 13: ". . . I wanted to be free—and I feel free, like a boy out of school, more free and independent than I have felt in six years." He described his tenting expedition to Æ, who kept trying to lure him to Donegal, where Æ annually "rejoined his soul" after months in Dublin. Æ wrote back that he had found two hill farmers who read all his verse and another who read Browning. The marvelous equability, the free-flowing vigor and kindliness, of Russell's letters continued to enrich Quinn's life. John Butler Yeats gave splendid expression to Russell's quality of mind and heart in a letter at the end of the year: "He has the most lucid, humorous and magnanimous mind I ever met. The rest of us will have to stay a long time in Purgatory to get rid of our ingrained vicious habits of unfairness, but Russell will be allowed to pass on." [14] That kind of letter was an enrichment, too.

By this time Quinn was busy once again arranging the tour of a visiting artist, Florence Farr Emery. Yeats had proposed that he and Mrs. Emery make a joint tour, but Quinn dissuaded him: "This is, after all, a provincial people. . . . for you two to come would be too risky, too easily misunderstood." [15] So the handsome actress was to come alone, bringing her odd new art of "speaking to the psaltery," chanting passages of prose or verse to the accompaniment of an instrument designed for her by Arnold Dolmetsch. Performances were arranged at several places in New York and Boston, as well as in Buffalo, Chicago, and Toronto. As Quinn had predicted, after she had appeared a few times she was quickly invited to take on numerous new engagements, many of them in private homes of elegance. She described one of these in New York in the middle of March:

> You were quite right about the Colliers and they were quite charming. He and I sat at one end of a long table & she & Mark Twain at the other & all the women were beautiful. Mrs. Cushing

the artist's wife with red hair & black dress and white Gibson Girl face. Mrs. J. J. Astor & two other tall wonderful things in gold and black.

They got me to chant a few different specimens for about 40 minutes and all filed out shaking hands & [Norman] Hapgood said he'd call to give me letters to Boston and Collier was most intelligent about it all & they sent me home in an "electric"—I thought it was all over; I'd received so much praise and fervour. Lo! and behold next day a check arrived for $200.

Quinn and Florence Farr Emery warmed to each other and became at least sufficiently intimate to discover a mutual liking for stories of some raciness. When she sailed for home in April they were fast friends, and Quinn encouraged her to go through with her plan for a second American tour in the fall as "second" actress to Mrs. Patrick Campbell. But by that time she had received an offer to write weekly dramatic criticism in London and abandoned the idea of a tour. She and Quinn never met again, though they corresponded warmly until her death.

Julia Anderson was preparing for her first child during this winter of 1906–7, with the baby expected in April. With the four recent deaths in his family weighing on his mind, and convinced that at least two of those could have been prevented by intelligent medical diagnosis and care, Quinn took an anxious part in the preparations. He made a special trip to Fostoria in February to urge his sister to spend at least the final weeks of her pregnancy in a hospital. She agreed—fortunately, as it turned out. She had hardly entered a Cleveland hospital when eclampsia developed, with severe convulsions, and her little daughter was born on March 16. Julia was very ill, and Quinn stood tensely by as godfather while a priest was baptizing the child in one room and the husband and nuns and nurses sat with the unconscious mother. But all came right soon. The baby was christened Mary for her grandmother, and Quinn dubbed her also "the little actress" in honor of the stage favorite Mary Anderson. His new niece moved into his heart at once, and stayed there.

For Quinn and for his Irish friends the cultural crisis of 1907 was the bitter contest over the presentation in Dublin of John Millington Synge's comic masterpiece *The Playboy of the Western*

World. Quinn counted Synge a friend and liked him as a man, and on the basis of what he already knew of his work considered him the real genius of the new Irish theatre. He had strongly recommended Synge's work to his friends among New York literary journalists, especially to James Gibbons Huneker, Paul Elmer More, and Frederick James Gregg. He had also extended to Synge his flourishing if unofficial copyrighting service for Irish writers, getting out small private editions of *The Well of the Saints, In the Shadow of the Glen*, and *The Playboy of the Western World*. (In printing *The Playboy* the reference to the woman's undergarment, a "white shift," which had angered the Dublin audience, appeared in Quinn's working typescript as "shite shift," was altered by the American printer to "night shift," and finally set right.) When Quinn wrote to Synge to ask for manuscripts to add to his collection, Synge's reply shed interesting light on his methods of composition:

> As to my manuscripts, I work always with a typewriter—typing myself—so I suppose it has no value? I make a rough draft first and then work over it with a pen till it is nearly unreadable; then I make a clean draft again, adding whatever seems wanting, and so on. My final drafts—I letter them as I go along—were "G" for the first act, "I" for the second and "K" for the third! I really wrote parts of the last act more than eleven times, as I often took out individual scenes and worked on them separately. The MS., as it now stands, is a good deal written over, and some of it is in slips or strips only, cut from the earlier versions—so I do not know whether it has any interest for the collection.
>
> [*September 5, 1907.*]

Of course Quinn wanted the manuscript. Unfortunately, his friendship with Synge was given a short lease by Synge's tragic illness and early death. He had been ill since the *Playboy* riots of the winter with what Yeats diagnosed as bronchitis. Synge himself wrote in September in terms which pathetically suggested the real nature of his malady, Hodgkin's disease, which was to take him off in 1909 at the lamentably early age of thirty-eight: "I have been only middling the last six months or so, and I have to go into an hospital and have some swelled glands taken out of my neck in a few days. . . . After that, they say, I will be better." [16] Reporting on October 4 of the "success" of the operation, W. B. Yeats said that Synge's first words on coming out of the ether had delighted his doctor who knew his plays: " 'May God damn the English, they can't even swear without vulgarity.' "

Yeats wrote on February 18 to thank Quinn for his help to Florence Farr Emery and to report details of the *Playboy* row of the week of January 26, and its aftereffects, which had extended into the District Councils, one of which, far away in Gort, had passed a resolution forbidding the local workhouse children to picnic any longer on Lady Gregory's grounds, in reprisal for her share in Synge's insult to Irish dignity and propriety. Yeats was inclined to welcome the fight. "It has been for some time inevitable that the intellectual element here in Dublin should fall out with the more brainless patriotic element, and come into existence as a conscious force by doing so," he wrote. Summoned from a lecture in Scotland by Lady Gregory's telegram after *The Playboy* had been shouted down, Yeats had hurried back to Dublin and opened the theatre for a raging three-hour debate with the "patriots." He took a peculiar pleasure, as did Quinn, in the image of his old father addressing the hostile crowd as citizens of "a land of saints—of plaster saints." Later the image was to decorate his great poem "Beautiful Lofty Things." A copy of the play had strayed by unexplained chance into a convent school in Dundrum; the girls' plan to attend the play and thank Synge in a delegation was frustrated by the nuns who got wind of the affair. A doctor said to Synge at the second performance of the play: " 'I wish medical etiquette permitted me to go down and stand in front of that pit and point out, among the protesters in the name of Irish virtue, the patients I am treating for venereal disease.' " [17] The janitress of the theatre, who had been horrified by the appearance of the word "shift" in the play, said to the stage carpenter: " 'Isn't Mr. Synge a bloody old snot to write such a play?' " "I sympathize with injured innocence," Jack Yeats wrote in reporting the last incident to Quinn in a letter of March 12. "If you can't be innocent you can be injured anyway."

Such were the ironies of the situation, and it was easy to see them as comedy; but the issue was a crucial one for the theatre and for the new intellectual movement. W. B. Yeats was anxious for an American tour for the Abbey Company, and he earnestly hoped that Irish-Americans would not duplicate the shallow but violent animosities of the Dublin patriots. He proposed that Quinn publish *The Playboy* in America with a special introduction "explaining," perhaps a bit disingenuously, that

> the play means that if Ireland goes on losing her strong men by emigration at the present rate and submitting her will to every kind of political and religious dominion, the young men will grow so tame that the young girls will prefer any man of spirit, even though he has killed his father, to any one of them.
>
> [*February 18, 1907.*]

Yeats hoped that "American respect for intellect" would ultimately bring acceptance for the candor and thoughtfulness of Synge's work; on the other hand he feared that the sentimentalizing tendency of the American "exiles" might make them even more prone than the natives to take umbrage at any unflattering image of Ireland, which they tended to see "through clouds of tenderness."

Months of reflection on the incident convinced Yeats that the reaction against Synge was deeper in its roots, and more fundamentally intellectual, than they had at first supposed. "Nothing is ever persecuted but the intellect," he wrote Quinn sadly on October 4, "though it is never persecuted under its own name." What the people hated in Synge were exactly those qualities Yeats had thought would make him their truest artistic "personality": his "harsh, independent, heroical, clean, wind-swept view of things." Yeats hoped that Quinn might lead the American Irish to value that candor and integrity and throw away the worser cause. It was a good deal to ask, but the Dublin Irish had come to think of Quinn as a sort of miracle worker. On a visit home to Ireland in the summer of 1907 Francis Hackett visited the theatre and introduced himself to Synge and the Yeatses and to the players as an acquaintance of John Quinn's. He reported to Quinn on August 16: "W. G. Fay told wondrous tales about your Energy, Despatch, and Force. I foresee a John Quinn Myth."

In New York Quinn had already been involved in "fight after

fight" over the play and the sequels to its Dublin performance. The American Irish papers had reprinted the *Freeman* attacks, and quarrels ensued, even though hardly anyone had yet seen the text of the play itself. Returning to Manhattan on the train from a dinner party at Judge Keogh's, Quinn gave a copy to John Devoy, doughty editor of the influential *Gaelic American* and about to become Quinn's habitual antagonist, and tried to persuade Devoy to look at the play in a fair literary context, as mature comic art. After a trial, Devoy still found it disgraceful. Quinn was enraged now, as he always was, by amateur "criticism" of a work of art on largely irrelevant grounds, such grounds as the present political and moralistic ones. He sent Yeats on August 23 a sweeping condemnation from which he did not even bother to except Yeats:

> An Irishman can't ever be a sane critic. He can't criticize anything without thinking it fair to make it the basis of a personal attack. The true critic dissects a thing lovingly and carefully. The Irish critic goes at the subject of dissection like a drunken sailor, and with a shillelagh and a sledge-hammer batters the poor corpse all around the room, and when he has mashed the poor thing into an unrecognizable pulp, or thinks he has, he points to the poor mass and says it is only jelly or calls it poison, and then he thinks he has done something great. They are not critics; they are only scavengers.

When Yeats wrote on October 4 that ordinary Irishmen preferred "their clerical conservatory where the air is warm and damp," he spoke directly to one of Quinn's own prejudices. With his now customary violence and inclusiveness, Quinn attacked the Church as "the greatest curse in Ireland." [18] He saw the Irish branch as a travesty and a betrayal of the ideals of the true Church, and felt that it had disastrously twisted the Irish character, straitening the intellect, making Irishmen fearful and incapable of rational self-rule. "It has made moral cowards out of them," he had written Yeats on August 23,

> so that now nine-tenths of the Catholics' chief idea is to cringe their way into heaven on the coat-tails of some priest, and the most unworldly of churches, the follower of Him who said that

His kingdom was not of this world, has become autocratic and domineering and grasping.

It was the repressive "medievalism" of the Church, as he saw it, that kept Irishmen emotionally and intellectually immature and made them liable to run panting after a succession of chimeras. To Judge Keogh on July 3 he denounced what he called the "tinkering" habits of Irish thought, and he listed four of the main current gadgets: Plunkett's agrarian "fresh butter philosophy"; Hyde's "philological spring toward true happiness"; Yeats's and Lady Gregory's inspiring examples of ancient heroes; the priests' and Christian Brothers' "insurance company method, giving them paid-up soul policies for another world."

At the same time to Keogh he attacked his main political target of the moment, the nationalistic Sinn Fein movement, newly invigorated with the slogan "Ourselves Alone," which he viewed as a mere apotheosis of habitual Irish proviciality and anti-intellectualism. "Sinn Feinism, summed up, is simply organization taking the place of intellect," he said.[19] Set off by an article in the *North American Review* by Seumas McManus (called "Shame-us" by Quinn and other enemies), Quinn sent denunciations of the Sinn Fein theory to all his Irish friends. Not all of them agreed with him. T. W. Rolleston replied that at least Sinn Fein was doing the wholesome work of crippling the Parliamentarians (the Irish members of the British Parliament), whom he saw as the chief obstacle in the way of Home Rule. The temperate Æ wrote that the Sinn Feiners were at least doing more practical good than any other Irish party, and he defined the movement as "a substitution of an individual patriotism for patriotism by proxy, which is what parliamentarianism means." [20] Jack Yeats wrote pacifically that he admired the principles and the energy of the movement, though he found many of the individual Sinn Feiners hard to like. He cautioned Quinn against blanket generalizations about the Irish. "In a word, or in a lot of words," he wrote on September 16, "Ireland consists of drunkards, murderers, thieves, humbugs, ex-policemen, Unionists—and honest men." He went on to draw up, according to the typical "mistake of the English," a burlesque table of international stereotypes:

The French	Cowardly, untrustworthy, and light-minded.
The Spanish	Lazy, cruel, guitar players, and untrustworthy.
The Germans	Fat, and very untrustworthy.
The Americans	Unprincipled, rushing, untrustworthy, and very nasty.
The Japanese	Imitative.
The Irish	All the above, with the addition of not being funny any more.

In the prejudicial violence and inclusiveness of his antipathies Quinn was of course guilty of the same anti-intellectualism of which he was accusing the Irish. But his distaste had gone beyond the point where he could be swayed by such gentle counsels as Jack Yeats's or Russell's. He had been brought up by his father in Ohio to a general reverence for everything Irish, but his own exile's "clouds of tenderness" were now already pretty well dissipated. His early general affection was shrinking to a deep and loyal affection for a small circle of friends, whom he saw as untypical Irishmen. The *Playboy* disgrace, the repressiveness of the Church, and the squabbling factionalism of the Irish at home and in America had nearly wiped out his old uncritical admiration. "I used to think that I would like to live in Ireland sometime," he wrote to Lady Gregory on August 2, "but I don't feel so strongly that way now." He continued:

> If I went to Ireland I should take some place where I could come to see you occasionally, and where I could have Yeats and Russell stop with me at times. I wouldn't want to hear the chatter of Dublin. When I think of how you and Yeats have been treated, it makes me very discouraged about things Irish generally. . . . I

suppose Yeats has made up his mind that those cattle will not understand him and that he doesn't mind.

In several further pages he went on to specify at length the grounds of his disenchantment. Finally, he expressed a tepid hope that he might be able to come to Ireland for a visit in September.

His transatlantic cultural exchange continued during 1907, but at a pace diminished by the demands of his first year of private practice. He exported his own current enthusiasms by sending gifts of William James's *Pragmatism* and the five volumes of Santayana's *The Life of Reason*. Æ expressed appreciation of the James but characteristically preferred his *Varieties of Religious Experience*. Quinn had read Mrs. Florence Farr Emery's copy of Yeats's *Deirdre* when she was in New York, and Yeats had sent him his new version of *The Shadowy Waters*. Quinn was bold enough to suggest some structural flaws in *Deirdre*, and in *The Shadowy Waters*, amusingly, he singled out for objection the liquorice-root image that Yeats had introduced so gaily as a sign of his new realism; Quinn judged such lines "too homely for a dream play." Requesting the *Deirdre* manuscript from Yeats, he listed some of the manuscripts that would keep it company in his collection: three of William Morris's, John Davidson's *Ballads and Songs*, several Dowsons, William Carleton's *Autobiography*, page proofs of Lady Gregory's *Gods and Fighting Men* (Yeats's own gift to Quinn).

Quinn's collection of Irish paintings grew rapidly, especially through continued wholesale purchases of works of Russell and Jack Yeats. He ordered a new portrait of W. B. Yeats by his father; it had been six years since the earlier portrait, and he wanted an image of the new "more robust" Yeats. Lady Gregory sent him a photograph of Mancini's portrait of her for her nephew Hugh Lane's new gallery, another of the pictures Yeats was to praise in his great poem "The Municipal Gallery Revisited"; and Quinn was charmed by Yeats's account of Mancini's presenting him with a large chrysanthemum and the ejaculation in French, " 'The master is very tall—very beautiful.' " [21] Quinn also asked Yeats to pose for a major portrait by Charles Shannon, and he bought a portrait drawing that Augustus John had done for an etching to adorn Yeats's forthcoming eight-volume collected edition. John's drawings, Yeats said, exaggerated "every little hill and hollow of the face till one looks a gypsy, grown old in wickedness and hardship." [22]

So Quinn first heard of John, who became one of the most important persons in his life as a collector. Yeats presented John as a vivid half-wild creature with earrings and hair to his shoulders, who had been living "in perfect harmony" with two wives and their children. At Coole he had climbed to the top of the highest tree in the garden and carved a symbol that not even the athletic Robert Gregory could reach and read.

Young Gregory—whose death in the First World War would rouse Yeats to the most moving elegy in English since *Lycidas*—had recently taken a wife who came, like Augustus John, from Wales, and her youthful air of aristocracy had touched a fundamental sympathy in Yeats. He described Margaret Gregory's type to Quinn in the letter of October 4: "I sometimes think that the combination of joyous youthfulness with the simplicity and conscious dignity that make up what we call the great lady is the most beautiful thing in the world."

By August of 1907, when Quinn set up his vacation tent at Sheepshead, and what Rolleston called his personal "Act of Separation" was a year old, it was apparent that his independent law practice was to be a success. Æ was already wondering if it was too early to include him in the category of "rising millionaire." His first winter had been a busy one and Quinn was much in court, making his reputation as a brilliant compositor and deliverer of legal briefs. His office was a small one, and never grew large by Wall Street standards, but it was not, as he made clear, a "small-case office." His was the kind of practice that depended on the close acquaintance and warm personal and professional faith between himself and the officers of a few banks and commercial houses, whose affairs were anything but small. His work in the banking panic of the fall and winter of 1907–8 solidified the reputation as a financial lawyer which he had established in the Equitable Trust contest. "My bank," as he called it, the National Bank of Commerce, second largest in the country, had placed him on a handsome annual retainer, and he was hectically involved on its behalf in the crisis set off by the failure of the Knickerbocker Trust

Company, for which his bank was clearing agent. He hoped to be named one of the receivers of the Knickerbocker Trust, and was enraged when his friend Bourke Cockran maneuvered the post for his own father-in-law. "If I had got it I could have afforded to subsidize the Abbey Theatre for a year myself," Quinn wrote to Lady Gregory on December 10. The panic that followed the Knickerbocker failure Quinn blamed on "yellow journalism and yellow magazines and yellower statesmen." [23] In the midst of it all the big Arnold Print Works of North Adams, Massachusetts, of which the National Bank of Commerce was secured creditor for $2,200,000, went into receivership. The bank's security was attacked, and Quinn feared that the argument might have to go all the way to the Supreme Court. Father Jeremiah Quinlan lightened the tension a bit when he wrote from Illinois: "I see that money is tight in New York, but Hell is loose." Quinn thought the *mot* good enough to quote to most of his correspondents. Professionally all this was gratifying, but physically and psychologically it was exhausting, and it meant hard demanding labor every day and often into the small hours of the morning. Quinn began to apply to himself the favorite epithet of later years: he was "driven."

1908-1909

AT the end of the year the only members of the Yeats family who had not made the pilgrimage to New York were on the high seas. J. B. Yeats wrote in November to ask Quinn to receive him with his favorite, Lily. He was strongly minded to set up, at nearly seventy, in a new career in the new world. Quinn tried hard to talk him out of the idea, but the old man had "strong feeling" of his success and came ahead, using a purse provided for him by his Dublin friends. Quinn met Mr. Yeats and his daughter at the boat, saw them through customs, and established them in the Grand Union Hotel, near Grand Central Station. He continued to see as much of them as he could in this busy time, taking them about the city, entertaining them at his apartment, and introducing them to his friends. In January he gave a dinner at the Belmont for them and a party of twelve. On January 28 he reported to Florence Farr Emery that J. B. Yeats and Lily were proving themselves admirable visitors, taking America as it came, not complaining, like most travelers from Britain, of overheated rooms or iced water.

Quinn arranged for Mr. Yeats to sit at the end of the jury box to sketch Mrs. Evelyn Thaw while she was giving her testimony in the Stanford White murder case before the state Supreme Court; but when he went into the room at the end of the day Quinn found Yeats happily sketching from the distant seat where a court attendant had put him, having forgotten all about his reserved seat. Lily Yeats left for home in early June, after nearly six months in the city. But the elder Yeats lingered, reluctant to abandon the new life. He was getting a few commissions, often engineered by Quinn,

56

for portraits, especially for his velvety pencil drawings, which he did fairly easily and could offer for modest sums. And he was finding a market of sorts for his perhaps greater gift, his marvelous fund of pointed, original, and endlessly fluent talk. In the middle of February he lectured to the Sinn Fein Society of New York, and Quinn had Thomas Curtin take down his talk in shorthand. Mr. Yeats corrected the copy, and it was published in two columns of the editorial page of the *Evening Sun* with an appreciative editorial comment. On the evening of Sunday, March 25, Quinn and Mr. Yeats shared a platform to speak on Irish drama to the American Playgoers' Association, an audience of five or six hundred in the ballroom of the Astor Hotel. Quinn thought Mr. Yeats tended to sensationalize the rows in the Dublin theatre, and he did what he could to play them down, emphasizing the smallness of the points at issue.

Quinn himself was now drawn marginally into one of these rows. In the middle of February 1908, the New York papers announced that there would be coming from Ireland "the National Theatre Company, with W. B. Yeats, who acts with the company in the leading role." It was baffling news: when had Willie turned actor, and why had he sent no news of the tour? Quinn and J. B. Yeats and Lily went loyally down to meet the boat, and found not W. B. Yeats and the Abbey Theatre company but a small secessionist group of players headed by William Fay. Quinn had arranged a dinner and theatre party of eight for the first performance, and they went through with it, seeing eventually what Quinn thought was a very poor rendering of Yeats's *The Pot of Broth*. Quinn sent news of the affair to Yeats at once. Both he and Yeats were angry that the splinter group were trading on the reputation of the Abbey company, and putting its name in peril. Quinn taxed Fay with this motive, and secured his promise to make the identity of his company plain. He then began to harass Fay for royalty money for the plays of Yeats he was using, and things dragged on irritably this way for several months. Quinn quarreled by mail with Francis Hackett in Chicago because he blamed Hackett for complicity in Burns Mantle's interview with William Fay in which Fay said that he had quit the Abbey because the three established playwrights who headed it, Synge, Yeats, and Lady Gregory, were inhospitable to the work of new playwrights. Yeats printed a blunt refutation of the story on May 21 in the Dublin *Evening Mail*. Quinn demanded a correction of the Chicago version, and Mantle printed a second piece stating both "sides."

Though nobody knew it yet, J. B. Yeats was in New York to stay: he remained there until his death in 1922. He and Quinn became firm if not easy friends. Two natures so vivid and so different were bound to clash, and they did so frequently, with no fundamental damage to their mutual respect. Mr. Yeats called Quinn " 'the crossest man in the world and the kindest,' " [1] and in one of his frequent letters to Quinn he wrote on June 30: "I never in my whole experience was treated with so much kindness and *tenderness* as by you." In this spring and summer, still thinking of Mr. Yeats as a visitor, Quinn saw the old man as often as he could, introduced him to prospective clients, and gave him commissions of his own of various sizes. He entertained father and daughter often at dinner, and he sent Jack Yeats an account of one party that lasted until two-thirty in the morning. His guests were the Yeatses, the painters Ernest Lawson and George Luks and Luks's wife, Quinn's Harvard friend Townsend Walsh, and his journalist friend F. J. Gregg. Luks provided the main entertainment with imitations of a German band.

Quinn had bought J. B. Yeats's portrait of George Moore though it was not really finished. Now Quinn sat for portraits to Yeats's friend Luks and to Yeats himself, in pencil and oil. Like everyone else, he wanted a portrait to be a "likeness" which would also be a compliment; he liked none of these pictures, though he bought them. J. B. Yeats had promised to paint Quinn in two or at most three sittings. After "eight solid Sundays" of painting and repainting with no real progress, Quinn rebelled and issued an ultimatum: he would allow one more hour for the eyes, one hour for the hair, and so on. Mr. Yeats promised, but soon started painting out again. Quinn exploded and threatened to stick a knife through the picture. After further promises, mutual apologies, and cigars, the picture was "finished," though a friend said of it, "It has a rather worried look." [2] Quinn liked better Yeats's portrait of his houseboy, Sadajiro Kumatani. For portraiture Mr. Yeats liked to place his sitter at a considerable distance from his easel and walk back and forth between them—a style which had afforded him many opportunities for fine harangues back in his Dublin studio. Things went better, Quinn thought, after he insisted that subject and artist be brought closer together. Jack Yeats was amused to hear of Quinn's stratagem; he calculated that his father had walked thousands of miles while painting portraits.

Quinn's magisterial manner did not always work so well. When Quinn tried to direct Yeats's painting of his "visiting wife," Dorothy Coates, the old painter was so upset that he could not go on with the picture. Writing to Quinn on August 17, some days after the incident, he showed himself forgiving and conciliatory but still shaken:

> After a while it will dawn on you that it is only a Goth or a Philistine or *a man blinded* by too much *friendship* (like a fond mother with her growing boy) who would try to deprive an artist of his right to paint his own way.
>
> It will soon be revealed to you that the right is *inalienable* and that he *cannot be contracted* out of it.

Though he signed himself "Now yours in undying regard," his postscript showed the wound was deep: "Do you know that the other day my hands trembled so much I could scarcely hold my brushes, and even now on this recollection I can scarcely guide my pen—and it was nervousness not anger."

It was a lesson in manners and in the ways of art which Quinn's habit of command very much needed. He and J. B. Yeats progressed in friendship by trial and error. J. B. Yeats wrote Quinn frequently, sometimes several letters in a single day when he was intent on pursuing an idea, and these messages were of a quality to enrich any life, outflowings of a large and genial intelligence. Still, whereas his presence was a joy it was also a bother and an anxiety. Quinn felt responsible to him and to his children for the old man's well-being in America, and it was a care for which he had little enough time. When he wrote to the Yeats sisters at the end of 1908 to report that their "Pilgrim Father" was happy and well, he also said plaintively: "I didn't know that he intended to stay on here for the winter." [3] Æ, who found Dublin "desolate" without J. B. Yeats, suggested on October 1 that they cable him:

" 'Family all dying. Come to receive last messages' "; but nobody believed even that would bring him home.

Clear signs of the gravity of Synge's illness darkened the year for Quinn and for all his Irish friends. Synge sent him the *Playboy* manuscript in January, making little of its value and inviting the "Noble Buyer," as Jack Yeats had dubbed him, to set his own price. Quinn was also trying to work out a means of giving Synge fuller and more formal publication in the United States, and offered to guarantee the cost of plates if a publisher could be found. He also offered, to Yeats, to pay the cost of a stenographer for Synge in order that he could get as much as possible on paper in the time that was left him. Synge had begun work on a three-act *Deirdre* in prose and was finding the "saga people" fascinating but "remote" and difficult; he was trying to resist the temptation to "fall into rhetoric" as a substitute for intimate acquaintance with his personæ.[4] He promised Quinn the manuscript of the play when it was done. Quinn agreed to scrutinize the publishing contract with Dutton. In the spring Synge had been well enough to conduct rehearsals in the theatre, but on May 1 Yeats reported ominously that he was back in the hospital for the removal of "a lump in his side." In the middle of June Lady Gregory found him cheerfully eating roast beef and potatoes; but he was by no means well enough to accept Quinn's invitation to conduct his convalescence in New York. In a letter of June 10 to Yeats Quinn spoke of him gloomily but accurately as "doomed." Yeats was still resisting the idea that Synge must perish. Thinking sadly of his friend's illness and his ill success in Ireland, his history of pearls before swine, Quinn quoted Lecky on Flood: " 'The curse of Swift was upon him, to have been born an Irishman and a man of genius and to have used his talents for his country's good.' "[5] It was probably the helpless wasting of the life of Synge, a man so valuable and so near his own age, that moved Quinn to a confused but interesting piece of synopsis and sentiment which he sent to Yeats on August 5:

> . . . I see things a little more clearly than I did some years ago. Poetry and the arts and books and pictures and statuary and music and even a wife and babies now seem to me to be the opium of life. The real persons that I honor are men of science and physicians and surgeons, who work for the relief of humanity's suffering

and pain and who live unselfish lives . . . for the good of others.
. . . if I were beginning life over again, I would train myself to
be one of these men. . . . I haven't joined any religious order and
I haven't broken down in health and I am not yet an old man. I
am just at the threshold of early middle age, and this isn't a
whine or an appeal for mercy; it is simply the recognition which
comes to everybody in the middle of the fight that after all very
little matters and that the great things in life are not justice or
success but kindness and mercy.

Yeats was being much limned in connection with the forthcoming eight-volume A. H. Bullen edition of his works. Quinn had
bought and given away about two dozen sets of the American two-
volume edition, and he now placed a preliminary order for four
sets of the new edition. He also purchased for his own collection
virtually all the new Yeats portraits that were going. In addition
to the Augustus John and the second J. B. Yeats, he now bought
the Shannon oil and a Sargent chalk drawing. When he ultimately
received the Sargent he admired its clarity and precision "like a
piece of marble." [6] Shannon also had done a fine drawing, but
Yeats said that unfortunately it looked "most damnably like
Keats." [7] Yeats had enjoyed all the picture-making, especially the
sittings for John, Mancini, and Sargent. Sargent he described on
April 27 as "good company, not so much like an artist as like some
wise, wealthy man of business who had lived with artists." Yeats
playfully proposed to group four of the portraits, his father's
"emaciated" version seen "through a mist of domestic emotion";
Mancini's Yeats, "half bandit-half cafe king"; John's "sheer tinker,
drunken, unpleasant and disreputable"; and Shannon's "idealist."
Then he would write an essay describing them as "all the different
personages that I have dreamt of being but have never had the
time for." [8]

W. B. Yeats had been happily busy for months on the texts of
his poems and plays for the big new edition. Always a restless
and brilliant improver of his own work, he now discovered with
delight the device of appendices, which let him continue revising
right up to press time. But he was writing an occasional lyric also,
and was working at *The Player Queen* for Mrs. Patrick Campbell,
stimulated by her offer to post herself at his elbow to advise on

practical questions of stagecraft. In the fall her performance of his *Deirdre* gave him his first big success in the theatre, with "great audiences and great enthusiasm," [9] and Yeats was touched and excited. He wrote to Quinn of these matters and to report on the new general prosperity of the Abbey. And he spoke of the continuing irony of the composition of their audience: "All the praise we have had from the most intellectual critics cannot bring the Irish educated classes and all the abuse we have had from the least intellectual cannot keep the less educated classes away." [10] But Quinn was out of sympathy with the theatre now. It was killing Synge he thought, and keeping Yeats from his "real work," lyric poetry. "Damn the theatre, anyway!" he wrote to Florence Farr Emery, who was soon to turn her own back upon it dramatically.[11]

George Russell had taken his annual painting holiday in June in a cottage on a hill in Donegal from which he could see seven seas. He reported that he was painting happily from morning to night, without news or ideas, and with "the healthy stupidity of a cow." "I find myself sinking deeper into the life of the rocks and the people," he wrote on June 23, "understanding them without thought." He tried the experiment of showing some of his prolific production in London and found that his pictures sold equally easily and at three times the prices of Dublin. And he recounted a half-hour's conversation in the Dublin National Gallery with an animated elderly man whom he thought "an immensely intelligent person," and whom he later identified as George Bernard Shaw, passing through Dublin for the first time in thirty-five years.

Quinn yearned for more of the landscapes of Nathaniel Hone, which were much admired in his New York apartment, and which he found particularly satisfying to his own spirit. They were images to which he could return for a "pure" view of Ireland. He asked Russell's help, and Russell agreed, but warned Quinn that Hone was wealthy, painted slowly, liked his own pictures, and sold them far more easily than he wished. Quinn wrote directly to Hone of his admiration, reminded him of his visit four years earlier in company with J. B. Yeats in which he had bought Hone's *Bundoran Rocks,* and asked permission for Æ to select three or four new pictures within a range of thirty to fifty pounds each. Hone agreed to relinquish five canvases, and these, with *Bundoran*

Rocks and two others acquired in intervening years, gave him a total of eight first-rate works of the old academician who had trained with the Barbizon painters.

Both Russell's and Yeats's letters of this period to Quinn are sprinkled with half-angry, half-amused references to George Moore's "farewell book," which was rumored to be a parting curse upon Ireland to take the form of a "novel" with real characters all appearing under their own names. Moore was allowing titillating glimpses at the manuscript of what would be in a few years the three volumes of the discursive and delightful *Hail and Farewell.* Æ called it good-humoredly "the most impudent book of the century" [12] and retailed Moore's boast that half the people in Dublin were afraid they would appear in the book and the other half were afraid they would be left out. Yeats's more malicious gossip estimated that Moore had only two friends remaining in Dublin, Russell and John Eglinton, "the two most virtuous members of the community." [13] He described Moore (who likened Yeats to an umbrella left behind at a picnic) as looking "more and more like a sick chaffinch or starling, I don't quite know which, for a starling isn't right in the colour and a chaffinch has not the perfect droop of the head."

Lady Gregory tended to stand outside all this sniping. She was busy with her own writing and with the life of her son and his new bride. Quinn had secured the American copyright of her play *The Gaol Gate* by inducing John Devoy to print it in the *Gaelic American,* and he had tried and failed to sell to American magazines her essay on the making of myths. She wrote in late June that she felt the need of notepaper stamped " 'Grateful thanks to John Quinn,' " [14] and her letter of a month later is headed in capital letters, "THANKS TO JOHN QUINN FOR. . . ." [15]

In July, wearing what he described to Florence Farr Emery as "a long, passionate-looking, yellow pongee duster and motor-car coat," [16] Quinn made the long train trip to the Democratic National Convention in Denver. As an elected delegate of New York and a Tammany stalwart, Quinn went west a week early to do a bit of pre-convention lobbying among southern and western delegates. He hoped for the nomination of a fresh candidate, such as Governor Johnson of Minnesota, but feared that the choice

would again be Bryan, whom he dismissed in the language of convention rhetoric as "nothing but a champion of lost causes and an
apostle of defeat." [17] Quinn's political ideals were far more than
merely partisan. Writing to Rolleston on June 25, the day after
the death of former President Grover Cleveland, he looked back
to Cleveland's administration as admirably dignified and strong-
minded. Compared to Cleveland, he felt, even his friend Roosevelt
had conducted public affairs in a rather noisy and vulgar fashion.
Still, when the "windbag" Bryan was nominated, Quinn went to
work for his election. Hearing of these activities, Æ took them as
fulfillment of his prophecy that Quinn was destined to turn to a
career in politics. "I had a kind of clairvoyant vision of your future," he wrote Quinn on October 1, "pulling endless wires with
unending energy. . . ." But Quinn had already made a resolve never
to become a candidate for office. His reasons are visible in the terms
of his congratulations to Rolleston, who had just refused a public
post: "It is wonderful how free a man becomes and feels when he
throws away ambition to be elected to office. . . . A man who has
got the office-holding habit or is afraid of public opinion, really
isn't a free man." [18]

Back in New York after the convention, Quinn was embarrassed
by reports in the *World* and the *Sun* that he had been "advising"
the Tammany chief Charles F. Murphy in Denver. The accounts
had been phrased, apparently, by journalistic friends wishing to
give a puff to what they took to be his political aspirations. Quinn
hastened to write to Judge Victor J. Dowling and other Democratic regulars to deny both the aspiration and the responsibility
for the writers' view of his role. A month or so later he was
approached by Murphy and Daniel Cohalan and pressed to accept
the chairmanship for the east of the Democratic National Committee. Quinn was flattered and tempted, but still more fearful. To
take the post he would have had in effect to abandon his practice
for several months, and he was by no means sure that it would be
there when he came back. Officers of the Equitable Trust advised
him against the move, and that was enough to confirm Quinn's
misgivings. At the end of August he declined the offer, but agreed
to serve on the national Advisory Committee, which meant a
"mere" few hours' work a day.

Quite clearly, with the presidential campaign stacked on top of his law work, Quinn could hardly dream of another trip abroad in the summer or autumn, though he was if anything more strongly tempted than usual. Dorothy Coates was in Paris, and Maud Gonne had looked her up at Quinn's suggestion, and they were touring the museums and picture galleries. He would have liked to join them, or to see Florence Farr Emery in London. And Lucien Pissarro sent him an attractive invitation in June to make an entrée into the London art world by means of meetings at Walter Sickert's co-operative studio in Fitzroy Street, gatherings of artists and amateurs including the great Augustus John. Ireland drew him far less seductively now. But it was all out of the question anyway. He had had another hard, successful year, and it was not easy to extract himself from the press—and he trusted nobody to take his place. An arch but suggestive glimpse at the texture of Quinn's days, at least of some of them, is afforded by a letter of June 1 from William Bulfin, journalist and author of one of Quinn's favorite books of Irish travels, *Rambles in Eirinn*:

> I wonder if you ever read how you struck my observation, what time we floated around Broadway and adjacent territories fixing up some cotton catastrophe? You did the fixing, I the attendant admiration thereof. We talked sagas, and Irish-Ireland, and the prose of Lady Gregory, and the loveableness of intellectual Ireland, and the sins of the New York snow, and the poetry of Yeats, and one thing and another, while we went from office to office.

When Quinn invited John Butler Yeats on December 20 to join a dinner party at Delmonico's for Sir Horace Plunkett, he said that the three days' rest he hoped for at Christmas would be his longest rest in a year.

Death came at last to Synge on March 24, 1909. Quinn did not learn of it until a week later, and then casually from a man in his office who had had a clipping from Dublin. He was hurt that no one in Ireland had thought to cable him. But he set to work to secure appropriate American notice of Synge's life and death. By now Quinn had collected a little group of newspaper men on whom he could rely for publicity: John Devoy of the *Gaelic American*, William Bulfin of the *Southern Cross* in Buenos Aires, Francis

Hackett of the Chicago *Evening Post,* Paul Elmer More of the *New York Evening Post,* James Huneker of the *Morning Sun,* and Yeats's old school friend, now one of Quinn's closest intimates, Frederick James Gregg of the *Evening Sun.* He got Huneker and Gregg to work on commemorative articles, and he himself dictated a hasty memorandum in appreciation of Synge which he sent off unedited to Gregg, who printed it as it stood. Quinn sent a clipping of his notice to W. B. Yeats, and the people of the Abbey Theatre liked it so much that they printed it in their program. He asked John Butler Yeats to come to his office and dictate a statement, and that too Gregg printed in the *Evening Sun.* Of Huneker's Sunday *Sun* article on Synge Quinn bought fifty copies and sent many of them abroad.

Quinn owned two drawings of the playwright by J. B. Yeats, one of them especially impressive and engaging, showing Synge looking handsome and Black Irish, ironically robust with arms folded across his chest, and the face full of humor, intelligence, and brooding force. Quinn offered the drawings and a sum of money in the hope that the people in Ireland would commission a bust for the Abbey Theatre or the National Gallery. W. B. Yeats was preparing his eloquent diary of the death of Synge, and was otherwise busy with the dead man's affairs, which were in a parlous state because of Synge's confused instructions. Members of his family who held his papers were Plymouth Brethren, the fundamentalist sect so hauntingly presented in Edmund Gosse's *Father and Son.* They talked of suppressing or censoriously editing what remained in their hands. Synge had sent for Yeats to make final disposition of his writings, but had died in the night before Yeats was to arrive. Now Yeats was struggling with the manuscript of the "magnificent" but still unfinished *Deirdre.* Quinn had an interest in that too, which it was awkward to express, for Synge had promised him the manuscript when it was finished.

Quinn now tried to persuade Jack Yeats also to write on Synge, as the man who knew him best in his habit as he lived. He cited again his favorite quotation from George Borrow, which he had appended to his letter in the *Sun,* and which he was likely to introduce in any hospitable context: " 'There's a wind on the heath, brother. Life is sweet. Who would wish to die?' " [19] For Jack

Yeats Quinn recalled dining with Synge at John Butler Yeats's house in Dublin, driving with him in a side-car to Russell's for an evening of fine talk, then walking with him back into Dublin after one o'clock in the morning. In his letter of April 15, he suggested the kind of thing Jack might write:

> . . . something to show what a simple, natural man he was; something to dispel the idea that he was decadent or morbid, and to show that he really loved the people and that his observation of them was true and just and honest, and how he disliked buncombe and the flattery that is so prevalent in Irish affairs, self-flattery and flattery of others.

It is one of the most winning of Quinn's own statements, and full of an unconscious wistful self-reference. Doubtless it owed something to J. B. Yeats's opinion in a note of April 4: "He was the very reverse of decadent. He respected all the Commandments, even the much-abused Seventh. He was essentially an orderly man, with unlimited indulgence for the disorderly."

In the midst of weeks of hard legal work on the merger of the Equitable Trust and the Bowling Green Trust, Quinn found time to serve the name of Synge in America by bringing out another of his little copyrighting editions. He took the text of Synge's *Poems and Translations* from the Yeats sisters' Cuala Press edition, "corrected" the punctuation as he always felt constrained to do, and ordered it done by his own printer in an edition of fifty copies, forty-five on handmade paper and five on vellum. When he saw the result he found new errors in the text, bought more paper, and had the whole thing done over. Now he sent copies of his elegant little edition broadcast among his friends and Synge's, taking particular pleasure in the vellum copy that went to Synge's fiancée, the Abbey actress Mollie Allgood.

The life and death of Synge had moved Quinn with a poignancy that is surprising and suggestive. It is clear he not only liked and admired Synge but also subconsciously saw in him a form of himself. The Irishman and the artist *manqué* in Quinn reached out and identified with Synge and found there a nature and a view of the world which he recognized, or wished to recognize, as his own. Quinn's vein of latent, perhaps Irish, self-pity was tapped by the

circumstances of Synge's career, as he saw them. Writing to W. B.
Yeats in mid-April he was moved by the death to draw up a melancholy little rollcalling statement on the passage of time and his own
homely ethical view:

> All we can do is to do our own work, write as well as we can,
> give a lift to a friend when we can, do as little harm as we can,
> see that nobody is worse off or has suffered by our existence, and
> try to play the part of a man.   [*April 16, 1909.*]

Quinn's typically Irish mistrust of Ireland made him see Synge
as a victim of Irish, specifically Catholic, hatred of intellect. He
saw Synge as a martyr, a kind of lay Christ-figure. He wrote to
Frank Hugh O'Donnell:

> He gave her what she needed—the truth as he saw it. He was not
> a liar, nor was he a flatterer, and so the Irish turned on him and
> abused him and assailed him as bitterly as though he had betrayed
> his country. . . . But because Synge didn't paint all Irishwomen as
> the milk fed lambs of the convent schools and Irishmen in green
> breeches and with Robert Emmet's dying speeches on their lips,
> he was reviled as a bad Irishman and as a traducer of his country-
> men. . . .   [*? May 1909.*]

In fact Quinn had begun to take a romantic satisfaction in mor-
bidly overdrawing Synge's difficulties. With his usual good sense,
Æ warned him away from that view, argued that Synge had never
been widely unpopular or personally persecuted, and reminded him
that *Riders to the Sea* had been applauded every evening before
The Playboy of the Western World came on. Russell reasoned that
the *Playboy* itself would have been found quite acceptable if the
actors had played it more for poetry and fantasy, less for realism.[20]
But Quinn would not have it so, and he felt his reading of Synge's
case confirmed in the subsequent maltreatment of the *Playboy* in
the United States.

Quinn's personal anti-clericalism was being further heated by
what he heard from abroad of the Irish Bishops' efforts to make
sure that the new National University would take the form of a
Catholic and parochial institution. T. W. Rolleston wrote him
sweepingly of the power of Maynooth:

Its really amazing, when you come to think of it, how stead-
fastly and consistently, since the cursing of Tara to the latest
pronouncement on the Irish language in the University, the
Church in Ireland has set itself to enfeeble and devitalize all Irish
secular life. Will there ever be a day of awakening and of reckon-
ing?   [*January 28, 1909.*]

A heartening sign of awakening appeared in the appointment of
Douglas Hyde to the chair of Modern Irish Language and Literature and of John MacNeill, his second in the Gaelic League, to
the chair of Early Irish History, both against strong clerical opposition. Hyde began at once to push the Gaelic League ideal of making the Irish language a compulsory course of study. Quinn was so
interested in the struggle, which raged through the first academic
year, that he sent repeated inquiring cables. Hyde was able to report triumphantly on June 26 of 1910 that from 1913 on every
matriculating student would have to prove his command of Irish,
which meant that the language would have to be taught in the
schools. He considered it the greatest victory of the Gaelic League,
and attributed it largely to the American money Quinn had helped
him to raise. The members of the League wanted to present Quinn
with a banquet and an address, and Hyde begged him not to slip
out of Dublin again without showing himself for this honor.

Quinn's letter of January 14, 1910, to Hyde revealed some of
his own demanding views of higher education. He was proud that
he had been required to present for matriculation at the University
of Michigan, "in that wild and uncultivated and money-grubbing
. . . country," four years of Latin, two of Greek, and four of
mathematics, that all three were required studies in the first year,
and that only one of them could be dropped in the second year.
He was contemptuous of the elective system at Harvard under
President Eliot and felt that Harvard was turning out a great many
half-educated men. Hyde's victory on the language question was
grounds for congratulations in so far as it might promote intellectual rigor—though Quinn suspected that Hyde's doctrinaire insistence on the language was anachronistic and would prove imprac-
tical. The true issue in any case, he insisted, was intellectual liberty:
would the University grant freedom of inquiry or would it submit
to clerical domination?

At the beginning of 1909 Quinn had paid Charles Shannon £100 for his portrait of Yeats, which was also to serve as a frontispiece for one of the handsome A. H. Bullen volumes. Yeats was surprised to see that Shannon's likeness brought out his resemblance to his mother and her family. "This is often so with paintings where there has been sincere work," he wrote to Quinn. "The painter seems to rummage through all one's ancestors." [21] In this year Quinn also bought from Shannon for £360 two additional paintings, *Summer* and *The Sapphire Bay*. His purchases were moving into a higher bracket. The paintings which Æ had extracted from the reluctant Hone were sent over in the spring, though Æ liked them so much himself that he was sad to see them leave Ireland. Russell was pushing another of his literary protégés, James Stephens, for Quinn's patronage, and sent him as a sample Stephens's *Insurrections*. Quinn was interested and ready to see more of Stephens. Russell continued his nervously humorous account of George Moore's progress with his "farewell book." Moore told Æ that he had just written 2,000 words about him but refused to show them. "Anyhow," Æ wrote, "we are good friends and I don't think he intends to say anything very hard. I think probably he is keeping most of his satire for the Church and W. B. Y." [22] Moore had visited Jack Yeats's show at a Dublin gallery and they had "swopped compliments," as Jack put it in his letter of May 21: Jack told Moore how much he admired *Esther Waters*, and Moore told him how much his painting reminded him of the novel.

Quinn was determined to get abroad in 1909. It was five years since his last trip, and this year he had been steadily overworked—"driven"—and intermittently ill. Writing in January, Lady Gregory chided him for letting himself get caught up in politics. "There are plenty of politicians," she said, "and there is but one John Quinn, the sympathetic, large-hearted, intellectual and gracious helper and providence of some at least who are worth it." [23] When she invited Quinn to "come back here and get strong and well and put new life and courage into us," she suggested something of Quinn's look to his Irish friends and something of their reason for valuing him. He was the man of energy from the new land, counted upon to work tirelessly at home for their common causes and to bring abroad an occasional charge of his miraculous force. This was what Francis Hackett meant by "the John Quinn Myth." But

Quinn and his Irish friends knew it was too simple and too sentimental a view of their relationship. Quinn was aware that his intellectual hunger was feeding richly, and that he took at least as much as he gave in his Irish affections. Equally it was clear, hypochondria aside, that he would soon have to cut down on his unselfish services to Irishmen and their personal and public causes. He was too busy and too tired. W. B. Yeats's warning of January 12 was both kind and prophetic: "Do not give so much time to the mechanism of life that you have no time for life itself. You will be a millionaire when you are fifty, but you will have spoilt your digestion. . . ." Quinn's digestion of things Irish was already more dyspeptic than even his best Irish friends realized. "I am sick of the Irish," he wrote bluntly to Townsend Walsh on July 20.

> They are suspicious, vindictive, uncertain in temper, ungrateful, lying. Ten years ago if a man said that to me I would feel like knocking him down. Five years ago it was told to me and I resented it. Today experience has taught me that it is the fact.

Most of this experience, of course, was New York experience. In New York, it seemed to him, he found the Irish chiefly in attitudes of supplication or vilification.

Since the beginning of the year he had been trying to persuade John Butler Yeats to abandon his American venture and accompany him back to Ireland, Quinn paying his passage. On January 18 Mr. Yeats "accepted" Quinn's offer and thanked him in handsome terms: "You are generous in such an ample way and with such superfluity of consideration for my feelings as well as interests, which makes me love your lawyer-like precision." But he soon began to hedge and to predict success for himself if only he could get a fair start-off. The Americans were "a swift people," once moved. Though he was far from paying his way, he seemed to be making a miniature career as a lecturer, to club and college audiences, on painting, on Ireland, on good and bad conversation. Quinn told Gregg, rather unfairly, that J. B. Yeats measured conversation as good or bad according to the proportion of acquiescence and dissent to his own views. J. B. Yeats's was a positive, optimistic nature, and so long as there was opportunity to talk and to paint he required very little of the ordinary furniture of life. He was quite capable of living whole days on nothing but apples. But at dinner in the middle of May Quinn found him looking cheerful and natty in a new blue suit, a new soft brown felt hat, and new shoes, all of unexplained provenance. Quinn wrote on May 15 to W. B. Yeats that his father might easily have made a good general, with Wellington's tenacity and the buoyancy of Chesterton or Shaw. In the end Quinn sailed without him.

Planting trees at Coole for her new grandson, Lady Gregory had written that what Quinn needed for a restoration of soul was to spend a summer there as she and Yeats did, alone with the fields, the woods, and the lake. But Quinn told Townsend Walsh that if he went to Ireland at all it would be for only a day. He had only three weeks to spend, and he aimed to divide them between Paris and London and to see as much as he could of painters and paintings. Though he was as yet barely aware of it, the plan expressed a fundamental shift in his own taste: away from Ireland and toward the Continent, away from literature and toward art. He promised Huneker, however, that he would see Arthur Symons in London and George Moore in Dublin. He sailed for Cherbourg on the *Amerika* on July 24 with a parcel of books of George Borrow's for his stateroom.

In the upshot London took most of his time. Quinn was particularly concerned about Arthur Symons, who had gone out of his head in Italy and was thought to be dangerously ill. Yeats had visited him in his nursing home in London in January and predicted that he could not live more than a few months. Symons was weak and raving, and one of his delusions was that he was in Paradise, charged with preparing a reception for Swinburne—who in fact died about a month later. Quinn wrote to Yeats to offer to contribute to the support of Rhoda, Symons's actress wife. But by May Symons was improved enough to go about with a "keeper," and by midsummer he was circulating freely again, though still considered vaguely doomed. (He lived on till 1946.) Quinn diagnosed syphilis. In August he saw Symons constantly in London, and he described him to Townsend Walsh in September as "as sane as I am," though more egotistical and impatient of his own will than formerly: "I defined him to a friend of his and mine as a Little Lord Fauntleroy satyr." [24] The friend might have been either Augustus John or Agnes Tobin, the young poetess from San Francisco who had formed intimacies with many writers and artists in

England. Quinn had made John's acquaintance promptly and warmed at once to the man who would soon be a good friend and a tutor of his taste. To Walsh he called him "one of the most interesting men I have ever met," and rated him as "probably the greatest painter in England after Sargeant [*sic*]." [25] Quinn introduced John to Symons. To meet Symons was to meet Agnes Tobin, who was constantly with him. The four of them quickly clubbed together for tours of studios and galleries as well as for a great deal of more or less sedate conviviality. The Café Royal in Regent Street was their most frequent resort.

John made a number of drawings of Quinn, one of which was called by a friend the portrait of a hanging judge, and Quinn soon commissioned him to do a formal portrait in oil. Quinn had had a troublesome tooth crowned in New York before sailing and in London it became abscessed and finally had to be extracted, leaving his jaw swollen and uncomfortable. This and other circumstances complicated the sittings, of which there were four. On the fourth day, when John was to finish the picture, Quinn came to the studio with Symons and Agnes Tobin. Symons planned to have John do a drawing of him. John had hardly picked up his brushes to resume work on Quinn's portrait, according to Quinn's story, when Miss Tobin glanced at the canvas, declared it perfect, " 'at the razor's edge,' " and begged John not to touch it further. Symons begged for his drawing, then John got drunk, and the portrait was perforce "finished." [26] The portrait presented Quinn at two-thirds length, seated, with his left hand on his hip and his right hand extended, resting on a cane. It is not an engaging likeness. Both face and figure seem bulbous and out of scale, and the countenance stares ahead with an air that is curiously vague and coarse at the same time. Quinn felt baffled and unhappy about it, but Symons and the painter pronounced it splendid, and he tried to make the best of it. The painting after all was an Augustus John, and it behooved him to like it. Quinn, John, Symons, and Agnes Tobin resumed their gay rounds. "Seven taxis in one day!" Symons exclaimed, marveling at Quinn's energy and his largesse. Miss Tobin made the suggestion, full of consequences, that Quinn look into the possibility of acquiring manuscripts from Symons and from another friend of hers, Joseph Conrad.

In his brief time in Ireland Quinn could not go to Coole or

Galway. He stayed entirely in Dublin and spent his time in buying pictures and talking art with Æ, Hone, Jack Yeats, and Sarah Purser, whom he called "the cleverest woman in Ireland." Miss Purser acted as "referee" for a conversation of several hours with Sir Walter Armstrong, Director of the National Gallery in Dublin. On September 3, after his return to New York, Quinn summed up for Townsend Walsh his altered views as a collector.

> I am going to stop putting hundreds and in fact some thousands a year into books. In fact I have got my collections about complete and I am not going into new lines of book collecting. I am going in for some good art, however. After all a picture is a more living thing than a book. It represents life or a moment of life and the older we get the more interest we ought to show in life and the less in a printed transcript of it.

It is not easy to see the ethical difference between a printed and a painted transcript; but Quinn always felt more comfortable when he had a rationale. His solid but conventional taste in art at this point is shown by his purchases in London and Dublin: five landscapes by Hone, "the greatest landscape painter Ireland has ever had, and one of the great landscape painters of the world"; four landscapes by Lucien Pissarro; eight paintings by George Russell; two water colors by Jack Yeats; ten Shannon lithographs; twenty-two etchings, fourteen pencil drawings, two water colors, and his portrait by Augustus John. When he reached New York on the *Lusitania* on September 2, "after a record run in the finest ship afloat—four days and five nights from Queenstown!", Quinn paid a customs duty of $535 on his art works and on "clothes and overcoats and fur coat and gloves and things of that sort that I bought for my friends." [27]

On the whole it had been a fine vacation, though the matter of the portrait rankled rather sorely and a grievous quarrel with W. B. Yeats more sorely still. Quinn and Yeats had come to bitter words and a loud parting over Dorothy Coates. Quinn thought Yeats had been gossiping loosely and injuriously about his relationship with her, and he charged Yeats with trying to take over his mistress for himself. Their friendship ceased at once. Quinn's furious but veiled account of the affair to John Butler Yeats left the old man mystified and distressed. Dublin, he warned Quinn, was a place full of "idle and excitable tongues," and Quinn himself the kind of man who must learn to expect notoriety: "You are a sort of *figure*. You loom on the eye. *You excite legend*—people can't help themselves." [28] But Quinn was placated neither by such flattery nor by the touching pleas which closed the letter: "Forgive me, forgive the Irish babbler, forgive your enemies, and which is harder, forgive your friends." He and W. B. Yeats had no further commerce for five years. And he had to find a place for Shannon's portrait of the poet, which had been on exhibition at Clausen's Gallery on East 35th Street, where his father had seen and approved it. But he did not repent having given James Huneker the eight handsome A. H. Bullen volumes of Yeats, in exchange for a review in the *Sun:* Yeats and his poems were separable matters.

At the end of October Quinn moved from his apartment at 1 West 87th Street, up three flights of stairs in an old-fashioned building without elevators, to 79 Central Park West, between 69th and 70th Streets, In his former apartment he had made himself locally famous for bad temper. He got tired of some tenants' habit of ringing the doorbells of other apartments when they got no answer to their own bell. The wires to all the doorbells ran through the dumbwaiter shaft, and Quinn opened it one day and with a hatchet "cut every damn wire there was." [29] Hearing the noise the tenants in apartments below him stuck their heads out into the shaft and protested at what he was doing. Quinn shouted: " 'Stick in your heads or the hatchet may fall on you.' " [30] After that bells were rung with finer discrimination. The new apartment offered elevators and rooms with larger wall space for his pictures. In 1908 and 1909 he made his first significant purchases of American painting, buying *Morris Heights* and several other landscapes from Ernest Lawson, thereby showing a New York version of his fondness for Hone's Irish scenes —a taste still homely and literary. He was fond of Lawson and frequently advanced sums of fifty to a hundred dollars to the chronically needy painter, most of which Quinn would subsequently collect in the form of additional pictures. While *Morris Heights* was still on show after Quinn had bought it, Mrs. Gertrude Whitney saw it and suggested that she might give Lawson $1,000 for it. Quinn agreed to give up his title if she would promise to give the canvas to a public gallery as she had said she would. But the issue hung suspended for months while she dallied.

On September 18 Esther Pissarro wrote to warn Quinn that she had given an introduction to him to May Morris, the spinster * daughter of William Morris, who was coming over for a series of lectures about the Kelmscott craft ideals. She predicted that they would like each other, and Quinn was charmed to anticipate knowing the daughter of one of his earliest idols. Mrs. Pissarro also offered him a chance to buy a Camille Pissarro *View of Havre* for £250. Quinn hesitated, feeling strapped for money after his purchases abroad, and not quite sure of his feeling about the work of the impressionists. His paintings were already a large heap, and he wanted to begin thinking of them as a collection, with limits and a purpose and some lines of internal logic. At the end of November Mrs. Pissarro wrote of seeing Augustus John's portrait of Quinn on show at the New English Art Club, "very well hung & we all think it is extremely good."

Catching up with some of his many periodicals late one night in the winter in a Pullman berth on the way to Chicago, Quinn "howled with glee" to find the following account of his picture in the January *English Review:*

> The peculiar note of hardness which Mr. A. E. John has could not have had a better subject than "The Man from New York." It shows exactly that hardness which we look for and find in this type of American.

What tickled Quinn, as he wrote to John on January 31, was to see the English critic *looking* for American hardness. Yet he could feel enough truth in the judgment to sting. The more he thought

---

* Such at least was her public figure. "The most beautiful of women" had been much admired in the eighties by G. B. Shaw when he was young and poor. After having "very carefully and quite deliberately made a gesture of assent with her eyes," registering in heaven a "Mystic Betrothal" to Shaw (Shaw, "Morris as I Knew Him"), she turned about and married an acolyte of her father's, H. Halliday Sparling, in 1890. Shaw then lived with the young couple, apparently innocently and happily, for some time in a *ménage à trois*. May Morris's marriage to Sparling—whom W. B. Yeats denounced as "that little wretch Sparling, with his atheisms and negations" (letter to Katharine Tynan, April 11, 1888)—was unhappy and was dissolved by divorce in 1898. Thereafter she tried to expunge all evidence of his name and of her marriage.

about John's view of him the less he liked it, and finally he condemned it altogether:

> He painted me as though I were a referee or umpire at a baseball
> game or the president of a street railway company with a head as
> round and unexpressive and undeveloped as a billiard ball. Thirty
> or forty years of life in school, college, university and the world
> has I hope put a little intelligence into my face. Intelligence is not
> predominant in the John painting of me, but force, self-assertion
> and a seeming lack of sensitiveness which is not mine.

Still, he could not bring himself to banish the painting and it hung
unloved over his mantelpiece as long as he lived.

From London John reported that he had seen much of Symons
and Agnes Tobin since Quinn's departure. Symons was still given
only two or three months of life by his doctors but was proving
an active invalid. He was showing an "embarrassing" affection for
John and read to him copiously from his new poems, "which are
all hell, damnation & lust." [31] John went on:

> The other night occurred a row as we came out of a restaurant. In
> order to cope the more successfully with the exigencies of Symons'
> society, I had, before meeting him, taken on a considerable ballast
> in the way of drink, and was thus, although the more seaworthy
> in respect to plain sailing on an even keel, rendered less competent
> to oppose the squall that followed. Well, as I said, when we got
> outside some man started buffooning me, holding out his hat and
> asking for alms. I regarded him for about a minute, then gravely
> and neatly knocked his hat halfway down the street, upon which I
> was set upon by his companions, a man and a woman, armed with
> an umbrella, and, the first man returning, I was in the thick of an
> ignominious struggle in which I stumbled and knocked myself or
> was knocked senseless on the curb. Miss Tobin was holding in
> Symons, and she got some of the assembled multitude to put my
> limp body into a four-wheeler. She drove me home. I had regained
> consciousness very soon and my first words were, "Has anybody
> got a cigarette?" I still have an aching jaw from that encounter. I
> think Miss Tobin enjoyed the affair, on the whole.

In addition to such racy journalism John sent photographs of his
wife and children, as Quinn had requested. Quinn showed them
about to his friends in New York, and he sent back the painter
Robert Henri's salute to John's wife Dorelia: " 'By God, I could
paint a woman like that all my life.' " [32]

1910

O N January 1, 1910, Quinn and John Butler Yeats saw the new year in with dinner, wine, and cigars at Quinn's apartment. The case containing Charles Shannon's *Summer* and *The Sapphire Bay* was opened and the pictures admired by both.

Earlier in the winter Quinn had nerved himself to propose his first formal patronage arrangement. He offered to guarantee Augustus John £300 a year in return for paintings to that approximate value. He wished both to free John from crude financial anxiety and to add to his collection work that he liked and that he was sure would increase in value. John accepted the proposition on December 18 "with the utmost gratitude":

> I can't say well what I think of it. One thing, were I alone, I would ask nothing better than to work for you exclusively, and would think it an ideal plan of life. As it is, I find myself infinitely fortunate in your friendship, and will always be stimulated and encouraged by it to merit it more and more.

With Quinn's subsidy in pocket and in prospect, Augustus John elected to spend most of 1910 in France and Italy, in Provence and on the Riviera. Quinn approved but felt entitled to send him a great deal of monitory advice: drink moderately, do not squander your energy, beware of venereal disease, especially among Italian women. Whenever John ran low on money and wished to move on, Quinn came through with an increment. In addition to practicing his own art, John aimed to study the work of the Italian masters, and to make acquaintance with the gypsy bands of the continent, especially with the Russian branch, whom he found "the most staggering looking crew imaginable." [1] For long Augustus John had made of the gypsies an adopted race; he spoke Romany, and in Britain he often traveled with his family for weeks at a time in a gypsy caravan. Now near Marseilles he was collecting songs, tales, and dialect and sending off articles and drawings to the *Gypsy Lore Journal*, to which Quinn had dutifully subscribed.

John was disappointed in Italy to find no modern painters with the energy and nearness to life of the men of the Renaissance; he cited Signorelli particularly as an example of the power that had been lost. In himself he felt a new access of vitality and passion and clear vision which he credited to being truly alone among new and earthy people and among great old pictures. On March 3 he wrote from Martigues: "I feel *nobody*, dead or alive, is so near the guts of things as I am at present—and its devilish hot." Far from succumbing to drink, he looked ahead to a near future when "I shall be able to get as drunk as I like on green tea." He praised the strength and beauty of the local women: "I see many powerful women, erect and unintimidated, whose essential nudity no amount of clothing can disguise." Quinn was delighted to get this kind of talk in return for his money, though he hoped also for pictures.

In Martigues John was fascinated too with his neighbor, Albert Bazin, the French airman, savant, and philosopher, who had bogged down for lack of funds on the eighth model of his flying machine. Obviously hoping that Quinn himself would oblige, John wrote again and again asking him to try to find a moneyed American "collaborator" for Bazin—who might be reminded, he suggested, that Bazin had a comely daughter of eighteen years.

Quinn cheered on all this from the distant sidelines, urging on the painting, sending books and clippings and occasional sums of money. In May John admired "the large, genial and comprehensive outlook" [2] of Quinn's friend Huneker's *Promenades of an Impressionist*, one of Quinn's gifts. The book made him see, he said, how far he had succumbed to the "finicking intellectuality" of London when he should have been trusting his own instincts and working away: "An artist has no business to think except brush in hand." Quinn soaked up all John's gusty talk of art and life; and he quickly accepted his recommendation of three artists who were to matter a good deal to his future as a collector, Jacob Epstein, Wyndham Lewis, and John's sister, the fey genius Gwen.

Esther Pissarro's inquiries in the fall as to whether Quinn was seeing May Morris in New York have a matchmaking sound. Indeed there was much logic in the notion: why should a forceful, personable bachelor and a lovely and lonely woman, with many tastes in common, not make a match of it? "I heard from Miss Morris how very kind & charming you had been to her," Mrs. Pissarro wrote on February 22. "We were sure you would like one another." They did like each other but not, unfortunately, to the same purpose. William Morris, the man and the work, was an early and lasting admiration for Quinn, as Morris was for Yeats who called him "my chief of men." [3] His daughter would embody the Morris ideal, and when Quinn met her in November he was warmly drawn in the flesh to the haunting Pre-Raphaelite beauty that May Morris had inherited from her mother who was a favorite subject of the painters of that brotherhood—the body slim, erect, and graceful, the face and head finely outlined, with deep still eyes and yellow hair in a great loose knot on the back of her neck. She and Quinn began to make acquaintance, which warmed and warmed. They toured the city, dined out, and were much together at Quinn's apartment. Early in January they were engaged to attend a reception at Columbia for Ambassador James Bryce of England, but a great snow fell and Quinn hired a double-seated sleigh with a pair of horses and bells, and instead of going to Columbia they drove for hours at night about the streets. When May Morris went west and into Canada on tour, Quinn wrote ahead of her to acquaintances in each city, making sure that she would be cosseted wherever she went. She returned to New York and again they were constantly together. When she sailed for home in early May Quinn's Pol Roget champagne was in her stateroom.

Miss Morris was in love, but Quinn had been in love and was out again, though she did not know it yet and would be slow in finding it out. The affair limped on till 1917, in a tragicomical, Chekhovian way, with affections in syncopated relationship. It is not pleasant to watch, in their correspondence, and Quinn does not come out of it well on the whole. He had already rejected May Morris, though he had used her, and to a point would continue to do so. Quinn was now nearly forty, and there was much in his psychology to confirm him as a bachelor. He liked being free to order his establishment entirely as he preferred it. His habitual hypochondria and the tense state of his nerves made him see himself as a bad physical risk for any woman. The deaths in his family and his own fear of sickness and death tempted him to keep his intimate circle as small, as little vulnerable, as possible. He had too the Irish tendency to define "the family" as that in which one had been a child, a hot clannish loyalty and sense of primary obligation to one's parents and siblings; when Julia Anderson had to undergo a minor operation early in January, Quinn felt no doubt as to where his duty lay: he left Miss Morris behind and spent several days at his sister's bedside in Cleveland. And there was always the latent inverted puritanism of the Irish about sexual life, fearing it when it is formalized, and so being slow to take a mate.

The friendship between them continued, more and more embarrassingly *diminuendo*, in a touchingly unequal correspondence. Quinn saw her a few more times, but he took care they met "socially" and intellectually, as one connoisseur to another, never again as man and woman. Her letters were prettily, sometimes painfully, feminine. In early stages they were candid and timorously confident of his affection; with time they moved toward drab neutrality, baffled injury, well-bred complaint, finally a barely concealed disgust. Quinn's letters were always dictated and typewritten, though in the first year after her return he sometimes wrote in the salutation by hand: "My Dear." Aside from that he never sent a truly personal word. A good lawyer and a coolheaded though not a cynical lover, who liked to quote Dion Boucicault's warning: "'Never fornicate through an ink bottle,'" Quinn kept his letters resolutely Platonic from the beginning. He wrote less and less frequently as time passed, and after a few years satisfied himself with a cable or a Christmas barrel of apples.

Miss Morris's friends told her that she had come home looking plumper and improved in health. Quinn assured her that was always the way with visiting Britons: all were terrified in advance of the horrors and dangers of America, all liked it, all went home fat and happy. He instanced Yeats and Hyde. Writing from her house on the river in Hammersmith Terrace on May 19, May Morris addressed him as "you, to whom I can talk of everything conceivable." She had just begun, she said, to realize the loneliness of her life, and she longed to show him her poor unpretentious house: ". . . it will be so good for a lordly person like yourself. . . ." Her letter of July 1 begins: "I must have a few words with you tonight. . . ." On August 14 she sent a brief note to accompany an unpublished poem which William Morris had written in his two daughters' copy of *The Earthly Paradise*. "I've been dreaming a great deal lately—radiant dreams . . ." she wrote, and closed plaintively: "I'm afraid you must be terribly busy." Quinn assured her that he was indeed busy, "driven" in fact. He described in detail all his classical symptoms of nervous tension: irritability, headaches, a bad stomach, sleeplessness, night sweats. He explained the dangers of bad feeding: "autointoxication," "fermentation," "making a distillery of the stomach." He had discovered the marvels of the Metchnikoff sour-milk diet, was virtually living on Zoolak, had lost seventeen pounds, and was feeling much better. He loudly defended boxing and other violent sports which she had deplored: "The occasional head cracked in polo or man killed in flying in the air is the price which the race pays for vigor, headship and command." [4] She begged him to come abroad, as he had promised to do, but Quinn said he could not come; he was too "driven," too unwell.

Writing on October 17 from Kelmscott Manor in Gloucestershire, she described the famous old family home and her lonely present life there in vivid and charming detail. She still heard without surprise, she said, her father's voice or the sound of his feet on the gravel of the garden, and she recalled the past:

> I have waked sometimes and lain watching his gable, at right angles to mine, listening to the chanting which accompanied the poetry-making. How the sound seemed wedded to the fragrance of the night in that enclosed garden!

She sketched for Quinn the pathetic contrast between her mother's life at Kelmscott and her own:

> She, married so early, the anxieties and griefs that must come into the happiest of human existences all softened by this atmosphere of love and tenderness; and I—not much to be said, but that I've

lived in a desert of loneliness and have set my teeth and endured it with a sort of dogged courage that has sometimes surprised myself.

Then a phrase worthy of Emily Dickinson: "After dinner we play a dreadful game called Patience." It would all interest Quinn, she suggested, if he were "less distracted and had leisure to be interested." But Quinn was proof against even such artful coals of fire.

May Morris was hard at work, and would be so for years, at the immense task of editing, with her own introductions and commentary, her father's writings in an edition for Longmans which was planned to run to 24 volumes. As she progressed she sent Quinn proof sheets of her father's texts and of her own introductions, which he promised to collect and have elegantly bound, as he had done with the several important manuscripts of Morris's he owned. Quinn seized upon this matter of the edition as another means of avoiding real intimacy, and he made it the chief subject of his letters to her. But he was quite genuinely interested as well; he worked hard at his sub-editing, and sent May Morris frequent advice that tells one something of his own knowledge and taste. As an earnest of his right to speak he estimated that he had read thirty books on Shelley and all the important studies of Blake. Now he cited Arthur Symons's *The Romantic Movement in English Poetry* as a model of scholarly but graceful criticism—much preferable, he thought, to such pedantry as Courthope's *History of English Poetry*, the last volume of which, on the Romantics, he had been reading. He used the posthumous publishing history of Shelley and Meredith to support his advice to Miss Morris to be free and inclusive in choosing her father's texts. And in repeatedly urging her to make her introductions as directly personal and full of biographical detail as she could, he advanced the examples of Lady Ritchie's 13-volume Thackeray and Cook's 37-volume Ruskin. All this testifies to a considerable bookishness, to say the least; and it shows Quinn's bias toward biography, which may be the only thing he shared with Dr. Johnson. " . . . You cannot be too personal," he wrote on September 1; " . . . to persons who love and admire a man's work everything personal about him is interesting."

Though Quinn was laboring to avoid a commitment he had in some sense already made back in New York, he was also unwilling to let go of a literary association that was of value and interest to him. May Morris was another means of being in touch with greatness, and he used her as such. She came to know it, but her loneliness was a fact, and she held on as best she could, too long, playing the dreadful game called Patience. At the end of it all she wrote him coldly on New Year's Eve of 1917: "I have received no letter since last February twelve-month, nearly two years ago. A few months back came a long envelope which I welcomed, but found to be a reprint of a public letter of yours." And by then she had for several years been giving his Christmas apples to the poor—with, one supposes, a complex satisfaction.

Quinn had at first promised both Augustus John and May Morris, as well as the numerous Irish friends who still remained after the death of Synge and the break with W. B. Yeats, that he would be coming abroad in July 1910. He revised the promise to August, and finally, under pressure of work in New York and unavoidable journeys to Washington and the midwest, he once again abandoned the annual dream. Actually conditions in his office were more stable than they had been thus far, with Thomas Curtin in control of details and with the addition of Paul Kieffer (who was to prove Quinn's only durable partner, to survive him, and to continue his business down to the present day). A newly made lawyer looking for an opening, Kieffer had heard of Quinn as a rising man but had fought shy of him because of his Tammany associations. A friend had advised him to see Quinn anyway: " 'He's a bully good Irishman.' " [5] Kieffer joined the office at once and found in Quinn a brilliant tutor and performer in the law, a fair if strenuous and exacting colleague, and a staunch friend. In addition to his established connection with banks and insurance companies, Quinn was now chief counsel for the financier Thomas Fortune Ryan, and Ryan's work meant at once a large access of responsibility and a handsome annual retainer. Quinn was making, and spending, a great deal of money. From the labor came the money, and the tension. Quinn hated the telephone but submitted to it as a useful tool. Once he had mastered the use of the telephone, the secretary, and the "typewriter" (stenographer), he boasted, he had been able to "treble and quadruple" his own output of work. When he reported to Nathaniel Hone how his symptoms had driven him to the Metchnikoff sour-milk diet, the old painter remarked drily: "I think that you Americans work a great deal too hard. I suppose that it is a matter of climate and that you cannot help it. In this lazy Island we find it quite easy to be idle." [6]

Quinn's lover's quarrel with the lazy Island continued. In January Judge Keogh honored him with the resonant compliment: "You are altogether the most clearly patriotic, most unselfish and intelligent Irishman I know." [7] Presumably he was thinking of Quinn in the context of American politics and American Irishry. All year he talked and wrote to Keogh, a more loyal Catholic, about the Church in Ireland. On June 25 Douglas Hyde cabled to Quinn: "Compulsory Irish carried in the University. Great victory." The victory, Quinn considered, was over the powers of darkness embodied in the Church. He wrote to Keogh on July 12: " . . . we Irish have about come to the pass where everything that Irishmen think is good is damned by the priests and bishops, and most of the Irish victories consist of the defeat of Irish bishops and priests in their efforts to thwart national aspirations." His attack on the Roman hierarchy of the Church drew from Keogh a shocked response on August 11: "Your contemptuous designation of the rulers of the Universal Church as 'Dago Ecclesiastics' is, even if merited, most audacious, irreverent and severe. I am glad you exclude the successor of Peter. . . ." Sadly, he accepted Quinn's estimate of the situation in Ireland: "I know no other man but yourself who has penetrated every cranny in the nature of the Irish political priest." [8]

A more positive piece of Irishry was his little American edition this summer of Synge's posthumous *Deirdre*, in form parallel to his printing of the same writer's *Poems and Translations*, of fifty copies, five of them on vellum. As usual he felt that the Dublin edition had been carelessly done, poor in spelling and punctuation, and with some actual distortions of the text. So he worked directly from Synge's unfinished manuscript, and he promised Lady Gregory that his edition would be worthy of any German scholar. Finding errors still in the first printing, which had cost him $250, he ordered a second printing which cost him an additional $123. He wrote irritably to Shannon on the nineteenth of August: "I have met but few Irishmen who cared to punctuate or knew how to spell. But then they are above such petty things and live in the higher realms of pure patriotism."

He compensated for his lost holiday abroad as best he could with brief outings to places in reach of the city, especially Sheepshead Bay, Fisher's Island, and Coney Island. At Sheepshead he was joined by Julia Anderson, and John Butler Yeats made the first of many drawings of "the kid," Quinn's beloved little red-gold niece Mary Anderson, now three and a half. Over the Fourth of July he took Mr. Yeats with him for an exploration of Fisher's Island at the head of Long Island Sound, involving a train trip of seventy-five miles, eight miles by boat through the fog to the island, afternoon and evening about the military installation, overnight in a good hotel, next day inspection of the twelve-inch guns and a motor trip about the island, then back to Manhattan. Back in the city on July 6 J. B. Yeats sent Quinn a note thanking him for two dollars that Quinn had paid him on a bet and commenting on Quinn's pale citified look among the soldiers:

> At Fisher's Island I had got rather unhappy about you. I even spoke to Major Watson about your looks—but he said you looked thin, but that your colour was healthy—afterwards in the train I recovered my composure—it was only the bronzed and fatted cheeks of those sunburnt warriors that by comparison made you look fragile & delicate—away from them you looked normal.

He decorated the bottom of his page with a pen sketch of himself and Quinn looking rather dim and overshadowed standing in a group with three burly men in uniform.

An all-day party on a Saturday in early August brought together a notable group that included John Butler Yeats, his friend the painter John Sloan, and his son's friend the young American poet, not yet confirmed expatriate, Ezra Pound. Much later Ezra Pound recalled that day in a letter to Quinn: "I have still a very clear recollection of Yeats père on an elephant . . . smiling like Elijah in the beatific vision, and of you plugging away in the shooting gallery. And a very good day it was." [9] In addition to the elephants, the shooting gallery, and the Shoot-the-Chutes, Quinn had treated Mr. Yeats and the Sloans to a surprise motor ride back to their homes in lower Manhattan. The sensation was new enough in 1910 to move Sloan, in his thank-you note of August 16, to consider the

Wednesday — 317, W 29ª N York

My dear Irmun

many thanks for the 2 dollars —

any one before and I bet I would won it — 6/5.
from Jack Nelthhp on a quotation from Shakespeare —
I would not have been equally _____ Jeffries. but
I knew that he was Irish — he was son of an
Irish methodist minister — Jim said he was Irish
but had not the details — I hope you had not
bet much —

I have had a good letter from John Schuler
who Treads it Typro — about the play _____
Chestatins.

At Father Island I had got rather unhappy
about you. I even spoke to major's Watson about
your looks — but he said you looked thin —
but that your colour was healthy —
afterwards in the train I recovered my composure
— it was only the bronzed _____ dinhs of these
sun burned warriors that by comparison made
you look fragile & delicate — away from
them — you looked normal —

psychology of motorized travel in a way that is still amusing and acute:

> ... I fear that the physical consciousness that the driving power is underneath me would be bound to result in an arrogant point of view. When drawn by horses or engine or any force applied ahead of the vehicle the human being must to some degree feel dependent, but when riding above the motor force he's bound to feel superior. A man on horseback can be commanding, haughty; the power is beneath him. Surely no general could command from the seat of a buggy! The automobile is therefore the first vehicle which has trained humans to arrogance. Think of the possibilities of the airship! a haughty race we will soon be!

On hot summer evenings Quinn liked to foregather with Gregg and James Huneker and his wife, Josephine, at the roof garden of one of the Manhattan hotels, the Majestic, or the Belmont, or the Astor. In practice Huneker was "visible" only on Saturday nights, when he liked a spree. He was a hard and prolific worker, a slave to his task. But he drank immense quantities of Pilsener, and Gregg matched him with Scotch whiskey. Quinn drank little, usually a dry wine. But there were cigars for the men, and a light supper for all, and quantities of good talk as they relaxed among the dancers and the music. They called themselves "the quartet." At the Belmont on October 16 Quinn was excited to see Henry James at dinner "with two gentlemen and one lady." He felt a reverence for James all his life, and he wrote at once now to Mrs. Keogh to beg her to invite James to her house with himself and John Butler Yeats. But nothing came of the idea, and he never met his hero.

Of course Quinn was not writing to W. B. Yeats, but he sent regular reports of the faring of John Butler Yeats in New York to the other Yeats children and to Hone and Russell and Lady Gregory. The great old man was much missed in Ireland and his presence and his habits remembered with affectionate exasperation. "Poor old J. B. Y.," Lady Gregory wrote on January 3, 1909:

> It is wonderful how hopeful, how cheerful, how impossible he is. I admire him immensely at a distance, and I think him the most trying visitor possible in a house. Space and time mean nothing to him, he goes his own way, spoiling portraits as hopefully as he

begins them, and always on the verge of a great future! I should lock up his paints and only allow him a pencil, and get occasional rapid sketches from him.

And Nathaniel Hone remarked with his customary laconicism: "Though it is a good thing in painting to be never satisfied with your work, the sitters should be considered." [10] Mr. Yeats had no thought of altering either his painting habits or his optimism. He had now found his spiritual home in America, the boarding house at 317 West 29th Street run by three Breton women, the sisters Petitpas. He was to live out his days there, illuminating that place and making it locally celebrated by his animated and gaily serious presence, his witty, nourishing talk flowing in a rich stream. When weather allowed, the boarders and their guests would dine in a sort of pavilion, an open, roofed shed in the back garden. It is in this setting that John Sloan painted him in 1910 in *Yeats at Petitpas'*, with a group of friends about the table, the white-bearded old man in an attitude reminiscent of his son's poem, "his beautiful mischievous head thrown back" ("Beautiful Lofty Things"), his teeth clamped on a long black cheroot, his eyes focused on a sketch pad on which he is drawing. Van Wyck Brooks, one of the young men at the table, memorialized such occasions in a moving essay the title of which he borrowed from Sloan's picture.

J. B. Yeats was Quinn's frequent guest at dinner, at the shore, or on Sunday rambles, or strides, on the Jersey Palisades across the Hudson. And his frequent short letters continued to enliven and instruct. On May 14 of 1910, for example, he questioned the definition of "virility" in an address of Theodore Roosevelt, the apostle of the strenuous life. "The man most human is the man most virile," was his own view of the matter. He went on to pay Quinn a compliment which, since he was no sycophant, carries value as evidence: "You are an eminently virile man in *my sense* of the word. Although you are a man of law I know no one who has so little legality in his composition, for which I give God Almighty my personal thanks." Boswell would have judged it "thousand-pound" praise.

Outward signs, at least, of the cultural life thickened visibly about Quinn. He had been in this new apartment at 79 Central Park West for less than a year when he told Charles Shannon on

August 19 that "every foot of its walls is filled with books and pictures. I keep on making a little more room, but not so much as necessary for incoming books and pictures." Quinn was buying books at the terrific rate of eight hundred to a thousand a year. Of Russell's pictures alone he already had "thirty or forty." Now he paid Shannon £360 for his *Doña Ana*, a portrait of Granville-Barker's wife, Lilah McCarthy, wearing Charles Ricketts's gorgeous gown designed for a performance of Shaw's *Man and Superman* at the Court Theatre in London. Quinn had now waited for more than a year while Mrs. Whitney procrastinated about Ernest Lawson's *Morris Heights*. He wrote Lawson at last on June 10 that he "didn't much care for the position of taking the leavings of a rich woman" who couldn't make up her mind. He had advanced Lawson $800 at this point, and he now proposed to pay him an extra $300 and take over both *Morris Heights*, which he figured at $600, and *Hoboken Heights*, at $500. Lawson closed with the offer next day. By August 11 he was advancing Lawson another $100, in ten-dollar bills. "Good heavens I hope my financial chaos will end some time," Lawson wrote piteously. "You have saved my life a number of times." [11] It was probably true.

Quinn had been attracted by Augustus John's account of his sister, Gwen, living skimpily in Paris with her friend from the Slade School, Ruth Manson. At the end of July he sent Gwen John £30 as the price of any painting of her own execution and choice. On July 28 she wrote that she had not been able to bring herself to send the picture she had chosen for him. "People say it is so ugly I am sure it is," she said. She was doing him another for the same £30. She signed herself: "Yours obediently and sincerely, Gwendolen John." On Christmas day she wrote again: "I am so much ashamed of not having your picture done by now. I have been working but I am not yet satisfied with what I have done. . . ." In tone, rhythm, and content the little affair thus far was a miniature of Quinn's frustrating and exhilarating experience with her in coming years.

That Christmas, and every Christmas, Quinn found "a damned bore," as he described this one to his old friend Eddie Robinson, a civil servant in Washington. Christmas of 1911 cost him over $2,500, including $550 to Tiffany's for an enameled watch set with pearls for Julia Anderson, $260 for an enameled watch and chain for Ada Smith, and $45 for a jewel case for Annie Foster.

He was busy, prosperous, and irritable. Weeks in the winter were taken up with the proposed merger of the Madison Trust and the Equitable Trust. He added and subtracted partners and clerks. Most of them he found incompetent and infuriating. "I do get weary of conducting a post-graduate Law School and training men to be lawyers, and at the same time paying them for the training," he wrote to May Morris on March 24. Paul Kieffer was a help in the office, and Thomas Curtin a salvation. A vacancy had opened for a United States Senator for New York, and Quinn was considered for the nomination by Democratic leaders, but was put aside as too close by reputation to Tammany Hall. Then when Judge O'Gorman was elected to the vacancy Quinn was urged for O'Gorman's former post on the state Supreme Court. He refused to be considered; his practice was large enough, yet young enough, so that he felt the move would be professionally more expensive than he could risk. Instead he put forward the name of his friend Daniel F. Cohalan and organized an elaborate campaign of supporting letters. Cohalan got the appointment.

Banking, tax, and insurance affairs of his clients took him frequently to Washington, and he sometimes combined these trips with visits to Thomas Fortune Ryan's Virginia estate, Oak Ridge, where he liked to take long horseback rides over the Blue Ridge foothills. In April he took J. B. Yeats along to Oak Ridge, first fitting him out with appropriate new clothing. "The old pirate," as Quinn privately called Ryan, was building a domestic chapel to add to his house on Fifth Avenue. His taste ran to thirteenth-century marbles and enamels, but Quinn took him to the Durand-Ruel show in May on the chance that useful decorations would appear. He told Ryan that if he would buy the $12,000 El Greco on sale he would come to Ryan's chapel for Mass some day. At the same sale Quinn took his first deep plunge into French art and into expensive art when he bought Manet's *L'Amazone* for $4,000. His mouth watered for the same painter's *Au Café* at $25,000, but that was far too steep.

"I have done very little reading this winter," he wrote in the middle of February to the wife of his good friend James F. Byrne;

then he went on to recite a sufficiently imposing list: the first four parts of *Jean Christophe*; Chamberlain's *The Foundations of the Nineteenth Century* in two volumes; Lafcadio Hearn's *Japanese Letters*; Mackail's *Lectures on Greek Poetry*; Heine's *Memoirs and Letters*, two volumes; "a dozen or so" novels by Arnold Bennett; Aulard's *French Revolution* in four volumes; Lord Acton's *Lectures on the French Revolution*; Ezra Pound's *The Spirit of Romance*; Goldwin Smith's reminiscences; Pierre Loti's *Egypt*; Santayana's *Three Philosophical Poets*; William Sharp's life by his wife; Lady Gregory's *Kiltartan Molière* and *Kiltartan Wonder Book*; a great many plays. Quite obviously he was a serious and phenomenally rapid reader. Most of these works had been gone through in bed late at night and in Pullman berths en route to Washington and the midwest.

1911

THE year 1911 was to be a critical one in the definition of Quinn's taste and in the sharpening of his appetite. Though he had not met Gwen John, he had begun to write confidentially to her, charmed by the candor and naïve grace of her letters. To her on January 5 he made a crucial pronouncement: "I like to be a man of my own day and time." He did not have, and did not expect to have, the kind of fortune that allowed one to collect the famous art of the past. What money he had would go farther, and do more good, if he confined his view to recent work, more especially to strictly contemporary work. He could not afford Old Masters, and anyway their ground was already tiresomely traveled over by generations of connoisseurs and moneyed men. "There is more real pleasure in the recognition and appreciation of a contemporary who is doing fine work . . ." he wrote to Gwen John.[1] The point was multiple, and perfectly conscious: the money bought more; there was more sport, more raciness, more "rigor" in the game of contemporary art. Furthermore one could feel the warming sensation of taking part in art, helping it to be born, in some sense *making* it, when one bought the work of living men.

About American art too Quinn had made up his mind, as he said to Gwen John: it was inferior to European art and interesting at all only in landscape. So he bought Lawsons, and when he discovered the work of Walt Kuhn at the Madison Art Gallery in the spring, what he bought first was *Salt Mists* for $300 and *Frozen River* for $200. Quinn's ideas about art were coming clear, he thought, but in fact his taste wavered now for some time, and his purchases tended to lag behind his theory. He still felt more comfortable and safe with landscapes, with a homely element. Three more Hones, chosen and shipped by Russell along with pictures of his own, gave him a total of seventeen Hones. John Butler Yeats admired them greatly on Quinn's walls, and that was both gratifying and obscurely troubling. In February he paid $1,075 for Camille Pissarro's *Apple Trees in Blossom, Eragny*, at the sale of the Julius Oehme collection, and next month gave Lucien Pissarro £200, £30 less than had been first asked, for his father's *Havre, the Harbor*. Buying the Manet *L'Amazone* for $4,000 had been a modestly bold step; but in October Quinn retreated from it and traded the picture back for one-third of the $12,000 needed for Puvis de Chavannes's *The Beheading of St. John the Baptist*, taking at the same time seven Puvis de Chavannes drawings. The air of chaste sentiment, mystery, spirituality of the Puvis de Chavannes was what still attracted him to the Russells. Yet by March 19, in a letter to Augustus John, he had begun to discriminate more boldly, to condemn aesthetically what he might love sentimentally, the alien literary appeal of such paintings. Russell's pictures, he said, were full of poetry: "But poetry in painting is not the same as the poetry of paint." It was one of his many pronouncements of this period, of no great profundity, on the value of "technique" as compared to "subject" or "conviction." He was trying out a new vocabulary, with less of sophistication than of his characteristic dogmatism.

Early in the year Quinn gave J. B. Yeats an order for a new self portrait, and the old man set to work cheerfully on what became in time a sort of sad joke, a picture painted and overpainted and still unfinished when he died, the paint a half-inch thick. Quinn went to hear him give a public reading of his son's play, *The Green Helmet*, in the middle of February and wrote to Lily Yeats on February 23 that he had found the whole thing unsatisfactory. He disliked to hear a play read, outside its natural setting in the theatre: "The whole of acting, the whole of drama, the whole of painting a picture, is convention." The judgment sounds more sophisticated than it actually was in Quinn's mind. By "technique" or "convention" in painting he meant little more at this time than sober academic discipline, rigorous school training and practice, knowl-

edge and systematic application of the fundamental skills of drawing, anatomy, and composition. J. B. Yeats, a gay but stubborn
humanist, was happy to argue this or any other question with him.
On March 8 Quinn had placed at his disposal for a tour with a
prospective client his rooms, his pictures, his tea and cigars, and his
Japanese houseboy, Sadji. Writing next day to thank him, Mr.
Yeats wrote of himself and of the general question: "I am a real
portrait painter and a man with convictions. . . . How shall you
know your painter to be an artist of convictions? In many ways,
yet by one infallible way—if people who do not share the convictions *condemn the technique*." He praised his friend John Sloan
as "the only artist in America who has convictions." Quinn liked
Sloan as a man and had no objection to his frank socialism; but he
feared Sloan's "conviction," socialism, was overpowering his technique as a painter, and the result was simply bad art. But on the
general question Quinn retreated to an unassailable position, writing the next day: "I don't think you can divide up the problem.
Trying to define what constitutes great art is like attempting the
philosophical thing of defining what is the *summum bonum*." He
had only paused in his dogmatizing.

At the same time he wanted to know about art as he felt he already knew about literature. He collected the opinions of his
friends abroad of the Post-Impressionist Exhibition which was
fluttering the London art world. Russell was sufficiently agitated by
the show to make an untypical uncharitable judgment: "I don't
think I ever saw anything so stupid in my life as the vast majority
of these pictures." [2] Augustus John, on the other hand, was "powerfully impressed" by Cézanne, Gauguin, and Van Gogh. About
Matisse he was more than dubious, writing on January 11, "He
is what the French call a *fumiste*—a charlatan, but an ingenious
one." May Morris, protesting that she was no judge of the matter,
thought the work was difficult and unpleasant to live with, but
certainly serious and exhilarating. She saw nothing posed or frivol-
ous in an orange-haired Christ or a blue dog with orange eyes. Her
overriding impression of the handsome vitality of a room full of
such pictures was one that particularly interested Quinn: " . . . the
general effect in the exhibition rooms was far more striking and
decorative than the effect of a collection of what one may call *sane*

pictures would be, with their silver tones, their blacks and greys, and general discretion and propriety!" [3] Why not? Quinn thought; he liked the sound of it. He wrote to Miss Morris on February 3 of a passage he had been reading in one of Lafcadio Hearn's letters from Japan: "He has one wonderful letter . . . upon Japanese eyelids and colours of various races. As I read it I said to myself, 'This fully justifies the Post-Impressionists'; for Hearn too saw green eyes and blue skins and purple hair. . . ."

The wish for light and for color, high bright color, was beginning to grip him harder and harder. It was a taste that led him straight to Matisse, among others, in spite of Augustus John's doubts. Quinn now felt that his Shannon portrait of W. B. Yeats, for example, was too dark, dim, and restrained to satisfy the eye and the mind. He wrote bluntly to John on May 19:

> . . . I think artists are beginning to learn more and more that their pictures should not look as though they were painted in a coal cellar or in a prison cell with very little light coming through a small hole in the wall. . . . I am sick of the old-fashioned, "dark chamber" style of painting. Whether this later painting in a higher key will endure and keep the high key, time only, perhaps, will tell. . . . These "dark chamber" pictures seem to me to be open to two objections: first, that it is easy to get results that way; and secondly, that they don't represent life. Most of the portraits with a black or very dark background should be entitled, "A Man Emerging from a Fog," or "A Lady Coming Down the Corridor of a Prison," or "In the Park at Midnight," or some such tag as that.

John happily reported that his own palette was turning lighter and brighter in recent work. And if Quinn wanted animation, what of John's scheme to come to America to paint the geysers in Yellowstone Park? He had found a symbol for his own personality. Life around John was only too bright. Wakened one morning by loud screams, he had found his servant maid running upstairs for help with her hair and clothing blazing. He had leaped out of bed and enveloped her in the loose dressing robe in which he had been sleeping, smothering the fire and saving her life, at the cost of painful burns on his own body in highly strategic areas.

John cut short Quinn's enthusiasm for the sculpture of Eric Gill, but persuaded him to buy four water colors by his own young protégé, J. D. Innes. When the pictures arrived Sadji pointed out to Quinn their Japanese influence. From John himself Quinn had ordered twelve of the studies in oil that he had done in Provence, "all in pure colour," and he was trying hard to get possession of a capital work, *The Way Down to the Sea*. John had given him first refusal of the work, pending a sight of it in London in the summer, and he had fended off Hugh Lane, who wanted it too. Then he had sent it for exhibition to a show at the White City, where a price tag of £500 had been inadvertently affixed. It was snapped up at once by a buyer who turned out to be Mme. Frida Strindberg, wife of the Swedish dramatist, with whom John had been intimate and who wished to possess him body, soul, and art. He described her in a letter to Quinn on August 16 as "the walking hell-bitch of the western world." The problem was how to get the painting out of her grip.

Quinn had recently paid $700 to Dodd and Livingston of New York for the autograph manuscript of the first draft of William Morris's translation of the *Odyssey*, in 470 leaves written on one side, plus nine leaves of a translation of a portion of the *Iliad*. Before going abroad in late August he sent the manuscripts to May Morris for use in preparing her big Longmans edition, along with four other important Morris manuscripts he already owned: *The Glittering Plain, The House of the Wolfings*, the *Æneid* translation, and a later draft of the *Odyssey* translation in a bound volume. In the spring and summer he kept booming Miss Morris's work to his journalist friends Gregg, Huneker, Hackett, and More. The books had begun to appear, and on August 19 he praised to Miss Morris herself "your stately and beautiful edition of your father's works." He called the volumes "almost too beautiful to read." He foresaw that seeing May Morris in London was going to be a problem, after a separation of more than a year, and she with her dream of a romance to be resumed.

In Ireland in January of 1911 George Moore had finally carried out his long threat to take his ceremonial leave of Dublin for London. His friends were desolate. Susan Mitchell, who liked Moore, "big baby and little devil" as she called him, lamented his passage—though she felt J. B. Yeats had been a still greater loss to the vitality of the city: "Conversation has become a lost art in Dublin since he left it; people only gabble now." [4] She threatened to come to America and bring Mr. Yeats back by the hair of his head. Moore's departure left Æ lonely and sad, especially when Moore's at-home evenings came around. "I miss him very much," he wrote to Quinn in the middle of February. "For the last two Saturdays I have wandered about trying to find a way of spending my Saturday night, which for seven years I spent with Moore." [5] He suggested that "George Moore" be made "a generic title, like Pharaoh, King of Egypt," to be vested in qualified persons in turn, those who showed signs of his gadfly virtues of animated irreverence and general satirical intelligence. Compared to Moore, Æ felt, most of the Irish writers he was seeing showed little but anemia, prejudice, and poverty of ideas. "There is nobody bold or broad enough to take his place," he mourned. [6]

By the end of the year Moore's first volume, *Ave*, was out and the second running in the *English Review*. Russell reported on December 7 that normally tepid Dublin was "seething" over the book, "frothing and fizzing for the last month as if somebody had flung a powder into it." Everybody "detested" the book and read it enthusiastically. Æ expressed a half-serious terror of what Moore might make of him as the work progressed: ". . . the Lord alone knows what controversial theology he may make me talk." So far he had fared well in Moore's hands, and he had little cause to worry: Moore told Quinn that he conceived Russell as "the Christ" of the work. The book in general, Russell thought, was "a desperately reckless and clever caricature. . . . one can see clever people struggling with the adversity of a brilliant historian." He summed up with his standard generosity: "Yeats, Hyde, myself and other literary folk will never get so vivid an account of ourselves and our follies written by some more sympathetic critic." To Francis Hackett, who had asked for his opinion, Quinn pronounced himself bored by *Hail and Farewell*. Apparently it was too slow and luxurious in plan for his impatient temperament. He read it in bed, he wrote Hackett on April 4: "and the only emotion that I can truthfully say it gave rise to was that of slumber." And generalizing on Moore's "egotism" he pronounced one of his occasional pompous and inscrutable dogmas: "All people with imagination are egotists, more or less." What Quinn really liked in Moore, he said, was his lack of pretense. He remembered observing with sympathy, on an earlier trip to Dublin, Moore's open suffering as his friends sprawled about his beautiful eighteenth-century house, spilling whiskey and cigar ashes on his mahogany and kicking the legs of his Chippendale tables. It had struck him as a dramatization of the built-in vulgarity of even cultivated Irishmen.

Moore was one of the persons Quinn wished most to see this summer of 1911, and he was happy to have him out of Dublin and in London; he did not intend to go to Dublin. He fell into his bed on the *Mauretania* at nine o'clock on the morning of August 23, having worked straight through twenty-one hours with a half-dozen other men in his office to clear his desk for departure. He sailed for home a month later on *La Savoie* from Le Havre. In the interval he had spent ten days in London, an equal time in Paris and Provence, and a final day or two in London. His snubbing of Ireland and his courting of France showed his new cultural directions, which this trip did much to define. Because Quinn left a fragmentary diary of these days, it is luckily possible to follow him in some detail. The feature of the whole thing was his close but not always easy companionship with Augustus John. John too wrote of their association, patronizingly, in his vivid, careless autobiographical notes, *Chiaroscuro*.[7]

In London Quinn stayed at the Ritz, and his first diary notes, for September 3, record a leisurely morning with breakfast and the Sunday papers in his room. May Morris joined him at the hotel for luncheon, bringing maps for their motor trip in the afternoon. They talked of her work for Longmans, and Quinn was shocked to hear that they were paying her only £10 per volume for all her work of editing and commentary: "So she gets less than a typewriter. . . . " In a big touring car they drove first to the Tate Gallery, where he admired the Turners but thought the sculpture collection "very very bad." Miss Morris pointed out Dante Gabriel Rossetti's portrait of her mother. Quinn considered it "a magnificent thing. . . . a splendidly rich picture of a beautiful woman." After less than an hour in the Tate they drove on through Chelsea, Richmond, and Twickenham to Windsor. The castle struck him as depressingly anachronistic and prisonlike. After tea they returned by the Hounslow Road to London, Miss Morris taking her leave in Hammersmith.

The evening was passed in the Café Royal with Augustus John, "sober but normal looking," according to Quinn's cryptic note, Innes, George Moore, and Jacob Epstein and his wife, Margaret Dunlop. The talk was of art and artists, and John gave an account of the hectic current condition of his affair with Mme. Frida Strindberg. In the latest of what he called in *Chiaroscuro* "a long series of grotesque and unedifying adventures," [8] seeking to terminate the affair, he had gone to see her in response to four or five pleading letters, and had found her (according to Quinn's notes) a "wild woman," who "clutched and raved." John told her she had forced herself upon him from the outset and had made herself a nuisance for two years. He refused to accept the letter she pressed upon him, directing the White City authorities to turn over to him her check for *The Way Down to the Sea*. At length he broke away and left her. " 'If I had only kissed her she would have dreamed a more peaceful dream,' " he supposed.[9] After John's story he and Quinn talked of their coming trip to Provence, thinking of Aix, Avignon, Arles. The general talk turned to writers and their religion: Hyde, Newman, Pascal, Verlaine, Huysmans. Quinn quoted Newman, pressed his familiar argument that the weakness of Ireland was due to the poor education of its Catholic men, and concluded bewilderingly that Moore was neither Christian nor pagan but "everything by turns."

Next morning May Morris conducted him to the shop of William Morris and Company, which had carried on the manufacture and sale of her father's kind of artifacts. Quinn approved of the tiles but disliked the carpets, wallpapers, and tapestries. Proceeding alone to John's studio at 181 King Street in Chelsea, Quinn learned that Mme. Strindberg had attempted overnight, with unwonted efficiency, another of her serial "suicides." She had taken poison, and her doctor doubted that she would last out the night. John was visibly shaken but determined to break with her if she lived. It developed that he had sent £350 of her money to Albert Bazin, the French birdman, and later repaid her. So Quinn judged, dubiously, that he was "out of pocket by her." He advised John to depart the country if Mme. Strindberg died, and entertained John and Innes, who had joined them, with an impersonation of Augustus John in the witness box. Innes had brought with him several small oil studies and one large picture, much influenced by John, Quinn thought. He selected two of the small pictures and paid Innes for them on the spot, £10 each. John had now committed himself to the Provence trip, and Quinn accompanied him to the Chenil Gallery to buy painting supplies. Quinn lingered after John left and picked out seven pencil drawings and one in charcoal to add to the fifteen Welsh and Provençal studies in oil for which he had already agreed.

Quinn took his taxi to Parkenthorpe's in Ebury Street, where John had told him both the clerks were homosexuals. "They looked it," he decided, after inspection. He bought half-a-dozen bibelots and examined a beautiful old Queen Anne cabinet of polished walnut. He sensed a flirting move by another patron and later described the Edwardian episode: ". . . a beautiful Englishwoman with a fat husband. She was all in white lace over pale print, and in a big white hat. She moved about and looked at me across the screens of lacquer and the cabinets and from around the cabinets." Back at the Ritz and tired out, he lay down for a half-hour before driving to Elkin Mathews and to Hatchard's, where he bought some books for the French trip and others to be sent to New York. At Elkin Mathews he enjoyed a colloquy with a clerk about Aleister Crowley, the black magician and satyr, "the wickedest man in England": Elkin Mathews had published one book of his " 'and we had a very 'ard time getting him to cut things out of it.' " Crowley was away now, " 'out of England because of something he had done.' " What was the trouble? " 'We don't know, Sir, only he has got himself dreadfully talked about—we don't know about what.' "

Back at the hotel Quinn telephoned to engage May Morris for dinner, taking care to specify that he had a nine-thirty appointment. She invited him to take pot luck at her house. As he was leaving the hotel John dashed up in a taxi with a girl whom Quinn recognized from the drawings as one of his models, and appointed a meeting for ten o'clock at the Café Royal. In Hammersmith Terrace May Morris looked

charming in a simple gown of Greek pattern but not white—pale pink stripes in cream-coloured body. The moon was up and the little garden looking out on the river was very fine. The tide was out and there was a fine tang of the salt water coming into the open windows from the river.

The house had no gas or electricity, and Quinn and Miss Morris shared by candlelight "a deliciously simple meal" of chops, potatoes, salad, cheese straws, stewed peaches and fresh fruit with Rhine wine, and Turkish coffee. They talked of her father, for the most part. Miss Morris told of his casual gifts of illuminated manuscripts to Lady Burne-Jones. When May Morris had told her that she wished her father would give her some of such things, Lady Burne-Jones replied: " 'Oh, that would be like keeping them oneself.' " She had managed to keep hold of some of her father's stained glass; but a big window which she had coveted had been broken up at the works after his death by persons who had thought she would not be interested in designs of Homer and Pericles and " 'other such Johnnies.' " She and Quinn talked of furniture. Miss Morris said: " 'You seem to think you can buy anything with money.' " Quinn "disabused her mind of that notion." With her permission he smoked a big cigar in her chaste drawing room, then walked down Hammersmith Terrace with her until a taxi appeared. During the evening he offered to make her a present of a pendant watch; but she preferred a little ring. " 'Make believe it is serious,' " she said.

At the Café Royal Quinn found George Moore in company with "a cultivated German looking man. . . . a keen-cut well dressed man of about 42 sandy mustache," who turned out to be Max Meyerfield who had translated Moore and Wilde and Synge into German. Moore wanted to know where Quinn was getting his Corona cigars at twenty-six shillings per box of twenty-five— and, predictably, "took one of mine." Moore sniped for a time at Yeats, and then they talked of Synge, with whom Meyerfield had corresponded at length. Innes played chess nearby with Daviel, the engraver. George Moore proffered several burlesque "subjects" for paintings: " '1) Time kissing the big toe of Eternity; 2) Life bridging the chosen of death; 3) The last Pope administering extreme unction to God.' " Augustus John, coming in with his model, pronounced for the third. The girl was Lillian Shelley, who generally was called by her last name only. John sat staring at her, trying to hypnotize her. Moore left in mid-evening but Meyerfield stayed on to talk with Quinn, who found him "a delightful, accomplished man." Mrs. Euphemia Lamb entered with young Howard, nephew of the Duke of Norfolk, handed him the Pekingese she was carrying, and walked across to kiss Shelley. When the party broke up at twelve-thirty, John and Daviel walked back with Quinn to the Ritz where they inquired about trains for Paris and made plans to shop for their trip. Tired but exhilarated, Quinn closed his entry for the day: "John very gentle & calm & bright. I came up here and wrote all of this from 12:30 to 2:30 & then turn in to eat the sandwiches before me & then to bed. Sorry I hadn't made notes every evening of the days of last week."

Tuesday morning Daviel came in by appointment to show him proofs of his engraving of a John drawing. Quinn liked it and paid him five pounds and nine shillings for a second copy: "Beautiful flesh tints—satin finish on belly of the kid." May Morris came for lunch at the hotel. Quinn put her into a taxi and took another to an engagement in the City. Looking about at the Inns of Court he decided he would not wish to practice law there: ". . . out of date—would not want to be there."

Back at the hotel he paid John £190, making a total of £200 he had paid for the Provençal studies. They shopped for bags and suitable caps and coats for the coming automobile journey, then after tea went again to Parkenthorpe's where Quinn bought "16 or 17" more bits of bric-a-brac and for £24 the Queen Anne chest that had caught his eye the day before. He went with John for a visit to a gypsy camp in an unnamed suburb, and circulated a box of cigars of which the "king" kept over half. They returned to the hotel past a "lovely citron sunset." There they found Quinn's New York friend Bourke Cockran with his cousin Winston Churchill and Churchill's American mother. John assured Quinn privately that Churchill was " 'a self-advertiser—a camera with every scene' "; and Lloyd George was " 'a successful man but no statesman.' "

At the Café Savoyard in Soho ("delightful little french place") they met Innes, Howard, Shelley and Shelley's lover "young Valentine." Most of the party had been at the gypsy camp, and Howard was very drunk. Quinn had a good dinner of sole and chops and considerable Chablis. Shelley addressed him from time to time as "father," "papa," "lawyer," "detective." In mid-evening the party moved on to the Café Royal, where they again found George Moore and Meyerfield. Quinn wrote Meyerfield a letter of introduction to Epstein, whom he described as "an honest fellow." " 'You seem to have honest fellow on the brain today,' " Moore remarked. Quinn told him that John planned to take Shelley to Provence, and asked what Moore thought of Quinn's taking Mrs. Lamb. " 'She is very beautiful; take her,' " Moore advised. Quinn put the question to Mrs. Lamb, and she agreed at once.

Around midnight the party removed to John's studio, "two divans full," "all drunk." John entertained with singing, dancing, and pantomimes. Daviel gave his approval of the Provence scheme but only for one week. Then all went by taxi to Howard's flat. Before returning to the Ritz Quinn gave Mrs. Lamb £5 in gold for the needs of the morning, and John changed £20 into French currency, explaining that he did not want to be a sponge. The four Provençal travelers agreed to meet Howard for breakfast before setting out on their journey. Quinn doubted that the ladies would appear in time. During the evening Quinn reflected that praise he had had from John was "the highest compliment I ever had." He was under the spell. He concluded his entry: "A rather busy day from 10 a. m. to 2:30 AM. I drank a lot of Chablis. Hope the trip will be pleasant."

The last morning in London, that of Wednesday, September 6, was spent in packing, getting money, paying bills. Quinn met May Morris for a melancholy luncheon. When he said he hoped to come back to London, and to spend more time with his friends, she cried: " 'For heaven's sake don't give all your time or spare me some of your time—or I'll go crazy.' " Quinn commented flatly in his journal: "The only outbreak she made this time."

Quinn made no record of the crossing to France or of the stay in Paris, but John set down a spectacular account in *Chiaroscuro*. Quinn had apparently carelessly revealed details of their trip to Mme. Strindberg, now back on her feet, and she appeared on both the train and the channel steamer. John locked himself in his cabin, but Quinn carried the huntress a cup of tea and made an appointment to see her in Paris. On reconsideration he decided not to meet her, and she committed another "suicide." From Quinn's scrappy notes it appears that Lillian Shelley and Euphemia Lamb did not cross to France with them and never appeared there. "Girls did not turn up"; "No girls"; a telegram, " 'Bill can't come' " (Shelley was also called Billie and Bill), are some of the pathetic entries—and finally: "Girls missing this—and so are we missing them."

For their trip to the south, Thomas Fortune Ryan had agreed to lend them his big seventy-five-horsepower Mercedes touring car with Ewald Brenner, "the best chauffeur in Europe." They found Ryan in Paris occupying "most of the Hotel Bristol." [10] John escorted the two Americans to the Bal Tabarin for the evening, but found them too grave; under Ryan's influence Quinn reverted to the heavy American type. John returned them to their hotel and went back to investigate a young Kabyle woman who had eyed him at the café. "The person of this dusky beauty exhaled the fragrance of musk and sandal-wood." [11] Next day he took Quinn to Vollard's and tried to interest him in the work of the new French painters, but found him not forthcoming, his taste still too timorous. Later Quinn mused in his notes that it was "wonderful how the Jews collect art. Two in Paris have a fine coln. of nothing but new men." He had heard of the Steins, evidently, and did not yet foresee that he would soon rival them as a collector of the new men. Now his nerve still had to stretch a bit to take in late nineteenth-century work. He visited Durand-Ruel's and James Durand-Ruel granted him a tour of his private collection in his rich apartment. Quinn was dazzled by the many Renoirs and Monets but did not plunge, fearful of both his taste and his purse. He did buy seven Manet drawings, and his plunge when it came was backward. He coveted the Puvis de Chavannes *Beheading of St. John the Baptist*, but the price was daunting, $12,000. When Durand-Ruel agreed to take back his Manet *L'Amazone* for a third of the Puvis de Chavannes, the deal was made and Quinn at last possessed a capital work of the painter he then considered the greatest of the century.

"John and I had a great time in France," Quinn wrote to Huneker after he returned home.[12] But it was not all so easy as that sounds. John was sometimes sullen or even insolent, and Quinn could never be sure when he would take off after a girl. John's own account in *Chiaroscuro*, written many years later and after disaffection had intervened, borders on the contemptuous. Quinn, he said, liked all the wrong things, from clothing to castles, and with his American bourgeois taste felt really comfortable only in the shelter of a luxury hotel. Quinn's private journal shows this to be unfair. It shows him working seriously at the instruction of his taste, perfectly willing to consider and to learn, and taking far more pleasure in the vicissitudes of the journey than John gives him credit for. Certainly he was enjoying it more than John was. John's position was difficult, and he filled it with little grace. He had done all this before, in freer more independent circumstances, and if he was to do it again he would have preferred it to be for a different motive and probably in different company. He simply did not like Quinn as much as Quinn liked him, and they needed each other with a difference that made a difficulty and turned John surly and ungracious.

Their journey was a long, hurried ellipse from Paris to the Mediterranean and back again; in little more than a week they "did," as Quinn put it, Chartres, Tours, Amboise, Blois, Montélimar, Le Puy (twice), Orange, Avignon, Aix, Marseilles, Martigues, Aiguesmortes, Arles, Nîmes, St. Étienne, Moulins, Bourges, and Fontainebleau. Obviously there was not time to do anything very reflectively. But Quinn enjoyed both the moving and the pausing, and felt himself to be reveling in good food, good drink, and good talk. In drinking he let himself go as never before or again in his life: ". . . we had two and sometimes three quarts of champagne a day—champagne for lunch, champagne for dinner, liqueurs of all kinds, vermouth, absinthe, and the devil knows what all," he told Huneker on November 15. Their route took them twice through the heart of the Cévennes, and with the roads and machines of 1911 this could be harrowing travel. Descending a mountain road one night in a dense fog, Quinn, according to John, showed the edgy state of his nerves by throwing himself bodily out of the vehicle: ". . . in one masterly leap precipitated himself clean through the open window," [13] to everyone's surprise rolling over unharmed. Quinn's journal says nothing of this.

Quinn's general object in the trip was not to see pictures, which needed more leisure, but to know in John's company a beautiful and historic countryside with its towns and buildings, and to talk at ease of life and letters with Augustus John. On the whole he was content, in spite of the strain of their pace and John's sporadic rudeness. When Quinn spoke of George Russell as a mystic who sometimes starved himself, and John growled: " 'What does that prove?' " Quinn mildly replied: " 'Nothing—I'm trying to prove nothing: I'm on my vacation now.' " When Quinn pressed his favorite attack upon the "dark" palette in painting, as too easy, John growled: " 'Nothing is easy.' " When Quinn suggested that copying frescoes such as those at Avignon would be good discipline for a painter, John said it was more important to express oneself: " 'It's better to be a live dog than a dead liar.' " John was bored, but he was not yet ready to dispense with a patron of Quinn's means and readiness. Ordinarily things went well enough. Of all they saw what moved Quinn most deeply were the tapestries at Aix. Predictably it was their brightness and purity of color that excited him. "Paint looks like tar compared to them," he jotted, and "cool—fresh—not sticky." That luminousness, he thought, was the secret of great painting, of the work of Puvis de Chavannes and of John himself. Enthusiasm for the tapestries and for Puvis de Chavannes John fully shared, for he too was an academic.

Impressionism, John argued, had reached its highest achievement in *pointillisme* and was now essentially dead. The Impressionists had thought in a way now outmoded of "episodes"; the episode would persist but the really creative painters were now striving toward "absolute" or "abstract" beauty. He and Quinn discussed the matter, and one feels Quinn again generalizing on the evidence of his sense of himself:

> Women quicker than men at that. I agreed as to the folk. In men the natural instinct for beauty killed or deadened by the struggle for life. Above the folk—among the bourgeois nothing—among others often a profound admiration or instinct for beauty—the appeal to the eye—not to the intellect. Few women have it; J. thought it instinctive. I said no—it could be—& often was—cultivated.

Their talk was of literature as well as art. John had now turned savage on the subject of Huneker, called him a poser and a phrasemaker and a man with no true taste or standards: he " 'swallowed

everything,' " and " 'admired things that killed each other' "; he
was not a critic but a " 'paid whore.' " Quinn could say in defense
of one of his best friends only that Huneker was too vulnerable
economically to afford real candor or strength of mind. They
shifted to safer ground. Quinn admired Baudelaire's criticism, his
appreciation of Wagner and of the free spirits among his contem-
poraries. John and Quinn came together firmly in admiration for
"the clarity and sanity of the French mind." John said he always
read French books, never English. Quinn cited Meredith's love of
France and the French language, and said that he himself never
read an American book—an untruth, and a disingenuous one. The
conversation trailed off into anecdotes of Oscar Wilde. John had
heard William Rothenstein read a letter from Robert Ross describing Wilde's last days. Wilde had been depressed and unwell and
descended one morning looking particularly ill; he had dreamed
he was in the middle of hell and it was terrible: " 'Never mind
Oscar said Turner I am sure you were the life of the party. That
seemed to cheer Wilde up.' " John told of Jack Nettleship's asking Wilde why he did not live with his wife, and Wilde's answer:
" 'Who could go to bed with a woman who slept in a flannel night-
gown?' "

It was entertaining to poke about John's old haunts with him,
especially in Marseilles and Martigues, where he was known to
many of the natives. Quinn accompanied John to restaurants and
cafés and at least once, evidently, to a brothel, which he found
drab: "no kick," he noted cryptically. At Martigues he explored
John's old studio, and at last met the elderly airman Bazin. He
showed no interest in Bazin's "machine" but admired his personal
dignity and handsomeness. The young daughter struck Quinn as
pretty but stupid.

There was no time left for Paris and very little for London,
where Quinn rushed through two last days shopping for pictures
and presents and paying bills. He did not see May Morris again.
On board *La Savoie* going home he spent most of his time in the
smoking room and got through two books a day. He particularly
liked Chesterton's "Ballad of the White Horse," and in a letter
of November 15 he quoted for Douglas Hyde the speech of the
Irish chieftain:

His harp was carved and cunning
  His sword was prompt and sharp,
And he was gay when he held the sword,
  Sad when he held the harp.

For the great Gaels of Ireland
  Are the men that God made mad,
For all their wars are merry,
  And all their songs are sad.

He was reminded of the Irishman who said: " 'If you have coffee give me tay, and if you have tay give me coffee, for I must have a change.' " Chesterton's grave jingle rattled about in his head for a long time, and he repeatedly quoted the lines, or variants of them, in application to vicissitudes in Irish affairs, his own and others'.

Though he continued to fulminate against the procession of begging Irishmen who came across the water, the "envoys" on "missions," it is clear that Quinn's heart and his purse were still open to many kinds of appeal. When Maud Gonne commenced painting, for example, Quinn loyally bought her rather amateurish decorations. He had a special respect for her as Yeats's Helen and daughter of the swan, and as a selfless patriot and free spirit. They had met only a few times, but she remembered his help in her "great trouble," and they addressed each other as "My dear friend" in a correspondence of many years. She tried hard to reconcile Quinn and Yeats. Willie, she said, was a careless gossip but not willfully malicious. Quinn was unpersuaded, though he continued silently to buy Yeats's books as they appeared, in lots of ten or more copies to be given to friends. Now he contributed generously to Maud Gonne's fund for feeding poor children in Irish schools: if the new generation were going to inherit Home Rule at last, it was well that they should not be weakened by starvation. It was largely thanks to Quinn, she said at the end of 1911, that her group had been able to give one hot meal a day to 250 children.

Even when he approved of an Irish "mission" he reserved the right of direction and correction, as Shane Leslie learned when he came to the United States in 1911 as emissary of Douglas Hyde and the Gaelic League. In time Quinn came to like and respect Leslie, who was a cousin of Churchill's and brother-in-law to Bourke Cockran, but on first view he was unimpressed. Leslie's performance at the Carnegie Hall meeting for the Gaelic League in November was one more "17th of March oration," a piece of standard Irish sentiment and rhetoric, when what the pragmatic Americans needed was a straightforward account of what the Gaelic League was actually accomplishing, especially for education and industry.

Quinn agreed with Æ that the Irish needed to work out their national salvation at home, and that the consequences of American-Irish dollars, by postponing self-dependence, might be debilitating and pernicious. He was thinking and writing a good deal at this time about the Irish in the United States. Knowing and deploring their shortcomings, their factionalism and bigotry, he still saw them as an able and generous race. On March 12, 1911, he wrote oratorically to Frank Hugh O'Donnell:

> . . . no country in the world can show an example of sacrifice and generosity toward the land that gave them birth, or gave their fathers and mothers birth, at all comparable to the generosity and sacrifice of the Irish and sons and daughters of Irish who found for themselves a fair measure of success in this country. They didn't come here equipped, as the Scotch are equipped, for the struggle for life. Most of them came here uneducated; many of them unable to write. They had little to be thankful to Ireland for, and many of them remember it as a place of poverty and squalor; and yet they have been generous and have remembered.

Quinn was thinking primarily about men like himself and his New York circle of emancipated and successful Irishmen, Dowling and Byrne and Cockran and Cohalan and Keogh. These were men of modest wealth who could still be depended upon to put their hands in their pockets for a hundred or five hundred dollars for almost any good Irish cause. And he recognized that theirs was an Americanized generation, a qualified Irishry. He knew from experience, too, that there were many Irishmen of grander fortune in America who could be depended upon to behave meanly.

Quinn thought of the decade from 1885 to 1895 as the high point of pure and sound Irish influence in America, best exemplified by General Patrick A. Collins of Boston. A letter from Lady Gregory elicited from him on March 22 a more commonplace patriotism. She remembered in her childhood home a case of stuffed birds that had been given to her grandfather by General Washington, and she mused humorously that Theodore Roosevelt might have given her a bear's paw from one of his outings "to carry on the tradition." Recent reading in Gertrude Atherton's *The Conqueror* and Trevelyan's *The American Revolution* had made her feel the tension and heroism of those times in contrast to the humdrum present. In his turn Quinn recalled his own boyhood when the American Civil War was a near echo and when the Revolution was made vivid to his imagination by lithographs of "The Spirit of '76." And he went on to list the numerous officers of Irish origin who figured in the Revolution and the War of 1812. "All through the history of the country," he concluded, "you will find Irish names prominent, if not the leading ones."

Before going abroad in August, again pressed for space for his books and pictures, Quinn had signed a lease for a much larger apartment which turned out to be his final home. At the end of September when he returned to New York he moved down the Avenue a short distance to the Georgian Court, at the southwest corner of 66th Street and Central Park West. Henceforth John Quinn was at home at 58 Central Park West. His new rooms were spacious and choicely situated at the top level, the ninth floor of the building, with drawing rooms across the front, looking out without obstruction across Central Park, the city's only sizable natural landscape. There was a long high corridor which he filled from floor to ceiling with bookshelves. He estimated his library now at "six or seven thousand" volumes. Four big bedrooms made space for himself, for guests and a servant, and up to a point for pictures. Quinn had not bothered to count his pictures, and there were still far too many for the larger wall space. Many had to be stacked in a bedroom and in closets. Purchases from his European trip were already complicating life. In November he wrote to Epstein of his rage at Parkenthorpe's for sending over a heavy oak chest empty and his delicate Queen Anne chest filled with fragile or heavy objects, damaging them and the chest itself. His first communication from Epstein had been a cable on October 31: "Could you advance money for stone bust." Quinn answered the same day: "Cabling sixty pounds," and wrote later: [14] ". . . sculptors I suppose, like women, sometimes have to live on their busts."

The whole idea of sculptured busts was sourly associated in Quinn's mind with Jo Davidson, the busy bust-maker, whom he despised.

The work of Gwen John was far from crowding the new apartment. Though Quinn had still not received the first picture for which he had paid her £30, he offered her on November 11 a further £50 for a second. She wrote on November 28 that her first picture had been hung at the New English Art Club in London and she had had "several press notices" about it. "I don't quite know what that means, but I suppose it means something," she said. She congratulated him on his new Puvis de Chavannes: "Surely he is the greatest painter of the century?" In her letter of August 22 she had been the first to call to Quinn's attention the work of a painter who was to matter to him in the highest degree, "a man named Rousseau," who had recently died and whose pictures she had seen at the exhibition of the *Independants*. Her primer prose style unconsciously caught much of his flavor: ". . . he was a douanier and at 50 years old he felt he must paint and so he painted, not knowing at all how to paint. His pictures are very remarkable works as you can imagine, but they are works of art."

Quinn had formed a qualified resolve to cut down on his book and manuscript dealings, but he was far from through with literature, and he found opportunities now that he was not even tempted to resist. Agnes Tobin, who was a friend of Symons and of Conrad, carried to both of them Quinn's offer to purchase manuscripts. She arrived in Symons's cottage in Kent just too late to prevent Symons and his wife, Rhoda, from burning as rubbish a pile of his prose manuscripts. "We must never speak of it—they feel terribly, poor things," she wrote to Quinn on March 29. But Symons's poems and plays in verse were intact, and he was heartened to hear of unexpected cash. The Conrad association, which ended in one of the saddest experiences of Quinn's life in the arts, began well and continued auspiciously for a dozen years. The lawyer and the writer commenced a correspondence which resulted, over the years, in Quinn's acquisition of nearly all of Conrad's manuscripts.

Inasmuch as Quinn was later accused of profiteering at Conrad's expense, it is well to note now that all their arrangements were open and amicable, and they proceeded to the apparent satisfaction of both men. The prices Quinn paid, from forty to a hundred and fifty pounds for a work, now seem very low; but he was dealing honorably in a different market. He made his offers when nobody else was coming forward, and he did not haggle. Conrad could have refused in part or whole; in fact he showed himself well pleased. "I would much rather you had my MSS. now than any one else—later on," he wrote Quinn on November 3. He said he was proud to form part of Quinn's "notable collection." [15] In setting a price for one item he said, ". . . pray don't think you have fallen upon a shark." And he repeatedly included extra short manuscripts as a compliment to what he called Quinn's generosity. Time made a shrewd thing of Quinn's good taste, but he was not guilty of sharp practice. And he was moved throughout by a deep admiration for Conrad as a man and a writer.

The affair began in August 1911 with Conrad sending Quinn the manuscript of one of his earliest novels, *An Outcast of the Islands* (1895), and that of his latest, *Freya of the Seven Isles* (1911). He had wished to send his first novel, *Almayer's Folly*, but the sheets of Chapter ix had unaccountably disappeared. He enclosed as a gift the eleven-page manuscript of the then-suppressed, now-famous preface to *The Nigger of the Narcissus*. Quinn had been following Conrad's new novel, *Under Western Eyes*, serially in the *Monthly Review*. On a train trip to Ryan's Oak Ridge estate in Virginia in the fall, he took along a copy of the English edition of the novel and reread the book as a whole. He sent Conrad an appreciation on November 15:

> It is quite worthy to rank with the best of Tourgenev's [*sic*]. . . .
> In reading most novels one is tempted to go through them with
> a pencil in hand and cancel the pages and paragraphs of padding
> . . . marking out . . . whole pages and entire paragraphs of stuff
> that didn't really add to the story. There is not a page or a para-
> graph that could be spared from your book.

He asked Conrad to autograph and send to him a copy of the latest number of the *English Review* which held a portrait draw-ing of Conrad by William Rothenstein. "I should like to have the drawing framed and hang it with photographs of Meredith, Wil-liam Morris, and one or two others of my favorite authors." He sent Conrad a volume of miscellaneous writings of William James just published in New York with the comment: "Everything that James writes is interesting and suggestive." Before the year was out Quinn possessed the original pages of a half-dozen major works of Conrad, including the immense heap, more than 1,300 pages, of *Under Western Eyes.*

The good and the bad in the Irish nature were given a prolonged dramatization in Quinn's circles during the fall and winter. The Abbey company had been invited to come to America and to make stands of some length in New York, Boston, Washington, Philadelphia, and Chicago. W. B. Yeats came with them. He had recently been honored with a Civil List pension of £150. Rolleston noted that the grant was twice the size of O'Leary's, a proportion which did not suit his own notions of relative worth. Quinn and Yeats of course did not meet, and Yeats in fact returned home early in the tour, to be succeeded by Lady Gregory. In the upshot Quinn saw a great deal of her, as he went to the aid of the players in several cities, and as she stayed at his apartment in intervals in New York. Later she called their association "a rapture of friendship." Quinn had already been a steady and useful friend, but henceforward their relationship was one of close and warm affection.

Quinn admired the players, and Lady Gregory herself, as almost the only Irishmen who came to America not to beg but to trade, to offer their art candidly as value received. He knew the plays, the players, and their leaders, and he tried to explain to the New York Irish the simple naturalistic motive that shaped their performances. He wrote on November 13 to Mrs. James F. Byrne, for example:

> These plays are given in a lower (and I think a finer) key than the people here are accustomed to, even if they are not great plays. An appreciation of the art of these players is a little like an understanding of Chinese painting or old tapestries, a matter that does not "grab" hold of one at the first jump.

He went on to say pessimistically that the American Irish rarely went to serious plays of any kind, and he had little hope now of a civilized response. He sensed too that the "pathriots" had been waiting impatiently for a chance to stage an exile version of the

Playboy riots of 1907. "That old fool" John Devoy worked hard in the *Gaelic American* to stir up hatred of Synge, especially, as unchristian and unpatriotic. Devoy quoted disingenuously, for example, a line from the text of *The Playboy* which referred to a woman's suckling a black ram to fatten it for the bishop's table. Quinn knew that the line was never spoken in performance, and he remarked to Judge Keogh that if the scene were ever actually staged in New York they would need a larger theatre than the Maxine Elliott, where the players were appearing; he suggested Madison Square Garden. He was politically and aesthetically outraged at the boorishness of his compatriots. He described their attacks to Hyde in a letter of November 15 as "the most bitter I have read in Irish papers since the last days of Parnell." What particularly infuriated him was that works of art were being denounced often in pure ignorance of their contents and by persons and principles that bore no relevance to art: "Everybody whose name happens to be Kennedy or Shaughnessy or Murphy or Moriarity seems to think he is a born critic of the drama."

Rolleston and Russell were moved to interestingly similar second thoughts about *The Playboy* by rumors of the hurly-burly abroad. Rolleston wrote Quinn on October 31:

> Synge's humour is often brutal. But the thing as a whole is great, and the impression of the West of Ireland folk which it leaves on the mind, though very unlike the sentimentalized peasant of the popular tales, is anything but disagreeable or vicious; on the contrary, one sees in these people a turbulent but powerful life, a sort of geyser bursting up from unknown depths. They are pathetically ignorant, wrong-headed, tremendously impressionable, and with no power of choosing what impressions should move them and what they should be impervious to; but they are richly, intensely vital, and, with any sort of decent chance to grow straight, this should save them in the end.

And Russell on December 7:

> When [Synge] invented or discovered Pegeen Mike, Christy Mahon and the rest he thought them, in all sincerity, glorious beings. He liked them better than any other kind of people, preferred their society to any other society, and had so little idea of running down or depreciating Irish peasants that I am firmly con-

vinced that he thought he was picturing a glorious society almost comparable with the society in Plato's Banquet, only his people were natural humanity at their highest as Plato's were cultured humanity at their highest. If Irish people only realized that Synge loved his characters and thought he was placing them in the most favorable way to show their vitality, their genius for speech and their naturalness, I am sure there would be no rows at all. Irish people never hated lovers of Ireland. They hate people whom [*sic*] they suspect sneer at Ireland. They were told by mistaken critics that Synge was sneering at the people he wrote about, and hence all the trouble.

Quinn had little hope for this kind of sanity and forbearance among the Irish in America. And what both sides seemed to have lost the power to see was that Synge was writing in the full spirit of comedy, in the love and dismay of a brilliant and robust comic intelligence.

Quinn attended the first three performances of *The Playboy* at the Maxine Elliott at the end of November. The first night was a shambles. The players could not be heard after the first few words. All the traditional vegetables were hurled onto the stage, and stink bombs and sneezing powders dropped in the audience. There was hissing, booing, loud coughing, and stamping of feet. Supporters of the play stood up and called for order. Ordinary neutral theatregoers looked on in fear and astonishment as men scuffled in the aisles and balconies. Policemen ejected some of the worst of the rowdies and peace was finally restored, but the evening lay in ruins. The morning papers reported these events in detail, some with shocked disapproval, some treating it with condescension or disgust as another piece of Irish ebullience or Irish barbarism. On Tuesday evening Quinn dined with Lady Gregory, Theodore Roosevelt, and Colonel Robert Temple Emmet before the play. He was astonished at Lady Gregory's unshaken calm: she had been through it all before. The second night went much better than the first. The audience appeared chastened by the newspapers' dismay at the behavior of the preceding evening, and further chastened by the presence of a great many burly policemen, many of them Irish of course. A few men were ejected for coughing, sneezing, or hissing, but things were generally quiet, and after a few awkward scenes the players could at last be actually heard. Roosevelt applauded loudly and often. Next night the rowdies confined themselves to grouping about the stage door and insulting the actresses as they appeared: " 'Ah, ye sluts, ye' "; " 'Ah, ye bitches, ye' "; " 'Ah, ye whores, ye.' " Quinn wrote to Daniel Cohalan after the third performance:

> Wednesday evening with the tension of the audience relaxed, the actors much more at their ease and the audience permitted to enjoy the play, there was laughter and fun throughout the entire evening, and it was obvious to everyone, as it would have been obvious to most of the disturbers on Monday night had they any sense of humor and had they ever listened to the play, that it was as it was called on the title page "A Comedy" and as its very name "The Playboy" implies, and not a chronological fact or history.
>
>   [*November 30, 1911.*]

Trouble followed the company from city to city, though Lady Gregory remained temperate and indomitable. When she was invited to address the Gaelic Society in Washington a Jesuit weekly charged that the invitation was forged and that it had been repudiated by the society. Quinn, in possession of the original invitation and printed programs bearing Lady Gregory's name, offered to donate a thousand dollars to charity if the charges were proven, the editor alternatively to make public apology. Nothing more was heard of the matter. In Chicago the Board of Aldermen passed a resolution asking the mayor to suppress the play. Quinn went to Chicago and persuaded the authorities to take expert opinion as to its content. The mayor, thus advised, decided the play was "stupid" but otherwise unobjectionable. Still more infuriating were the numerous anonymous letters, obscene and insulting, usually directed to Lady Gregory. One letter threatened her life. Quinn called in Federal postal authorities and hired private detectives, without result. In Philadelphia the company was arrested, on the warrant of a liquor dealer, and charged with putting on a sacrilegious and immoral performance. Quinn went twice to the city for periods of several days and secured a writ of *habeas corpus*. In the hearing he savagely cross-examined the complaining publican, his brother, a priest, and another priest, and elicited testimony that the fact that the play showed a boy and a girl alone together, in different rooms of a public house, was presumptive evidence of immorality; that nothing indecent transpired on the stage " 'while the curtain was up' "; and that " 'a theatre was no place for a sense of humor.' " Judge Carr took the book under consideration and dismissed the charge. "I skinned them alive," Quinn wrote in triumph to Rolleston.[16] At a farewell party before the players sailed for home, they presented him with a large low silver cup, a replica of the ancient Chalice of Ardagh, engraved with lines from Lady Gregory's play *The Image*: "He had a gift of sweetness on the tongue. Whatever cause he took in hand it was as good as gained." Quinn preserved it proudly.

1912

THE Philadelphia adventure, Quinn remarked to Townsend Walsh, made him think of the old vaunt that in Ireland a woman could circumambulate the island " 'without losing her virtue *even once.*' " He had been occasionally exhilarated by the fight for the players, but had found his own part in it degrading professionally and far more shaming than amusing. The whole disorderly business of the rowdy harrying of the players had disgusted him deeply. In time he was able to think of it all as a contest for orderly democratic process against a tyrannical rabble. "The fight here was not whether people liked it or not," he wrote to O'Donnell on February 23, 1912. "The fight was whether a few cowardly ignoramuses should be permitted to prevent the American people from seeing the play and determining for themselves whether they liked it or not." Less philosophically, he was moved to new personal animosities and thrown back upon his old biases. The affair was a kiss of death for the remnants of his first uncritical reverence for everything Irish. He was furious and disgusted at Hyde for weakly sending two messages repudiating any endorsement of the Abbey company in America by the Gaelic League—threatened by the Clan-na-Gael enthusiasts that they would otherwise sabotage the League's appeal for American funds. He quarreled conclusively now with John Devoy, with whom he had been sparring irritably for years. One of the Yeats sisters had published in an Irish paper a portion of a private letter in which Quinn had spoken of Devoy's " 'churning up the Irish patriots,' " and Devoy had reprinted the piece in the *Gaelic American* and called Quinn himself a coward for publishing the statement without his own signature.

As always, Quinn felt that the ultimate villains were the priests and the Irish darkness of mind that followed from Catholic education. "The whole fight against 'The Playboy' was ecclesiastical," he wrote sweepingly to Rolleston, who would be certain to agree.[1] To Æ, who had sent on to him a vision of noble temples blossoming in the Irish landscape, he objected:

> You will never get marble temples on Irish hills or the works of beauty that made the glories of Greece . . . until you have pagans, freed from the leading-strings of parish priests and parochial ignorance, and released from terror for their damned little immortal souls. . . .   [*May 15, 1912.*]

His own vision, expressed to O'Donnell on February 23, was bleakly Joycean:

> If the Irish are to drive all ideas, all thought, out of Ireland, if your "Irish peasants with fifteen centuries of Catholic faith behind them" [quoting the phrase in which O'Donnell had defended the instinct to attack Synge] are to attempt to stifle all thought except what is harmonious with their own provincial or parochial patriotism or their parochial ideas of what patriotism ought to be, then it seems to me it doesn't make any difference whether the Irish language is revived or not. Thought—fine, high thought—art, literature, poetry, painting, music, the arts generally, will go elsewhere.

While the players were in New York Quinn commissioned John Butler Yeats to make pencil drawings of six of the men and two of the women of the company. Mr. Yeats decorated one of his letters home with a pen sketch of Quinn bringing Bourke Cockran backstage to see the actors.[2] In a discussion continuing into the autumn of 1912 Quinn and J. B. Yeats argued the relationship of the Irish people to the Church, with the Protestant Yeats taking far the more tolerant view of graces and flexibilities in the union. His position was that the understood symbolism of Catholic dogma shielded its young communicants in a way denied to the more literal-minded Protestants. Among Catholics, he said, "the very infants know how to handle the mysteries," and young Catholics listened with delight to sermons on the terrors of hell. He told of an incident in his daughters' workrooms at Cuala Industries: when a group of young girls was sitting working quietly and seriously, one had broken the silence by exclaiming: " 'Sixteen years in boiling oil—God Almighty' "; and the whole group had shouted with laughter.[3] Quinn agreed that he would still enjoy a good Catholic priest's anatomy of hell "as a sort of archaeological survival"; [4] in fact he remembered being already amused and unfrightened by such sermons as a boy of eight or ten. But he was convinced that the Firbolg mind of the typical Irish peasant took the whole thing literally and lived out its time in bondage to the priesthood. It is easy to see why in a few years Quinn found Joyce's work so quickly familiar and congenial.

The Abbey tour had not all been an expense of spirit. Quinn had found a more genial satisfaction than in priest-baiting in the enrichment of his friendship with Lady Gregory. He had admired her serenity and commanding good sense in all the squabbling, had placed his office and his staff at her disposal, and luxuriated in their private times together. Before she sailed in March he accompanied her to Boston, where she was to lecture at Fenway Court, the famous "Venetian" mansion of Mrs. Isabella Stewart Gardner. After the lecture Mrs. Gardner gave them a tour of the house and the collection. Quinn was both charmed and impressed, and he showed his pleasure in the account he sent to Augustus John on March 7. "All the pictures seemed to be at home," he said of the Old Masters, and of their hostess: "She is a woman of wonderful taste and cultivation." In the evening they went to hear Marie Gay in *Werther*. Calling on Mme. Gay in her dressing room after the performance, he told her she was the image of the main figure in John's *The Way Down to the Sea* (for which John's wife Dorelia had served as a model). In France, she said, she had been likened to a Manet. From Coole Park Lady Gregory wrote on May 6: "Just two months today since I said good-bye to America and to you!" She complained of uncommon depression. "I have felt more profound loneliness than I have felt for many a year. I know that is just paying for past happiness, that rapture of friendship that so possessed and satisfied me." She sent as memorial an ancient seal ring for Quinn and a rosary for his sister; but they went down with the *Titanic*. "Perhaps I am as well off without the ring," Quinn wrote darkly to John.[5]

May Morris sent an entertaining note of an evening with the Irish Players during their visit to London in the summer of 1912. She went with a friend, she told Quinn, and both being short of cash, they sat in the shilling gallery,

> which at these plays is *very* intellectual—all the women in loose, flowing gowns, and the men with broad, thoughtful brows. And I'm sure in between they don't munch Rumpelmayer chocolates but nut-sandwiches and various brain foods.   [*July 17, 1912.*]

But *The Countess Cathleen* was as magical as ever. Things were soon back to normal in the theatre in Dublin. Now there were attacks upon St. John Ervine's short play, *The Magnanimous Lovers*. "Oh it is a long fight against insincerity and organized stupidity," Lady Gregory moaned in a letter of October 22. Life went on in ordinary ways as well. She directed Quinn to use money she had left in New York to pay for the American washing machine he had sent over for Coole. She told of a gay note she had had from J. B. Yeats about his self portrait for Quinn: " 'who is to pay me *any price I like to ask*. Under these circumstances a self-portrait becomes a colossal business, a wild labyrinth of infinite effort.' " Soon Lady Gregory was on Quinn's list for a Christmas box of American apples, and their relationship had settled into its cordial and homely future form.

In the spring of 1912 Quinn put down his disgust with things Irish long enough to join other Irish-Americans in cabling to John Redmond, leader of the Irish party in Parliament, urging him to work for the latest Liberal bill for Home Rule. The bill was an imperfect compromise, Quinn felt, but he was swayed by America's experience with her own constitution, "a thing of shreds and patches, plastered with compromises," [6] to view the Liberal bill as a *modus vivendi* which could be lived under and improved with time. He also hoped, as he confessed to Russell, that any Home Rule bill might put an end to "the painful spectacle" of Irish "envoys" on "missions" to America, pleading for money to carry on the struggle, promising victory year after year, like "Sarah Bernhardt's or Henry Irving's farewell tours, or poor old worn-out Patti . . . perpetually repeating their farewell. . . ." Accompanying his attack with a substantial donation, he wrote in the same harsh

strain to Padraic Pearse, the young schoolmaster and poet marked
for death in the Easter Rising, who was trying to raise money for
his school, St. Enda's College in Rathfarnham. Led on by Hyde's
careless " 'Oh, if John Quinn took you up it would be all right,' "
Pearse proposed a "mission" to America and asked Quinn to arrange it. Quinn bluntly declined. Pearse wrote back that he thought
he would come anyway; he stoutly questioned, furthermore,
whether the American Irish were either so much badgered or so
generous in response as the native Irish. Pearse did come on his
mission, and spent a winter evening at 58 Central Park West that
Quinn recollected emotionally four years later when Pearse had
been executed for his leader's part in the Rising of 1916.

In the spring of 1912 Quinn arranged to sell a large group of
his manuscripts to Henry E. Huntington for his great new library
to be established in San Marino, California. Before going abroad in
August 1911 Quinn had deposited his manuscripts for safety in
storage in the Equitable Building, and he had removed them later,
by chance, shortly before a disastrous fire in that building. The
whole experience had made him think how perishable and what a
constant care such papers were. That feeling, the perennial need
to find space at home, and his increasing interest in art had joined
to determine him to sell. Writing to May Morris on March 6 to
ask for the return of her father's manuscripts which he had lent to
her, he said: "My regret at selling the manuscripts is tempered a
little by the fact that they will not be locked up or be the property
of any one individual." In any case, he explained, he would sell
none of the manuscripts which had come to him as gifts, only
those he had bought. In the event he sold the papers to Huntington
at cost plus interest, what he had paid for each item plus what the
same sum would have earned in interest in the period of his possession of the manuscript.

Characteristically, Quinn quickly bought other manuscripts to
fill the space of the old. In April he paid Arthur Symons £35 for
the pages of an article on Conrad, and in August £40 for his
translations from Catullus. Conrad's own manuscripts were coming
on in an uneven stream, and his letters were a joy to Quinn, with
their glimpses of the writer's domestic and professional life. In the
spring Conrad touched Quinn by presenting him with the manu-

script of Stephen Crane's "Five White Mice," which had been given him in friendship in Crane's last days in England. Quinn had known Crane briefly in New York before he went to Cuba and before he made his name with *The Red Badge of Courage*. He remembered vividly the end of "The Open Boat," "the swift end and the limp figure of the man drowned just as the boat was beached," [7] though he had not looked at the story for years. When Quinn demurred at the gift, Conrad said he chiefly wished that "these few pages from Crane's best days" might rest in an appropriate place: "Let them go back to their native country and rest under your protection." [8] If Quinn preferred, he could consider that Conrad had not given him the manuscript but deposited it with him "for safekeeping and future disposal."

Of his own manuscripts Conrad sent in March the whole of *The Secret Agent* and the truncated *Almayer's Folly* "in the original wrapper as it was put away a month or so after the pubn. of the book"; [9] also the stories "Karain" and "The Brute." Conrad wrote on March 15: "The story *Karain* belonging to that parcel will be sent to you by the next mail. My wife can't lay her hand on the MS at the moment, and I don't want to miss the Saturday's ship." In fact, "Karain" went on the *Titanic* and sank with Lady Gregory's seal ring and her rosary. Conrad sent another story, "The Informer," in its place. In his own letter of April 15, after asking permission to address him as "Conrad," Quinn recollected reading *Almayer's Folly* when it came out in 1895 and mused sadly: "I seem to have had time in those days to read everything." Thought of Conrad's book, of his own past, and of his own present moved his mind obscurely to Hardy's *Jude the Obscure*: "I often think of the end of Jude, the stone-cutter, with his dog-eared and thumbed classical books and the open window and the summer day and the hand-clapping and the noise from the college commemoration."

The idea of his letters' being read by Conrad, an eminent artist whom he did not know personally and of whom he stood in a considerable appropriate awe, put Quinn into a more systematically reflective posture than was normal in his correspondence and made him take more thought for the quality of his normally execrable businessman's prose. His letters were invariably dictated, and they retained the wordiness and the droning rhythm of a busy man speaking in a hurry, but these letters to Conrad often showed passages of touchingly unconscious "literary" derivation and impulse. On March 27 Conrad had sent him a gratifyingly intimate account of finishing the long and for him unusually sustained labor of his new novel *Chance*: " . . . on the 25th March, the last words being written at 3.10 a.m., just as my working lamp began to burn dimly and the fire in the grate to turn black. . . . I went out and walked in the drive for half an hour. It was raining and the night was still very black." Quinn wrote back on April 15 that Conrad's account "made me think for a moment of Gibbon walking out after he had finished his work and recalling the time and mood in Rome when he resolved to begin it." He reflected that nine months and twenty-three days was a long time to give to one piece of work (Conrad had called it "my *quickest*"), but that he had spent comparable periods on law cases, "and as I look back there are very few of my law cases or law matters that give any real satisfaction or pleasure." Again he was feeling the wistful envy of the artist *manqué.* He was sending Conrad two volumes of Lady Gregory's folk history plays, and he pointed out that the second volume was dedicated to himself.*

Conrad was gracefully eager to turn his papers into cash ("I hope you won't think that I am trying to push my wares on to you. . . ."), and was searching everywhere among his effects. Jessie Conrad's silent prudence through the years had made it certain that he would find more than he expected: "How all this wreckage got preserved all these years is what astonishes me most." [10] In the bottom of an old sea chest he and his wife found *Falk* complete and a welter of loose leaves which yielded most of *Typhoon* and fragments of *Lord Jim, Romance, Nostromo,* and *The Nigger of the Narcissus.* Late in May Conrad sent Quinn the long manuscript, nearly 1,200 pages, of the recently completed *Chance.* He begged Quinn not to read it in its serial form in the *New York Herald,* but to wait till he could read it as a whole book. He told of beginning the novel in 1906, then setting it aside for five years before the final push.

---

* Lady Gregory, *Irish Folk-History Plays,* second series, New York, G. P. Putnam's Sons, 1912. The dedication runs: "To Dear John Quinn Best Friend Best Helper These Half-Score Years on this Side of the Sea."

Out of the "chaos of loose pages" in the sea chest, after two days of disentangling, Conrad was able to send forward *Typhoon*, "Amy Foster," and "To-morrow." For those he asked and got £70; and he offered to throw in some 300 pages of *Nostromo*, "Heart of Darkness," and *Lord Jim* "for an extra fiver." "And then," he wrote on October 27, "you shall be in possession of *every scrap* of Conrad's MSS. up to date, with the knowledge besides that you have befriended him in a time of difficulty." He promised Quinn that he would never sell or give away to others any of his manuscripts in his own lifetime, so long as Quinn kept his collection intact: "You have made a corner in Conrad. . . ."

But the story was not over. Conrad later turned up the manuscript of his only play, made from the story "To-morrow," for which he asked £40 and a typed copy; and he engaged to give Quinn free the manuscript of any play he should happen to write in the future. Then Jessie Conrad looked into an old cardboard box unopened for years and exclaimed: " 'Here's the *Nigger*!' " Conrad was deeply moved to rediscover the manuscript, bearing Edward Garnett's penciled notes in the margin, of the work he considered "the story by which, as creative artist, I stand or fall, and which, at any rate, no one else could have written." [11] He put a price of £80 on the manuscript, and said that but for need, "no money would have bought it." "Old, old days!" he mused.

> I began writing it in Brittany on our honeymoon and it was finished before we had been twelve months married. I haven't seen these pages for sixteen years and they looked to me strange, as if written by some man I used to know in the past and just could remember dimly.

The same cardboard box yielded the 113 pages of "The Return." When Quinn accepted these manuscripts he was assumed to possess every surviving autograph manuscript of Conrad's except *The Mirror of the Sea*, which had been largely dictated: ". . . there can be no further discoveries because there is nothing more to discover," Conrad wrote at the end of the year, on December 8. Even this was not quite true: odd bits, or alternative forms, of other works still turned up sporadically. But by and large, henceforward Quinn had to wait for new manuscripts until Conrad wrote them. The collector had drawn abreast of the creator.

Conrad's motives in these transactions were clear. He respected Quinn's collection and was glad to be a part of it. But also he was a writer working for bread and medicine, racing against need. Thanking Quinn for a draft in a letter of February 9, 1913, he wrote: "The hundred pounds will pay last year's doctor's bill and cover my overdraft at my bank. They save me from the necessity of putting aside the work I am busy with now to write a couple of silly stories for the magazines." For Quinn, to receive the many pages of Conrad's handsome script, to box and catalog them elegantly, was to taste the satisfaction of close and serviceable contact with genius, in Conrad a lofty yet humane genius. It was a pleasure, for example, to have such a man write to him so familiarly of another they both admired: "I see in my paper that Henry James is going to be made a Litt. D. of Oxford. *Honoris causa*. Well done, Oxford! He's a grand Old Boy." [12] Quinn wrote back on June 18, "Henry James . . . is the best this country has turned out or away as a novelist in my time." For a man with Quinn's tendency to feel sorry for himself, it was a pleasure to hear genius being confidentially grumpy, as Conrad was in his letter of July 1:

> . . . I am far from ascribing to literary work any sort of special merit—or special difficulty. I am only getting a little tired of it. After sixteen years it is excusable; for, in that lapse of time, illusions get tarnished a bit and one's imaginative machinery begins to show signs of wear. It works, but it creaks—which is annoying, and also a little alarming for a man who has to depend entirely on it for everything. I can't go on living on my reputation, as some great business firms contrive to do for quite a long time after the inspiring spirit has departed.

Quinn's side of the correspondence was, like himself, clear-headed and systematic on the practical side, busy, rangy, and unprofound in philosophical ideas, full of crotchets. Conrad's gout, like his brain-fag, was real, and so was Jessie Conrad's wretchedly lame knee. Quinn prescribed for both of them at length, and rehearsed his own symptoms and the exhausting trials of his professional life. Untroubled by any sense of incongruity, he indulged in his favorite game of *ex post facto* "editing" with Conrad:

> I amused myself on the train by making chapter headings and cross-references [in a copy of Conrad's *A Personal Record*] as I

would with a law brief by one of the juniors in the office who
had run his points together. My first chapter ran from the beginning to the bottom of page 32. My chapter two started at the top
of page 33. . . .   [*February 11, 1912.*]

Madame Delestang's warning to Conrad: " 'Take care not to spoil
your life,' " cited in that book, gave Quinn a chance to recall in
the same letter a Jamesian interval in his own past:

> The same words must have been said to many others. I know
> they were to me, over twenty years ago, by the widow of a dis-
> tinguished general. She was about forty; I was about twenty. I
> knew her in Washington. She advised me to take care not to spoil
> my life, while her younger sister, about thirty-five and a widow,
> was trying to charm me. Both were good women and both very
> human. . . . One offered councils of prudence and wisdom, the
> other of experience and affection. One was wise and unselfish, the
> younger courageous and beautiful.

Making use of ideas picked up recently from J. B. Yeats and years
earlier from W. B. Yeats, he kept trying to enroll Conrad among
the admirers of Meredith's "reticence." He wished Conrad to know
his own friends in England and introduced Arthur Symons and
Augustus John to Conrad from across the Atlantic on June 18.
"Symons is a charming man, a very sensitive man, but his illness
has made him self-centered. The only sign that I ever saw of his
illness was fearful impatience of contradiction. . . . You would
like John immensely. He is a remarkable man and I am very fond
of him."

John continued much in Quinn's mind and in his pocketbook.
In March the Chenil Gallery in Chelsea sent him a bill for £754
for two works of Spencer Gore, two of J. D. Innes, one of Gwen
John, and fifteen of Augustus John, the Welsh and Provençal
studies. Quinn was touched to hear of the illness and death of
John's little son Pyramus, whom Knewstub of the Chenil Gallery
described to him as "the most lovable of all his sons," and in July
he paid John E. Slade £200 for Augustus John's *Caspar and Pyramus*, a painting of two of the sons, which Slade had bought from
John's exhibition of December 1911. He had sent John an advance
of £100 to hold the large decoration *Forze e Amore* which he had
admired in an unfinished state the preceding autumn; and he was

working hard to get *The Way Down to the Sea* away from Mme. Strindberg. In October 1912 he finally got his way, after a complicated strategy conducted through John Slade: Quinn anonymously put up £600 for a loan to Mme. Strindberg, with the picture as security, to be sacrificed if she did not repay the money by an early date. It was tacitly assumed by all parties that she could not meet the deadline, and so it proved: Quinn had his picture, but it had cost him an extra hundred pounds and a great deal of nervous expense.

The Gore and Innes pictures of his Chenil purchase he had taken in compliance with Augustus John's loyal enthusiasm for the work of his friends. The Gwen John purchase, if it should ever be consummated, Quinn thought of as his own enthusiasm. John had led him to Jacob Epstein, and there Quinn had willingly taken possession. He had seen Epstein hard at work on his Oscar Wilde Memorial in the fall of 1911 and thought it a work of high promise. In the spring Epstein was excited and energetic, with the feeling that he had brought off a triumph in the Wilde memorial. He wrote Quinn on March 22: "I don't want to rest with the Oscar Wilde but go on & do new things: no work no matter what the scope would appall me, the larger the better; I want to carve mountains." Quinn sought a modest mountain for him by recommending him to friends on the Committee of Fifteen charged with planning the New York Building at the San Francisco Fair. But the puff accomplished nothing, and by the summer of 1912 Epstein was in sad trouble with the Oscar Wilde work.

Florence Farr Emery wrote Quinn on June 18: "Epstein has made a great monument to Wilde & I have been delivered of the following septet upon it.

> Neither in Anuradharpoura,
> Nor Nineveh, nor Babylon,
> Nor cut in porphyry at Itzalan,
> Nor carved for Khefren's tomb in diolite
> Has a wrought stone
> Set prouder seal of silence on the dead,
> Than that enchanted, winged hermaphrodite.

The apparent equivocal sexuality of the figure, in the context of Wilde's famous habits, had caused a sensation when the statue was installed in the Père Lachaise Cemetery in Paris. The work was covered with a tarpaulin "on moral grounds" and the *conservateur* of the cemetery demanded that Epstein normalize his image. Epstein was of course enraged and crushed at this reception of what he felt to be a masterpiece, and tried to fight his case in London and Paris, adamant against any change. When Quinn was in London briefly in the middle of September 1912 Epstein appealed to him for an advance of fifty pounds to enable him to stay in Paris and conduct his resistance. Quinn gave the money at once.

Nineteen twelve was election year again, and Quinn was active as never before and never subsequently. As in 1908 he was a delegate from New York to the Democratic National Convention meeting in Baltimore in late June. Anticipating the event in a letter to Russell on May 15, he vowed to stay and campaign if the party nominated "a sane and conservative man"; but if they settled on Bryan "or some other wind-bag of that kind" he meant to go abroad in July. Quinn's personal candidate was a dark horse, Oscar W. Underwood, leader of the party in the House, whom he considered one of the few true statesmen he had met in America, in an acquaintance that included all the presidents and most of the cabinet members of the past twenty years. "Underwood has poise, great courage, foresight, good temper, and dignity," he assured Augustus John on May 24, and praised Underwood as a student of economics and of constitutional law. "Underwood has a mind like mine," he wrote John on July 8. "He comes to the facts." A fact they had come to in the interval was defeat.

Quinn spent June 22 in Washington working with Underwood on an anticipatory platform, and then was continuously at work in Baltimore until the third of July. Quinn and his friend Judge Daniel F. Cohalan were in effect running Underwood's cause, under the nominal leadership of Senator Bankhead of Alabama. "We had the fight won three times," Quinn said,[13] and he was certain his man would have won through but for a failure of nerve on the part of Bankhead, who released the southern delegates to Woodrow Wilson, weakly, in Quinn's view, at a point when resoluteness would have forced the other partisans to clear a way for Underwood to come through. Never a graceful loser, Quinn described Bankhead brutally as "nothing but a digestive tract, a voice, a sweaty, tired old face with a bunch of hair above each ear, glazed eyes, and no will." [14] Quinn could find nothing good to say of Wilson, the convention's choice. For Wilson he felt only the contempt of the professional, the politician and man of affairs, for the amateur, the type of the academic idealist. "The strong men in college do not become college tutors, college professors, and finally college presidents," he wrote of the Princetonian to J. B. Yeats on August 22. To Conrad he described Wilson's speeches as "a mixture of Morris' essays, Emerson's essays, and Samuel Smiles on 'Self-Help.' " [15]

As well as money and labor, the convention had cost Quinn the friendship of Francis Hackett. Hackett had given up his newspaper post in Chicago and was struggling to write a novel. Quinn helped him with money and in the spring of 1912 housed Hackett, more or less on his uppers, for a month at his apartment. He took Hackett along to Baltimore in June as one of his personal aides in the campaign for Underwood, then in the heat of the fight on the convention floor turned on him and denounced him as "yellow" and a "quitter." Hackett was irreparably insulted.

Chagrined and angry as he was at Underwood's defeat, Quinn still felt exhilarated at having been at the center of a big struggle over big issues. He had plunged headlong for ten days, sleeping about three hours a day, going to bed at anywhere from four-thirty to eight-thirty in the morning, yet he felt that he could easily have gone on so for another two weeks, "enjoying the fight." He had "got into the rhythm of it," [16] and finished fresher than he had begun. Enlivened by adrenalin and large issues, he had found the hectic interval less exhausting than his normal life in the law with its "distractions of clients, telephones, and office mistakes." "In that sense, this work of being on my feet and talking or listening twenty-one hours out of the twenty-four was almost a vacation," he wrote to John. "That will give you a little idea of what my time in the office is, when I honestly tell you that the time at Baltimore was restful compared to what it is in the office." [17]

As usual, he was "dreadfully driven." In the summer he had sloughed another partner, whom he had described to May Morris as "slipshod," "incompetent," "lazy," "conceited." [18] This particular "experiment in partnership" had cost him more than ten thousand dollars, he estimated to Conrad.[19] In a letter of June 18 he gave Conrad a picture of his normal situation in his personal office, with a large desk behind him, a long table in front of him, and clients' chairs on the opposite side of the table to keep callers at a distance: "I do hate to have people come up and attempt to 'paw' me or stand over me and talk down on me or get too close to me. . . . On the table are the different matters that I am attending to, just as a chemist has his different bottles and tubes in the laboratory watching the progress of different cultures or experiments." Agnes Tobin was in town in the autumn, and Quinn had taken her for a Sunday drive up along the Hudson with his sister Julia Anderson and her daughter, Mary. A few days later Miss Tobin telephoned his office while he was busy in court to say that she wished to take tea with him that day at the St. Regis. Quinn phrased his response to Conrad:

> She little knows that I am a laboring man. And, above all things, I hate to explain. But in about ten days I suppose I shall get myself up to the point of explaining that I am in the treadmill, that the courts are now open, and that I am busy. If she had a glimpse of my office today, with stenographers going and clerks on the jump, papers being dictated on the rush, and so forth, she would have fled, glad to get out without thinking of tea at the St. Regis or anywhere else.   [*October 29, 1912.*]

He felt so harried by August that he had about given up his plan to go abroad. With the nomination of Wilson he had cried curse upon American politics and resolved not to work for the nominee, though he was sure that any Democrat who could prove temperature, pulse, and respiration would be elected. Business was enough to tie him down. He had dreamed of reversing his plan of the preceding summer, going first to France to motor slowly to Aix and back, then to England to motor about with Augustus John and Miss Tobin, particularly to Kent to visit with Conrad and Symons. He wished to avoid cities, especially London, where he anticipated "late hours, cigars, and general weariness." Writing to Conrad on August 10 of his scheme, and pledging him to secrecy, he said: ". . . there is only one safety for me in London, and that is to get in and out before too many persons know I am there. Otherwise I will have telegrams and notes and invitations to dodge and explanations to make for dodging them."

Circumstances altered his plan with tragicomical perfection. After he had decided he could not go at all, he was peremptorily summoned to France by a cable from Thomas Fortune Ryan. Sailing hurriedly on September 3, Quinn landed at Cherbourg on the ninth, and took a night boat train which put him down in Paris at four in the morning. Ryan's affairs would not let him leave Paris, and this time he found the city "hellish"—rainy and cold, like his own mood. He wrote of it to Conrad after his return: "Paris is like other things, and people, and women, I suppose. Sometimes it appeals to one and sometimes it does not. This time it was hateful to me and everything in it." [20] He was nervous and peevish, and so tired physically and spiritually that on several of his eight days in Paris he went to bed in mid-afternoon in his hotel. For the third year he tried and failed to meet Gwen John, missing her in both Paris and London. Maud Gonne he did see in Paris, and with her toured one of her favorite retreats, the weird little Musée Gustave Moreau, stuffed with Moreau's drawings and his immense spectral decorations. In two days in London he saw something of Augustus John and May Morris, but before he could make the trip to Kent to meet Conrad in the flesh he was summoned home by cables announcing crises in the office. "A most unhappy trip," he summed it up. His friends told him he looked worse than when he left home.

Yet he made a daring purchase from Vollard in Paris of three pictures which were the true nucleus of the John Quinn Collection as it took shape in the coming years: a Cézanne portrait of his wife, a Gauguin Tahitian scene, and a Van Gogh self portrait. And, though he had not met Gwen John, he had at last seen at Chenil's in London the picture she intended for him. "It is a perfect little gem and I am very much pleased to have it," he wrote her on November 1. Forthwith he handsomely offered her a subsidy of £100 annually, for which she might do for him one, two, or three pictures, as she chose: "This is not trying to monopolize your work or anything of that sort. . . . I think we both might possibly be the gainers from it, I in the assurance that I should have two or three pictures a year from you, and you possibly in the reliance that you would have that much certain from your work." Gwen John wrote back promptly on November 17, with the modesty that had engaged him to her in the first place: "I find it difficult to thank you as I wish to for your offer to buy my pictures regularly and to send

me the money regularly. I cannot decide on my answer now but
will in a few weeks. It would be very good for me to have money
regularly and so be able to have models but I am not sure at the
moment whether my pictures will be good."

Quinn's major enthusiasm on the literary side at this time was for
the letters of an old god of his, George Meredith, which had recently been published in two volumes. Quinn praised the letters
to his friends and sent them as gifts to many, including Lady
Gregory, Florence Farr Emery, May Morris, and Æ. Meredith
figured largely too in Quinn's rich epistolary dialogue of this year
with John Butler Yeats. He sent the Meredith volumes to Mr. Yeats
with a peremptory summons to return first editions of Whitman
and Swinburne, previously lent. The old man had misplaced those
under a pile of clothes in a drawer. Commending the Meredith
letters, Quinn recalled approvingly Stevenson's statement that
Meredith was " 'built for immortality.' " He himself habitually
referred to Meredith as "the immortal." "These letters are the best
letters in the English language; infinitely more interesting to me
than Fitzgerald's letters," he wrote J. B. Yeats on October 26, and
moved on to beg the question: "These letters are great because one
feels that there was a great man back of them, and Meredith was
a great man."

Old Mr. Yeats's speculations about such matters were altogether
more complex and philosophical than Quinn's, and he pursued ideas
into areas where Quinn gave up trying to follow him. Ideas tended
to matter and carry meaning for Quinn when they were attached
to personalities and events. Thus he handled Augustus John's ideal
of "abstract beauty," expressed the summer before, as philosophically a cant phrase, comprehensible only in terms of its empirical
working. He wrote of this in a July 25 letter to J. B. Yeats:

> John has real intellect, I often think, more intellect than imagina-
> tion, but above all he has a fine idea of beauty, abstract beauty.
> It is hard, of course, to define "abstract beauty," but it is the thing
> that Keats placed above all, and Shelley.

Quinn had long abandoned his reading in theology. Though he
leaned more to history, biography, criticism, he still read a good
deal of philosophy—but preferring those works, as in Nietzsche,

William James, and Santayana, where the emphasis was ethical or aesthetic. With pure thought Quinn was soon bored and uncomfortable. He had, after all, little enough time for speculative thinking, and it says much for his mind that he kept up such a correspondence as this with J. B. Yeats in the midst of such a summer and autumn as this of 1912.

Always an eager and able controversialist, John Butler Yeats had been invited by his son to set down his ideas formally in letters which would be published at Cuala, and he was trying now to think in a broader range and in more consecutive form than was common for him. It is his posture of formal *philosophe* which complicates and enriches his correspondence of this year with Quinn. When he began to expatiate upon one of his favorite speculations, the relation of "the ego and the infinite," Quinn's pragmatical gorge began to rise. He wrote on August 24:

> I did enjoy your letter of the 15th. But I can't follow you when you say that in art "beauty and the infinite are identical terms." I don't quite know what the infinite is. Emerson overdid it, and about ten years ago I came across a book by a man named Ralph Waldo Tryne called, "In Tune with the Infinite." I have never been able to read much of Emerson since.

Quinn's praise of Meredith's "manliness," his fullblooded size and roundness, the depth of his roots in life, was one of the starting points of this general argument. Like many of his deepest affections, Quinn's admiration for Meredith dated back to his boyhood. One of the most deeply satisfying of his manuscripts was the 300-page record of Meredith's reports as a publisher's reader for Chapman & Hall. Both Quinn and J. B. Yeats had recently been reading Strindberg's grim play *Miss Julie*, and for Yeats talk of Meredith and Strindberg was made to lead into another main current interest, the work and the personality of Goethe. Quinn too had read a good deal of Goethe in the past; he recalled *Conversations with Eckermann* from twenty years earlier in Washington. What Yeats was trying Platonically to understand was the relationship of the self, the world of things and real experience, and "the infinite," the sense of ultimate wholeness and radiant impersonal significance. He saw that the ego was the source of all impulse and effort, the

locus at once of triumph and anxiety; but the ego was blessed with
capacity to feel a mysterious range of cosmic emotion, of inchoate
but inclusive significance, the breath of the universal. This contact
with ultimate beauty, he argued in a letter to Quinn, is "the God or
the Divine within us. It is also the holy spirit of the Gospel." It is a
consciousness that can be excited by many kinds of impulse, great
or small, happy or sad:

> Now this restless ego is suddenly quieted when we feel the in-
> finite—the far horizon, the starry sky, a line of verse, music, a
> beautiful woman, and thousands of things big and little, and among
> them this play of "Countess Julie" and that poor girl's woe.[21]

But the exciting impulse is always "things," realities of this
world. Music creates feelings but offers no trustworthy images;
paintings make images but they are mute; hence the richest art is
poetry, which moves the ego by images and sweet sound toward
the infinite:

> When feeling is very deep and strange and wonderful, as in a per-
> sonality like Goethe's, it cannot be put into words that would be
> intelligible. So Goethe, as it were, turned away from his friends
> and threw the whole thing into imagery and into a series of pic-
> tures, while at the same time playing to it an accompaniment on
> his harp, which is verse, so as to heighten the effect and excite his
> feelings to higher flights.[22]

Yeats agreed that Goethe had much of the robustness of presence
and of thought that Quinn was ascribing to Meredith. But when
Quinn kept praising Meredith's "reticence," Yeats was moved to
complex doubts of both the meaning and the value of the idea. He
compared Lamb and his letters to Meredith's, and found Lamb
more nourishing:

> His personality is interesting and enchanting, because he had the
> strength that was just sufficient and no more to keep together all
> his *faults and not lose one of them*. When the strong man weeps
> it is his *weakness* which is valuable.

Quinn's notion of Meredith's reticence, he wrote Quinn, was altogether too simple, a piece of cant criticism; thus:

> C. Lamb was essentially reticent, and for that reason always really
> poetical. Meredith was reticent on *principle*, but *essentially* anx-

ious to expand and explain his feelings. That is to say, eloquent rather than poetical. I have always thought the same of Browning. Hence, in both a certain restlessness and a curious straining after queer words. Meredith and Browning are trying to get *at* their readers, talking directly to them, which is the way of eloquence, not of poetry. You *hear* rather than *overhear* them. It was J. S. Mill who made this a test. [*November 1, 1912.*]

J. B. Yeats was developing, by trying it out on Quinn, a concept of "weakness" as a virtue: as a source of deep feeling, a valuable avenue to the infinite. When Quinn queried the term he defined it: "By '*weaknesses*' I meant all those vulnerabilities and sensibilities which cannot be exposed, being by their nature unintelligible except in closest intimacy. . . ." [23] Touchingly and entertainingly, he explained to Quinn the idea under the figure of marriage, which itself needed to be understood analogically:

When people marry it is not as the vulgar vainly imagine, that they may bring strength into union with strength. Marriage of that sort is not a marriage at all, no tenderness on either side. Marriage means that two people are bringing into the common stock all their weaknesses, and there are two comparisons possible. Marriage is sometimes like two drunken men seeing each other home. Neither can reproach the other or refuse sympathy or help. The other comparison is this: Marriage is like two mortal enemies (the sexes are enemies) meeting on the scaffold and reconciled by the imminence of the great enemy of both. [*October 27, 1912.*]

"So," he summed up in a rebuke that had grown unconscious in the exhilaration of argument, "in the individual man one likes to know where he is *sensitive*. Any fool can admire his strength. It is quite obvious where it shows a palpable menace." [24] And he closed with a gay apology: "Excuse my dogmatic way, which is never Lamb's or Goethe's way. I belong to the lower type, the pedagogic type." So he did, doubtless, in his own strict terms, "try to get *at*" his hearers, follow the line of eloquence rather than that of poetry. So did Quinn, a far less interesting hortatory type, though well enough in his way. The long line of thought had made Yeats think of Quinn at several junctures. Speaking of Goethe's satisfaction in controversy and in anger, he slyly instanced Quinn's way of thriving on irascibility. But he placed Quinn in a handsome light against the spectrum of the ego and the infinite:

. . . I think of all men I have ever known and watched you are the man in whom the Ego is oftenest quieted by passing into the infinite—this affection and that sudden sympathy or idealism—a whole apothecary's shop of herbs and simples you carry within you to keep yourself in health.   [*September 1, 1912.*]

That he meant something other than mere dreamy sentiment is shown by the idea that immediately ensued: "A good hatred, for instance, has in it a touch of the infinite." All in all it is a view of Quinn more sweetly charitable than one usually gets from other sources. Margaret Anderson, one of the editors of the famous *Little Review*, for example, remembers him as "the most irascible man I've ever known." [25] Van Wyck Brooks may have been the only person ever to describe Quinn publicly as "bland." [26] Quinn was a man of fierce feelings, a fierce lover and a fierce hater. J. B. Yeats's letter home to his son the poet in the first year of his transplantation in New York puts Quinn's case in a plainer and probably a more objective way, and shows Yeats's insight into the way Quinn's emotional possessiveness gave rise to equivocal behavior: " . . . sometimes it is a little lonely now that Lily has gone. Quinn is like a son to me. He is the crossest man I ever met and the most affectionate—affection and crossness go together with him, as with animals when they have their young with them." [27] J. B. Yeats's view of Quinn was colored by affection; but that affection, on the other hand, was inspired by Quinn's behavior.

It is perfectly clear, in any case, that it was worth one's while to puzzle out John Butler Yeats's tiny scrawl—which Quinn now habitually turned over to a secretary to be copied on the typewriter before trying to read it. The letters were a marvelous leaven in the mailbag of a busy law office. Quinn valued them as a stream of civilization flowing generously in, and he performed his part in the correspondence in a manner appropriate, if not equal, to the quality of his good fortune.

Quinn's intimacy with J. B. Yeats led to acquaintance in turn with the old man's friends among New York artists, especially the seminal group known as "The Eight," at the center of which were a group of friends and students of Robert Henri who had emigrated from Philadelphia. Quinn knew Henri, Ernest Lawson, George Luks, William Glackens, John Sloan, and Arthur B. Davies. With his prejudice against American art he was not buying many of their pictures, and Lawson was the only one of this group of whom he then owned capital works. Davies would soon come to be a good friend and valued adviser and one of Quinn's few enthusiasms among American artists. But at this point, late in 1912, John Sloan being most intimate with Yeats was best known to Quinn—though he saw most of The Eight with some frequency at Petitpas' or as guests at his own apartment. Quinn bought a complete set of Sloan's admirable etchings, which he found more pleasingly abstract and less troublesomely full of "convictions" than his oils. Sloan's socialism was all right with Quinn, so long as it was candid and so long as he kept it out of his painting, though Quinn's own political position was far more conservative. Sloan was on the board of the socialist organ *The Masses* and pushing hard for its success, and Quinn helped out in 1912 and 1913 with six contributions of twenty to forty dollars each. As a veteran propagandist himself he offered advice on January 1, 1913: "You ask me what I think of the magazine. I think it is too bitter in tone to make converts. Bitterness in propagandist literature may keep those already converted but it does not bring converts." On April 20, 1913, thanking Quinn for a doubled contribution to *The Masses* for the month, Sloan regretted the fact that J. B. Yeats's increasing deafness was beginning to take away some of his pleasure in conversation. He decorated his page with a pen drawing of W. B. Yeats wearing heavy dark pince-nez glasses on a long black ribbon and another of his father conceived as wearing a large forward-pointing funnel in each ear, and he wondered why one appliance should be thought any queerer than the other.

Other friendships, of greater or less intimacy, of course continued. The life of the handsome and worldly Florence Farr Emery was about to take a surprising tack. She wrote to Quinn from London on June 18: "I may go off to Ceylon the end of this year to end my days in the "society of the wise" as the Vedanta books say one should." By August she had gone back to her old school, Cheltenham Ladies College, "to find out the latest modern ideas in education," and had heard there and approved of the Montessori System: "It is exactly what I have always thought ought to be done." By the end of the year she was "Principal Mrs. F. F. Emery"

You asked about Mr Yeats — I saw him last about a week since — he was right well — deafness seems to be growing on him as you have perhaps noticed. This I think depresses him a bit it takes off the joy of conversation. Does it not seem strange that in these days when a man with a tiny defect of sight may look like this

W B. Yeats

and be regarded not abnormal

John Butler Yeats

A man with defective hearing would be regarded as a freak if he were gotten up so —

John Sloan to Quinn, April 20, 1913. Appliances: W. B. Yeats and J. B. Yeats.

of the Ramanathan College at Jaffna in Northern Ceylon, super-intending the education of eight hundred Tamil girls. The young Irish writer Brinsley MacNamara turned up at 58 Central Park West one morning at breakfast time and stood about looking mutely needy. Quinn gave him ten of the eleven dollars he had in his pocket, and later another twenty-five. On New Year's Eve John Butler Yeats was proud of having been kissed by all the girls at the party at Petitpas'. He said to Quinn: "The years bring their privileges." Quinn replied on January 7: "I think opportunity is the word." On Christmas Eve Quinn cabled to May Morris: "Sent you barrel pippins by Baltic nineteenth. Best wishes. Been dreadfully rushed. Hope you are well." It was cold comfort for a woman in love.

Frequent trips to Washington on political and legal errands, on top of his years there in the early nineties as law student and assistant to Secretary Foster, had given Quinn a bad stomach for "art" in that city. He sent Arthur Symons on April 15, 1912, a diatribe on the sameness and conventionality and general lifelessness of official art. If he could be made Commissioner of Fine Arts in Washington for six months, he said: "I would outdo the record of the French Revolution in cutting off heads—of bad statues. . . . The canvases wouldn't be worth much, but they might be varnished up and made into tarpaulins for government delivery wagons or small grocers." He was particularly offended by what he liked to call "contract sculpture" which he found in heaps in Washington and New York—works thrown together from stock elements, expressing standardized sentiments to order. Such work on a smaller scale he would dismiss contemptuously as "stove-ornament" sculpture: Paul Manship, for example, was a "stove-ornament sculptor." A favorite object of his rage was the big incoherent monument to the victims of the *Maine* sinking, in Columbus Circle at the entrance to Central Park, a few blocks from his home where he was forced to look at it every day. The memorial had been financed by popular gifts, in response to a sentiment egged on by William Randolph Hearst. To Quinn it seemed an embodiment of the disaster which was sure to follow from trusting art to popular taste. "It is that sort of thing that makes one feel that a man like William Morris, who thought that Socialism would bring back the fine arts of life, didn't think very far," he wrote to Epstein on May 22, 1913. Epstein suggested that the Suffragettes might be induced to blow it up.

Such feelings and such remarks offer a context for understanding Quinn's excitement over the great Armory Show of February and March of 1913, and his passionate commitment to its processes. The genesis of the event came in late 1911 and early 1912 when a group of New York artists, having abandoned hope of any progressive leadership from the National Academy of Design, began to hold meetings looking toward a new organization, "an association of live and progressive men and women who shall lead the public taste in art rather than follow it," as Henry Fitch Taylor put it in the meeting of December 19, 1911.[28] An ultimate group of twenty-five formed what was officially called the Association of American Painters and Sculptors when Quinn put through their incorporation on July 1, 1912. At their head were officers he identified to Augustus John as "some of the better young men here"[29]: Arthur B. Davies as president, the sculptor Gutzon Borglum as vice-president, Walt Kuhn as secretary, and Elmer L. MacRae as treasurer. Davies and Kuhn were acquaintances of Quinn's, as was Walter Pach, who did very important work of selection and propaganda in Paris and behind the scenes in New York; and Frederick James Gregg, who handled the major publicity chores, serving, like everybody else, without pay, was already one of his closest friends. Thus Quinn was drawn into events, as was so often the case for him, by a combination of personal loyalty to the principals and philosophical loyalty to the ideas at stake. The labor and excitement of carrying out the show brought Quinn close to Davies, Kuhn, and Pach, and they became part of his inner circle of personal and professional regard.

The Association of American Painters and Sculptors barely survived its first year of life, and it performed really only one function. But that single service, the presentation of the Armory Show in New York, then in Chicago, then in Boston, granted it immortality. For the Armory Show was the Continental Divide of American art, beyond question the most important event in the history of American taste in painting and sculpture, a rude push of American artists and patrons into the main stream of world art. The officers of the Association resolved at once on an exhibition, then on a large exhibition, then on a large international exhibition. The definition of the character of the show, its dominant shaping toward continental art, was largely the work of Davies's taste and his energy and quiet stubbornness. It was a direction perfectly congenial to Quinn as his own taste was beginning to take form. When he wrote to Augustus John on December 7, 1912, to urge him to send his work to the exhibition (as he also urged Jack Yeats), he suggested a grand portmanteau title for the Association, one which proved prophetic: "the Society for the Diffusion of Knowledge of Contemporary European and Particularly French Art in the United States." Within the built-in limits of American tolerance, that work of diffusion was precisely what the Armory Show attempted and achieved.

Davies had some money of his own, and mysterious sources of funds among his friends, and he sent Kuhn abroad to "collect" for the show, later joining him abroad. It is at least probable that money of Quinn's helped out now and later. The envoys visited Holland, Germany, and France, and finally England. In nine weeks of search, persuasion, and rejection they "nailed down" for the show immense quantities of European, especially French, art. But Quinn exaggerated by approximately 100 per cent when he set the figure to John at nearly 3,000 paintings as well as quantities of drawings and sculpture. Their way in Paris was smoothed by Walter Pach, later more important as a critic and historian of art, but working then in Paris on his painting, who had formed a wide and warm acquaintance among artists, dealers, and patrons. Quinn was enthusiastically aiming to lend as liberally from his own collection as the selectors would allow, and he wrote urgently to dealers and artists who had works of his on hand, trying to gather as many as possible in time for the opening. In Paris in September he had agreed with Ambroise Vollard for Cézanne's portrait of his wife, Gauguin's Tahitian scene (*Promenade au bord de la Mer*), and Van Gogh's self portrait. These were obviously prime material for the show, and on January 25 Quinn cabled Vollard 12,000 francs on account, promising the remaining 37,000 in quarterly installments. On January 14 he sent Gwen John £20 as the first payment on his promised subsidy of £100, the remainder to come in equal quarterly sums. "I *know* your pictures will be fine," he encouraged her. "I fell in love with the one I saw in London." He urged her to send liberally of her work to the show: "It has been organized by *men who know.*" Her pictures would have the company of her brother's, including *The Way Down to the Sea*, extracted from Mme. Strindberg. He instructed her to cable him how many paintings she would send, and offered a hopeful paradigm:

> QUINLEX NEW YORK
> FOUR (OR THREE)
> GWEN JOHN.

On January 24 she cabled back:

> QUINLEX NYK
> ONE
> GWEN JOHN.

Davies and Kuhn had not been able to see Augustus John or Jack Yeats in England, as Quinn had urged, and Quinn was anxious for those artists and other protégés of his to stand out in the show. On December 28, 1912, he wrote to John Knewstub of the Chenil Gallery, who had been assembling his purchases for shipment in a mass, insisting that he send at once everything he had on hand. Knewstub cabled on January 13: "Fiftyfive works . . . arriving Mauretania Saturday next. . . ." Quinn tried to hurry Epstein, but his *Euphemia Lamb* reached the show two weeks late, though then much admired. Quinn paid the Chenil Gallery £180 for it on February 6. Quinn remembered Mrs. Lamb's blonde beauty vividly from London, and was surprised to find her dark in the bronze form.

It was all intensely exciting. Quinn's loan would be by far the largest to the show, if not the most varied or daring. "All told I am to have about 75 or 80 pictures in the exhibition," he wrote Knewstub on February 5, twelve days before the opening. Of Knewstub's painters he said there would be many Johns, three Derwent Lees, and six Inneses. Milton W. Brown's *catalogue raisonné* of the actual exhibition lists the following works as lent by John Quinn: one Mary Cassatt water color; the Cézanne portrait; Auguste Chabaud's "sheep picture," *Le Troupeau sort après la pluie*; five works of Charles Conder, including two of the nine big paintings on silk panels done for Bing the Paris dealer, for which Quinn paid Martin Birnbaum $12,000 in early February, with the thought that they might some day decorate the music room if he ever bought a house; the Epstein *Euphemia Lamb*; the Gauguin Tahitian scene; a Goya miniature on ivory; two Nathaniel Hone landscapes; four oils and two water colors by Innes; fourteen drawings, three works in tempera, and twenty works in oil by Augustus John, including *The Way Down to the Sea* and *Caspar and Pyramus* and fifteen of the so-called "Provençal studies"; the first two paintings received from Gwen John, *Girl Reading at the Window* and *A Woman in a Red Shawl*; three oils of Derwent Lees; thirteen works by Puvis de Chavannes, mostly drawings but including the oils *La Décollation de St. Jean Baptiste* and *Femme Nue*; two oils by George Russell, a single water color by Jack Yeats. All these works were cataloged as "Lent by John Quinn" and of course listed as "not for sale." Quinn's loan totaled seventy-seven items. The list is not a true index to the emphases of his collection as a whole at this point: the selectors had taken what they thought would fit best in the general design of the exhibition, modernist and European. In quantity Quinn's list is impressive; in quality not strikingly so. The general drift is homely, solid, traditional. Only the Cézanne, the Gauguin, and the Van Gogh could be called truly capital and truly modern. His list offers only one piece of sculpture. His predilection for Puvis de Chavannes is obvious, and those pictures must have been particularly congenial to Arthur B. Davies, whose work at this time bore so many affinities to that of the Frenchman. Augustus John's presence and his influence are very heavy. Quinn's old Irish loyalties show through, but weakly on the whole, in the few works of Hone, Russell, and Jack Yeats. The single Quinn water color by Jack Yeats is a surprise, in that his work should have sorted well with the general tenor of the show. But Jack had also sent five oils himself (of which he sold one). The little Gwen John studies were among the quiet successes of the show, to Quinn's gratification. He wrote her on March 18, 1914, when the pictures had completed their travels and come back home, of the first one, charmingly Vermeer-like in pose and feeling: "Your little picture of the "Girl Reading" is invariably picked out in my apartment and immensely admired."

Quinn helped arrange for the renting of a home for the show, the big new armory of the 69th Regiment of the New York National Guard. It pleased him that the regiment was known as "The Fighting Irish." In his proprietary way Quinn came to think of the show as "his." At the opening, he wrote John on December 7: "I am going to have the Mayor of the town, the Governor of the State, and United States Senator Root and the French Ambassador, Jusserand. . . ." He explained to John how he would apply his own courtroom strategy in the interview he was preparing for newspapers:

> They want me to give out an interview in about a week. I am dreadfully rushed, but if I can spare the time I will do it. I am going to begin . . . with the statement that, apart from the old masters, there are not over twenty pictures out of the hundreds in the Metropolitan Museum that are worth wall space; that, aside from its old things, if those twenty pictures were removed from it, it would be negligible among the galleries of the world. I find in court that the way to do is to attack the other side, so that the opposition has to take up its time in *defending*. The man who comes out and *asks to be heard* is generally attacked. The right way to do is to demand that the other fellows be wiped off the map and then they may *defend* themselves.   [*December 7, 1912.*]

The immense bare hall of the armory was simply but gracefully treated for the show. Festoons of greenery, evergreen branches, and whole pine trees were spread about liberally, expressing, as did the pine-tree emblem of the publicity material, the strenuous "freshness" of the show. Broad strips of pale yellow and pale gray drapery eased the harsh lines of the ceiling, and on the floor eighteen octagonal "rooms," assigned to rather loosely designated "schools" of art, were formed by panels of plain brown burlap. In a letter to Walter Pach on December 12 Kuhn described Quinn as "our lawyer and biggest booster," and one "strong for plenty of publicity." Quinn had said "the New Yorkers are worse than rubes, and must be told . . . . our show must be talked about all over the U.S. before the doors open. . . ." [30] The preliminary fanfare had been efficient enough to draw 4,000 visitors to the opening on the evening of February 17, 1913, and they were ready to mill as Quinn delivered the brief address of unveiling. He was typically assertive

and categorical, but not ungraceful, as he praised the artists of the
Association for their labor, nerve, and unselfishness, and praised
the exhibition as in effect America's artistic Declaration of Independence: "epoch making in the history of American art, . . . the
most complete art exhibition that has been held in the world during the last quarter century." It was at once a sign that "American
artists—young American artists, that is—do not dread . . . the ideas
or the culture of Europe," and Americans' first big chance "to see
and judge for themselves the work of the Europeans who are creating a new art." Quinn's aggressive psychology was sound in the
context of the exhibition's propagandist motive, and his inclusive
claims probably accurate. It was probably "literally true," as he
assured Æ on March 2, that the Armory Show was the greatest
exhibition of contemporary art ever held to date—true if size was
the measure, certainly, and true down to this date for America, by
any measure.

1913

QUINN was in high key throughout the month's run of the show. John Butler Yeats called him "wildly happy" in a letter home on March 16, and said he had bought "a whole heap of pictures." [1] Quinn attended tirelessly, giving a part of every day when he was in the city. He dragooned all his own friends and every useful celebrity he could lay hands on. Mrs. Jeanne Robert Foster, who was to become the dearest friend of Quinn's last years but who was keeping her distance at this stage because she had been warned that Quinn was a dangerous man for young women to know, recalls following a group that focused on Quinn leading Theodore Roosevelt about the show, and hearing TR's invariable comment as he moved from picture to picture: " 'Bully!' " [2] One Sunday afternoon Quinn made the rounds with John Butler Yeats and Lady Gregory, who had come back with the Abbey Players for a second, more peaceful, American tour. Mr. Yeats showed little interest in the strange new pictures; he praised the Hones, then gave himself over to animated talk with other visitors. But in his letter home he expressed a temperate enthusiasm and set it as usual in a grand ethical and aesthetic frame:

> All the Americans think it overtops creation, and it is extraordinarily interesting, but I think artists who have lived and studied abroad, in France and England, are not so much astonished and impressed. . . . The exhibition is interesting to me because of some fine things at once new and fine. "The world is saved by the extraordinary" said Goethe, and here it is in fine form and *some of these Quinn has bought*. His judgment is really sound, if at times

it goes wrong. One must do extraordinary things, *yet long for the sober and the conformable.* With this impulse and this discipline comes spontaneity—a river flowing between its well-kept banks.[3]

It is heartbreaking to think now what a collector with nerve and a long pocketbook could have accomplished at the Armory show. Quinn's nerve was at least better than anyone else's. Though the exhibition attracted in the neighborhood of 90,000 visitors in New York, and even more than that, with the aid of free tickets, in Chicago,[4] total sales for all three cities came to the shamefully low figure of $44,148.75.[5] Quinn spent $5,808.75 at the show, including $6 for a Gauguin lithograph for Dorothy Coates which he ordered from Chicago. The Metropolitan Museum topped Quinn's figure with a single reluctant purchase, paying $6,700 for Cézanne's *Colline des Pauvres,* the first work of Cézanne's to make its way into an American museum. But the only private collector to approach Quinn's modest investment was another lawyer, the engaging Chicagoan Arthur Jerome Eddy, who laid out $4,888.50 for eighteen paintings and seven lithographs. Brown accurately describes what Quinn got for his money as "a varied selection, which reflects no deep commitment to the more experimental phases of contemporary art."[6] That commitment was not far off, but it was yet to come. Quinn's was a mixed bag, of no great daring, and surprising in some of its inclusions as well as in some of its exclusions. He gave $540 for Alexandre Blanchet's *Deux Amies;* $486 for Derain's fine *La Fenêtre sur le Parc;* $486 for two bronzes by Raymond Duchamp-Villon, the sculpturing member of the three artist brothers; $270 for an oil and a gouache by Pierre Girieud; $600 for Walt Kuhn's *Morning* and $350 for his *Girl with Red Cap,* Kuhn's only pictures in the show; $202.50 for Manolo's bronze *Femme Nue Accroupie;* $359 for an engraving, two water colors, and three drawings by Jules Pascin; $675 for the Odilon Redon oil *Initiation à l'Étude,* $12.50 for his lithograph on the same subject, and $20 for his lithograph of *Maurice Denis;* $162 for three drawings of nudes by André Dunoyer de Segonzac; $360 for three water colors by Paul Signac; $540 for three oils by Jacques Villon, another of the three artistic brothers; and $340 for the oil *En Été* by Eugene Zak. He also bought a scattering of minor works, ranging from Renoir prints to water colors by Edith Dimock, the wife of his friend William Glackens.

Reviewing the list one sees that the emphasis is almost exclusively French or artists who would be identified with Paris. The American works he bought were attributable to personal loyalties. The Redon purchases are interesting as an expression of the endurance of Quinn's unconfessed mystical bent. Redon is one of a number of artists in this group who moved onto the list of Quinn's permanent enthusiasms: Derain, the Duchamp brothers, Kuhn, Pascin, Segonzac. In some ways the Pascin purchase seems the most suggestive, the purest and most cerebral of the lot. Quinn bought nothing of Brancusi's, though he would soon be deeply and happily involved with that artist, and there were some of his most attractive things available. Of Cézanne he took only inexpensive water colors and lithographs; prices on his oils were set at a level that demanded time for reflection. He resisted Gauguin, Manet, Renoir, and Van Gogh on the same grounds; but also Dufy, La Fresnaye, Marie Laurencin, Matisse, Picasso, Rouault, Rousseau, and Toulouse-Lautrec, all of whom he was soon to be pursuing with varying degrees of eagerness. He was one of 200,000 persons who resisted the beautiful mantis-figure of Lehmbruck's *Femme à Genoux* at $2,160. For Quinn it would be enough that the sculptor's name sounded German. Quinn's list was that of a man who knew where he was not going, and vaguely where he was going. He was not going German or English or Irish and only very selectively American. He was going French, but he was not sure how far— how far back or how far forward, in time or taste, or how deep into the purse.

Probably Quinn did not know himself how deeply he was committed. The excitement of partisanship was what had drawn him in, and what still gripped him. He was only beginning to find words for his feeling about art. His response to the modern work was neither technical nor sophisticated. He was working subjectively, as was natural and right. But, in fact, at the Armory Show he had taken a step beyond the men he had previously trusted as mentors, Æ and Jack Yeats and even Augustus John. Russell had recently seen the big Post-Impressionist exhibition at the Grafton Galleries in London, and was still unimpressed: "the second childhood of art," he called it in his letter of February 7. Jack Yeats had the kind of originality of vision that would make his own work always "radical"; but this was not his sense of himself, and he mistrusted the fanfare accompanying the "new." He thought the wild new men were useful liberators, efficient enemies of convention, but he felt no need of their services, being, like his friend Synge, a "realist," a mere honest looker. He wrote Quinn on December 15, 1913: ". . . these gay souls will do good in unshackling painting. But, so far, they do not shake me in my plans, which are only to paint what I have seen happen."

In letters to Russell and others Quinn began to demand painting that had "radium" in it. Russell translated the term as "electricity." On March 2, in the midst of the Armory Show, Quinn wrote to him: ". . . after studying the work of the Cubists and Futurists, it makes it hard to stomach the sweetness, the prettiness and the clawing [*sic*] sentiment of some of the other work." He did not recognize the respectable element of sentiment in his own taste. His subjective criterion of "radium," his visceral response, his location of it in his "stomach," shows a nature trying to assert its pragmatism, unaware of its own ingrained romanticism. But the great thing about contemporary art for him, as he was beginning to understand, was its *presentness*: it was alive, ongoing, a part of one's own vitality; and the closer it came to one's own days, the better one could lay hold on the illusion of sharing in the creation. It was not a thing done but a thing doing. It animated. "It is a refreshing thing to be there," he wrote to Æ on March 2. "I enjoy a visit to the Armory with its pictures more than I would to an old cathedral. This thing is living. The cathedrals, after all, seem mostly dead or remind one of the dead." And the pictures in the immense rude hall had awakened him to a Feininger-vision of the real-abstract world of the streets:

> When one leaves this exhibition one goes outside and sees the lights streaking up and down the tall buildings and watches their shadows, and feels that the pictures that one has seen inside after all have some relation to the life and color and rhythm and movement that one sees outside. [*March 2, 1913.*]

"It was a genuine refreshment to me," Quinn wrote to Conrad on March 30, after the show had moved on to Chicago. "I never got tired of going around." He had never been so much *of* the world of art before, and he found life in the Armory a far purer pleasure than a Democratic convention hall or a courtroom. He described for Conrad his involvement. Two weeks after the opening he attended an artists' ball, dressed with absolute irony as a Roman cardinal: ". . . scarlet gown, sash, stockings, slippers, cap and all, including a gold chain around the neck and a big crucifix. I felt like a play actor during the first part, but about one or two o'clock, when I had three or four drinks of whiskey and had thrown the wig in a corner, I felt like a real cardinal." [7] On March 8 he had sat at the head table and made a speech at a dinner for the gentlemen of the press at Healy's Restaurant, dressed like everyone else in a long white apron. And on the closing night of the show he demonstrated in the least mild of these "three mild sprees," the only ones in which he had indulged in years:

> . . . the artists and their friends, including about a dozen policemen and twelve or fifteen watchmen, formed a procession led by a band, with a tall artist about six feet four [actually Putnam Brinley, said to have been nearly seven feet tall] as drum major, and I directing him, and we marched in and around the . . . rooms of the exhibition, winding our way in between statues and bronzes and figures and groups, and cheering the different American artists, cheering Augustus John, cheering the French, cheering the "Nude Coming Downstairs," cheering Odilon Redon, and so on. Everybody enjoyed himself.

Speeches and champagne, some of the former and all of the latter supplied by Quinn, went on till three-thirty in the morning. When someone proposed a burlesque toast: "To the Academy!" Quinn sprang up and said: " 'No, no! Don't you remember Captain John Philip of the *Texas*? When his guns sank a Spanish ship at Santiago, he said, 'Don't cheer, boys, the poor devils are dying!' ' " [8]

The weeks before and during the show had offered a rich feast of excitement, but they were overlaid upon a routine already hectic, and the combination took a heavy toll. Quinn was exhausted, and he found little relief as the year moved on. He thought enviously of Huneker's habit of suspending his routine every two or three years for a long period of rambling and gourmandizing in Europe. In a letter of February 14 he grouped his feelings in an omnibus complaint to Conrad: "The passion for having things and collecting things and doing things and being something is a cursed, damnable passion after all." But passion was only too accurate a word for the temper of Quinn's multiple ambition, and whereas he could curse it he could not let it go. He was collecting not only books, but also manuscripts, and not only art but also artifacts, and not only modern art but also ancient Chinese and African art. At the period of the Armory Show, for example, he was also busily pursuing Chinese landscapes, portraits, and porcelains, and paying out as much for these as for modern painting and sculpture. All this added up to a career in itself, but it had to be managed with the left hand, while the right and the left were frantically busy with the law, the "being something" that made the "having things" conceivable. Quinn had no money but what he directly earned or what his earned money could realize on investment. He was an arch-American victim of ambitions and his own nature, a driving yet uneasy perfectionist temperament that dared not trust anything but itself.

John Butler Yeats's first glance had been a shrewd one when he called Quinn a "new world Puritan" in 1902. The work in his office was thriving, but Quinn had to dominate it absolutely to be at all comfortable with his prosperity, and so his "partnership" turned unevenly and dangerously on his own obsessive axis. Francis Hackett reported in Dublin that Quinn was engaged in "a demoniac pursuit after efficiency." But Quinn was pursuing efficiency less than the illusion of omnipotence. He was reluctant to delegate labor or trust, and almost never satisfied with the way a job was done by anyone but himself. Whenever he left his office he left the most minute instructions for his subordinates' tasks in his absence; while he was away, he felt, nothing was done, or done well; when he returned he had all their work to do over, with rage and vituperation. On one of the rare occasions when he treated the matter humorously, he told Symons that the operation of his office reminded him of Abraham Lincoln's story of the steamboat with a big whistle that used so much steam that the boat stopped every time the whistle blew. One of Quinn's grievances against W. B. Yeats was his busy retailing of the "myth" that "Quinn is a man of tremendous energy," laying him open to endless appeals from the Irish. But of course it was no myth: the energy was real and what it accomplished was almost incredible. It was not always pretty

International Exhibition Modern Art

New York

To our
Friends and Enemies
of the Press

The Association of
American Painters and
Sculptors, Inc.

BEEFSTEAK DINNER 1913

March 8th   *Healy's—66th St. and Columbus Ave.*

MENU

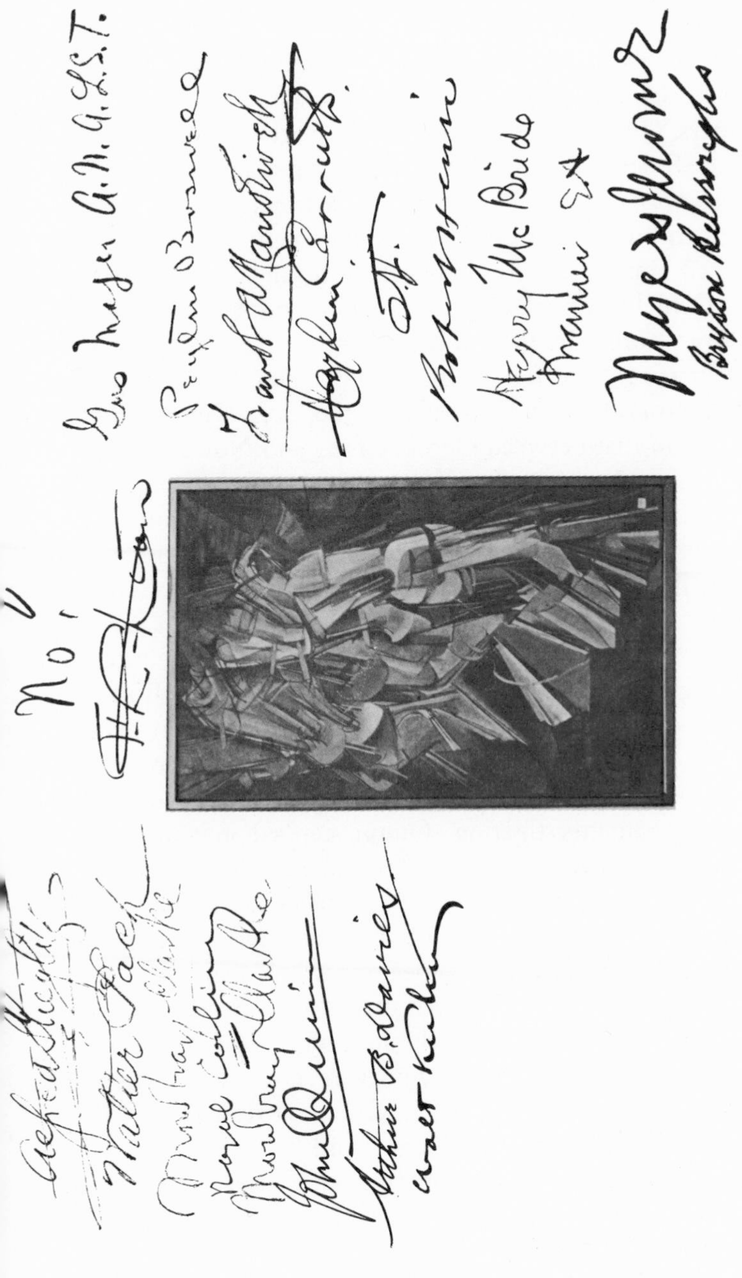

to watch in operation, but its achievements made an astonishing and daunting spectacle.

In addition to his established work for Thomas Fortune Ryan and for the banks and insurance companies who paid him large annual retainers, Quinn was now counsel on matters of tax law for the New York Stock Exchange. In the spring and summer of 1913 the Exchange was under federal and state attack, which meant repeated trips to both Albany and Washington. In May and June Quinn involved himself heavily on behalf of his old Irish and Tammany friend Daniel F. Cohalan, whose appointment to the Supreme Court of New York Quinn had engineered after declining the post himself in 1911. One John A. Connolly, who had been president of the Victor Heating Company in the city, claimed in the *New York World* that between October 1904 and November 1906 he had paid nearly $4,000 to Cohalan, who was then rising to be the chief lieutenant of Boss Charles F. Murphy of Tammany Hall, for Cohalan's use of his influence in getting Connolly contracts for work for the city. Connolly further claimed to have paid Cohalan another $4,000 in 1911, after Cohalan rose to the bench, to get him a political post which had never materialized. In editorials *The New York Times* demanded that Cohalan clear himself of the nasty charges or resign from the Supreme Court. Cohalan denied everything but otherwise remained silent, and he refused to appear before the Grievance Committee of the New York Bar Association, which undertook an investigation. Quinn stepped in and bullied Cohalan and his advisers into demanding an investigation by the state Legislature, a move which "saved" Cohalan, as Quinn saw it, convinced of Cohalan's innocence. Quinn gave five weeks to the defense, culminating in a week of appearances in Cohalan's hearing before the Joint Judiciary Committee of the state Senate and Assembly. What was proven was less the innocence of Cohalan than the untrustworthiness of Connolly, who was shown to have spent time in a mental institution and to have made a deal with Ralph Pulitzer of the *World* to receive money and a job in return for substantiating his charges against Cohalan. After an emotional final appearance by Cohalan, surrounded by four sons and wearing mourning for his dead wife, his exoneration was recommended unanimously by the Judiciary Committee and passed by a large majority in both houses of the Legislature. On the same day, July 18, 1913, Cohalan sailed for Ireland on the *Adriatic*.

Somehow in the midst of all these activities Quinn found time to initiate and to conduct entirely through his own office, in a contest that occupied most of the year, the struggle for removal of the federal customs duty on works of art. Though he could not know it now, this was the first engagement of a running battle which broke out again and again down to the day of his death. The issue was an old and sore one with Quinn. The idea of a tax on art he loathed in principle and in practice, in its general and in its personal application. He pointed out to Huneker that the United States was "the only civilized country in the world" which penalized the importation of art. It was one of the habits that made him doubt the civilization of this country. Furthermore he was finding the customs duty a heavy expense and a grievous nuisance in his own dealings for painting and sculpture, and he had tacitly evaded it for years as far as he could, with a clear conscience. Since the Tariff Act of 1909, specifically, "antiquities" had been allowed to enter the country duty-free, whereas works of art up to twenty years old were levied at 15 per cent. Quinn saw that the effect of this was to penalize "living art" and to indulge art which had become a commodity, safe and staid, with no living relation to its creator, and now material for trade between merchants and speculators, most of whom he was sure were Jews or Germans or both. The customs duty was one of the sorest trials of the men who were putting together the Armory Show, and it was probably his experience of it at work there on a large scale which carried Quinn's anger from the sullen to the active stage.

He followed his habitual strategy of attack rather than defense. Realizing that new tariff measures would be moving through the Ways and Means Committee, and that its chairman, Oscar W. Underwood, had old debts to him, Quinn mounted a heavy campaign for the virtual reversal of the tariff philosophy on art. He wrote to many of the most important living writers and artists and urged them to send him considered statements in support of the ethics and the aesthetics of his position. He published these piecemeal in letters to newspapers, sent them to influential members of Congress, and incorporated them with extended arguments of his own in a series of printed briefs which he broadcast in several thousand copies to the press and other interested parties. He had had himself nominally retained by the American Free Art League, the Federation of Art Museums, and the Association of American Painters and Sculptors, but only, as he explained to May Morris on December 16 after the issue was settled for the time: "because I wanted a peg to hang my brief on and wanted to represent some art body other than myself." He represented these bodies in the sense that his interest coincided with theirs, but he served without fee, and in fact the initiation, the conduct, the labor, and the cost of the cause were all Quinn's. The body he really represented was himself, but that was a formidable body. The triumph, too, he felt should have been his, and when it was all over he was both angry and amused to see other bodies quietly accepting congratulations.

"I have stirred up a hell of a row here over the subject," he wrote Knewstub of Chenil's on the first of June, when he was in mid-flight on the issue, having already sent out over 1,200 copies of his first brief and written "countless" letters. He was virtually commuting to Washington, where he was widely acquainted in Congress and known as a candid and powerful lobbyist for causes near his heart or his purse. On February 4 he described for Huneker, with relish, his first argument before the House Ways and Means Committee: "I never spoke better in my life;—no vehemence, no heat, no haste, no gestures. All the goods in the shop-window and nothing but intellect and the highest kind of statesmanship and the broadest sweep of vision from start to finish. The whole thing was cold, lucid, convincing." In Chairman Underwood Quinn had an able ally, and the House measure incorporated Quinn's wishes for exemption of new art from duty. When the bill moved to the Senate Quinn submitted a second brief. But the Senate, motivated, he supposed, by "the idea that foreign art is a luxury like jewelry or diamonds or precious stones or foreign wines or tobacco," [9] was against him and sought to restore the old invidious discrimination against new art. Quinn got out 2,100 copies of a third brief. Then the issue was sent to a Conference Committee of both houses, and Underwood's influence gradually prevailed in the direction of Quinn's principles. Quinn interrupted his vacation in the Adirondacks to spend several days in Washington conferring on the final stipulations of the bill.

"Underwood did it for me," he wrote May Morris on December 16, presenting the legislator as executive agent for Quinn's one-man show:

> I started the fight; I made the only argument before the House; I submitted the only brief to the House; I submitted a brief to the Senate; I interviewed the Senators, and finally, I submitted a final brief after the Senate had acted. I started the propaganda, sent the stuff to all the newspapers, collected the newspaper editorials and cartoons; my office sent out all the circulars. . . . I bore all the expenses of the campaign. . . . In addition to that, I read into the law for the first time the word "original," so that it now provides that only original paintings in oil, water, pastel, and original drawings, and artist proof etchings unbound, and engravings unbound, and original sculpture and not more than two replicas, come in free. All copies are taxed fifteen per cent. I did that deliberately to put the importers, largely Jews, I am told, of fake Corots and Raeburns and so on, out of business. And the result has been precisely as I planned. For example, the other day a Sir Joshua Reynolds was sent over valued at $50,000. It was sent as an original. The examiners examined it and pronounced it to be merely a copy and levied a duty of fifteen per cent, or $7500. . . . Result: the New York dealer sent it back to the London dealer and America is relieved of that fake. . . . I had got rather tired of people on the other side poking fun at America because of the number of fake Corots here and fake other things.

Beyond the initiation, the argument, and the framing of the measure, Quinn's influence had reached on to legal interpretation of its work in practice.

> I might add [he continued to Miss Morris] that my legal opinion construing the law has become the official one of the Department. In other words, I drew the law and my interpretation of the law has been adopted by the Department just as I planned. That of course is not known publicly, because I passed on my opinion to the examiners, who passed it on to the Legal Department, and it was adopted in that way.

"So that I have done that much for the freedom of American art and for the purity of American art," he concluded. Quinn's vaunting immodesty is a fact that must be faced, but the "free art fight," as he came to call it over the years, was one case in which it is easy to forgive a certain amount of self-celebration. From the point of view of living art, he was surely on the side of the angels, and he had fought a brilliant campaign. He was moved by respect for the artist and the buyer in what he saw as a free, daring, and co-operative enterprise. By "the freedom of American art" he meant freedom to learn from and to compete with the best contemporary art being made anywhere in the world. By its "purity" he meant protection from corruption by examples of work which was not original but fabricated from pure models for commercial motives.

On March 4, 1913, Woodrow Wilson was inaugurated, and Quinn recalled sourly that twenty years before he had stood six feet behind Grover Cleveland on his inaugural platform. The Armory exhibition, greatly diminished in size, had moved on to Chicago, where it drew crowds and jeers but few sales and little enlightened commentary. "It's a rube town!" twice underscored, Walt Kuhn headed a letter from Chicago to Elmer L. MacRae on March 25.[10] Quinn could have told them so. New York was bad enough, but he still saw it as the only partly civilized American city. He wrote to Epstein on April 28: "The artists hated Chicago and thought it ignorant, bumptious, conceited, arrogant and hateful in every way." In June Quinn refused to lend Epstein £200 to help him to buy the cottage in Sussex where he had been living and working, but offered to send him £100 or £150 to shop for African sculptures for Quinn in Paris. His Armory purchases were only a fragment of his current dealings in art. In January Knewstub billed him for £701 and 15 shillings for three Augustus John paintings. The nine Charles Conder panels had cost him a round $12,000. On March 2, with the Armory Show in full career, he plunged for his costliest purchase to date, $28,000 for two very large oil paintings, *La Rivière* and *Le Vendage*, which Puvis de Chavannes had made in 1866 in preparation for his frescoes in the Picardy Museum at Amiens. Puvis de Chavannes had sold them to Durand-Ruel in 1894, and then they had passed into the collection of the Prince de Wagram. The French government had selected them for showing at the Paris Exposition of 1900. Quinn took them from Turner and Gardiner of Fifth Avenue, who were agents in turn for Levesque et Cie. of Paris, after he had been warned that the Worcester Museum was about to buy them. He found the combination of painter, pictures, provenance, and rivalry an irresistible one. From Gwen John, on the other hand, all Quinn's patient eliciting for several years had drawn only two small pictures, though those were among the nearest to his heart. She wrote him miserably on June 27: "Please do not send any money again in advance. I am so ashamed of never keeping my word."

In a small way Lady Gregory was running a show competitive to the Armory in the spring of 1913. In addition to presiding over the second American tour of the Abbey company, she was begging on behalf of a new gallery in Dublin to house, as a nucleus, the notable modern collection of her nephew Hugh Lane. Quinn warned her not to hope for money from the American Irish: they had no love for art and no understanding of it. In the middle of March he gave her a luncheon to which he invited a number of American art lovers, among them Judge Gary, Henry Clay Frick, Alexander Cochran, and Otto Kahn, whom he identified to Russell on March 2 as "a Hebrew of culture who buys pictures"—again his ugly invidious phrase. In a weirdly schizophrenic way, Quinn was quite capable of fulminating against the Jews as grasping vulgarians in the same paragraph in which he was praising Otto Kahn or Max Pam for giving generously to a cultural cause in which he was interested. In early April Quinn could report that Lady Gregory had collected $5,000 in Chicago, $5,000 in Montreal, $5,000 from the players, $5,000 from Alexander Cochran, and $250 each from Andrew Carnegie, Bourke Cockran, and himself.

Especially in his letters to Russell, Quinn continued his railing at the Irish. With his dislike for the English, the Irish, the Germans, and the Jews, things were getting to the point that only the French were left him to admire. Having heard from Francis Hackett of Quinn's "demoniac pursuit after efficiency," Æ wrote to console and chide. Quinn wrote back that he dreamed of a wholesale dynamiting of fools. Favor-seeking Irishmen were among his sorest trials, he said, in a rage at their egocentricity, their rationalizations, their short-sighted fondness for the easy job, their self-indulgent assumption that they were racially exempt from the difficult apprenticeship and discipline needed for success in the professions or in business. He rehearsed his feelings of the previous year during the *Playboy* fuss—on the one hand the bigotry and meanness of the attack, on the other the vitality and purity of the object of attack, as he had recently again seen the company on arrival in New York:

> But when I stood on the dock and saw the bright, clean faces of that little company of Irish boys and girls, their fine, clear eyes, their quick intelligence and their sympathy and understanding and the freshness of it all, the youth of it, I felt like embracing all of them.[11]

He had to admit that both images were real and both were Irish. He was furious at the race, but he had not abandoned it, indeed he could not. Here, as habitually, he was showing the habit Lily Yeats had marked in him years earlier: to knock a man down with one hand and pick him up with the other.

The exasperating paradox of the Irish character was on Æ's mind, too. "I am damnably tired of Irish things," he wrote Quinn on New Year's Day of 1913, "and yet I love the people and the country and could not endure the surfaces if it were not that I divine the depths." But the depths were not getting into the writing in Ireland, and he spoke impatiently of its slightness and facility:

> The flaw in our literature is that it is too instinctive and has little intellectual basis. We imagine too easily and think too little and are too easily content with what nature has done for us and add too little art. I would rather have an Irish Carlyle than a score of poets. We want somebody to stir us to the depths of human consciousness.

Quinn judged that Standish O'Grady had come closest to qualifying as the Irish Carlyle. But he feared the times were not propitious for any kind of Carlyle: ". . . styles have changed. Carlyle's preachings would not do now. We would send him to a stomach specialist and he would turn out a Scotch Bernard Shaw." [12]

Russell cited Lord Dunsany as a classic case of the Irishman of genius, making his effects all too easily, turning out work of much imagination but little heart, and writing a play in an afternoon— "God forgive him." Still mourning the loss of George Moore and his Saturdays, Æ was trying the young man James Stephens in his place as boon companion. Stephens's *The Crock of Gold* had been the Irish literary success of 1912, and Æ thought him the best of the coming men. Quinn promptly put in a bid for the manuscript, and Stephens sent it across in six little notebooks, followed by a note to say that it might "cock its tail and brag of its lodgings." [13] Quinn had naturally been seeking manuscripts from Æ himself, but there his luck was poor. Typically, Æ had given away some, thrown away others, and had none to sell for the moment.

After a week's visit to London late in January, much like one of Quinn's, in which he had seen much of George Moore and his cronies of the New English Art Club, the literary men Ralph Hodgson, Laurence Binyon, and F. S. Oliver, and the politicians Asquith, Birrell, and Balfour, Russell found that he loved Ireland more than ever. He had been appalled by the bustle and conglomerateness of London. "The more humanity crowds together the more inhuman does it seem," he wrote Quinn on February 7. He approved the Greek idea of limiting a city to the number of persons who could hear a single orator; and he would have liked to see a free Ireland, detached from "all the big imperial rascalities," and willingly self-divided into "independent county kingdoms" about the size of Sligo. He stated his own modest and winning version of the general Irish dream: "I believe in the intensive cultivation of humanity." According to Maud Gonne's more grandiloquent dream, the British Empire was about to disappear, and "a great Celtic Federation" would take its place.[14] Standish O'Grady's contemporaneous vision was much like Russell's, though lacking his humor and charity. O'Grady was seeking a means of public return to "the primal sanities," and he thought the way might lie through small "fraternal" states. He wrote stoutly to Quinn on January 7, 1908: "There is really no difficulty save the necessary change of mind and thought, which I shall do my best to bring about." Quinn picked up Æ's reference to the Greek city-states in a characteristic way. He advised the learned Irishman, "sometime when you feel like putting your teeth in a bit of serious reading," to try Zimmern's *Greek Commonwealth*; and he cited the nominating conventions of the American political parties as the closest modern counterparts of the Greek citizen assemblies.

Quinn's feminine correspondents were behaving loyally. When

Florence Farr Emery wrote from her college in Ceylon that she had picked up a Jacobean chair for six rupees and a beautiful old satinwood dining table for fifteen, Quinn put her on notice to look out for fine things for his apartment: "anything that you think is really beautiful and decorative." May Morris went in July for a rest in Majorca, and she sent Quinn long letters, enchanted but not enchanting, of her primitive life there. In her Christmas letter from Hammersmith she described herself mournfully as "an anchorite," but also described entertainingly a Fabian meeting chaired by Shaw and addressed by Anatole France, who turned out to be "rather a dear . . . he kissed my hand and said pretty things about my Father." And she came through with the kind of sympathy and admonition which Quinn's complaints of his life demanded in responding letters: "It is the old story of work, work, and overwork, and disregarding doctors' orders—it is grievous to people who are fond of you." [15]

Writing on the same line on October 13, Lady Gregory quoted Quinn's favorite "sailor's commandment":

> Six days shalt thou work as long as thou art able;
> On the seventh holystone the deck and scrape down the cable.

She was still struggling, with diminishing hope, for a Dublin gallery for Hugh Lane's pictures, and she enclosed for Quinn a draft of W. B. Yeats's bitter new satirical poem on the subject, "To a Shade," in which the ghost of Parnell was summoned to observe this new instance of Irish bigotry and niggardliness. She reported that Abbey audiences had been heavily reduced by the big Dublin tramway strike of the summer and the subsequent lockout of thousands of workmen. Maud Gonne was in a rage over the mess in Dublin and the suffering of the poor, and consoled only by the fact that general misery had led to the spread of her school-feeding program throughout the city. After Christmas she wrote to thank Quinn for his check for the poor of Dublin, and for the annual barrel of apples. And Lily Yeats thanked him for trying to persuade her father in New York to allow his reminiscences to be "taken down" in Quinn's office. She had at last succeeded in collecting and photographing all the Yeats family miniatures and portraits, and she coveted her father's memoirs "in his own fine and often beautiful language," though not in his execrable handwriting.[16]

Involved as he was with the "free art fight" as well as with more remunerative legal affairs, Quinn had no hope of getting abroad in the summer of 1913. Instead he had invited Kuhn and Gregg to go as his guests for a month in the Adirondacks, where he hoped he could be detached yet available for emergency summonses. He wrote to Arthur Symons on August 18:

> I am going away to the woods where I hope to rest and get some exercise and be away from law cases and telephone messages and politics and friends and Irish beggars or Irish self seekers. . . . They seem to think that because I haven't a wife and seven babies I have time to do all these things and money for all their needs.

Resuming the same letter two days later he reported that he was still on the jump, working with several stenographers to put affairs in shape for his absence: "If I don't get away tonight something will burst." Realizing that he was writing to stylists, Quinn apologized to both Symons and Conrad for his own bad epistolary prose. "Dictation of course spoils any possibility of style unless one goes very slowly," he wrote Conrad on July 29, "and most of my stuff is dictated as fast as I can talk." Similarly to Symons he wrote on August 20: ". . . I find that in dictating letters in a rush they get longer than if one stops and thinks and dictates short sentences. In fact short sentences take more time than long sentences." Of course he was right, and his shame was real in one who cared about language; but he did not allow himself to brood about it; he did not have time for that. His bad style, ironically, was one of the tools which let him get more work done. A fixture of Quinn's routine was "the bag," a thick leather brief case which an office boy carried home for him at night filled with personal letters, letters about dealings in art, books, and manuscripts, as well as unfinished legal matters that were preying on his mind. He panted along behind the quantity and the variety of his commitments. In the evening he would pore over the contents of the bag, making notes, and often would arrange for Thomas Curtin or another stenographer from the office to come to the apartment to take his dictation in counterpoint to his morning processes of shaving, dressing, and breakfasting. At about nine o'clock an office boy would arrive to pick up the bag and carry it downtown with its completed and uncompleted work. Quinn himself would follow more slowly, arriving at ten or ten-thirty or eleven, often having stopped once or twice en route at a gallery or a studio where there was work in which he was interested.

In times of emergency or special tension, Curtin would often be joined by Quinn's other favorite stenographers, Florence Thompson and Ida Odes, and sometimes also by a girl from Miss Celia Lape's secretarial agency, or even by Miss Lape herself. Personal letters were particularly hard to keep up with, and they often traveled back and forth in the bag for days or even weeks before Quinn could find time to dictate a response. As life thickened about him through the years, Quinn formed the habit of collecting the personal letters of several weeks for treatment in a mass, usually on a Sunday, when he would dictate to several stenographers more or less concurrently, each handling a separate correspondent. One of the economies of the process was that he could compose paradigm paragraphs of his own personal news and opinions which could go into all the letters written at a given time. Such letters naturally suffered from the discursiveness and irritation of the circumstances in which they were made, and they tended to formlessness—rambling, repetitious, wordy, dully oratorical, too long for their essential work. Eight to ten pages of double-spaced typing was a sort of standard length for such letters, but they often extended to fifteen and occasionally to thirty pages. Quinn took a keen pleasure in correcting his own style when it was important and possible to do so, as in law briefs to be printed, and then his habit was always to clarify, tighten up, diminish, cut away. A few years later when his niece, Mary Anderson, began to write letters and stories, it was Quinn's godfatherly pleasure to subject them to an editorial eye which was mainly alert for waste matter or unclearness. But there was no time to edit his own letters: others were waiting.

One of Quinn's motives in going to the Adirondacks in this summer of 1913 was to be near Dorothy Coates, who was seriously ill with tuberculosis at Saranac. He visited her there several times a week in August and September, after he finally got away from New York. When Maud Gonne heard of the illness of Miss Coates, whom she had known in Paris, she wrote on September 4 to assure Quinn that the disease was curable: she herself had nearly died of it at one time but now was all right. She had been so far gone that

W. B. Yeats had written her epitaph, which he showed her after she improved.* But Quinn was much shaken in his nerves, as he always was by the illness of anyone close to him, and turned even more fearful, edgy, and irascible. After only two days in the mountains he was summoned to Buffalo where he had to try a case which had been wretchedly prepared by one of his partners. This meant sending to New York for a stenographer, hours of dictation in his hotel room, uneasy hours in court where he was unsure of his material, and little rest or sleep. When he returned to the mountains he felt too weak and short of breath to play tennis, and found that climbing the smallest hill set his heart to pounding alarmingly. After a few days' rest, however, he was able to begin golfing and then he ate and slept better. He returned to the office still underweight but feeling calmer and more optimistic. Then he was plunged into two long cases which he felt had also been botched in his office in his absence, and had to try those "on his nerve." Soon he was in his old lamentable state: ". . . nervous, weak, troubled with my throat, night sweats about every other night, and feverish." [17] He began to have afternoon fevers, and of course his mind went back to Saranac and tuberculosis. He fired his doctors and got new ones, forced himself to eat and rest at least a bit, and gradually improved. In December he managed to get away for a few days to Hot Springs in Virginia, where he got real rest and found much relief in the hot baths. He wished his own father had had the advantage of a "boiling out" for several weeks once or twice a year. And when Conrad continued to complain of his gout Quinn wrote back on August 31: "Lord! my Friend, *that* can be cured. If you showed a sign of it here, I'd pack you off to Hot Springs, Virginia, where hot baths for two or three weeks would make you so free and limber and eager for exercise that you'd gallop around the golf course. . . ."

Conrad congratulated Quinn on his victory for free art, and marveled at his finding time and energy for such extraordinary concerns: "I envy you your power and your temperament, and that mental mastery of yourself which enables you to multiply your activities to this extent outside your appointed calling." [18] The formality of his phrasing lends it a certain dutiful and per-

---

* See also Yeats's lyric, "I dreamt that one had died in a strange place."

functory air, and one may feel some dryness in the tone with which he joins the long line of sympathizers for Quinn's overworking: "The insight you give me into the toil and tribulations of a man of affairs commands my appreciative sympathy." He placed Quinn's difficulties within the general perspective of the human condition: "Man is born to trouble, as sparks fly upward." [19] Conrad had his own troubles, and he mentioned those seriously but casually, as data for casting up accounts on the state of his career. At fifty-three, with sixteen years of writing behind him, he could pass on to his wife and his two young sons only his civil list pension of £100 and £1,600 on his life insurance. The past three years of hard labor at his desk had reduced a debt of £2,700 to £600; but he was still subject to crippling attacks of gout that made the future seem shaky. He thought "with terror" of the contract for three new novels he had just signed with Dent: he doubted whether he still had three novels in him. Conrad could not know that his novel *Chance*, then in the press, was to bring him his first great popular success, his first real fame and fortune. Now he wrote in terms touchingly diffident about the future of his literary reputation. It heartened him that young French writers were following his work: "They write to me, they write about me—and what they have discovered that's so very wonderful I'm hanged if I know." [20] And, with a wistfulness that time would make ironic: "Later on, when I am no longer here and some literary searcher wishes to write an analytical study of Conrad's work (more unlikely things have happened), you will give him access to your collection, I have no doubt." [21]

In a diminishing but still considerable flow, Conrad items continued to join Quinn's collection. In a letter of January 1, 1913, Quinn demurred for the first time at one of Conrad's prices, £80 (about $384) for the manuscript of *The Nigger of the Narcissus*. He had recently bought manuscripts of Gissing, Meredith, and Rossetti, and he thought Conrad's price a bit steep, comparatively. But he admired *The Nigger* unreservedly, and after grumbling mildly, he paid up. He sent a draft for £100 "on account," figuring *The Nigger* at £80, "The Return" at £15, and the play "Tomorrow" at £40, and offered to pay the other £35 at once if Conrad would promise to use the £135 windfall for a real trip to the south of France.

Quinn had expressed an interest in hand-revised typescripts of Conrad's works, as well as in actual manuscripts, and Conrad sent on many of these, at nominal prices, typically five or ten pounds. He was also presenting Quinn with inscribed copies of his works as they appeared in foreign translations; for example, on March 16, 1913: "I am sending you two of my novels in their French dress: *Le Nègre du Narcisse* and *L'Agent Sécret.*" And then there were the manuscripts of his current writings, and still, occasionally and unexpectedly, a few bits of his older work. The manuscript of *Smile of Fortune*, which had been on loan in France, came home to Conrad and went across to Quinn. Some 135 pages of *The End of the Tether*, all that survived of a manuscript that had been burned before publication in an accident with a lamp, turned up and was sent on as a supplement to the collection of fragments Quinn had bought in 1912. Then there was the first pencil draft of *Youth* in a little black notebook; Conrad remembered writing it lying on his stomach under a chestnut tree in the garden of his home in Essex before the birth of his first child. This went for £15 and *Freya* for £25. Various short stories changed hands, usually at £15. On July 17 Conrad sent in one huge parcel the corrected typescripts of *Almayer's Folly* and *Chance*, his earliest novel and his latest: "If you think that they are worth £5 apiece then send me that money—or whatever you think is right."

Two other fragments of particular interest materialized: 190 pages of Conrad's part in *Romance*, in which he had collaborated with Ford Madox Ford (then Hueffer); and 39 pages of *The Sisters*, a "true fragment" the circumstances of which Conrad recalled poignantly. It was to have been his third novel, following *The Outcast of the Islands*, but it was "abandoned in despair of being able to keep up the high pitch . . . and *The Nigger* came instead." "I wonder whether I *would* have done it," he mused, "if I had not got scared off it thinking it out ahead, one winter evening, alone in my lodgings, a fortnight or so before we were married." [22] As always, he recollected events in his creative life against the calendar of his marriage. Asking £20 for this fragment, Conrad said he would have given it to Quinn if the past year had not been so hard. As the story was to have been about a painter, he thought it appropriate that Quinn should possess it. In any case, he wrote in the same letter, ". . . it seems a sort of necessity that you should

have every scrap of my handwriting now. Fate has willed it."
Conrad wrapped the rolled manuscript with a note conveying the
copyright to Quinn. After he was dead, he suggested, Quinn might
publish the fragment "as a literary curiosity—and the blessed critics will babble about it." Quinn accepted the copyright, but only
"in trust." He had a typed copy of the manuscript sent back to
Conrad, and suggested that he think back through the story and
note down a summary statement of the projected action of the
novel—to round out the item for Quinn's collection.

The long-distance cordiality of the two men continued throughout the year. Conrad was pleased that Doubleday, Page & Company had taken up his last novel, *Twixt Land and Sea*, and the
forthcoming *Chance*; and Quinn advised him in detail on the management of his affairs with United States publishers. It was due to
the Doubleday association that Quinn first met Alfred A. Knopf,
then a young editor in that firm. Knopf called on Quinn for permission to dip into his Conrad collection for publicity material for
American editions, and Quinn granted permission for photographing manuscript pages of *Chance* and *Lord Jim*, the manuscript notebook of *Youth*, and Conrad's letter to Quinn describing the finishing of *Chance*. All year Quinn kept pressing Conrad to take a
holiday journey to America and be his guest in New York, promising him a key to his apartment above Central Park and a quiet
room with two beds for the writer and his wife. Conrad was
attracted, debated the idea throughout the year, and gave it up
at last under pressure of work, debt, and uncertain health. Writing
on October 25 to enclose an autographed photograph of himself,
Conrad had this to say of Quinn's letters: "Don't imagine though
that I don't appreciate to the full the friendliness, the interest, and
the wisdom of your letters. Your (written down) voice has become a part of my existence. I look forward to it."

1914

IN the first month of the new year Quinn tried to get at Conrad
through his wife, pressing Jessie Conrad to send the great man
over to him for a "boiling out" at Hot Springs. He attributed
Conrad's condition to bad diet, especially too many fried foods,
and he promised to have him looked over by specialists and a
regimen of diet and exercise prescribed to "knock out the gout." [1]
Mrs. Conrad had written of her two sons, and Quinn replied in a
plaintive and teasing vein: "I wish I had a couple of boys of my
own. Only then one would have to have a wife, too, for the boys'
sake, and that might sometimes be embarrassing." Jessie Conrad's
reply suggested that her family would work out their own salvation, including diet. [2]

To Conrad himself Quinn sent clippings of newspaper accounts
of his triumph over Anthony Comstock and the Society for the
Suppression of Vice in the obscenity case against *Hagar Revelly*,
a novel by Daniel Carson Goodman, heard before Judge E. C.
Thomas in the Federal Court from February fifth to ninth. He
identified Comstock as "the man . . . that Shaw has taken so many
kicks at" and felt that his verdict, "although the judge was dead
against us," was "the first big set-back" administered to Comstockery. [3] Quinn's argument, characteristically, amounted to an
attack on Comstock himself, in a vein of *Honi soit qui mal y pense*:
the dirtiness was not in the book but in the mind of the reader.
Reporters at the hearing made much of the presence among the
spectators of the six-foot beauty and famous suffragette Inez
Milholland Boissevain, chewing gum and wearing a tam-o'-shanter

and accompanied by her Dutch husband who wore, suspiciously, a wristwatch.

In his letter of March 10 Conrad spoke again of the special pleasure he found in the "invariable friendliness" of Quinn's letters. It was always a shock to him, he said, to realize that they had never met: "Your kindly sagacity in what you say on life, conduct and work fits my case so perfectly, always, that years of intimacy could not make it more so." Quinn had advised him on February 25: "Don't overdo your work. Don't press the machine too far"— counsel, as he noted, too often ignored by himself. Conrad's country life, he judged, happily preserved him from certain city distractions, especially "those two temptations of wine and women" which he feared were endangering the career of Augustus John. He proposed to commission a portrait of Conrad by John to add to his gallery of writers, and Conrad promised to sit out of regard for both the patron and the artist. Quinn expressed his delight that Conrad had at long last reached a popular success: *Chance* had reached its sixth printing. As a true and loyal bibliophile, he had ordered his bookseller to send him a copy of each printing.

In July Conrad sent over the 1,100 pages of his new manuscript, *Victory*, representing the better part of two years' work. "Poor show," he thought, "very poor. And yet I haven't loafed over my work." He asked £60 for the manuscript and the first version of the typed copy; if Quinn thought that exorbitant, he would throw in the manuscript of his next short story. In late July Conrad took his first holiday in years, going off with his wife and sons for what was planned as six weeks in Poland. He hoped to be in New York by October. "And then at last I shall behold you in the flesh, which will be a very great pleasure." [4] But by October the world was at war. From Ogunquit in Maine Walt Kuhn sent Quinn a "War Bulletin" on August 30: "It is reported that the Germans have taken Peruna"—gaily signed "Lydia Pinkham."

In this summer of 1914, after the appearance of a study of Conrad by the novelist's friend Richard Curle, occurred a characteristic and embarrassing episode in Quinn's career as a passionate and able, if often officious and overbearing, amateur of letters. Quinn appraised Curle's judgments, especially his comparisons of Conrad to other novelists, with a skeptical eye, and he sent Curle on July 9 a letter of nine pages correcting his taste. Quinn's own comparisons, as in his letter of the same day to Huneker, of Conrad to Meredith, Henry James, Hardy, Tolstoy, and Turgenev, were general but shrewd. Quinn corrected, however, not only Curle's taste but his English style—a risky venture for one whose own epistolary style was so inelegant. He sent Curle a copy of Curle's own book in which he had marked the presumed barbarisms, chiefly overused co-ordinate conjunctions. "He may or may not thank me," Quinn wrote Huneker on July 9, "but I have told him something." Curle's reply on July 21 was elegant indeed, expressing a kind of temperate rage but withal a willingness to accept Quinn's strictures as disinterested and fundamentally kind. He answered some of Quinn's objections and would have answered all of them, he said: ". . . but I really don't know whether you want answers or are simply making statements." He pointed out the "didactic tone" and "peremptory style" of Quinn's letter. The "corrected" copy of his book he would return unexamined "with many thanks."

Quinn's prompt reply, on August 5, was of a kind to do him credit. He had written originally, he said, because he was sorry to see a good book disfigured by little blemishes: "It was because I liked your book so much that I wrote you as I did. . . ." He assured Curle that he had bought several copies of the book and had given one to Huneker, hoping that might lead to a useful critical notice. He was "surprised" that Curle had found his tone "didactic"; he had meant only to be modestly helpful. Perhaps he transferred to Curle's book his disgust with Hueffer's new book on Henry James, which he had thought "priggish, slovenly, carelessly written." At the same time he chided Curle for attributing to him an attitude of condescension to a neophyte: "I wrote not knowing or thinking or caring whether you were twenty or thirty." But if his letter had struck Curle in that way, his "exasperation" was "quite natural." Still it was unbecoming in any writer to condemn the counsel of one who after all knew a good deal about his subject:

It may be, if you return the book to me *"without your seeing it"* that you will do it "solely from motives of common sense." But it will seem—pace your thirty years—a young indignant man who does it.

Finally he assured Curle that he had read and enjoyed his book on Meredith and his book of stories, *Life Is a Dream*. With Quinn's temperate and dignified reply, Curle began to feel that he had himself been guilty of the arrogance he had been finding in the other. He wrote to apologize and over the next tense weeks he kept Quinn informed, as well as he could, of the difficult fortunes of the Conrad family, trapped in the continent at war.

Curle's epithets, "didactic" and "peremptory," applied more accurately to Quinn's epistolary manner than to his general personal presence. Unquestionably his was a temperament which required to dominate, needed to feel itself in command of a situation. Quinn rather savored his accumulating reputation as a Mr. Bang of legal circles and of the world of practical connoisseurship. Both his tense nervous economy and his notions of efficient conduct led him to behave in hectoring and explosive ways. Æ's young protégé Padraic Colum, now settled with his beautiful young wife in a little apartment overlooking the East River, found Quinn irascible and unsympathetic, and Mary Colum later spoke of him in *Life and the Dream* as "Very dictatorial, of the type lately depicted in books as Nazi. . . ." [5] Augustus John, on the other hand, compared him favorably with Hugh Lane in a letter of February 9, 1914: ". . . Lane is given to haranguing and you are not. . . ."

Equally, Quinn was capable of great personal sweetness and warmth, when things were going well, and of infinite practical kindness whether things were going well or ill. Letter writing tended to call out the worst in him: when he dictated he was likely to be dictatorial. His epistolary bluster at its worst can be seen in a letter of this year to Laurence J. Gomme, a knowing bookman who had innocently offered him a chance at a de luxe Blackstone. The great jurist, Quinn asserted, "wrote damned badly," and he ranted on:

> He has been responsible for a lot of vague thinking by lawyers and judges, because they have taken him as a model for high sounding phrases and magniloquent expressions and "the gladsome light of jurisprudence," and a lot of other high sounding twaddle such as that "justice has her feet in the bosom of God," or something

of that sort, wholly unscientific. Oh no, no Blackstone ever again for me. . . . I take great pride that I have not a single law book in my library of twelve or fifteen thousand volumes, nor, may I add, have I an atlas or an encyclopedia, so Blackstone is not alone in his exclusion. [*December 7, 1914.*]

What is the point of the harangue, all this excitement in excess of cause? On the one hand he seems to suggest that his taste rises above the realm of merely empirically useful books; on the other he seems to profess that his own pragmatic modernity of means is equal to every challenging event. One part of Quinn was a familiar kind of simple bully.

But his more humane and engaging side, his outgoing warmth and generous energy, was always available, too. When old Standish O'Grady arrived in New York in mid-January of 1914 Quinn was absent in Ohio at the funeral of a cousin, but he had his clerk Watson meet O'Grady at the boat, see him through customs, and install him in Quinn's apartment. When he returned to the city he made sure that J. B. Yeats would be much in evidence so that the two old friends could have an extended reunion. Quinn wrote to Mrs. O'Grady in Ireland on January 24: "Mr. Yeats looks the same as ever, and your husband said that it was just as though he had turned the corner and resumed a conversation today that had been broken off yesterday, although it has been over five years since they met." On January 29 he wrote to Judge Keogh to describe the hectic process of getting O'Grady off for his return to Ireland. Following a dinner for his guest downtown they returned to the apartment so that O'Grady could change into his "Irish clothes." Then they set off for the dock with Mr. Yeats in a taxi through a dense fog:

A ship, the sea, Ireland—all these things were entirely out of his mind. He was talking as though he were wandering in a nice wooded garden on a summer's day with an abundance of leisure, and Mr. Yeats was wandering there with him; and I was sitting nervously in the taxi, apprehensive on the one hand that if we went too fast we would run over somebody in the fog, and if we didn't go fast we would miss the boat.

Back home O'Grady wrote to send thanks for "the extraordinary and quite princely way" in which he had been entertained.

He estimated that Quinn must have spent a hundred pounds upon him.

> I saw you give a dollar to the boy who carried my two little traps from your automobile into the steamer; and I noticed, too, that you regarded all this princely hospitality as a mere trifle, save for your desire to do something for the pleasure and entertainment, while with you, of an Irishman who once gave a very little time and labour to the interests of the poor old country.
>
> [*March 15, 1914.*]

Quinn tried to extend his generosity to the "Irish Carlyle" yet further: he offered the old statesman an outright subvention. But O'Grady was able to refuse with grateful thanks, as "an independent man" with means adequate to his needs. "He is an old thoroughbred," Quinn wrote Russell on June 2, "and everybody that met him liked him." O'Grady urged Quinn to carry out his dream of a "Sabine farm" in the Adirondacks, a refuge from the strain of the city, with "a nice Irish girl as the Queen of it." About the queen Quinn was noncommittal, but agreed that such a retreat would appeal to him—if it were near the city and if it had a wing for painting and sculpture.

And Quinn had now, in Russell's phrase, "made it up with Yeats." Dorothy Coates, over whom the two men had quarreled in 1909, seriously ill with tuberculosis had written from Saranac to urge Quinn to make peace. Hearing that the poet was coming to America for another series of lectures, Quinn wrote on February 9 addressing him as "My dear Yeats":

> . . . I have always felt that apart from intellect you were always generous in your sympathies and full of humanity and that your heart was in the right place.
>
> So if the suggestion appeals to you, I should be glad to shake hands with you and let by-gones be by-gones.

Yeats replied on March 11 from the National Arts Club in New York, welcoming the placatory gesture and proposing lunch. Within a week he was installed in Quinn's apartment for a ten days' stay. Old Mr. Yeats, Russell, and Lady Gregory were relieved at the reconciliation; the quarrel had made difficulties for all their friends. "I am more glad than I can tell you that peace is made with Quinn," Mr. Yeats wrote to his son on March 16. "Quinn is a man of genius—not a touch of the commonplace or any other kind of prose in his whole composition, and yet an eminent lawyer —who also sticks to his work." And on March 24, after a Sunday passed at Quinn's apartment in company with the two younger men, he wrote to his daughter Lily to express his satisfaction at their restored intimacy: "It was pleasant to see Willie and Quinn like brothers together. They seemed to have the same thoughts and the same interests. What one said was echoed by the other."

Quinn noticed gray in Yeats's hair but thought him otherwise more robust than when he had last seen him and "as interesting and as keen on things as ever." [6] To Huneker he described him as "as charming and agreeable a man as you ever met," with a strain of natural humor not easily visible in his writings.[7] They talked of George Moore's *Hail and Farewell* and Yeats scribbled a satirical quatrain:

> What wonder that so vain a creature
> Mastered by the old deceit,
> Mistook an impulse of ill-nature
> For art's deliberate heat.

Then he altered the second line to "Being jealous of the very wind" and the fourth to "For art's deliberate mind." After an evening with W. B. Yeats and Huneker Quinn remarked that Yeats had shown nothing of "that droop of the head and apparent abstraction" which was a defensive posture for him, "a mere mask that he puts on when he is bored or doesn't know people." [8]

Bourke Cockran and his wife gave a luncheon for Yeats at the St. Regis, and Quinn tendered the poet a large dinner, with thirty-eight guests, on April 1, the night before he sailed for home. Quinn's publishing friend Mitchell Kennerley, wishing to offer him "something special in the way of place cards," printed a little edition of fifty copies of a pamphlet, "Nine Poems Chosen from the Works of William Butler Yeats, Privately printed for John Quinn and his friends, April First MCMXIV," in blue paper covers and with a studio portrait photograph of Yeats by Arnold Genthe. There were brief speeches by Augustus Thomas, Bourke Cockran, and Yeats. "Yeats' speech was very personal," Quinn wrote Huneker next day. "He gave more of his real self, of his theory of sincerity in poetry, than I had ever heard him give." But Judge Keogh, assured by Quinn that Yeats had "really meant" what he said at dinner, exclaimed: "'Why John, he must be a regular pagan!'" Dinner was over by eleven o'clock and was followed by a mass gathering of most of the males of the party at Quinn's until two in the morning. Subsequently Quinn sent copies of the Kennerley pamphlet to his friends in Ireland. Lily Yeats sent thanks from G. K. Chesterton's house in Beaconsfield, where she was a guest. She wrote to Quinn of her host's charm as a talker and of his odd but productive habits of work:

> He does not come to breakfast; I think he picnics in his room. Yesterday morning he sent down for a cup of hot milk and a bible. The first he got at once; the latter had to be hunted for.
>
> [*May 13, 1914.*]

Later in the spring, tired from his lectures and his renewed work in the theatre in Dublin, Yeats was taking a holiday by visiting Maud Gonne in Paris. He and Maud went to Poitiers with Everard Fielding, secretary of the Society for Psychical Research, who had been authorized by the Vatican to investigate a reported miracle, a "bleeding" oleograph of the Sacred Heart in the chapel of an old priest. Yeats was happy to be in the presence of anything conceivably supernatural; but Quinn warned that samples of the "blood" should be carefully collected and scientifically analyzed. If the substance proved to be genuine saint's blood, he wrote Yeats on June 3: "a real discovery will have been made in the anatomy of the saints, for science will then for the first time be able to tell the relative number of red and white corpuscles in a saint's blood." Quinn was also urging Yeats at this time to accept from him an annual payment in exchange for all his available manuscripts:

> . . . I will pay you so much a year for them, depending upon the quantity and the different things, taking articles as they are or poems as they are. I would put them in separate cases, and I would pay you a reasonable price for them, more perhaps than you would get of any dealer, who would pay you only a small price and then shop them around at a high price.   [*April 28, 1914.*]

Yeats, however, demurred at the idea of a fixed figure:

I would not like to arrange with you for an annual sum for my MSS. for if I did that I would always be afraid that you might tire of your bargain or that I might not have enough MSS. I will gladly however send you all I have and you can give me a price for it according to the measure. [*July 9, 1914.*]

The first bit would be a portion of his autobiography, which he had carried down to his twentieth year. The preservation of Yeats's early manuscripts, like that of Conrad's, was due to the foresight of a loyal female, in this case his sister Lily. "I just saved them from destruction long ago and kept them safe," she explained to Quinn, "being something of a magpie in these matters." [9] Eventually Yeats and Quinn agreed that sums due for the manuscripts would be paid over to J. B. Yeats as an allowance to keep him more comfortably in New York, where his children were now resigned to leaving him at least for the duration of the war.

When Arnold Genthe was making the portrait photograph of W. B. Yeats for the Kennerley pamphlet he made another of Yeats and Quinn, posed together in a grave and stately fashion, both full face, Yeats seated and Quinn standing at his shoulder. Quinn sent a print to Lady Gregory, and she reported flattering reactions with a mischievously conscious disloyalty to her great friend: "I said to Hugh Lane, 'John Quinn is the beauty of these two,' and he said, 'Yes, and the intellectual one!' " [10] She was back from five weeks in London with the Abbey company, and she explained that she had not written from there because she was without her typewriter and had not wished to inflict her inscrutable handwriting upon him: ". . . but I felt lonely not writing to you sometimes. It is not talking, but just better than nothing." [11] She had lunched with Shaw and heard amusing stories of rehearsing Mrs. Pat Campbell in *Pygmalion*. Theodore Roosevelt, in London for a few days, asked her to tea and talked of his grandchildren. Then at lunch at 10 Downing Street she had sat next to Asquith who thought Roosevelt a bore: he had "lectured" on the American constitution at a luncheon party that included James Bryce, the British authority on the subject. Lady Gregory recalled that Gladstone had used the same tactics when he wished to avoid a particularly uncomfortable subject.

George Russell was dissatisfied with Lady Gregory's account

of the history of the Abbey Theatre in *Our Irish Theatre* (1913), and he wrote to Quinn to set the record straight as he knew it. "She centralises herself a great deal too much and gives too little credit to the Fays," he thought.[12] He recognized that Yeats, Edward Martyn, and George Moore had set going the literary side of the movement, splendidly augmented by Synge and Lady Gregory. But it was the brothers Fay, Frank and Willie, who had really founded the Irish school of acting, and they carried it on for years, hand to mouth, before Yeats and Lady Gregory entered the picture. Russell recalled the trouble he had had in persuading Yeats to give them *Cathleen ni Houlihan* for performance. It was at the request of the Fays that Russell had drawn up the rules of the National Theatre Society; and the young Dublin amateurs had subscribed sixpence each a week to hire a little hall in which to rehearse. Russell wished Frank and William Fay noticed as the true founders of the theatre as a practical affair: when the writers came with their plays they found a working theatre ready to their hand. Russell agreed that the writers had given the theatre its intellectual base and made it famous; but "histories of movements ought to be generous to those obscure folk who worked at the foundations and did all the hard work unthanked when nobody looked on or praised them."[13]

The third volume, *Vale*, of George Moore's *Hail and Farewell* was now out, and Quinn on the whole disliked it, though he thought it beautifully written like everything else of Moore's. He considered Moore's treatment of Douglas Hyde and W. B. Yeats unfair, especially his imputation of ingrained snobbery to Yeats; and Quinn described as "horrible" Moore's candid but actually gentle and winning presentation of the young woman he called "Stella." Æ wrote of Moore with his usual mixture of affection, amusement and exasperation, a bit acidified now by time and habit. He agreed that he had "escaped with a halo" from Moore's scrutiny, but feared that "halos fixed on one's brows by the wicked don't add to one's glory." He had heard that Moore, having "re-anointed himself with the oil of his old sins," was off to Palestine to soak up atmosphere for a romance about Christ (*The Brook Kerith*): "Having desecrated one Holy Island he is now going to desecrate the Holy Land in Asia."[14]

Having lost Moore to London and Palestine, James Stephens to Paris, and Padraic Colum to New York, Æ was feeling hard up for friends and even for protégés. "I have been losing friends this way all my life," he wrote plaintively on July 8, and he lamented Ireland's famous inability to keep her able men. But he himself felt no temptation to leave her, not even for the American visit which Quinn had been urging upon him. In the July 8 letter to Quinn he wrote:

> I never want to leave it myself. I love Ireland and I love the people. . . . I admit they are not modern, but they are human, and business and science and finance have not removed from them some flavour of ancient romance and beauty in mind and form. I know Ireland better than most people. Its faults are all national and public. Its virtues are private and personal and need intimacy to appreciate rightly.

In his present loneliness Russell was delighted to espouse a new protégé of Dunsany's, the poet Francis Ledwidge, a young country boy who had been discovered working as a road mender. Russell's account of him was attractive enough to shake Quinn's dyspeptic resolve to "help" no more Irishmen. Quinn wrote on July 2:

> I have quit that sort of thing now, and God knows I should not want to volunteer to get into it again, but from what you write of this young chap—"mending roads in Meath," only twenty-two, a loveable creature, with a feeling for natural beauty, and his sensitiveness—I feel moved to do what I can to help him.

He offered, as a starter, to try to find an American publisher for Ledwidge if an Irish or English publication were arranged. In the upshot, Dunsany took over, and no calls were made upon Quinn. Ledwidge was to die in the war in 1917 after Dunsany had helped him to publish three volumes of verse.

George Moore hoped that no one could call him a really bad man in the face of the fact that for ten years Æ had been his friend. He had nominated Æ as "the Christ" of *Hail and Farewell.* Russell might more accurately have been called the Saint Paul of Irish life, with his Pagan and Christian mingling, his fluent fusion of spiritual and practical power, his missionary apostleship, the range and beauty of his vision, and the earthy strength of his working presence. He was showing all these qualities in the spring of 1914. He had intervened on behalf of the workers in the bitter Dublin strike and lockout of 1913, and he was trying now to compose a book which might serve as a testament of a genuine labor movement in Ireland. He was in a Swiftian rage at the ancient impoverishment of the masses in Ireland:

> Nobody seems to care a damn in this cursed country about the poor. Everybody tramples on them. They are housed worse than swine. The church bullies them. The press lies about them. The law is weighed heavily against them.[15]

Russell was well aware of the irony of the involvement of a person such as himself, "originally shy, intended to be an artist or a poet," in such rude affairs of the market place, but his strenuous morality rationalized the phenomenon quite simply: "It is not my job but I've got to do what I can or be ashamed of myself." And he concluded with his habitual sweetness: "But I suppose it is all right and one won't go back empty-handed to the stars." [16]

The beautifully complex character of Russell was used as evidence by J. B. Yeats in a fine letter of September 25, 1914, to Quinn:

> It is the defect of A. E.'s [poetry] that one feels he has never lived in the finite world at all. At least he does not use it in his poetry—why, I have never been able to understand, for he lives strongly in the finite.

The same unworldliness made the ethos of Russell's paintings, and it helps one understand why he looked forward with such homesick longing to his painting holiday in Donegal every year. The balance of strength and sweetness, the fertile tension so finely obvious in Æ's life as a man, though so overweighted toward spirituality in his life as an artist, was one John Butler Yeats's son understood very well, and embodied in some of the greatest of his poems—in such figures as the lion and the honeycomb of "Vacillation." As he tried once again to advance his speculations about "the Ego, the finite, and the infinite," the engaging old amateur metaphysician J. B. Yeats had arrived at certain impressive psychological and ethical insights. He announced now the "doctrine (my own discovery) that neither virtue nor pleasure nor happiness is the end of life but growth, and that is so not merely as regards the whole man but as to each individual feeling." [17] Thus, when Rachel was weeping for her children, it would have been a moral and psychological error to ask her to control her grief. Rather the finite grief should be exploited "poetically," in art and life, as a means to touching its infinite reference, the beauty of its universal truth:

> Rather should one seek in every way to enhance her grief by dwelling on the subject of her loss, expatiating on the beauty of the children and on the extent of her desolation, only doing it in such a way that some sense of harmony and of what is called beauty might steal into the picture. In other words, there is no consoler except poetry, and religion so far as it is poetry. But let the practical man keep away.
>
> The poet helps growth by stimulating and intensifying humanity, and if the finite world—this close room with the low ceiling —be too small for us he opens the windows and lets in the air of infinity. . . .
>
> In a work of art we find the finite constantly being melted into the infinite, and so melted that the finite is not lost but that it colours and stains the infinite. When a lovely girl dies it is precisely then that one would know every detail of her life and her dying. All of which explains why the great poet in his work is as rich in the finite—in that which can be observed, tasted and handled—as he is in the infinite, the infinite being the impalpable which cannot be expressed except in suggestion, by symbols and by rhythm.

And his conclusion, Keatsian in nature and in stature:

> Happiness comes to a man when the principle of growth within works unimpeded. Grief itself turns to happiness if only the tears come in sufficient abundance and the whole heart melts. It is this sudden melting of the heart that we call the *sense of beauty*.[18]

Such letters, clearly, contributed to the immense available richness of Quinn's life. And they mattered greatly to W. B. Yeats, to whom his father was regularly sending versions of the same ideas. Their thought and style is visible in Yeats's poems and his prose, as he had acknowledged several years before "with some surprise." [19]

The great event of the year, for Quinn as for everyone else in

the western world, was the outbreak of world war. It was soon
the obsessive subject. Lady Gregory reported that W. B. Yeats
had gone to his favorite London astrologer to get the Kaiser's
horoscope and found the man out—gone to the public library,
" 'where they take *all* the papers.' " [20] Russell wrote that little was
to be expected of artists for the time; the war news was far more
sensational than anything the imagination could fabricate. May
Morris first suggested that Quinn send her money for war work
rather than his annual barrel of apples, then resolved to let the
apples come—she would send those to the men. Maud Gonne had
gone to nurse the wounded in French hospitals. Gwen John was
stoically fixed at Meudon outside Paris, with no intention of
moving:

> I didn't leave Paris. I thought I should at first but when the danger
> got nearer I found I wouldn't. . . . It is very high there and we
> can see all Paris. We saw the chase of the aeroplanes when the
> enemy dropped a few bombs those afternoons.[21]

The influence of the war apart, W. B. Yeats was feeling a general
disenchantment with the progress of the arts, toward vulgarity
and away from his own romantic and aristocratic ideals. He wrote
to introduce a young woman painter to Quinn as "one of those
new people who have overthrown my world by substituting sensation for sentiment." "The generation of the mangel-wurzel has
followed that of the green carnation," he grumbled bitterly, "and
I am growing old." [22]

Before the outbreak of the war Ireland was conducting her private rehearsal in a new confrontation, built on centuries of ani-
mosity, of northern and southern, orange and green, Protestant
and Catholic parties. Both sides were arming, and Ulster said she
would fight for political partition of the island rather than submit
to the dissolution of the union with England. Æ reported in March
that Edward Carson had a hundred thousand men armed and
trained in Ulster, "all stark, raving mad with hatred of the Catholics, whom they regard as Hottentots." [23] In July he was back from
his painting holiday in Donegal, lovely and peaceful as usual: "But
across the bay at Downings there were Ulster Volunteers and National Volunteers, both lively folk, and some of them were doing

a little gun running." [24] He enjoined a plague on both their houses. "The Ulster folk have less brains but more character and will. The Nationalists are clever but have no character," he judged; and marveled: "I don't know what sin this nation has committed that it was born with blind guides." He foresaw the violent wreck of the kind of work to which he had devoted twenty years' labor, for a reasonable statehood, a sound economy, and an enlightened culture; but he was bitterly resigned to the fatality of events: "There must be bloodletting to get rid of the congestion of political and religious blood to the head." He felt that with time the motives of the rabid Nationalists had turned merely negative, destructive, and full of hate: ". . . they are no longer Irishmen but simply anti-Englishmen of the most frenzied type." [25] For the announced religious motives on either side Russell felt no more respect. They showed nothing of what he beautifully understood as religion: "Ireland is rotten with rotten sects. There is not a decimal fraction of real religion in either party, but they are all, both of them, blind with bigotry. . . ." And if partition was to be the price of Home Rule, Russell preferred to live without it.

The crisis roused Quinn's dozing Irish partisanship and left him dismayed and enraged. When the parliamentary Home Rule bill came through with its rider for the exclusion of Ulster, he spat with fury at Edward Carson and John Redmond and with contempt for the whole of Anglo-Irish politics. He praised Ulster bitterly: they had played a strong and clever hand. "I take my hat off to the Protestants in the North of Ireland," he wrote to Russell on July 2. "I regard English politics and even Irish politics, outside of those few Protestants of the North, as simply beneath contempt, weak, flabby, cowardly." He felt some slight hope that "some of the idealists, men like yourself, Standish O'Grady, Yeats, Hyde, Plunkett and others," might yet be able to woo and argue Ulster back into the fold. But he gloomily foresaw that neither he nor Russell would now live to see Ireland free and united.

The arch-criminal, Quinn felt, was the leader of the Irish Parliamentary Party, John Redmond, who should have put an early stop to Ulster's arming, so that she might not now rattle her saber so intimidatingly. Finally, when world war had erupted, Quinn went so far as to blame its outbreak largely upon Carson and Ulster:

they had assured the Germans that the threat of Ulster arms would keep England from opposing Germany in the war. So he wrote to Russell on November 9:

> I believe that the Kaiser, conceited fool that he is, and his general staff, counted upon the fact that England was divided, was on the brink of civil strife and civil war, that her army was honeycombed with treason and rebellion, and that England being in that condition . . . she would not take part in the war, and that Germany felt that England would be out of it, and that Ulster had more to do with it as a contributing cause than any other cause, outside of Germany and Russia. If I am right, the Ulster braggarts, boasters, and treason mongers have a damned heavy burden upon their consciences.

Clotted with partisan guesswork and newspaper rhetoric, it was the argument of a passionately concerned and disappointed man. The war was a general human disaster, and the proposed partition of Ireland the destruction of a dream long postponed and apparently at the point of realization.

The war offered a complex test of the loyalties of Irishmen and men of Irish sympathies. Loyalty to England and opposition to Germany was not then for Irishmen the obvious course that time has made it seem to a spectator. But Quinn and Russell made up their minds quickly. "I am rather detached but my sympathies are with the Allies," Russell wrote on December 10. He went on:

> The old lion has got rather kindly to Ireland of late, and the new young German lion is ravenous and bureaucratic and despotic and vain and is as vulgar as Great Britain, rather more so, I think. What it calls culture is really a mechanical education.

Quinn had already written him a month earlier: "I have no sympathy with the Irish in this country and in Ireland who are on the side of Germany." [26] On the last day of the year he summed up his feelings for Hyde in crudely neat antitheses:

> . . . if I were an Irishman I would have been on the side of England because I prefer English civilization to German civilization; England's idea of freedom to Germany's idea of imperialism and military government; England's notion of liberty to Germany's notion of machine government; individual freedom to bossism; French culture and French ideals to German sentiment and German beer.

He sourly reflected that German occupation of Ireland for a year or two might not be a bad idea: "It would teach the Irish industry, order, efficiency, economy, cleanliness, and it would shut up a good deal of the mouths-almighty who are in the habit of killing the enemy with their mouths." [27] The Irish would soon be happy to return to the English brand of oppression.

But it was his new love, the French, who were pleasing Quinn most at this stage, going about their heartbreaking business with little parading of "culture" and few claims to exclusive possession of God's grace. "The spectacle of France's standing up quietly, unboastfully, without panic, and fighting her best, has been wine to my soul," he wrote to Hyde. [28]

Quinn's loyalties met a peculiarly personal and complex test in the summer of 1914, and for two years thereafter, in his close relationship with Sir Roger Casement. Casement had arrived in the United States with a commission to raise money for one of the southern parties, the Irish National Volunteers, especially to buy arms; following the beaten track of fund-seeking Irishmen, he made his way at once to Quinn's place. Quinn housed him for a month, gave money to his campaign, and helped him to approach other potential donors. "Again a hundred thanks for all your companionship, cheering words and kindly acts to me since I met you," Casement wrote back on July 30 after he had moved on to Philadelphia. "You are a fellow countryman—if ever there was one." Quinn liked Casement, though he grew quickly dubious about his motives and his tactics, and eventually about his sanity. Casement "seemed to get more and more excited as the war went on," Quinn wrote to Hyde quite early in the story, on December 31, 1914. In effect if not in fact, both Casement and Kuno Meyer, whom Quinn also liked and admired as a companion and a scholar, were German agents from the outset of the war, Casement from that sort of negative patriotism and hatred of England which Æ found so dangerous. "I know Casement," Æ wrote Quinn with his profound good sense:

He is a romantic person of the picturesque kind, with no heavy mentality to embarrass him in his actions. A thousand years ago he would have been a knight errant doing wild things, hunting for the Holy Grail or spitting dragons on his spear. I am dubious about the nationality of men who cannot live in Ireland but must always be inventing grandiose schemes for us at the other ends of the earth. *[December 10, 1914.]*

Casement was stumping American cities on behalf of the Volunteers, addressing rallies in Philadelphia, Baltimore, Buffalo, Chicago, and fighting off the challenge of the rival Redmondite canvassers, who were following a policy of emergency loyalty to Britain. Casement expressed his own line in a letter to Quinn from Philadelphia on July 30—his second letter of that day:

> Everything looks like a war, with John Bull pulled in; and, if so, I think we should lose no chance to arm the Volunteers, so that we may be able to repeat 1782 [when Henry Grattan's "Volunteers" convened at Dungannon and secured concessions from the English] over again. Bull will want our help, and it should be given only on terms that we get freedom at home, and if we have the men armed we can ensure a greater measure of respect for our claims.

A month later, his prophecy of war fulfilled, Casement had formed a new scheme: instead of begging guns or buying them clandestinely, then attempting to smuggle them into Ireland, why not found a company and send a good businessman as an agent to Ireland to sell guns openly? "A new development of American commerce!" he exulted. "To capture the Irish rifle market!" He wanted Quinn to act as American legal agent for the scheme "and put it up to Bryan & Co. in Washington to *assist* American trade in a new market. . . . A grape-juice Secretary of State [William Jennings Bryan] should appreciate that." [29]

In September he asked Quinn's advice about circulating a manifesto he had composed against the enlistment of Irishmen in the English forces, in which he called England's latest Home Rule proposals a "promissory note (payable after death)." He was advised by Quinn, and by men closer to his own sympathies, such as John Devoy of the *Gaelic American*, not to circulate inflammatory anti-British documents in the United States. He gave in, but grumbled:

> There is too much "Anglo-Saxon" here, too much "Evening Post" (a weak imitation of the "Westminster Gazette"); and I think, with John Bull Redmond on his recruiting mission in Ire-

land, it is time I got back and helped to save some of the poor
boys from this abominable sacrifice of Irish manhood to English
mammon.[30]

But Casement's route of return to Ireland was devious and pitiful
and ended in a "traitor's" grave. He had been talking obscurely for
some time of going to Berlin, and Quinn had tried to dissuade him;
now, a month later, Kuno Meyer brought "secret" messages that
he had already made his way to the German capital. Casement himself wrote Quinn on Christmas day a long incoherent letter in
which he referred to England outright as "the enemy." In Germany, he said, he had found "a fortress of soul, a unanimity of
patriotism, an unkillable courage in this land and people that not
all the world in arms against them could overthrow. *They* are the
true battlers for European freedom, and please God they win right
thro'." He believed that he had made "a strong, brave friend for
our poor, defrauded little country," but at the cost of making himself "a refugee, an outcast." He was convinced that the English
had put a price of £10,000 on his head. Incongruously mingled
with these melodramatic matters were requests to Quinn to find
him a publisher and to negotiate a contract for a book on " 'Germany from within during the war,' " and to send him a copy of
a work by Trevelyan which Quinn had told him made a flattering
reference to him. Quinn wrote of all this to Hyde on December 31,
apparently not yet realizing the full fatality of Casement's behavior: "It was a silly thing to do. It has absolutely cut him off from
any usefulness in Ireland." Russell thought so too, and took a long
visionary look at the war and the future beyond:

> . . . I think it will be a long war, and the sole result will be to
> make the centre of power shift from Europe to U. S. A., which
> will boss the world in future until Asia in a couple of centuries
> gets organized again.[31]

Neither war nor business nor politics nor literature had markedly
slowed Quinn's expanding new career as a collector and propagandist of painting. At the beginning of 1914, with the Armory
Show still a warm reflection, he wrote Arthur Symons of his turn
from book and manuscript collecting to art: "One is a hobby and
the other is art. . . ."[32] In buying a painting or a piece of sculp-

ture, that is, he could have the feeling of participating in the creative process. In the first weeks of January 1914 he happily allowed himself to be drawn into the *Evening Telegram's* campaign to secure the opening of the Metropolitan Museum much more freely than the established single evening each week. On January 5 Quinn gave out an approving interview: "It is only where the public has an opportunity to see and to study examples of good art that the hope may be felt that people will learn in time to turn away from meretricious and bad art." He quoted Henry James (in "The Art of Fiction") to the effect that " 'Art lives upon discussion, upon experiment, upon curiosity, upon variety of attempt. . . .' " He pointed out that among his arguments in Washington against the duty on living art was that "art should be brought within the reach of people of modest means and not remain the trading commodity of wealthy art dealers or become merely the hobby or the exclusive possession of the rich. . . ." And he recalled the efforts of Ruskin and William Morris to "bring art to the people." On January 16, as "a taxpayer and private citizen," Quinn spoke at length before a committee of inquiry on the question. He advocated an experiment of freer opening not for one month, as had been proposed, but for three years. He could see nothing against the idea except the cost, estimated at $37,000 a year, and suggested that the city cheerfully appropriate the money. He argued that an appreciation of art had to be slowly fostered through generations; and he spoke of the value to skilled workmen, and ultimately to the national taste, of having available a concentrated view of "form, design, color and so forth." He reminded the committee that in one month there had been 90,000 paid admissions to the Armory Show. At the end of Quinn's little speech Robert W. de Forest, President of the Metropolitan, said: " 'The public and all the Museums of the country owe a debt to Mr. Quinn, as it was under his leadership that the fight for free art was won and that the provisions to that end were incorporated in the new Underwood Tariff Law.' " Quinn reached over to shake his hand: " 'With your earnest and efficient cooperation, Mr. deForest.' " In this diplomatic situation, Quinn did not press his usual claim to exclusive credit for the establishment of "free art."

Quinn's personal collection moved ahead, but hesitatingly, at nothing like the pace it would reach in a few years. He sought advice from men he considered expert, especially from Augustus John in England and James Huneker and Walt Kuhn in New York. He accepted Huneker's judgment that old English art was "painted dolls," and was impressed with his rating of John, Epstein, and Matisse as the "three biggest talents" of living men whose work he had seen.[33] On January 15, on John's recommendation, he bought for one hundred guineas Epstein's *Head of Romilly John*, a study of John's young son. He corresponded with Epstein also about his beleaguered Oscar Wilde Memorial in Père Lachaise Cemetery in Paris, and heard from him on August 12 that the work, after alteration, had at least been unveiled. "I can feel only bitterness," the sculptor wrote, "that the work to which I gave 10 months of hard labor, after being hid for so long, mutilated and made a scandal of, should at last be sumptiously [*sic*] unveild [*sic*]." And in the spring of 1914 at the Photo-Secession Gallery of Alfred Stieglitz Quinn made his first of many purchases of capital works of Constantin Brancusi: on March 19 the marble head of *Mademoiselle Pogany* for $1,200; on May 2 the marble *Bird* for $600.

The first rift in the lute of Quinn's friendship with Augustus John appeared about this time in the course of an exasperating series of events surrounding John's picture *Forze e Amore*. John had painted the big decoration for the entrance hall of Hugh Lane's house in Cheyne Walk in Chelsea; then, after a quarrel with Lane, he had sold it to Horace deVere Cole, from whom he had extracted it for Quinn. Quinn agreed on a price of £1,200 of which he paid £900. Hugh Lane appeared about this time at Quinn's apartment and offered to buy John's portrait of William Nicholson and then trade it to Quinn for *Forze e Amore*. Quinn wrote to John to explore the idea, and John wrote back to say that he had painted out the picture and was doing *The Flute of Pan* over it. He was sorry Quinn had been "so set" on the original picture, but assured him that he had been "merely conscientious" in painting it out; he would offer the new picture at the same price and he was confident that Quinn would like it better. [34]

It was high-handed behavior, and Quinn naturally never forgot it. He watched darkly for signs in support of his suspicion that John's dissipations were undermining his morals and his craft.

"Poor Symons" wrote on June 20 of a gala outing in London occasioned by the prospect that his "Tragedies" might be both published and performed. At lunch at the Cavour John congratulated him in his deep voice: " 'Symons, fame and money—both.' " They went in a taxi to Pachmann's concert, and afterward backstage John, lounging with his pipe in his mouth, said: " 'Let's have a drink.' " From five to eight they drank at the Café Royal "seven absinthes, with cigarettes and conversation. In spite of that we got few sensations." John ordered dinner for them and a third man who had joined them. After dinner, with whiskey and soda, they were joined by "Little Helen," an artist's model, just seventeen years old. Finally Symons took a taxi to his hotel "in some confusion." Next day he had a headache but was otherwise well. Quinn was amused and titillated and passed on the story to Huneker in a note of July 9: "There is a good honest story of a good honest drunk, and I hope a good honest screw with Little Helen. . . ." He imagined that John was carrying on this way more or less constantly; but he was still willing to buy, and on June 1 he paid a bill of £841 to the Chenil Gallery, mostly for Augustus John items.

Quinn was also having trouble extracting pictures from Gwen John, but with that lady, whom he had never met, he felt a good deal more patient, being charmed by her modesty and the reticent prose of her letters. In July she sent him a painting by her friend Ruth Manson, and Quinn paid £8 for it in December. Gwen John was so dissatisfied with one picture she had sent him that she hoped it had gone down on the *Titanic*. By September Quinn had finally received from Chenil a shipment of two drawings and the third painting of hers to reach him, *Study of a Woman*. But the anticipated flow was turning into a trickle, and Quinn's proposed annual payment to her of £100 was tacitly suspended for the time.

His purchases of American work were also sparse and hesitant. On February 26 he paid the Montross Gallery $1,925 for seven paintings by Arthur B. Davies, Walt Kuhn, Maurice Prendergast, and George F. Of, and in July he bought Kuhn's *The Cyclist* and *White Tights* for $250. Quinn was pretty well willing to take anything Kuhn offered him, out of friendship as well as confidence in his art. But his eye was really turned abroad.

He felt tense and unwell throughout the year, and complained in the spring of indigestion, sleeplessness, night sweats, and chills. The war put an end to his dream of a cure at Dr. Dengler's sanitarium at Baden-Baden, followed by an art-trip to Paris and London, and in the upshot his only vacation was a few weekends in the Adirondacks and at the shore. He was working hard and making money but felt entirely unable to relax within his professional well-being. He had been named special counsel for the Comptroller of the State of New York in inheritance tax proceedings against the estate of John Jacob Astor, drowned on the *Titanic,* and he was furious when his large anticipated fee was reduced by more than a third.[35] In a letter of November 25 to Judge Keogh he quoted the "Gladstonian compliment" he had received from Frank Hugh O'Donnell, in America on one of the Irish "secret missions," after Quinn had refused to give him introductions to the President, the Secretary of State, and other government officials:

> "I never admired more your magnificent detachment from politics than in your inability to help me to a single introduction after crossing the Atlantic. I suppose more lawyers are built that way— hard money making and tranquil hedonism—than any other profession."

It was a direct and detailed attack, and Quinn thought it over, though defiantly. "Hard I am not," he wrote to Keogh; "tranquil very seldom. Money making—I wish I could make more of it. Hedonic, yes, insofar as money making and debts would permit me to. I'd be a Sybarite if I could as well as a Hedonist." [36]

These and other motives drove him—pride in his talents and the wish to excel, obligations to friends and family and to his Irish heritage, the wish to achieve and to deserve a high position in the social and cultural life of the time. "Some people think that I am a good lawyer," he wrote to Mitchell Kennerley on October 31. "I know that I am a good business man. Few men know the banking business or credits as well as I." But it was never a position in which he could rest; he drove himself to reach it and then to hold it and advance upon it. In the general tension he found some relief in luncheon chats with cronies at the Bankers' Club. Visits to galleries were at once a relief and a different challenge. He spent a good many evenings talking life and letters with James Huneker, though he gave up hope of matching Huneker's consumption of wine and Pilsener. The *Sun* had let Huneker go, and when he signed on with *Puck* Quinn ordered six subscriptions "beginning with the date of Mr. Huneker's first weekly article," [37] having three copies sent to himself, one to Dorothy Coates, one to Annie Foster, and one to his sister Julia Anderson. His preoccupation with business and with art gave a disingenuous air to his statement to Huneker on July 9, celebrating "life":

> Good God, yes, rum and music and for me *women,* if we can stand all three or anyone of them for long, beat art any day, just as the living, breathing, pulsing beauty of a girl, her skin, her eyes, her hair, figure, form and movement, move one and draw one more than any damned oil painting or drawing that ever was; so life is bigger than art. . . .

It was to Huneker that Quinn reported at the end of the year of his meetings with Aleister Crowley, the celebrated sensualist and Black Magician, "driven out" of England by his notoriety and now on his uppers in New York. Quinn bought all Crowley's books but had not read them; his clerk Watson looked into them and called them " 'the limit,' " " 'both erotic and blasphemous.' " [38] Crowley sent word that he would like to have a look at the portrait drawing of him by Augustus John, which Quinn owned. Subsequently he came several times to the apartment, and Quinn helped him out by buying several of his manuscripts. On the whole he found the wicked man a bore, especially at the price of $700. Yet he asked him to Christmas dinner at the apartment, along with John Butler Yeats and Frederic James Gregg, who, like Huneker, had left the *Sun* and was now one of the main contributors to *Vanity Fair.* The four men smoked Quinn's big Christmas cigars and drank rye, Rhine wine, and Chartreuse. When W. B. Yeats learned of Quinn's meetings with Crowley he sent on a gaily malicious account of his own experience with the man:

> I knew him 16 or 17 years ago but dropped him on finding that he lived under various false names and left various districts without paying his debts. Lord Middlesex was one of his names, another was that of a Russian nobleman. I was also in a case against him.

He dropped the case rather than go into the witness box. He is I think mad, but has written about six lines, amid much bad rhetoric, of real poetry. I asked about him at Cambridge, and a man described him being dragged out of the dining hall by a porter, thrown out, struggling, because of the indecency of his conversation. He is an English and French type. You I think have nothing like him. [*March 21, 1915.*]

1915

AS far as Quinn's life was concerned, Crowley was just passing through. Gregg ("El Greggo") and J. B. Yeats were organic and welcome, functional members near the center of his life. Old Mr. Yeats had recently made portrait drawings of Dorothy Coates, at the Majestic, her hotel near Quinn's apartment, as she passed through the city on her way from Saranac to continue her convalescence in Asheville, North Carolina, and of Mary Anderson, Quinn's beloved seven-year-old niece, posed a bit stiffly in a parlor chair in a homespun linen dress, woven and embroidered at Cuala in Dublin. Young Mary marveled at and rather resented Mr. Yeats's appetite at Quinn's dinners; when he was at table, others had to fight for their rights. She found long sessions of posing for him a trial, too, and sometimes locked herself in the bathroom to escape him, where Moto, Quinn's new Japanese servant, would bring her sympathetic plates of ice cream. J. B. Yeats carried on happily if parlously in New York, on erratic earnings from portrait paintings or drawings, lectures, bits of journalism, sums from Willie and occasionally from Quinn, who found him as personally enchanting and occasionally exasperating as ever. His health remained good, though his hearing continued to fail. He walked about the city with his head high and his eyes straight ahead, and he would step off curbs with no thought of the motor cars which were no longer infrequent. In the spring of 1915 he was knocked down in the street and painfully cut and bruised; but he was soon out again and campaigning with his customary ebullience.

It was agreed by Quinn and W. B. Yeats that the £50 for the

manuscript of "Reveries," the first portion of Yeats's memoirs, should remain in Quinn's hands for the use of J. B. Yeats in New York. Quinn received the copy, in manuscript and typescript, in June 1915, and a month later he "corrected" the typed copy and sent it back to Yeats, who ignored it. Out of affection and sympathy, Quinn was also still regularly buying batches of manuscript from "poor Symons," whose letters came with such frequency that Quinn saved them up to answer a half-dozen at a time. Rhoda Symons, whom Yeats described as his "beautiful, hard, innocent wife," [1] wrote to thank Quinn for the pleasure her husband found in sums from him, going up to London for sprees at the Savoy Hotel and the Café Royal. Rhoda Symons had been predicting her husband's dissolution ever since his mental collapse in Italy in 1909. On April 6, 1915, she wrote to Quinn: "Alas! he is getting terribly thin—wasting—and he is very much in a state of vibration—but he is happy. . . ." Doctors had predicted that Symons would live on for years, becoming gradually "more infantile." Since she and her husband "must" live apart, Rhoda Symons begged Quinn to help her find a way to earn £100 a year so that she could keep her flat in London.[2] Symons, meanwhile, had promised Quinn the dedication of *The Life and Adventures of Lucy Newcome*.[3]

In treating for manuscripts with Yeats and Symons, Quinn was running counter to his newly established movement away from Ireland and England and toward France, and away from literature and toward art. He told Yeats he was resolved to buy no more manuscripts except those of a few living men whom he cared about personally, such as Conrad, Symons, James Stephens, and Yeats himself. In testimony to his new emphases he had, in the process of raising $28,000 to buy *La Rivière* and *Le Vendage* of Puvis de Chavannes, sold manuscripts of Meredith, Morris, Swinburne, Gissing, Henley, Rossetti, and others to Henry E. Huntington for his library. (He inadvertently included in the shipment his fragment of Conrad's *Nostromo*, and had to ask for it back.) The connoisseur's career which had begun with an Ohio schoolboy buying contemporary first editions was beginning to find its ultimate direction. Now in January 1915 Quinn felt rudely and personally attacked when he read in the *New Age* of January 21 an article in which Ezra Pound, lamenting the needy situation of an artist such as Jacob

Epstein, struck out at "American collectors buying autograph
MSS. of William Morris, faked Rembrandts and faked Van
Dykes. ..." Quinn suspected, apparently with some justice, that he
was Pound's model for the brainless retrospective American collector.

Having admired Pound for years and read everything of his he
had seen, Quinn was hurt by the unfair and inaccurate image of
himself, and on February 25 wrote in a manly strain to set the
record straight. He reminded Pound that they had met when Pound
returned to America in 1910, dined at Petitpas' with Mr. Yeats,
and joined Quinn's party for an evening's sport at Coney Island.
He vowed not to resent Pound's slur, applauded his "habit of hitting straight from the shoulder," and proceeded to defend himself
in the attacking posture that they both preferred. He told of
selling his older manuscripts to buy the works of Puvis de Chavannes, and asserted the liveliness and modernity of his collection:
"If there is a 'liver' collector of vital contemporary art in this
country, for a man of moderate means, I should like to meet him."
As for poor Epstein, he already possessed a half-dozen examples.
He summed up the current state of his collection:

> I have bought and own a fine Cézanne—a portrait of Madame
> Cézanne; one of the best Van Goghs in the world; a first-rate
> Gauguin; more than one painting by Derain; three or four fine
> Picassos—three of the blue period and two of his latest cubistic
> work; two important Matisses and a large number of lithographs
> and etchings by Matisse; paintings by Rouault and ceramics by
> Rouault; paintings in oil and water-color by Dufy; paintings by
> de Segonzac, by Chabaud, by Jacques Villon and by Marcel
> Duchamp; besides having perhaps the largest collection of paint-
> ings by Augustus John in the world; and works of the Americans,
> Walt Kuhn, Maurice Prendergast, Arthur B. Davies, Ernest Law-
> son, and other living American artists.

Far from being a buyer of "faked" work, Quinn reckoned that he
had done more than any other person to put an end to the American trade in fakes when he had drafted the new tariff law, of which
he claimed to have written "every word and line" and the detailed
construction of which was based on his legal opinion. "I inserted
the word 'original' in the law, so that only *original* works of art

come in duty free, that is, works of art really by the artists that they purport to be by." All in all, Quinn supposed, he was "as much alive to good art" as anybody in America, and he had done more practical service for modern art than any other man then living. Demonstrating that his eyes were fixed forward, he asked how he could get hold of some of the sculpture of Gaudier-Brzeska which Pound had praised in his article. Finally he suggested that Pound begin contributing to the new American weekly, the *New Republic,* which he described as dull but "the best we have."

Clearly Quinn's notion of his function as connoisseur, patron, and activist was already programmatic and detailed. Pound was not slow to scent in Quinn a kindred spirit and a potentially serviceable ally. Himself the most unselfish and efficient midwife to modernism in the arts, Pound kept his antennae always in motion seeking assistance for himself, his friends, and protégés. His reply, dated March 8, 1915, was an archetypal Poundian document and the first in a vivid series that continued until Quinn died. He recollected that when they had met in New York Quinn had been in the middle of his affair with May Morris, and of the evening at Coney Island called up the image of J. B. Yeats riding an elephant and Quinn "plugging away" in the shooting gallery. Having scotched the tariff on art, he suggested, Quinn ought now to do the same for books, especially "non-commercial" writings. He promised to send photographs of available works of Gaudier-Brzeska, then in the trenches. He then went on to develop a character of the patron which became a part of Quinn's notion of himself and his ideal modes of behavior. Pound declared himself shocked to hear of a man's paying $30,000 for two pictures. The true patron would consider not the commercial or exchange "value" of works of art, but how much work of living men he could underwrite with what money he had: ". . . NO artist needs more than 2,000 dollars per year, and any artist can do two pictures at least in a year. 30,000 dollars would feed a whole little art world for five years." Pound continued:

My whole drive is that if a patron buys from an artist who needs money (needs money to buy tools, time and food), the patron then makes himself equal to the artist: he is building art into the world; he creates. . . .

A great age of painting, a renaissance in the arts, comes when there are a few patrons who back their own flair and who buy from unrecognized men. In every artist's life there is, if he be poor, and they mostly are, a period when £10 is a fortune and when £100 means a year's leisure to work or to travel. . . .

Besides, if a man has any sense, the sport and even the commercial advantage is so infinitely greater. If you can hammer this into a few more collectors you will bring on another cinquecento.

Diplomatically, Pound deprecated the bitterness of his *New Age* article. He recalled that in his eight months in America he had earned just £14, "my exact fare from Philadelphia back to Paris. Oh I was in a fine mood to appreciate the purchase of old mss. . . ." He remembered too that he had been on the verge of a real as well as a figurative attack of jaundice. All in all, Pound's letter made the honest statement of an honest man; but it also offered the subtly drawn outline of a relationship that Quinn might gracefully choose to occupy with Pound and his friends: the patron as creator, his "equal" part with the artist in the production of enduring work, the sport of the chase, the generosity that might turn out to be good business, the image of the modern Medici. Those rosy ideas Quinn grasped frankly, and thereafter he was not only a friend of Pound and his enthusiasms but a Poundian patron of the arts in general. Pound had "put style upon" Quinn's half-spoken image of himself.*

In January Quinn placed on indefinite loan to the Metropolitan Museum four of his capital pictures of a traditional sort: Augustus John's *The Way Down to the Sea* and Puvis de Chavannes's *La Rivière, Le Vendage,* and *La Décollation de St. Jean Baptiste.* Aleister Crowley told him that he had been asked by a charming lady: " 'By the way, have you seen Mr. Quinn's huge John?' " [4] Quinn wrote to John on March 10 to describe his picture's handsome effect: "It glows and outshines any of them, and you can see it a hundred yards off down the corridor and through two rooms into

---

* George Moore accused W. B. Yeats of "putting style upon" Lady Gregory's Irish peasant dialect stories, and of wishing to "put style on" Moore's own plays. *Ave,* p. 267.

the room where it hangs." Quinn thought it a triumphant demonstration of his ideas of right painterly color. Robert W. de Forest
now nominated Quinn to be an Honorary Fellow for life of the
Museum, and he was elected at the annual meeting in the middle
of February. No doubt accurately, he considered his election as
mainly a tribute to his successful campaign against the tariff duty
on art. He reviewed the case to W. B. Yeats:

> They had spent thousands and thousands of dollars in 1909 in their
> campaign for free art, but they succeeded in getting the duty
> off only on old art; and until I entered the field all art less than
> twenty years old had to pay 15% duty. I got all art free of duty
> and I paid the bills of the 9-months campaign, over £500.
>
> [*February 15, 1915.*]

When Quinn sent Gwen John a copy of the *Bulletin of the Metropolitan Museum* with news of his election, she reacted in a characteristically oblique manner: ". . . I love the picture on the cover,
the last communion of St. Jerome. . . . St. Jerome is so beautiful in
it." [5]

Of course such recognition, or Pound's instruction in the art of
patronage, or even the growth of his collection, did not turn Quinn
into a connoisseur. He possessed a strong, true natural taste, but
one that remained fundamentally inarticulate, more visceral than
verbal. His buying grew rapidly bolder and sounder, but he never
really learned the trick of talking artfully about art. His established
practice, ordered by Pound's image of the patron, along with his
own taste and the counsel of trusted advisers, gave him a frame-
work within which he could work with increasing coherence and
confidence, in a simple and humane program warmed by sentiment
and limited by modest means. At this time he still tended to classify
anything experimental as "cubistic," and he showed an uneasy need
to defend such work and his own liking for it as "intellectual,"
"sincere"—not charlatanry or frivolity. Sending Theodore Roosevelt four volumes of Masefield and the catalog of an exhibition of
contemporary French art at the Carroll Galleries on East 44th
Street, he wrote:

> Many of the pictures are pure cubism. They are all interesting to
> me. These artists have got away from mere Sargent brush work

and from the mere repetition of technique and tones of Rembrandt
or Velasquez, and have tackled new problems, mostly hard intellectual problems, a little like higher mathematics. . . . Not all
the cubists are sincere, but three or four of the men whose work
is shown there are sincere, intellectual men.   [*March 15, 1915.*]

Quinn was not only disarming the strenuously "sincere" Roosevelt
but also ventriloquizing a line of derivative salon and studio patter
which had little to do with his own direct feeling for the work of
art. To Maud Gonne, in the same way, instead of phrasing his own
sound and potent pleasure in the work of Brancusi, he had rationalized his taste in the language of other artists' admiration.[6] Far more
impressive was his note of April 3, 1915, to Huneker in which he
set down his reflections on Royal Cortissoz's attack upon the idea
of the artist's painting to please himself, published in the *Tribune*.

> If he paints to please someone else he paints to order, and a man
> who paints to order is no artist. The difference between an artist
> and a tradesman is that the artist paints to please himself or satisfy
> his conscience, and the tradesman supplies goods to order. The
> man who makes his goods to order—"Anything to please the gen-
> tleman"—"Something nice and tasty"—is a waiter or an artisan. . . .
>   The question is: Is the result a beautiful one? . . . Is there any
> abstract beauty in it? Is it alive? . . . Does it give one a sensation?
> Could one come back to it in three months with a renewed feeling?
> And again after three months would it move one? Not is it new.

Quinn's art talk was rarely so direct or so sound. He liked Brancusi and the "cubists" because he liked them, and the permanent
base of his amateur aesthetics was something warmly subjective and
fortunately trustworthy.

Situated as he was, a fanatically busy working lawyer of moderate means, trying to conduct a virtually full-time career as an
amateur of art, letters, and politics in evenings and on Sundays,
without even occasional access in wartime to European galleries,
still shaping his own taste, Quinn wisely and necessarily leaned
hard on the advice of men he trusted as experts: in New York he
consulted Kuhn, Davies, Huneker, and for the time Marcel Duchamp; in London it was still Augustus John and now Pound; he
lacked and badly needed a resident French adviser. In deciding
whether or not to make one or another purchase, especially when

he could not see the work in question, Quinn frequently sought a triangulation by collecting two or more opinions. When Pound wrote that in buying Epstein's *Birds* he must "for God's sake get the two that are stuck together, not the pair in which one is standing up on its legs," [7] Quinn wrote in haste to the sculptor for reassurance. Epstein replied that he was indeed getting the stuck-together birds, but he wondered by what right Pound was commenting on his work with such vehemence: Pound might mind his own business.[8] When Quinn asked John to take a look at Epstein's *Rock Drill*, the painter sent back the following description: "He's turning the handle for all he's worth and under his ribs is the vague shape of a rudimentary child or is it something indigestible he's been eating? Altogether the most hideous thing I've seen." [9] Quinn did not buy the queer piece, now in the Tate Gallery; but the truth was that his own taste had now moved beyond John's brilliant romantic academicism.

Of his own work Epstein had again written grandly and pitifully: "I dream of great commissions, works of heroic dimensions, but after the Oscar Wilde monument I don't think I will get anything of that sort to occupy me." [10] Epstein was feeling complexly alienated in London as an artist, an American, and a Jew. In the winter of 1915 his four pieces in the show of the London Group at the Goupil Gallery had been harshly criticized. "The scribblers have been emboldened by the war," he wrote Quinn on March 28, "and wish to take an unfair advantage of creative artists by declaring that now we are at war artists have no business to be anything but normal; that is, mediocre. Queer argument that. In abnormal times be normal." In the fall he wrote that windows in his house had been smashed by explosions in the Zeppelin raids; and letters of his had been stolen: "no doubt due to private detective work on the part of the other tenants, who imagine I'm a German." [11] In the summer Epstein offered his bronze head of Lillian Shelley for £100, and Quinn was attracted at once, sending back a counter-offer of £70; eventually they agreed on £80. Quinn remembered Lillian Shelley vividly from his London spree of the summer of 1911, when she and Mrs. Lamb had agreed to accompany Quinn and John on their tour of France, then reneged. He wrote of her to Huneker on August 8: "She was a beautiful thing four or five years ago, red lips and hair as black as a Turk's, stunning figure, great sense of humor." When the piece arrived he savored it as art and as memory, and wrote to the sculptor, ". . . I am glad to have it as a companion piece to the head of Mrs. Lamb. Two birds of a feather, at least in one respect, whether they still flock together, in fair or stormy weather, and so on." [12] Having lost the birds in the flesh, it was evidently some comfort to possess them in bronze.

Pound's main enthusiasms of the moment were Wyndham Lewis and Henri Gaudier-Brzeska, and he lost no time in trying to sell them to Quinn. In a letter of March 18 he puffed Lewis as the man who was to enrich the art of the West with the power of the old Chinese painters. When Lewis entered the army, before Quinn had bought any of his work, Quinn cabled him £30 in response to Pound's cable of December 17: "Lewis enlisted needs money debts." Pound's high opinion of the work of Gaudier-Brzeska Quinn checked with that of Augustus John, who wrote: "G-B is a man of talent. His things look as if they'd been sat on before they got quite hard. Some of them look like bits of stalactite roughly resembling human forms"; [13] and with that of Epstein, who wrote after Gaudier's death, " . . . I feel a sympathetic and keen intelligence is gone, and there are few of that sort here." [14] When Pound sent word on July 13 that Gaudier had been shot in the head in a charge at Neuville St. Vaast and had died instantly, Quinn wrote back swiftly on July 27: "Poor brave fellow. There is only the memory now of a brave gifted man. What I can do I will do." In a burst of sentiment he ordered Pound to buy for him everything of Gaudier's he could lay hands on. And he guaranteed to underwrite the cost of a New York show of the Vorticist group, especially Lewis and Gaudier, at Montross or any other gallery; at the same time he ordered twenty copies of the Vorticist publication, *Blast* No. 1 and No. 2. He sent drafts of £10 and £30 for deposit on such Gaudier-Brzeska items as might be available. "It's a man's letter and I thank you for it," Pound wrote back on August 11. He said it was his first experience of spending another man's money and he wished to proceed with care; but he promised Quinn some sculpture even if he had to spend a portion of the advance on firearms as persuaders. He went round to Roger Fry's Omega Workshops and deposited £30 to "hold down their little lot," and by October 9 he had Sophie Brzeska's receipt for £30 for six drawings "and a further sum of £10 on account of further purchases. . . ." [15] It was the beginning of a protracted and frustrating negotiation with Gaudier's informal relict which ended in Quinn's possession of little art and a deep exasperation.

On October 10, 1914, Augustus John had written: "I must send you over some pictures soon or go bankrupt." Quinn was still John's steady sustaining patron, buying virtually everything offered him, though they had not met since 1911 and much of the early warmth had leaked out of the relationship, on both sides. "He generally promises when he is hard up," Quinn wrote sourly of John to Walt Kuhn on August 30, 1915. He was still angry at John's painting out of *Forze e Amore* and at his failure to deliver the immense eighteen-foot decoration of *The Mumpers*, though Quinn had paid him £600 for it. In March Quinn wrote to inquire about the big picture, to send the Metropolitan Museum bulletin with news of his election to an honorary fellowship for life, and to describe his pirate costume at the recent annual ball of the Kit Kat Club, his only regular spree since the Armory Show: fake blood and scars, a painted scowl, a pair of old Spanish pistols, and a pirate cutlass. John was holding onto *The Mumpers*, he said, to do some repainting on it. At last he unrolled the huge canvas, repainted one head, and rolled it up again; it was finally shipped at the end of the year rolled on a ten-inch cylinder. "Its big and rather uncouth, but I may say I still like it myself . . . ," John concluded.[16] Quinn was not amused to hear that John, needing ready money, had let Hugh Lane have his new portrait of Iris Tree, "a fine wench, with pink hair," [17] daughter of Beerbohm Tree, the actor and producer. John was doing portraits of soldiers for war charity drives and a portrait of Lloyd George for the Red Cross, but feeling peevish and uneasy at being no more intimately involved in the martial bustle all around him. Oliver St. John Gogarty had paid him a visit and John had found Gogarty's celebrated ribald wit untimely and trying: "The Dublin people I've met are altogether too strenuously Rabelaisian." [18] John was still pecking spasmodically at Hugh Lane's decorations in London, and he was at Coole Park with Bernard Shaw when word came that Lane, a nephew dear as a son to Lady Gregory, was among the missing passengers on the *Lusitania*. Lady Gregory "behaved with wonderful restraint and went off alone by night to London," [19] refusing the company of John who crossed after her with the Shaws in a boat along with an American woman who had lost her husband and her father in the tragedy and had spent five hours in the water herself.

Quinn was finding his correspondence with Gwen John more engaging than that with her brother, though even less productive of art for his walls. In March she was flurried by the loss of a draft of money from Quinn: "I must be the sufferer if it has been collected because I might have let it fall and in the other case the post-man is more mine than yours." [20] Quinn wanted her to get to know Maud Gonne and had written to urge Gwen John to make overtures: "Always we'd have the new friend meet the old," as Yeats was soon to write.[21] After she had mastered her shyness enough to arrange a meeting, Gwen John wrote on May 5: "I am so happy to have met her. She is very beautiful and charming." But she was "frightened and chilled" by Maud Gonne's account of the war and her experience in the hospitals. Of her general correspondence with Quinn she wrote touchingly on July 26: ". . . Your letters give me pleasure and your friendship it is something my art has brought me unexpectedy [*sic*]."

In New York Quinn had been seeing a good deal of the painter and critic Walter Pach for about a year; he admired Pach's talent and his knowledge and liked him as a man, and they became friends. By February of 1915 Pach had become a trusted adviser, and he was one of several persons who helped him out with translations of his correspondence with French artists and dealers which was already copious. On April 30 of 1915 Quinn recommended Pach as art critic to Allan Dawson of the *Globe and Commercial Advertiser* as "a gentleman of cultivation and learning and an artist of fastidiousness," "a learned man of art," an expert judge and critic, widely acquainted among living artists and learned in the traditions, agreeable but incorruptible, one who "would make the art criticism in The Globe notable." Pach had painted in Paris before the war and was indeed conversant with the artists of the new movement there. Years later Quinn's French friend and adviser Henri-Pierre Roché recalled meeting Pach occasionally before the war at the Lapin

Agile on the Butte Montmartre; on request, Pach would sing "savage melodies," at rather tiresome length.²² In 1914 Harriet Bryant of the Carroll Gallery had commissioned Pach to make a trip abroad to solicit contemporary work, and he had shipped back the materials for a large and notable show. Quinn admired Harriet Bryant's nerve in carrying on undaunted in wartime, and he was generally attracted by the gallery and its spirited, long-legged mistress. He patronized the gallery and kept an eye, at first amiable then exasperated, on its affairs. The strange new French works sold poorly, and it began to seem that Quinn was nearly the only buyer. He began to think that Miss Bryant was not pushing the show properly, that she was proceeding with a generally unbusinesslike fecklessness, and finally that she was turning the proceeds from sales of paintings to the use of the decorating part of her business, rather than paying off the artists and dealers. Quinn reacted characteristically by angry letters to Harriet Bryant and by buying more and more hectically. When the formal show was closed in the summer with many works unsold, he continued to make offers at a third or a half off the asking price for groups of paintings and sculptures—bearing in mind the labor, cost, and danger of shipping in wartime and seizing the opportunity to add notably to his collection with a reasonable outlay. But he was buying hard at other galleries as well, and buying American as well as French art. In February he paid the Carroll Gallery $4,700 for sixteen oils and water colors of Maurice Prendergast. To the Montross Gallery he paid in March $2,200 for Matisse's *Cyclamen* and *The Hat with the Roses;* in April $2,805 for works of Davies, Kuhn, Charles Prendergast, Morton Schamberg, and Charles Sheeler; in June $3,500 for two paintings by Maurice Prendergast, one by Kuhn, and one by Davies. Charles Prendergast was making numerous hand-carved frames for him, now and later, for which Quinn often paid as much as a hundred dollars.

On February 26 Quinn wrote to Vollard and offered 21,500 francs for six Picassos at the Carroll Gallery: *The Sad Mother* and *Old Man* of the blue period, *Woman* of the rose period, a woman with her hands under her chin (probably the stunning blue period *Woman at Table*), a black cubist figure, and a still life—provided Vollard was willing to accept four quarterly payments. *The Old*

Man was badly cracked and looked to Quinn as if it had been painted on the top of a paint table, and *The Sad Mother* had runs down the side; he thought the 500 to 750 francs it would cost him to get them put right would partly justify his delay in paying. Vollard cabled his agreement on March 11. On March 9 Quinn agreed with the Carroll Gallery for $700 for four oils of Raoul Dufy, *Still Life, The Studio, Promenade,* and *The Belfry of St. Vincent,* for which $1,000 had been asked. Next month he paid $5,460 plus $2,015 gallery commission for seven Picassos, one Duchamp, one Gleizes, and three Jacques Villons.

On one day, August 24, he made a large sweep among the works left at the Carroll Gallery: 1,275 francs for a painting and four drawings by André Dunoyer de Segonzac, of whom he had bought *The Man Reading* and two drawings during the scheduled exhibition; 4,150 francs for five sculptures of Raymond Duchamp-Villon; 1,916 francs for two more paintings and nine water colors by Dufy, all that remained in Miss Bryant's hands; 1,700 francs for three pictures of Chabaud; 1,550 francs for a porcelain panel, a ceramic *Nude,* and two paintings, *Poor Creatures* and *Woman's Head,* by Georges Rouault. Shortly, remembering that his *poussée* to French art had commenced with his purchase of Chabaud's "sheep picture" in London in 1911, and that the artist was now a soldier at the front, Quinn sent him a supplementary 400 francs. He wrote on August 24 to Pach, manipulating his counters of "sincerity," "intellect," and "sentiment":

> There are many other things that I like better than Chabaud's work. But his mother wrote such a touching letter and he hadn't sold any of his things and he is evidently such a sincere man that I felt like making an offer to him. But I know that isn't the way to buy pictures. One should be guided by one's intellect and not by sentiment.

There was trouble over Rouault's ceramics with baffled customs officials, who wanted to call them "objects of utility" and assess them at a 40 per cent duty. Rouault wrote to Quinn on September 26 to express his gratitude to a new patron and to describe the current state of his career. He was curator of the weird and charming little Musée Gustave Moreau in Paris, keeping the post more to honor his (and Matisse's) old teacher, Moreau, than because of the remuneration, which came to only 2,400 francs a year. He considered his craft "uncommon and subtle" already, but dreamed of "infinite" progress to come; and, though he tried to be a "disinterested" artist, he had to bear in mind that he would soon have "4 children and no money."

The Carroll Gallery affair had been frustrating and costly to Quinn, but it had rewarded him with a large increase in the size and variety of his collection and a large access of new friends and correspondents among the French artists. His guess of August 11 to Vollard: "I think I have bought more modern art this year than anyone else in America," was almost certainly accurate. Quinn had stepped up his pace, not only because his interest was intensifying and his taste sharpening, but also because he wanted to do as much as he could to help out artists, American and European, whose small market had been further constricted by wartime pressures. "The war has been hard upon American artists," he wrote on July 31 to Epstein who had complained of the situation in London.

> . . . The old soft, sweet, flabby, academic fellows sell occasionally, and here and there museums occasionally buy. But the advanced men, the courageous, younger, progressive, honest fellows, are not bought at all. Some of them have said that I saved the art season last year by buying together with one or two others a few examples of the best men's good work. The number of buyers of modern, advanced, courageous stuff is limited at best.

The transplanted Frenchman and hero of the Armory Show, Marcel Duchamp, was now living in New York, staying for the time near Quinn's place at the home of his friend Walter Arensberg, who was also a friend of Pach's. Quinn liked Duchamp and occasionally had him in for breakfast or dinner. He bought from Duchamp for $120 his study for the *Nude Descending the Staircase* in order to possess "a personal souvenir of the Armory Exhibition." [23] When he thought Duchamp looked tired and thin in August Quinn gave him a railway ticket and a hotel reservation for a week's holiday at Spring Lake. Because Duchamp wanted to find a way to earn his living at something other than painting, so as "to keep his mind free of any consideration of money in thinking about his painting," [24] Quinn used his influence with his friend Belle Greene, librarian to J. P. Morgan, to secure for Duchamp an appointment as librarian of the Institut Français.

When Walt Kuhn sent a postcard message from Ogunquit on July 29, "comfortable shanty fine grub—glorious air mais toutes les femmes sont vielles [*sic*]—Triste!" Quinn could only smile. He was held in the city again this summer by the pressure of his law practice (especially the big Timothy J. Kiely will case in which he represented the widow, for whom he got a judgment giving her the whole of the $2,000,000 estate), by his art dealings, and by dickerings for a major new "folly," a house in the country. He did manage an occasional weekend at Yama Farms in the Catskills, often with one or another girl friend, and he liked to hire a car and a driver and take a party of friends to the Jersey shore where they would swim or play tennis and wind up for dinner and the evening at the Ross-Fenton Farm, near Allenhurst, which he described to Kuhn as "one of the best places of the kind in America, not formal and yet not rowdy, excellent food and fine nigger waiters." "The Quartet," Quinn, Gregg, James Huneker, and his wife, Josephine, would go often to one or another of the Manhattan hotels which offered a roof garden and music for dinner followed by leisurely talk over cigars, light wines, and Pilsener. Huneker's *Ivory Apes and Peacocks* was out with a dedication to Quinn who bought fifteen copies and sent them to friends in America and abroad.

The country house to which Quinn succumbed this summer, always referred to in the family as "Purchase Street," was the old home of the Westchester Hunt Club, set on a rise six hundred feet above sea level with a fine view of Long Island Sound. The big white frame house was about sixty years old, and there were a well, a pond, a tennis court, and dozens of fine old trees, on an estate of 80 acres in a rectangle shaped "like a barn door," as Quinn put it in a letter to Kuhn on August 30. Down the road 300 yards was "The Olympia," the "Hygienic Institute" of William ("The Great") Muldoon, a cavalryman under Custer in the Civil War and a former prize fighter and trainer of John L. Sullivan. His stationery promised "Rational Hygienic Treatment for Cure of Dyspepsia, Neurasthenia, Constipation, Insomnia and Nervous Prostration," and asserted: "Men consume too much Food and too little Pure Air.

They take too much Medicine and too little Exercise." Muldoon often sauntered down to cast a critical eye over the complex processes of Quinn's occupation of Purchase Street. Quinn set out to install new porches, a new roof, new hardwood floors, new plumbing, tanks, and electrical fittings, hot water heating instead of the existing hot air system, and to scrape down and repaint the woodwork inside and out. By September he had a dozen men at work and was frantically trying to keep hold of details there along with his other work. He was convinced that the foreman and the men were "robbing him blind" on time and materials. Quinn paid $42,500 for Purchase Street in the summer of 1915, and when he abandoned it two years later he estimated that the venture had cost him $26,000 "for the sake of a few Saturdays." Neither his temperament nor his career was suited to the life of a country gentleman.

On the whole Quinn's general health seemed better this summer than it had been for several years; he was so busy that he hardly had time to feel sick or to complain. His suspiciousness and irritability were a concomitant of his ambitiousness and his energy, inevitable properties of a nature no more deeply secure than his. "Patience is sometimes greater than genius," as he wrote to Symons on August 9. "I wish I had more of it." An old drawing of Quinn by Augustus John had been reproduced in *Vanity Fair*, and Arthur Symons was happy to find it there as a memento of both artist and subject. He admired John as the man who "of all living men, has lived his life almost entirely as he willed to live it," [25] and John's representation of "the penetrating eyes, firm mouth, and strong chin" [26] of Quinn brought back to life for him the friend and patron he had not seen for four years. Maud Gonne, who had seen the same drawing in an earler reproduction at Douglas Hyde's house, wrote Quinn to ask for a copy of the picture which "looks harder than you do generally, but I have seen you look like that occasionally." [27] Quinn's "strength and determination," visible in the drawing, made her "feel wild that you do not belong to Ireland entirely, for you would have led the people and made history as Parnell did." Her mind was given to such passionate leaps.

Far from wishing to lead the Irish people, Quinn continued in angry and profane retreat from their importunities. In a letter to

W. B. Yeats in February he marveled sardonically that Padraic Colum had been in New York two months without announcing himself to Quinn. After a new appeal from Padraic Pearse for money for his school, St. Enda's, Quinn wrote in a rage to Judge Keogh: "I get nothing but cheek, touches, and gall from the Irish. . . ." [28] He was moved to an interminable and intolerable piece of doggerel.* He was sorry that he had not thought to recommend that the War Revenue Bill incorporate a tax on Irishmen coming to America for any purpose but to take up citizenship: they might be levied per capita or at 15 per cent of what they collected on their "missions."

* Damn, damn, damn the Gaelic Leaguers,
  Damn the Parliamentarians too.
  Damn, damn, damn the Clan-na-Gaelers
  Damn all the Irish missions through and through.
  I am sick and tired of their stories
  Of all their hard luck tales and plaints;
  I think that they have become a race of spongers,
  And have long since ceased to be the land of saints.
  I am neutral of course;
  I don't care a pin
  If the Germans are licked
  Which of the Allies win
  Redmond is senile,
  Carson's heroics a bore,
  The Volunteers are flabby
  The Parliamentary Party a whore.
  Let them come to America,
  If they don't want to fight.
  To see them at work here would be a delight.
  Perhaps Dr. Wilson
  Ought to be told
  That the way to make peace
  Is for Germany to hold
  The land of the saints
  When they will speak only Dutch,
  And won't dare to breathe in Irish
  Which they all love so much.
  Then the Casements, the Crowleys, the Pearses,
  The Redmonds, the Carsons, the Healys, the Kellys and all
  Can send their appeals in high and low Dutch
  To Berlin and Cologne and Munich and such.
  And thank God and the saints that we here
  In benighted U.S.A. will be free
  From their damned appeals by night and by day.
  In the language of a bill in equit-ae
  For this your orator will ever pray.

Lady Gregory and Hugh Lane, who visited the country separately in the winter and spring of 1915, were of course exempt
from Quinn's irritation. Lady Gregory arrived in the middle of
January for her circuit of lectures, and she visited with Quinn
regularly when she was in the city. He was trying to arrange for
a third tour by the Abbey Theatre company, and he warmed her
heart more intimately by laying preliminary plans for a New York
showing of the paintings of her son, Robert Gregory. In March she
spent her final two weeks at Quinn's apartment. He persuaded her,
for safety's sake, to sail on an American rather than an English
vessel, and put her on board with an armload of presents including
Conrad's *Victory*. From the U.S.M.S. *St. Paul* she wrote on April
3 to thank him for the "encompassing kindness" which gave her the
feeling of "having lived in summer time." She was going home
happy at having done her work well, at having paid her debts and
put money by, and at the prospect of showing her son's pictures,
"which is what I care about more than all the rest."

Meeting frequently in the city in April, Quinn and Lane got
on warmly, though they had divergent tastes as well as common
ones. Quinn entertained Lane in his usual energetic way, with
dinners, a play, a motor ride, and visits to exhibitions and sales of
pictures. At one sale Lane tried to interest him in some of the
older pictures, Raeburns and Wilkies, but Quinn resisted: "I have
made up my mind to buy only the work of living men, with the
possible exception of Gauguin and Van Gogh and maybe Cézanne,
if I can get another good example of each at a reasonable price," he
wrote of the incident to W. B. Yeats on April 24. On "modern art"
Quinn's and Lane's opinions met head on, in a classic confrontation.
When Quinn told him he had bought "five or six" Picassos, Lane
called them "rubbish." In Lane's view "sanity," "normality," and
"health" were the property of traditional art and artists; the new
experiments were the work of weak and disordered imaginations.
(It is important to remember that in Britain Hugh Lane passed for
a champion of modernism.) Quinn conceded that "of course" the
present period was "rather an age of experiment than of accomplishment" in literature as well as art. But he reasserted his faith in his
own men, in his usual terms: "Many of them are highly intellectual
and are honest." [29] Among the pictures at the sale was Benjamin
West's apocalyptic *Death on a White Horse*, the same that had

moved Keats, negatively, to one of the most important formulations in his letters: ". . . the excellence of every Art is its intensity. . . ." [30] To Hugh Lane Quinn argued that West's picture was "quite cubistic or futuristic"—a judgment that needed a loose definition of those terms. Quinn summed up their standoff:

> I told Lane that the whole question turned on how one defined art, and whether one wanted to limit it to what had been art and to keep it in the lines of tradition. His only answer was that painting was too beautiful a thing and too fine a medium to be distorted.[31]

Lane boarded the *Lusitania* against the advice of Quinn who had heard that the German Ambassador had boasted that the vessel would be torpedoed. Before he left Lane sent a farewell note of thanks and an invitation to return the visit in the summer. Lane hoped to have a Hupmobile, and they could "run about looking at pictures and places." [32]

It was in fact a cable from Quinn that arrived when Augustus John and Bernard Shaw were at Coole Park with the news that Lady Gregory's beloved nephew had been a passenger on the torpedoed ship. Stunned but stoical, she set off for London to open the Abbey company's season there, not yet knowing whether Lane had lived or died. "Oh, my heart is as if stopped still and everything seems so empty, and the visit to London a nightmare!" she wrote to Quinn as she left Coole on May 9. By May 18, when she wrote again, it was clear that Lane had perished. Lady Allan, who had been saved herself, though she had lost her two young daughters, told her of Lane's standing near them, pale and calm, without a life belt. " 'This is a sad end for us all,' he said, before he went off to try to assist other friends just before the ship went down." Quinn had already described Lane's death to Charles Prendergast as "murder," and he praised the dead man emotionally:

> He was one of the best men I ever knew, not a self-indulgent or selfish person. . . . He was a man of the greatest charm, had a great sense of humor, a droll way of telling things, a man of great social gifts, a helpful person, interested in many things, with a profound knowledge of old and modern art, a great fastidiousness and sensitiveness, courage, with an intellect as swift as an eagle, but with it all a lonely man.   [*May 10, 1915.*]

Attention now turned to the disposition of Lane's estate, especially the important body of modern paintings which he had tried for years to give to Ireland on terms satisfactory to himself. Bored and angry at the squabbling philistinism of the Dublin Corporation, Lane had a few years previously altered his will so as to devise the pictures as a nucleus for a modern gallery in London. Lady Gregory now instituted a search of his papers which turned up a codicil, later in date but unfortunately unwitnessed, again leaving the collection to the Dublin Municipal Gallery, provided the city made available an appropriate site and an appropriate structure to house them—Lady Gregory to judge. Who was really entitled to the pictures: England or Ireland? The question was to agitate W. B. Yeats and Lady Gregory and the public press for years. "It is wonderful the amount of toil and intrigue one has to go through to accomplish anything in Ireland," Yeats lamented. "Intelligence has no organization whilst stupidity always has." [33]

Yeats was in London with his players, their audiences much diminished by the war. But he reported that a successful performance of *On Baile's Strand* had given him a new access of creative energy: "The result is that I am full of new poems—dramatic and lyrical. All my mythological people have come alive again and I want to begin the completion of my heroic cycle." [34] He judged, most inaccurately, that he was "free at last from the obsession of the supernatural": that obsession, like his obsession for Maud Gonne, would last as long as life for Yeats. He was "keeping" Monday evenings for the discussion of poetry at home and Friday evenings for the discussion of painting at Charles Ricketts's house. In the midst of the generation of the mangel-wurzel, he had discovered a new genius, Ernest Albert Cole, and considered that if his sculptures measured up to his drawings "in the style of Michelangelo" the event would be comparable to the publication of *Paradise Lost* "in the very year when Dryden announced the disappearance of blank verse." [35] At the end of the year he wrote of raising £208 for the Theatre by a lecture, and of plans to go again to a cottage in Sussex with the Pounds, where Ezra would read Landor to him in the evenings: "He has a beautiful young wife who does the housekeeping, and both treat me with the respect due to my years and so make me feel that it is agreeable to grow old."[36] Yeats had reached the half-century. He liked the country life and wished he could avoid London altogether; but he was tied there, he said, by "bad eyesight and the need of a woman friend."[37] The city was now looking its best, he thought, hiding from the Zeppelins with its lights out. Of the war Yeats wrote loftily: "It is merely the most expensive outbreak of insolence and stupidity the world has ever seen, and I give it as little of my thoughts as I can."[38] He went to his club to catch up on the war news and ended up reading Keats's *Lamia* instead.

Others were taking the war a good deal harder. Florence Farr Emery wrote on April 5, "We are having the experience of centuries packed into our lifetimes, aren't we?" Like Yeats, May Morris wrote on June 4 to describe her visit to the forest cottage of her beloved Fabian friend, Philip Webb, to pay last respects to his dead body. She told of her war work, sewing, knitting, organizing food supplies, sending food and clothing to hospitals, and of her disgust at seeing in London "smart young women peering into shop windows." The sinking of the *Lusitania* had appalled her: "Human life has always seemed to me so sacred, and now humans are of no more account than swarms of flies." Like Yeats, however, she was able to feel a certain reluctant aesthetics of the Zeppelin; she described an October raid on London as "a wonderful experience."

> It came on a still night of the most wonderful starlight I've ever seen, after a lovely sunset, with a delicate, crescent moon. Across the water opposite a huge booming (of the biggest gun round the city) travelled up the great path of light that was searching the N. E. sky, and there, among the stars, were little sparks and morning stars—the anti-aircraft aeroplane guns (what do they call them?), worrying the big monster. I was not in the least alarmed, it was all too strange, but spent the night in a state of intense excitement, wishing (foolishly enough) *for more*—the murder of quiet folk being all over in seven minutes and the "gallant crusaders" off again to their country.　　　[*December 31, 1915.*]

Joseph Conrad had returned after many trials from his wartime journey to Poland, ill and depressed at the plight of his old country. He broke his promise to Quinn by giving the manuscript of the articles he had written about the trip to Edith Wharton to auction for the benefit of Belgian Relief. "You can hardly make a crime of it," he wrote to Quinn. "I had to do something and I wasn't in a state to write anything original for her." [39] It did not matter; Quinn bought the papers in the sale. Conrad's older son, Borys, was a lieutenant in Mechanical Transport, where he was known as "The Boy." He expected to be seeing service before his eighteenth birthday with a brigade of heavy howitzers before Ypres. Epstein wrote of the return of his friend, the philosopher T. E. Hulme, with a shattered arm. Maud Gonne and her daughter Iseult had already seen service in four French hospitals, nursing and scrambling for supplementary food for the wounded. Quinn sent her 500 francs, then another 250 francs. The beautiful Iseult said theirs was " 'an *abrutissant* life and leaves no room for the intellect,' " but she was a faithful nurse and much beloved of the soldiers.[40] Maud Gonne's sister, who had been nursing with them, had broken down with shattered nerves and a bad lung after the death of her son at Neuve Chapelle. "All the young art and intellect of France is being killed in the trenches," it seemed to Maud. Lily Yeats wrote of taut nerves in Dublin. At a performance of Synge's *Riders to the Sea* there had been sobbing all through the audience. "Death all about us—so many we hardly mention it when we meet, partly because most one meets have sons or brothers at the front." [41]

For Quinn in New York the Germans were displacing the Irish as objects of corporate hatred. "I am beginning to loathe and hate the German idea," he wrote Gwen John on January 15, 1915. A dozen years before he had started W. B. Yeats reading Nietzsche, and even this year he persuaded Walter Pach to read Georg Brandes's book on the German whom Yeats called "that strong enchanter." [42] But now he was growing ashamed of his own taste. "Ten or fifteen years ago I was rather taken with Nietzsche and with the philosophy of the strong conquering man and with the notion that the conquering nations were the great nations," he admitted to Gwen John in his January 15 letter. "But I realize now that that is all wrong." In the winter he wandered into Frank Harris's "anti-English Pro-German" lecture in a hall lent him by Mitchell Kennerley. At the end of the lecture Quinn stood up and asked Harris whether Germany's "progressiveness" gave her the right to invade and plunder her neighbors. He reported the ensuing dialogue to W. B. Yeats on February 25: Harris: " 'The gentleman's question implies a quarrel with God.'" Quinn: "'Ah, yes, you ape the Kaiser 'Me unt [*sic*] Gott.'" Harris: "'No, I mean you quarrel with the law of evolution.'" Quinn: "'. . . the law of the brute.'" But the sinking of the *Lusitania* and the death of Lane focused his disgust, drove it deeper, and extended it to all of German lineage. On June 7 he wrote to Gwen John:

> The Germans have been acting like demons and after their massacre of the Lusitania victims we can and should believe the worst of them. I am in favor of boycotting them in this country, of making them ashamed of their nationality and their blood and their names. They ought to be made to feel it so that generations should elapse before the stain is wiped out.

Throughout the war and until he died his hatred of everything German grew only more savage and sullen.

The thought of any sort of alliance between the Irish and the Germans was intolerable to him. He heard from Maud Gonne and from others that Kitchener and Carson had made a secret agreement guaranteeing that men of the Ulster Volunteers would not be sent to posts of danger in the war, and he wrote in a rage to Russell, himself originally an Ulsterman:

> Other Irishmen by the thousands have died in France and Belgium and in Gallipoli; and if these Ulster Protestants have been kept back and trained and drilled and organized and disciplined and their health improved and so on, but have not seen fighting, if that monstrous thing be true, then I want to see England licked, because that would not be decadence, it would be abominable treason, unspeakable betrayal.   [*September 23, 1915.*]

Æ investigated and reported the rumor false. The Ulster Division had been held back because it needed further training, because equipment was short, and because it was to go as an intact division. Even as he wrote on October 11, word came that the Ulster soldiers were off to the front.

Russell observed the war with a sense of apocalyptic horror, troubled as much by its omens for the future as by its present murderousness. He wrote Quinn with a terrible clairvoyance on January 13, 1915: "The German upheaval will multiply images and shadows in men's minds of the power of the organized state, and we are in for a hundred years of militarism and bureaucracy and everything abhorrent to the free spirit." But with typical calm, largeness of vision, and undaunted sweetness of temper, Æ was working at even larger ideas, trying to trace out the design of a mysterious "cosmic consciousness" or "planetary spirit" or "Over-soul," moving toward a spiritual definition of the nature of men so large and slow and inclusive that even wars and "national ideas" appeared small stations on a long way. German militarism and vain-glory, for example, might be "accidentals of its idea, a local colour-ing, not an essential." [43]

A blunter, hotter, shallower thinker, Quinn heard these ideas patiently as coming from a valued and peculiar friend; but he could feel no fundamental sympathy. Of Russell's "mysticism" Quinn wrote crudely to May Morris:

> The only mystic that I ever knew that amounted to anything as a man was George Russell, and he is now getting fat and living bet-ter, and is the able and successful editor of the Irish Homestead, perhaps the best agricultural paper in the world, and is an author-ity upon farming and agricultural banks and agricultural credits. I imagine he doesn't see as many visions as he used to in the days when he ate less and his blood was thinner. [*June 18, 1913.*]

The implication, clearly, is that Russell "amounted to something as a man" in the degree to which he turned toward being a man of Quinn's own type. But in fact Russell never left off seeing visions. Quinn understood Russell's line of thought, and he was not unfamiliar with it as a kind of thinking, but he simply did not find it useful. "I am not at all sure that I believe in an oversoul," he wrote, "at any rate an oversoul that is in direct relation with this world *as we know it*." He went on: "I cannot see any 'world spirit' evolving out of this brute contest. This war is no different from other wars except that it is more wide-spread and destruc-tive." [44] The war was the absolute pragmatic confrontation of two irreconcilable political ideologies. Martial and monarchical, Ger-many embodied "science plus slavery" (as he had expressed it to Yeats). To abolish the monarchical principle was to abolish war, he argued. Russell rebuked him gently: "I don't agree with you about the adequacy of the common sense view of the militarism in Germany and the struggle. . . . People really do not sacrifice life in millions for superficial reasons, but are caught in a net spread by the spirit. . . ." [45]

Meanwhile Quinn had sent to Æ, as to all his most valued friends, his gift book of the year, the speeches of Justice Oliver. Wendell Holmes—eminently a man of affairs, but withal an artist in the fine stylishness with which he went about affairs. Quinn's writing and thinking about the war were making patent the dualism in his nature which had never lain far beneath the surface. It was the running conflict between the practical and the aesthetic sides of his temperament, the drive to live and do opposed to the drive to make or, failing that, to appreciate. It was the ambivalence that made him think of a law brief as a literary composition, of an argument as an oration, of a courtroom as a theatre. It was what led him to push his way into print in a post-hoc creative way, the only way really open to his limited talent, in letters to editors and journalistic commentaries on events; and to "edit" the copy of primary creative spirits such as Conrad and Yeats and Sherwood Anderson. The boy with an eye on the main chance, driving hard toward a career, who yet collected first editions of Walter Pater, who as a law student read thirty books on Shelley, became the man who led strenuous fifteen-mile Sunday hikes on the New Jersey Palisades, insisting that the whole party carry sketching pads, and would lead about a golf course in France a group including Constantin Brancusi, Erik Satie, the composer, and Henri-Pierre Roché.

Much of this passionate dualism was gay, most of it was innocent, all of it was comprehensible, and in Quinn's management it was productive and, in sum, admirable. It made him an interesting man, though it did not make him a happy one. His intersecting courses were the sign of a deep and imperfectly satisfied desire— an elaborately, perhaps brilliantly, sublimated obsession. It was the case of the man with all the artist's drives and urges but few, or only rudimentary forms, of the artist's powers. Quinn had a Platonic conception of himself, like F. Scott Fitzgerald's Gatsby. But he escaped Gatsby's victimization, because he had the good sense to instate in his life the naturally dominant side of his temperament, that of the man of practical affairs; to subordinate the naturally recessive side, that of the artist; and then to sublimate the failed artist as appreciator, connoisseur. If he could not make art he could possess it, and a successful practical career could be used to bring art into being through the hands of others, the ones with the full gifts. It gave him a power, though not the one he wanted most. His was not an easy nature nor an easy life. The tension was always there, and it made a psychology subject to extremes of stress and excitement—gaieties, triumphs, glooms, rages. Within Quinn the conflict could never really cease between the lawyer and the artist. The power of his will and the force of his practical intelligence brought the conflict under fairly comfortable and generally profitable equipoise. But the unconfessedly romantic, subjective, and sentimental coloring of his aesthetic judgments was the price of his redefinition of the rudimentary artist within. He carried about with him always the tension of a nature that had never had its say in an original and creative form fully satisfactory to itself.

Thus it is interesting to watch Quinn and Russell confronted on the issue of the war and its human significance. For Russell's nature too was a warring union of swordsman and saint, as he well knew. It is significant that Russell was fully aware of the conflict and its potential ironies in behavior, and that he could speak of it so sanely. In him the antinomies stood in dynamic harmony, a rare and graceful balance that gave him serenity and poise in both sides of his nature and made both capable of efficient action. But the rudely dominant pragmatist in Quinn showed itself in his hardly veiled suggestion that whereas men like Æ had their uses and were not likely to do much damage, in these strenuous times they should give way silently before the commissars:

> I agree with you that artists and poets ought to try to create a spiritual empire in the minds of men. That is the business of artists and poets. That doesn't mean, though, that there should not be statesmen and philosophers and warriors attending to the business of the physical world, the real world. The poet and artist will always be rare enough and they won't be in sufficient numbers to dilute the sanity and the judgment and the foresight and the vision and the wisdom of the men of affairs into weakness and inaction and passivity. . . .   [*June 8, 1915.*]

But even as he was committing this drab journalism, he was forming friendships, some of which lasted for years, with a visiting group of Indian scholars, scientists, and public officials, Ananda Coomaraswamy and others. "I liked them all," Quinn wrote to W. B. Yeats. "There is a serenity about them that I liked." [46] At the same time he was ranting against the conduct of American

public affairs by such men as Wilson and Bryan, yogis in a time
that required commissars:

> Mr. Wilson, the president of this country for the time being, is a
> theorist, a mere essayist. He won't fight. Bryan, the Secretary of
> State, is a wind-bag. He has about as much sense as a Methodist
> parson and talks and thinks like one. He has been for years one of
> the peace-spouters, a fifth-rate man in a big place and a tragic
> misfit.*

Again at the same time Quinn was expressing the wistful hope
to Russell, as to Yeats and Maud Gonne, that artists might be
allowed to go on fulfilling their role in spite of the war. "The world
needs the flower more than the flower needs life. And the world
needs the artist and the poet more than they need the world." So
he expressed it to Maud Gonne in a letter dictated the same day as
that to Russell; and he suggested that good artists, in the event of
conscription, ought to be permitted to hire substitutes, as in the
American Civil War. Still at the same time, he ordered his annual
complement of Æ's misty poetical canvases, and asked him to look
out for likely things by Jack Yeats.

Russell's various selves worked harmoniously ahead: he was
editing the *Irish Homestead*; pushing the agrarian co-operative
movement; propagandizing for a coherent Irish labor policy; writing a "mystical book" (*Mother and Child*), a "political book" (*The
National Being: Some Thoughts on an Irish Polity*) drawing on his
theories of the "cosmic consciousness," and selecting from his essays
of twenty-five years a volume to be called *Imaginations and Reveries*; anticipating, to his own surprise, a new volume of poems ("I
find to my astonishment, also, that I have some faint tricklings of
poetry still in me. . . ."); [47] and he persevered, humbly, in his painting: "I go on painting, though I know I will never get over my

---

* To George Russell, June 8, 1915. Bryan resigned before Quinn mailed
this letter to Russell, and in a postscript he noted that Bryan had now begun
to attack Wilson. He commented, in a spectacularly mixed figure: "Bryan
always has been an unfair fighter, and when Wilson took him to his bosom
he must have known that sooner or later Bryan would try to stab him below
the belt." Quinn always believed that Bryan had been given the cabinet post
as a prize for making way for Wilson at the Democratic nominating convention of 1912. He was unconsoled when his former partner, Bainbridge
Colby, whom he considered "an idiot," was later made Secretary of State.

absence of early training. People like the pictures, badly drawn and painted as they are, for some kind of fancy in them." [48] Punning elegantly in a letter of April 16, he commented on his habit of retreating from practical affairs into "something lawless like poetry or painting." Quinn made a revealing response to Æ's acute guess:

One can't live by business alone or by law alone. And politics often is a trying business. My interest in literature and art is not altogether that of a reaction, but it is a keen, deep interest. If I had the time I should like to take up painting, and if I had more time I should like to take up writing. And if I had the money I should quit practicing law and would like to edit a paper and to gather some live young men around me, only, young men who would have the courage to say things and speak out, damn society and damn success and damn the circulation. [49]

It was the voice of the wishful artist speaking plainly at last, with no trepidations as to talent, and no audible misgivings about the fact that one cannot "take up" writing or painting as one takes up stock farming or even law. Otherwise it was a fair and reasonable review of Quinn's conflicting impulses, and a roughly accurate suggestion of their proportionate force.

The would-be editor in Quinn got a bit of vicarious play in certain further dealings with Ezra Pound in the latter half of 1915. On May 21 Pound wrote that he thought he might get hold of "an ancient weekly," which turned out to be the *Academy*, to edit. He was immediately attracted by the prospect of a new international journal of letters under his own control. He believed he could give Europe and America a chance to talk with each other intellectually, a privilege currently denied them in existing journals. He wondered what support he could expect in the United States: "Who is there in New York (with the sole exception of a certain J. Q.) who has any gutttts?" Quinn wrote back encouragingly, but the *Academy* prospect soon evaporated, leaving Pound in a rage: ". . . je m'emmerde du public, they want shit and they get it, and they smack their dung smeared lips and holler for more. And when a good thing comes they hate it." [50]

Pound now broached the idea of a new fortnightly journal in English on the model of the *Mercure de France*. He noted that Remy de Gourmont, a stranger, had written him when approached on the *Academy* scheme: " 'Je vous servirai autant qu'il sera en mon pouvoir' " *; and he shouted typographically, "IT IS A DISGRACE THAT THERE IS NO ENGLISH OR AMERICAN PUBLICATION THAT CAN BE READ BY AN INTELLIGENT AND WELL INFORMED MAN." [51] W. B. Yeats and Ford Madox Hueffer had offered what help they could in London. All he really asked, Pound said, was a chance to discuss life and letters in literate English prose, without mumbling; decent prose was quite possible to write, he argued, if one knew what one wanted to say and was willing to say it without a frock coat and a mouth full of black gloves.[52] He still dreamed of finding in England and America the kind of disinterested and civilized support which seemed for the time to be peculiarly French, and which alone could make his kind of journal possible. Quinn had heard from Mitchell Kennerley in New York that he was about ready to abandon his sponsorship of the *Forum*, and he tried at once to secure it for Pound, as a more or less going concern which Pound could alter in his own image. Quinn was all ready with a new title, *The International Forum*. Pound had misgivings about dealings with Kennerley, who had a reputation of being slow to pay, and who had for Pound more serious limitations: he was stuck, intellectually, in the nineties, and he liked to keep people dangling about, waiting on his decisions, as a demonstration of his importance.[53] Still, Pound thought, if the journal was to take a monthly form, the *Forum* might be as good a place as any to start: ". . . a perfectly good stump to sprout out of. It could be changed into a live article in a month or two." [54] But at the end of August Quinn had to report that Kennerley had changed his mind and would keep the status quo on the *Forum*.

Meanwhile Pound had sent over his first introduction of a new protégé, the young American expatriate T. S. Eliot, who would soon join the brood who sheltered at least intermittently under Quinn's wide if bony wing. Pound presented Eliot as a quiet chap with more "entrails" than one might suppose. He had returned briefly to America and Pound hoped he might find his way to some useful cash: he knew Mrs. Jack Gardner was interested in Eliot. He pressed Quinn to call the young man in and confer with him before he returned to England.[55]

With the *Academy* and the *Forum* out of the running the

* "I will serve you as far as is in my power."

thought turned to an entirely new organ, and Pound's energetic letters came in a busy stream, at some periods almost daily. He cited the example of Harriet Monroe's *Poetry*, which was able to print all the good verse concurrently being written in English, as well as a good deal of bad verse, in a magazine about the size of a Sunday School card.[56] He reminded Quinn that *Poetry* had been underwritten by a hundred guarantors, each of whom promised $50 a year for five years; the monthly journal of 128 pages he now envisioned could subsist, he reckoned, with a thousand subscribers and a guarantee of $2,500; or with 2,200 paid subscriptions he could run it from his own flat "till doomsday."[57] He defined his own notion of success: " 'BIG' future to me does not so much mean circulation to 70,000 fools, but circulation among 4000 really intelligent men."[58] As a candidate for the American editorship of the putative journal Quinn and Kennerley suggested Willard Huntington Wright. Pound feared Wright's fustiness of taste and lack of nerve, and wrote on September 17 to warn that they must find a man who would not immediately put off writers of the caliber of de Gourmont and W. B. Yeats. He himself preferred Orrick Johns, unless, as he feared, Johns had turned into a hopeless drunkard. In any case, he felt, in early stages everything except straight news items had better pass through his own editorial hands in London, until he could see more signs than he had yet found of a knowledgeableness about writing among New York literary men.[59] Before the end of the year Quinn had committed himself to round up guarantors of $10,000, beginning with Otto Kahn.

Earlier in the year Quinn had also involved Otto Kahn in consideration of a grandiose scheme presented to him by Gordon Craig, the brilliant artist and visionary stage designer who was the illegitimate son of the actress Ellen Terry. Acting under the impression that Quinn was a professional or at least habitual lecture agent, Craig first wrote to ask Quinn to act as his "representative" in arranging lectures, shows, productions of unspecified kinds in America. Vehemently and circumstantially but not unkindly, Quinn disposed of that idea in his reply:

> Years ago I helped my friend W. B. Yeats in his first lecture tour in this country. That was a great pleasure. But I have paid for it since because about every Irishman or Irishwoman that believes he or she has capacity or qualifications for a lecturer has thought

that I was a sort of lecture bureau and has made himself or herself an infernal nuisance to me. This extends to lecturers, writers, poets, priests, patriots, actors, artists, philanthropists, politicians, liberators, soldiers, rebels, parliamentarians, nuns, school teachers, college presidents, hospitals, and St. Patrick only knows whatnot if St. Patrick is paying any attention to Irish affairs these days. It doesn't do me as a busy practicing lawyer any good to be regarded as a lecture impresario. [*February 16, 1915.*]

Quinn went on to suggest that Harriet Bryant of the Carroll Gallery might be willing to act as Craig's agent, in which event he offered to "advise" her. It now struck Craig that if Quinn was too big to act as his bear leader he might be useful for higher things. He proposed to Quinn that he undertake the promotion of the main scheme he had had in mind: an extravaganza production of Bach's *Passion according to St. Matthew,* operatic and dramatic, with a scenario, full orchestra and chorus, in a huge amphitheatre probably to be constructed in the hills along the Hudson River in New York State. Quinn felt a bit baffled and stunned by the idea, but attracted, and he put it up to Otto Kahn, who was a major backer of the Metropolitan Opera Association. Kahn too was interested, and the two men lunched over the idea several times, advancing so far as to agree each to offer Craig $500 to cover the cost of his coming to America to explore the idea and its problems in person. But it was eventually agreed to postpone any action until the war was over, and in time the whole impulse quietly died.

The second act of the pitiful and tragic drama of Sir Roger Casement had been unfolding throughout 1915. It was now generally assumed that his associate Kuno Meyer was an outright German agent. "Kuno Meyer's game we all understood," T. W. Rolleston wrote Quinn on May 19. Quinn believed that Meyer's American lectures were only a thin screen for systematic German propaganda. Augustus John was convinced that throughout his years in England as an honored Celtic scholar Meyer had been spying and sending home reports of English "weak spots." [60] All but the most rabid Irish Nationalists had by now come to believe that Casement was either mad or a victim of wildly deluded idealism. Rolleston's statement was representative of temperate opinion: ". . . it seems difficult to believe that any quite sane man can sincerely think he is doing Ireland a service by entangling her in this war on the side of Germany." [61] In a cable of March 15 and a letter of March 20, Casement in Germany asked Quinn to institute an action for slander, asking damages of $100,000, against the *New York World* for publishing the assertion that he was taking pay from the German government. He denied that he had ever taken a penny from the Germans, and charged that the story was a planted lie of the British government, making use of "the elemental weapons of British warfare against an Irishman—the Black Lie and the Silver Bullet." [62] He was in no sense a German agent, Casement maintained: "I came here only for one thing, and that alone—for the sake of Ireland, and no one knows that better than Sir E. Grey and the British government."

The "Black Lie," he believed, had been fabricated in Downing Street following British embarrassment at the failure of their "Silver Bullet," the attempt by Sir Edward Grey and his minister at Christiania, M. de C. Findlay, to have Casement assassinated or kidnapped. Casement had written Grey in February threatening to expose this "plot" to Norwegian authorities, and he believed that Grey's fear of such exposure had led to the lying counterattack in the press. In his March 20, 1915, letter to Quinn, Casement made a sweeping denial of the charge that he was hiding in Germany as their paid agent:

> I have never received one cent from the German government, but have refused to allow them to contribute in any way to my expenses, even in my fight against Findlay. They offered to pay *all* my expenses. It cost me 6,000 marks, and they (the German government) knew I was poor and that John Bull had collared all I possessed and they offered privately to bear all that expense. I refused. I have refused every form of "assistance." I have never been "in hiding," but staying in the principal hotels in Germany and visited by scores. My name is a household word through Germany today. At this moment I am the guest of the Baron and Baroness von Nordenflycht—he is the German minister at Montevideo, and was my former colleague at Rio de Janeiro.

He had turned down, he said, repeated chances to profit from his German popularity—offers from publishers, from lecture and cinema agents, from a tobacco company which wanted to bring

out a new cigar bearing his name and picture. He was not a British
traitor but a loyal Irishman; and after the war, said the homeless
and apparently hopelessly disoriented man, he would flee to the
United States and become a citizen of that country.

On March 29 Casement received Quinn's message that he considered a slander action hopeless. A month later he wrote that he
had seen a letter of Quinn's to a friend, dated March 22, in which
Quinn made it plain that he had refused to represent Casement because he was certain that he was "acting for Germany." Once
more Casement resumed his defense, and he dismissed Quinn's
pusillanimity in lofty terms when he wrote to him:

> No action of mine since I arrived in Europe has been an act for
> Germany—any more than, say, to cite a very notable case, Wolfe
> Tone acted "for France" when he tried to get French help for
> Ireland in a previous great Continental war. However different the
> circumstances may be in many respects, my action and the motives
> inspiring it have been the same; and I had thought that every Irish-
> man would understand, at least, that much, even if a restricted
> patriotic development might not permit him to sympathize with
> the end in view.   [*April 29, 1915.*]

Sensing Quinn's timidity and anticipating his refusal, Casement
said, he had in any case already instructed another lawyer to act
for him. He had given up Quinn, and on Casement's part the rest
was silence: he never wrote to Quinn again. Though Quinn's feeling about all this grew a great deal warmer later on, it was now, as
expressed to Rolleston in June, perfectly crisp and cold: "I told
him that if he wanted to serve Ireland his place was in Ireland. He
has written me two or three letters. I have answered none of them.
He sent me pamphlets and circulars and so on. I have acknowledged none of them." [63] Quinn accepted Casement's protestations
of good faith, but he believed his course mad and wrong. His own
commitment to the Allied cause, his affection for France if not for
England, and his hatred of Germany were now so fixed that he
could feel no sympathy for behavior which seemed to him to show
a hysterical dislocation of values, personal and political. And he
was not the kind of lawyer who willingly undertook lost causes.

1916

CASEMENT'S adventure in Germany turned rapidly toward *opéra-bouffe* and tragedy. His Wolfe Tone scheme of recruiting an Irish Brigade among Irish prisoners of war in Germany, most of whom had become seasoned and loyal British soldiers, was the kind of idea that could occur only to "a victim of the gods, blinded by *Hybris*, and lured towards his doom by *Nemesis*"—as Walter Starkie wrote.[1] According to Shane Leslie, the fifty-two Irish prisoners Casement managed to "enroll" and to uniform in green and gold got drunk in Berlin, rolled arm in arm down Unter den Linden singing "Rule, Britannia," and gave three cheers for the King.[2] Casement had wildly overestimated his personal popularity and the general propitiousness of his affairs in Germany. The hardheaded Germans, in the final irony, suspected that they were entertaining either a madman or a British spy. By the winter of 1915–16 Casement was in despair; he concluded that England's sea power must bring her eventual victory, that the Germans meant to destroy him and Ireland, and that the best he could hope for was to be landed in Ireland with a handful of outmoded and useless arms. When news reached him of the rebellion planned for Easter Sunday, April 23, 1916, he resolved at once to go to Ireland. He no longer dreamed of leading, or even of augmenting, the revolt; his hope now was only to prevent a helpless slaughter by persuading the leaders to postpone the outbreak. From a German submarine he was sent ashore in a collapsible dinghy, landing on Banna Strand. Before he was captured he managed to send to John MacNeill, the Chairman of the Irish Volunteers, by a Catholic priest he met on the shore, his frantic plea for delay. By Saturday, April 22, the German ship *Aud*, bearing arms for the rebels, was trapped and scuttled off Queenstown (now Cobh), and MacNeill forbade the rising to proceed. But initiative had been seized by a radical party of the Executive Committee of the Irish Volunteers, they countermanded the orders of the Chairman, and on Monday, April 24, the pathetic and terrible Easter Rising began.

"Did you ever hear or know of such a piece of childish madness?" Lily Yeats asked when the firing had ended. "There is not one person in the whole of Ireland that is not the worse for this last fortnight's work." [3] "All Dublin seemed in flames. . . . 160 civilians were killed in the streets. . . . Sackville Street from the Bridge to the Pillar is a ruin, still smoking," she reported. Walter Starkie, who as a young Trinity College student roamed the streets on foot and bicycle, making one in the crowd, attributed the fact that civilian casualties outnumbered the military to the famous insatiable curiosity of the Dublin populace: when they were not looting the shops the people stood about amid the firing as if it were all a circus providentially provided. The brutality was real enough. Francis Sheehy-Skeffington, a fearless pacifist idealist who had been going about in the city appealing for order and helping the injured, was arrested as a hostage and then shot by order of the insane British commandant, Captain Bowen Colthurst. The captured rebel leader James Connolly, who had been shot in both legs, was executed while strapped in a chair when he could not stand to face the firing squad. The rebels had dreamed that their action would be the signal for a tremendous popular revolt in their support, and that they needed only to hold out for a couple of weeks while help was mysteriously coming from Germany and America. When Eamon De Valera was arrested he was heard to lament: " 'If only the people had come out with knives and forks.' " [4]

When the general firing had ended there followed the excruciating days of single volleys, as the leaders were condemned one by one and led out for execution and the martyrdom they had half anticipated and half desired. All Ireland was appalled at the bravery and the waste. Among those most deeply stirred and shaken was W. B. Yeats. For years he had been writing poems of insult to ordinary Irishmen, slanging their cowardice, their crassness, their coarseness of mind. But now the Easter events struck him as a kind of secular miracle, in which the operative word was "transformation." He was equally moved by the beauty of the sacrifice and horrified by the brutality of the waste, as he was haunted by the thought that his own writings, *The Countess Cathleen*, for example, had moved men to their terrible deeds, or that things he should have written might have prevented them. "We have lost the ablest and most fine-natured of our young men," Yeats wrote to Quinn a month after Easter Monday.[5] "A world seems to have been swept away. I keep going over the past in my mind and wondering if I could have done anything to turn those young men in some other direction." Looking sadly about the new rooms he had recently taken in Woburn Buildings in London, he resolved to abandon them for Dublin, "to begin building again."

Among the less fine-natured of the Sixteen Men was Major John MacBride, who had led an Irish contingent against the British in the Boer War, the swashbuckling soldier who had succeeded where Yeats had failed with Maud Gonne a dozen years before, then mistreated her and been divorced by her. Even he, Yeats felt, was changed utterly in the general terrible beauty.* Maud thought so too, writing to Quinn on May 11 from Paris: "He has died for Ireland and his son will bear an honored name—I remember nothing else." After Quinn had sent her a poem on MacBride's death, she wrote again on August 15: "He made a fine, heroic end, which has atoned for all. It was a death he had always desired."† In old days

---

* "This other man I had dreamed
A drunken, vainglorious lout.
He had done most bitter wrong
To some who are near my heart,
Yet I number him in the song;
He, too, has resigned his part
In the casual comedy;
He, too, has been changed in his turn,
Transformed utterly:
A terrible beauty is born."
     (from "Easter 1916")

† Maud Gonne sent Quinn a copy of a letter she had had from the Franciscan, Father Augustine, who attended MacBride before his execution: " 'He prepared for the end like a good Catholic and met his fate with a most admirable fortitude. After having heard his confession we prayed together in preparation for holy Communion which he received with the most beauti-

Maud had been foremost among those who would, in Yeats's phrase, have thrown the little streets against the great: in her long residence in France, essentially an exile, she had grown a bit more detached about Ireland's grievances. But now she lived it all again in the struggle of MacBride and the bravery of Constance Gore-Booth, Countess Markievicz, her dearest friend, who had put aside the silk kimono of Yeats's Pre-Raphaelite recollection of her [6] and put on the rumpled rebel uniform. On May 22 Shane Leslie wrote Quinn that he had had an account of the Dublin fighting from "the O'Kane," who was "horrified at his old friend and pupil the Countess picking off mutual acquaintances as they looked out of club windows! But the general note is more ghastly than we imagined." Like Yeats, Maud felt she must now return to Ireland to rear and educate her son as an Irishman. In a massive subterranean way the farcical rebellion was beginning to accomplish its work after all.

Quinn's response to the news of the rebellion was complex, if not simply confused, and he spoke about it in several voices. On May 1 he wrote Conrad: "I have been disgusted and depressed by the horrible fiasco in Ireland. . . . The whole thing was sheer lunacy. . . ." The practical man and the Allied partisan in Quinn were contemptuous of the "misguided" affair as treasonous and madly romantic, and he traced it all back to "the essential falsity of Irish life; listening to the big speeches, the worship of Robert Emmet, the refusal to face facts, preferring talk to acts and expecting miracles to happen." [7] He scornfully supposed that before the first shot was fired every one of the Sixteen Men "probably had a speech from the dock up his sleeve." [8] Again the practical politician, wishing well-being both to England and to Ireland, and the preservation of the good name of both in the United States at a critical time, was appalled at England's tactical "stupidity" in executing the rebel leaders. He wrote Conrad on May 13:

I am a pure pragmatist in politics, in international affairs and in war. . . . There are no "eternal principles" in politics or in diplo-

---

ful dispositions, and then we said together the prayers in thanksgiving. He was quite calm, gave me some money for bread for the poor and felt very glad when I told him I would be by his side when he fell to anoint him.' "
(September 4, 1916)

macy. . . . If England had announced after the revolt had been quelled, as it was within three days, that technically the lives of the leaders were forfeited but that she did not propose to imitate Germany, that they would be imprisoned during the term of the war, that the rebels would be deprived of their arms, that would have made an impression in this country that nothing could have effaced.

But then the Irish patriot and the romantic in Quinn spoke in the letter he sent to Mrs. Theodore Roosevelt along with his gift of a volume of the writings of Padraic Pearse, one of the executed rebel leaders. Quinn recollected in a glow of sentiment an evening in his apartment several years before when Pearse had been in America soliciting money for his school, St. Enda's College:

> I remember his sitting near a window in my drawing room and looking out into Central Park, covered with snow, about twelve o'clock at night, and talking about his hopes and dreams for Ireland; and I remember well, and often think of it as I look at that chair and out of that window, his saying, quite simply, "I would be glad to die for Ireland . . . any time." That was the faith by which he lived, and for which he died. However much one may differ from his political beliefs, one must admire his ideality, his undaunted spirit, and the purity of the motives that always moved him. [*August 15, 1917.*]

Finally the Irishman, the sentimentalist, the pragmatic politician, the guilty idealist, and the conscience-stricken friend in Quinn all spoke in his efforts to save the life of Roger Casement. On June 29, confidently and prematurely, he announced to Conrad: "Casement . . . won't swing."

The last act of the tragedy of Casement, his trial, conviction, and execution in England, was also the last formal movement of the drama of the rebellion. Seeking to prevent the revolt, Casement had been the first of the rebels captured, and he was the last to die. As his imprisonment and his trial continued, the immense sweep of romantic and elegiac feeling set moving by the Rising came to focus on his lonely, pitiable, oddly imposing figure. With his bearded, haggardly handsome face and patrician bearing, his contempt for the power of authority, his history of fearless service to the downtrodden, Casement had always been the kind of figure about whom legend accumulates. Now, quixotic and intransigent, he seemed to many Irishmen to be playing out in a symmetrical and poetical form the embodied legend of Ireland's bitter past. "He was really magnificent-looking," Mary Colum remembered of Casement from happier days, and she went on to quote Stephen Gwynn's description: " 'Figure and face, he seemed to me one of the finest-looking creatures I had ever seen, and his countenance had charm and distinction and high chivalry.' " [9] Quinn believed Casement at the very least "honest and honorable," and in his personal life "a man of the utmost austerity and purity." Quinn remained convinced that Casement had "never touched a penny" in German bribery.[10]

Prodded by Quinn's excitement and pity, Joseph Conrad sent him his own far more disenchanted recollections of Casement. At Matadi in the Congo in 1890 the two men had shared a room for three weeks, and they had made several trips together to arrange with village chiefs for porters for the caravans going to Leopold-ville and Kinchassa. Then Conrad had gone into the interior to take command of a stern-wheel steamer, leaving Casement behind: the situation of Conrad's great story *Heart of Darkness*. Six years later they met again by chance in London at a dinner of the Johnson Society, and Casement was the Conrads' guest overnight in the country. "Certain Liberal circles were making rather a pet of him," Conrad understated Casement's celebrity; "well-connected Irishman, Protestant Home-ruler, of romantic aspect—and so on." [11] About 1911 they had met for the last time, again by chance, in the Strand, when Casement was on leave from his post as British Consul in Rio de Janeiro, and seemed "more gaunt than ever and his eyes still more sunk in his head. There was a strange austerity in his aspect." Conrad concluded:

> We never talked politics. I didn't think he had really any. A Home-ruler accepting Lord Salisbury's patronage couldn't be taken very seriously. He was a good companion; but already in Africa I judged that he was a man, properly speaking, of no mind at all. I don't mean stupid. I mean that he was all emotion. By emotional force (Congo report, Putumayo, etc.) he made his way, and sheer temperament—a truly tragic personality: all but the greatness of which he had not a trace. Only vanity. But in the Congo it was not visible yet. [*May 24, 1916.*]

The whole Casement story, in fact, with the revelations and refutations that would stir sullenly for the next fifty years, was the material of a perfect Conrad novel.

In going to Germany, as Quinn saw, Casement had acted in the traditional spirit of the Irish maxim: "England's difficulty is Ireland's opportunity." Though Casement held unshakeably to the conviction that he acted not for Germany but for Ireland, there could be little question that as a British citizen seeking the help of the enemy to discomfit England in time of war, he had been legally guilty of treason. And even had he gained his immediate objective it was hard to see any long-term logic in his action. Conrad wrote Quinn, commenting on his irrationality with scorn:

> One only wonders, in one's grief, what it was all for? With Britain smashed and the German fleet riding the seas, the very shadow of Irish independence would have passed away. The Island Republic (if that is what they wanted) would have become merely a strongly held German outpost—a despised stepping-stone towards the final aim of the Welt-Politik. *[May 24, 1916.]*

Quinn accepted Casement's technical guilt as clear; but he thought there was a chance of saving his life, and it was to that end that he labored: writing to the newspapers, writing and cabling to persons of power abroad, arguing with British officials in New York and Washington, working frantically to collect American opinion behind an appeal for clemency. He sent a twenty-four-page memorandum to the British Foreign Office arguing for a reprieve on grounds of strategy and humanity. In two days of telephoning he collected the signatures of twenty-five prominent Americans for a cablegram sent to Sir Edward Grey, the Foreign Secretary, late in July:

> The undersigned, American citizens, all of whom have been and are pro-Ally in their sympathies, respectfully appeal in the interests of humanity for clemency in the case of Roger Casement, and are profoundly convinced that clemency would be wise policy on the part of the British Government at this juncture and in this great crisis in the history of our race.[12]

Largely as a result of the pressures Quinn had amassed, the United States Senate requested the State Department to cable on behalf of Casement, and this was done.

Quinn took the position that Casement's design to work "for Ireland, not for Germany," was humanly exculpatory if legally worthless; that it would be tactically dangerous for England to make Casement into a martyr; that England must do everything possible to avoid alienating American opinion at a critical period in the war. By late July Quinn saw the case as hopeless, and he believed England was about to kill Casement out of guilt and fear: "I think he knew too much." [13] Quinn saw himself as having "kept peace" thus far, but now he sat down and dictated a long statement praising and excusing Casement, lamenting his end, and attacking the English action. He wrote on August 12 of the piece and his motives in it to Pound: "I meant to hurt, and I think I have hurt. There is no style about the damned thing. . . . In fact it was dictated, and dictated in a devil of a rush, done in about six hours. . . . He was a damned fine fellow." Quinn's elegy for Casement appeared in *The New York Times Magazine* as the feature article on Sunday, August 13, 1916: "Roger Casement, Martyr: Some Notes for a Chapter of History by a Friend Whose Guest He Was When the War Broke Out." But by then Casement was dead, having been hanged on the morning of August 3. On August 2 Quinn had cabled Gavan Duffy, Casement's solicitor: "Have exhausted my efforts for weeks in behalf of clemency. I sincerely hope you will see Casement and shall be greatly obliged if you will give him my love." Both this and a similar cable to Alice Stopford Green ("the Widow Green"), Casement's bravest champion in England, arrived too late for the prisoner to hear them.

With Casement's life gone Quinn labored to salvage his memory. Rumors had been circulating for weeks that Scotland Yard investigators had found in locked trunks in Casement's London flat handwritten diaries demonstrating his "degeneracy"—homosexual proclivities and behavior extending over the years in which he had been forming his image as the champion of helpless subject peoples. When these tales reached Quinn he flew into an augmented rage. In the first place, he refused on the basis of his own experience to believe that Casement could be a homosexual. He wrote emphatically on August 22 to his friend and fellow lawyer, Frederic R. Coudert, of his impressions of Casement in the weeks they had spent together in Quinn's apartment two years before:

"Never by word or act, by tone of the voice, by a gesture or the slightest syllable or letter was there a shadow of a shade of anything of a degenerate about him." He assumed that the diaries were forged documents, and his mind flew at once to the analogy of the proven Piggott forgeries against the good name of Parnell: the British were cooking up another Black Lie. Quinn was further angered at British timing of these allegations, and he demanded to know why they had not brought forward the evidence of the diaries when Casement was free in Germany and might hope to defend himself. "But not until he was arrested, in their power, dead or all but dead, did they attack him, when he could not reply or fight back or defend himself or bring an action." [14]

Quinn warned British officials whom he knew in New York and Washington that he would fight back with "a second battery" if they continued to circulate innuendoes about Casement's private life. He threatened to make a public charge of forgery and to reveal Casement's "evidence" of a British plot against his life.

I will rehearse for the American people the whole Piggott-Times forgeries, and wonder whether England didn't then get her bellyful of forgeries. I will denounce the diary as a forgery. I will call attention to the fact that it was not used when Casement could fight back. I will print the facsimile of Casement's letter in which Casement charged he had the evidence that the British Ambassador at Christiania had offered money to have Casement kidnapped or knocked on the head. I will print the facsimiles of Casement's letters to Grey. And I will leave the American people to draw the conclusion from the facts which I give that Casement was to be put out of the way not because he was a rebel, but because he knew too much, and that these loathsome, vile insinuations are being made now to blacken his memory because he had caught the Ambassador at Christiania in the act of attempting to have him assassinated. I have got the material. If they stop, I will stop. [15]

Finally, and a good deal more temperately and logically, Quinn wondered what earthly relevance the charge of Casement's "degeneracy" bore to the charge of his treasonous disloyalty.

In the upshot Quinn's friend Sir Cecil Spring-Rice, the British Ambassador in Washington, defused his anger artfully and quickly. The British problem was to prevent a cultish accumulation of sentiment, strong enough to alienate American sympathy for England, about the romantic figure and dramatic history of Roger Casement. Quinn's own deep allegiance to the Allied cause, his impatience with the pro-German Irish in America and Ireland, made it easy for him to accept the force of the English motive. Further, Spring-Rice told Quinn, he had had peremptory instructions from Sir Edward Grey that the diaries were to be given no general publicity: they had in fact been shown or mentioned in confidence only to a few persons who were in danger of taking a line on Casement potentially embarrassing not only to England but also to themselves—if all the facts were known. Finally, as a person about to take such a dangerous line, Quinn was shown by Captain Guy Gaunt, Naval Attaché of the British Embassy in New York, documents which were said to be photographic facsimiles of portions of the Casement diaries. Quinn was charmed by Gaunt and convinced, after comparing his knowledge of Casement's handwriting with the facsimiles, that the diaries were authentic. The whole question of their relevance to the primary charge against Casement apparently went by the board, in Quinn's mind as well as in others'. The whole affair made a characteristic and Quinnian sequence: within forty-eight hours his rage had risen, expressed itself, taken action, and been assuaged. He now resolved to let *The New York Times* article stand as his last public word on Roger Casement.

The New York Times article, reprinted in full in the Philadelphia *Ledger* and the Boston *Herald,* brought praise from all sides, some of it, like Huneker's, distastefully fulsome and sycophantic. Huneker in a letter to Quinn called it the most "relentless, logical, and powerful polemic" yet published during the war, and lauded its style and feeling: "As a document of rhetoric it is a classic; but its periodic sentences, so admirably adapted for the expression of pious indignation, would only be rhetoric if not backed by your tremendous sincerity." [16] He warned Quinn to be on guard for attacks from "foreign" spies. Even Padraic Colum, who had never warmed to Quinn and whose Irish Nationalist position was a good deal more radical, wrote generously: "More than any other article connected with the insurrection, I am glad that yours was written." [17] Michael Monahan said the paper recalled "the Grattans

John Quinn in 1921

Mary Quinlan Quinn

James William Quinn

Julia Quinn Anderson

Father Jeremiah Quinlan

Mary on "Dandy"

John Quinn delivering Lafayette Day address, 1917

John Quinn as a boy   John Quinn on shipboard

Golf of sorts: Brancusi, Mrs. Foster, Roché

Fontainebleau, 1923: Picasso, Mrs. Foster, Mme. Picasso, Quinn

Paris, 1923: Joyce, Pound, Quinn, Ford Madox Ford

Jeanne Robert Foster

John Butler Yeats: the unfinishable self-portrait

William Butler Yeats

George W. Russell

George Moore

Standish O'Grady

Courtesy of the National Gallery of Ireland

and the Currans, the noblest traditions of Irish patriotism and its canonized utterances." [18] Shane Leslie wrote more ambiguously of "your remarkable letter, which nobody else in the world could have written." [19] James Byrne told of overhearing at a picnic the daughter of an Englishman say that the piece had made her wish to drain off her English blood and leave only the French. In good Capitol Hill idiom, Quinn's old political hero, Oscar W. Underwood, wrote to praise "a splendid article, forcefully and clearly expressed, painting a word-picture that, once conceived, will never be forgotten." [20] James Stephens did not come across the piece until late in September, when he wrote at once to Quinn:

> It is a most eloquent, brave, and moving piece of writing. . . . Indeed, I think it is the best piece of writing and feeling which this lamentable war has brought forth, and our poor friend is justified anyhow in some part of the earth. [*September 28, 1916.*]

But doubtless the encomium Quinn valued most was Lady Gregory's:

> Your wonderful defense of your dead friend has very much moved and touched me. It is so clear, so logical, so passionate. If you could have been his advocate at the trial I believe you might have saved him, if anyone could have done so. Anyhow you have with this "Elegy, or Friend's Passion" lifted his memory to a higher plane. And is not that the greatest service one can do? [*September 3, 1916.*]

All this was grateful to the ear of a would-be artist, and hardly less grateful was Æ's reference to the article as "extraordinarily moving and eloquent," and "the best expression of your character and intellect I have yet seen." [21] Russell was especially impressed that Quinn had not been shaken from his larger personal allegiances by the event he so passionately deplored. Sharing Quinn's Allied sympathies, Russell too had written to Asquith, admitting the legal validity of the charge of treason but pleading for mercy on grounds of "high policy and humanity." [22] Whereas he was "spiritually antagonized" by the "mechanic materialism" of Germany, Russell was in hopes that the "deepening" experience of the war would lead England to meet Ireland's needs and aspirations in future with greater wisdom and charity. In the meantime, with typical largemindedness and foresight, Æ had been trying to form committees to think ahead systematically toward a rational constitution for Ireland after the war. But the spiritual and political climate in Ireland seemed darker and more ominous than ever; as James Stephens put it: "Here everything is wrong and set hard for worse. . . ." [23] Four months after the Rising, the country seemed to Russell even more "disintegrated" politically than before: "There is emotion and prejudice in plenty but little thought." [24] "The psychology of the rising interested me," he wrote blandly. People exposed to the noise, danger, and destructiveness of Easter Week, he felt, had reacted with a form of "dilated consciousness," a deep, half-conscious, irrational excitement that showed itself in striking ways. A sober businessman got himself a revolver and threatened to shoot dead the first man who did not do exactly as he was told. A young lieutenant was convinced, quite without basis in fact, that he had shot a man lying in bed asleep. "Lord, what creatures we are!" Æ mused. "We must rewrite psychology when the war is over." [25]

Even more gratifying than Russell's praise was his spontaneous decision to dedicate his major volume *Imaginations and Reveries* to Quinn—especially, as Quinn wrote, since Æ was one of the few Irishmen of his acquaintance who had never plagued him for favors and for whom he had never "done anything." [26] Quinn at once ordered thirty copies of the American edition and ten of the Dublin edition to distribute among his friends. He hoped Russell would at last cease to subdivide his energies so prodigally and concentrate more on his writing and painting. He cited his own bad example:

> I have allowed myself to be pulled and dragged here and there and to be interested in this and to give time to that and to help this and to be a member of that, and so on, and have done nothing permanent.		[*January 13, 1916.*]

Then, with no sense of irony, he once more pressed Russell to allow him to arrange with Pond's bureau for a course of American lectures. Ironically it was the multiplicity of Æ's powers and interests that he praised when he sent Theodore Roosevelt a copy of *Imaginations and Reveries* on January 26: "He is not as great an artist or a poet as Rossetti was, but he is a bigger man, for he is a man of action and of affairs, a practical man as well as a poet and a mystic." The praise was bent, that is, to suit the auditor.*

Douglas Hyde wrote on March 19 to send thanks for Æ's book, though he found the prose "a little too sublimated" for his taste. In 1915 Hyde had resigned "in the odour of sanctity" after twenty-two years as president of the Gaelic League. In the inclusive political hysteria of the day, he felt, the movement was being shifted from its proper cultural base and turned to serve more narrowly political ends. Half a year later he wrote that the League had been "steered on the rocks by fools." [27] The general outlook in Ireland seemed to him "as black as can be," and Hyde's depression was intensified by the unexpected death of his daughter Nuala, only twenty-two, whom they had thought cured of tuberculosis. He took some formal comfort in the Celtic ceremonial of her burial, in which she was carried to her grave by twenty-four young un-married men.

But the kindest word and the handsomest praise from Ireland, of this or any year—in response, for a change, to thanks *from* Quinn (for the gift of *The Brook Kerith*)—came from George Moore: "You are, of all men I have ever met, the most willing to help your fellows, whether they be lame or sound, over the stiles of life, and I fancy you must have helped a great many." [28]

Both Ezra Pound and W. B. Yeats wrote of their activities during the weeks they spent together in early 1916 at Stone Cottage, Coleman's Hatch, in Sussex. The area was "prohibited," and Pound discovered after a time that he should have registered as an alien. Yeats reported that after his third visit from a police-man Pound had flung out of the house so violently that he had torn the coat hook from the wall. Yeats himself was happy at having at last finished *The Player Queen* after years of what he called "puzzle-headed work." Mrs. Pat Campbell had "ordered" the play five years before, assuring him with casual arithmetic: " 'You will

---

* A few months before he had accepted an invitation to sit on the plat-form in a lecture by Theodore Roosevelt at Carnegie Hall sponsored by the Knights of Columbus, then reneged when it occurred to him that his pres-ence there might be interpreted as indicating that he was a member of the society, which required going to confession and communion at least once a year. (To James G. Huneker, October 22, 1915.)

write it in a fortnight and I will send you two dozen of champagne, a bottle for each day.' " [29] Yeats had refused the champagne, fortunately. "It has blundered into one bad construction after another," he reflected, "and instead of turning out the most poetical of my plays in verse, it is almost a farce." [30] "Yeats is brrring in the next room," Pound reported on February 26, rewriting a lyric for one of his short Noh-plays. Pound felt honored by Yeats's having consented to write an introduction to the volume Pound was preparing of his own versions, adapted from those of Ernest Fenollosa, of the Japanese plays Yeats was using as a model. Pound had led Yeats to the study of the classical Noh dramas of Japan, and their spare symbolic style was striking him with the force of revelation. The two men were sharing another pleasant chore, making a volume from "the high and mountainous parts of old Pop Yeats' letters. Some of which are quite fine." [31] As Quinn well knew. And Pound's mind returned once more to old Mr. Yeats atop the Coney Island elephant, "smiling with apostolic joy of a pre-christian prophet." [32]

On April 2 the "new playlet," *At the Hawk's Well*, the first of W. B. Yeats's Noh-inspired plays, was in rehearsal and Yeats wrote of his excitement and exhaustion. He explained the Noh as an "aristocratic" form, intended for a small élite audience and capable of presentation in an ordinary room with a minimum of stage paraphernalia. He stated his current aspiration:

> I hope to create a form of drama which may delight the best minds of my time, and all the more because it can pay its expenses without the others. If when the play is perfectly performed (the music is the devil) Balfour and Sargent and Ricketts and Sturge Moore and John and the Prime Minister and a few pretty ladies will come to see it, I shall have a success that would have pleased Sophocles.

The play was being done with masked actors and a simple musical accompaniment, and it pleased Yeats to think that in his play masks were being seriously used in western theatre for the first time since the classical drama. The room chosen for the performance was not quite ordinary—Lady Cunard's drawing room. Edward Marsh, who was present, described the event in a letter to Cathleen Nesbitt:

I find I can manage quite well without *any* scenery at all—but they had been a little too careful not to disturb the room, and I couldn't help being disconcerted, just when I had persuaded myself that I had before me a wild mountain tract of semi-historic Ireland, to notice the characters skirting round a Louis XV table covered with French novels. The actors wore masks made by Dulac, awfully good, and I found it quite easy to accept the convention. But I had an odd sensation just before the play began. Harry Ainley [the principal actor] had a mask very like his own face, and I didn't know it wasn't his own self till he came up to me roaring with laughter and not a *muscle* of his mouth moving, it was quite uncanny. The play began with very atmospheric "keening" behind the screen and a man in black solemnly pacing to the front—he got there, made an impressive bow to the audience, then started, and said "Oh we've forgotten to light the lanterns!"—lighted them, retired, paced solemnly forward again, and began his speech.[33]

By midsummer of 1916 Yeats was well into the second portion of his "Autobiographies," carrying the narrative from the close of "Reveries" down to the turn of the century. He had gone to stay with Maud Gonne in Calvados to work on the book, and wrote Quinn that he was sounding her memory of the period as well as his own. He meant to write a "perfectly frank" account of the writers and men of letters who had turned the century in England and Ireland, and he feared the volume could not be published until perhaps twenty years after his death. "I will lay many ghosts," he wrote on August 1, "or rather I will purify my own imagination by setting the past in order." He found that sorting and ordering the characters of the recollected drama was "like writing a play." Two weeks later Pound reported that Yeats was still in France and when last heard from was feeding young rabbits with a spoon.[34]

Cordial and somewhat better-spirited messages, as well as portions of manuscript, went forward from Conrad throughout 1916. On February 27 he thanked Quinn for the annual "supremely delightful" Christmas apples, sent on the final typewritten state of *Victory* and the manuscript of *The Shadow-Line*, and promised shortly to send the manuscript, about sixty pages, of the story "The Humane Tomassov." He pointed out again that Quinn would possess "every scrap" of his extant completed manuscripts. For these

three items Conrad asked £60, and he hoped Quinn would send
the money at once without waiting for the unfinished story: he
was hard up and still unable to work regularly. On January 25
Quinn had bought the manuscript of "Poland Revisited," the first
bit Conrad had allowed to slip away from him, in an auction for
war relief at the American Art Galleries of the manuscripts Edith
Wharton had collected for "The Book of the Homeless." Two
friends of his bid against him and ran the price up to $320, a sum
Quinn was happy to pay in a good cause and in order to keep his
Conrad collection absolute. To ease Conrad's fiscal situation Quinn
urged him to undertake a tour of lectures or readings organized
by J. B. Pond's Lyceum Bureau, and he promised to throw his own
weight and experience behind the enterprise. He cited the examples
of Masefield's thirty to forty engagements at $100 to $150 each,
Lady Gregory's clearing £700 in three months, Douglas Hyde's
gain of seventeen pounds in flesh.[35] But Conrad refused to entertain the notion and explained why in a letter of March 14:

> You are very good to take such friendly interest in the improve-
> ment of my affairs. There's nothing I would have liked more
> than to give readings from my novels—but it's impossible. About
> 5 years ago after an attack of gouty throat I lost my voice com-
> pletely. It fails me even in ordinary conversation if it is at all
> prolonged. A sustained effort such as a lecture or reading is out of
> question.

As a confirmed admirer of the work of Henry James, Quinn inquired about the fate of the manuscript of a brief paper Conrad had
written on James some dozen years previously. Conrad replied that
the manuscript was lost, that he had never seen it in print, and
that he had now no recollection of what he had said in it: "Perfect
blank," he summed up.[36] Quinn dug up the issue of the *North
American Review* which had contained the article [37] and sent it
on to Conrad with a query as to whether, if writing now, he
would "pitch the note higher." Conrad thought he could hardly
do so: "I said he was great and incomparable—and what more
could one say?" [38] He went on to review his personal and professional relationship with James.

> The only time he did me the honour of speaking of me in
> print (about 2 years ago) he confined himself to the analysis of

method, which he rather airily condemned in relation to the methods of two young writers. I may say, with scrupulous truth, that this was the *only time* a criticism affected me painfully But in our private relations he has been always warmly appreciative and full of invariable kindness. I had a profound affection for him. He knew of it and he accepted it as if it were something worth having. At any rate that is the impression I have. And he wasn't a man who would pretend. What need had he?—even if he had been capable of it.

In February Conrad had confided his plan for a postwar Edition de Luxe of his complete works, to be called the Orlestone Edition after his home village in Kent, now being negotiated by his agent and good friend J. B. Pinker with the London firm of William Heinemann. The scheme was for 1,000 sets in the English edition, and Conrad asked Quinn's advice as to the feasibility of printing a simultaneous American edition of 1,500 sets. The project lay close to Conrad's heart, for he foresaw it as the only certain legacy of consequence he could leave to his wife and younger son, John. His other son, "The Boy," Lieutenant Borys Conrad, had been home for a pitifully brief leave before going to the front; he had called the big guns with which he was serving " 'simply lovely things.' " [39] Conrad asked Quinn to keep an eye on his practical interests in negotiations for the edition with his American publisher, Doubleday, Page, and Quinn undertook the task with an enthusiasm that ultimately both Conrad and Doubleday found hard to take. The energy, or officiousness, of his mediation in this affair was apparently the beginning of his later mysterious alienation from Conrad.

Quinn evidently interpreted his mandate as total. He corresponded copiously with Doubleday and was soon sending advice in both directions on such matters as titles, typography, format, paper, illustrations, bibliography, binding, quantity, price. Doubleday envisioned a "Sundial Edition" of Conrad's collected works in eighteen to twenty volumes, a limited, numbered edition to sell at $5 per volume. Quinn insisted, and Conrad agreed, that the original order and grouping of Conrad's publications must be followed in the new edition. Conrad also heartily approved Quinn's suggestion of three illustrations, a photograph, a recent portrait drawing by William Rothenstein, and a new portrait by Augustus John which Quinn would commission: "No pencil sketch of your home, no art student's art. I hate it," Quinn directed.[40] In the middle of June he journeyed out to Garden City to confer with Doubleday, taking along Walt Kuhn as aesthetic adviser. They were impressed with the "garden" aspect of the Doubleday operation but not with the publishing aspect. On June 29 Quinn sent Conrad a letter running to fourteen pages on these matters. On the following day F. N. Doubleday sent Quinn a confidential note complaining of Pinker's poor co-operation on the venture; he had waited more than a year for an answer to one of his proposals. He cited the wartime problem of rising costs and scarcity of paper. The timing of the edition was the main issue, Doubleday wishing early publication, Conrad and Pinker from the outset wishing to delay. Quinn intervened again, eliciting a cablegram from Pinker insisting that the collected edition must wait, probably till after the war. Conrad had reasons "both of the sentimental and of a practical order" for waiting, and he did not see why Doubleday could not understand that. He refused "to run my life like a cinema-film, regardless of anything but time, to please anybody's temperamental idiosyncrasy."[41] He was angry too at any criticism of Pinker, who had handled his affairs efficiently for years and who had been a loyal friend in more than one financial or emotional crisis.

Of Quinn's part in the negotiations to date Conrad wrote gratefully and consolingly:

> The thought and time you have so generously given to the Collected Edition are not lost. We appreciate it too much on this side, as a matter of taste and knowledge alone, to let it go to waste; and I personally look upon it as an evidence of friendship to which I attach the highest value. All your suggestions will be carried out, your letter containing them being the top-document on the file relating to that affair. [*August 10, 1916.*]

But, he still insisted: "In business there is rush but there is foresight too." Doubleday and perhaps Quinn were pushing too hard for rush in a time which needed foresight. "Both Pinker and I myself," he wrote sardonically, "have made it as clear as our European intellects allowed us to make it that publication would take place after the war."[42] Quinn bridled a bit at the implied scorn of American overbearing, answering on August 25: "Whatever English people may say, many people here that are really worth while are really too damned modest." The question of the edition was left to simmer for the time, and eventually it was settled along the lines of Conrad's original plan. By that time, apparently, Conrad and Doubleday had agreed to blame some of their difficulties upon Quinn.

But in midsummer 1916, on the easier side of the old relationship, Conrad could assure Quinn that the manuscript of the new book, *The Rescue*, was "growing into an enormous pile." [43] And there were other gentle matters to talk about. Quinn wrote happily or furiously, depending on the current condition of things, of his progress with the Purchase Street estate. James Huneker, their mutual friend whom Quinn called "one of the kindest of men," [44] had come safely through a long bout with rheumatic fever in the winter, and attributed his recovery to a lifetime of drinking Pilsener rather than whiskey. Conrad praised the "mental agility" and the "flexible liveliness of style" of Huneker's *Ivory Apes and Peacocks*, dedicated to Quinn, which Quinn had sent him.[45] Jo Davidson, the international bust-man, was in Orlestone in the spring, making a likeness of Conrad, and they had talked of Quinn. News of this set Quinn off, for Davidson was one who, as a man and an artist, always drew forth his contempt and insult. He wrote of Davidson to Conrad on May 1:

Masterpieces aren't made with the lightning rapidity that he polishes off his photographs in plaster or in bronze. They are *photographs* and not art. I was amused at his statement . . . "that he knew me slightly." He knows me to the extent of £70 which he has owed me for several years and which he has never offered to repay or to give me sculpture or drawings for.

A few days later, as it chanced, Davidson made a fruitless attempt to pay off his debt. Quinn was dining at the Brevoort with Walt Kuhn and Horace Brodzky when "that little whelp" sat down uninvited at their table and "began to pose." [46] Davidson said he wished to settle his debt and Quinn answered, the sooner the better. Davidson said he meant to do a bust of Quinn to pay off the old $350. Quinn: " 'I wouldn't have you fool with a bust of me if you were the last sculptor in the world.' " Quinn was angered by the familiar way in which Davidson referred to Iris Tree, the exotic daughter of Sir Beerbohm Tree, as "Iris" several times in the course of his chat.

The Brodzky of this ugly little occasion was a young writer and painter who had been a minor member of the London Group of artists who had made his way to New York and to Quinn's acquaintance on the heels of a warning note from Knewstub of the Chenil Gallery, dated December 5, 1915. According to Knewstub, Brodzky had announced in the Café Royal and elsewhere that he meant to be "accepted in New York either as a genius or a madman." Knewstub thought he was neither, and Ezra Pound described him offhandedly as "an amiable bore with some talent." [47] When they met Quinn found he liked the little man and that there were ways in which he could be made useful. The dinner at the Brevoort was undoubtedly the scene of a more or less desperate exploration of ways and means of handling the Vorticist show in New York, another of the benevolent and frustrating enterprises in which Quinn was involved by the spreading sympathies and energies of Ezra Pound. Jo Davidson received some of the force of that frustration as well as that of Quinn's fixed dislike of him.

What with his proprietorship of a half-dozen careers aside from his own, Pound was having one of his more frenetic years, and he was writing to Quinn at almost daily intervals. "I have never been so rushed," he wrote on March 18. "I seem to be a universal committee for the arts. . . ." Among other things, he noted, he was supposed to be writing his "life work in verse"—the *Cantos*. "Well I shan't make 'il gran rifiuto,' " he characteristically resolved. "I shall take the papacy when it comes." At the end of his letter of April 23, after taking his oath to put some "kick" into the *Egoist*, he wondered if he had not overlooked a number of things that were entitled to his wrath. In early January he was ready to believe the Pound-Quinn magazine an imminent fact and offered to come to America at Quinn's signal. "I am ready to spew two weeks' meals into the north Atlantic whenever you think necessary." Yeats, he added, had "got hold of a new gang of plutocrats," but he suspected he would want "all the pickings for the Oirish Tee-Ater." If Quinn got "almost the *needful*" Pound thought he might be able to tap Yeats's new sources, though on the whole he imagined they would be "more useful as surplus than vertebrae." [48] On February 26 he said he had "took up again" with the *Egoist* with the understanding that he would contribute twelve free articles in exchange for £50 to James Joyce and £50 to Wyndham Lewis. His feelings about the lady editors of the *Egoist* were mixed. Dora Marsden, he thought, was mainly ballast, unfortunately not inert but antipathetic to his own line of thought. Harriet Shaw Weaver, on the other hand, was the classical type of the toughminded lettered Englishwoman, one of those persons, so often women, who kept cropping up to demonstrate the mysterious vitality of that people whose demise had been repeatedly predicted. Three days later, having heard from Quinn of a dinner with Roosevelt, he wrote: "BY THE WAY NEXT TIME YOU ARE EATING TEETHADORUS'S T. ROOSEVELT'S OYSTERS you might note that THE REAL TROUBLE WITH A LOT OF OUR COMPATRIOTS IS IGNORANCE, just BONE Abyssinian ignorance." Roosevelt could help make an inroad on American ignorance, he suggested, by working to abolish the "prohibitive" tariff on books and to institute an international copyright law. Quinn steadily ignored Pound's steady demands that he do something for literature comparable to what he had done for art in engineering some of the provisions of the Underwood Tariff Act.

On March 15 Quinn offered, if Pound were to occupy an editorial capacity on the *Egoist*, to subsidize him to the extent of £100 a year for two years "to make something of that paper"; or, "If it will make it more comfortable to have it £120, then let it be £120." [49] In a letter of April 5 the sum proposed had mysteriously increased to £150. Pound had written the day before to thank Quinn for his "bully offer" in regard to the *Egoist*. He had put the proposition to the editors and they were considering whether their dynasty could tolerate a "large armed body" such as Ezra Pound within the state. Five days later he reported that Miss Weaver was for him but Miss Marsden doubtful: "So I am calling things off." Meanwhile he hoped Quinn might send a gift of £10 to James Joyce, floundering in Zurich. Quinn directed his trusted Scottish clerk, John Watson, to send the money to Joyce and did not discover until August after Watson had departed that he had let that and numerous other bookkeeping matters slide into an untidy heap. "God damn Watson," Quinn wrote Kuhn. "I wish I could choke him."[50] Joe the office boy told him that it had been Watson's habit to rush out to the stock ticker and speculate whenever Quinn left the office. Quinn appended a cautious note to Joyce on August 11 to the small draft "which I am forwarding to you on Mr. Pound's suggestion":

> It came about in this way: I offered to stake Pound in a certain matter and he declined it, but did suggest that I stake you to this extent. I am not generally in the staking business. . . . But I send you this with pleasure. Really it is because I am interested in your work.

Pound had also entrusted to Quinn the much-traveled manuscript of Joyce's first novel, *A Portrait of the Artist as a Young Man*, and the book had been offered to B. W. Huebsch and to young Alfred A. Knopf, who had left Doubleday, Page to found his own firm. Huebsch made an offer, and on July 19 Pound instructed Quinn to let him have the Joyce novel "IF he is a reputable publisher." Quinn replied on July 29: "Huebsch is all right if he takes the Joyce book. He is a Jew but a fairly decent Jew."

In March Quinn ordered twelve copies of Pound's little book in appreciation of Gaudier-Brzeska as soon as it should appear.[51] In August, after Pound had seen American reviews of the work, he wrote that he had been reminded once more of "the outer utter barbarism" of his native land. Pound's frustrated efforts to secure Gaudier's work for Quinn continued throughout the year, chiefly in confusing attempts to negotiate with Sophie Brzeska, whom he described on March 1 as "a female of uncertain age, of race transcaucassian [*sic*], of temper difficile. . . ." When Quinn offered to have made for him a second cast of Gaudier-Brzeska's *Bird Swallowing Fish*, Pound thanked him but refused: he had tried all his life to own "nothing that won't go into a suitcase." He admitted that he had succumbed to the possession of a wife and a clavichord and felt that they filled his three-room apartment. Sophie's latest gambit was to refuse to ship anything across the Atlantic because of the war. Pound and Quinn had wished to feature the works of Gaudier in their proposed Vorticist show in New York; Sophie said no, she was planning a memorial exhibition herself. On March

12 Pound cabled that Sophie was now demanding £500 for nine sculptures, two of them to be cast in bronze at her expense. He was forced to send his message in general terms because the post office clerk told him no censor would pass a detailed message. Pound saw their point: he reckoned that he could have "betrayed seven empires" in a code made from the list of Gaudier titles and numbers.[52] Quinn cabled back promptly demanding a list of the works proposed for the sum, and Pound went back to the telegraph office next day carrying the proof sheets and illustrations for his Gaudier-Brzeska book to demonstrate his, Quinn's, and Gaudier's bona fides. This time he was allowed to send titles and prices of individual works.

Mutual suspicion, as well as Sophie Brzeska's difficult nature and her distracted state and the disordered condition of the dead man's studio, were making negotiations almost impossible. Sophie suspected Quinn of being a slick operator on the scent of a shrewd deal; Quinn suspected her of being an adventuress with a dubious right to the remaining works; Pound was uneasy about committing another man's money in a situation of unclear titles and murky motives. Quinn's feeling about Sophie softened after he heard from Horace Brodzky at the Salmagundi Club that she had always been "good to" Gaudier, a faithful wife in fact if not in name. But he still had a sore feeling that he was being treated with unwarranted suspicion and probably with canny feminine disingenuousness. He paid £150 for Gaudier drawings, as a lead to securing a representative group of his sculptures, and when the drawings arrived he estimated them as casual studio scrawls "not worth £50."[53] By August he had received from Pound and Sophie the Gaudier *Cat* and *Water Carrier*. From Frank Harris, now working in New York under the wing of Mitchell Kennerley, he had independently secured, for $350, a fine Augustus John drawing and Gaudier's marble *Dog* (now in the Phillips Collection in Washington). But he was far from content, and in September he asked Jacob Epstein to plead his case with Sophie:

> . . . I should be glad if you will tell her that I am not a dealer, nor an over-reached [*sic*], nor a liar, nor a thief, nor a crook, nor a naïve [*sic*], nor a man who takes advantage of women financially or otherwise, and that it is altogether stupid on her part to write to

me as though I was one, or some, or any or all of the things that she imagined I was. There is a great deal of canniness mixed up in her emotionalism.   [*September 8, 1916.*]

Quinn's ego as well as his heart was now fixed on securing a corner on the works of the young Frenchman of genius, romantically cut off at the outset of his career, and he felt obscurely wounded at being bested by a shrewd or hysterical female.

Beginning full of life in the winter of 1916, the Vorticist affair dragged on decrescendo for most of the year. Never in truth a school or a movement, Vorticism was really the fabrication and the expression of Ezra Pound, his dynamic affections and coruscating energies, a forcible collocation and rationalization of his dominant current enthusiasms. The work of Wyndham Lewis now stood or vibrated at the center of these. Writing to Quinn on March 10 in a room scattered with a dozen new drawings by Lewis, Pound was intensely excited. "The vitality, the fullness of the man!" he exclaimed. ". . . Nobody has any conception of the volume and energy and the variety." He was now sure that Wyndham Lewis was a better artist than Gaudier-Brzeska, better even than Blake, "that W.B.Y. is always going on about. . . ."; only Picasso of modern artists ranked in Lewis's class. He described the work as the manifestation of the pure spirit of the new "movement":

> It is not merely knowledge of technique, or skill, it is intelligence and knowledge of life, of the whole of it, beauty, heaven, hell, sarcasm, every kind of whirlwind of force and emotion. Vortex. That is the right word, if I did find it myself. Every kind of geyser from jism bursting up white as ivory, to hate or a storm at sea. Spermatozoon, enough to repopulate the island with active and vigorous animals. Wit, satire, tragedy.

What Pound was expressing in his prodigally generous and exclamatory prose was the mirror image of his own fertilizing creativity.

Quinn had promised to arrange, probably at the Montross Gallery and probably in the late spring of 1916, a New York exhibition and sale of paintings, drawings, and sculpture of the Vorticist "group" to include works of Gaudier-Brzeska, Wyndham Lewis, Edward Wadsworth, Frederick Etchells, Helen Saunders, and

Jessie Dismorr. On March 9 Pound wrote that because Lewis feared to trust all his work on one ship "in these torpedoing times" Knewstub of the Chenil Gallery would ship the Vorticist works in two lots. On the fourteenth he presented a new scheme to load half the show as luggage upon T. S. Eliot, who was to sail on April 1 to take Ph.D. examinations at Harvard. Pound would buy him an extra trunk, see him off, and pay any extra baggage charges; Eliot's trunk alone, he thought, would hold enough good art to justify the price of admission.[54] He trusted Quinn to send a clerk to see Eliot through customs in New York. But Eliot's boat was taken off at the last minute and that part of the scheme fell through.

Quinn had espoused the show not only out of loyalty to Pound and curiosity to see the work of Lewis, but also because he saw an opportunity to get his hands on the work of Gaudier in wholesale lots. When he heard that Sophie had refused to allow Gaudier's work to be included he sent Pound an order to cancel the whole affair. Pound was horrified: "Ma che Cristo. about the Vorticist show!!! I simply CANT stop it now. The boys have sent in the stuff, and if it don't go I can never look anybody in the face again." [55] After suggesting that Quinn accept the existing Vorticist material and delay the show in New York until Sophie could be persuaded to relent, Pound capitulated and held up the shipment at the last moment. When it was too late for a spring show Quinn relented in his turn and sullenly agreed to let matters proceed. Everything went to the packers in London on April 27, in an open wagon, to Pound's horror—but the day happened to be fair. By late June when the works arrived on the *Minnesota*, Montross had backed out of his offer to hold a summer show beginning on July 10, and Quinn was stuck with the bill of $328.58 for packing, insurance, and freight.

The shipment was delivered to Quinn's apartment where Walt Kuhn and Arthur B. Davies dined with him and stayed till midnight to help check through the items. Kuhn was unimpressed with the Vorticist works, found them " 'too literary.' " [56] Montross was "yellow," Quinn charged, and he resolved never to buy from him again.[57] It was decided to hold the show in the rather drab quarters of the Penguin Club at 8 East 15th Street, a newly established rendezvous of the group of artists centering around Kuhn.

Horace Brodzky would be put in charge. In addition to the "damnably high" freight charges, Quinn now made himself liable for the cost of framing and installation. Davies offered to bear half the cost of the show but Quinn refused, feeling that the obligation, like the misjudgment, was his only. He was pessimistic about the prospect of sales and felt that he had been obscurely victimized by the course of the whole affair. "You and I were both sentimental about Brzeska," he wrote sullenly to Pound on July 1. Among other things he felt he had made a bit of a fool of himself before his New York artist friends. Pound wrote back on July 19 to say consolingly that he thought none of the artists would be disappointed at poor public sales. They would be not unhappy merely to know that their work had been inspected by Quinn, the "recognized American public."

In fact Quinn was almost the only buyer. In the first week in August he took a painting and two drawings by Etchells for £35, a set of Wadsworth woodcuts for £12, and two Roberts drawings for £16. On August 19 he took his deepest plunge with £300 for twenty-four drawings and water colors of Wyndham Lewis; a week later he paid £75 for eight additional works of Lewis. On August 25 Pound wrote to thank him for "absorbing" the pictures so generously. On September 9, with Quinn's further draft of £46 in hand for works of Etchells, Jessie Dismorr, and Helen Saunders, Pound wrote again and said he wondered if Quinn had not absorbed as much Vorticism as was good for him. On October 13 came the last formal movement of the Vorticist performance, a note from Pound that he and Charles Langdon Coburn had invented the "vortescope"—"a simple device which frees the camera from reality and lets one take Picasso's direct from nature."

Alongside all this Quinn had also been more or less cheerfully involved in Pound's literary fortunes—the creative ones aside from the editorial ones. In his letter of April 29 Pound had announced that he was about to send off the text of a collection of essays on modern literature to be called *This Generation,* and he invited Quinn to send him notice of anything he wanted praised or attacked. Just two days later he was sending to the publisher Elkin Mathews the manuscript of *Lustra,* a volume of poems, and was about to relax a bit by teasing Yeats, pretending to believe he had been taking part in the Easter Rising in Dublin. Yeats, he said, disliked republics and liked queens, "preferably dead ones." Yeats having been absent from London for three days, Pound would twit him by assuming that he had been carrying on in Stephen's Green. At the end of May Pound reported that Mathews and his printer had "struck" against the raciness of his diction in *Lustra*, objecting to "whore" rather than "prostitute" and "cuckold" rather than "trompé." Yeats had gone to Mathews's office and "quoted Donne at him" to illustrate the historical freedom of speech of English poetry.

Quinn advised Pound in the middle of May—too late—against entrusting *This Generation* to the New York publisher John Marshall, who he warned was trying to run a small business with no capital. As he liked to do periodically, Quinn quoted Henry Ward Beecher: " 'I keep making mistakes, but I prefer them to be new ones.' " [58] Quinn tried several times to see Marshall about the matter, and after Marshall had broken two appointments, Quinn called in the publisher's friend Alfred Kreymborg, who revealed that Marshall had gone off heartbroken to Canada with his young bride who was dying of tuberculosis. Marshall's office was closed and the whereabouts of Pound's manuscript unknown. On September 11, when all hope appeared to be gone, Pound wrote in terms of surprising cheerfulness: if *This Generation* was gone with Marshall then it was lost for good; no other copy of the manuscript existed. Pound supposed there were just enough "white men" in existence to keep him going on in his innocent presumption of the honorableness of the race as a whole.

Lying a good deal nearer Pound's heart than the essays of *This Generation* was the project of publishing a volume of his poems in America, which Quinn had also espoused. What Pound offered were the *Lustra* poems in the English page proofs and a selection of poems from three earlier volumes. With Pound's approval, Quinn proposed the volume first to George H. Brett of the American branch of Macmillan's. On July 14 he had to report that Brett had turned him down. Pound was not surprised to hear it, but the incident was sufficient to release some of the accumulated frustration of the advanced creative spirit making its way against older tastes and entrenched interests. He wrote at length to Quinn on

July 27 to explain the reality and the "business sense" of the opposition among commercial publishers to new spirits such as Lewis and himself: "If all your capital is sunk in Leighton and Tadema you don't encourage Cézanne and Picasso." He supposed, bitterly, that perhaps a score of people would accept his work while he was living, and after he was dead his worst work would be entombed in a textbook for incompetent students.

Such were the major concerns of Quinn's friendly dealings with Pound during 1916. Of course, there were ordinary humane matters of mutual interest. Quinn continued to worry about the effect of the war upon the artists that both men cared about. The fact that Lewis was serving in the artillery was one thing that led Quinn to buy his work in quantity and with little reluctance, and it was with Gaudier-Brzeska's fate in mind that he wrote to Pound on April 5: "There ought to be something that a man of Lewis's brains could do besides stopping a damned Prussian bullet." Nor was he comforted by the wry tone of Pound's report on August 15 that Ford Madox Hueffer was laid up in a field hospital suffering "from shell shock, or nerve shock or something due to shell bursting too close for detached and placid literary contemplation of the precise 'impression and the mot juste required to render it.'" It was the experience so fundamental to Hueffer's great Tietjens novels written after the war. Far more homely and comfortable than these tense affairs was a visit at Quinn's apartment from Pound's parents, who came in from Philadelphia on September 9, took tea, chatted, and toured his collection. The elder Pounds kept up the warmest possible relation with their baffling and distant son, and Quinn liked them much. He considered the occasion sufficiently signal to justify a cable to Ezra in London.

Two major passions were meeting in Quinn's mind in these days. His standing affection for art and artists, his wish to foster and to possess fine new work of all kinds, confronted the general positive excitement of the war, his commitment to the Allies, especially the French, and his hatred of Germany. He wanted more art and he wanted a quick Allied victory, and there was no simple way to mediate such motives. His patriotism was simple and classical and so was his connoisseur's urge, and he wished not to qualify either. The death of Gaudier shocked him and yet the soldiership of

Lewis and Hueffer impressed and excited him. The conflicting motives were dramatized perfectly in a note of March 6 from Auguste Chabaud, scribbled in pencil "entre deux coups de canon." The young French artist-soldier thanked Quinn for his draft of 2,000 francs, and continued:

> Mais assez parle d'argent. Ce qui m'intéresse dans cette affaire ce n'est pas tant la question pécuniaire (dailleurs appréciable) mais le fait, que je place plus haut que tout, d'avoir trouvé un admirateur qui a éprouvé devant mes oeuvres l'émotion que j'ai à les faire.*

The circumstances and the message were at once frightening, touching, and exhilarating. Quinn wished such a man to be an artist, and to live, but he would not have had him be no soldier. On New Year's Day of 1916 Marcel Duchamp told Quinn that both his artist brothers were on active service at the front: Jacques Villon, the painter, was an infantryman in the front trenches and Raymond Duchamp-Villon, the sculptor, was a surgeon serving with the heavy artillery. Gwen John's description of wartime Paris to Quinn was primitive and terrible:

> Paris is sad. It is dreadful to see the maimed in the streets it is still more heart-rending to see a body of the blind (but it is a rare sight). A man goes before and cries Faites place! Faites place! and the poor men follow holding on to one another.
> *[March 17, 1916.]*

Such Brueghelesque visions wrung the heart even in New York, and Quinn reacted in hotly emotional ways. He wrote Conrad in April of his outrage at the pacifistic talk of such English visitors as Laurence Housman and "a little jack-ass named Norman Angell." He vowed to find means to insult them publicly if he met them in New York. And he reiterated his vengeful sentiments toward the Germans: ". . . by God I hope that the world will never cease hating the Germans. They ought to be stained to the tenth generation and marked as an outlaw nation, a nation of murder-

* "But enough talk of money. What interests me in this matter is not so much the pecuniary question (important as that is) as the fact, which I place above all others, of having found an admirer who has felt in my works the emotion which I felt in making them."

ers. . . ." [59] His feelings of the opposite order were stirred equally deeply in the first week of September when, as a member of the Lafayette Committee to receive Ambassador Jusserand of France, he sat on the stage in front of City Hall and listened to the patriotic oratory. He described the occasion to Walter Pach:

> I do not know when I listened to anything that moved me more than that hour of speeches. There was a great big Frenchman sitting beside me who had all he could do to control himself from a breakdown. He was sobbing during the speeches. Jusserand nearly got me when he stated that Lafayette had designed the French flag, the tri-color, "The flag of Valmy, of the Marne and of Verdun"! The history of a century from the revolution to today summed up in those few words . . .   [*September 8, 1916.*]

Yet in this same period Quinn was responding willingly to appeals for help from Jacob Epstein, who was threatened with induction in London, and more particularly from his Scottish wife, Margaret Dunlop Epstein. Epstein was a New Yorker naturalized a British subject, and Quinn suggested: "There might be some defect in the naturalization, or you might say that you had conscientious scruples against warfare and escape as the Quakers do." [60] Epstein was asking not for outright exemption but merely for delay to give him time to finish several major works which he had carried to a crucial stage and which he needed to sell to pay debts and keep his family going. He "hated" conscientious objectors, his wife said.[61] He believed, however, that he was being harried into the army precipitately by a coalition of enemies who were taking advantage of his rumored German origin. Most of the appeals to Quinn came from Epstein's wife, who said Epstein would have tried to stop them if he had known of them. She was signing her cables to Quinn "Margaret Dunlop" because, she said, all cables bearing the name of Epstein were held up by the censors.[62] Epstein's father had adopted that name in New York as easier to pronounce than his Polish name, Brubinsky. "I wish to goodness he had thought of say Macdonald instead," Mrs. Epstein wrote.[63] On June 25 she cabled to ask Quinn to send cables to the Director of Recruiting in the War Office and the clerk of the Exemption Tribunal in support of Epstein's plea for deferment to finish his large works in hand,

"Sungod Venus Man Woman Maternity and the Rockdrill," in order to avoid "exceedingly grave financial hardship." Quinn sent the cables at once and supported them with a letter on June 27:

> Mr. Epstein is a really great sculptor. His inability to finish the works that he has in hand would be not only a great loss to art and in particular to English art but would be a loss to the world, a loss comparable to which the mere destruction of property or buildings would be nothing. His work as a sculptor is extraordinary.

At the same time he suggested to Margaret Epstein that she ask Pound to enlist Yeats on her husband's behalf, as Yeats was "in the way of meeting important Cabinet men like Asquith and Balfour and so on." She reported that Lord Fisher had written to the Director of Recruiting: " '. . . as you exempt piano makers who make pianos for the rich poor why not exempt Epstein to make statues for the poor rich' "; and added that, Epstein having much work to do and he having none, he offered himself as a substitute. "As the fiery old warrior is nearly 80, this is very sporting of him don't you think," was her comment.[64] By this date, July 10, Epstein had been certified fit for active service, but on August 13 he was still in suspense, and Augustus John wrote: "I sincerely hope they'll let him off."

At least the half of Quinn that cheered on Epstein's art hoped so too. On March 2, after Epstein had cabled that the Grosvenor Gallery had had an offer of £150 "for Iris bust," his bronze of Iris Tree, Quinn cabled an offer of £300 for that work plus a painted plaster figure and the *Carving in Flenite*, which Quinn described to Pound as "the head with a body like a foetus." [65] Epstein accepted that offer, as he did the offer of £250 for the marble *Mother and Child* and two bronzes, *Head of an Old Woman* and *Head of an Irish Girl*. But Quinn had refused peremptorily the offer of a portrait bust of *Mrs. McEvoy*, recollecting the original: "I don't like that type of Englishwoman. . . . She is too damned typical, dry and uninteresting for me. I like them juicier looking." [66] Something juicier, the "fine wench" Iris Tree herself, came up to Quinn's apartment to inspect her portrait bust after it had been delivered. Both she and Quinn approved, and Quinn sent the bust on to Knoedlers for exhibition there: "That will help your name something [*sic*] here," [67] he wrote Epstein. He also followed his usual practice in giving photographs of the work to F. J. Gregg and Henry MacBride for publication in *Vanity Fair* and the *Sun*. At the end of the year Epstein was still free, still at work, and still in trouble. On November 30 he cabled: "I must pay urgent debt Judgement out against me Could you cable two hundred pounds." On December 12 came a second cable from Mrs. Epstein and on December 17 a third from the sculptor. On December 19 Quinn at last cabled the money and the message that he had been away from his office for several weeks. He had been absent in Florida and Illinois, combining business engagements and family visits.

Augustus John's good wishes on behalf of Epstein were ironical in that John was one of those Epstein suspected of stirring up trouble for him in the draft. Quinn continued to have his own troubles with John which were due partly to dissatisfaction with John's treatment of him, partly to a real shift in his own taste which made John's work less interesting to him than it had been. He wrote to Judge Dowling at the end of 1916:

> Now that John is commanding high prices and is very popular, I am not so keen on buying his things. My interest has turned to other more advanced things, things that are as advanced now as John was ten years ago. [*December 29, 1916*.]

He had begun to feel that John's pictures were simply not worth their high prices to him, and he suspected that with popularity John had ceased to honor their old understanding that Quinn was to have the first refusal of everything new and important among his easel pictures. In February of 1916 Quinn reminded John's agent, Knewstub, of the Chenil Gallery, that he had sent to John £300 since September with very little to show for it. "Frankly I am getting tired of responding to hurry-up calls for money from John and then getting second choice on pictures," he went on.[68] It appeared to Quinn that in the past couple of years before his death Hugh Lane had "got all the bargains." He was thinking particularly of the portrait of Iris Tree and that of John's young son. In a long letter to Epstein of May 19 Quinn inquired first about a large limestone figure of which Epstein had sent photographs: ". . . the woman with the big breasts exposed, which might be called 'Maternity' or 'Paternity' or 'Fecundity' or 'Whoring' or 'A Chinese Goddess.' She might be a Kwanin or a madame of a house or the mother of a patriarchal family or a Venus; and anything but a virgin." He asked Epstein to look into the prices and the quality of some works of John's on show at Dowdeswell's, and then went on to develop his grievances with John at length.

Confidentially I don't think John has played quite fair with me. I never beat him down in prices; I have given him money in advance of receiving work; I have been very generous with him, and yet he has given all the bargains and the good things to others and given me the small panels, of which I have enough and too many. He parted with the painting of "Iris Tree" to Lane, although I had asked for the refusal of it. He sold Lane the "Head of a Boy" at less than half I would have paid for it. And yet he keeps offering these small panels to me that he does very easily and which are not important. I am just therefore about at the breaking point with him. The whole record is a long one, but I think he has treated me badly. . . .

I paid £900 on a big painting called "Forze et [*sic*] Amore" to John some two or three years ago, and then he painted it out. Last autumn he wanted money at a time when money was real money, and I sent him £100 and again £100, and then a third £100 on account of two large nude panels which he had in his studio and which he said he thought were the best things he had done. I got a cable from him "panels shipped." . . . But lo and behold, they were two dinky little wooden panels that aren't worth $200 apiece. . . .

I dislike above all the Café Royal gossip. When I saw that little rat [Jo] Davidson the other night it all came back to me with a revulsion of feeling. One of John's greatest limitations is his obvious fondness for it and for the admiration of mere imitators.

Still three weeks later he agreed to pay the New English Art Club £600, nearly $3,000, for John's *The Girl by the Lake*, and in early July he paid a bill to the Chenil Gallery of £962 for twelve John drawings and four of his paintings (including *The Girl by the Lake*).

Quinn's correspondence with Gwen John continued in terms of gentle intimacy and trust, though of course they had still not met. Her timidity was even less productive of paintings than her brother's arrogance, but it was a good deal easier to take. On February 12 she reported that she had just left with Pottier in Paris for shipment to Quinn a group of nine gouaches and two oils, including *La Petite Modèle,* her likeness of a little neighborhood girl whom she had persuaded to pose for some of Quinn's funds. Gwen John had been procrastinating for more than two years over a portrait of the Mother Superior, *Mère Poussepin,* commissioned by the nuns of the near-by convent in Meudon. Quinn had promised to take the portrait if it ever came on her hands; and she now said: "Your offer to take the nun strengthened me against the nuns for a long time. But as the time went by and the picture was not done I fell into a discouragement about my work and felt the nuns contempt again." The naïveté and diffidence so transparently present in her letters called forth in Quinn a rare patience and sympathy; but it was with some querulousness that he noted at the end of the year that five years of dealings with her had produced only four oil paintings for his collection.[69]

The tone of this correspondence was much different from the desultory pathos of that with his other English art-lady, May Morris. Periodically Miss Morris still sent him long letters, but occasionally her pique at Quinn's coolness and neglect showed through. In April she thanked him for his gift of four books—one of which she had liked; she had delayed to acknowledge a bundle of *The New York Times* "as I was waiting so many months hoping to hear from you."[70] She was planning three additional volumes of left-over items for the big Longmans edition of her father's works, and she continued to send Quinn proofs of her introduction to each volume; she wondered whether he was still interested. Continuing as best she could the practical side of her father's work, she was making plans for an autumn exhibition of arts and crafts at Burlington House—thinking, as William Morris had always thought, of "the national art of the future." In memory of her mother she was building two new cottages at Kelmscott, and as part of her homely war effort she had turned the Kelmscott strawberry beds into onion beds—none of which offered much deep solace for a woman still hopelessly in love with an indifferent man.

With the closing of accounts on Harriet Bryant's disorderly show at the Carroll Gallery, Quinn's direct dealings in New York for French art slackened this year. He did put 3,800 francs into three final relics of that show, Jacques Villon's *Portrait de J. B. Peintre, Acrobate,* and *Portrait de Femme,* in midsummer.[71] At the Modern Gallery on Fifth Avenue he made a major Brancusi purchase, $1,050 for *The Penguins* on January 22. Two weeks later, before the squabble over the Vorticist show had time to develop, he paid Montross $2,250 for three Cézanne water colors. He was still buying the Rouault ceramics and still having trouble with customs authorities who wanted to classify the works as "articles of utility" or "decorated earthenware." Quinn was determined to "keep the customs door wide open and the threshold lowered," as he expressed it to the artist on January 17, and he stoutly refused to pay the duty imposed. Early rulings went against him, but he finally won his point in the next year when he carried a suit in the name of the Carroll Gallery to the Court of Customs Appeal in Washington. His central argument was that the painting of the ceramics constituted an original work of art and that the mechanical process of glazing and firing did not qualify the originality, that it had no more to do with the definition of the work as art than did the varnishing of a painting.[72] The whole litigation, as usual, was carried out at his own expense. Rouault was sending him, meanwhile, charming long ramshackle letters about his life, his painting, and his writing. Quinn was touched, for example, by his account attributing his shaky health to the circumstances of his birth, which he believed had left him with a "feeble" heart: he was born in Paris on May 27, 1871, in the midst of "civil and national war," and twenty minutes before his birth his mother's bed was shattered by a cannon shot.

Quinn's only other significant purchase of continental art, $1,115 for ten works of Gino Severini, the Futurist, came in March at the Photo-Secession Gallery, where he liked to deal because he approved Alfred Stieglitz's practice of showing advanced work for little or no commission to himself. Here he also bought bits of American work outside that of his usual small circle of favorite native painters. In February he paid Stieglitz $1,200 for four water colors by John Marin, in April $460 for three of S. Macdonald-Wright's "synchromy" paintings, in July $400 for two Marsden

Hartley oils. But none of this work really answered to his taste. A few months before his death he would return the four Marins to Stieglitz to sell for $800; but they did not sell and were returned to his apartment after his death.

Of his favorite Americans, especially Kuhn, he was buying fairly heavily. He had committed himself to collect a complete set of John Sloan's etchings, and he took them as they appeared, although Sloan's etching Number 24, *Silence*, which portrayed a dead man, spoke to one of Quinn's deepest phobias. "It seems to me horrible," he wrote to Sloan on February 7. "But as I want to have a complete set of your etchings I suppose I have to have it." He paid Walt Kuhn $500 in January toward the painting *Youth*, followed by $300 in April. In May the Macbeth Gallery got $2,090 for a purchase that included two carved panels by Kuhn, three carvings by Arthur B. Davies, and three drawings and two paintings by Jules Pascin, whose work Quinn had first bought in the Armory Show and who was now a friend in New York. In July he bought Kuhn's *Woman with White Hat* for $550, and in the fall he paid him $350 for five wood carvings, then a further $250 for five drawings. Loyalty to Kuhn also led him naturally to help underwrite the expenses of the Penguin Club for rent and equipment. A bill of November 22, for example, shows Quinn presenting two black benches at $25 apiece. And it was to Kuhn that Quinn expressed himself feelingly about Dorothy Coates's epistolary style, which was not improved by the enthusiasm for Henry James which she shared with Quinn: "When she talks about a snow storm being a miracle and that 'one saw the hand of God,' it makes one feel one shouldn't read her letters too soon after a meal. . . ." [73]

The letters of 1916 between Quinn and John Butler Yeats show the continuing closeness and cordiality of their friendship as well as some sharpening and new articulateness in Quinn's aesthetic standards. On February 14 Quinn wrote to invite Mr. Yeats to dinner with Captain Mitchell McDonald, long the intimate friend of another old idol of Quinn's, Lafcadio Hearn: Mr. Yeats could dress or not, as he pleased, and Quinn would send him home in a taxi. The letter resumed several subjects about which he and Mr. Yeats had been differing amicably. He argued that Mr. Yeats had failed to rise to ancient Chinese art not because he was immune to new sensations, but because he had never taken the trouble to understand the history and the aesthetics of that art. He needed to read Binyon and Fenollosa and Morrison. Quinn reprimanded the old portraitist for having asked a friend of theirs to "explain" the cubists: that was as bad as Kenyon Cox's asking Quinn at the Cosmopolitan Club to "define modern art." Even if a definition were possible, Quinn said, it would be no help in the crucial problem which was to distinguish good art from bad. It would be aesthetically useless as Herbert Spencer's "definition of life" was ethically useless—similarly incapable of separating good from bad. Value-judgment must remain subjective, empirical, peculiar to the instance.

> We know that the secret is there, we know that the thrill is there, we know that there is such a thing as color and form and masses in relation, we know that a certain thing moves us by its nobility of design or the suggestion of movement, we know that it has the radium in it, and what we call art.

Quinn returned to his old animus against dusky pigment in painting. He invited Mr. Yeats, as a concentrated experience of bad art, to have a look at the current show at the American Art Galleries on 23rd Street, where, aside from a few modern pictures and a single redeeming Puvis de Chavannes, he considered everything, even the Rembrandts, "a collection of dirty pictures"—bad art.

Taking advantage of Quinn's permissive tone, J. B. Yeats politely declined the invitation to dinner. He was growing old, and an expedition on a winter evening was no longer a light thing for him. "The nights are very cold, and it is an effort going out in the evening, and then there is the coming back to a cold and locked up house." [74] He rebuked Quinn for his oversimplicity in calling all dark pictures dirty and thus bad art: a brown picture was no more dirty than black and white pictures, such as Rembrandt's etchings or Abbey's drawings, were "sooty." What really distinguished excellence in a work of art, he contended, was its fullness and fidelity of "imitation." He tried out on Quinn ideas which were really a continuation and crystallization of his earlier thoughts about "the finite and the infinite" in painting, sculpture, music, poetry:

The business of every artist is to get as close as ever he can to the finite, *living* in what he sees and hears. To live in the finite is to have a soul. Modern poets, to their own undoing, are always getting away from the finite into what they call the infinite, and sometimes they call it the world of ideas.   [*February 18, 1916.*]

And he amusingly misquoted Keats's famous letter to Shelley: " 'Cut out the magnanimity,' said Keats to Shelley, 'and load every rift with ore.' " *

"A poet and artist must *love* what is about him and let nothing weaken his intensity . . . ," he continued. In the long run what makes true art is the intensity of the artist's imitation of the finite, for that is the true leading to the intuitive infinite. Again Keats is audible in his thought: "The excellence of every art is its intensity. . . ." J. B. Yeats recognized varieties of susceptibility and hence of "imitation": "A passionate susceptibility means a passionate imitation, an ironical an ironical, a humorous a humorous, etc."; but he demanded that each be intense in its kind. He drew instances from his eminent sons. Jack Yeats had been drawing all his life a horse that had been badly drawn for him by an aunt when he was a child—"a ramping, roaring, rearing horse of his infant mind." And he quoted four lines of W. B. Yeats's "Down by the Salley Gardens" as a piece of passionate imitation and a show of that *"intense orderliness"* which he thought was the life at the heart of verse.

"I will write to you about a very serious matter," J. B. Yeats began his letter of April 8—Quinn's corrupt use of "ass" when he meant "arse." He traced the corruption to the lazy work of the modern Englishman, too "debilitated" to pronounce the R. The Irishman spoke of "that intelligent but much misunderstood animal with the handsome ears" as an ass, whereas the Englishman had to call him a donkey for fear of embarrassing the ladies. "In Ireland ladies know the difference between arse and ass." He recalled with delight that Defoe had written a preface to a book called *Advice to Heavy-Arsed Christians*, and suggested that someone should do an *Advice to Heavy-Chinned Presidents*: "Roosevelt has

* "You I am sure will forgive me for sincerely remarking that you might curb your magnanimity and be more of an artist, and 'load every rift' of your subject with ore." (Keats to Shelley, August 16, 1820.)

a menacing chin, threatening the wicked. German bullies and American cowards tremble at his name."

At the end of the year the two were corresponding half-seriously about a play on which Mr. Yeats had been working in a desultory way. Sending Quinn some lines of verse from his fragmentary text, he commented: "Like Homer, I have written two poems, only his are much longer." [75] On Christmas Eve he reported that he had been punished for breaking his rule against dining out by an evening of the conversation of the American "half-educated" —"about as interesting and intelligible as the barking of a kennel of dogs. . . ." In England, he said, men were educated or uneducated and one knew where one stood; but America was amorphously full of the half-educated. The educated man he defined in Arnoldian terms: "He is a man who has acquired the habit of *intellectual disinterestedness*." Though the half-educated man may have "entered the world of ideas," he is "a ruffian" in "that temple of delight": "He has no reverence for it and no tenderness. With blackguardly insistence he defiles all the sacred places." He described the tortures he had endured until nearly midnight, with only Dolly Sloan, the wife of the painter, showing any glimmers of civilization. Finally, he paid Quinn a consolatory tribute, but one with a crucial reservation: ". . . in defining the educated man I have had you and some other Americans in my eye—you chiefly—tho' you are a little too forensic." The codicil again placed J. B. Yeats in the list of those who dared to call attention to Quinn's habit of verbal bullying.

Quinn was having his own troubles in finding satisfying conversation, though he blamed most of the difficulty on the presence of women. At a dinner party which he gave for Padraic Colum and Ernest Boyd, the Irish writer who was British Vice-Consul at Baltimore, and their wives (and probably Dorothy Coates), he had "realized again," as he put the case to Ezra Pound, "how women spoil conversation."

> Not one woman in a hundred knows how to carry along the conversation well. In their desire to get into the picture they grab at the chain of conversation as it passes and then swing into autobiographies about what convent they were educated at or how their father wasn't able to give them a dot or some other

damned bit of personal gossip that no one in the group is interested in.   [*August 25, 1916.*]

The less formal roof-garden gatherings of "the Quartet" were still
going on and they were easier to manage: Quinn, Gregg, and
James Huneker were powerful enough to keep Josephine Huneker
in her place. Socially and professionally, as well as aesthetically,
it was another busy and demanding year. Yet Quinn was still
behaving fairly comfortably, complaining less of ill health or of
being "driven" than before the war. He was likely to seem healthier
and happier while he was being willingly overworked in affairs
which required a total involvement, when his own deepest sympathies were fully committed. The war and the Casement affair held
this kind of fascination and excitement for Quinn. In the two years
since he had vowed to take his nervous stomach to Baden-Baden
he had been busier than ever and had grumbled less. Legal work
took him frequently to Chicago and more frequently to Washington. He often combined his Chicago trips with visits to the Andersons in Fostoria, Ohio, to his sister Clara at her convent in Tiffin,
Ohio, and to his beloved uncle Father Jeremiah Quinlan at his
pastorate in El Paso, Illinois. He described one of his Washington
trips to Huneker: leaving New York by train at 11:08, arriving
in Washington at 4:20, "on the jump" with legal matters till
midnight, catching a return sleeper that put him in New York at
6:00 on Sunday morning, changing at home for an hour's ride in
Central Park beginning before 7:00 o'clock.

He rode as often as he could, and he was a commanding figure,
elegantly habited on his black horse which he kept stabled at Durland's near the park. Occasionally on Sunday he played golf,
vigorously but unskillfully, at the Sleepy Hollow Country Club,
or he might go for a strenuous hike on the Jersey Palisades, often
with Walt Kuhn and "El Greggo": "Have mercy, Quinn!" Gregg
would pant. Rarely, he would spend a whole Sunday in bed, reading as voraciously as he walked. Or he might lie in bed dictating
by telephone to a secretary who had been commanded to stand by.
But his commonest Sunday practice was to summon two or three
secretaries to the apartment, seat them about a round table, and
dictate to them in turn, catching up with arrears of correspondence, especially personal letters and letters on art and literary

affairs for which he had found no time in the office and which might by now have traveled back and forth in "the bag" for weeks. Many of these dictated letters ran on for a dozen or fifteen pages or even longer.

The English literary and amatory adventurer Frank Harris was now rather tenuously established in New York as an editor of *Pearson's Magazine,* and he sought Quinn's help with his journalistic career and with anticipated suppressions of his longer works. Quinn read through his two volumes on Oscar Wilde and predicted that they would escape Sumner's prosecution. He did not warm to Harris personally, and thought of him as one more nuisance, writing to Harris's other protector, Mitchell Kennerley: ". . . this business of shepherding geniuses in trouble gets very irksome." [76] By contrast he grew quickly to like and respect the Indian savant, Ananda Coomaraswamy, who came several times to the apartment with his wife to take dinner with a small party of art or literary folk and to enjoy Quinn's growing collection of oriental art and artifacts, especially Chinese. W. B. Yeats had not given Coomaraswamy an introduction to Quinn "on the ground that two capitals pelt you with introductions," but he commended him as "a handsome man with an agreeable English wife," and a knowledgeable person.[77] On experience Quinn entirely agreed.

In an angry moment in the summer of 1916 Quinn had discharged his Japanese "boy" Moto, and he soon regretted the action. He described to John Sloan the disorder in the apartment, with books and pictures disarranged and the dozens of magazines to which he subscribed in tumbling piles. Moto, too, had mastered the art of "showing" the art collection, which had long since overflowed the available wall space. It had been a relief to Quinn to be able to send deserving inquirers to Moto and to be sure that he could lay his hands quickly on any works in question among the stacks and ranks of pictures in closets or bedroom. Quinn had the kind of nerves that were set jangling by disorder of any kind, and he resolved now to try the experiment of moving out to Purchase Street for the summer and turning himself into a country gentleman, or a commuting gentleman. For years Quinn had been trying to persuade his brother-in-law, Will Anderson, the pharmacist in Fostoria, to bring his wife and daughter and settle in the neighborhood of New York, where he could see them constantly. Seducing the Andersons to New York had formed a major motive in his decision to buy Purchase Street in the preceding year, and now they gratified him by joining him for a trial of the place in the summer of 1916.

The country experiment was pretty sure to fail, given Quinn's confirmed citified habits, his neurotic fear of wasted time, and his unwillingness to trust employees. The refurbishing of the rambling, graceful house and grounds was now completed, but Quinn found it hard to take much pleasure in the fact; the process had "nearly busted" him, as he phrased it to Conrad.[78] In fact he had already told Kennerley in June that he was ready to sell out, lock, stock, and barrel; he would ask $60,000 for the house and eighty acres and all the equipment, including a car and various animals—horses, a cow, chickens. In March Kennerley had offered him "the best cow in Westchester County," a Jersey guaranteed to give fourteen to twenty quarts of milk a day. Quinn sent his farmer, Edward Carman, down to Kennerley's place with a man in the back of the wagon to lead the cow home. But on trial Carman called the cow a poor thing, scrawny and unproductive, and Quinn paid only fifty dollars for her rather than the asking price of one hundred. In spite of Quinn's complaints, Mary Anderson remembered the cow and the summer in general as a great success. There were Sunday visits from Kuhn and Gregg and Mr. Yeats, and Quinn and Kuhn labored hard in laying out a rock garden near the garage " 'à la Cézanne,' " in Kuhn's phrase. After they had finished, their neighbor, the Great Muldoon, looking to Quinn "like an oak of the forest," [79] came over to make a general neighborly inspection, and remarked, " 'Now, those rocks are too big to be moved and so they will have to be blasted out.' " [80] But Quinn was unhappy, and after the Andersons left in August, he again resolved to clear out of the house and put it up for sale, meanwhile "camping" there occasionally, with an extra bed for "an alibi"—the alibi, not the extra bed, for Dorothy Coates.[81] In point of fact it took him nearly a year to dispose of the property, to the Sunshine Holding Company of New York. If he ever bought another, he wrote to Alfred Knopf, it would not be " 'a dear old place to make over,' accent on the 'dear.' " [82]

1917

D ON'T burn your candle so fast, dear Quinn," wrote old
Standish O'Grady, recollecting at the same time Quinn's
"noble dinner" of 1914 in his honor, at which he had sat across
from Sir Hugh Lane. "We only get one each." [1] On New Year's
Day of 1917 Quinn dictated an "infernally long letter" of twelve
pages to Jacob Epstein, much of it occupied with a harassed
account of the accumulated disorder left in his office by Watson
and the line of bookkeepers who had followed him. Quinn had
found his books and files in such a state that he was driven to try
to straighten out the mess himself. Persons kept calling him on the
telephone to ask why they had not seen him recently. "Most of
the time I did not explain," Quinn wrote. "I just cursed. It generally effectively shortens the interview." In January and February
he was working frantically in the interest of munitions makers who
were being subjected to "double taxation" in the federal emergency
revenue bill. In six weeks he put in thirty-four solid days, chiefly
in Washington, on what turned out to be a lost cause. [2]

Quite apart from the law, from family and social duties, from
Irish and American politics, and from dealings for pictures and
manuscripts, his affairs with Ezra Pound were enough to keep one
man and his office busy. "That boy of mine is always springing
some surprise," Homer L. Pound wrote plaintively from Philadelphia. [3] The smallest but most exotic surprise from Pound in 1917
was his request to Quinn to look up two letters of his in his father's
safe from King Ferdinand and Queen Isabella of Spain, dated 1491
and 1492, and to put them on the market: if they should bring

more than a thousand dollars Pound promised to put half of it into the *Little Review,* with which he was now associated.[4] Pound's own letters ranged over such a variety of subjects that Quinn found them impossible to file, and he finally directed Pound to write a separate letter about each of his concerns. Pound wrote back to say he had not realized he was so "departmentalized" in Quinn's files, and to propose despairingly that his letter sent the day before be filed under " 'Ezra Pound, MESS.' " [5] Quinn worked loyally and willingly for Pound, though their labors put little in either's pocket. He defended Pound to Vincent O'Sullivan, who disliked him—lifting phrases and opinions, without acknowledgment, from a letter of November 19 he had just received from John Butler Yeats:

> He is a powerful astringent. He may inflict pain, but his pain is salutary. It is wonderful how people who do not know him hate him. I sometimes think that opposition, even hatred, is the harvest he wants to gather.[6]

W. B. Yeats, his sister Lily said, looked upon Pound "as the cock does the rising sun," but otherwise Quinn's was the only voice she had heard in his praise: "After the Kaiser he seems quite the most hated man." As his printer at Cuala Press she had found his proofreading infuriatingly casual. And when she quoted to her brother one of Pound's epistolary extravagances, " 'Oh,' said Willie sadly, 'he is violent by conviction.' " [7] Violence by conviction, or from conviction, was a line of temperament that Quinn understood and warmed to; it was one of his own standard public postures. Pound's strategy of defense by attack was also his own. But above all he respected in Pound his candor, directness, and unselfishness. Pound's causes were demanding, and they took up time Quinn could not spare; but they were seldom trivial or self-seeking. It was easy to see, and impossible not to respect, the fact that a good half of his energy was being spent in the interest of others; it was only with the left hand, as it were, that he was writing "a new long poem (really L O N G, endless, leviathanic)" [8]—the *Cantos.*

Quinn had liked Pound's English volume, *Lustra,* and had sent copies broadcast among his friends, and Pound was glad that the work itself had pleased: "I have always wanted to write 'poetry' that a grown man could read without groans of ennui, or without having to have it cooed into his ear by a flapper." [9] Quinn was trying to groom Alfred A. Knopf as the American publisher for Pound and Pound's stable of protégés, especially Eliot, Joyce, and Wyndham Lewis. By early January of 1917 Quinn had had two conversations with Knopf about Pound's poetry and prose, and he wrote on the twelfth to present Knopf formally to Pound as "not a plunger," as "a man of his word," and one who was "in the business to stay." On the twenty-fourth Pound wrote back to say he was happy to be in the hands of the publisher of W. H. Hudson and to be associated with a contemporary, a young man unbound to nineteenth-century loyalties. Two days later Pound suggested that as soon as Knopf had his own work well in hand he should undertake Wyndham Lewis's novel *Tarr* and Eliot's "little vol. of poems," the manuscript of which had also disappeared with John Marshall into the Canadian wilds, and which as the Egoist Press *Prufrock and Other Observations* became the clarion call of modernism in English verse. Both Pound and Quinn looked upon Knopf as a promising and virginal beginner who might be molded in the shape of their own tastes. Quinn put it in this proprietary way: "I am anxious to have Knopf take 'Tarr.' Now that you have gone with Knopf, the more we build him up the better—the stronger we make him in modern work the better." [10]

Quinn mentioned to Pound in his letter of January 12 that he had just received that day from B. W. Huebsch, at the request of Joyce himself, a copy of *A Portrait of the Artist as a Young Man;* that much-traveled work had at last ironically found a home in the land of the Philistines, and the "good Jew" Huebsch was about to bring it out. Huebsch appended a note: " 'I think that this work very nearly approaches genius and I trust that you will find an early opportunity to examine it.' " [11] To date Quinn's benefaction to Joyce was limited to his gift of £10 in the preceding year; now, at the sound of the word "genius" he pricked up his ears again and inquired of Pound as to the state of Joyce's affairs. Quinn had had a letter from Joyce which thanked him and referred to "some government pension"; "So he is probably on Easy Street by this time," Quinn supposed.[12] Pound assured him that this was by no means the case. Joyce's grant of £100 from the last English government, which had been solicited by Yeats and others (as usual, egged on by Pound), had been "one lump sum, not a hardy annual," [13] and Joyce deserved and needed all the help he could find.

One way both to assist Joyce and to lay hands on a bit of genius was to buy manuscripts, and Quinn set about this. His first effort involved him in an ugly epistolary quarrel. He learned that in printing *A Portrait of the Artist as a Young Man* B. W. Huebsch had worked from the printed *Egoist* sheets, with some few autograph corrections and insertions of Joyce's, and that these had been brought to Huebsch by Byrne Hackett, instructed by Harriet Shaw Weaver at the suggestion of Ezra Pound. Hackett, a Clongowes schoolmate of Joyce, and now operating the Brick Row Print and Book Shop in New Haven, had taken back the *Egoist* sheets after Huebsch's publication. Quinn wrote to Hackett on March 3 proposing that Hackett set a price, perhaps of ten or twelve pounds, on the sheets; Quinn would buy them and remit direct to Joyce. Hackett wrote back two days later: "I am quite willing to have one-half of the fine piece of philanthropy you have in mind for James Joyce." He set a price of $100 on the manuscript, then astonished Quinn by suggesting that he pay half to Joyce, half to himself. On March 8 Quinn sent $50 to Hackett and promised to send the other $50 to Joyce; but he argued bluntly that the "manuscript" was Joyce's property and neither the Huebsch nor the *Egoist* office had any right to give it to Hackett. He scoffed at Hackett's reference to having been Joyce's classmate, and continued sardonically: "Just where the alleged 'warm-hearted Irish sentiment' that might be expected, has been diffused or evaporated, it would perhaps be useless to inquire. Possibly it is the cold Connecticut-Yankee-New Haven denatured atmosphere." Hackett replied stiffly and defensively on March 12: "If the manuscript in question is not my property I have no desire to sell it to you or anyone else. You impugn my good faith in the transaction ungenerously, I think." He enclosed a check to Quinn for $75, to cover Quinn's check for $50 to himself and half of Quinn's $50 cable to Joyce—if that had been sent. He directed Quinn to return the "manuscript" to Huebsch—presumably forcibly making of any payment to Joyce an outright philanthropy. On the nineteenth

Hackett wrote: "B. W. Huebsch must decide whether you are to retain the Joyce manuscript. As far as I am concerned you have absolutely no right to do so." Quinn did redeposit the sheets with Huebsch, but only until he could get from Joyce an acceptance of his purchase. "Mr. E. Byrne Hackett has no more right to them or in them than your office cat has," Quinn wrote to Huebsch on March 20. Huebsch agreed that the sheets were Joyce's property and that their disposal was his affair.

The wrangle with Hackett had at any rate accomplished the doubling of Quinn's first proposal of $50 to Joyce, and on March 19, ill in Zurich, Joyce received Quinn's cable offering $100. He accepted gladly and cabled Pound in London to cable Quinn. Pound's cable of the twenty-second read: "Joyce accepts; money to be sent via me." Quinn did not understand all this triangulation (probably motivated by Joyce's illness and his mistrust of wartime communications), and he at first suspected that Joyce's working through Pound implied lack of faith; but Joyce's grateful and forthright letter of March 19, when it arrived, made him regret his misgivings. Quinn now collected and sent on to Pound copies of the whole correspondence with Hackett, with the suggestion that he read it and send it on to Joyce. Pound replied in doggerel on April 19:

> The ex-Irlandais that hight Hackett
> Attempted to purloin Joyce's jacket
>> But the Godly J. Quinn
>> Forestalled him in sin
> And purloined Hackett's hindpart to smack it.

I do not use these classic forms with Joyce's ease and felicity. Aliter, try again:

> In a life so lacking in condiment
> I confess I am smitten with wonderment
>> At the curious neatness,
>> At the "lightness and sweetness"
> With which Q. has smacked Hackett's fundiment.

In early April Joyce was correcting misprints, "nearly four hundred" of them, in the text of his novel; he had been sent no revised proofs. He made the corrections "in view of a possible second edition during the century." [14] He was moved to a superior limerick of his own upon the subject of his hero:

There once was a lounger named Stephen
Whose youth was most odd and uneven.
    He throve on the smell
    Of a horrible hell
That a Hottentot wouldn't believe in.

In any case, he assured Pound: "I shall go on writing, thanks to the kindness of my unknown friend and also of Mr. Quinn." His unknown friend, who was paying him an anonymous subsidy, was Harriet Shaw Weaver of the *Egoist*. Quinn's £20 for the embattled "manuscript" finally reached Joyce through Pound on April 30, and Nora Joyce, with her husband ill of glaucoma and expecting to enter a hospital for an operation, wrote on that day to thank Quinn for the money and for his *Vanity Fair* appreciation of the novel. In view of the enforced doubling of Quinn's price, Joyce wished to throw in his seven pages of corrections for *A Portrait of the Artist as a Young Man* and his single page of corrections for *Dubliners*, which Huebsch had now also taken in hand. These scraps Quinn finally received from the publisher in June.

No Irish writing since Synge's had interested Quinn so personally and directly as did that of Joyce, and as always he was stirred by the thought of an art which was being denied an audience by ingrained prejudice. He bought "25 or 30" [15] copies of the new novel and sent them to his friends in America, England, and Ireland, and he puffed the book at every opportunity. Huneker wrote of the copy Quinn had given him in the *Sun*, a long laudatory review in which he asked " 'Who is James Joyce?' " [16] Quinn set himself to answer that rhetorical question in a dictated article, which was refused by the *Sun* as too long. He then revised the piece and sent it to *Vanity Fair* on February 24, and Frank Crowninshield accepted it. In writing "James Joyce and His Book 'A Portrait of the Artist as a Young Man,' " Quinn said, his motive was to help "poor Joyce." [17] Remembering Quinn's old reputation as a universal Irish propagandist, Crowninshield proposed in March to pay Quinn's $65 honorarium for the article to an Irish charity. But the new Quinn said no, let it be French, and the small sum helped two objects of his concern when it went to the Duc de Richelieu's Tuberculosis Fund.[18] In May when he took a $100 box for a concert by the Irish tenor John McCormack and sold another to James Byrne, half the money went to the French fund and half to Irish relief.

"I think *he* is launched all right enough," Pound wrote Quinn with satisfaction on May 5 after seeing in Miss Weaver's office a batch of Joyce's American press notices. Joyce took notice of "one slight inaccuracy" in Quinn's article: *Dubliners* was not " 'refused' " by the Dublin publisher. "It was accepted, set up, printed, and then the entire first edition was maliciously burned." [19] Quinn interested himself also in the question of Joyce's health. He collected from Pound an account of Joyce's symptoms and his past treatment and carried it to a specialist in New York, who naturally advised him to consult specialists on the scene. On May 25 Quinn sent Nora Joyce a long letter of advice about eye specialists and offered another gift of £10. By the middle of May Joyce himself was able to write that a new operation had been postponed for the time, to his relief: ". . . I dislike the idea of cutting out pieces of the iris at intervals." He was quite willing to co-operate with Quinn's desire for additional manuscripts, but hampered by his circumstances. The manuscripts of the *Portrait* and *Dubliners* and the only known copy of the burned first edition of *Dubliners* were in his desk in Trieste, but he was sending on the manuscript of his play, *Exiles,* through Pound in London: "I am much honored by your proposal of buying it and am well content to leave the matter in your hands." [20] More grandly, he suggested that the play might be retyped "over there" and then "submitted to my publisher in New York for his autumn list. . . ." [21] Quinn dreamed for a time that he might find a publisher, or even a producer, but in the end he failed everywhere he tried. At the end of May Joyce confessed to feeling "superstitious" at receiving an inquiry about *Exiles* from a New York agent named L. Bloom, "for it is the name of the chief character in the book I am writing *Ulysses.*" [22] Leopold Bloom is the great soft hero of the great hard novel on which Joyce was struggling to work—writing it, "as Aristotle would say, by different means in different parts." [23]

Of *Exiles* Pound expressed himself to Quinn in uncharacteristically dubious tones. He doubted Joyce's natural powers as a dramatist, and thought it unwise to expose an imperfect play to view when Joyce's fiction was beginning to make his name. But he thought *Exiles* might possibly be an affair for B. W. Huebsch.[24] Huebsch did not think so. Having had his fingers burned so often, Joyce was not surprised. He was quite willing to have Quinn go on seeking a publisher or a producer, but he was not optimistic or in a mood to temporize: "I want a definite agreement to publish or produce by a certain date, or a refusal," he instructed Quinn on July 10. He set down the melancholy history of his experience with publishers to date. In the two years since he finished *Exiles* in Zurich in September of 1915, it had traveled to publishers or theatre managers in Turin, London, Zurich, Berne, Chicago, London again, Dublin, London for the third time, and now to New York. He reckoned that difficulties over *Dubliners* had "consumed" ten years of his life.

> It was rejected by 40 publishers; three times set up, and once burnt. It cost me about 3,000 francs in postage, fees, train and boat fare, for I was in correspondence with 110 newspapers, 7 solicitors, 3 societies, 40 publishers, and several men of letters about it. All refused to aid me, except Mr. Ezra Pound. In the end it was published, in 1914, word for word as I wrote it in 1905. My novel [the *Portrait*] was refused by every publisher in London to whom it was offered—refused (as Mr. Pound informed me) with offensive comments. When a review decided to publish it, it was impossible to find in the United Kingdom a printer to print it.[25]

In the long run Quinn's only service to Joyce's *Exiles* was the purchase of the manuscript, and even that was not managed without difficulty. On August 18 he sent off his draft for £25 for the manuscript, but before that Pound had passed on to Joyce Quinn's casual statement that he was willing to send an advance against the purchase price; Joyce had apparently thought the money en route, had become exercised at its non-appearance, and had come back at Pound for an explanation. On August 29 Pound cabled to Quinn: "Joyce Broke." On the same day, on a sheet headed "Re/ Joyce NOT Rejoice," he quoted the cable, and commented that with cables costing a shilling per word his two-word message had probably conveyed "the simple sensuous heart-throb." But Quinn was not through trying to aid Joyce, and he determined to do everything he could for him short of outright charity, which was rarely Quinn's way. He expressed his general feeling to Pound: "Poor fellow, one can tell from his letters that he is a sick man and harassed and depressed. I will do the best I can for him." [26]

Pound's services to T. S. Eliot, as usual drawing in a willing Quinn, were for the time being fewer and simpler than those to Joyce, though not less useful. Pound had been dickering with Elkin Mathews for the publication of Eliot's maiden volume of poems, but when Mathews complained of cost and risk and demanded an advance payment Pound determined to manage the matter on his own. He promised Mathews that if he was unwilling to publish Eliot's poems without a great many conditions he would find somebody else to do it. Now "officially" the *Egoist* was doing it.[27] In fact Pound had personally borrowed the cost of printing and was "being the Egoist." [28] Eliot did not know of the arrangement, nor did anyone else save Dorothy Pound and Harriet Shaw Weaver, and Pound asked Quinn to keep it in confidence. Quinn at once offered to replace Pound as "the Egoist" and to guarantee the cost of publication, but Pound refused with thanks on May 18: he believed there was little danger that the volume would fail to pay its own way. In April Pound had been thinking he would reserve Knopf as an Eliot publisher until he could do a bigger volume of poems; but on June 12 he wrote to Knopf, with a copy to Quinn, to suggest that Knopf go ahead and undertake Eliot's "Egoist" book with the few additional poems now available; after that Knopf could do Pound's own *Pavannes and Divisions*. In early August Quinn himself sent on to Knopf a copy of Eliot's "Egoist" *Prufrock and Other Observations*, commending it to his notice and remarking that he liked everything about the volume but its title. Knopf wrote back on August 17:

> I have read Eliot's little book of poems with immense enjoyment. I do not know whether it is great poetry or not. I do know that it is great fun and I like it. I surely hope that he writes some more of it so that we can make a book of him over here.

The book's mere thirty-two pages of verse struck Knopf as too skimpy for a satisfactory volume, and he preferred to wait to see what further was forthcoming. It was not until 1920 that these twelve poems were incorporated in Knopf's *Poems by T. S. Eliot.*

Again urged on by Pound, Quinn began in March to agitate with Knopf for the publication of Wyndham Lewis's *Tarr.* To Lewis he identified Knopf as "the same man who is taking Pound's two books" (*Lustra* and *Noh*).[29] He told Knopf that in his opinion *Tarr* was "a bigger thing" than Joyce's *Portrait,* but that its appeal would be less wide. At lunch on September 14 Knopf agreed to publish Lewis's novel in the spring, and when Quinn sent the news on to Lewis on the twenty-first he remarked that Knopf had taken over the contract Quinn had drawn for Pound's *Lustra*: "the clearest and best arranged publisher's contract he had ever seen," and had had it printed for steady use.

To encourage Knopf to bring out the Pound-Fenollosa "Noh" book and the volume of Pound's poems promptly, Quinn promised to buy personally forty copies of one and fifty of the other. At the same time, late in March, he proposed to Knopf that they issue a printed pamphlet or brochure on Pound's work as a means of introducing him at once to a wider American audience. Knopf accepted the notion, with the stipulation that Quinn would pay $80 and Knopf $20 of the projected cost of $100. Quinn was irritated when Knopf confirmed in writing their telephone agreement to this effect.[30] Pound was naturally grateful to hear of these developments, and he wrote on April 17 with his standard candor: "I can only say that I appreciate the cash and energy you are putting into booming my stuff. I will try to give you a run for your money." Two days later he summed up his fiscal situation: ". . . my balance consisting of £7/15 belonging to Roberts, £6 belonging to the committee on the production of Japani-Celtic-mask-dancing-Ainley-Itow-Hawkswell drama, £1/17/6 personal." Pound promptly nominated Eliot to compose the text of the brochure but insisted that it must remain anonymous, a course for which he had his own good reasons: ". . . I want to boom Eliot, and one cant have too obvious a ping-pong match at that sort of thing. (Not unless one is Amy Lowell and J. G. Fletcher.)"[31]

Pound finally forwarded the text of the brochure, Eliot's later famous little essay "Ezra Pound: His Metric and Poetry," on September 9, and saluted it as a sound and unsentimental piece of work, if slow in coming. Pound himself had made three deletions in Eliot's text. He thanked Quinn again for "inspiring" the publication. Both Pound and Quinn wished to use as a frontispiece for *Lustra* and for the brochure the bold black-ink portrait drawing of Pound which Gaudier-Brzeska had made while they were friends in London before the war. But Knopf did not like the drawing and predicted that its "freakishness" would drive off buyers. With Knopf sitting in his office, Quinn dictated a letter to Pound detailing his objections.[32] Pound was angry and adamant. Knopf agreed to use the drawing in the brochure but not in the book of poems, but later withdrew that concession. Nor did he like the anonymous authorship of the pamphlet. Pound lashed out at publishers in a letter to Quinn late in the year: all publishers were bad in one way or another, and Knopf was merely representative; hence his own habit of falling back on Quinn's hospitality and energy.[33] But by this time both publications were in print, and the Gaudier-Brzeska drawing appeared in the pamphlet and in one hundred copies of *Lustra* which were specially printed and bound for Quinn. By November 20 too Quinn's part of the cost of the brochure had grown to $130, and on that day he offered Knopf another $30 as his share of the cost of binding the pamphlet in boards; next day Knopf agreed to his share.

The actual contract for *Lustra* had been returned by Pound to Quinn on March 24; details of the publication occupied the two of them during most of the year. Pound wrote at length on April 17 of the "long and comic" history of the English volume and of what he wished to accomplish and avoid in the Knopf publication. Elkin Mathews in London had ultimately supplied six sets of proofs of Pound's full text, 2,000 copies of a "privately printed" edition containing all but four poems, and the "public edition, castrated and useless." All this backing and filling had been made necessary by moralistic objections to Pound's text raised by Mathews and his printer. In order to persuade the American printer that he was being offered the actual text of Mathews's edition, Pound had "with low cunning" sent on to Quinn for transmission to Knopf a clean set of the six "undiluted" proofs. Pound charged Quinn to make sure that Knopf received, and printed, nothing less than the "uncastrated" *Lustra*— plus the intended additional poems from his earlier volumes. When this was accomplished Quinn was welcome to keep the Mathews proof sheets. The whole affair with Elkin Mathews, Pound thought, could one day make a part of his " 'Reveries over Asshood and Imbecility' or whatever else my reminiscences of a happy life are to be entitled." He was playing irreverently upon the title of Yeats's first volume of memoirs, "Reveries Over Childhood and Youth."

At the end of the Knopf volume would appear "Three Cantos of a Poem of Some Length"—Pound's "leviathanic" *Cantos* which now number well over one hundred and are still in process of composition in his old age. In an "onrush of vigour" in May Pound cut the long version of the poems which were to appear in *Poetry* in three issues beginning in June, from twenty-four to eighteen pages for the new book.[34] In his office Quinn had the manuscript retyped and set to work to edit it himself, making numerous suggestions as to punctuation, all of which Pound accepted as "improvements." [35] When Quinn queried his word "mælid," * Pound said the word was correct as written, and explained his reference. By discovering that mælids were nymphs of the apple trees he had taken over a bit of new property in Greek mythology, and had crowded out even Richard Aldington who had thought the word referred merely to ordinary, uninhabited apple trees.[36]

Quinn extended his editing, in fact, to the whole text of *Lustra and Earlier Poems*, and with a pertinacity that Knopf found trying. On August 14 he sent Knopf a twelve-page letter of suggestions and corrections on the proofs. He recalled how in the past he had served the texts of Yeats, Synge, and Lady Gregory in the same way. When Pound began to see the records of Quinn's assiduousness he wrote feelingly of his gratitude for the extraordinary pains Quinn was taking for the shape of his pages.[37] As Quinn con-

---

* Light: and the first light, before ever dew was fallen.
 Panisks, and from the oak, dryas,
 And from the apple, mælid,
 Through all the wood, and the leaves are full of voices,
 A-whisper, and the clouds bowe over the lake,
 And there are gods upon them,
 And in the water, the almond-white swimmers,
 The silvery water glazes the upturned nipple,
  As Poggio has remarked.
 (Canto III, lines 9–17)

tinued the minutiæ of his attentions Knopf began to levy charges for further corrections. Pound wrote on September 18 to express regret that Knopf had charged $20 for extra corrections, and to assure Quinn that any excellence in the book's appearance would be of his making. He appended a "Special detachable supplement":

> I hereby, being in my right mind, sound in wind and probably sound in limb, compos mentis, give to John Quinn, father of his country, unlimited right in making all such decisions re/ format, contents etc. of my books published in America, such decisions as have to be made in a hurry and which it is too damd a bother to wait writing to England about.

As Knopf continued to grumble at what seemed to him niggling alterations, Quinn admonished him: "A printer has not always the excuse of the girl who had the illegitimate child and excused herself because it was such a little one." [38] When Knopf wondered if Quinn had really considered one of his typically categorical judgments, Quinn wrote coldly that he never expressed an opinion on a piece of literature or a work of art without examining it: "My opinions are my own." [39]

Because he did not like their appearance on the page, Quinn paid Knopf an extra $25 to reduce to ordinary size the large initial capital letters with which the poems had been set up.[40] For three days in September the two bickered more or less amicably over the use of Knopf's "Borzoi," the engraved running dog which was already his emblem. Quinn wrote on the nineteenth that he did not like the symbol and did not want it on the title page of *Lustra*. Knopf replied next day: ". . . I have never published a book, and never will publish a book that does not have this dog on the title page. It is my trade mark. . . ." On the twenty-first Quinn wrote that he had picked up that day in Scribner's book shop a Knopf publication of 1917, William Archer's *God and Mr. Wells*, which showed no dog on the title page, "primo or verso, front, rear, middle, top, bottom, back or side." Knopf capitulated: "You've got me. There shall be no dog on the title page of Lustra." [41] On November 14 Pound held in his hands the first two copies of the book and was delighted with the look and feel of it.[42] He thought it "very handsome" of Quinn to fulfill his bargain to buy fifty copies of *Lustra*.[43] Quinn's copies were specially bound and included, in contrast to the ordinary edition, the Gaudier-Brzeska frontispiece; and he apparently bought nearer a hundred than fifty.[44]

En passant, as it were, during all of this Knopf had brought out in June, using sheets imported from the English Macmillan edition of January, the Pound-Fenollosa *'Noh' or Accomplishment: A Study of the Classical Stage of Japan;* and he had accepted for publication in 1918 the manuscript of Pound's collection of prose essays to be called *Pavannes and Divisions*, which Pound had sent at the end of August. With these matters Quinn had for the time little to do. Pound's new association with the *Little Review*, on the other hand, was a demanding affair for both of them. Bearing in mind Quinn's standing offer of £150 per year as a subsidy for any journal in which he chose to interest himself, Pound had gone on with the *Egoist* while sorting out his "varied and divergent propositions." [45] The *Egoist* ladies allotted him four pages each month, or eight pages if he paid an extra £3. What Pound yearned for was an organ in which he could speak freely for himself, in which he had a free hand editorially, and in which he could push the work of the men who interested him most, especially now Eliot, Joyce, and Lewis. The plan of Quinn's subsidy was to pay Pound himself a small steady allowance and to give him a modest sum which he could pay out for manuscripts. The young editors of the *Little Review*, Margaret Anderson and Jane Heap, (or jane heap as she always signed her name), sounded out Pound at the beginning of the year on the idea of acting as their European editor, and Pound scrutinized their journal and asked Quinn's advice as to their bona fides. Pound was attracted by the nerve of the young women in printing half the pages of one issue blank because they had not found work of a quality to satisfy them: such standards and such bravery spoke directly to him. But he wanted to be sure the *Little Review* girls were serious handmaidens of art and not mere spawn of a self-indulgent and unproductive American bohemianism. He shared with Quinn an old disenchantment with what they called "Washington Square" and what would soon stretch to "Greenwich Village." Quinn was particularly bitter about this phenomenon. It was not the hard center of art where he wished to work; and furthermore it had destroyed the usefulness, as he saw the case, of his partner Sheffield: dangling about "Washington Square" had ruined Sheffield as a lawyer and as a man. Quinn phrased his disgust at length in a letter of January 12 to Pound:

> I don't know whether you know the pseudo-Bohemianism of Washington Square. It is nauseating to a decent man who doesn't need artificial sexual stimulation. It is a vulgar, disgusting conglomerate of second and third-rate artists and would-be artists, of I.W.W. agitators, of sluts kept or casual, clean and unclean, of Socialists and near Socialists, of poetasters and pimps, of fornicators and dancers and those who dance to enable them to fornicate—But hell, words fail me to express my contempt for the whole damned bunch. They have neither culture nor reticence nor pride. All then [*sic*] can do is talk and talk about art and litera-choor. The women dress badly; their hair looks greasy and unkempt; and they're either whores or near-artists or fifth-rate kept ones, and they're altogether a pathetic and disgusting bunch. Words fail me when I think of them. A self-respecting real artist like Arthur Davies or Walt Kuhn wouldn't be caught dead within gunshot of the damned place. I'd rather scrape up manure on the street than endure their nauseating drivel at a table for an hour. That is the kind of stuff that Sheffield apparently wallows in, and naturally after hours of talk of that sort, and then dancing, and then fornicating, he isn't any good the next day, or the next day. There have been times when I couldn't stand him in the room, when his efforts to keep awake were painful to look at.

Pound wrote that he too was "suspicious of Washington Sq."; and he took note of Quinn's vehemence: "You seem at times a bit more than suspicious. Bloodydamdownright certain you seem sometimes about N.Y.'s bo-hemian talent." [46]

By late March, after the *Little Review* editors had proposed to give him a free hand as European editor and to print 5,000 words a month of his choice, Pound determined to give them a trial for a year or two, with Quinn's £150 per year to come directly to Pound as paymaster of his authors.[47] He already had promises of manuscripts from Yeats, Joyce, Eliot, Lewis, and Hueffer. By mid-May he had still not had a response from Thomas Hardy or Anatole France—"But then we have not set up as a journal of archæology." [48] Quinn cabled his willingness to come through with the £150 subvention, and on May 5 Pound confided his scheme for manipulating both the *Egoist* and the *Little Review* in the interest of his movement. He planned to install Eliot as proprietor of their mutual concerns on the *Egoist*, and to go on contributing "strengthening" articles himself; Joyce's work he would print in both the *Egoist* and the *Little Review*, thus securing both the English and the American copyright. He was thinking of the *Egoist* as his locus for argument, the *Little Review* as his locus for art. In March he was already sending in manuscripts to the *Little Review*. Yeats had promised eight poems for the June number and others later, and Pound reckoned those would help out with the "cultured" reader. He expected to secure parts of Joyce's current novel, *Ulysses*, and of Hueffer's *Women and Men*, which had been lying unfinished for six years. Lady Gregory promised a play. On April 18 he wrote modestly: "I think with Yeats' poems, Lewis, Joyce, Eliot, and the chance of a few 'young', the 'Little Review' is worth going on with." At the same time, "wroth with the editorial in 'Poetry' on the same topic," he had submitted an article scoffing at the notion that patrons could "create artists": "H. Monroe seems to think that if her Chicago widows and spinsters will only shell out she can turn her gang of free-versers into geniuses all of a once-ness." [49] He hoped Quinn would not be hurt by such remarks and would realize that he had in mind a cruder kind of patronage. But he did not hesitate to give a direct rebuff to Quinn, who had sounded out Huneker in New York for a contribution. He warned Quinn that he had no right to accept anybody's manuscript, though of course they would look sympathetically on his suggestions. If Quinn found himself under pressure, Pound suggested, he could excuse himself by explaining that Pound was a vile-tempered man who had insisted on "ABSOLOOTLY no INTERFURRENCE." [50]

In the same letter Pound sent on a charming anecdote of neighborhood loyalty to his concerns:

> The little, 55 year old old maid who keeps the cake shop round the corner, has subscribed [to the *Little Review*] and put up a placard. She looked at the placard:
> "But Mr. Yeats and Mr. Lewis don't go together, do they?"
> I said, no, only in that they are each of them the best of their kind.

"I *quite* agree with you," she says. Would that half the "intellectuals" knew as much. She has read the "Gaudier" and used it as Christmas presents to her friends. I think she objects to selling food to anyone who isn't "doing something." i.e. in one art or another.

And his anecdote of the treatment he received from the widow of Ernest Fenollosa showed the kind of company in which he wished to place Quinn. After three weeks' acquaintance, knowing that her husband would have wanted his work completed and that he cared more about the poetry than the philology, she had given Pound a free hand to edit and publish Fenollosa's papers, had given him the right to any profit, and had found £40 from somewhere for him to go on with. "There *are* some white folks in the world," he reflected.[51]

Pound was willing to put Margaret Anderson among the white folks when he discovered she had the nerve to refuse manuscripts, even some of the early ones he had accepted before he was certain he could enlist writers of the stature of Yeats and Lady Gregory. He reckoned they would be able to "pull together," and could make the magazine "good, not merely mediocre." [52] By now Quinn had come to know the *Little Review* editors and reacted in opposite ways to the two. Jane Heap he dismissed as "a typical Washington Squareite" but to Margaret Anderson he was sharply attracted. She was handsome and beautifully dressed and he guessed her age as about thirty: ". . . a woman of taste and refinement and good looking," he described her to Pound. He feared trouble to come, however, from temperamental hardheadedness: "They are both wilful women, not bad tempered, but just wilful, and I don't think they are very receptive to ideas." [53] When Quinn, Margaret Anderson, and Jane Heap got together there were three hard heads in the room. A few months later he was still warmly stirred by Miss Anderson, and one feels in his new description of her to Pound a yearning for a more intimate acquaintance: "She is a damned attractive young woman, one of the handsomest I have ever seen, very high-spirited, very courageous and very fine." [54] He was willing to extend his praise of Miss Anderson's spirit to her companion: ". . . it is all to their credit that they are making this uphill fight decently and almost alone. I don't know that I have seen any two women who were less maudlin, less sentimental and slushy about it, and more courageous."

Pound was soon caught in the inevitable crossfire between Quinn and the two young women. They complained to Pound in the spring of Quinn's penuriousness, doubted his aesthetic judgment, and noted the carelessness and vulgarity of his way of discussing art and literature. Pound's letter to Margaret Anderson defending Quinn and counseling modesty and patience tells one a great deal about both men and their true relationship. His letter begins with the caution: "ONLY don't go wrong about Quinn." [55] He continues: "Quinn made me mad the first time I saw him (1910) [the Coney Island episode]. I came back on him four years later, and since then I have spent a good deal of his money. His name does NOT spell Tightwad." He tried to explain that Quinn was not a rich man in the usual American sense of the term, but a man trying to do a great deal out of current income: "He has what he makes month by month, and most of it goes to the arts. I know part of what he does, and I know somewhat of how he does it. . . ." The £150, or $750, of Quinn's subvention, Pound informed them, had been "my figure, NOT his." His desire, as always, had been to keep his artistic and editorial "independence" as nearly absolute as possible, to carry on with an indispensable minimum of outside assistance: "The point is that if I accept more than I *need* I at once become a sponger, and I at once lose my integrity." Quinn was providing him with the indispensable minimum, and Pound was grateful: "I wish there were one or two more like him." He further warned Miss Anderson not to underestimate Quinn's cultural sense, or to mistake his bluster for ignorance:

> I think also Quinn may know more than you think. He works very hard and I think rather excitedly and his talk after hours may not have the precision a sentence would have if a man had nothing to do but write art criticism and if he took a day to a paragraph. . . .
>
> I don't know whether his talk about art is like all American talk about art, but his *act* is a damn sight different.
>
> Don't insist on his toning down his enthusiasms to a given foot rule.

Pound cautioned Margaret Anderson not to allow Jane Heap to "cheek Quinn too much," and since those two had taken a dislike to each other, he advised Miss Anderson to conduct any necessary negotiations with Quinn herself. If Miss Heap did meet Quinn she might bear in mind, whatever her own opinion of his artistic judgment, "that some of the best living artists think a great deal of it. NOT merely because he buys their stuff." Margaret Anderson still remembers John Quinn as "the most irascible man I've ever known." [56] On this count, at this time, Pound quoted "Old Yeats" who had called Quinn " 'The kindest, most generous, most irascible' of men"; and concluded for himself: "I have never known anyone worth a damn who wasn't irascible." All in all, a salutary and illuminating set of opinions. But they had little permanent effect upon the increasingly tense relationship between Quinn and the two young women.

"But they are not business women," Quinn had concluded his account of October 31, and that was the heart of the matter for him, finally. It was not only that they were casual and unsystematic in business affairs—Quinn could forgive a certain amount of slovenly bookkeeping; but he also thought they were philosophically bad business women, contemptuous of advice and immune to instruction and hellbent to achieve their ends, egoistic if high, with a lofty or muddling superiority to practical realities. For the time being Quinn played along more or less patiently. He interested Kuhn and Davies in taking over the "art side" of the *Little Review*, and set up a dinner for Kuhn, Miss Anderson, Miss Heap, and himself to explore the idea. But there were mutual misgivings, and the idea was abandoned. On September 21 Quinn reported to Pound that he had found the "girls" "hard-up" recently and had given them $150. He knew they had had another $150 from a woman in Chicago because they had come to his office to cash her check—having no bank account of their own. "I like the spunk of the two women, their industry, their courage," he still felt. He promised to do his best to round up supplementary donors to the magazine, a few men who would be willing to guarantee $250 or $500 each. On November 1 Walt Kuhn telephoned to say that the editors had just been in to see him at the Penguin Club and had begged $30 to take their new number to the press; Kuhn had "practically promised" the money, and so of course it fell to Quinn to send up the $30, by messenger.[57] Meanwhile Quinn was well enough pleased with the actual contents of the magazine, at least with Pound's side of it. To Wyndham Lewis on September 21 he expressed approval in a characteristic idiom: ". . . your things and Pound's and Eliot's contributions are alive and kicking and full of radium."

But trouble was impending, and it was actually a story of Lewis's which inaugurated the *Little Review*'s official difficulties. Quinn had been warning of possible censorship, but Pound was at first both stoical and defiant, writing to Quinn on October 4 that he preferred, rather than capitulate, to run boldly on for the two years of Quinn's subsidy and then give up if necessary. He figured that two years with no compromise would establish some sort of record anyway. The young New York editors took and held the same stand, though Quinn warned them insistently that they faced certain suppression unless they softened their editorial voice and voluntarily censored some of the texts they were printing. Now, when the October 1917 issue of the *Little Review* was suppressed, ostensibly for printing Lewis's "Cantleman's Spring Mate," Pound was in a rage: "I can not have literature stopped merely because Mr. Comstock suffered from a psychic disease, now accurately diagnosed by psychic-physicians; or because others follow in his arse-marks." [58] Yeats, he reported, gaily thought the suppression a piece of "great luck"—it would be the making of the magazine. Pound wondered what Quinn would make of it all, and he was afraid the affair would put him to a great deal of further trouble.[59] That much, in any case, was certain: Quinn would not only have to argue their courses with the editors but defend them in court. Quinn himself suspected that their troubles followed as much from their political position as from their censorable texts, from their defense of the radical Emma Goldman, for example, and from their general pacifist slant. These were views with which Quinn, with his traditional kind of patriotism, could not possibly sympathize; he saw them as cynical, irresponsible, muddle-headed—typical "Washington Square" stuff. Published views of their kind, he thought, were leading the federal authorities to look at every issue of the magazine with a hostile eye and to seek out any actionable material.

The *Little Review*'s most imposing achievement, and the grand cause of its difficulty, was just about to manifest itself. In August James Joyce's glaucoma had struck again with such force that he had after all to submit to an iridectomy on his right eye late in the month. Thereafter he was able, with difficulty, to complete the first three episodes of *Ulysses*, the great segment he called the *Telemachiad*, and these he sent in December and January to Pound for transmission to the *Little Review*. The force of the experience of reading them jolted Pound into his Artemus Ward idiom in his letter to Joyce on December 18: " 'Wall, Mr Joice, I recon your a damn fine writer, that's what I recon'. An' I recon' this here work o' yourn is some concarn'd literature. You can take it from me, an' I'm a jedge.' " [60] When Margaret Anderson received the *Telemachiad* from Pound in February she was properly ravished, and saluted it: " 'This is the most beautiful thing we'll ever have. We'll print it if it's the last effort of our lives.' " [61] Foreboding censorship, Pound had already been writing Quinn uneasily about Joyce's text. "The Joyce is worth being suppressed for," he wrote on December 29, but he was already troubled about its potential cost to Quinn: "I don't think it or anything else is worth taking up such swathes of your time defending." He proceeded to cases: "Also is urination lascivious. . . ." There was no question what Joyce referred to, "under the softened and refined term 'water.' " He went on plaintively, "Still I don't think this would lead to copulation by the reader, or accelerate such action on his part—or her part."

Pound's besetting pitiful desire, as he kept writing to Quinn, was simply to "print some good prose," and he knew he would never get his hands on a lither prose than Joyce's. He had begun to feel, he said, that Quinn and his own father were the only Americans capable of sympathizing with his motive.[62] What Pound meant by good prose emerges from several statements in his letters of this interval. Early in May, searching W. B. Yeats's rooms in London during Yeats's absence in France for a manuscript that was not there, he came across a heap of letters from J. B. Yeats in New York, and he pounced upon them with the thought that he could do a supplementary volume to the letters he had edited for the

Cuala Press earlier in the year.[63] Two weeks later, before he had
begun to study the letters, he wrote of his feelings about Yeatsian
prose and the problem of editing it. He thought W. B. Yeats had
been wise to name him to edit his father's letters: both father and
son had minds "a bit wooly at the edges," and if Willie had done
the editing he would have left "nebulæ." [64] But when he actually
got into the letters a few weeks later he was dismayed to see the
consequences of Mr. Yeats's seduction by the idea that he was now
writing for publication: he had now begun trying to "explain" his
ideas and the result was a fatal new "journalistic" wordiness and
abstractness.[65]

At the end of November, after Quinn had sent him some of the
lush effusions of his friend Michael Monahan ("Editor and Proprietor of *The Phoenix*, Norwalk, Connecticut"), Pound addressed
to "J. Quinn SHEET ANCHOR" a response which spelled out his
notions of right style:

> Somebody ought to tell him to TRY AT LEAST TO WRITE THE
> LANGUAGE HE TALKS. . . .
> Good prose is presumably just one's talk, with the edges
> trimmed, with the redundancies removed, with the order made
> perhaps a little simpler, a little more lucid, with chance am-
> biguities removed. . . .   [*November 28, 1917.*]

Early in 1917 Quinn tried to distinguish for Pound between the
two American artists who were trying to help him make something
of his show of Pound's Vorticist mates. Arthur B. Davies, often
referred to as "A.B.D.," was "a difficult person" but "one of the
best artists that we have"; whereas Kuhn was "a fine fellow, just a
great big boy," but one who would "go far." [66] The Penguin Club
at 8 East 15th Street had been formed by Kuhn and a few artist
friends after Kuhn had quarreled with the members of the Kit
Kat Club. Davies and Quinn helped to fit it out as a modest lounging place and show room, and it was there that the Vorticist show
finally held forth for three weeks in January, including the pieces
that Quinn had already agreed to buy. Horace Brodzky was installed as clerk of the works, and a few other young artists helped
with details, but essentially the affair remained Quinn's one man
show. He composed and proofread the catalog, saw to the sending

of two thousand publicity postcards, and bore all the new expenses, amounting to about $200. When the show closed the unsold works were returned to Quinn's apartment for storage; then they were carted downtown once more for an auction at the Penguin Club on November 10, when Quinn submitted to buy eighteen last items for $952.50.

The main beneficiary in this process was Wyndham Lewis, who had warmed Quinn's heart by writing from a severely functional address, "R.A. Mess, Hut Town, Lydd, Kent," shortly before going across to the front in France:

> . . . now let me say how much I appreciate your action in buying my drawings, and all the kindness and interest you have shown in my work and my friends'. . . . I see what it means for a man to be angel enough to find himself invariably on the side of the angels. Your support is at once a privilege and of incalculable use to the few artists with whom I am associated here: let me speak for them. [*January 24, 1917.*]

In addition to what he had bought the summer before when the works first arrived from Pound, Quinn now agreed to pay £100 for Lewis's *Kermess* and *Plan of War* and a further £61 for a group of drawings, and he promised to wait for subsequent work of Lewis's in a receptive frame of mind. When he learned from Pound that Lewis had done some "obscenities," he wrote for a selection of those to add to his small subterranean collection of such things: "I don't believe in obscenity for obscenity's sake in art. But I have got some peaches by Pascin, and if Lewis's are as good as Pascin's I should like to have them." [67] On August 21, Pound wrote that Lewis had been in and out of hospital and was now back in action: "Last note said he had his respirator on for two hours without break, parapet of one of his battery's guns knocked off, and general hotness." But late in the autumn Lewis was recommended by Lord Beaverbrook for appointment as a war artist, and Pound suggested that is might help to expedite the matter if Quinn cabled "congratulations" to Beaverbrook on the idea.[68] On the last day of the year Quinn did cable Beaverbrook at great length. Now Pound wrote that Lewis had been attached to the Canadian forces as a war artist for a three-month period, capable of extension, and

Quinn was well pleased. He still did not like the idea of artists facing bullets directly.

Of Walt Kuhn's own work Quinn continued to buy steadily. In January 1917 he took nineteen etchings for a total of $125, and in the next month gave $500 for two wood carvings, *Triptych* and *Head of Boy*. In August he paid $350 for two water colors and a pastel, plus a last installment of $200 for Kuhn's large oil *Youth*, making a total of $1,000 for this work which Quinn had possessed since June of the preceding year. In December thirteen etchings came to $130. From Kuhn's show at the Montross Gallery in March Quinn had taken the big canvas, *The Tragic Comedians*, four by eight feet, at a price of $1,250, but he did not pay for it until this winter—$750 in January and $500 in February. Thus his direct payments to Kuhn in just over a twelvemonth came to at least $2,655.

In April occurred one of the very rare sales from Quinn's collection when Martin Birnbaum, agent for Scott and Fowles of New York, disposed of the nine big Conder panels on silk which Quinn had thought of installing in an elegant music room some day. It was the end of that dream, but the $13,500 realized gave him extra cash to turn where he most wanted to turn, toward French art of the present and future. His taste was defining itself more and more confidently away from the sentimental and literary and illustrative in art, toward a more strictly abstract and painterly set of values. "The further I progress in my feeling for art," as he put it to Shane Leslie in his February 16, 1917, letter, "the less I care for subject pictures." In leaning toward French modernism and the School of Paris, he had now the patriotic motive as well, and America's entry into the war stirred him as much as anything else by the thought that the new civilization was coming to the aid of the old—an old culture demonstrating its perennial youth by the daring and vitality of its art. Quinn's correspondence of this period with the French artists repeatedly develops these themes. *"Art is eternal and war accidental,"* Georges Rouault wrote him on September 6; Quinn liked to believe that in buying French art in wartime he was serving both the eternity and the accident on the side of the angels. Quinn wrote Rouault that he believed himself to be the only person in America who had bought his work, including two paintings from the Bourgeois Gallery in the spring of 1916 and all of his works at the Carroll Gallery except one which had been presented to Walter Pach; but he predicted a better future: "Like many other fine artists, your works do not seem to have a wide, general appeal. But some day I think you will come into your own. I liked them very much." [69]

The desultory "show" at the Carroll Gallery dragged on, with Quinn virtually the only purchaser, and with Walter Pach finally taking over the custody and responsibility for the remaining works in September. Quinn had bought his first example of the mysteriously spiritualized works of Odilon Redon, *Roger and Angelica*, at the Armory Show four years before. Seeing more of Redon at the Carroll Gallery he was still attracted, and in February he took six new works from Miss Bryant at 16,300 francs. Then in September he took three of the four paintings remaining, *The White Bouquet* at 2,500 francs and *Apollo* and *Design for a Stained Glass Window* at 2,000 francs each. On November 19 he wrote to the widow of the artist, who had died the year before at 76, that he now happily possessed a collection of ten of her husband's oils, a "rather varied collection" though there was some similarity among the flower pieces. Sending back her thanks on December 16, she invited Quinn to make a trade one day if he wished: "Si vous trouvez que dans l'ensemble de votre collection d'Odilon Redon, vous avez trop de fleurs, vous pouvez, après la guerre, lorsque vous viendrez en France échanger chez moi des fleurs contre un autre tableau." * Of the works which the great Paris dealer Vollard had consigned to the Carroll Gallery Quinn bought in March Picasso's *The Women*, massive Negro-classical figures, at 6,000 francs, or about $1,200, and three paintings of Vlaminck at 1,050 francs. To Vollard he expressed his rage at the scrupulosity of the Allies in refusing to send their armies through the neutral countries: the Hun had been hampered by no such gentility.[70]

Sentimentally loyal to the Frenchman and artist Auguste Chabaud, although he had lost most of his interest in his work, Quinn

* "If you find that in your collection of Odilon Redon as a whole, you have too many flower pieces, you can, after the war, when you come to France, make an exchange with me of some of the flowers for another painting."

paid the Carroll Gallery 3,600 francs in February for the six Chabauds remaining after two years of the "show." Madame Chabaud wrote him of the pride and terror of having two soldier sons. Auguste Chabaud replied *aux armées;* incredibly enough, he was painting calmly in Paris during every brief leave, and he wrote: "I do not doubt but that my art, tempered in the sources of collective emotions, will come out of this war stronger than before." [71] By the end of May Quinn knew that the painter's brother had died at Verdun. To André Dunoyer de Segonzac Quinn sent 2,200 francs for the single painting and the ten drawings he had taken since his earlier purchase. Thanking him for both purchases, Segonzac wrote appropriately from a *Section de Camouflage.*

Aside from this gleaning at the Carroll Gallery Quinn had given $1,000 for Brancusi's marble *Portrait of Mme. P.B.K.* at the Modern Gallery in early March. A few days later he wrote to the sculptor himself to offer him 3,500 francs if he would make for him a bronze of the marble bust which Arthur B. Davies had bought two years previously at the Photo-Secession Gallery. Quinn gave the work the title of "The Woman with the Goitre." Brancusi agreed to the proposal on June 20 and enclosed a drawing of the goitre-woman. The work was properly called *A Muse,* he said, but he did not object to Quinn's title: "Muses always have something distinct about them." Brancusi's ravishing marble *Mlle. Pogany* already sat among Quinn's treasures, and the *Muse* would make her an admirable companion.

It was through Jules Pascin, the Rumanian-Parisian artist who had washed up in New York, that Quinn now met in March the man who quickly became a good friend and his most useful and trusted agent during what remained of his time as a collector. This was Henri-Pierre Roché, called by Leo Stein "the great introducer" —a French painter and journalist, in old age to become a novelist, who was widely acquainted in the European art world and a general operator among artists, dealers, and collectors. Pascin introduced Roché first to Quinn in his charming pidgin-English in a letter on February 28: "A french writer, who is at present on a government mission here and is an intim friend of all the french artists presentet in your collection and knows John, Epstein, Mme. Lamb etc to verry well, would like verry much to get a chance to see your collection." On March 6 Quinn entertained Roché at dinner at home along with the Pascins, Walt Kuhn, Mrs. Coomaraswamy, and Dorothy Coates. He liked Roché, who turned out to be a tall thin man with sleek red hair and big ears, well enough to wish to see more of him.

Quinn had bought enough of Pascin's wittily sensual drawings to owe him $1,500, and he paid off $800 of this on March 2. In the summer, when Pascin was hard up because he had ceased to receive remittances from abroad on his inheritance and feared he would have to turn to journalistic illustration to keep food in the house, he sent Quinn a pleasant humble letter in which he hesitantly proposed a semi-formal patronage arrangement—Quinn to grant him a steady allowance in return for art: ". . . if your interest in my work still subsides and if you dont feel, you have already done enough for me." [72] Quinn agreed to the arrangement. Late in October Quinn received another note, signed "Pascin the shortempered artist," in which the painter told of being unable to find an expressman to take three paintings to Quinn's apartment, carrying them there himself, and quarreling with Quinn's houseboy when he was ordered to take them around to the back entrance. Then at Christmas time Quinn heard from Pascin who had moved on to New Orleans: "I am awfully sorry you have been bothered in my behalf the day before our depart." Quinn had been summoned to vouch for him when Pascin was being roughly interrogated by federal agents who riffled through his drawings, called them " 'camouflage,' " and broke the crystal frame of a miniature made by Mme. Pascin, looking for " 'secret contents.' " Pascin attributed the crude inquisition to his wife's correspondence with a Belgian woman in Miami whose husband had worked in the Pascin family business in Rumania and was a German subject. [73]

1917 *Continued*

QUINN'S dealings with Jacob Epstein during 1917 were numerous and varied and some of them were hectic. On New Year's day he congratulated Mrs. Epstein on the fact that her husband had received another three months' exemption from military service. To the sculptor himself he apologized for his slowness in sending money owed, explaining that he was now suffering through his third bookkeeper in four months. Epstein had complained to Quinn, as if he were somehow responsible, because *Vanity Fair* had published photographs of works by Epstein and Jo Davidson on the same page. Quinn protested: "I never mixed you up with Davison [*sic*]. I hate the beast." [1] In correspondence with Epstein Quinn enjoyed insulting rival sculptors, for example calling the popular American Paul Manship "the stove-ornament sculptor." [2] For Jo Davidson he reserved his worst epithets and his most casual spelling: ". . . that pushing, thick-skinned, egotistical little photographer-in-mud who calls himself Joe Davison." [3] Of Epstein's own work Quinn wrote reassuringly but with a new note of warning: "I still believe in you and in your work, even though you apparently are on the way to popularity, which generally ruins most artists." [4] He had in mind the example primarily of Augustus John, whose craft and whose integrity, he believed, were being softened and twisted by easy success. But he had also begun to reluct at some of Epstein's new prices. When the sculptor asked £500 for his marble *Venus* Quinn wrote back bluntly: "I can't afford it." [5] Epstein, on the other hand, spoke his own word of caution about what he saw as a dangerous pattern of oversimplification in the tendencies of Quinn's taste:

I think you are inclined to over rate what you call advanced
work; not all advanced work is good, some of it is damn damn
bad. I say this because there is a tendency to slight work that
has any resemblance to natural objects. My own essays into
abstract art have always been natural and not forced. I make no
formula, and only when I see something to be done in abstract
form that better conveys my meaning than natural forms then
I use it. There is a solidity in natural forms though that will always
attract a sculptor, and great work can be done on a natural
basis.   [*February 11, 1917.*]

On February 17 Quinn cabled Epstein an offer of £400 for the
eight-foot marble *Venus* and £300 for the granite carving of
Mother and Child. He suggested that Epstein might wish to withdraw these works from his current show at the Leicester Gallery
and deal for them direct, thus saving himself the gallery commission. Epstein accepted the offer but preferred to work through the
gallery. Quinn instructed that the works should be shipped by an
American passenger vessel, believing that German submarines were
attacking only cargo vessels. When the *Venus* and the *Mother and
Child* arrived the heavy stones could only be stored in the basement of his apartment house. Writing to the Leicester Gallery on
December 3 to speak of their safe arrival, Quinn took the occasion
to write also at length—seven pages—of his troubles with Sophie
Brzeska over which he was still brooding sorely.

In February Epstein offered at £200 his new bronze portrait
head of Augustus John, looking like John the Baptist as tradition-
ally pictured, and specified that he was making "six copies one
only for America." But Quinn had in his hands a priced catalog
of the show at the Leicester Gallery which offered for sale six
copies of the bust of Iris Tree, six of Romilly John (son of Augustus), six of Euphemia Lamb, and six of Lillian Shelley. In purchasing these works earlier Quinn had ceded Epstein's right to make
and sell two copies of the Iris Tree, six of the Romilly John, three
of the Lamb, and four of the Shelley. Quinn now made his point
bluntly and immediately:

I think that six copies of a bronze are too many for a sculptor to
make anyway. Limiting them to one in America doesn't meet the
point, for a dealer or any Tom, Dick or Harry in England can

buy one or two or three and send them to America without your knowledge, consent or approval. Certainly dealers would ultimately be doing it. I won't want to be churlish about the matter but in your own interest I don't think there ought to be six copies of these bronzes made.   [*March 14, 1917.*]

That, he continued, was where Rodin "went off": he had "sold stuff like an old foundry maker," and Tiffany's in New York had had copies of Rodin's *Baiser* in bronze "as polished and as smooth as stove ornaments." If Epstein was going to make six copies of all his bronzes, Quinn wanted nothing more to do with them; and further: ". . . I think you ought to stand on your understanding with me as above detailed." Finally he made a counter offer of £150 for the Augustus John, provided Epstein made only three copies in all.

On April 5 Epstein cabled back to say that the generalized statement of the catalog had given a false impression: he was adhering strictly to his first agreement with Quinn as to numbers of copies. He refused the £150 offer for the Augustus John. Meanwhile on March 28 Quinn had written to couple that offer with offers of £80 each for *Meum No. 1*, *Meum No. 2*, and *The Tin Hat* (his British Tommy's bust), and £100 for *Lord Fisher*. On April 20 Epstein cabled his acceptance of the conglomerate offer, £490 for the five works.

In the summer Epstein fell into new and now inextricable difficulty with the military draft. The story is summed up in four cables from Margaret Dunlop Epstein to Quinn:

June 8:   Jacob exempted three months. Artists angry in press;
June 16:   Question asked in House. Military counter appeal to reconsider exemption because of artists anger. Cable what you think Director Central Tribunal Local Government Board Whitehall;
July 20:   Exemption refused. Further appeal impossible. Jacob called up sixth September;
July 25:   Would Jacob have any chance as artist in American army.

Once more Quinn loyally sent his cables to English officials, asking that, failing exemption, Epstein be assigned work as a draftsman or something of the kind to keep him out of the trenches. He inquired of American officials as to whether Epstein could be attached to the American army as a war artist, but was rebuffed on the grounds that the sculptor now held British citizenship. He sought also an interview with Lord Northcliffe in New York, who drily refused to intervene: his errand in America being that of trying to persuade Englishmen there to return home for military service.[6] Finally, Mrs. Epstein suggested that Quinn get behind a movement to summon Epstein home to America to do an official monument of some kind. Epstein believed that Augustus John had covertly led "a deliberate conspiracy in the press" against his exemption, and that John and his confederates had been motivated by professional jealousy: "To be attacked in the press is now my almost daily portion. I loom too large for our feeble small folk of the brush and chisel. Even my existence is a nuisance to them. They shall have their reward." [7] Mrs. Epstein's reconstruction was that the famous London practical joker Horace de Vere Cole, as a front for Augustus John, had egged on the lesser artists to protest.[8] Quinn continued sympathetic for some time, writing to Epstein on August 6:

> I am dreadfully sorry to know that your enemies have made that wretched campaign against you. . . . If you had not assured me of the cabals and intrigues against you I would have said that it was impossible for artists to be guilty of such dirty and cowardly acts merely because they disliked a man's work.*

But soon he began to question his own motives and to wonder at his own actions, especially as he thought about the number of his friends and artists of his acquaintance who had been helplessly or willingly involved in the war. Now he wrote Epstein with some impatience on September 12: "I have done all I can about getting you excused." Particularly on his mind was the news he had just had from Pound of the "general hotness" in which Wyndham Lewis was involved, and he spoke of this to Epstein: ". . . Lewis

---

* "I had to discover for myself how superficial is the world of art, and what a wretched lot of log-rollers, schemers, sharks, opportunists, profiteers, sycophants, camp-followers, social climbers . . . infest the world of art. It is a jungle, into which the artist is forced periodically to bring his work and live" [1908]. (Jacob Epstein, *Epstein: An Autobiography*, London, Studio Vista, 1963, p. 29.)

is out of the hospital and back in the thick of it. . . . I am afraid
that he will get done in, unless he gets a suitable wound first."
But the Epsteins scorned Pound and Lewis, and they had their own
candidate for heroism, T. E. Hulme. Quinn's letter elicited a long
cable from Mrs. Epstein on October 4:

> Epstein from camp writes cable Quinn to do nothing for me in
> army. So this my last communication. Epstein extremely an-
> noyed with your letter twelfth September especially as Pounds
> report from Lewis more brag than truth as we know. Epsteins
> greatest friend Hulme out since 1914 just killed. Epstein writing
> you.

Her husband's letter of October 1, dated from Crownhill Bar-
racks in Plymouth, developed these themes more explicitly:

> I have just had your letter of the 12th Sept. and am very as-
> tonished at your tone about the army. I feel angry with Mrs.
> Epstein for ever writing to you about it and asking you to do
> anything. I have never felt that I shirked my duty. While given
> time I worked (perhaps harder than any soldier) and when
> called I went. I shall do my full duty and in giving up the priest-
> hood of the artist, I know that personally as far as physical com-
> fort and peace of mind goes my life is easier. I wish to remain in
> the army and shall do nothing and hope you will make no effort
> to effect anything else. . . .

Epstein was contemptuous of the reputed heroism of Lewis, and
of the professional behavior of both Lewis and Pound. His own
grief was for the philosopher-poet T. E. Hulme who had returned
to the front after a severe wound and been recently killed: "He
had, I believe, the best brains in England and his nature was of the
most generous." Quinn perused these messages, evidently, with his
jaw dropping. "I am accustomed to ingratitude, large and small,
right and left," he noted to Mitchell Kennerley on October 5, "but
I never have had such a case as that of Jacob Epstein."

Ironically Quinn had just been in the middle of publishing his
praise of Epstein as a sculptor. In the summer Crowninshield of
Vanity Fair had received some new Charles Langdon Coburn photographs of Epstein works and had asked Quinn to write an appreciation to accompany them. Quinn agreed, and his article appeared

in the October number just as he was reading the last communications from the sculptor and his wife. Crowninshield had edited his text heavily, and Quinn described the article as "rather mutilated by having its feet decapitated." [9] He had mimeographed in his office the missing portions of his text, pasted them in copies of the magazine, and sent his re-edited article to a few of the friends whose opinion he valued most, especially to Gregg, Davies, and Kuhn. Jules Pascin wrote of it on October 9: "I had verry much pleasuer to read your article on Epstein. It is to bad that the editor cut parts of it out, but the article is even so a verry refreshing change after all these boudoir-causeries on gets mostly as so-called art articles." Nor did the squabble with the Epsteins put an end to the buying and selling of art. Before the bitter letters Epstein cabled to offer his busts of Bernard Van Dieren and Lady Drogheda at £175 for both, and Quinn accepted promptly by cable. In a cable on October 10 Epstein accepted in turn Quinn's offer of £100 for the bust of the Duchess of Hamilton. At the end of the year Pound told of meeting Epstein on the street in London and congratulating him on his lean and fit look under army training. Epstein held out his hands to a point two feet in front of his stomach, and said, " 'By God, I'd rather have a pot out to there.' " [10]

Meanwhile Quinn heard sporadically from Augustus John. "Hail, Columbia!" John wrote excitedly on April 20 to celebrate America's entry into the war. He went on to praise, in what seem the cant terms of European response, the formal statement of the man of whom Quinn wished to hear no praise:

> President Wilson's speech was a wonderful thing, the finest pronouncement so far made by any statesman, and the furthest reaching. He has lifted the whole struggle to a higher plane, given it a clearer meaning and a more definite and loftier goal.

He felt that the whole tide of the war was at last turning in favor of the Allies. "But what casualty lists!" he groaned, and listed nearly a dozen men lost from his own small circle of friends: "We must be bleeding white; and it seems the best go down always." One of his own sons was already a naval cadet and another would soon join him. John's art was moving ahead. He had painted in a single week a forty-foot decoration for the Arts and Crafts show at Burlington House, in which May Morris was also involved, and he was planning a summer show at Chenil's and a later one in America, which he was arranging with Martin Birnbaum of Scott & Fowles. With the offhandedness which Quinn found so exasperating, John explained why he had not after all sent over *The Girl by the Lake* as he had promised: ". . . on reflection I felt dissatisfied with it, and I've never yet sent you anything I didn't like myself." (Quinn had paid for the painting.)

Quinn's feeling about John had sunk into a smoldering personal irritation. He genuinely cared little now about having or losing the general run of John's pictures, which were too academic in feeling to suit his advancing taste. But there was still no denying John's bravura powers as a portraitist, and when Quinn learned that his new portrait of Arthur Symons was offered in his London show he cabled an offer at once. A gossipy letter from Symons himself on November 22 brought later news of John and of others in Quinn's big scattered circle of friends, many of whom he had not seen now for a half-dozen years. To supplement the unsteady income of "poor Symons," Quinn still regularly bought what manuscripts he offered, and he tried himself or through an agent in New York to place Symons's work with American publishers. This letter brought Symons's essay on Stendhal, much admired by Augustus John, he assured Quinn. He told of lunching at the Café Royal with John, now Major John in khaki, commissioned as a war artist and preparing to go next month to the coast of France. John had been unlike himself, brooding and somber and the uniform unbecoming. But the night before Symons had dined more gaily with John and Maud Gonne: ". . . five people and five hours! Much reading aloud of Baudelaire and Verlaine." Maud too had been brooding and impressive: ". . . majestic, speaking rarely, seeing always visions; still with some of her strange beauty; saying: 'I am old . . . old. My heart is for Ireland and my love for France.'" All of them, Symons said, had spoken kindly of John Quinn.

Maud Gonne had passed most of the year in France, dividing her time between Paris and Colleville on the Normandy coast. Her old implacable bitterness against the English had only been intensified by their refusal, even after the general amnesty and release of the prisoners taken in the Easter Rising of 1916, to grant her a passport to return to Dublin. She had heard unofficially through W. B. Yeats that she could have the passport if she would promise to refrain from political activity—a proposition which she scornfully refused. She was happy at America's declaration of war because she took that to mean that Ireland would now have a powerful ally against England at an eventual peace table. Her letters to Quinn told of civilian and military suffering in France— no men for farm work, food desperately short. At Easter time she was turning her orchards at Colleville into patches of potatoes and beans, and in July they were eating their crop. Sometimes they heard the sound of big guns at sea, and she and Iseult and Seagan, her daughter and son, patrolled the beaches gleaning for torpedoed fish and coal from sunken colliers. Quinn, she suspected, "still saw beauty in war," but her only wish now was for the end of it all: ". . . hospitals and broken hearts and the devastation and destruction of all art and beauty have changed me and I bow to every peace advocate." [11] Quinn's "generous cheque" she laid out in aid of needy French people around her, always carefully explaining that the money came from " 'an Irishman in America.' " She did not want to relinquish Ireland's right to Quinn, and she returned to her dream of Quinn as Parnell *redivivus*:

> What a strange place you will find Europe the next time you come! It will be good to see you, anyhow, and I hope it will be in Ireland. Come over and build up an Irish Republic. Think what a man like you could do there! America is so vast that the individual can do little to mould the country even with your immense energy and will. In Ireland think how it would tell!
>
> [*July 30, 1917.*]

Quinn sent her his sacred books of the year, Pound's *Noh*, Joyce's *A Portrait of the Artist as a Young Man*, and his own *Vanity Fair* article on Joyce. The Pound volume she liked in spite of an old prejudice against the "affectation" of its author, whom she had not yet met in the flesh. Now in September it was from Pound that Quinn heard of the descent of Maud Gonne's *suite* upon London: Yeats had brought back from Paris ten canary birds, a parrot, a monkey, a cat, Iseult, Seagan, Maud herself, and a fervent hope that she might be persuaded into some degree of political tranquility.[12] Pound thanked Quinn for giving Maud Gonne the *Noh*, which had served as his means of first introduction to her. Even the gay and skeptical Pound found himself stirred by her grand beauty and passion and force of will.

Yeats himself had written Quinn on May 16 to suggest that he pay over to J. B. Yeats in New York the value of an important group of manuscripts which he would send as soon as the seas were safer. He identified the papers as the text of a new volume of poems, " 'The [Wild] Swans at Coole' "; " 'The Alphabet: *Anima Hominis, Anima Mundi*,' " the little book of mysterious and beautiful philosophical essays, "an elaborate bit of writing" as he described it to Quinn, subsequently published as *Per Amica Silentia Lunae*; two plays, *At the Hawk's Well* and *The Player Queen*; and two long essays on "witchcraft, spiritism, etc.," which were to be appended to Lady Gregory's *Visions and Beliefs*. The same letter announced that, sick of the town and anxious to return to Irish roots, Yeats had just bought for £35 "an old ruin in Galway" which he intended to restore and occupy. In 1904 in Dublin Quinn had first heard Yeats speak of his dream of owning Ballylee. This was an ancient square stone tower, roofless and dilapidated, with a "broken" cottage at its base, within a few miles of the sea, of the town of Gort, and of the seat of the Gregorys at Coole Park. When the war was over, Yeats wrote, he hoped to entertain Quinn in "my ruined tower." He had "launched into these gaieties," as he put it, in anticipation of the money from another American lecture tour, proposed by Pond's bureau but now forcibly postponed by the war. A month later, with his own experience at Purchase Street in mind, Quinn predicted to Yeats that he would soon regret his impulsiveness. Practically he was right, as time proved; but with the tower Yeats had in any case acquired one of the most potent symbols for the great poetry of his late years, an image at once grand, various, fluent, and strong.

In France in the summer Yeats had proposed for the last time to Maud Gonne, and when refused he had proposed to her beautiful daughter Iseult, who also refused. In October, to the astonishment and scattered ribaldry of his friends, Yeats was married at fifty-two to Georgiana Hyde-Lees who was half his age. "It all seems very sudden and suggests that she is furniture for the Castle," Charles Shannon wrote Quinn when he heard the news.[13] If

Symons's account is to be trusted, Maud Gonne was moved to mirth and spite.[14] Pound saw this reaction quite differently. Maud Gonne and her family seemed to him quite pleased with the bride, and he thought Lady Gregory was satisfied as well.[15] Returning Yeats's favor of a few years before, Pound stood in for the couple at the secular ceremony in London, and he reported Yeats's "last exhortation" to him on taking leave: " 'Send a telegram to Lady Gregory. NOT one that will be talked about in Coole for the next generation. It's a place where the parson goes down to the post office every day to get the news off the post cards.' " [16] Quite clearly Yeats had had his wits about him when he was getting married. Pound was temperately optimistic. He thought Yeats might have done a great deal worse: the young woman seemed attractive and sensible and capable of counteracting some of Yeats's tendencies to spookiness; at least she would not be a "flaming nuisance [*sic*]." [17] He identified Miss Hyde-Lees as the stepdaughter of his own wife's uncle and as his wife's good friend—"so it is not an incursion." [18]

Quinn had sustained his own bachelor status, he remarked to Arthur B. Davies, "by great foresight, courage and iron determination." [19] He was a bit sorry to lose a notable bachelor among his acquaintance, but he was sure that the part of Yeats's head which occupied the ordinary world was level, and he preferred not to hear the event of the marriage sensationalized or sentimentalized. When Lady Gregory wrote him of her sententious wish for Yeats's "happiness" in marriage, Quinn was oddly irritated and wrote to E. E. Flynn: "Twenty years ago I got sick of the over-worked word 'happiness,' eighteen years ago of the words 'Celtic magic,' fourteen years ago of the word 'mysticism,' eleven years ago of 'imaginative.' " [20] He was satisfied to trust Yeats's common sense: "Yeats is a wise man and I doubt if he has made a mistake." [21]

Yeats himself wrote Quinn engagingly of his young wife a month after marriage. He was calling her "George," having found the usual diminutive, "Georgie," "not to be endured." [22] He had sent his only photograph of his wife to his father, and he directed Quinn to go there for a likeness:

> She is not so black-haired and white-skinned as it makes her, but brown-haired and high-coloured, and looks nearer to her 25 years than the photograph. She is a deep student in all my sub-

jects, and is at present deep in the astrological works of Pico della Mirandola.   [*November 29, 1917.*]

Mrs. Yeats soon proved to be more than a "deep student" of Yeats's "subjects"; she brought to this extraordinary and happy marriage those powers as a medium to which Yeats attributed the clarifying and codifying of his years of speculation in the "system" he was to call *A Vision*, his great strange book of 1925. But now he hoped, among other things, that his marriage would bring him still closer to Ezra Pound, as George was the close friend of Pound's wife, Dorothy, who was in turn the daughter of Yeats's great friend, Olivia Shakespear.

In New York "the father of all the Yeatsssssss' [23] had been a bit perturbed at his son's marrying such a young woman, but was reassured when he heard she was also tall—five feet and seven inches. "I think tall women are easier to get on with and live with than little women," he wrote to Quinn on December 6. "They have more sentiment and gentleness, and because they are more conspicuous are more watchful of themselves. The little women are constantly out of sight so that you don't know what they are up to." Having passed most of the winter with the Pounds in Sussex, W. B. Yeats did not expose his wife to his sisters in Dublin until March of 1918. But meanwhile Lily Yeats wrote tartly of other notable reactions:

> Lady Gregory and Maud both, I believe are pleased. And why shouldn't they be? They have both, so to speak, had their "whack" —the latter a very considerable "whack" of her own choosing, but she will live forever in Willy's verse, which is a fine crown and tribute to her beauty. Lady Gregory would, I expect, have liked to choose the bride, but Willie liked in this to be his own master.[24]

When at last the Yeats sisters did meet George they expressed themselves as well content with their brother's taste:

> We like her very much. . . . She is not good looking, but is comely, her nose too big for good looks; her colour ruddy and her hair reddish brown; her eyes very good and a fine blue, with very dark, strongly marked eyebrows. She is quiet but not slow, her brain, I would judge, quick and trained and sensitive. They

are most happy together. Willy I never saw looking so well. He is very brown, as if they had been in the open air a lot.[25]

Lily Yeats's was one of the most circumstantial and interesting of the responses to the new phenomenon of James Joyce which Quinn received this year from the numerous Dubliners who were indebted to him for a copy of Joyce's *Portrait*, set in that city of his hatred and love. James Stephens wrote only a blunt postscript to a note of July 30: "I don't like Joyce's work, but he can write." Maud Gonne thought Quinn had been much too generous to the novel in *Vanity Fair*. Predictably, she was offended by Joyce's remorselessly unromantic vision of youth, politics, and church in his native place, and she called his book "curious and interesting" only as the "self-analysis of a somewhat mediocre soul who has failed to see and to understand the beauty it has lived among. . . ." Joyce had turned the Dublin students, the vivid and high-minded followers of Pearce and MacDonagh of her own impression, into "uncouth nonentities," she said.[26] Lily Yeats had not yet read the *Portrait* but she had read Quinn's essay "twice, with much pleasure," and on reflection she had found Joyce's vision of the city and the citizens in *Dubliners* credible enough. She called that one "a never-to-be-forgotten book, a haunting book."

> At first I thought, "How gray, how sordid! Can such lives be lived even in the gray old houses about the north side of Dublin, built long ago for people who had leisure and money and talk, and now lived in by drab people?" I saw the elderly women coming out and slipping into the city chapels for mouthfuls of prayer, seedy men coming out and slipping into greasy public houses for mouthfuls of porter—but of their lives I knew nothing—what went on behind the dirty windows like those behind which James Stephens' charwoman lived,[27] which were so dirty anyone wishing to look out had to open them. Since I read "Dubliners" I feel I know something of their lives.[28]

She went on to give her recollections of Joyce himself, whom of course Quinn had never met:

> I remember Joyce. He used to be in and out among us all at the start of the Abbey and all its movements. I remember him one night—very cheerful, he thought drink would soon end his father,

and then he would give his six little sisters to Archbishop Walsh to make nuns of, leaving him free. Then I remember him—tall, slim, and dark, darting past me in a doorway in white canvas shoes.

Joyce's white canvas shoes seem to have registered in the mind of everyone who remembered him in these days. Lily Yeats later learned that her doorway epiphany had shown Joyce on the very day of his famous real and symbolic flight—away from Ireland, into Europe and the great world.

She wrote movingly of another exile, the father whom she had not seen for ten years now, and she spoke her gratitude for Quinn's continuing care and respect for the old man. By June she was able to say of J. B. Yeats's little book of letters with Pound's introduction, published by herself and her sister: "Papa's book is liked by all." [29] She was touched by the thought of the old artist, whose wonderful talk had casually enriched so many lives, publishing his first book at the age of seventy-eight, and wrote to Quinn:

> I appreciate very much what you say about Papa. Not only do I love him as my father but as my greatest friend. When I think of his age and the distance he is off I cannot keep away my tears, and then the thought of the sixty years of hard struggle he has had for the money that never came! He doesn't know what a success he is, how fine his work is, what a big man he is.
>
> [*December 10, 1917.*]

It was a just if partial judgment. John Butler Yeats was one of those men whose practical success always followed behind them, just out of present reach, and whose visible success, splendid but uncountable, lay in the act of humane association. And he wore always the nimbus of having fathered four brilliant and devoted sons and daughters.

Joyce and his *Portrait* loom large in J. B. Yeats's communications to Quinn at this period. He made his way into Joyce only after a struggle. Quinn described to W. B. Yeats his father's response to *Dubliners* when he gave him the book to read during his visit to Quinn's cottage on the Great South Bay of Long Island in the summer of 1914: "He read about half the book and then returned it to me, saying: 'Good God, how depressing! One always knew there were such persons and places in Dublin, but one never wanted to see them.' " [30] The *Portrait* first baffled and then deeply stirred J. B. Yeats, and he kept coming back to it. In June he returned general thanks to Quinn for regular supplies of books and magazines which kept him from "dropping back" intellectually; he found himself often rereading books Quinn had chosen for him. Joyce's was one such. "But it is a queer book," was his first response, in January. It reminded him of Balzac without the Frenchman's clarity. He felt Joyce as "a thinker, a man looking for a principle; his purpose other than mere mischief. And he is not a propagandist." He liked the "poetry" of the prose, "a stormy sort of poetry, cloudy and wild, like the Irish skies in the winter months." His reading, in contrast to Maud Gonne's, shrewdly divined Joyce's passionate intellectualism: "I fancy he is a great student, and that sometimes makes all the difference between the major and the minor writer." [31] Picking up the book again before he closed his letter, he was pleased to see it as a rediscovery of the animating principle of Dublin herself: "So much vitality, and no business to drain it off—that's the charm of Dublin, and doubtless it was the charm of Athens." In March his praise went extravagantly to Quinn himself for his *Vanity Fair* piece: "It is a splendid article and a revelation of *you*. You are really a great literary artist." [32] This was persiflage, as both men knew. When J. B. Yeats reread the book again at the end of the year his reservations were all gone; he told Quinn that the *Portrait* was a masterpiece:

> What a wonderful book it is! Not a sentence, not a line, not a word would I blot. And what a style he has! It mutters and murmurs and sometimes sings. I find myself saying over to myself many of his sentences. And he is never long-winded, never says too much. That book will live forever, preserved like a fly in amber by its incomparable style. . . . I don't think people have yet discovered that book. I have met many who have read it, but none of them had a guess as to its value. [*December 13, 1917.*]

Still he thought it better to withhold the book from a friend's seventeen-year-old daughter, a student at Vassar, who had asked to borrow it.

Mr. Yeats had been drifting for some time toward a peculiarly dialectical mood, and his letters of this year to Quinn were full of hurried but stimulating antitheses. In his first brief letter on the *Portrait*, for example, he compared Joyce to Balzac and to Æ's clever disciple, Susan Mitchell; the Irish to the French and the Spanish; Dublin to Athens, Belfast, and London; the eighteenth century to the nineteenth and twentieth. His letter of March 21 echoed another to his poet son in which he had argued that the antithesis to poetry was "discord," not science as was usually alleged. A few days later he was writing to attack argument or wrangling as the great enemy of real conversation: argument, he said, was only intensity of bullying. Dr. Johnson's way was not wrangling but "wit combats"—an entirely different thing, a matching of intellects. "Argument" (he argued) "is only for Methodist parsons, undergraduates, and the public house." [33]

In his letter of May 5 Mr. Yeats developed for Quinn certain ideas which he was making into a paper on Whitman as a dangerous ideal for Americans. He had mentioned his essay to his good friend, the young critic Van Wyck Brooks, a member of his circle at Petitpas', who had recommended it in turn to Maxwell Perkins, editor at Scribner's. As the end of this chain of influence J. B. Yeats expected to paint a portrait of Perkins's mother "forthwith, or as soon as I can get this article finished to my satisfaction." He had been thinking, in a loose and inclusive way, of the relation of "emotion" to "feeling," and of both to "personality" and "individuality." The trouble with Whitman was that he was "a man purely emotional" and thus a dangerously comforting image to a people already overinclined that way.

> I make a distinction between emotion, which is a quality purely agreeable and self-indulgent, and feeling, which is made of stronger material, more allied to pain than to pleasure. I contrast the portraits of such men as Milton and Dante with Walt Whitman's, in the latter of which I find something unbraced and relaxed.

According to the same distinction he separated heroes and statesmen—heroes being "purely emotional," "whereas statesmen are personalities compact of the pleasure and pain of *feeling*." All nations as such, he thought, were a form of emotional expression. But America had forced a peculiar subjugation of the individual into "a mere item in the national totality," in which posture the American dutifully admired Walt Whitman's poetry "with its pleasant chanting of (mostly lies) brotherly love and of the grandeur of American democracy."

Because of their cold mistrust of emotion the English struck J. B. Yeats as a less agreeable people than the Americans, but a race far more hospitable to real individuality; and the individual had always the private option of emotion, even in England. Thus "in their cold climate and on their inhospitable soil" the English had been able to produce the great poets. He offered a vision of the "future" of two of the great ones from whom time had withheld a future:

> Keats . . . emotional, but soon to be a personality, the firmly etched lines superseding the wavering lines of emotion. Shelley would have grown as stern-visaged as Dante. He was not emotional—ecstasy, an enthusiasm, a kindling of the whole personality, because of his passionate intellectualism would have finally frozen into the coldness of a polar sea, the magnificent calm of the North Pole.

Of the headlong emotionality of the French J. B. Yeats had just had a demonstration from the Petitpas sisters. They had been so pleased with his drawing of the beautiful young matron Mrs. Jeanne Robert Foster that they had enthusiastically set alight the house furnace, cold for weeks, and smoked him out of his room. It is the first audible mention of Mrs. Foster, whom Mr. Yeats had been trying to bring together with Quinn for several years. He had been telling Mrs. Foster: "Quinn needs a good woman to rest his head." She and Quinn did not meet until the following year, but thereafter she was the most important person aside from his family in what remained of his life.

In mid-June Mr. Yeats was commenting acutely on President Wilson's speeches and on the text of one of his son's plays, probably *At the Hawk's Well*, sent him by Quinn. Wilson, he said: "writes like an archbishop and as all archbishops have always written—slumberous, sonorous sentences all permeated with official dignity; but no life anywhere. Yet well done, by a man studiously accomplished." [34] He set that archepiscopal mode against the style of Quinn's hero Theodore Roosevelt: ". . . not an original thinker, just the thoughts of ordinary people; but the man himself is an original and so his sentences are full of life—sledgehammer blows, fierce thrusts, given in the heat of combat and with a *kind of happiness.*"[35] "Willie's play" he found "a most delicate piece of artistry and exquisitely inexplicable; trite as a summer's day, yet, like that day, all a mystery."[36] Quinn sent him Ezra Pounds *Lustra* as soon as that book appeared from Knopf in October, and he read in it from time to time in November and December, distracted as well by Alan Seeger's poems and the strong medicine of Joyce. Style as always was much on his mind, and he spoke of Pound's verse almost as prose, admiring its strong rhetorical structure. "Many of the sentences will stick in my memory," he wrote, because of "a queer kind of startlingness and challenge. . . . Who reads him will discard the loose phrase and the flabby paragraph."[37] It was precisely the effect Pound sought. Mr. Yeats was also excited and amused by Pound as a phenomenon of personality: "He is a powerful astringent. . . . It is his deliberate intention to inflict pain. And one does not mind, for it is salutary. . . . It is wonderful how people hate him. But hatred is the harvest he wants to gather—great sheaves of it, beneath a sky of disastrous moonlight. . . . He is a hair shirt to be worn next the skin."[38] He recollected certain other hair-shirt friends in his past: ". . . none of them came to much. I did not wear their hair-shirt and they died of it." He wondered if Pound was courting some of the same dangers; he thought Shakespeare's Iago had been a hair-shirt friend, and he "ended in becoming a very disagreeable person."[39]

Quinn had gone to Mr. Yeats, among others, for help in composing his argument in the "Cantleman case" against the *Little Review,* and Mr. Yeats wrote on December 3 to condole with him upon the adverse decision. Trained as a lawyer himself, he considered the decision of the District Judge "worthy of a police magistrate, for it is at once silly and monstrous." He wished for an appeal but thought it a waste of money, for he had concluded that the decision must have been founded in the hysterical psychology of war, not in the real point at issue in the case, and "War is the glorification of the animal so that everything shall be merely animal; just as poetry is the glorification of the entire man in his totality of body, soul and intellect."

The most moving of the year's rich antithetical images, his contrast of the "solitary" and the "social" man, is developed in J. B. Yeats's letter of December 13:

> The solitary we never criticize—we can't; he is outside our sphere. A baby while it retains its baby solitariness one is afraid to scold; we prefer to spoil it. Or a beautiful woman with the charm of a real solitariness. Or Hamlet. Even Falstaff is rescued from us by a certain solitariness. Lily, who hates drunkards, maintains that Shakespeare's drunkards are not drunkards at all, but hobgoblins, and so she likes them. Swift was a solitary; we not only put up with him but are fascinated. Walt Whitman was not a solitary but a social man, teaching and preaching and evoking criticism for and against. Poets, so far as and when they are poets, are solitaries, and, like women who are beautiful with solitariness, *charm but do not teach.* The social man teaches and convinces, but does not charm. Susan Mitchell, who—the rogue—practices every kind of charm, amusingly avoids teaching, even to giving advice, for which reason her eyes "rain bright influence." Swift's writings are the outspokenness of a solitary man inflamed by anger and passion. He is among the great solitaries. That was his confessed charm.

From a man so social and teacherly it was a fine bit of imaginative appreciation. Mr. Yeats's lifelong didacticism had its own kind of charm, and all this was heady stuff in a busy lawyer's morning mail. The old man's argument was like his art, with excellent powers of observation and analysis but poor powers of synthesis. His arguments rarely completed themselves, and his dogma accumulated in patches, like his self-portrait for Quinn, still "in progress" in his upper room at Petitpas'. As a correspondent and dialectical companion, Quinn panted along behind the stream of Mr. Yeats's letters which arrived almost daily, a page to a dozen pages of tiny scribble, often illuminated with witty and charming little drawings in ink. Quinn would "answer" several letters at a time, sometimes following out Mr. Yeats's train of argument, sometimes propounding dogmas of his own, sometimes falling back on ordinary news of the many persons and affairs they held in common. Quinn had by now pretty well abandoned his former habit of taking Mr. Yeats along to galleries and exhibitions; their tastes had moved apart

to a hopeless degree, and he found their disagreement too wearing, even when amiable. The old man was undoubtedly losing
some of the energy and animation which had been so winning. He
set down for Quinn his own view of his state:

> I don't like going out in the evening. In the morning I am a ra-
> diant youth of promise; in midday and afternoon a virile man;
> in the evening a depressed old fellow—like an old rooster I be-
> come somnolent. I don't eat much at dinner but drink two bottles
> (half bottles) of California wine, which makes me rather more
> somnolent, but with a cheerful quality, like good dreams. I
> breakfast every morning at 7:30 and go to bed between 10 and 11.
> [*May 5, 1917.*]

Quinn could still often get him out for Sunday midday dinner at
the apartment, or to Purchase Street for overnight or a weekend,
and occasionally for evening dinner when the company was seductive enough and he was promised a trip home by taxi.

In Dublin George Russell had liked his old friend's letters in
the Cuala Press edition and had reviewed the volume for the *Irish
Times*. With its editor he felt some impatience. Pound's habit of
writing about writing made Æ think of him as "a preposterous
literary creature . . . a mandarin of letters." [40] That image set him
off on a little dissertation on style, which to Russell seemed to
reduce itself to a concomitant of fundamental intellectual honesty
and unselfconsciousness:

> Style is truth telling at its root. It is saying exactly what one feels
> or thinks, and if one does that, adding nothing, exaggerating
> nothing or sophisticating nothing, if the thought, feeling or
> imagination is good the literary expression will be good. That is
> my gospel, briefly, and the folk who write learnedly and end-
> lessly about style bore me. Rossetti called this "literary incest,"
> literature begetting literature on itself, and I feel he is right.[41]

But then Quinn's gift of Pound's *Noh* arrived, and Russell, admiring it, admitted that the mandarin "had his uses." [42] His description
of Pound as "the keeper of a literary museum" might have shocked
Pound as an inclusive description of himself, though it certainly
pointed accurately at his casual mandarin side, his accumulation
and exhibition in his writings of vortices from all times and places.

Rising promptly to Russell's bait on the issue of style, Quinn returned a competent qualification and rebuttal:

> Imitation, of course, will not make great art, nor fine writing make great art, nor taking thought as to style. Neither will truth-telling produce great art. While you may not like to read things about style, or on how things should be written, you have unconsciously thought about style, and you have a style of your own, one of great eloquence and beauty. At the same time, matter is not everything, and that is why probably very little of what G. B. Shaw has written will live. It produces its immediate effect, as Voltaire and as Ibsen did. It takes the miracle of style for a work of art to be really living, whether painting or poetry or prose. But that doesn't come by thinking over-much of style.
>
> [*June 19, 1917.*]

Quinn's pursuit of living art in manuscript continued, in its diminished and desultory way, now less a passion than a habit and an exercise of personal loyalty. He kept urging Æ to send him his pages, which he promised to value and to pay for at a fair going rate: if Russell did not like the thought of taking pay for his manuscripts Quinn invited him to give the money to his wife or child or to charity. Russell promised to make the effort, though he found the whole process a bit pretentious and distasteful. He described for Quinn his manner of working on his new book (*The Candle of Vision*, 1918) on "all kinds of psychological problems of vision, imagination and intuition," of which he had already sent Quinn the final version of the first chapter. To "make most difficult and intricate subjects easy reading," he had rewritten some of the chapters six or seven times. When finally he was satisfied with a chapter and had it typed, he "flung" the manuscript into a corner of the room and went back to work on remaining chapters. Since no one was allowed to disturb his papers, he assumed that the complete manuscript could eventually be mined from that corner. But he felt little sympathy for the project: "I never understand this feeling for MSS. myself." [43] He was shocked when the manuscript of his review of W. B. Yeats's *Reveries Over Childhood and Youth* which he had written for nothing was sold after a month for £4. With his moral and spiritual attitude toward the function of writing, Russell could feel none of the mystique of the thing, the artifact—the mere script. Perhaps he was "a vandal" with "a narrow soul," he mused, but it appeared to him that the main business of a book was to be clear and portable: ". . . I prefer print and would not, for reading purposes, exchange a good, clearly-printed edition of 'Hamlet' for the original MS. . . . First editions mean nothing to me unless they are the most convenient to read and one can slip them into a pocket." Russell's personal mystique was one of matter and not of manner. He went on to list for Quinn his own sacred books: ". . . if I have these I regret nothing else."

> I want four or five Platonic dialogues, Patanjali, Yoga Aphorisms, the Tao of Laotse, the Gita, the Upanishads, and, for light reading, Walt Whitman, to keep me in touch with the sun and wind and grass, and I am completely equipped with the wisdom of the world. I have an Irish .love for O'Grady's Bardic History, i.e., the Cuculain saga. I love also the Mahabharata. With all these I could go equipped into a cell and feel that, so far as thought was concerned, the world had not much chance of going ahead of me while I was in confinement. . . . One is always in advance of the moderns, even the latest fashions, if one reads the great ancients.
> [*May 23, 1917.*]

In addition to those of Symons and Yeats, manuscripts also arrived with some regularity from Æ's young friend James Stephens. Quinn asked him for the manuscript of *Green Branches*, but Stephens had lost it and sent him *Spring* instead. He also sent first copies of numerous short poems, lovely simple lyrics which he was turning out with great facility. In one "almighty fit of writing" of twelve days, Stephens reported to Quinn in August, he had composed twelve stories and twenty-five poems.

> It was a good harvest, but just now I am leaning against a rail with a straw in my mouth and feeling very contented with myself. By George, I mean, by Saint Patrick, its a great thing to be able to do work, and to have done it. I praise the gods, and entreat from them another twelve days and a similar load to stagger under.   [*August 8, 1917.*]

With happy results, Stephens had been trying the device of composing upon a single line of the blind Connacht poet Raftery, whose work and image had also excited Yeats: ". . . I hooked up one line out of the decent man's Irish, and I played on that line the way Pan plays on his pipes, only better." [44] Stephens was also one of those who regularly received Quinn's standard gift books of a given period, at this time Pound's *Noh* and Joyce's *Portrait*. To the Pound volume he reacted ambiguously: he had read it with "a kind of complicated pleasure." [45]

The flow of manuscripts from Joseph Conrad had dried up for the time. The scattered caches of old work appeared to be exhausted at last, and Conrad had no completed new work to offer. The cordial correspondence continued. Wilson Follett's little book on Conrad [46] was another of those Quinn bought in numbers as gifts for his friends, his motivation supplied by Conrad's surprised and delighted praise of the book when he came across it. Conrad had written: "I can be no other than profoundly grateful to the man for this work of sympathetic insight. He *has* understood me, as a writer, and in great part as a man too." [47] F. N. Doubleday, Conrad's and Follett's publisher, arranged a lecture on Conrad by Follett in Chickering Hall, in the Lord and Taylor Building, on the afternoon of May 29, and asked Quinn to preside over the gathering. Quinn was pleased with young Follett, who had come down from his duties at Brown University for the occasion. In his talk Follett compared Conrad favorably to H. G. Wells, Arnold Bennett, and John Galsworthy, the other great names among English novelists of the period. In his chairmanic remarks after Follett sat down Quinn pursued the case of Wells, who he said had taken up in turn Science, Humanity, Herbert Spencer, Agnosticism, and finally God. He described the scene ebulliently for Conrad in England: ". . . I added that he had literally taken God to his bosom, in fact, that it might be said that 'he had a liaison with God.' It would have amused you to see the jerks of some of the ladies' heads when I threw that at them. It was perhaps irreverent but I could not help shooting it out." [48]

Of his own work Conrad could offer only an inscribed first edition of his new novel *The Shadow-Line* and the corrected typed copy of *Victory*, and even these he was holding back because of the submarine menace: "Nothing's safe for 5 minutes at sea just now." [49] Quinn's Christmas apples of 1916 had got through. Conrad wrote at length of his young son Borys, home on leave at his nineteenth birthday after a full year of active duty on the French front. He had been gassed slightly and had been knocked down by the same shell concussion that had felled General Gough; both were unhurt but Borys had had to wipe his driver's blood and flesh off the general with a rag. His parents were impressed and amused by his new maturity, "a sort of good-tempered, imperturbable serenity in his manner, speech and thoughts—as if nothing in the world could startle or annoy him anymore." [50] Conrad thought his son had developed an aptitude for war and for "the other two Ws also." In May he was glad to welcome Quinn's country among the Allies; but he was drily unimpressed with the flowery idealism of American expression of motives:

> Here we don't fight for democracy or any other "-cracy" or for humanitarian or pacifist ideals. We are fighting for life first, for freedom of thought and development in whatever form next. For the old, old watchwords of country and liberty, in fact. The army has no doubt about it.[51]

America's entry into the war had excited Ezra Pound to write to Quinn on April 30 to sound him out on ways in which he might be put to use in American service in France. Pound knew he would be thought a queer figure in the United States herself, but the French would know what to make of him: "My profession will not be against me, with the French, nor even my appearance." The Irish Carlyle, old Standish O'Grady, wrote proudly of the fighting feats of his son, Standish Con O'Grady, a young engineer whom Quinn had met in New York: "Connie for his fighting and flying has been made Captain Flight Commander, and has won the military cross 'for valour.' I believe he has seven Hun aeroplanes down to his credit and has saved several lives by daring and judgement." [52] Such tales of valor all around him only intensified the simplicities and heated the passions of Quinn's patriotic excitement. His strongest feeling was negative, hatred of Germany and the Germans, a lust to see them beaten and humbled and rendered permanently impotent, a rage at any expression of opinion less than implacable. Such feelings made him loathe the "pacifism" and "socialism" of the *Little Review*, and brought him finally to the point of affronting Jacob Epstein. On April 11 an invitation from Walt Kuhn to hear a luncheon address by Bernard Ridder, editor of the *Staats-Zeitung*, the leading German-language paper in the United States, at the "Recruiting Hall and Headquarters" on Chambers Street of the "Mid-Day Recruiting Committee of New York City" ("Your Lunch Hour for Your Country!") reduced Quinn to sputtering profanity in his reply:

> I will be God damned if I will go to a meeting addressed by Mr. Bernard Ridder. . . . I am no more anxious to rehabilitate Bernard Ridder than I am George Sylvester Vierick [*sic*]. . . . I say again, I will be God damned if I want to have anything to do with a movement that will give him a certificate of loyalty.
>
> [*April 11, 1917.*]

In August the Vatican proposal of terms on which peace might be negotiated with Germany brought to a union his anti-German and anti-clerical prejudices. "Damn the Pope and damn his peace proposals!" he wrote to Conrad. "He is a damned meddling old crook, that's my view of him." [53] Quinn wanted no negotiated peace, he wanted Germany overrun on her own soil and beaten to the point of sterilization if not annihilation. He was convinced that German Catholic influence about the Pope had made him a virtual creature of German interest, that in effect he now spoke as a German. This argument he propounded in more circumspect terms in other quarters, in writing to Shane Leslie, for example, confining himself to drawing up a table of "deadly parallel" specifications in the papal and German terms. He was exercised about both the morality and the legality of trade between American and German commercial interests in other countries after America's declaration of war, and he took the most positive personal steps he could conceive to put an end to the traffic. In *The New York Times* of September 6 he published a long letter denouncing the practice as illegal and wrong. As chief counsel to the officers of the National Bank of Commerce, the second largest bank in the nation, Quinn forbade any further transactions with German interests. "I sealed my bank's transactions up hermetically," he wrote on September 13 to Cecil Spring-Rice, the British Ambassador. "And I don't hesitate to tell you that I never dictated an opinion with a great many 'don'ts' and 'illegals' in it with more pleasure."

A Trading with the Enemy Act was tied up in the Commerce Committee of the Senate. Quinn went to Washington, had interviews with the Deputy Attorney General and with the chairman and two other members of the Senate committee, and gave himself much of the credit for the passage of the bill in the Senate on September 12.[54]

At the same time, on Lafayette Day, September 6, Quinn spoke for Allied patriotism and Irish nationalism at the Lafayette Monument in Union Square; he had listened emotionally to Ambassador Jusserand on this occasion a year before with a big weeping Frenchman at his side. He enclosed a copy of his speech in the letter of September 12 to Epstein in which he said: "I have done all I can about getting you excused." He had been one of a committee seeking a "representative Irishman" to counter the effect of "the soapbox asses who advertise themselves as 'friends of Irish freedom,'" and had been drafted to speak himself after Colonel Robert Temple Emmet and Judge Victor J. Dowling of the New York Supreme Court had declined the honor.

In all these affairs Quinn was trying to conduct himself as an Irish-American, patriotically in pursuit of the best interests of both nations, and doing so in a public and exemplary fashion. Consequently he was outraged two weeks later to see in the *New Republic* a letter from the Irish expatriate Padraic Colum attacking the hysterical "Vigilante" psychology of wartime America which heard the Hun behind every voice of even moderate dissent. Quinn did not want to hear this kind of talk from anybody, and certainly not from an Irishman. It sounded to him like the old Clan-na-Gael line of collaboration with Germany, cynically willing in the name of Irish nationalism to accept the help of anybody who would do England in the eye—the voice of John Devoy and Daniel F. Cohalan in New York and of more high-minded and more helpless German dupes such as Roger Casement. Quinn hotly sent off a bitter and insulting letter stating this view of the case to Colum, who replied in terms graver but equally bitter:

My dear John Quinn,

I have read your letter with the greatest astonishment. It is so obviously full of dislike of me and of all my doings that I feel there can be no more friendly intercourse between you and me.

I want to say just one thing more in this letter: the people who continually talk about others receiving German or British or French pay are mentally prostitutes—their whole mind runs on the idea of hire. *[September 21, 1917.]*

Colum signed his letter: "Yours sincerely and terminatingly." Quinn was shaken enough to soften his indictment in a second letter: he did not think Colum was a real German sympathizer but only a young man who had been led astray by corrupt persons about him. Colum found this reading of his character and motive little more palatable than the former, but perhaps entitled to a more systematic refutation. He replied on September 26:

I think your second letter was written to me under just the same misapprehensions as the first. You seem to think that I have been touching upon politics here. You are mistaken. I find that the job of earning a living by writing is as much as I can get into a day. I wrote about the Vigilantes, not as anyone interested in politics, Irish or American, but as a literary man who was shocked to hear the old platitudes of hate, the old ravings of national assertion that Europe is so heartily sick of (you never see them in an English journal now outside of "John Bull") being brought up here. You are mistaken in thinking that any of the people I associate with influence me—I know very few people here—and I am very well able to save myself from being influenced by anyone.

The kind of behavior from which Colum dissociated himself emerged with sensational publicity at just this time, on September 23, with front page headlines in *The New York Times*: "Cohalan and Other Irish Leaders Named in New Exposé of German Plots; Von Igel Papers Bared Wide Conspiracy." The federal Committee on Public Information was releasing an account, an "official exposé," of the workings of German intrigue in America, prominently involving, on its Irish side, Judge Daniel F. Cohalan of the New York Supreme Court and John Devoy of the *Gaelic American*. The events described were a year and a half old, coinciding (hardly by chance) with the Easter Rising in Dublin and long antedating America's formal entry into the war. According to the account, Secret Service agents in April 1916 had raided an "advertising office" in Wall Street and had trapped a Nordic giant named

Wolf von Igel in the act of trying to destroy papers which showed numerous acts of complicity between German agents and American sympathizers aiming at sabotage and general troubling of the sentiment for Allied unity. Among the "documents" was a copy of what purported to be a message from Cohalan to Count von Bernstorff, the German Ambassador and super-spy, dated April 17, 1916, a week before the Rising, advising the Germans to bomb the English coast, to land arms and officers in Ireland, and to seal off the Irish ports from English access: to promote the rebellion and to help accomplish the eventual defeat of Britain.

When Quinn, whose Irish politics were after all temperate and comparatively conservative, read these "disclosures" he had little doubt of their truth; nor was he altogether sorry to believe that Cohalan had at last gone too far. Quinn took the position that he had "saved" Cohalan once but that this time he would leave him to suffer a deserved fate. As an Allied loyalist and categorical anti-Teuton, Quinn could only see the "exposé" as a shocking stain upon the good name of Irish-Americans. But Devoy and Cohalan fought back toughly and shrewdly. It was no secret that Cohalan and the old Fenian soldier Devoy stood at the head of the Clan-na-Gael, the most radical and intransigent of American fighters for Irish independence; and there was little doubt that they were the American sponsors of the Dublin Rising, that Roger Casement was in effect their agent. The fact that they were willing to use Germany to do England in the eye in the cause of Irish freedom did not, they argued, in April 1916 make them agents of Germany or disloyal Americans. The "martyring" of the Sixteen Men had created in America a good deal of disgust for Britain and admiration for the reckless bravery of the Irish Republicans. Now Cohalan and Devoy proclaimed their sympathy with Casement and the Rising; both denied any contact with Germany or German agents; both asserted a pre-eminent American patriotism. They pointed out the suspicious timing of the "raid" in Wall Street, and wondered publicly if the "betrayal" of the Rising and the arrest of Casement might be attributed to information laid by American authorities. Cohalan denied any knowledge of von Igel and called the "message" to von Bernstorff an outright forgery. He was attacked editorially in the press, assailed again in the Legislature, and denounced by Theodore Roosevelt in a speech at Carnegie Hall. He was "disowned" by Tammany Hall, and defiantly applauded by the Boston Clan-na-Gael. He kept on flatly denying his guilt and reasserting his American patriotism. Ultimately Cohalan won his own point, with no help from Quinn, asked or offered. He sued the Mail and Express Company of New York for $750,000 for libel, for printing as facts the present charges and the old Connolly bribery charges, and accepted on December 2, 1918, a judgment for $5,000 damages and an abject public apology. Quinn was still perfectly convinced of Cohalan's and Devoy's disloyalty to the Allied cause and of their moral cynicism in chumming with Germany, whatever their "higher" loyalty to Ireland, and their names were anathema to him henceforth.

Padraic Colum's second letter had expressed thanks to Quinn for his gift of the "Irish convention book," and a promise to read it at once. The little volume, *The Irish Home Rule Convention: with an Introduction by John Quinn,* appeared in September and was one product of Quinn's resolution to try one last time to do something himself for Irish nationalism. Since the summer of 1916 Quinn had been scheming sporadically with Shane Leslie to find a way to bring pressure upon English authorities for the release of John MacNeill, Douglas Hyde's Vice-President in the Gaelic League, Professor of Ancient History at the National University, and Chairman of the Irish Volunteers, from his imprisonment under a life sentence following the Easter Rebellion. In January Quinn and Leslie were trying to enlist forty or fifty American scholars and professors who would be willing to put their names to a petition for MacNeill's release. Cecil Spring-Rice had promised to forward it to England with a strong recommendation of his own. In February Quinn learned that in Ireland Douglas Hyde had submitted a petition signed by about fifty scholars and historians, asking only that MacNeill be allowed free use of his books in prison. Quinn drafted his own proposal, asking outright liberation upon MacNeill's engagement to abstain from political activity, and sent it to Hyde to be presented to MacNeill for approval. As Hyde had anticipated, the prisoner forthwith rejected the reservation against political action—with thanks to Quinn for his good intentions. The general amnesty extended to the prisoners of the Rising soon freed MacNeill in any case, after having given him time to learn Spanish and brush up his Greek. Within a week of his release he was with De Valera in County Clare, campaigning for Irish "independence." When in the autumn MacNeill was asking for re-appointment to his ancient history professorship, Hyde hoped for the best but noted drily, ". . . many people think he is too much engaged in making modern history to think much of, or work much at, the ancient thing." [55] His mild involvement in the Mac-Neill affair had, however, put Quinn back in the posture of caring about and working for Irish Home Rule, and one of his reasons for welcoming America's participation in the war on the side of Britain was that it lent force to Irish-American pressure for Home Rule. He cared enough about the writer and his purpose to send Shane Leslie an eleven-page letter of suggestions on September 6 for his chapter on "Irish America During the War" for his book, *The Irish Issue in Its American Aspect.*[56]

Hyde wondered what MacNeill really meant in demanding an "independent" Ireland. If a republic was what he intended, then Hyde thought nothing short of revolution in England could bring that about. Or he thought MacNeill and De Valera might be only trading, "like a man in a fair, asking more than he expects to get." Hyde was afraid of the whole agitation as muddling and badly timed political tactics, and by no means expressive of the national mood. "Colonial Home Rule would amply satisfy nineteen-twenti-eths of the race," he estimated, "and I don't care to see a republic preached lest, when real grievances are settled, the demand for *it* should persist and throw things into confusion." [57] Quinn accepted this conservative tactical logic. "Independence for Ireland is a dream—nothing more," he wrote to Theodore Roosevelt, and he went on in his letter of August 13 to adopt Hyde's argument, his arithmetic, his figures of speech, and most of his language:

> Of course, there will be no independent republic in Ireland ex-cept as the sequel to a rebellion in England. . . . they [the Sinn Feiners] are like a man at a fair, probably asking more than they expect to get. Colonial home rule would, I believe, satisfy nine-teen-twentieths of the Irishmen throughout the world. On the other hand, the preaching of a republic is perhaps not whole-some, because when real grievances are settled the demand for a republic may persist and throw things into mere confusion.

"Ireland is the spectre of the British Empire," Shane Leslie's book would pronounce in its first sentence.[58] The ancient "Irish Question," the question of the form to be taken by an Irish government and its relation to Britain as a whole, the old spectre now vaguely and inclusively known as Home Rule, was again particularly pressing after the Rising and as a problem of the war. A Home Rule Bill had slumbered in the parliamentary books since before the war, held up largely because of the apparently irreconcilable claims of Ulster and of southern Ireland. Quinn was violently opposed to the idea of a divided Ireland and contemptuously dismissed both the claims and the fears of Ulster. But T. W. Rolleston, who agreed with him that "the Ulstermen ought to take the risk and quit them like men," thought Quinn was treating the Ulster case much too lightly and simply, and wrote to persuade him that Protestant Ulster had good historical and logical reason to fear severance from England and domination by a Catholic majority under Home Rule:

I don't think you fully appreciate the strength of the Ulster case. You say the "Popery cry" is "absurd." Are you so sure of that? On the surface, the Ulstermen have every reason to think it a serious danger. The Church has, right down to the present day, constantly and emphatically asserted its claim to coerce religious opinion. It has singled out for anathema every principle on which the modern world is based. . . . Remember that in Ireland, alone, I believe, of all countries in the world, mediaeval Catholicism is still in full bloom and vigour. You do not know that, but the Orangemen do, and they do not appreciate the long-distance point of view that nothing would prove a greater solvent of this mediaeval Catholicism than self-government. At least, that is my own hope and expectation. . . . Political cooperation of any genuine kind is not merely an affair of Cabinet meetings and Parliamentary divisions. It must have a basis in solid life, in mutual knowledge and regard. All this is exceedingly difficult between the rival sects in Ireland. The Catholic Church has now succeeded in segregating itself from all intercourse with the Protestant world through all the stages of education right up to the end of the university career. . . . The result is that Catholic and Protestant form two separate worlds and have scarcely any knowledge of each other, so that the basis for a true cooperation in national work is lacking. [*October 30, 1917.*]

Partisan political feeling, always violent in Ireland, grew more and more heated as Home Rule began to seem imminent at last. Southern Ireland was not only opposed to Ulster but divided within itself. John Redmond and the Irish Parliamentary Party had been declining steadily for years in power and prestige, in local faith. Sinn Feiners were now beating them at the polls, then sardonically boycotting the whole parliamentary process, refusing to take the seats to which they had been elected. The situation was explosive, and it was to explode for the next five years. The Sixteen Men had built better than anyone knew. ". . . Ireland is more exciting than I ever remember it," Æ wrote on July 28, and James Stephens wrote in the autumn: "We are not the folk we were in August, 1914. We are harder, more careless, and very ready to live or die as opportunity serves or demands." [59]

Quinn's view of the situation was essentially that of most of the conservative thinkers in Ireland. He believed that the wise and proper solution for both Ireland and England was a semi-autonomous Irish dominion in familial relation to England. But he wanted a whole Ireland, with no division of counties between north and south, all one in relation to each other and to England. He looked upon the Ulster leader Carson as a cynical special pleader, little better than a bandit. But he agreed with those who saw Redmond and his party in Parliament as disqualified by a history of pusillanimity and compromise with England—though their statutory position still seemed to him the one from which Irish political action ought to proceed. When T. P. O'Connor came to America in the summer of 1917 on the latest Redmondite "mission," Quinn did what he could to help him raise money; but he judged Redmond's cause already lost in both Ireland and America. He held to the view that the solid success of Home Rule would be best achieved by persistent but reasonable diplomatic pressure upon English statesmen, and he worked to that end all during 1917, as indeed he had done for years as opportunity offered. In the large sense, the MacNeill petition was a piece of these tactics, as his labors to save Casement had been.

Quinn pressed his case at every opportunity with Cecil Spring-Rice, already a friend and general sympathizer, and with every British official whose ear he could reach in New York and Washington. In April he elicited from Theodore Roosevelt a powerful statement in favor of Home Rule for Ireland and caused it to be widely published in England and America. Shane Leslie secured the public backing of William Howard Taft. These moves Quinn followed up in the first week in May by organizing a deputation to urge the case with Arthur Balfour in Washington. His party consisted of Father John J. Wynne (an old Jesuit friend in New York) and Father Sigourney Fay "representing Catholic Irishmen"; Colonel Robert Temple Emmet and Lawrence Godkin "representing Protestant Irishmen"; and Morgan J. O'Brien and Quinn "representing American neutral Irishmen but nationalists." The awkward categories suggest at once some of the complexities of Irish partisanship and Quinn's definition of his own role as Irish-American patriot. The purpose of the delegation, as of all Quinn's related actions, was to dramatize and argue before the British, looking ahead to their general relations with America after the war, that there were large and considerable bodies in the United States who would be displeased unless something humane and statesman-like were finally done about Ireland's ancient and valid grievances. Just as Shane Leslie would subtitle his book "A Contribution to the Settlement of Anglo-American Relations During and After the Great War," so Quinn played again and again upon the theme of generosity to Ireland as sound British policy. Both Spring-Rice and Balfour's aide, General Bridges, told Quinn that Balfour had been strongly impressed by his argument. Quinn was confident that he was making an impact, and in letters to Lady Gregory and others he expressed his satisfaction that he was well known and seriously considered in English cabinet circles. He was expressing, after all, only a temperate Irish nationalism which sorted very well with the feelings of most English political men; caught in an exhausting war and anticipating complex international problems to follow, and long heartily sick of the Irish Question, they were delighted to pacify the Irish if a way could be found to do so without embarrassment or danger to security.

In fact the English now took a boldly civilized step, inviting and challenging the Irish to find a shape for their own polity—to convene representatives of all the contending Irish factions to try to draw a generally agreeable design for the island's future government. Quinn at once threw his energies behind the plan, pressing in all quarters for the inclusion in the deliberations of the men he considered the ablest and most temperate spirits, Douglas Hyde, George Russell, and Sir Horace Plunkett. To make a more direct personal contribution he undertook to circulate two monitory essays by Russell and Plunkett, whose influence he wished to see disseminated at once as a guide and check upon partisan opinion. He thought first of publishing the two essays as a pamphlet with a brief covering letter from himself. Then he decided to offer the essays for publication in the *New York Evening Post*, which kept them ten days and then wished to print a curtailed version of the texts. Quinn now took the material to Brett of Macmillan's in New York, and he agreed to publish the small volume if Quinn would write an introduction. When Quinn set out to dictate his brief statement, he found himself going on for an ultimate ninety pages. He finished the draft in two afternoons, partly revised it in the second evening just before leaving for Washington, and telephoned final revisions from Washington in time to catch the printers.

What emerged in September 1917 was a neat little blue-backed volume of 183 pages, *The Irish Home-Rule Convention*, with Quinn's opinions and expositions filling seven chapters and half the pages, Æ's "Thoughts for a Convention" filling sixty pages, and Plunkett's "A Defence of the Convention" filling only twenty pages. Quinn summarized his major purposes in the operation to James Byrne on September 24:

> . . . I had two or three objects in mind in writing the introduction. One was an experiment in suggestion in politics. Every leader has recognized the value of suggestion but only the big ones practise it. I tried to practise it in an elementary way on the English in regard to this convention. I dictated it with the thought in mind that Englishmen, even Lloyd George and Balfour, to whom I have sent copies of the book, after reading the introduction would say: "Great God, we have got to do it this time, for America expects it."
>
> I also wanted to take a fall out of the stupid pro-German Irish in this country, and I wanted to put the Irish right in this country so far as I could in the introduction. I said nothing that could be offensive to an Englishman, nor to an Ulsterman.

He despatched two hundred copies of the book hastily to all possible quarters of influence, English, Irish, and American, as well as to his usual list of book-receiving friends. Thanks and felicitations, of varying temperature, poured in during the autumn. Theodore Roosevelt thanked him for "that capital little book" and promised to use it thenceforth as his "Confession of Faith on Home Rule." [60]

Russell was made a member of the committee to nominate a chairman of the convention; he proposed Plunkett, who was warmly approved and elected by the delegates. Æ himself had accepted service as a civilized obligation, though he felt little faith in solid results from the convention. "I accepted Lloyd George's nomination," he explained to Quinn on July 28, "because I could not have it on my conscience that I refused to help to bring about an Irish settlement if there was the ghost of a chance. I think there is the ghost of a chance and I will stick on it." Something, he thought, might be accomplished by private reasoning with "these Northerners," the Ulster delegates. Quinn's Dublin lawyer friend, Richard J. Kelly, writing on November 12 to thank him for his "admirable little book," expressed the same kind of wistfully qualified pessimism:

> All that is sensible and reasonable in the country anxiously asks for and wants a settlement. The times favour a broad-minded and bold measure of autonomy. England has declared her willingness to accept and ratify a full measure, and the only difficulty lies with ourselves: our once irreconcilable Orange crowd—dour, determined and desperate—and our growing mass of discontent comprehensively designated Sinn Feiners.

James Stephens wrote on August 8, the second day of the convention's sitting in the Regent House, "that last infirmary for noble minds," to phrase his homely version of the "mandate" from the country to the delegates: " 'Let ye talk about Colonial Home Rule, and if ye don't talk about that then shut your gobs and go home. . . .' " By the middle of October Stephens had pretty well abandoned hope that a positive program could emerge from the convention. But he was full of admiration for the conduct of his master, Russell, who seemed to him to be quietly dominating the proceedings with his integrity, his clarity of mind, and his unpretentious eloquence of speech. "He has had to wait a long time," Stephens wrote, "for something to come along which would stretch him out to the full, and he is proving himself the man we always said he was." [61]

May Morris's ritual New Year's Eve letter made a sad coda to the year. After having had the care of her invalid sister during the year, she had come to Kelmscott House in Lechlade for a rest at Christmas with a spinster friend, then fallen ill with influenza herself. Now she was well enough to iron the soldiers' socks knitted by her circle of village girls. She pointed out that she had not had a personal letter from Quinn for nearly two years: "A few months back came a long envelope which I welcomed, but found to be a reprint of a public letter of yours." It is a sad letter from the daughter of a powerful and original father—confirmed in gloom and loneliness, busy about her good works, writing drably to the man who had chosen not to transform her life, or, finally, to value her affection. She never wrote again.

1918

QUINN had appeared fairly well during 1917, or perhaps he had merely been too busy to complain. In April he did, however, have a painful fall while riding his horse in Central Park. The horse had stumbled and thrown him to the ground on his left side; when he tried to remount the horse shied, and Quinn fell again on his right side. Shaken but stubborn, he walked the animal back to Durland's, calmed him down, and continued his ride for another forty minutes, but found his left arm was of no use to him. In court on a criminal case during the morning he suffered considerable pain, and an X ray taken in the afternoon showed that the radius bone in his left arm had been split at the end.[1] Earlier in the same month Quinn had been differently shaken by the death of Annie Foster, daughter of his old master Governor Foster, and his first love—long quieted but full of residual feeling. When the galley proofs of his *Vanity Fair* article on Joyce arrived with a border of black ink on each page, he took scissors and cut off the borders before he could bring himself to work at the text. As a sentimental gesture at the end of the year Quinn had brought out, privately printed by Mitchell Kennerley in an edition of one hundred copies bound in blue buckram with gold lettering, the undistinguished poems of his dead cousin Katherine Quinn. One feels a small current of morbidity in such actions.

Not surprisingly, too, his irascibility accumulated with the number and variety of his tensions, especially the pressure of persons demanding help. He wrote to Keogh on January 18 to let off steam after a long trying session with "a young lady . . . brown habited, fur hatted, brown gloved, smiling, but persistent, oh so persistent," who pleaded with him to "help" *Pearson's* magazine. To Quinn her smile had felt chronic and remorseless and seemed to transmit itself to his own features: "And, having eased my feelings, I now have a persistent smile and pass it on to you." To Knopf he wrote at about the same time: "I learned years ago that people appreciate what they pay for. Very few people have the sense to appreciate what is given to them. That applies both to love as well as [*sic*] to literature. In fact I think it is a universal principle. It applies also to legal advice." [2] Also at the same time he sent a nineteen-page letter to Jacob Epstein in the course of which he summed up his chief distractions and irritations:

> If I attempted to help all the people that were referred to me, men who want commissions in the army, and men who are pinched in the draft and want to be excused, and some of the most deserving cases, I'd have to open up a war department as an annex to my office. Then while I was in the war business, I might open an Irish annex and a Home Rule annex, and a hard-luck annex.
>
> [*January 21, 1918.*]

To Joseph Conrad a month later he cited the case of Mrs. Sheehy-Skeffington, widow of the unfortunate casualty of the Easter Rising in Dublin, as an example of the kind of thing he was constantly being called upon to accomplish for others; she had been "smuggled" into the United States by Irish "patriots" who, when the time came for her return, begged Quinn to manage her clearance by means of his influence at the British Embassy: "And I did it." [3] Quinn's irritation was general as well as specific; the letter to Epstein, for example, refers less to Epstein's own case than to the general tenor of Quinn's life. Collectively things were beginning to seem unbearable. The quantity and variety of Quinn's labors during 1917 had been staggering by any standard; when one realizes that all these things had been accomplished by a man with cancer, the record seems nearly incredible.

In the last months of 1917 and the first weeks of 1918 Quinn had been troubled by stomach and intestinal cramps. He had interpreted these as his usual symptoms aggravated by overwork and had carried gamely on with his ordinary extraordinary regimen.

Only his trusted friend and clerk T. J. Curtin knew how unwell he was feeling. About the beginning of December Quinn began to suffer bleeding from the rectum. He put up with this until late in January when he submitted himself to Dr. John F. Erdmann at the Post-Graduate Hospital for a full examination. Dr. Erdmann suspected a malignancy and advised immediate surgery. Quinn asked for a second opinion, which was corroborative. He then asked only for a few days in which to put his affairs in order, and the operation was set for Tuesday, February 5, giving him five days in which to work. His doctors did not hide from him the fact that the matter was serious, but they estimated he had an 80 or 85 per cent chance of surviving. Quinn wrote to the Andersons in Fostoria to ask them to come to New York to stand by, and they arrived in the afternoon of the day before the operation. Shane Leslie sent him from Washington on the second a mingled Christian and pagan prayer which Quinn was willing enough to echo: "God guide the leech and keep you from Tir nan Og awhile." He spent his five days constantly at work in his office, going over cases on hand with the other lawyers and bringing his immense correspondence up to date. Most of his letters made no mention of the impending operation. Dr. Erdmann's work on the morning of the fifth Quinn called gratefully "a miracle of success-ful surgery." [4] He described the operation graphically for Conrad: "It consisted in removing a bleeding ulcer from the lower abdomen, about ten inches up the rectum, cutting out a section and bringing the sections together, and splicing them. . . ." The incision was abdominal, and the appendix was removed along the way. Dr. Erdmann told Quinn that he had also held his gall bladder in his hand and been of two minds whether to take that as well, but had finally dropped it back. "I'm glad you left me something," Quinn said. All seemed to have gone well, the only seriously troublesome consequence of the operation being a phlebitis in his left leg which lingered for several months.

But the shock had been a severe one and full convalescence was a slow and lingering affair. Quinn remained in the hospital for five weeks, with a metal frame to keep the bedclothes off his bad leg; then rested for two weeks at his apartment with two nurses on duty; then went for two further weeks to the Buckhill Inn in the

Pocono Mountains, accompanied by his sister Julia Anderson, her eleven-year-old daughter, Mary, and a single nurse. Quinn was back in New York on April 11 and back in his office, on a limited schedule, on April 15. Two months later he still felt weak and unwell, "frightfully shaky in the legs and all over," suffering from rheumatism in his neck and throat, and subject to fits of extreme nervousness.[5] He was still taking a massage for an hour every afternoon. He now wore, and would wear until he died, a canvas vest or corset to support his back and abdomen, into which he had to be laced each morning by his new French manservant, Paul. He did not feel physically competent until late in the summer. By the end of September he was able to sustain, and to profit by, eight days of action and inaction in Hot Springs, Virginia, with golf, motoring, hiking, milk and eggs morning and afternoon, and one and often two Negro servants in close attendance.

In his five days of grace before the operation Quinn had behaved with surprising calm and efficiency. He was forty-seven years old, in the prime of life as he felt it. He knew that his life mattered to a great many others as well as to himself, and later he was quietly proud of the way he had met the obligations of his own usefulness. "I worked hard and fast those days," he recalled in writing to W. B. Yeats. "I had to think and dictate and arrange things quick." [6] On the same day he wrote to Lady Gregory: "I felt that there was so much I wanted to do that I could only do a few things to make life easier for others. If ever I lived selfless days, those five days were selfless." [7] He knew that he might die and that he did not want to die. His early reticence about the crisis soon began to turn *vibrato* with a characteristic tone of candid sentiment and self-dramatization. He had faced death bravely, he thought, but not unfeelingly: "But to face it when one is strong and full of life and the love of life, and I love life very much, and full of the love of family and friends, and with many hopes and plans still to be carried out, that is a bitter thing, more bitter than any words can tell." [8] He used the current martial metaphor: "I was like a man going over the top, only I had no company." [9] He felt he had had a transforming experience, and a spiritual experience. "One looks at things out of hospital windows very differently from what one does out of other windows," he phrased it on April 16 to Mrs. Conrad, who knew about hospital windows. Quinn's mind had always run much, reluctantly, on the idea of death, and now death forced itself to the top of his consciousness and stayed there. In his letters of this interval he kept making occasions to quote Turgenev's line: " 'Death is the only irreparable thing.' " Like many another in similar crises, he found his skepticism quailing: "Extinction is a horrible thing to think about," he mused to Arthur Symons, "—passing out into the dark, even *through the dark*. I believe that it is *through the dark*, and not into the dark." [10]

Quinn had found his first serious illness a humbling and softening experience, and he wrote to W. B. Yeats of this new look of things from hospital windows:

> My illness has made me horribly sensitive and tender of suffering in others. Before, when I did kind or considerate things, they were perhaps mostly intellectually kind, kind without tenderness, except of course to my sisters and my parents and my brother when he lived. But tenderness must be felt. It cannot be described. It does not mean sentimentality. I never before realized what a power for good money could be if there were tenderness and love as well as intellect in its use. [*September 15, 1918.*]

These were new words as well as new ideas for Quinn, and they faced fairly bravely a crucial deficiency in the spirit of his benevolent actions. They tell one, of course, more of his past than of his future, and it rested with time to tell whether he had suffered a deep change of spirit. Tenderness takes time as well as impulse, and Quinn had had and would have little enough time. During this year when he was forcing himself to slow down his hectic pace, tenderness and indeed sentiment are often visible and audible in his conduct of affairs, as, for example, in his condolences to Mrs. Roosevelt on the death of her son in France: "The loss of your son Quentin hurt me almost like a personal grief, and my heart went out to you and the Colonel, although I felt that your pride in his bravery and gallantry was some consolation for your loss." [11] He reminded her that her husband had gone under the knife on the same day as himself, in the hospital named for Roosevelt, and told her how he had been cheered in his own convalescence by bulletins of his strenuous friend's quick recovery.

A few days after Quinn's operation, when all seemed to have

gone well and the prognosis appeared favorable, Thomas Curtin sent cables announcing Quinn's illness and recovery to his friends in England, Ireland, and France. Æ wrote back on February 11: "It is only when one hears of a friend's illness that one realizes how much one likes, relies on and trusts that friend. I am sure with you it is due to overwork, and not work for yourself, at that." Ezra Pound put the same sentiments in his own idiom: "I hope you are well and out of the hospital by the time this reaches you. You will certainly die with your cheque-book in your hand, paying the debts of some irrelevant artist, and may that day be long hence." [12] Among the letters Quinn dictated in the hurried days before the operation was a long one to Lady Gregory on the affairs of an educational fund which she had set up for her grandson Richard Gregory and of which she had made Quinn trustee. In February, still in the hopsital, he received her news that her son Robert Gregory had fallen to his death in his plane on the Italian front, leaving his wife and three small children and, of course, his mother, crushingly bereaved for the second time by the war. Quinn had known Robert Gregory as a brilliant young man, and his affection for his mother was such as to make him feel the death almost as a loss in his own family. When Yeats, moved by Gregory's death to the most passionate and eloquent elegy in English since *Lycidas*, published "In Memory of Major Robert Gregory" in the *English Review* in August, Quinn enclosed a copy of the poem in his letter of sympathy to Mrs. Roosevelt, similarly bereaved.

Over the next months Lady Gregory conducted her grief nobly and gracefully, in a manner that exemplified John Butler Yeats's theory of the right expression of such feeling, fluent and unembarrassed, the "infinite" finding its voice in the free exercise of the "finite." Quinn followed the story with eager understanding. She had been at her writing table at Coole Park when a friend "came slowly, slowly in" with the news that a telegram awaited her at the post office: ". . . I think I knew what was in the telegram before I saw the word 'killed.' " [13] It is notable that she sent Quinn "a little line" on the next day: he was among the few to whom she wished to speak first. Her first and hardest trial lay in carrying the news to Robert's wife, Margaret: "I could hardly stand but had to go and take the train for Galway to bring it to her. When she saw me she knew what it was, and I was able at last to cry and cry. . . ." [14] Lady Gregory was comforted that her son had died in Italy, and that he had been buried by comrades in Padua, in a portion of the cemetery saved for "those who have come to die for Italy." And she found an odd inverted pleasure in a letter from Bernard Shaw, who had seen Robert Gregory in a visit to the west front, when, " 'in abominably cold weather, with a frostbite on his face hardly healed, he told me that the six months he had been there had been the happiest of his life.' " [15] Sorrowing and admiring letters were reaching her from her son's comrades, and those hurt and helped. "But my heart is very sore for my fair-haired son, so gentle and affectionate to me through all his life. . . ." She noted the sad continuity of her life, as she went about her work at Coole: "Last month I was planting for Robert, now I am planting for Richard."

"Dear John, I hope I have not tired you with all this," she said at the end of this long *cri du cœur* of February 10. It was the first long letter she had written, and she sent it partly in expression of Robert Gregory's gratitude for Quinn's long kindness to his mother. She wrote in ignorance of Quinn's own grave illness, but when she wrote again on February 22 she had had letters of January 28 and February 4 from Quinn and Curtin's cable of reassurance, and now she admonished: ". . . you must not neglect yourself again. You were always thinking of others and leaving no time for that." She had begun to pick up her work in the theatre again, and going on with the old fight to recover Hugh Lane's pictures for Dublin, but everything related itself against her will to the lost son. When Quinn's gift of Henry James's three autobiographical volumes arrived, she could only recollect James in the company of Robert Gregory: "He was kind to Robert, was the only one of my visitors long ago who used to kiss him when he came into my London drawing room as a child, and came later, much later, to his first picture exhibitions in London and spoke so nicely of them." [16] By March she felt that she had herself in hand, except when relics of her son in life kept tapping the sources. "That is what happens; one gets on well for a while, and then something—his palette hanging in the studio or his coat in the hall—does away with all reasoning. . . ." [17] Her will to creative work was gone forever, she thought, but she was able to work at secondary tasks, translations

of poems and tales from the Irish, her Kiltartan History, and a loose
and tentative autobiographical collection which she was referring to
as her "education," after Henry Adams. At the end of the long
year her work still seemed to her mainly a screen between herself
and the "thought of that late death"—in Yeats's phrase. But work
had helped, and she determined to keep on with "some work
beyond that of the day, something that makes a background for the
mind." [18]

But it was the nobility of W. B. Yeats's public response that
turned this death, among so many thousands, into myth, turned the
finite toward the infinite. It was the young man's multiplicity and
fullness, the Renaissance roundness of his humane masculinity, that
had impressed itself on Yeats's mind and left him now with the
sense of stunning waste. "He was the most accomplished man I have
ever known; I mean that he could do more things well than any
other," Yeats wrote to Quinn on February 8. Of that thought he
made the iterated image of the poem:

> Soldier, scholar, horseman, he,
> And all he did done perfectly
> As though he had but that one trade alone.

Quinn naturally made use of his convalescence as his first chance
in a long while to do some systematic reading, and before he even
left the hospital he had gone through Conrad's *The Inheritors*,
Romance (with Ford Madox Hueffer), *Almayer's Folly*, *Tales of
Unrest*, and *Mirror of the Sea;* Whibley's *Political Portraits;* Chesterton's *History of England;* Yeats's *Per Amica Silentia Lunae;* and
Pierre Loti's *India*. Among the letters he read in the hospital was
one from Joseph Conrad in which he included a genially condescending note on the author of *Lustra*, a gift from Quinn:

> E. P. is certainly a poet but I am afraid I am too old and too
> wooden-headed to appreciate him as perhaps he deserves. The
> critics here consider him harmless; but as he has, I believe, a
> very good opinion of himself I don't suppose he worries his head
> about the critics very much. Besides, he has many women at his
> feet; which must be immensely comforting. [19]

Harmless was perhaps the last thing Pound would wish to be called;
he would have been much happier to hear J. B. Yeats's judgment

that he wished to reap a harvest of hate. Also in the hospital Quinn read Pound's letter of January 29 making the welcome and appropriate suggestion that he accept the dedication of *Pavannes and Divisions*, now in the works at Knopf's. To urge Knopf along Quinn had already agreed to advance the sum of $150 with the understanding that he could take back that value in copies of *Pavannes and Divisions* or other works of Pound's published by Knopf.[20] Pound suggested the inscription " 'To John Quinn,' " then, "if the fancy takes you: *Americanus non moribus.*" Then he began to wonder if *Americanus* should have been made dative; he looked up Dante's epistle to Can Grande, which was his model, and amended his phrase to "*Americano natione non moribus.*" Quinn carried the grammatical question to his scholarly friend in Brooklyn, Vincent O'Sullivan, who voted for the dative case, but went on to question the good taste of the whole idea: "At these times I should think it rather tasteless, to say the least, to be thus complimented at the expense of all the rest of my countrymen by an American living abroad and not, as I understand it, engaged in any sort of work for his country." [21] Quinn rather tamely acquiesced, and said he had already reached the same conclusion himself. When the dedication appeared it read simply "To John Quinn."

Quinn had committed himself to read proofs on Pound's volume, as he had done for *Lustra;* the proofs appeared while he was in hospital, and he set them aside until late spring when he felt up to the task. Then he went to work with his usual thoroughness on the page proofs. As Lily Yeats had done, he found Pound's own work on the galleys negligent, and he wrote to call him down. Pound wrote back to say he was sorry Quinn had had "so much fag" with the task, but protested that he had read the proofs and had had them read by two others; but he realized he was poor at the trade: his tendency was always to get caught up again with interesting problems of style and content and to overlook the mere mechanics of the printed text.[22] The text met further difficulty when the British censors held up Pound's cable suggesting the title "Tergenda" for items to be appended to the end, "meaning matter to be ultimately rubbed out, or polished up, or polished off." [23] The censor suspected code, and protested that the word was "in Latin"; that, Pound admitted, was "incontrovertible." [24] When the book appeared at the end of June "Tergenda" had metamorphosed drably to "Appendices."

The Pound "brochure," T. S. Eliot's "Ezra Pound: His Metric and Poetry," had also appeared from Knopf before Quinn entered the hospital. Quinn saw that a hundred copies were sent to Pound in London, kept two hundred for distribution himself, and consigned the rest to Knopf for publicity purposes. His bill for four-fifths of the cost finally came to $117.92. Quinn had again read the proofs, and he was pleased with the final appearance of the pamphlet. It remained anonymous, with Eliot's authorship unspecified as Pound had insisted, and the Gaudier drawing of Pound was in as a frontispiece.[25] Pound wrote to Quinn of his satisfaction after he had seen his first copies:

> I am delighted with the format, you certainly have done me proud, and it is very crafty to present me in gold and old rose maddar [*sic*], as if I had just that graceful and saddened tonality that the American "patron of the perfumed shelf" has so long desired and been accustomed to. . . .
>
> Certainly if America finally decides to pay my rent, it will be your doing. *[April 7, 1918.]*

Pound's comprehensive obligations he expressed not only to Quinn but also to Margaret Anderson, who had been complaining of Quinn again:

> Re Quinn, remember: Tis he who hath bought the pictures; tis he who both getteth me an American publisher and smacketh the same with rods; tis he who sendeth me the Spondos Oligos, which is by interpretation the small tribute or spondooliks wherewith I do pay my contributors, WHEREFORE is my heart softened toward the said J.Q., and he in mine eyes can commit nothing heinous.[26]

Quinn's "disciplining" of Knopf struck Pound as one of his more important and delightful functions. He wrote Quinn on January 29: "Knopf wrote on Jan. 4 and on Jan. 7, before and AFTER Quinn. Contrast extremely amusing"; and on February 17, "[Knopf's] letters to me BEFORE *and* AFTER his last dose of QUINNine were a very, very, VERY amusing contrast." The *Little Review* had issued a printed appeal for funds, and Quinn corrected its form and helped to send it about. Just before his operation he wrote Pound that he had gone himself to his usual coterie of reliable donors to his causes, and had secured $400 each from Otto Kahn, Max Pam, and Mrs. James Byrne. Kahn had said that he would have given $600 had he not disliked the American contributions to recent issues. In addition to his own standing subsidy of $750, Quinn now promised to match the other $400 gifts.[27] At the end of the year he noted to Pound that he had made the *Little Review* ladies a further "loan" of $200, but by that time he was so angry at the way they were behaving that he resolved to give nothing more beyond his original subsidy, which had always been a tribute to Pound himself.[28] "1600 broad 'pieces of eight,'" Pound exulted when he heard of the new gifts. He was touched at these new signs of Quinn's loyalty and thoughtfulness in the midst of a serious illness and a serious dissatisfaction with the magazine itself and thought it admirable of him to have rounded up guarantors in spite of his own irritation at the editors' courses.[29]

Pound's own situation was as always perilous, animated, and interesting. He informed Quinn at the end of April that he had sent Margaret Anderson "a sort of ultimatum, very mild and friendly, as indeed it should be,"[30] that the magazine must achieve a sound basis within the year or he would have to abandon it. He cited his labors on the forthcoming French and Henry James issues of the *Little Review*, which should have been the work of several years but were being accomplished in a few months. Meanwhile his rent was "being paid by continuous journalism." He was contributing regular columns to Orage's *New Age* under pseudonyms, writing on art as "B.H. Dias" and on music as "William Atheling."[31] Of Quinn's £150 subsidy to the *Little Review* Pound was keeping only £5 a month or £60 a year, and using the rest to pay his contributors. When Quinn now offered him personally a further "£25 or, mon dieu, £50,"[32] Pound refused with thanks: what he wanted was not more money from Quinn but a more stable base for his life generally. He restated his philosophy as to the subsidy, the magazine, and his personal function. To have taken more than £60 out of Quinn's first £150 would have "spoiled the spirit of the thing." He needed to be able to point out to contributors that he was getting only a pittance and they could not expect a higher rate. The contents of a review, he argued, were a testimony to an editor's ability to collect and hold a group or "vortex" of articulate spirits: with Pound these had been first Lewis and Gaudier, then Lewis and Yeats, and now Ford Madox Ford, Romains, Joyce, and Eliot.[33]

Quinn's annoyance with Miss Anderson and Miss Heap was accumulating all the time, and he kept telling Pound that the magazine was heading for serious and probably fatal trouble from the unkempt business habits and the arrogant editorial attitudes of "those two rabbits," as he liked to call them. He was angered at what seemed to him Miss Anderson's rude and lofty treatment of his friend Georgette Passedoit, whom he had recommended to correct certain French texts for the magazine; he was only slightly mollified when Miss Passedoit received a letter of thanks after two weeks.[34] Miss Anderson told him that the installments of *Ulysses* she was receiving and printing were "very frank," and Quinn warned Pound that the language must be "toned down." He reminded them that different standards of censorship obtained for books and magazines, that books could get away with things that would draw quick suppression upon a magazine, and that the *Little Review* was already under constant suspicious scrutiny. When he read in the hospital a draft from Pound of a proposed attack upon Judge Augustus N. Hand's decision in the "Cantleman case," he angrily "chucked it out." [35] On March 2 he wrote Pound that Jane Heap had shown him proofs of a short article by Pound denouncing the Hand decision. He had advised her and now advised Pound against printing it, and Margaret Anderson had promised Thomas Curtin to suppress the piece. He cautioned Pound against lining up himself and the magazine with what he called the "sex literature" advocates. Quinn had no intention of mounting a crusade on principle against the censorship laws, as doubtless the *Little Review* editors would have liked; he spoke to Pound pragmatically, as a workman trying to make the best of a fallible trade:

There are many provisions in the law that are absurd. I have run up against them. But, Christ, I haven't wasted my time in trying to reform them. I have left that up to the long-haired nuts of the bar associations. . . . Nobody ever regarded the law, common or statute, as perfection, and the man that discusses it on the assumption that it is a perfect instrument shows his inexperience.   [*March 2, 1918.*]

When Quinn wrote again on March 14 he had just read the March number of the *Little Review* and was in a furious state: after soliciting his advice the editors had ignored it, and had printed the Pound letter after promising to omit it. Pound had directed his attack less at the decision than at the law—"the law, the amazing, grotesque, and unthinkable law of our country"—and had inveighed against subjecting literature to the same set of interdictions (in using the mails) as were applied to contraceptive devices: ". . . the inventions of the late Dr. Condom." [36] Quinn conceded that the letter had been toned down a bit, but he felt that the Pound piece and the contributions of Joyce and Lewis were all open to successful prosecution. To their *défi* on the cover, "Making no compromise with the public taste," they should add, Quinn proposed: " 'or commonly accepted ideas of decency and propriety.' " Quinn had his own sympathies with the censorship, as well as with the realities of the law and the logic of tactics. Now he objected particularly to Joyce's rich epithets, "scrotumtightening" and "snotgreen." That the March issue had already gone through the mails when he wrote was "not due to the fact that it was not stoppable," he thought, but merely to the general wartime rush of things.

Pound was trapped again, among his wish to placate Quinn, his own reluctant recognition of practicalities, his respect for his own editorial integrity, his hatred of censorship in principle, and his immense admiration for Joyce's work. He fought back as stoutly as he could, but with good temper. He conceded that Joyce wrote with "a certain odeur-de-muskrat," but insisted that such *odeur* was vital to his intention and to his achievement: "I don't think the passages about his mother's death and the sea would come with such force if they weren't imbedded in squalor and disgusts." [37] Such work as Joyce's he looked upon as necessarily strong medicine which he was prescribing for American moral anemia: ". . . America will never look *anything*—animal, mineral, vegetable, political, social, international, religious, philosophical or ANYTHING else —in the face until she gets used to perfectly bald statements." But Quinn had frightened, persuaded, or bullied him enough so that he had "deleted about twenty lines" in Joyce's fourth chapter, recently

received, before sending it on to New York, and had written Joyce
of his action.[38]

Quinn felt that his gifts of money and time gave him certain
rights of criticism over the magazine, and he did not hesitate to
exercise them. He disapproved Pound's selection of Jules Romains
as chief of the "French number," for example. But what drew him
out more positively and at greater length was the prospect of an
issue devoted to Henry James, one of his own oldest and most
passionate enthusiasms. Quinn had been reading and rereading
James since boyhood, and had been newly moved by the old
writer's strong Allied partisanship in the war as evidenced by such
gestures as his adoption of British citizenship before his death in
February 1916. "And he made a fine finish!" he exclaimed to Pound
on March 14. The fullness and accuracy of his knowledge of James's
work is another of the tastes and the capacities that make one think
hard about the native quality of Quinn's mind. He was learned in
the whole long canon, and it stirred him often to comments that
were deeper and fuller than the common run of his literary remarks.
Now the thought of the commemorative issue excited him again
to an exclamatory mood: "Don't under-value Henry James!" he
commanded Pound. "He was one of the best writers the United
States has ever had. What style, what genius for arranging and
amassing his facts! What lucidity! And what happy turns of
phrase! . . . No damn German vagueness about him!" [39]

Quinn had read James's recently published posthumous fragments, *The Sense of the Past* and *The Ivory Tower*, each with a
few completed chapters and a scenario of the remainder, and
praised them to Pound for giving "a great artist's method of work
to perfection." [40] He noted the rich variousness of James's career:
"the novelist, the critic, the historian, the cosmopolitan man of
letters. . . ." He found James's autobiographical volumes, *A Small
Boy and Others* and *Notes of a Son and Brother*, "infinitely more
interesting . . . than Morley's two big volumes of reminiscences,
which I have just been dipping into," and thought "the picture of
that cosmopolitan family . . . one of the best things in English."
Pound or Joyce or Lewis, Quinn supposed, might condemn James
for the narrowness of the social range in his novels; but he went on
to rationalize astutely that very selectivity:

James would admit it. He might justify himself by Meredith's dictum in his "Essay on Comedy," that comedy was only possible in persons of a certain type. Humor, yes. Horseplay, yes. Comedy, no! You must have the background. So James chose society of a certain degree of finish for his background.[41]

For Quinn, James could do no wrong. He even admired James's youthful paintings, done under Saint-Gaudens, which he had taken the trouble to seek out and examine.

Pound listened politely and again spoke his mind. He thought James great early and late, weak in the middle of his career; and he did not believe in over-inclusive and uncritical praise. "I don't believe it will do any good to overlook his limitations," he wrote on April 3. "Nor that one's praise will be effective if one doesn't recognize the defects, or the great stretch between his best and his worst." The early pages of *A Small Boy and Others*, for example, he found "disgusting," and he thought James, "when he isn't being a great and magnificent author," frequently "a very fussy and tiresome one." Almost in passing, Pound tossed in an insult to another of Quinn's idols: "Meredith is, to me, chiefly a stink."

Writing to W. B. Yeats on September 15 Quinn put a more sanguine face on the affairs of the *Little Review*. He still thought the magazine would be hard put to survive the year, but he felt it would have justified his subsidy in any case by publishing work of such quality as the French number, the Henry James number, and Joyce's *Ulysses*. Quinn fully confessed the power of Joyce's work, though he still marvelled that it had not been suppressed. And Yeats was quite willing to agree that this time Quinn had got his hands on an authentic genius, "a most remarkable man," who "surpassed in intensity any novelist of our time." He was impressed by Joyce's narrative method, the fluent and mordant interior monologue of *Ulysses*, as "an entirely new thing—neither what the eye sees nor the ear hears, but what the rambling mind thinks and imagines from moment to moment." [42] "The same thing had occurred to me," Quinn wrote back. "The style is just as one imagines things when one is walking the roads, and is interrupted by turns and one's thoughts are broken, or when one is recovering from illness and in a reverie." [43]

In his letter of April 3 Pound agreed with Quinn that the March issue of the *Little Review* was "too much on one note," and he explained various problems of timing in his receipt of manuscripts that had made it hard for him to vary the tone. But he still felt that their function was to print the best available work, and that they were doing so: ". . . who is there apart from the group of writers we are printing who is writing or can write??" Pound was sorry to see Quinn annoyed in the midst of an illness, and he apologized for the "general gloom and cantankerousness" of his defensive letter; but he came back to the incontrovertible point: "After all, it is something to get Joyce, Hueffer and Lewis into one number of one magazine. . . ." Pound's moderate glooms were eddies in the flow of his more characteristic energy and ebullience, the youth of spirit that would not be put down. He noted to Quinn in August that he had only recently "got over noting signs of 'LAD WANTED' in windows, and wondering if it is an opening." Two months later he proposed that Quinn get himself elected President of the United States, after which he could make Pound Secretary of Fine Arts: between them they might yet save America.[44]

Quinn of course continued to be involved, and more or less willingly, with Pound's group of writers in need of American assistance. Proofs of Wyndham Lewis's *Tarr* came to him in the hospital from Knopf at about the same time as those of Pound's *Pavannes and Divisions.* He saved the Pound proofs for himself but farmed out the Lewis proofs to healthier friends, Vincent O'Sullivan and Georgette Passedoit, and paid them $50 each for the job. When *Tarr* appeared in the summer he bought thirty copies to be sent to his usual gift list. Yeats had sent him the manuscript of his play *The Dreaming of the Bones,* and Quinn offered it to the *North American Review* for publication. When they refused it on the grounds that they were "chock-up" with more practical kinds of texts, Quinn offered it to the *Dial* if they would pay $150 for it. When Pound heard of these negotiations he wrote quickly to forestall them: he had paid Yeats £20 for the play and he wanted it badly for the *Little Review.* Quinn then extracted it from the *Dial* editors, although they were eager to print it, and it went on to the *Little Review.*

Alfred Knopf's intention to publish a volume of T. S. Eliot's verse was still waiting for Eliot to produce additional poems. Quinn heard in the winter a rumor that Boni & Liveright were planning to "pirate" the *Prufrock* volume, and he investigated to see whether the scheme existed and needed stopping. He found the rumor false, and he blamed Margaret Anderson and Jane Heap for setting it going. Eliot wrote to thank him for his trouble: "I appreciated it the more because I knew you had recently undergone a serious operation; I do not think that there are many people who, under such conditions, would bestir themselves so actively even for personal friends, still less for a man who was personally unknown to them." [45] Eliot lamented his small output of verse and accounted for it in part by the demands of his regimen: a full time job at Lloyd's Bank, regular editorial work for the *Egoist*, two evening lectures on English literature for working people each week. He judged that Pound's recent quarrel with Harriet Monroe of *Poetry* was on the whole a good thing, in that it meant all his new poems could go to the *Little Review*, and it freed him from a basically unsympathetic editor. Eliot recalled sorely how Pound had labored to persuade Miss Monroe to publish "The Love Song of J. Alfred Prufrock," and how she had deleted without his permission the whole line containing the word "foetus" in printing "Mr. Apollinax."

Pound finally sent Eliot's manuscript to Knopf in early September, and wrote to Quinn to say that Eliot had been so busy that he had to put the manuscript into final shape himself. Eliot had been pronounced unfit for military service because of an old hernia, and he was now trying to get into the United States Intelligence Service abroad. In a letter which reached Quinn's office on October 1, Pound asked Quinn to cable to London in support of Eliot's application and, if possible, to "get two other big pots to counter sign the recommend." Eliot sent his own similar plea to Quinn on September 8. Quinn cabled to what he judged appropriate quarters of influence. With his usual grave courtesy Eliot wrote to thank him on November 13: "I must say that your kindness to me, who am personally unknown to you, has been quite extraordinary, and such as I am not likely to forget." The Intelligence Service scheme had fallen through: "Everything turned to red tape in my hands." After collecting testimonials for Army Intelligence, he had been sent for by Navy Intelligence and offered an appointment as Chief Yeoman

with a promise of an early commission. Eliot had arranged for a
two-week delay to enable him to clear out his duties at Lloyd's
Bank, resigned there, and returned to take up service. He was told
to wait for confirmation from Washington. After another week he
was put off again. Finally he returned to the bank. By now the
Armistice had intervened. On November 15 Pound wrote that he
was nursing a cold contracted in walking about London in a drizzle
of rain to watch the response of the city crowds to the Peace. He
had stood within a few feet of King George's open carriage as it
passed through Piccadilly "with no escort save a couple of cops.
Poor devil was looking happy, I should think, for the first time in
his life."

    After *Pavannes and Divisions* was attended to, there was nothing
else of Pound's own on Quinn's horizon for the time. In January
Pound had sent off by registered mail his text of Arnaut Daniel,
the Provençal poet, to the Reverend C. C. Bubb of Cleveland, who
had appeared out of nowhere with an offer to do a private printing
of the book. The manuscript had cleared the British censors, but it
failed to appear in Cleveland in due time, and Pound at last concluded that it must have fallen foul of the American censorship; he
pictured it as being "decoded by some asst.-sec. of the N.J.
Y.M.C.A." [46] He thought that by the time the American censors
had discovered that they were dealing with the text of a trouba-
dour, they would also have decided that "troubadours are bad for
the public puberty." [47] By the first of September the text had still
not reached "the reverend printer" in Cleveland, and Pound wrote
to ask Quinn to do what he could to trace it in the halls of the
censors. Quinn tried and failed. Pound once more apologized for
troubling him with his personal affairs after an illness: carrying
always his only image of Quinn as a man firing a rifle at targets at
Coney Island, it was hard for him to see Quinn as a sick man; and
thinking of Quinn as the only man of full sympathy and energy he
knew in America, he feared he was making himself a constant
nuisance.[48]

    By winter, at least, Quinn was well enough to laugh heartily
again. Reading the November number of the *Little Review* in bed
in the evening of December 10, he came across Jane Heap's reference to some of Pound's editorial work as foreign to her taste—

" 'foreign to courtesy, foreign to our standards of art.' " "That sentence," he wrote Pound next day, "made me roar." At about the same time, T. S. Eliot was brooding more seriously about the general problem of American taste, as he wondered why a journal such as the *Little Review* found it so hard to gain ordinary subscribers. "I sometimes think," he wrote Quinn on November 13, "that with us (Americans) the serious has to be the pedantic, and that only the pedantic and the cheap are understood. . . ."

The affairs of Maud Gonne were also much bruited in the correspondence of Quinn and Pound in the fall and winter of 1918. She was still denied permission to return to Ireland and was living in Yeats's old rooms in Woburn Buildings with her son and daughter. Iseult was doing typing and copying for Pound three days a week, and Seagan was in the hands of a Catholic tutor. Pound wondered if she meant to ruin her son's mind.[49] Then Maud slipped across to Ireland in disguise and picked up where she had left off years before, among other things holding a meeting in Dublin "to express sympathy with the Russian Bolsheviks." [50] When she returned to London later in October she was placed under "preventive arrest," along with a good many other persons of suspicious Irish sympathies. A "German plot" was suspected and another Rising, or worse, was feared. Maud fell ill and appeared to be in danger of a recurrence of her old tuberculosis. Quinn heard of this state of things and was frantically upset, as always when someone dear to him was threatened with illness, especially with tuberculosis. He wrote excitedly to Pound and hurriedly cabled to everyone in London and Dublin who might have influence in the matter. Maud was sent to a nursing home in London, which she left after five days, unopposed, and still refusing to promise good conduct. Quinn believed that he had secured her release; "I . . . got a quick decision releasing her," he wrote Æ on November 26. Pound doubted this interpretation: "Personally, I don't think the release was obtained by a policy of worrying officials. I think the health report did it on its merits, plus a little amiable influence." [51] In any case Maud was free again in London, breathing fire and again demanding a clearance for Ireland—which, as Pound remarked: "had never been considered a health resort for consumptives." [52] On November 19 at Quinn's request Pound dutifully carried to Maud his cable advising her that the Irish climate was "unsuitable" for her. He reported the result: "Peals of laughter from that unfortunate female." [53] Quinn saw nothing funny in his cable, in Maud's reaction to it, or in Pound's account; he reminded Pound that it was his reports of Maud's illness and arrest that had set him off.[54] On December 2 Pound reported that Maud was gone again: ". . . did a bunk to Ireland nine days ago." But he had just had a note from Iseult to say that she (Iseult) had "fixed it up with the Lord Mayor and that Maud is to be left in peace." Pound himself was unamused by the course of events. He thought the threat of Irish treachery to England was real enough and the preventive arrests quite justified in the circumstances. Maud's "only constructive political idea," so far as he could see, was that "Ireland and the rest of the world should be free to be one large Donegal Fair." [55] He had no hope at all that Maud would change her ways if given freedom of action in Ireland. "I give it up," he wrote several times. Maud seemed to him "fanatic" if not "lunatic" on the subject of Irish politics—sane enough on most subjects, but a bit mad on that one, "just like Yeats on his ghosts:" [56] ". . . I notice with Yeats he will be quite sensible till some question of ghosts or occultism comes up, then he is subject to a curious excitement, twists everything to his theory, usual quality of mind goes. So with M.G." [57] In Dublin, in her new disguise, Maud had knocked at the door of her own house in Stephen's Green, which she had turned over to Yeats and his bride, and he had turned her away in a confused and noisy scene. But the quarrel was soon made up.

In the previous winter the spottily and crankily educated Yeats, feeling the need for systematic study as he thought his way deeper into his "philosophy," had rented a house in Oxford in order to be near the Bodleian Library. The new Mrs. Yeats found local society cause for wonder: "My wife never knows which to be more surprised at, the hats or the minds of the Dons' wives, and is convinced that if we live here every winter, which is possible, she will be driven to great extravagance by the desire for contrast." [58] Yeats had completed four short plays in the "Noh" manner and was plotting a fifth. In conceiving and presenting these plays he had hoped to keep them free of the full theatrical hurly-burly, to treat them more as masques, reserving them for a sort of domestic "court" performance which might occur equally well in a drawing room or a barn. But he wrote in the summer that he had felt obliged to release *At the Hawk's Well* for a performance in the theatre by his friend the Japanese actor Itow and his troupe, and he was sorry: "I had thought to escape the press, and people digesting their dinners, and to write for my friends." [59]

At Easter Yeats went with his wife to Coole, to be near Lady Gregory in her trouble, and to proceed with the rehabilitation of the "castle" and its attendant cottage. He took a primitive pleasure in the roughness of the scene and of the work. He bought the wreckage of an old mill for rebuilding materials, "great beams and three-inch planks and old paving stones," [60] and employed local artisans to do the work. The local builder, Raftery, "a morbid man who cries when anything goes wrong," was in charge, and "the drunken man of genius, Scott," had provided designs for two massive beds.[61] As his own contribution to the country artisanship Yeats had prepared verses to be inscribed on a large stone set in the castle wall near the main door, and he transcribed for Quinn the current form, later much altered, of his powerful numbers:

> I, the poet, William Yeats,
> With common sedge and broken slates
> And smithy work from the Gort forge,
> Restored this tower for my wife George;
> And on my heirs I lay a curse
> If they should alter for the worse,
> From fashion or an empty mind,
> What Raftery built and Scott designed.
> [*July 23, 1918.*]

The loneliness and ancientness of the place delighted Yeats. They had found one stone in the cottage carved with the date 1657.

In the summer young Seagan MacBride was staying with the Yeatses in a separate cottage they had rented to be near the work and near Lady Gregory, and they found him "a gentle, solitary boy." [62] Yeats was impressed both with the boy and with his sister Iseult—whom after all he had wished to marry; he thought them a vindication of Maud Gonne's peculiar ideas of education: "The boy, like the girl, has a great sense of justice, and both have strong, gentle minds. The girl is very beautiful." [63] Jeanne Robert Foster remembers being told by an old woman in Dublin: " 'I met Iseult Gonne in the street and I fell on my knees, she was so beautiful.' " [64]

By early September the Yeatses' own cottage was ready to receive them, though the tower still lacked such fundamental members as roof and floors—it was "half dead at the top." [65] Yeats was very happy—with his wife, with his writing, with his strange house that spoke to deep needs in his nature. Of George Yeats Æ had written Quinn in February: "I gather she will write for him, read for him . . . communicate with the dead or living for him, and will make the ideal poet's wife." [66] Yeats's own letters to Quinn were now being dictated to his wife. Of the house itself he wrote: "We shall have a wonder house, a house full of history and yet quite without pretence—a farmer's house in dreamland"; [67] and earlier: "I am making a setting for my old age, a place to influence lawless youth, with its severity and antiquity. If I had had this tower of mine when Joyce began to write I daresay I might have been of use to him, have got him to meet those who might have helped him." [68] His tone was half-serious, his meaning wholly so, and complex. No doubt his mind was running on his own youth and on his masters, Henley and Morris, surrounded in their own place of work by a company of the able and eager young, acolytes of genius. The tower might be a *salon* in the rough country seacoast, savagely elegant, "severe" and "antique," in touch with the oldest bases of being. It would suck from the stream, the road, the hills, the sea, and the sky, and from its own stones soaked in history. It was a place where a man could work all alone with his own passion and experience, or could send his mind out to meet his own ghosts and the ghosts of his race. The complex and impassioned mystique of the tower grooved itself into Yeats's mind, and from this time on it showed itself everywhere in his themes and his symbols. His thought of himself as the host of a sacred place, where friends of genius could meet in fraternal and creative mystical union, would be best specified in "The Tower" of 1926. It is striking that it was Joyce who came first to his mind as the type of the needy creative spirit who has missed this chance, and sad that these two greatest Irish geniuses could not have meant more, directly, to each other. They had met, of course, and Joyce had apparently said something like " 'You are too old for me to help you.' " [69] But Joyce had his own tower, also real and symbolic, and in view of the work his difficult life produced it is hard to wish the life different.

It had been George Russell who had brought Yeats and Joyce together in Dublin in 1902; Æ had had his own difficulties with the prickly and brilliant young man, and had watched him since with wary admiration. Quinn kept Russell supplied with the material that came out of his association with Pound and the *Little Review*. He put Æ down for a subscription to the review, where he could watch Joyce's *Ulysses* unfolding in successive issues, and he sent him Lewis's *Tarr*, Pound's *Pavannes and Divisions*, and Eliot's "brochure" on Pound. As always his gifts paid rewards in Russell's responses. On February 21 Æ took advantage of Quinn's unprecedented immobilization to send him a little treatise on sound in poetry, stimulated by Eliot's analysis of Pound's poetic technique. In Pound's verse, Russell thought, intelligence got in the way of imagination and learning obstructed music. He praised "the harmony of dusky sibilants" in Blake's lines: ". . . speak, silence, with thy glimmering eyes/ And wash the dusk with silver,' " [70] and thought Swinburne had been right to call this the loveliest bit of pure sound in English verse. Æ went on to quote for Quinn, and to analyze with diacritical markings, verses of his own, of Yeats's, and of Ferguson's. He was trying to work out "a theory of opposites in sound to supplement the law of harmonies," the "pattern of vowels and consonants within a line, which is the essence of musical utterance." [71] This "highest technical excellence," he argued, could not be achieved by such often mechanical manipulations as Swinburne's; it rose naturally in a profound intensity of feeling, a true inspiration, "which gathers to itself consonants and vowels in assonance and harmony with themselves and it." [72]

Lewis's *Tarr*, Æ felt, "really might have been called 'Pitch'. . . . By itself sex is a bore and the cleverest mind can't make it art." [73] He recognized Joyce's tower in the early pages of *Ulysses*, and recognized that young Dedalus's companion there was modeled on Dr. Oliver St. John Gogarty, whom he went on to praise thus handsomely: ". . . the most brilliant and witty person in Dublin, and really much more amusing and human and interesting than

James Joyce ever was." [74] The manifold Pound he considered, shrewdly, "a little too wide for his depth," but conceded that he was "always entertaining and intellectually exciting." [75] "All these moderns," he summed up Quinn's new favorites, "are a damned sight too clever." [76] He found them something unconvincing and a touch hysterical: "Their intellect has got something akin to St. Vitus' Dance, and they are so restless that they tire one." He had prepared his "anti-toxin": ". . . to lie for a month on the sand-dunes at Dunfanaghy or on the hillside and do absolutely nothing, loaf, in fact, and tell Nature it is up to her to amuse me. I find the Earth talks to me in a kind of lordly way whenever I have sufficient awe of her to shut up my noisy intelligence and prevent its speaking in the society of its betters." [77]

The Russell who wrote in February of the harmony of Blake's "dusky sibilants" was a poet who had labored hard at being a public political man and then returned willingly if sadly to being a poet and a citizen. Early in that month he had quietly resigned from the Irish Constitutional Convention, judging it a hopeless cause. He was sure that the violent Unionism of the North and the violent Nationalism of the South were two irreconcilable bigotries, too polar and too stubborn to come together yet in a rational and humane common government. "I like them both personally," he wrote Quinn on February 11, "but I feel when I talk to a Sinn Feiner or an Ulsterman that I am yelling back through the centuries to men whose ideas ought to have been dead and buried long ago." By early August he had lost everything but "a far-off, philosophical interest" in the political question, and was waiting hopelessly for disaster: "I watch like a doctor the patient for the development of the disease." [78]

Russell's philosophic book, *The Candle of Vision*, had been interrupted so often that he began to fear he might die before he could finish it. But by July it was done, and the manuscript chapters were salvaged from his study corner as he completed his revisions and sent across to Quinn, to whom he wrote on August 8:

> I think it is well written, but it will destroy my hard-won reputation for sanity and will embroil me with the churches and all "sensible" people, so I may be left alone and get more time to go on with a new book as nobody will ask me to lecture, speak

or write for a considerable time, for which I will be heartily glad.

Quinn sent his reactions to the book on November 26. He was familiar with a good deal of mystical literature, he said, and understood the tradition within which Russell was writing. "The beauty of your book is that you do not treat it technically," he thought. He had preferred the first two-thirds, the less "technical" portion:

> When you got down to the symbols and the letters representing the elements, I could not follow it, although I daresay that they meant a great deal to you. That part of the book I want to read again. But, aside from those two or three chapters, the rest of it is a beautiful thing, and I congratulate you on doing it.

Some of the ambivalence of Quinn's feeling for mystical thought is there. The homesick Platonism latent in Quinn's nature showed itself in many ways: in some of his literary preferences, such as Shelley, Blake, Morris, Pater; in his taste for the painting of such artists as Russell, Redon, Davies, and for Oriental art generally; in his drawing toward his small circle of Indian friends. But it was a leading opposed by the whole pragmatic drive of his life, and a taste to which he did not like to confess. He preferred to believe that the appeal of art and thought to him was "man to man," hearty and tellurian. Thus in this same spring he wrote to Vincent O'Sullivan in praise of Synge's motive in art, which he read as a wish to return Ireland to "decent, clean savagery," and in contemptuous rejection of the mystical side of Yeats and Russell: "Synge was as much opposed to the fairy interpretation of life and to fairies in poetry (as in many of Yeats's things) and to the vague, mystic interpretation of life (as in George Russell's things), as you or I could be. He was a realist if there ever was one." [79] It was a coarsely condescending reading of two great writers, and the manly "you and I" robustiousness is irritating; one should recognize too Quinn's willingness to speak out of one or another side of his mouth, depending on his audience. But Quinn was a good deal more knowing and intelligent than he sounds here, and much more genuinely drawn to the thing he was attacking. The "realist" was doubtless the dominant personality in Quinn, but the "mystic" was there too, hesitant and shamefaced, half developed, half understood. * It frightened and embarrassed him in himself, and so he had to reject it when it grew "technical"—which is to say when it began to show itself systematic and serious.

At the end of March, looking forward to the Convention's report, Æ had lost his little lingering hope that the small measure of agreement possible among the sectarian delegates would have "any soothing effect" on Irish politics. Five months later Ireland seemed to him to be "squirming like a terrier on whose tail an immense foot has trodden. . . . I do wish the Lord would send us a man," he lamented. He predicted that the "delightful rank and file" of the Irish, their leaders shot or imprisoned, would now lead themselves into jail. He was meditating "a futurist tale, a hundred years from this," a kind of Symposium in the style of a Platonic dialogue on the theme of nationality: ". . . and to keep it on a high level I will imagine all my characters condemned to death and discussing the ideals which led them to that pass." [80] Russell in fact was "sick" of the Irish Question and did not see how anyone else inside or outside Ireland could fail to be sick of it too.

Quinn had hoped that the Quinn-Russell-Plunkett book on the Irish Constitutional Convention would help to produce agreement on a basis for a united new Ireland under Colonial Home Rule. It was a large hope and only a little time had proved it empty. Now he was troubled not only about the long future of Ireland but about her current image in the eyes of the world—especially the new world. He shared Russell's view that America would emerge from the war as the dominant nation in the world. On the day of the American declaration of war he had lunched at the British Embassy with the French philosopher Henri Bergson and the British Ambassador Sir Cecil Spring-Rice. Spring-Rice had sat through the long hours of debate in Congress, and he told Quinn that he felt as if he were witnessing " 'the final act in the drama that would result in the transference of power in the English-speaking world from England to the U.S.A.' " [81] Quinn's fear was that Ireland had blackened her image in the eyes of America as well as England by her flirtations with Germany and by her refusal of

* "Quinn for all his material success and his associates is entirely spiritual. . . ." J. B. Yeats to W. B. Yeats, February 25, 1913 (*Letters*, p. 156).

conscription. "Ireland has backed the wrong horse," he said repeatedly in his letters of this year. "I doubt very much whether history will justify Ireland's course in refusing to take part in this war of civilized men against organized brutes," he wrote on October 3 to Russell, who had just published an eloquent letter on the opposite side of the question, defending the necessity and rightness of Ireland's course. Quinn's political thought, especially in wartime, tended to move in black and white terms, unshaded. The loss of fifteen or twenty thousand men out of a hypothetical force of a hundred thousand seemed to him a price worth paying for the world's good opinion—and, he estimated, not seriously crippling to a fertile nation:

> I, personally, have a greater confidence in the philoprogenitiveness of the Irish race than to believe that such a loss would mean the extinction of Irish manhood or the death of the Irish race. So long as the Catholic church is supreme in Ireland and the diet is not exclusively confined to potatoes, there is not likely to be a scarcity of Irish babies. . . . [82]

But he held onto his hope, in any case, that American opinion could be held in favor of Home Rule and that that opinion could be brought to bear with greater force on England in the new balance of power after the war.

Russell had asked the Lord to send Ireland "a man," and Standish O'Grady set the same feeling in a general context in a letter of October 27:

> We are awfully backward, every way, as well as absurd, and want —We want everything. O'Keefe of the War Office just with me, and says "a Despot". . . . Still I think *all* the nations have a lot to learn from each other. Would that we Irish had something to teach. We certainly have a lot to learn.

If Russell was sick of the Irish Question, so was Conrad, and he thought all England shared his feeling as the Irish Constitutional Convention quarreled away its civilized opportunity. "I will tell you frankly that we don't think much about Ireland now," he wrote on October 16 to Quinn, who had been rehearsing for him the ancient Irish grievances. Conrad continued:

I, who have seen England ever since the early eighties putting on the penitent's shirt in her desire for conciliation, and throwing millions of her money with both hands to Ireland in her remorse for all the old wrongs, and getting nothing in exchange but undying hostility, don't wonder at her weariness. The Irishmen would not be conciliated. . . . they took the money and went on cursing the "oppressor" with renewed zest.

What could be done with "a people that, being begged on bended knees to come to some understanding amongst themselves, is incapable or unwilling to agree on the form of its free institutions"? Conrad's own heart was too sore at the condition of his native Poland, where wrong was not only historical but also present and deadly, to consider the Irish case with patience: ". . . I, who also spring from an oppressed race where oppression was not a matter of history but a crushing fact in the daily life of all individuals, made still more bitter by declared hatred and contempt." Russell would have had the patience, the subtlety, and the command of fact and psychology to point out the simplistic character of England's expectation of quick orderliness from a nation as confused and vehement as the Irish after centuries of proprietorship. But Quinn did not, though he remonstrated with some skill with Conrad for his denunciation in a letter of December 13. He was stung by the bitterness of Conrad's tone, by the force of his comparison of Ireland and Poland, and by the implication that he, as an American Irish patriot, was guilty of provincialism and narrow views. In a letter to Conrad he defended his own course vaguely but spiritedly:

I wish I could be over there. I have done a great many things for the English, some very crucial things. I used to work very closely with Spring-Rice, the late British Ambassador here. I could not go to the front, but I have done my duty and done it in no provincial spirit, but as a citizen of the world, and I have done good and valuable things for the English, and some of them took courage, and I did not do them with a band.

[*December 13, 1918.*]

On February 6 Conrad had sent Quinn an extraordinary letter in which he described his meeting with a pathetic group of Polish intellectuals in Cracow in August of 1914. " 'Have no illusions,' " he had warned them:

> "If anybody has got to be sacrificed in this war it will be you. If there is any salvation to be found it is only in your own breasts, it is only by the force of your inner life that you will be able to resist the rottenness of Russia and the soullessness of Germany. And this will be your fate for ever and ever. For nothing in the world can alter the force of facts."

In the context of such ancient and hopeless misery, the plight of Ireland, looking plump and unscratched in time of war, could only impress Conrad as factitious and unreal. The awful weight of the war, "the bitterness of lost lives, of unsettled consciences and of spiritual perplexities," had gathered upon Conrad's spirit with apocalyptic force. In the frame of apocalypse, the optimism and idealism of Wilson and his admirers struck him as false and dangerous:

> There is an awful air of unreality in all the words that are being flung about in the face of such appalling realities. For the closer they are looked into the more appalling they are. And the devil of the situation for all the hearts that are not the Devil's or the Angels' but those of Men truly worthy of the name, is this: that they can't contemplate either Peace or War otherwise than with an equal dread.

The letter reached Quinn at the time when both he and Theodore Roosevelt were in the hospital, and he was enough impressed to send it on to Roosevelt as a guide to statesmanship.

At intervals during the difficult year Conrad wrote of the continued survival of his soldier son, of his own wretched health, of his wife's painful and unsuccessful operation on the knee that had lamed her for fifteen years, and of her satisfaction in her own correspondence with Quinn: "She hopes that one of the first pleasures after the war will be to actually behold you in your proper person under our roof. May it be soon!" [83] The typescript of Conrad's latest and as yet unpublished novel, *The Arrow of Gold*, "corrected, scored and interlined in ink," [84] all but the first thirty-six pages dictated rather than handwritten, was offered to Quinn in October. Quinn's slow response to the offer was soon to make trouble.

Doubtful and troubled about his father's financial state in New York, W. B. Yeats sent him occasional substantial checks and again asked Quinn to turn over to his father the value of the manuscripts he was sending from Ireland. Quinn did so, and also made the old man periodical presents of money to fill out his comfort. John Butler Yeats was ostensibly at work on his autobiography, and his son was anxious for the success of the project, as Quinn was. W. B. Yeats hoped to have it published by Macmillan, with reproductions of the work of the old painter himself and of Potter and Wilson and especially some of the symbolic designs of Nettleship, which he had been finding potent in his own arcane musings. He thought such a volume might return a very fair profit to his father, and he further valued it as a document in the social and cultural history of the recent past—the kind of steeped savoring of the mind's history that he himself had recently been setting down. As he put the case to Quinn: "The book should have its value as telling people something of distinguished men who are not yet historical enough to be common knowledge. It is always the past just before our own time that we know least of." [85] Well knowing his father's disinclination to systematic work, Yeats proposed a scheme whereby Quinn would pay J. B. Yeats a pound for every thousand words of manuscript delivered to his office, W. B. Yeats to repay Quinn in cash or in manuscripts of his own.

Quinn wrote of these matters in September. His affection for J. B. Yeats was undiminished, and he saw him often and kept up their busy correspondence. He thought the old man was sometimes lonely but in general good physical and spiritual frame: "He has lost some weight and has grown whiter, but he is cheerful and hopeful and as alert, mentally and physically, as ever." [86] J. B. Yeats had been surprised and moved by the praise accorded his published letters, especially in England. Of the projected memoirs Quinn wrote with guarded optimism. Old Mr. Yeats was "at work" on the manuscript, and Quinn hoped for an eventual volume of 150,000 to 200,000 words. Now and then Quinn solicited manuscript, but there had been no inundation. Mr. Yeats feared that if he went too fast the work would be "thin." Quinn reminded W. B.

Yeats that his father still showed no signs of finishing his self-portrait after seven years; he had urged J. B. Yeats to drop "work" on the portrait and concentrate on the memoirs.

Lily Yeats wrote in the spring to felicitate Quinn on his good progress after the operation and to thank him for his check for a Cuala Industries screen, embroidered in one of the designs the sisters had learned in William Morris's studio, and replacing another screen which had gone down at sea. She had been thinking again, tremulously, of her aged and distant Pilgrim Father: "He will be 79 this week, on St. Patrick's eve. He was born the year of the big wind, 1839. I wish he were even ten years younger, even five." [87] In October she recalled her visit to New York with her father, now ten years past, when together they had seen so much of Quinn, and when she had seen her father for the last time: ". . . I would take my visit to America again just as it was. It was the time fullest of good things of all my life. I look back at it with the greatest pleasure. I was free from anxiety. I was with Papa, and so I had a companion, the best of companions." [88] Quinn had asked Lily, J. B. Yeats's favorite and the family squirrel, to search out old writings of her father's that might be blended into the memoirs, and a bundle had gone forward from Cuala. She thought that the news that Willie and George were expecting a child would keep the prospective grandfather at his task: "I hope it will, because we will all be so old and remote by the time he or she is old enough to be interested that it will only be through the written word they will get any knowledge of us and those before us." [89]

Lily Yeats's association of her father with the famous big wind of 1839 was doubtless casual, but it made a joke he would have appreciated. Certainly his letters to Quinn in 1918 showed no diminution in the copiousness, the generous range and vigor of his mind as he approached four score. "And here is the mental thing I want to introduce to your illustrious attention," he announced breezily on May 27—introducing a little lecture on why the arts flowered in Italy in the time of Michelangelo. Quinn was able to savor in the hospital a letter of January 24 in which, under cover of a formal judgment of Pound's *Lustra* and the painting of Arthur B. Davies, J. B. Yeats worked out further aesthetic concepts—pithy, original, and useful definitions of wit and humor and the "appointed agony" of artists. Pound's volume, J. B. Yeats concluded, showed "wit touched with fantasy, and . . . better still, fantasy touched with wit—(there is no fantasy in G. B. Shaw's wit)." He elaborated:

> A wit is hated by his contemporaries—Sterne was hated, so was Oscar Wilde—for contemporaries are their victims. But the posterity enjoy it (quite forgetting that they themselves in due time will also be ancestors). But all men love fantasy and for its sake enjoy the wit, as the bitter which adds savour to the sweet. Humour may be described as the wit of the many, but "the wit" is one against thousands, against the mob. Contrast the position of Mark Twain with that of the unhappy Oscar! Wit is aristocratic and humour plebeian. Shakespeare carried both in his quiver of arrows.

J. B. Yeats's definition of Davies as "an artificer rather than an artist" was a judgment grounded in his own humanistic faith:

> Before a man can be an artist he must be a student of life—as father or brother or husband or wife or statesman or lawyer or perhaps, which is more universal, as a poor creature trying to survive, the self-preservative instinct within the root from whence spring all his thoughts. Then let him paint or write poems and everything coming from him will be heavy with knowledge, self knowledge or world knowledge.

He could distinguish no sign of this struggle, none of this blood-knowledge, behind the work of Davies; it had all come too easily to "a happy and amicable man." Davies's exhibition had made him think of Tiffany's, with young society women shopping. J. B. Yeats saw only one appropriate frame of mind for a true artist, the consciousness of ideal failure:

> The true artist when he paints a sunrise or sunset knows that he has failed—of one thing only certain, that the copy resembles hardly at all the original, however much he be consoled afterwards by his friends who tell him he has surpassed Turner or Constable or Rembrandt. This sense of failure is the melancholy of artists. It is their appointed agony.

One understands why J. B. Yeats followed a single landscape with his despairing brush through the whole cycle of the seasons, and why the paint would be a half-inch thick on his unfinished self-portrait when he died in 1922. Lily Yeats had found the right simple epithet when she said that her father did not know how big a man he was.

By April 18 old Mr. Yeats could thank Quinn for a "cheery" letter, following his operation. "There was a time when I felt anxious as to what might happen," he admitted. The rest of a fairly long letter he devoted to analysis of certain writers and statesmen who interested them both. John Morley reminded him of Quinn's favorite Meredith, in that both, coming into high society from outside, "adopted all its conventions with the zeal of the novice." The strain of that factitious conventionalism, he shrewdly argued, marked all Meredith's novels. Rossetti, by contrast, seemed to him an example of that true "personality" he kept adverting to with admiration, the integrity of a nature intuitively whole in itself. "Rossetti had no formulas and no conventions, not even the conventions of unconventionality, and was a marked personality." J. B. Yeats might have been describing himself. He went on to cite Cromwell as the type of "the man of personality, the natural man turning away from the abstract that he may take hold of the concrete." Gladstone he saw as a man of intermittent "personality": "Gladstone's occasionally forgetting his opinions and showing the real man, as in his hatred for Chamberlain, I would compare to a knight in battle raising his visor so that you see into his eyes." He contrasted Shakespeare, "personality through and through," with the abstract and opinionated Milton: Shakespeare created Juliet "as a poet," "but no one knows what he *thought* about her. He did not know himself"; Milton would have started with an "opinion," an abstract, and fabricated Juliet to illustrate it.

A month later J. B. Yeats attached two codicils to a letter contrasting Belfast and Dublin. He was continuing a discussion of tragic catharsis which had been the matter of the previous day's conversation with Quinn. His thought on that ancient crux again deserves quotation at length. Speaking of the cleansing of the passions in tragedy, he said to Quinn:

> I omitted the best illustration of all—the Hebraic conception of Jehovah: He is the image of Terror—terror itself—but so overwhelmingly magnificent that the beauty of the conception cleanses

away all the pain, and as the energy of the terror inspired so is the intensity of the feeling of Beauty. Prostrating themselves in abject submission, these Jews were and are penetrated through and through with the delirium of Beauty. It is that which inspires the psalmists. [*May 19, 1918.*]

In his second addendum he corrected the famous Aristotelian formula itself:

Aristotle says that tragedy by terror and pity cleanses the passions. It should have been that the beauty of the tragedy cleanses the passions of pity and terror inspired by the story of the drama, so that there remains no suffering. . . . However, these presumptuous people who deny that art is imitation are more daring, and besides they are utterly and everlastingly wrong. Art is imitative, said Aristotle; and I say that the more intense the imitation the better the art. David puts forth all his strength in describing the merciless awfulness of Jehovah. A tropical thunderstorm is more beautiful than any other, because more terrifying. [*May 19, 1918.*]

The copiousness of this correspondence continued, often with several letters passing back and forth in a week, or even two in a single day. Mr. Yeats's tiny scribble had to be translated and copied in his office before Quinn would deal with it. Both men hated the telephone, and Mr. Yeats's growing deafness also made writing pleasanter. Something of what their correspondence meant to them is suggested by J. B. Yeats's letter of October 28, which is about letters themselves. "Letters are the children of idleness," he wrote. "It is only the idle, the discursive and the chatty mind that can write them." He meant, of course, "good" letters, easy social and intellectual commerce. Quinn's letters, he felt, were "thunderbolts" —hardly letters at all in his sense. Quinn certainly came off second best—or, from the other point of view, profited more—in the interchange. J. B. Yeats had the advantage of relative idleness, as well as a different and a better mind. Quinn tried to keep pace, within the little time he had, but he always lagged a step behind, and fell a cut below, the nimble old man. It is clear too that Quinn unconsciously tried to write in kind to J. B. Yeats, to imitate his graceful discursiveness and easy didacticism. But that was not the way his mind naturally moved, and he would quickly fall into the "thunderbolt" style, the rather hectoring insistence, what Mr. Yeats would have called "argument," "a bit too forensic," and into unmodulated recitations of data—a finite only too obviously out of touch with the infinite.

Early in November the Petitpas sisters called Quinn to say that the old man seemed unwell, and when Quinn saw him he was alarmed by his weakness. Doctors diagnosed first influenza, then pneumonia, but with careful nursing he had come round by the end of the month. This illness was the mechanism which brought Quinn the dearest companion of his last years, Jeanne Robert Foster. He knew of Mrs. Foster as a devoted friend of Mr. Yeats, and he telephoned to beg her to superintend his nursing. She agreed at once, she and Quinn met in the sickroom, and Quinn had found the "good woman to rest his head" that J. B. Yeats had been prescribing for years. She was a bronze-haired beauty in her middle thirties, living with an older, invalid husband in an apartment at the Elmsford, 300 West 49th Street. Of French-Canadian and English stock, she had grown up in the Adirondacks and married a family friend while still a young schoolteacher in her teens, after which she had gone on to brief careers as a student, actress, model, and writer. She had published several volumes of verse and fiction and had been for several years now a writer and editor for the *Review of Reviews*. She had traveled abroad and knew the New York art and literary world, and she was already acquainted with many of Quinn's friends in Ireland, England, France, and America. She would doubtless have met Quinn long since had she not avoided him because of his reputation as an eater of females. Their experience, their tastes, and their temperaments dovetailed beautifully, and they came together now with mutual delight.

During the month of Mr. Yeats's illness Quinn cabled frequent bulletins to the younger Yeatses in Ireland and all of them sent back their anxiety and their gratitude to Quinn. Jack Yeats, from whom Quinn heard least frequently, though the warmth of their early friendship remained alive, had written also in September from his lodgings in the home of a sea captain's widow at Covetown, County Wexford. He was enjoying the honest primitiveness of the waterfront ship painters, admiring especially a painting of a three-masted schooner entering Holyhead in a gale. The realism and earthy good sense which drew Quinn to Jack Yeats came through in his reflection:

> It is indeed a good, hard picture, and much better than the kind of simplicity pictures which the clever ones with their tongues in their cheeks try to do. The odd thing about doing anything with the tongue in the cheek seems to be that the fact of the tongue in such an abnormal position becomes the most interesting part of the spectacle, and people who stick their tongues in their cheeks generally have large, coarse tongues.[90]

J. B. Yeats had made a resilient recovery, but Quinn had been newly troubled to feel responsible for the old man in whom his distant children, all middle-aged themselves now, had made such an investment of feeling. Quinn began again to plead with them, especially with Willie, to bring the father home from his ten years' exile as soon as he was strong enough to travel. J. B. Yeats's illness had spanned the Armistice, and Europe was again in reach.

Among the notable letters of the summer of 1918 from J. B. Yeats was one which Quinn solicited when he was called upon once more to plead the cause for the relief of art from taxation. A new war revenue bill before Congress proposed a virtually annihilatory tax upon works of art and objects of art, and Quinn quickly picked up that old challenge, even though he still felt physically unequal to the strain. He was being unwillingly drawn back into the full tide of his former life, and the old demands brought their old irritations. When Walter Pach wrote to him about the tax problem, Quinn wrote back explaining the situation at length but concluding sourly: "Your letter was one of 14 outside matters that came yesterday, Monday, and a rotten Monday it was. I came damn near tearing them *all* up in a bunch and throwing them away." [91] As only properly constituted organizations, not individuals, were allowed a hearing before Congress, Quinn hurriedly formed an association of artists and declared himself their spokesman. He asked Mr. Yeats to set down his own thoughts on the principle involved as an aid in preparing his brief. J. B. Yeats responded with a long, good-tempered, and unsentimental attack upon the mercantilist view of artists as triflers in luxuries, and a defense of their moral and intellectual seriousness, their useful citizenship. Like Shelley, he saw artists as unacknowledged legislators—educators, teachers of the true unstated patriotism that rests in affection for one's land and its people and is visible in the artist's loving images. Quinn put these ideas to work. He was confident that he would win out, and wrote Pach that it would be "a tremendous victory for the artists" if he did so: "They ought to be eternally grateful to me for making that dividing line"—the old dividing line between original works of art and reproductions and a new one between sales by dealers and sales by artists of their own work.[92]

The measure was called for hearings before the Ways and Means Committee of the House, whose chairman was John Nance Garner and one of whose prominent members was Nicholas Longworth, son-in-law of Theodore Roosevelt. To plead their particular cause the Antique Dealers' Association engaged Mr. Barnett Hollander. Quinn was contemptuous of Mr. Hollander at the time, describing him as "a Jew lawyer . . . who knew little about the subject and who was not known in Washington, whereas I am known to the Committee." [93] As it began to appear that Quinn could not gain his whole point, the total exemption of original works of art, he began to maneuver for the smallest possible general tax on sales of such works and no tax at all on artists' own direct sales; and he saw the argument as a direct contest between himself and Hollander. In terms far more generous than Quinn's, Mr. Hollander recalls making his plea before the full committee and the delegations of interested persons, then giving way to Quinn. He remembers Quinn's appearance, pale and elegant, "tall, distinguished, slender, ascetic appearance, aquiline nose . . . a typical New York lawyer, if ever." [94] He reports Quinn's opening gambit, characteristic in language, in emphasis, and in offensive strategy: " 'My friend, Mr. Hollander, comes before you to speak for dead art. I come to speak for living art and living artists, so poor that I organized them to qualifying here and at my own expense.' " [95]

Quinn won his final point. The general tax on original works was set at the reduced figure of 10 per cent, and sales by artists were wholly exempted. Quinn saw the result as a victory for himself, and for artists, and as a defeat for Mr. Hollander personally and for the dealers, administered by himself. "Get it straight," he wrote Ezra Pound on October 30. "I put the knife into the dealers. . . . I 'did' the dealers. . . . And why in hell should not the dealers pay the tax? There is more bunk and more fraud in art sales than there is in Monte Carlo." In his ranting letter to Walter Pach on August 13, while the argument was still pending, Quinn set down his view of the situation and his part in it, with analogies to the 1913 affair:

> I am not merely a personal friend to many members of the Committee but am known to them as a man who knows about art. My brief shows what a fine chance they ["the dealers"] have now —of being taxed. I have refused to have extracts from my brief printed. I am conducting a still hunt. It is the result I want and not interim advertising. . . . There is no reason why I should enlighten them. I made the fight for free art in 1913, and then all sorts of people wanted to claim the credit for that, including the Free Art League and the Association of American Painters and Sculptors and others. The agitation was my idea, and while I used the name of the Association in conducting the campaign, I made all the briefs, made all the trips to Washington, made the arguments and paid all the expenses. But no damned association or free art league or committee will be able to claim that they won this victory, for I raised the question and made the trip alone and paid all the expenses. The Secretary of your Society [The Society of Independent Artists] formally authorized my appearance on behalf of your Society, not that it amounts to a damn, for I could have gone down and made my argument just as effectively on behalf of living artists generally. . . .

After his "still hunt" was over Quinn was glad enough to break silence. He sent copies of his brief, or of the Bulletin of the Metropolitan Museum containing excerpts from his brief, to all his important friends. It was the kind of thing May Morris would receive in lieu of a love letter.

Quinn's illness and convalescence caused a marked diminution in his dealings for art of his own in 1918. What there was of it still showed a pronounced leaning toward the French. In the spring, when he was just beginning to move about the city a bit once more, he happened to see French, Australian, and English troops on the street, and what seemed to him the superior animation, intelligence, and manliness of the French soldiers warmed his old prejudice in favor of that nation.[96] His only important American purchase of this year was $3,600 for works of Maurice Prendergast on exhibition at Miss Bryant's gallery. Three days before his operation he agreed to take four paintings from Raoul Dufy, of which the painter had sent photographs, for 3,800 francs.[97] A month later he bought four paintings and five ceramics by Rouault, from his dealer Vollard, at about 800 francs each.[98] In May Walter Pach came to him to offer at "half-price" a Marie Laurencin water color owned by Albert Gleizes, who was hard up after losing the money for which he had gone surety to a friend in a business venture. Quinn refused the picture and gave Pach a check to give to Gleizes as a loan to tide him over; but Gleizes refused the money with many thanks: he had a horror of borrowing.[99]

André Dunoyer de Segonzac wrote in March that he was in the habit of reading excerpts from Quinn's letters to his comrades in the army, finding Quinn's "broad conception of events" a relief from the standard tone of the French press.[100] After the Peace, and after having seen Noyon "taken, lost, then retaken," he wrote with joy from Paris of seeing old friends who had survived, taking up again the life in art. The poet Guillaume Apollinaire, after surviving fearful head wounds and a trepanning, had succumbed to influenza. La Fresnaye had gone to the south of France with what appeared to be tuberculosis. But Segonzac had seen Picasso, Braque, Derain, and Léger, and he announced the birth of a new school, "Le Purisme." [101] It was from Walter Pach in New York that Quinn learned in October of the death of Raymond Duchamp-Villon, the sculpturing member of the three French artist brothers, of anemia following an emergency operation.[102] In the summer Brancusi sent thanks for Quinn's check in payment for his bronze *Muse*, and instructions for preserving its patina: it was to be wiped often with chamois skin, and not by professionals, "for professionals sometimes know more than is necessary." [103] The widow of Odilon Redon complimented Quinn on "the concise way in which you do business": "It is all in such perfect order, and so agreeable, that I must thank you for it." [104] In June she sent thanks for a check, along with a lament for a passing generation: "Rodin, Degas, gone also after Odilon Redon. That great and beautiful period of art which gave so much joy will soon be over. Renoir holds good in spite of his 78 years." [105] In December, acknowledging yet another check, Mme. Redon spoke of her happiness at the coming of peace, at the survival of her soldier son "with all his limbs," and at the visit of President Wilson, whose "grave and smiling face" had "conquered the Parisians." It was not the kind of thing Quinn wished to hear of Wilson. More to his taste was her response to the Americans' laying flowers on the tomb of General de Lafayette, who had been godfather to her grandmother and a legend of her own childhood. The American gesture, she was glad to say, had reawakened French interest in their forgotten hero.

Despite his resolution to cut back his purchases from Augustus John, Quinn cabled on February 20, two weeks after his operation, to Knewstub of the Chenil Gallery to offer £400 for John's portrait of Arthur Symons, which had been priced at £500. He had already agreed recently for John's *Madame Réjane* at £400. Thus his payment for the two works came to about $4,000. Major John had been "pushed out" of France along with other official artists when the big German offensive began in the spring. Now he was back in London and working on a big war landscape for the Canadians. His letter of November 22 was the first to Quinn in over a year, and he had not heard from Quinn in so long that he had begun to fear that Quinn bore him a grudge. It was Gwen John who told her brother of Quinn's serious illness. Augustus had found her looking seedy in Meudon, and feared that she did not bother to eat regularly. He could not persuade her to join him in England, but did manage to get her off to Brittany for a rest and a change of air. He thanked Quinn for his continued support of his talented and difficult sister. Quinn had written Knewstub of a rumored loan show of John's work in New York, and of this John grumbled to Quinn: "Well, I have heard nothing of it and it won't have my sanction. There is nothing I have in America I set any store by beyond what you have in your collection." [106] Knewstub later wrote that the huge charcoal cartoon for John's Canadian War Memorial, twelve by forty feet, would be on view at the Royal Academy in January. Quinn cabled "Not interested. Entirely too large." [107] At a mere eighteen feet *The Mumpers* had turned out to be enough of a nuisance.

Matters with Jacob Epstein had been pretty well patched up at the end of 1917, and he and Quinn were dealing cordially together again. Quinn was still angry at the treatment of his Epstein article, in *Vanity Fair* in October 1917. As he saw it, Crowninshield had cut "three or four of the best paragraphs at the end" of his piece, then printed a laudatory article on the "stove-ornament sculptor" Paul Manship on the facing page in "a deliberate ambush." [108] Actually Crowninshield's cuts had been moderate and in good taste, and had been made necessary by lack of space in the pages at the back of the magazine. Crowninshield replied sweetly to Quinn's elaborate letter of protest and sent him a check for $50 for the article. Quinn promptly endorsed it over to Mrs. Benjamin Guinness for her favorite charity, and wrote Epstein on January 21 that he had "had nothing to do with Crowninshield since." Quinn liked the photographs Epstein had sent of his heads of Lieutenant T. E. Hulme and Muirhead Bone, and he offered £150 for the two. He remarked that he knew Hulme's French translations and his book on Bergson. Epstein's *Venus* and his *Mother and Child* were still resting in the basement at 58 Central Park West. The big stones had had to be handled by windlass, and they were so heavy that the building superintendent had been afraid to allow them in the elevator or to stand in any room of Quinn's apartment. He liked the *Venus* and called it "a very fine and distinguished thing," [109] but was disappointed in the granite carving, of which he had not seen a photograph and which he had confused with another work of which he had seen a photograph. He asked Epstein to "finish" the work when he came over after the war, or to exchange it for the carving he had thought he was getting: "a little like a Chinese figure, with a sort of hood on her head, and partly nude, carved down to the waist, showing the arms and hands and breasts." [110] Epstein agreed to an eventual exchange for the piece he supposed Quinn had had in mind, his *Mother*, which he had stored with a friend while he was in the army. Epstein was still mourning the loss of his dear friend Hulme, with whom had also perished, apparently, Hulme's manuscript for a book on the sculptor.

On February 21 Margaret Dunlop Epstein sent Quinn a graceful apology and explanation for her unfortunate cable in the autumn. Her purpose, she wrote, had been only to retire from the correspondence between Quinn and her husband which she felt would explode after Quinn's letter of September 12 refusing to act further for Epstein's deferment and citing the bravery of other artists. She, too, wrote a feeling appreciation of Hulme and regret for his loss. On May 18 Quinn cabled an offer of £80 for Epstein's bronze head of his wife and was promptly accepted. Mrs. Epstein cabled on May 27: "Epstein very well in hospital Plymouth." On July 20 Epstein himself cabled to ask for £400 which was now overdue. He was still in the hospital. Ten days later he cabled to say he had been invalided out of the army, and to offer for £100 ten drawings of wounded soldiers he had made in the hospital. In his letter of July 26 he explained that he had suffered "a complete breakdown" and had spent five months in the hospital: "I haven't been allowed to see letters and my state has been a bad one altogether." By early August Epstein was sufficiently recovered to wish, as in earlier days, for something big and demanding to be asked of him: he still dreamed of carving mountains. He was again depressed by the pusillanimity of the audience for art in England and their niggling expectations, and he now saw Quinn as a rare and valuable point of light:

> If I produced babes heads to the end of my days I would be thought wonderful, but anything large, grand and terrible, fit for our times, is timidly shrunk away from in the timid and tepid atmosphere of our art world here. . . .
>
> I hope Quinn, you are not unwell. There are too few like you in the world. Scarcely one out of a million has insight and courage, and that is what is so disheartening. In the old days popes and princes knew something about art. Today the artist is a solitary worker.[111]

In May Brown and Philips of the Leicester Galleries in London at last opened the Gaudier-Brzeska memorial exhibition for which Sophie Brzeska had been holding out since the sculptor's death in 1915. Ezra Pound wrote the preface to the exhibition catalog. With no further maneuvering, Quinn closed swiftly for three major works, the *Stags* at £260, *Sleeping Woman* at £200, and *Birds Erect* at £100. By being systematically difficult, Sophie had had a shrewd last word with Quinn, to the tune of nearly three thousand dollars. It was hard for Quinn to concede that a woman had bested him in an art dealing, and he tended to comfort himself with the idea that Ezra Pound had been obscurely at fault in the affair.

Quinn feared that the war and its residual feelings would "give a tremendous push to sentimentality in art," and he suggested sardonically to W. B. Yeats that it might be a good idea to negotiate an international moratorium for ten years on the erection of public monuments and statues of all kinds.[112] He continued to fulminate against the big monument to the victims of the *Maine* disaster at the entrance of Central Park, which he had to pass, suffering, almost every day. As the end of the war approached, then arrived, Quinn was still breathing fire. He was far from pleased at the drift of events, especially at unrevengeful views of the enemy. He wrote Wyndham Lewis in the middle of September: "To think that the war may be ended by Germany joining a league of peace would be much like liberating murderers from prison upon their joining the Young Men's Christian Association and taking the pledge and promising in the future to be good." [113] He was one of many who wanted the war carried violently and punitively into Germany "to teach the Germans a lesson" on their own soil. Quinn wished to see the Germans sterilized if not destroyed. "I am not thinking of what is good for the Germans when I regret that they have not felt what war is at home, but of what is good for the world," he wrote Russell two weeks after the Armistice. "Now they will be a hideously vindictive, a hideously brutal, a hideously sullen, a hideously unreformed lot of brutes." [114] Quinn had tended to accept atrocity stories at face value, and he had never sympathized with what he saw as the weak and sentimental distinction between the German people and their rulers. They were a sanguinary and rapacious breed, all of them. "They all loved the war and rejoiced in its atrocities and were willing to participate in the booty." [115] Standish O'Grady reminded him that he had once heard Quinn say that no problem could arise which the United States could not solve.[116] But with the country committed to a "soft" peace and her destiny, perhaps that of the world, in the hands of Woodrow Wilson, Quinn foresaw only revenge lost and confusion renewed. Having always disliked Wilson, he took a sour satisfaction in the wrongness of his course, his disgusting talk of disarmament and a generous peace "free from anger." Quinn had long been planning to write an essay on the subject of "How Phrases Kill Thought," and he now listed the Wilsonian phrases that he would enjoy attacking: " 'making the world safe for democracy,' " " 'peace with honor,' " " 'freedom of the seas,' " " 'no annexations and no indemnities.' " He never wrote his essay, but this disgusting lenity to the beaten Germans was a theme upon which he grew only more rabid as time passed.

By natural stages, by the end of the year Quinn's life had drifted back into its old multifariousness. His week in Virginia in July had been his only formal vacation since his return to the office in April, but he had closed his apartment and taken a house at Elmsford, on the Tarrytown Road a few miles from White Plains, for the period from July 15 to October 1. Julia Anderson and Mary, now a leggy eleven-year-old, were with him, and he found the suburban living and commuting pleasant enough when they did not involve the anxiety of an expensive place of his own. By October he could say to Russell: "I'm feeling better and getting stronger every day. I like life and the world." [117] He was trying, with fair success, to "train" himself to resist pleas and demands upon him; he cited to Brancusi the Maeterlinck story of the lighthouse keeper who gave away all his oil so that his vital light went out.[118] Before Christmas he set aside all his cares for a week's idyll in a visit to the little prairie town of El Paso, Illinois, and the parish of his beloved uncle, Father Jeremiah Quinlan, now seventy-eight years old. He described the interval and his pleasure in it to Frank Harris:

> I have had some peaceful days, freedom from telephone calls, from personal calls, from invitations, from friends, and from self-seekers, and I have talked and smoked corncob pipes of tobacco with him, and walked and looked at the red squirrels, who balance themselves with their tails, leaping like lightning up and down and among the trees. [*December 21, 1918.*]

It was an idyll stolen from work on one of the most strenuous and important legal cases of his career, the Botany Mills case, which had been brought to test the constitutionality of the Trading with the Enemy Act, and which involved the question of the legality of the government's selling formerly German-owned property valued at many millions of dollars. This lengthy affair had just got under way at the end of the year. Meanwhile Quinn's other lives were continuing. He wrote to Jack Yeats of attending Bryson Burroughs's lecture on Puvis de Chavannes at the Metropolitan Museum, with slides including Quinn's own three big Puvis de Chavannes paintings. "Certainly he was the greatest decorative painter of modern times," he still felt: [119] it was one of his older tastes of which he did not repent. To Gordon Craig he reminisced about one of the great collectors of the preceding generation, "Mrs. Jack"—Isabella Stewart Gardner:

> Twenty years ago she was a handsome woman. She had courage in art matters. Berenson was her adviser. She had beautiful eyes at one time and a beautiful figure, and she knew it and made the most of her eyes and her figure, and her husband did not seem to object. But she is now very late Renaissance. [*October 11, 1918.*]

Like Epstein, Craig yearned for a chance to do something monumental, to create a thing that would make an epoch in theatrical history. But war, distance, and the misgivings of Quinn and Otto Kahn joined to discourage Craig's scheme for a spectacular production on the upper Hudson. Quinn continued to correspond with Craig, bought his designs, and kept him on his list for gift books. Craig wrote from Genoa in December to thank him for Lewis's *Tarr* and Pound's *Pavannes and Divisions,* and to comment on the gift as a gesture peculiarly Quinnian and American. In Europe, he said, artists occasionally made such presentations but ordinary men never—". . . whereas with you men over there, no matter what branch of work yours may be you still are strong enough to relax." [120] The statement shed a queer and interesting light on Quinn's habits. "Relax" seemed an odd word to apply to Quinn's strenuous and programmatic avocations, yet from one point of view it was accurate and revealing. His activities in art and literature, for all their restlessness and systematization, were the intense relaxation of a nature discontented and self-exhausting without them, a nature not really capable of pure rest. Standish O'Grady wrote Quinn in the autumn: "I note you have a critical period to pass through, after which I trust you will for many years go ahead with your valiant and strenuous life. Only, *festina lente.*" [121] Ultimately it was a vain plea, to a man who even in the pursuit of health understood only strenuous means. From now on, naturally, the great fear was a recurrence of the cancer; but about that one could only watch and wait.

1919

QUINN'S long-distance friendship with Joseph Conrad, sustained for eight years by Quinn's admiration, his systematic acquisition of the manuscripts, his occasional friendly representation to Conrad's American publisher, and by Conrad's own apparent general satisfaction with the relationship, began to go to pieces in 1919. There occurred a series of troublesome little shocks, which seemed to have been absorbed in friendly and forgiving fashion on both sides, but which left sore spots behind them. The trouble really began in the autumn of 1918, when Quinn for some reason did not respond promptly and explicitly to Conrad's offer of the largely dictated typescript of his novel *The Arrow of Gold*. But the consequences of this did not show themselves for nearly a year, and in the interval other awkwardnesses developed. On April 10, 1919, Conrad wrote to ask Quinn to turn over to Doubleday, Page the brief unpublished preface to *Almayer's Folly* which he wished to use in the Collected Edition on which the publisher was at last going to work—after the war, as Conrad had insisted all along. At the same time Conrad announced his intention to dedicate to Quinn the new novel, *The Arrow of Gold*, which was about to be brought out by Doubleday:

> . . . the substance of it is so closely related to me personally that it can in fitness be inscribed only to a friend. I hope that after more than eight years' intercourse (though we have not seen each other yet) your kindness has given me that status towards you.

Proofs of the novel, with dedication "To John Quinn," had already been mailed to Doubleday, and Conrad invited Quinn to remonstrate with the publisher if he did not wish "to be compromised by any public association with that unspeakable Conrad."

All this was gay, warm, and gratifying, and Quinn set to work. He got out his copy of the preface to *Almayer's Folly*, had it carefully copied in his office, and read proof on it twice, exchanging manuscript and copy with his typist, before sending it on to Doubleday. But when he spoke by telephone with Doubleday about the proposed dedication he discovered that a first edition of 15,000 copies of *The Arrow of Gold* had been printed by April 12, before the arrival of Conrad's corrected proofs with the dedication to Quinn, and that edition stood dedicated "To Richard Curle." A second printing of 5,000 copies was ready for the press and that could be made to carry the dedication to Quinn; but of course that struck Quinn as unseemly procedure. "I am sure you would not want that," he wrote Conrad on May 1, "for your sake or for Curle's sake or for Quinn's sake. It would be almost like literary Mormanism [*sic*], you being the Morman [*sic*] and the two dedications of the one book being the plural wives; or perhaps polyandry might be the symbol." Quinn asked Doubleday to hold work on the second printing while he cabled Conrad to explain the situation and to suggest that the dedication to Richard Curle ought to stand. Conrad cabled back at once, agreeing, and promising: "My Napoleonic novel [*Suspense*, 1925] shall be for you." [1] Meanwhile Doubleday, who was naturally reluctant to alter the dedication of *The Arrow of Gold*, had suggested that Conrad might dedicate his next forthcoming work, *The Rescue*, to Quinn.

All these matters Quinn set down, with utmost cheerfulness, in a long letter to Conrad dictated piecemeal over four days from April 28 to May 1. In the same letter he awarded Danzig to the Poles in the peace settlement, and spoke at length of his sympathy for Mrs. Conrad, facing another operation on her lame leg, comparing her feelings to his in his own operation, and applying his phrase-of-the-year, Turgenev's "'Death is the only irreparable thing.'" He had just finished reading *The Arrow of Gold*, and he was full of praise: "*The Arrow of Gold* is a very great book, and Joseph Conrad is a great wizard in the telling of tales." A great work of art was "a miracle," he considered, and this novel one of those miracles. He was especially impressed with the character of

Rita, and he thought this novel ought to put an end to the "absurd legend" that Conrad was no good at creating females. He had urged Doubleday to advertise the book generously and to emphasize this point. As for the dedication, he was touched by the thought that Conrad had wished to salute him in a work that meant so much personally to its author. But he thought "our friend Curle" perfectly deserving of the same honor, and he was glad the dedication to Curle should stand unaltered in any edition. He looked ahead to his own turn: " 'Twill be a great honor to have your Napoleonic novel dedicated to me."

Before receiving Quinn's long letter Conrad wrote hastily on May 3 to explain the "curious embroglio of which the fault was entirely mine"—though he also blamed Doubleday for not allowing enough time for return of corrected proofs before printing. He explained that he had long intended to dedicate to Quinn the "Napoleonic novel" which was due to follow *The Rescue*, now nearly finished. "Then, while passing the first proofs of *Arrow*, it occurred to me that I would not keep you waiting and that the *Arrow* was perhaps good enough to be inscribed to you." *The Rescue*, he said, was out of the running, for that had been mentally consecrated for five years to the honor of F. C. Penfield, the American Ambassador in Vienna who had managed the release of the Conrad family from Austria in the crisis of 1914: "His name will be gratefully remembered as long as there is one of the Conrad tribe alive." Conrad wrote again on May 26 with Quinn's letter now in hand: "Thank you very much, my dear Quinn, for your friendly, wise and indulgent behaviour in the miserable imbroglio about the *A. of G.*" He thanked Quinn also for his "enlightened appreciation" of the novel. The "Napoleonic novel," he said again, had been tagged in his mind for years as " 'Quinn's book,' " before he had had the unlucky impulse "not to keep you waiting for that sign of my regard." With the shift to Quinn, he had thought, he could give Curle the dedication of his next volume of short stories: but now he would return to his first resolve, the "Napoleonic novel" for Quinn. The last words of *The Rescue* had been set down on the preceding day; but that must remain "Mr. Penfield's book." *

* When *The Rescue* was published in 1920 it carried the dedication: "To Frederic Courtland Penfield Last Ambassador of the United States of Amer-

All this was embarrassing but so far harmless. But in the summer Doubleday had misgivings and second thoughts about his arrangement with Conrad, and came to Quinn with proposed changes in the publishing plans. Quinn, who had no official brief to act for Conrad, wrote to him of Doubleday's new schemes and offered to serve as a "buffer" between the writer and the publisher, but pointed out the demands all this was making upon his time, sufficiently occupied. Conrad was annoyed at Doubleday's vacillation and at his gratuitous approach to Quinn as a legally unconcerned party, and at Quinn's peevishness about an issue not of Conrad's making: ". . . frankly, you need not have pointed out to me the multiplicity of your occupations and the value of your time. I am quite aware of the demands your position in the world makes upon you." [2] In parts of his letter Quinn had spoken in the querulous tone common to his "driven" moods. Conrad felt no need of a buffer. He was quietly determined to hold to his original agreement with Doubleday, for whom he felt a cordiality which he expected to continue. One of Doubleday's suggestions, that a special grouping of his "sea" books be issued, Conrad found repugnant. "How would poor Thackeray have liked a set labelled Mr. Thack.'s 'society' novels?" he wondered. He went on to speak with noble resonance of his understanding of his own work: "The sea is not my subject. Mankind is my subject, and 'imaginative rendering' of truth is my aim." It was plainly a testy letter, but its irritated tone was softened by new expressions of regard for Quinn, and it was signed: "Always gratefully yours."

In June Quinn made the surprising but perfectly serious suggestion that Conrad authorize him to try his hand at a dramatization of *The Arrow of Gold*. He had been attracted to the idea by his own near association with the novel, by Conrad's pleasure in the stage success of Macdonald Hastings's adaptation of *Victory*, and by his keen interest in the romantic conflict at the center of *The Arrow of Gold*. ". . . I should like to have it understood that I can have a hack at it," he wrote on June 19, and went on to sketch out a workmanlike scenario in four acts. He had discussed the idea with Walt Kuhn on a weekend in the Adirondacks, and Kuhn had

---

ica to the late Austrian Empire this old time tale is gratefully inscribed in memory of the rescue of certain distressed travellers effected by him in the world's great storm of the year 1914."

called the scenario melodramatic; but J. M. Kerrigan, an old Abbey actor, had been "enthusiastic." His play would "catch the women," Quinn imagined, "for they would all applaud Rita's self-sacrifice, although very few of them are built that way themselves. . . ." [3] Conrad crowded his response to Quinn's "interesting suggestion" into the end of his letter of July 31: "I am certain that Quinn's dramatisation of Conrad would be a great success of curiosity at the very least," he wrote, and went on to be gently discouraging. He could not answer Quinn's request definitely, as he was negotiating for general dramatic rights in his work. In any case he considered *The Arrow of Gold*, "which consists not of action but of shades of intimate emotions," almost the least naturally dramatic of his novels. But Kuhn's judgment of the novel as melodramatic roused him to an elegant definition of his own: "A melodrama is a play where the motives lack verisimilitude, or else are not strong enough to justify a certain violence of action, which thus becomes a mere fatuous display of false emotions. Violent action in itself does not make melodrama." Then at the end of September Conrad wrote in confidence that he meant to try his own hand at dramatizing certain of the novels. Quinn now quietly dropped his whole scheme, representing himself as persuaded by Conrad's doubts of the stageworthiness of *The Arrow of Gold*.

Again, awkward but not particularly distressing. The more serious *contretemps* began to develop in the autumn when the London journalist Clement Shorter, inspecting Quinn's Conrad collection in New York one evening, told him he had heard that the novelist had recently disposed of certain manuscripts to the eminent bibliophile T. J. Wise—not yet unmasked as an eminent literary forger. Bearing in mind Conrad's repeated promise not to sell manuscripts to anyone else so long as he kept his collection intact, Quinn wrote to question Shorter's story. Conrad bluntly confirmed it: "What C.S. told you is perfectly correct. I sold the typed first draft of *A. of G.* and also the incomplete MS. of *Rescue* (completed in type) to Mr. Wise because I wanted the money at once for a specific purpose." [4] He went on to explain his reasoning at length. He had thought, for one thing, that Quinn might have "had enough" of Conrad's manuscripts in general. And he suspected that Quinn would be less interested in these works which had been dictated and typed, not written by hand. He reminded Quinn that his collection already possessed the perfect unity of containing "every line of my pen-and-ink first drafts," and he argued further that Quinn's collection had "a double character of completeness in so far that it is *all* pen-and-ink Conrad and *all* pre-war Conrad"— Wise having taken two post-war pieces. Conrad himself "would prefer to have a smaller thing absolutely complete, both in time and kind, than a larger but not complete collection." He now offered, though he felt "a delicacy" in doing so in the circumstances, forty-five pages of autograph manuscript of two articles written during the war. And he promised Quinn, as a gift, what was to be Mrs. Conrad's final discovery: sixty small typed pages of a "mixed draft" of *Falk*, "corrected, altered, and in many places altogether re-written," which had turned up in the bottom of a drawer. Conrad could not now remember, what was in fact the case, whether Quinn already possessed the handwritten first draft: "But in any case they belong to your period and notwithstanding their mixed character I am going to send them to you without of course any question of payment arising between us in that respect."

Conrad had clearly broken a repeated emphatic promise to Quinn, and for reasons not satisfactorily explained: his rationale sounded lame and disingenuous. Quinn's tardiness in rising to the offer of the manuscript of *The Arrow of Gold* was no real excuse for turning to Wise: Quinn had invariably accepted, in due time, every previous offer from Conrad, and there was no reason to suspect him of real reluctance now. Conrad did not bother to explain the "specific purpose" that had led him hastily to Wise. He did make it clear that he had profited by the change: because of the "mixed character" of the two manuscripts in question, he had felt free to ask more of Wise than he would have asked of Quinn. Conrad's account of the affair could not have comforted Quinn very warmly. Conrad does not emerge very creditably from the episode. It is hard to avoid the feeling that he was chafing under the bonds of a more or less established scale of pay with Quinn, and that he had been rather easily tempted by the prospect of higher prices. The prices Quinn had paid all along had been those set by Conrad. No doubt Conrad's manuscripts were "worth" more now than they had been eight years before. But it was surely open to him to make that point to Quinn, to have offered him the refusal of the pieces at a price satisfactory to himself—distasteful as it might have been to commence bargaining at this stage of a relationship so long established and heretofore so candid. At the end of 1918, then, matters between the two remained apparently amicable but actually subtly troubled.

Conrad was one of those to whom Quinn expressed himself violently and at length about the international situation that continued to prey on his mind, the shape of the peace that was to follow the war, his unappeased hatred and fear of Germany. On April 28, 1919, for example, he wrote to Conrad:

> I am sick of the twaddle about the league of peace. In my opinion, the armistice was the greatest blunder in history. If the war was fought to end German militarism, the best way of ending German militarism would have been the destruction or capture or unconditional surrender of the German army, with only its broken remnants escaping across the Rhine. The greatest opportunity in all the world to inflict such a lesson in applied psychology upon the Germans was lost when the French and the English weakly and, I think, stupidly agreed to grant an armistice to the Germans on Wilson's ambiguous fourteen points. The politicians nearly lost the war. . . . Without any treaty of peace Germany cannot fight for ten or twenty years, but unless she is now permanently disarmed, not temporarily demobilized, and unless there is a perpetual inspection by an allied commission with diplomatic powers of her forts, arsenals, munition plants and all other factories capable of making munitions, in thirty or forty years she will re-arm those seventy million brutes in the heart of Europe, still worshipping only force, and again try to crush France and Belgium and menace the peace of the world.

If Wilson's grave and smiling face had conquered the hearts of the Parisians, as Mme. Redon had said, the more fools they. "I am sick of the word 'idealism,' " Quinn went on in his letter to Conrad. "Kindness and ideality may sometimes be nothing but stupid credulity." To André Dunoyer de Segonzac he denounced Wilson's speeches as the "vague vaporings of a vain, arrogant, ambitious pedagogue." [5] To John Butler Yeats he interpreted the Armistice as a comprehensive Allied crime of weakness and deceit, and one aimed primarily at his beloved France: "It is the greatest betrayal of the ages. When Judas betrayed Christ he betrayed one being, but the betrayal of France by England and the United States is the betrayal of a race and of millions of the dead." [6]

Conrad, still broken-hearted for Poland, was inclined to agree. But the same line of talk to the temperate George Russell brought only a gentle reprimand; it suggested to him the hysteria of fatigue: "I think your extreme statements about the Germans show that you want a holiday," he wrote in midsummer. "When I am fagged out I get ferocious in my judgements." [7] He hoped that Quinn's proposed vacation in the Adirondacks would make him feel like Emerson: "who got gay and found wisdom went from the berries." He demurred, as he had patiently done for years, at Quinn's sweeping and denunciatory interpretation of the character of nations: whereas there was a reason in nature why acorns grew into oaks and not into elms, with human beings the thing that made the difference was environment and training. The Germans were not congenital brutes but "human beings shaped by their environment." Quinn's own country, he pointed out, was a laboratory proving the power of a place and an atmosphere to shape the nature of persons—second and third generation immigrants of many countries turning out sound indistinguishable Americans. "Bring up in U.S.A. the children of German emigrants, give them an American education, and they will be average American citizens," he argued; and the same principle could be made to work within Germany herself—a changed environment altering human motives and acts.

Russell wrote in the light of his own inner peace, also in the reminiscent glow of his annual return to the earth, a month's painting holiday in Donegal. To keep them safe during the war, Quinn had stored for some time the pictures which Russell had sent for exhibition at the Chicago Art Institute in 1916, and these he now returned. Oddly, and to Æ's own surprise, his painting had turned into his chief source of income. His approach to the matter was typically unstrained. He had had a little early formal training (sharing classes with W. B. Yeats, as it happened), but felt that he had never really learned to draw with any accuracy. He painted for pleasure and renewal, quickly and easily, with little public expense of passion, and took little thought for the sale of his wares, which seemed to walk off his walls of their own accord. He had not held an exhibition in England or Ireland for several years, but persons still came in an orderly file, unbidden, and took away his gentle, mysterious, rather amateurish pictures at a fair price.

Æ's attitude toward Irish politics continued for the time similarly quietistic. He was watching and waiting, in temperate pessimism, for a time and a way to be useful:

> I do not intend to take any part in Irish politics or argue for anything or propose anything. I will wait to see if the Government makes a firm offer and if it is a workable scheme it proposes I will use what influence I have to get it a fair hearing. Nobody supposes here that I am either a creature of the Government or an agent of theirs or of any party, Sinn Fein or Republican, and I think that they believe I am disinterested and honest in my political judgments which I am because I am bored with politics and loathe them and if we had any kind of government of our own I would never write a line of political matter if I remained myself but would confine myself to art and literature and economics.[8]

Meanwhile he supposed the Sinn Feiners might as well "have their chance . . . to move the government by making Ireland ungovernable." The bloody "Troubles" which would make Ireland hideous for the next few years were getting under way. But Russell thought talk thus far was exaggerated, and he advised Quinn not to take rumors of anarchy too seriously: there were still more murders in London in a month than in all of Ireland in a year. The recent murders of policemen were "horrible," but he thought not surprising among a people "maddened by military rule" and "treated as a slave people."

Æ recounted a "friendly chat" of the preceding evening with W. B. Yeats, an old friend whom he now rarely saw, passing through Dublin on his way to his "castle," Thoor Ballylee. Yeats had been full of a new prose work, which Russell identified as his "philosophy of mysticism": that great queer book, *A Vision*, was being conceived. Russell was amused and skeptical to hear that the text was coming to Yeats through his own and his wife's "automatic" writing: "But I believe there is a lot of humour accompanying these manifestations of mysticism. His mind is subtle but never very clear in its thought"—a penetrating analysis before the fact. It had again struck Russell that Yeats was thinking too much, too consciously, of style as something apart from and anterior to matter, and he recapitulated for Quinn his earlier definition of true style as the organic vestment of a given matter and mood. He summed up:

> My favourite scripture is the Tao-teh-king of Laotse, which is the gospel of being natural. When I do not feel inspired I don't try to keep any atmosphere of poetry about me. I would feel a sham. The spirit comes and goes. When it comes it is better to let it speak for itself. When it goes it is best to behave as if one were an ordinary citizen, because you feel like that.
>
> [*July 10, 1919.*]

All in all, in its high-minded and luminous common sense, Russell's had been a beautifully characteristic letter, high pay for storing a few pictures and making a rant against the Germans.

Quinn had been keeping such close tab on J. B. Yeats in the winter after his illness that the old man had begun calling him "the schoolmaster." Quinn kept on urging the family to force their father to come home. He was still deeply afraid of Mr. Yeats's dying on his hands, and of having to deal with a dead body and funeral arrangements—"all of which I shrink from horribly," as he candidly phrased it to Willie in a letter of January 16. Discovering that Mr. Yeats owed the Petitpas sisters a bill of $453 for room and board, Quinn tried to use the fact as a lever, promising to pay the bill but only on condition that Mr. Yeats agree to return to Ireland.[9] One of the things that got on Quinn's nerves in the situation, and indeed in J. B. Yeats's conduct of life generally, was the old man's *insouciance*, his refusal to be flurried or hurried—in fact that general freedom from nervous anxiety which galled a man of Quinn's hectic temperament. It irritated him unreasonably, for example, when the painter refused to have his hair and beard trimmed because he was "working" on his self-portrait and did not want to alter his image. The work had now been in progress for eight years.

W. B. Yeats did his best to persuade his father to return, but when he failed, he refused in his turn to get as excited as Quinn was by the problem. In a letter of January 21 W. B. Yeats took up the issue of Maud Gonne's derision, as reported by Pound, at Quinn's cables warning her to stay away from the "unsuitable" Irish climate: "Now about Madame Gonne. Pound must have been mistaken about the laughter—I imagine all she meant was that it was incredible to her that Ireland should be bad for the health. She looks ghastly. I heard a young English officer speak of her the other day as a tragic sight." He quoted Pound's description of an aunt of George Yeats's: " 'She is so old she is an atheist,' " and applied the thought gaily to his father: "When my father comes home he can be put into the University Club where he can talk to the other atheists and my sister will give him the bodily comforts." And he reflected, philosophically: "If we live long enough we shall all be trials. . . ." Yeats now determined that it would be better to separate the cost of his father's keep from his manuscript dealings with Quinn, and he sent a check for £234 to pay up all the accumulated debts.[10] He and George had made a return to Woburn Buildings in London and packed up the manuscript material there. He thought he might bring some manuscripts with him on his trip to America on the *Carmania*, planned for January 1920, but he promised to mail a bundle in advance, which Quinn could look over and "give me what you think right for it." [11] Passing through Dublin en route to Ballylee on the same visit of which Russell had spoken, after George had gone on ahead with her new daughter Anne to catch trout, Yeats wrote that he had at last sent off the manuscripts of *The Wild Swans at Coole* and *Per Amica Silentia Lunæ*. He awaited news of their safe arrival and of Quinn's reaction before sending others, being reluctant to trust the Gort post office, always "a happy, inattentive place," and recently robbed three times by "enthusiastic patriots." [12] "We are reeling back into the middle ages without growing more picturesque": so Yeats summed up his feeling about Ireland at the onset of the Troubles. For the moment he was cheerful, but his image took on an altogether different coloring in the great violent poem which he titled, according to the year, "Nineteen Hundred and Nineteen."

"It looks as if I may have a spirited old age," Yeats wrote Quinn in what time would prove a gross understatement.[13] He had been invited to lecture at a Japanese university for two years, and the

idea drew him with its Yeatsian union of antiquity and novelty.
He imagined himself happily settled for life in "some grass-grown
city, scarce inhabited since the tenth century," while back home
the Sinn Feiners stored arms in his Norman tower and lads from
the school broke his fine new windows. But he did not want to
abandon his tower, a noble place to rear a child, "full of history
and romance," before he had finished making it into "a fitting
monument and symbol." [14] At the end of the year Ezra Pound
wrote irreverently of the "vision" that was coming out of the
fitting monument and symbol: "Bit queer in his head about 'moon';
whole new metaphysics about 'moon,' very very very bug-
house." [15] And at the end of the year Quinn was paying John
Butler Yeats's bill for $100 for a complete set of false teeth [16]—
to be worn in New York, not in Dublin.

The early months of 1919, with big jobs on his hands and no
recurrence of his malign ailment after a year, were on the whole a
sanguine and happy interval for Quinn. Some of his ebullience
showed in his letters to J. B. Yeats, who was already embodying
the spirited old age of the Yeats family. On January 6, congratulating him on his recovery from the pneumonia, Quinn said he
would not repeat his warnings about care of health, then went
ahead and repeated them: be moderate in use of wine and spirits
and keep warm and dry, especially the feet. He plunged into a
polemical denunciation of the polemical side of Tolstoy, whom
they had been discussing: "Tolstoy was not a thinker. His book,
'What is Art?' was an absurdity. He lied when he said his object
was 'not to reform society,' for he was attempting to reform society
for years." In the kind of unconscious comedy into which his
contentiousness kept leading him, Quinn paused to quarrel with
Mr. Yeats's favorite charge that Americans were too much given
to "verbal wrangle." When he returned to Tolstoy he showed that
he was soundly conversant with his work and alive to the quality
of the novels and tales. The letter closed with a moved lament for
the passing of Theodore Roosevelt, who had just died at Roosevelt
Hospital. Quinn had called on him several times at the hospital and
had spent an hour and a half with him before leaving for the
midwest at Christmas time. He had lost a friend of twenty-five
years: "I could not believe it this morning when I heard the news

of his death. He seemed to be a great elemental force, like Niagara or the Hudson River." Quinn had lost too, as he felt, one of his own pragmatical kind, and the type of the tough-minded hero-statesman, as he was careful to point out to his French correspondents who were inclined to be seduced by such charlatanry as Wilson's. He wrote of Roosevelt to Mme. Redon, for example: "He was straight-forward and honest and courageous, and believed in facts and not in words, in deeds and not in theories, in acts and not in cheap phrases." [17]

A letter of May 19 to J. B. Yeats recorded an example of Quinn's kind of cultivated social evening. He had served dinner to J. B. Yeats and to three English guests Clement Shorter, H. W. Massingham, and C. C. Burlingham, and the talk had turned mainly on politics and art. Mr. Yeats had left the party early to go home and rest, and Quinn in his letter was courteously summing up for him the conversation of the remainder of the evening. Quinn agreed with Massingham in denunciation of Lloyd George as " a thorough-going scoundrel and publicly-confessed liar," and he thought that Asquith's defense of George in the Marconi scandal had sealed Asquith's political fate. "If I had been Asquith," wrote Quinn grandly, "I should have turned George out and thus got rid, once and for all, of that dangerous, unscrupulous, dishonest rival. All for the good of England, of course! A leader has no right to make mistakes. The price of leadership is freedom from mistakes." He cited John Redmond as a leader who had lost power by one small error after another. Quinn passed on to Mr. Yeats the pleasant things Massingham had said of him after he left: " 'How pregnant his questions are!' 'How much to the point his statements were!' Also, and this will astonish you: 'And what a good listener he is!' " Quinn, who considered himself a good listener, appreciated "the exercise of the art by a master." When Quinn had treated his guests to a show of some of his prize works of art they had returned him only gay ridicule. They had jeered at Matisse's *The Cyclamen* and at Brancusi's marble *The Sleeping Muse*, which Quinn called "one of the most sensitive and subtle works of art in existence," so blatantly that he thought even Mr. Yeats, who was no admirer of such things, would have been tempted to their defense. Quinn was amused to notice that his

guests ignored entirely the dozen or so African masks and statu-
ettes on top of his grand piano—"things that artists and sculptors
rave over." In closing Quinn recalled his obligation to the Yeats
family to keep the old man busy about his memoirs: "You see, I
am like a rent collector or a banker who does not refer to money
due him but who never forgets collection day. I have not mentioned
memoirs to you for months, but now I am around collecting. I
should like to know how many thousand words you have typed
and revised and ready for delivery."

Quinn's next letter, four days later, revived another matter of
amicable contention between them: he offered to send round a new
canvas for Mr. Yeats's self portrait. On a beautiful sunny spring
morning, Quinn saluted the day in a way rare for him, and saluted
Mr. Yeats for the use he had made of his days: "I congratulate you
upon having learned to live so many years ago, so early in life, and
having lived each day." [18] He was full of his own love of life,
and he recalled his joy in the aspect of simple things when he left
the hospital the year before: "It was a grey, winter afternoon, but
I loved the streets and the automobiles and the faces of the people
and the houses and the noises, and everything seemed delightful."
Much of his present excitement, it is clear, sprang from his pleasure
in two new paintings from Matisse, a woman (probably *Figure of
an Italian Girl*) and a great still life of apples. For days he had been
busy taking out and inspecting and sending off for framing some of
the paintings he had bought in the past two years but had had time
only to stow away in bedrooms and closets. Now he listed for Mr.
Yeats some of the purchases of that period: "eight or nine" Derains;
six Vlamincks; one Segonzac; four Rouault oils, five of his ceramics,
and thirty of his water colors, including fifteen of his *Ubu Roi*
illustrations; four post-war paintings of Raoul Dufy; and nine
gouache drawings of Gwen John. He closed this unwontedly gay,
spring-inspired letter with a Prohibition joke and a reminder to
Mr. Yeats that if he went back to Dublin he would be returning to
one of the world's most graceful drinking cities.

The works listed were by no means all he had bought in those
two years, and it is obvious that Quinn chose to single out what
were closest to his heart, works by Parisian artists of what he now
identified as "his" period. But he was narrowing his range still

further, buying from a relatively small group of contemporary French painters and sculptors whose work emanated the "radium" or the "acid" he was always on the scent of. At the beginning of 1919, for example, he turned down with hardly a second thought a chance to buy the most famous painting of the Armory Show, Marcel Duchamp's *Nude Descending a Staircase*. Frederick C. Torrey of San Francisco had originally bought the canvas out of the show for $324; and Walter Pach now came to Quinn with the news that Torrey, troubled by the "high price of gasolene" and other staples, was ready to part with it for $1,000.[19] Quinn refused at once. He thought five or six hundred dollars would be nearer the value of the work, but in any case he would not make a counter-offer: he was more interested in other works. He commented on Torrey's representative American values: "He is evidently willing to place Henry Ford's product ahead of Duchamp's work. In that, of course, he has the support of the vast majority of his fellow countrymen, nine hundred and ninety-nine out of a thousand of whom would inevitably prefer a motor to a work of art." [20] Mme. Lucien Pissarro, just back from six weeks in France with her husband—where they had been renewing war-broken ties and had seen, among others, Claude Monet, hale and hardworking at seventy-nine, painting huge light-struck studies of his own lily ponds—offered Quinn a chance to buy at a reasonable figure two major works of Camille Pissarro which they had recovered from hiding. She sent photographs of the pictures, Pissarro's only night scene from nature and his view of the Seine and the Louvre through a haze of mist and snow; Quinn was drawn to these two beautiful bits of Impressionism but finally refused them, holding to his resolve to patronize the living. He was even more strongly tempted by the offer from Percy Moore Turner of the Independent Gallery in London of the big Gauguin masterpiece *D'ou Venons Nous . . .* at 100,000 francs, but felt he could not afford the price. He tried to persuade the officials of the Metropolitan Museum to buy it, but they could not agree, and the work went to Copenhagen at a still higher price.[21]

Nor was Quinn a universal salesman or enthusiast for art, even for modern art. He refused, for example, to donate any pictures to Howard University, the Negro University in Washington. He was opposed to "art propaganda" or to trying to "bring art to the masses"; he preferred to expend his energies privately or in public ways that seemed to him ultimately more useful—in building up his own collection, that is, and in working with Congress and with museums.[22] When Walter Pach urged him in the spring to do an article on American art for the *Dial*, Quinn refused with gratuitous scorn:

> Apart from a few men, men that one could name on the fingers of one hand, American art does not interest me at all. I have not the inclination to say it this summer, in print, and in *The Dial*. I may never say it publicly. After all, when one demonstrates to another that he has been guilty of rudeness or bad manners one is doing a favor to that person, and I do not think enough of the 999 painters in America out of the 1000 to tell the public what bad and rotten painters they really are.[23]

In point of fact Quinn's whole dealing for American art reduced itself in 1919 to two large pictures by Walt Kuhn, priced at $1,125 each, *The Harlequin* and the painting of three women which Quinn referred to as " 'The Caucus' " or " 'The Cock-us.' " [24] He paid for these relatively costly works piecemeal; with a $300 credit standing at the beginning of the year, he paid $700 in January, $600 in May, the final $650 in June, then $200 in November as "a further payment on account in advance." [25] He still loyally admired Kuhn's art, but some of the warmth had gone out of their old personal friendship. Quinn had begun to feel that Kuhn occasionally "used" him as Augustus John had done, both as friend and patron. Now when he felt like inviting a masculine companion to Ogunquit or the Adirondacks it was still likely to be Kuhn but leavened by F. J. Gregg or his old friend Eddie Robinson, who came up from Washington when summoned.

Gwen John wrote on April 25: "When I last saw my brother, it was more than a year ago, he said he thought you took no more interest in his work. He doesn't understand that he makes it sometimes difficult for one to show one's interest." When John's dealer Knewstub wrote in February that John was off to France again, this time with a commission to paint the members of the Peace Conference, Quinn showed no interest whatever. His last dealings with John had been in the preceding year, when he had tentatively accepted the portraits of Arthur Symons and Mme. Réjane at £400 each. Now in April Quinn returned the *Mme. Réjane* outright, and in paying for the *Arthur Symons* he deducted £283 and 16 shillings which he figured John owed him for money paid in advance. In order to make the understanding as plain as possible he made the payment direct to John rather than Knewstub.[26] When John's new etchings went on show in the winter of 1919–20 Knewstub reserved a good selection for Quinn, but when he was slow in ordering, went ahead and sold the etchings to other buyers. After March 1920 Quinn ceased to correspond with either Knewstub or John. In ten years of intermittent dealing with John, Quinn had invested in the neighborhood of $50,000. He had grown dissatisfied both with the prices and the quality of John's painting, and felt the quality had gone down as the prices were going up. To Conrad he grumbled that the £400 for *Arthur Symons* was "just about £200 too much. . . . John's latest things lack intensity . . . there is no pain in them, no struggle." [27]

Symons himself wrote in November, announcing his discovery of the art of Gwen John and offering to send photographs. Posessing already four important oils of hers and twenty of her drawings, and standing ready to purchase any of the pictures she so reluctantly let go, Quinn was amused by Symons's suggestion. He told Symons how he had failed to see Gwen John in both 1911 and 1912 on his visits to Paris, and how much he admired her art and what he could divine of her personality from her work and her correspondence over eight years. To meet her in person was one of the motives that urged him to go abroad again as soon as possible. He was sure she was a better artist than her famous brother, and he expressed his discontent with Augustus John in terms such as those he used to Conrad:

> John is entirely too facile. He is a wonderful draughtsman, but there is no acid in his work. Confidentially, he is such an accomplished painter that he ought to be ashamed to paint the way he does. There is no harshness, no acid, no pain, in his work. He is in the Slade tradition of fine draughtsmanship, but fine draughtsmanship alone is nothing . . . but fine draughtsmanship! [28]

He applied the same terms, and apparently the same standards, in seconding Symons's praise of Toulouse-Lautrec:

> I think Lautrec was a great artist, and in his best work a greater artist than Degas, for Lautrec had more ideas than Degas and more harshness, more acidity, more torment and pain in his work than there was in Degas.[29]

As art talk such phrasing is not very satifactory and helps one little to get at the bases of Quinn's values. When so many judgments are expressed in the same limited vocabulary, and when work after work is praised or dismissed on apparently the same grounds, the words cease to carry much meaning. There is an effect of echolalia, and Quinn was in fact echoing not only himself, but also the empty *salon* lingo that had stuck in his head as generally useful: "The Slade tradition of fine draughtsmanship," for example, was a threadbare bit of London *salon* cant. Quinn kept rattling off words like "radium" and "acid" and "pain" and "harshness" as if they were objective counters, conveying real judgment and real information, whereas they really seemed to testify to a basic inarticulateness before a work of art. One understands and respects Quinn's meaning when he asks for "pain" or "acid" in a painting: he did not want pictures "about" suffering but pictures that persuaded one by their power that they had not come easily, that they had cost the artist some expense of soul. It is a respectable criterion but not an easily demonstrable one. Quinn's taste was a natural one, and an excellent one, but it was subjectively based and not easy to rationalize. It is not quite accurate to say he groped for words to express it: rather he tried to express what was better silent, and to do so satisfied himself with a small number of rather crude and emptily conceptual terms. His problem was partly that of the pioneer of taste: as an American collector of European modernism in the first quarter-century, and as a man who was otherwise a hardheaded and efficient man of affairs, he was constantly being called upon to justify his natural and instinctive courses by words —words which he really did not possess. He commanded the passion and the judgment of a connoisseur and was a genuinely qualified amateur of art, but when he tried to talk like a professional the result was distressing, and made one wish that he had rested content with the evidences on his walls.

Quinn continued to "beg" Gwen John for pictures and got fewer than he liked, as she painted on slowly and with excessive self-doubt. She described for him the little old Chateau de Vauxclair near Pléneuf where she had recently lived and painted: "It is not fine or grand. It has rather a humble beauty, and an atmosphere *un peu triste*." [30] The castle had been bought cheaply by cattle merchants, who were planning disastrous improvements, and was thought to be still for sale at a modest price. Quinn was distinctly attracted by the idea and corresponded with Gwen John about it during 1919 and 1920. The Purchase Street failure had not cured him completely, and now his old dream of a country estate in Ireland had naturally given way to a dream of a country estate in France. With Mrs. Gardner and her Boston mansion in mind, he pictured himself as the genial host of a house preferably in reach of Paris, filled with books and pictures, a place of gracious resort for artists, bibliophiles, and connoisseurs. But nothing came of the Vauxclair scheme, or ultimately of the general idea: life got in the way again for Quinn.

Having come to another sweeping conclusion, that the only good sculpture was carving, Quinn had discouraged Epstein from sending him any more of the bronzes which were that artist's main current interest. Coupled with his disenchantment with Augustus John, this meant that only Wyndham Lewis among the English artists was left to compete with the French; and in fact Quinn's loyalty to Lewis was mainly a loyalty to his friend Ezra Pound. When Lewis's post-war show opened at Marchant's Goupil Gallery in London late in January 1919, Pound and Lewis made independent rounds of the gallery, each marking a catalog to pick out the works he thought Quinn would want, then compared their lists.[31] Ultimately Quinn bought seven drawings at the considerable price of £245. He expressed his dislike of the big spring show of English and Canadian War Memorial pictures at the Anderson Gallery in New York in letters to both Lewis and Epstein, and this time he let himself go in a relaxed personal judgment that was a good deal more interesting than his usual critical talk. He told Lewis the only thing he had liked was "your large picture of a gun battery, which is realistic in treatment, and is done in harsh colors and is a big thing and has harsh vigor to it and looks like war and like a real battery." [32] To Epstein he wrote of the show as a whole: "They are thoroughly banal, domestic, sentimental and the trace of Orpenism is over them all. They look like pictures of mimic wars staged in Algiers by Belasco for the moving pictures." [33] In another letter to Epstein he expanded the judgment into a rationalization of the whole trend of his taste: "In fact I don't care too much for English art at all. It is too domestic, too heavy, and it lacks the brilliance and style and chic quality of the best French art." [34]

Late in May Epstein wrote that the composer Bernard Van Dieren was doing a book on his work to be published by John Lane, and asked Quinn to send him photographs of certain works in his collection of which he did not have a satisfactory likeness. Quinn was driving hard to order affairs in his office so that he could get off for a vacation in the Adirondacks, and he undertook Epstein's chore with poor grace. Charles Sheeler, who seemed to him the best man to make the pictures, was located in Philadelphia only after several days' pursuit, and returned to New York. Men had to be hired to move the heavy stones into satisfactory position for photographing. Two men moved the *Birds* but seven men could not move the granite *Mother and Child* and that part of the enterprise had to be abandoned.[35] When Van Dieren's book appeared in the following year it included fourteen plates of major works held by Quinn, and showed him to be by far the sculptor's most significant collector.*

Quinn's friendship with one artist of French provenance now came to a mysterious and distressing interruption. After periods in New Orleans and Havana, Jules Pascin was now back in New York. He had made a portrait sketch of Quinn, and Quinn urged him to complete the likeness in oil. Pascin replied that he thought the sketch execrable and begged Quinn to destroy it. Nor would he undertake the portrait on any terms. His theory of portraiture was that it must be done "from inside out": the painter had to

---

* 1. *Cursed be the day wherein I was born.* 2. *Venus.* 3. *Mother and Child.* 4. *Carving in Flenite.* 5. *Head of a Boy.* 6. *Mrs. Jacob Epstein.* 7. *Euphemia Lamb.* 8. *The Late Lieutenant T. E. Hulme, R.M.A.* 9. *The Countess of Drogheda.* 10. *Bust of a Girl.* 11. *Iris Tree.* 12. *Augustus John.* 13. *Bernard Van Dieren.* 14. *Old Italian Woman.*

assume the role of his subject, like an actor; and Quinn, he felt, was "the type the most difficult for me to impersonate." Pascin wrote in these terms on April 23. Apparently at about the same time he sent Quinn another note charging him with " 'calumnies, slander and insults,' " for Quinn wrote him at length on April 25 denying any guilt of such behavior. Pascin did not reply at all, and Quinn, who owed the painter $600 for work he had accepted, finally returned his *Landscape with Figures* to cancel his debt. There were no further dealings between them.

In fact Quinn's dealings for art of any kind, even the French, continued moderate in 1919. He was buying fewer works at higher prices, and most of them were sculptures for the moment. Brancusi, recently released from the hospital where he had been laid up with a broken leg, wrote at the end of January 1919 to say that he was sending two marble carvings, as well as photographs of two new wood carvings and a marble bird designed for Quinn which had got broken. He feared Quinn would find his new prices rather steep but he justified them by the amount of effort that had gone into them, including the woods, which he carved as lovingly as the stone. If Quinn rejected the woods, he wrote: "it is neither my fault nor yours, and I am not in the least offended." [36] The two marbles were evidently the *Prometheus* and *The Sleeping Muse*, for Quinn paid Brancusi 3,000 francs and 4,000 francs, respectively, for those two works on October 25. In November he bought through the dealer Marius de Zayas Brancusi's bronze *Head* for $500. It was also through de Zayas that he obtained the two Matisse paintings which excited him so, the *Figure of an Italian Girl* and the still life of *Apples*, for which he paid $2,400 and $3,200. De Zayas agreed to accept in part payment, for $1,500, Brancusi's wooden door, bench, and lintels. Quinn rarely traded in this way, and in fact rarely parted with a work he had once accepted; but he was trying more and more consciously to narrow and sharpen the range of his collection, and he had concluded that his basic kind of sculpture was to be carving in stone.

He had obtained through the great Paris dealer Ambroise Vollard four *Views of London* by Derain at 6,000 francs, and on October 25, when he was in a bill-paying mood, he closed with Vollard for four paintings and three ceramics by Rouault at 4,800 francs. In his letter of June 28 to Vollard he took pains to explain at length the results of his labors in the "free art fight" in 1913 and again in 1918: Vollard should be aware that the exemption from taxation of the first sale of a work of art by an artist applied also to a first sale by a dealer. He expressed once more his aggrieved view of his own experience in the matter:

> It is needless to say that I was never paid a penny by any artist or art association for the work that I did in 1913, which extended over a period of nearly nine months, nor for the work I did in the summer of last year, nor indeed have I ever had any recognition from the artists or thanks from them for what I have done for them, largely because, I imagine, they haven't the wit or sense to understand what was done for them.

Moved to sentiment by the death of Raymond Duchamp-Villon, Quinn had bought through Walter Pach for 800 francs a Gallic cock in plaster and wood which the sculptor had made as a decoration for a theatre behind the lines. To carry the gesture a step further, Quinn had the decoration cast in bronze in the summer of 1919, in two copies, and he sent one of these to the widow of Duchamp-Villon with a note explaining that he intended it as a personal memorial to an artist he valued.[37] Both Quinn and Pach, who had been the sculptor's personal friend, lay on watch for other memorial gestures they might make.

Though his dealings with other French artists were quiet for the moment, Quinn continued to correspond with those he cared about. Segonzac, for example, wrote of how it felt to take up painting again after five years' interruption by the war: "I found myself to be somewhat like a beginner, working too nervously, wanting to undertake too much at one time, and lacking in method. It is all coming back little by little."[38] Isadora Duncan was dancing again and had offered to pose for him again: "She dances now with less joy and movement, but what she creates is more human—very profound and moving." He listed the "painter comrades" he had lately seen in Paris: Picasso, Gleizes, Metzinger, Léger, Van Dongen, Derain; but La Fresnaye remained very ill with tuberculosis in the south of France.

In the autumn of this quiet year for his collection Quinn took a step which was to focus, animate, and enlarge his dealings for

French art. Henri-Pierre Roché had been back in New York, and the two had again met cordially several times. Roché looked over Quinn's collection more systematically, and they began to speak of ways in which they might be of use to each other. On September 17, the eve of Roché's return to Paris, Quinn sent him a note specifying in general terms what he expected: Roché was to function as a scout, looking out for available works he thought Quinn would like and sending over photographs with descriptions, specifications, prices, and his own advice. He was to look primarily for "works of museum rank" which might be within the reach of a man of modest pocket. Roché replied next day "Au Bord de 'France' ": "Dear Mr Quinn, Before the boat leaves I wish to tell you that your letter gave me great interest and pleasure—that I quite approve your plans—and that I shall be glad to help them as much as I can." He would of course receive some sort of friendly honorarium for his services as middleman between the buyer and the artists and dealers, but the specific rate of pay was left in genteel suspension.

French artists were among the many who sent Quinn congratulations in the autumn after he was named to the French Legion of Honor. News of his nomination was carried in the New York papers of September 7, and Quinn sent clippings to friends at home and abroad. Georges Rouault welcomed the event because "c'est un lien de plus avec la France." [39] Segonzac wrote on October 12:

> Bien cher Monsieur—
> J'ai été tres heureux d'apprendre votre nomination dans l'Ordre de La Légion d'Honneur.
> Je sais combien cette haute distinction est justifié après l'appui que vous avez donné à la France à des heures critiques et cruelles et pour l'aide si généreuse que vous avez été à l'Art Moderne, malgré toutes les attaques dont il est l'objet.*

The "red ribbon," Walter Pach wrote, "will make a very nice note in your color scheme." [40] Michael Monahan addressed Quinn

---

* Dear Sir—I was very happy to learn of your nomination to the Order of the Legion of Honor.
I know how that high distinction is justified by the support which you have given to France in critical and cruel hours and by your generous assistance to Modern Art, in spite of all the attacks of which it is the object.

henceforth as "Mon Chevalier," and Ezra Pound wrote on the first of October addressing Quinn as "M. LE CHEVALIER" and asking him to present his compliments to the Legion of Honor for having shown such good taste. Quinn had sent him the *Sun* and *Herald* of September 7 with news of his election. Lady Gregory congratulated him upon the honor "so well deserved," then noted rather dauntingly that her family possessed one such decoration presented by Napoleon as well as that won by her dead airman son in 1917.[41] "You will find it a practical help on your next visit to France," she wrote; "it makes a real difference in railway journeys and the like."[42] Standish O'Grady pitched his comment at a higher level: "Such a feather in your cap inserted by that Queen of Nations, La Belle France."[43]

Of his own airman son O'Grady had written at the end of July. This one had survived the war and was camped with his wife in County Mayo, between a lake and the sea, and fishing in both. O'Grady had recently suffered his second mild cerebral shock in two years, what he called a "fall," and guessed that he might "tumble for good next time"; he faced the thought of death with fine sanity and feeling: "I confess I don't like leaving, would rather not, but am not in the least alarmed or afraid. I know that to leave is as essential, natural and right as coming in and being in."[44] Quinn had described for him at length the Adirondack country in which he was going to spend his vacation, and O'Grady accepted the account as a representation of the American ethos: "Great woods, the Blue Mountain Lake, sister, brother-in-law and child; it all sounds delightful; fishing, shooting, a possible bear in your bag; and all that in a state with New York as chief town. You have a marvellous country and are truly too a marvellous people."[45] James Stephens wrote to inquire: "What is an Adirondack?"[46]

Quinn's holiday in the mountains lasted a good five weeks, from late June to early August. It was his first extended rest since 1913, and he managed for once to keep the cares of the office fairly well off his mind. The Andersons were with him, and he loved the sense of living with them as a family in a relaxed frame. O'Grady's account sounded a good deal more strenuous than the reality; Quinn wanted only to sleep and eat, take long walks, and play a little golf. When he wrote to Epstein from the city again on August 7 he was in a much better temper than when he had been wrestling with photographers and heavy statues. He apologized for the tone of his last letter and set down his view of the state of his nerves: "Pure work without mental worry or strain never hurts anyone. It is worry and strain and irritation and sometimes anger, recurrent fits or prolonged anger, that upsets men." Epstein had been complaining of neuritis and insomnia, and Quinn sent him extended advice which boiled down to two main points: get hold of a good general practitioner and watch diet carefully. Too many people, he said, "make a distillery of their stomach," and he recollected the jingle in which old Dr. Spitzka, who had "cured" him of chronic sleeplessness and stomach trouble, had phrased his index of forbidden foods:

"Pork, pickles, pastries, pies,
Fish, fritters, fats and fries."

It was one of the calmest and most satisfying years of his life. He was famous in the city for having fired five law partners in a single year, and he fired one this year, his senior lawyer Sheffield, the "Washington Square" type; after that things went better for the time. The Andersons had yielded to his wish to have them in the city after his illness and settled in an apartment at 37 West 93rd Street. Mary, now nearly twelve, came in to breakfast on Quinn's forty-ninth birthday on April 24. He renewed his lease on 58 Central Park West, but agreed for only one year rather than three, disgruntled by a rise in rent from $3,200 to $3,500 per year. His housekeeping was in the satisfactory hands of a French couple in their middle thirties, Paul and Marie Bertranne. The Volstead Act infuriated him, as an invasion of privacy and as unenforceable legislation. Abstemious himself, he still refused to be told that he could not serve wine at dinner or spirits with his cigars, so he bought much of the stock of the Manhattan Club when it had to close its bar. On May 1 he paid a bill for three cases of "Jameson Five-Star" Irish whiskey, from an unspecified source. Mrs. Jeanne Robert Foster was much in his company, and one of her unromantic duties was to read over his law briefs to him before he appeared in court; usually she would read through a brief twice, after which Quinn never consulted it again: he remembered it almost verbatim. Mrs. Foster was present when Huneker brought Mary Garden around in April to take tea and tour his collection. Quinn described to Huneker his chat with Miss Garden and her mother at a lecture. She asked whether his pictures were old masters, and Quinn answered: " 'No, all modern. All as modern as you. I don't go in for antiques of any kind.' And Mary laughed a merry laugh." [47] Before she arrived at the apartment he took care to move to one side Brancusi's *Princess X* which usually faced the entrance in his foyer, and which many guests found immediately and heroically phallic. But when she entered she spied it at once, and cried out: " 'My God! What is that?' " [48]

Some of the chief frustrations of the year as well as some of the satisfactions arose from Quinn's part in the affairs of Pound and Eliot, both of whom were much on his mind. He still approved of both of them, as good artists and honest men. Of Pound he remarked to Horace Brodzky at the beginning of the year: "Pound is frank above all things. One need not read one of his sentences twice to learn its meaning." [49] In his dryer, more academical way, Eliot was equally direct and candid. Both men recognized Quinn as their best American ally, in fact almost their only one. Two troubled letters from Eliot to Quinn in January of 1919 showed him in the role of a classic American type, the young man in the grip of Puritan family pressure. On January 6 Eliot explained that he had settled abroad in 1914 against the opposition of his family "on the claim that I found the environment more favorable to the production of literature." For some time the family had been letting him feel that it was about time for him to produce some literature; a visible book would help "toward satisfying them that I have not made a mess of my life, as they are inclined to believe." When Eliot wrote again three weeks later he reported that his father had died in the interval, but his mother remained to be pleased.[50] Quinn was carrying the American responsibility for an important manuscript of each writer: Pound's *Instigations*, a collection of his own critical papers plus a work dear to his heart, Ernest Fenollosa's essay on "The Chinese Written Character," edited and annotated by Pound; and a collection of Eliot's composed of his poems to date, still few, and prose critical pieces

many of which had been written for the *Egoist* or the *Athenæum*.
Eliot recognized that the poems made a scanty show, and he had
misgivings about the scattered and occasional character of the
essays; he would have preferred to represent himself in a more
unified and decisive way, but still it was important to him to get
out a book of some kind soon. Meanwhile he continued to send
Quinn additional pieces, both prose and verse, to add to the proffered manuscript.

During the summer and early fall of 1918 Pound's prose collection and Eliot's bundle of prose and poetry had been placed in
Knopf's hands, partly by Pound direct, partly by agency of Quinn.
At the end of January Pound heard from Knopf that he had decided to reject both of the proffered volumes. Pound wrote to
Knopf directing him to turn the manuscripts back to Quinn, and
wrote to Quinn on January 30 in a state of anger and depression.
He asked Quinn to try his own manuscript on Huebsch, but remarked bitterly that if Quinn and the elder Pound would look
through the manuscript it would have been exposed to three-
quarters of its potential American audience. *Instigations* and "Mr.
T.S. Eliot's manuscript" reached Quinn from Knopf's office on
February 13. He carried them not to Huebsch but to Boni & Liveright. At the end of April he wrote Eliot that they had accepted
Pound's work but were dithering about Eliot's. Meanwhile Knopf
had written that he would like to publish Eliot's poems but not
his prose—his position on the matter from the outset.[51] Eliot wrote
on May 25 to thank Quinn for his pains and to say that he still
hoped to expand and improve his manuscript with new poems and
essays. When Quinn replied on June 30, the bad-tempered day of
his departure for Blue Mountain Lake, he was enraged because
Liveright had still not made up his mind about Eliot's manuscript.
He was convinced that Liveright had delayed in order to force
Quinn to offer a subsidy of a hundred or two hundred dollars. He
had extracted the manuscript and turned it over to Mrs. Foster to
offer to the American office of John Lane, and he told Eliot he
would if necessary offer Lane $150 as a subsidy.[52] By late August
the matter was sorted out at last. Lane had refused the manuscript,
and Quinn had accepted Knopf's proposal of a volume of poems
and no prose.

On July 9 Eliot had given Quinn a free hand and renewed thanks:

> . . . I leave it in your hands in all confidence, but with the always stronger feeling that you ought not to accept or have forced upon you so much disinterested labour. My only justification is that I do not know anyone else with either the influence, the intelligence, or the generosity necessary to undertake it. It is quite obvious that, without you, I should never get anything published in America at all.

Quinn suggested the title "Poems by T.S. Eliot," thinking it better to avoid the "Prufrock" in the title of Eliot's first English volume.[53] On September 29 Eliot sent Quinn an important new poem, "Gerontion," listed the poems as he wished them to appear in the book, and asked Quinn to execute a contract with Knopf on the lines of those he had arranged for Pound with the publisher. On the whole Eliot was well pleased with the way things had turned out, glad to have a book of his verse in the works for America, and glad to be able to plan his prose book more carefully. On November 5 he approved the contract with Knopf and asked Quinn to return the prose that was once more in his hands: "It is in fact a great relief to me that it will not reach print in the form in which you have it." He intended to revise and supplement the group of essays for publication by the Egoist Press, after which he might again offer them to Knopf. Once more he thanked Quinn warmly and gracefully: "I earnestly hope that my affairs will not take any more of your time and thought; if you took no further interest in them whatever you would still have earned my lifelong gratitude, which, I assure you, you shall have." And he made his first veiled reference to the gestation of his most famous work, *The Waste Land:* "I hope to get started on a poem that I have in mind."

Pound's affair ran a roughly parallel course. Boni & Liveright accepted *Instigations* in April, and Quinn arranged the contract before his holiday in June. Pound wrote his reaction on August 6: he found Quinn an abiding comfort and he thanked him for an excellent contract. Without Quinn, he said again, he would never have been published in America. Quinn's dealings with these publishers were far from sweet, however. Something in Liveright's way of doing business brought out all Quinn's anti-semitism; he liked to refer to him in letters as "Liverwart," and he bullied Liveright or his agents whenever he got a chance.

On April 28 Quinn had sent Pound £60 as an increment in his *Little Review* subsidy, and Pound at once laid out £20 to Yeats and £20 to Joyce. At the same time Quinn offered to continue his annual grant to Pound if he chose to go to a new magazine. The *Little Review* and Joyce's *Ulysses* were again in mutual difficulty, as Quinn had been certain would happen. Joyce's eighth episode, "Lestrygonians," scraped by its first mailing to subscribers, but the Post Office Department forbade the mailing of any additional copies. The editors capitulated to the extent of making some deletions before printing episode IX, "Scylla and Charybdis," in the May number; but Miss Anderson appended a haughty footnote: "To avoid similar interference this month I have ruined Mr. Joyce's story by cutting certain passages in which he mentions natural facts known to everyone." But the May issue was stopped anyway. Quinn wrote Pound on June 17 that "It would be perfectly hopeless to take the matter into Court." But he wrote a brief on the matter which he sent to the Solicitor of the Post Office Department in Washington. When Pound read a copy of it he thought it a superlative defense not only of James Joyce but also of realist literature in general.[54] Pound wanted it printed, and sent it to Eliot for publication in the *Egoist* if Quinn would grant permission. That permission Quinn refused, both to Pound and to Eliot. He said that his brief had been too hurriedly composed to merit printing. In fact, he did not wish to appear popularly as a defender of "license" in print. Pound was disgusted at the *Little Review* suppression as one more evidence of American fear of the mind: "It is typical that they should have hit on Joyce's best and most intellectual chapter; typical of the way America spews when given any real food for the intellect. . . ."[55] But again he agreed with his wife that the root of the fear was not prudery but the horror of vitality itself: it was "the energy" in Joyce, Lewis, and Pound that "upset people," and indecency was only a name they gave to it.

When Pound wrote on October 25 he reported that he had just been fired "in most caddish possible manner" after "two opulent weeks" as drama critic on the *Outlook,* and was feeling vengeful, he said, for the first time in his life. But he was also feeling uplifted and exhilarated from reading the manuscript he had just received from Joyce of the great fourteenth episode of *Ulysses,* "Oxen of the Sun." He described the passage: "Parody of styles, a trick borrowed from Rabelais, but never done better, even in Rab." He went on with typical generosity and gusto: "Our James is a grrreat man. I hope to God there is a foundation of truth in the yarn he wrote me about a windfall. Feel he may have done it just to take himself off my mind." It was not the kind of gesture to which Joyce was given. Joyce's windfall was real, and sizable, and it did not come from Quinn.

Eliot wrote on July 9 in praise of the forbidden ninth episode of *Ulysses,* which he thought superb: ". . . I have lived on it ever since I read it." He considered the suppression a national American scandal, and wanted to give it wide notice in England. But he recalled too that the *Egoist* had been unable to find a printer willing to set up *Ulysses,* and he had to admit that English public opinion as to Joyce had been no more enlightened to date than the American:

> . . . I have found it uphill and exasperating work trying to impose Joyce on such "intellectual" people as I know, or people whose opinion carries weight, in London. He is far from being accepted, yet. I only know two or three people, besides my wife and myself, who are really carried away by him. There is a strong body of critical Brahminism, destructive and conservative in temper, which will not have Joyce. Novelty is no more acceptable here than anywhere else, and the forces of conservatism and obstruction are more intelligent, better educated, and more formidable.

Joyce himself wrote Quinn from Zurich on August 3. After ten years of frustration, he was looking forward to the world premiere of *Exiles* in Munich in a week's time, and he hoped that Quinn might yet succeed in persuading an American company to put on the play. Alerted by Pound, Harriet Shaw Weaver of the *Egoist,* who was Joyce's still anonymous patron, had written him of what Pound called Quinn's "magnificent defense" of *Ulysses,* and Joyce thanked him. He set down his reaction to the affair in a sardonic postscript: "It is extraordinary that American law allows an employee to penalize a citizen for *not* having committed an offence.

I allude to the penalizing of Miss Anderson on account of suppressed passages." Quinn had written him that the Solicitor's judgment was based on the general contents of the May issue and on
"the cuts contained therein." "Cuts" referred not to excised texts
but to reproductions of four nude drawings by James Light; the
term confused a good many people. Meanwhile the great work was
moving slowly ahead in its massive members, four or five months to
a chapter. Joyce estimated that he might barely be able to finish
the novel by the end of 1920. Pound wrote Quinn that in spite of
his anticipated "windfall" Joyce had "no money in view until
January," and Quinn now proposed to buy the complete manuscript of *Ulysses* when finished, and cabled an offer of an advance
of $125. He found Joyce's cables cryptic and hard to deal with, as
for example, that of October 15, from Zurich, which he quoted
to Pound: " 'Starting cable maximum advance manuscript Ulysses
via Sanita two Trieste.' " To Pound he wrote: "I am willing to
cable him another $100 in addition to the $125 mentioned in my
cable, which ought to tide him over until January. I had not heard
anything about his windfall. I shall be glad to help him out." [56]

Elsewhere in his letter of November 9 Quinn sounded less
benign. The Adirondack euphoria had long since worn away and
he was driven again:

> I had hoped that I could be able to take Saturdays and Sundays
> off this autumn and get some exercise, but not a single Saturday
> have I been away. I have had to do hard traveling to Washing-
> ton and other places, and this letter is dictated in my apartment
> on Sunday afternoon at the end of a whole day's work with
> Mr. Curtin. So there are compensations, my dear Pound, in being
> a poet and an artist.

Pound had written a month earlier to suggest, gaily, that Quinn
abandon the American professional treadmill and retire to Europe,
with whatever competence he could collect, while he was still
young: Quinn already knew everybody who amounted to anything in Europe, and he could pass his time happily in endless converse with his "friends and debtors." [57] He listed other roles Quinn
could play if he wanted to "vary the bowling": "J.Q. loafer;
J.Q. critic; various J.Q.s perfectly capable of emerging from J.Q.
barhister and councillorrrr at lar, and owner of three museums.

J.Q. with no possessions save a very small cheque-book and a tooth-brush." Pound's own dilemmas at the end of the year were in-teresting but hardly disastrous. He wanted an American passport and was having some trouble in getting it, as he could no longer claim to "represent" either *Poetry* or the *Little Review;* he sug-gested that Quinn might name him as his "representative" for one or another semi-official function.[58] And he had a feeling that his major original work in verse, still young but grown large, was tending to slip its hold on life: "I suspect my "Cantos" are getting too too too abstruse and obscure for human consumption." [59]

With his obsessive concern for the Peace settlement and the putting-down of Germany, and with the admission of the fruit-lessness of his direct flurry in Irish politics in the *Irish Home-Rule Convention* book, Quinn's interest in Irish political affairs re-treated into a bored and sullen watchfulness. T. W. Rolleston kept trying to persuade him of the justice of the Ulster Unionist cause, but Quinn would hear of nothing but a united Ireland under Colonial Home Rule. The Ulster leader Carson he called "one of the most sinister figures in modern history." [60] But it was to Lady Gregory he said this, not to Rolleston. During the year she had to thank him for persuading Putnam's to print her *Kiltartan Poetry*, a thought of his own, as well as for the usual flow of gift books, including *The Education of Henry Adams* which he had sent on the hint that she found her own memoirs taking the form of "an education." She spent much of her Christmas holiday writing a play for her grandson Richard to take back to be performed at his school, but most of her general leisure, as for twenty years, was spent in supervising the planting of the young trees she thought of as "for Richard" but which, after the destruction of her house in 1941, would become part of the national forests of Ireland. Lady Gregory was one of those who for the time felt optimistic about the future of Ireland. She believed in the idealism of the Sinn Fein party, and believed that their success at the polls must call forth their latent sense of responsibility and with it a feasible politi-cal policy. "Responsibility is what we want for the whole country," she wrote at the beginning of the year, "not to be alternately spoon-fed and whipped." [61] Writing in September James Stephens saw a different scene. He noted that Irish policemen were now being armed with bombs "so as to make other lives as hazardy as their own," and he summed up his impression of the national temper: "The fact is that no one in Ireland cares the least rattle of a dying damn for anything any longer. . . ." [62] The problem, of course, was that too many people cared too much about too many different things.

Simpler, pleasanter Irish notes came from Jack Yeats. He expressed his pleasure in an old travel book of Mexico by Madame Calderon de Barca in terms that revealed his own homely and pragmatical tastes and the substructure of his art: "She gives plenty of what people eat and drink and say and not a great deal of what they look as if they were thinking." [63] In the autumn, after felicitating Quinn upon his "red ribbon," the Legion of Honor, he went on to describe his bay-haunting habits: "I have never yet got too much of rowing to a quay, going ashore, making the boat fast, exploring the land, coming back to the quay again, casting off, and rowing away." [64] It was an order of actions which made a ritual and an idyll, and made a picture of life and of Ireland at which Quinn could only stare in bemused fascination.

1920

DURING 1920 Quinn's relationship with Conrad continued to be troubled in ways both obvious and subtle, though both men behaved with sufficient politeness and accommodation to finish out another year as seeming friends. Quinn had received Conrad's letter of July 31, 1919, in which he complained of Quinn's "pointing out the value of his time," in late August. He had passed the letter on at once to Doubleday, who returned it a few days later. Quinn did not trouble himself to answer the letter for nearly five months, and apparently it simmered angrily in his mind all that time. Quinn's letter of January 20, 1920, was the only acrimonious document ever to pass between them, and its tone was one Quinn soon regretted. "Dictation," as he put it to W. B. Yeats, "is often thinking with one's ears or with one's tongue and not with one's mind or inner consciousness." [1] Unfortunately he wrote Conrad now at a time of peculiar general tension. In another letter Quinn described his law business to Conrad as "of a highly technical and specialized kind, consisting of bank work and corporation work, intricate and large taxation questions, contracts, international exchange, acceptance credits, etc." [2] Involvement in such affairs meant that the weeks at the end of one year and the beginning of the next were always the most crucial and harassing period in a twelvemonth's work. At the beginning of 1920 Quinn was involved not only with his annual crisis, but with another reorganization of his partnership arrangement, and with the imminent decisive moment in one of the most important cases of his career, the Botany Mills case on which he had already spent months of labor, and which involved millions of dollars and a constitutional issue. These were "days of painful stress" in which he worked "under dreadful pressure and strain," [3] and he feared he might lose his case in spite of all he could do.

It was while thus harried that he picked up Conrad's letter of the summer. His experience in interceding between Conrad and Doubleday, he said, reminded him of the couplet, " 'They that in quarrels interpose/Will often wipe the bloody nose.' " He had entered the situation, he said, out of good will to Conrad and because he had been invited in:

> From an impulse of friendliness, and *specifically* because Doubleday requested my cooperation, I interposed. But never again! . . . I don't know what I could have been thinking of that June afternoon when I dictated my letter to you about acting as a buffer. I cannot be a buffer for the simple reason that I must be on your side.

He denied that he had meant to complain of Conrad's inroads on his time, and maintained that there had been nothing in his letter to wound Conrad's "amour propre." His feeling had been that Doubleday "had been working and wishing for your fame enthusiastically and that in spite of this he was met with doubt and suspicion." Unstated in Quinn's sentence was his and Doubleday's suspicion and dissatisfaction with James B. Pinker—the agent and generous friend against whom Conrad could bear no complaint. Quinn restated his general position: "I interposed in the matter specifically because invited to do so by Mr. D. and because, being a lawyer and therefore a friend of peace and concord among mankind, I thought I might help in the business." He assured Conrad that Doubleday was "most enthusiastic" about his new novel, *The Rescue,* and he had promised to send Quinn advance proofs: "But I have not heard from him and I am glad not to hear from him and I hope I shall not hear from him about your work or affairs ever again or ever again call upon me for any reason." In his condition of rhetorical afflatus Quinn had lost hold of his usually trustworthy grammar. In spite of his renunciation, he wrote to the Doubleday editors on March 27 to ask for a set of the final corrected proofs of *The Rescue.* The manuscript had already gone to T. J. Wise, but

Quinn still cared enough for his Conrad collection to keep it as full and as close to the manuscript state as was possible in the altered circumstances.

When Quinn wrote again on February 15 it was in a much more temperate and pacific spirit, though he took up the affair of the manuscripts in a plain-spoken way. He did not "follow," he said, the rather disingenuous logic of Conrad's division of his manuscripts into pre-war and post-war, penned and typewritten; and he stoutly reminded Conrad of their old and plain understanding:

> You and I had an agreement that I was to have the first offer on all your MSS. I was not bound to take what you offered and you were at perfect freedom to put your own price upon what you offered. But I was to have the refusal at the price named by you.

At last he made the point that might have avoided much of the current and future awkwardness if he had made it earlier: "I knew of course, as you knew, and know, that manuscripts by Joseph Conrad today are not what they were eight or ten years ago when you and I began the business." Conrad had advanced his prices to Quinn over the years, but moderately, on a scale by no means commensurate with the advanced "value" of his name in the world of popular letters. Quinn would have been wise himself to offer the larger sums that were hard for Conrad to ask of the man who had first sought him out then loyally adhered. The heart of this letter of February 15, in any case, was its message of pained but generous forgiveness: "It is entirely all right about your MSS. I *did* hope that I might have the MS. of *The Rescue*, which your letter states you also sold to Mr. Wise. . . . I was naturally disappointed. But what is done is done."

Conrad suavely left it at that. In his reply of March 2 he expressed his and his wife's "sympathetic interest" in Quinn's "difficulties and the fine single-handed fight against adverse circumstances," and went on to phrase formally and elegantly their general respect and good will:

> Our best wishes for a less strenuous but not unoccupied life in your distinguished position, in which you could find both material reward and the continued praise of men at less cost to your splendid vitality and your mental force. One does not like to

think of a friend for whom one has a great regard and a man of
an established great reputation so hard driven by circumstances.

He refused to reopen "all that Doubleday matter" which, he said,
had been amicably settled some time since; he had signed a new
formal agreement with the publishers a week before, and they
were "going ahead in their usual whole-hearted manner." The
problem of the manuscripts Conrad now treated again, repeating his
arguments but in terms more satisfactory, at once gentler and more
explicit, and duly emphasizing the uncertainty of affairs during
the war:

> Whatever promises may have passed between us in the years from
> 1911 to 1914 I plead that the conditions of the war, which have
> affected so many other transactions, apply to my action too.
> As I have said before, I wanted money in the first instance for
> a specific purpose which could suffer no delay. In the conditions
> of the unforeseen insecurity and disorganization of all means of
> communication I went to the man on the spot [Wise]; and under
> the prolongation of those same circumstances I went again to the
> man on the spot. The state of war brought unexpected calls on
> me, as on many others, and I was bound to attend to them. It so
> happened that this period coincided with my abandonment of
> handwriting. Thus you found yourself in possession of everything
> of mine drafted in pen and ink. You say, my dear Quinn, that you
> do not take that point; and, probably, from a collector's point of
> view there is nothing in it. But, frankly, I didn't advance it as any
> sort of excuse. I am an idealist in my way, and the fact that all
> MSS. written completely by my hand will be in America while
> all the others, drafted differently, may remain in England seems
> (since division was unavoidable) to have a sort of fitness.

So he sent on to Quinn the handwritten manuscripts of the two
wartime essays he had mentioned in September 1919. "That infernal *Falk* fragment" had gone underground again, mislaid in
moving the Conrad household from Wye to Bishopsbourne. But
astonishingly the bulk of the manuscript of *An Anarchist* had
turned up "mysteriously," as had a few further pages of *Romance*
in the handwriting of Conrad and Hueffer. All these were Quinn's
if he wanted them.

The "Mediterranean ['Napoleonic'] novel," Conrad promised

once more, "will be dedicated to you all right if I live long enough to finish it—and even if I don't." Should he not live to finish it, he would take care to leave the dedication page for publication with the fragment. Conrad was feeling sad and unwell, depressed by his inability to work. "The gout clings to me like ivy to a decaying tree," he lamented in his March letter, and on July 5 he noted that he had done virtually no writing in a year and a half. He stood in mortal dread of "impotent old age"; but he reflected that he had already lived through "two hard lives"—his careers as seaman and writer, Pole and Englishmen. He could at last be sure, at any rate, that his copyrights would be of value to his wife and his sons, Borys and "your namesake" John.

In a letter of March 2 Conrad also notified Quinn that he would shortly be called upon in New York by J. B. Pinker, his literary agent and his generous and loyal friend, the man who had seen him through his hardest days. Pinker would be bearing "messages from me personally of friendship and regard for you." Conrad reminded Quinn that Pinker's "manners and moral character" had satisfied Henry James, John Galsworthy, Arnold Bennett, "and a host of other men of worth and standing." Pinker called promptly, and on March 20 he and Quinn shared a leisurely Saturday lunch followed by a long afternoon talk. Quinn was converted and congratulated Conrad on possessing "such an able representative and such a good friend." [4] In his letter of June 30 Quinn at last struck an entirely sweet-tempered and pacific note. "No more about our old arrangement re MSS.," he promised and counseled. "You and I will never have any differences about that old arrangement or any other matter. You are perfectly right in stating that unforeseen conditions altered the understanding, and justifiably so." He hoped that Conrad would one day offer to him the manuscript of his "Napoleonic novel": "which is to be dedicated to me"—but he gave him free leave to dispose of the manuscript otherwise if he chose. Conrad thanked him for his forbearance—"I am glad you take my arrangements as to the MSS. so well"—and went on to explain, still mysteriously but as fully as he ever intended to do, his motives in turning to Wise: "I had many claims on me, and I have some still (in another country now)—not to speak of my wife's prolonged disablement. . . ." [5] And he spoke yet again the hope that the Conrads might at last meet Quinn "de visu" when next he crossed the Atlantic.

Quinn's letter of August 15, dictated just before leaving for a holiday of three weeks in Ogunquit with Julia Anderson and Mary, was again sympathetic and reassuring. He felt sure Conrad would never face an impotent old age: "You are far from the end of your time." And his position, Quinn assured him, was already unassailably "brilliant": "There is no one writing fiction today who is to be mentioned with you. You are one of the leading writers living in the world today and still producing work that is worthy of your best." Speaking as an old friend who had "learned by bitter experience what it is to overwork and to drive one's body more than it can stand," he passed on his standard advice to ailing friends: take more holidays, get a good general practitioner and a specialist for special problems, pay attention to food and exercise. Whereas, Quinn said, he had himself thought very little in the past about old age, his serious illness of two years before had forced him to think ahead to a time when he could not perform as he had done for the twenty-five years in which he had "worked hard, had made some money, and spent it or given it away without thought."

He cited *The Rescue* as evidence of Conrad's continuing strength of powers: "There is no falling off there! It is a fine thing, one of your best things." Quinn had finished it recently in the small hours of the morning after a late night's work at the office. Once again he had been especially impressed by the psychological accuracy of Conrad's treatment of women—a subject that seems to have been much on his own mind at this period. "But you make her interesting," he wrote of the handling of Edith Travers. "Women won't like the finish. They like to feel a sense of power over men and to exert it. Nothing displeases a woman more than to treat her as one would a man, in a friendly, courteous way, for then she realizes that she is not dangerous to that man, and that annoys her for it makes her feel that her power is going or has gone." The relationship of Edith Travers and Lingard in the novel reminded him of the poem "Never Give All the Heart" which W. B. Yeats had written in his apartment sixteen years before, during that first lecture tour arranged by Quinn.

Quinn's reading of *The Rescue* was also productive of some

fairly heavy comedy with Walt Kuhn. One of his habits, he wrote Kuhn on August 14, was to send special delivery letters to persons he disliked very much, about five in the afternoon, knowing that they would be delivered at home after midnight. Now Kuhn had sent him a telegram which reached him at 12:30 a.m. as he lay in bed finishing *The Rescue,* and Quinn tried to phrase his disgust in Conradese; the front door bell, he wrote:

rang out in the stillness of the night and in the darkness of the front room. It broke the stillness, as Conrad would say; it shattered the quiet, it woke up the darkness and split the blackness that enveloped all the front part of my apartment. It seemed to penetrate to the door where the bell was, through the whole front of the apartment, into every chink and corner and out through the open windows into the blackness of the night; a blackness relieved by no moon or stars; a blackness damp, oppressive, without a stir or a murmur, relieved only by the faint yellow glimmer of a few of the park lights visible from the hot, steaming mass that seemed to rise up endlessly from the dark below. It rang out, I say, on the stillness of the night, a stillness not diminished by the low murmuring of the tram cars from the trolley line nine stories below, and in the stillness of the still night the very steels of the tracks seemed to turn to rubber, and the customary shriek from the tracks and clamor of the wheels did not rise; did not rise up; did not rise to the ninth floor apartment where the stillness abode, and so the stillness was shattered.

" 'Oh Hell,' " said the hero, and shuffled out in his bare feet and pajamas, down in the elevator to pick up the telegram that had been slipped under the front door of the building. Later Kuhn painted a comic water color on the theme of *The Rescue,* and Gregg suggested that Quinn send a reproduction to the novelist; but Quinn demurred: ". . . I told him that Conrad was incurably romantic and I did not think he would see the fun that you had made, though perfectly legitimate fun, over his serious romance." [6]

One of the earlier letters in this sequence to Conrad, that of February 15, had announced the presence of W. B. Yeats in New York: "I have known him for twenty years and, great artist that he is, he is as much of a boy as he ever was, and one of the most delightful companions I have ever known." For Quinn and Yeats it was a reunion after six years. Yeats was returning to America as one of the world's famous men of letters, with several motives in mind: he needed cash, especially for the expensive renovations on his tower, still "half dead at the top"; he wanted to show his young wife to his old father; and he wanted to try directly to persuade J. B. Yeats to return to Ireland before it was too late. Husband and wife reached New York on Saturday, January 14. Quinn visited them at the Algonquin that day, and next day they came to his apartment with J. B. Yeats for midday dinner and the afternoon. He described the scene for Pound: "Yeats seemed to be devoted to her, and she seems to be interested in and devoted to Yeats. And the old man beamed upon both of them, and was evidently pleased and delighted with the wife. So all of them ought to be happy, and I think they are." [7] But he noticed sadly that Yeats's blue-black hair had turned gray. His note to Gwen John a month after the arrival again emphasized the pleasure of Yeats's personal presence: "Tete-a-tete he is one of the most pleasant companions I ever knew and one of my best friends. . . ." [8] He tried to rephrase for her some of the speculations arising in the birth of Yeats's new "system":

> He seems to think we may be on the eve of a great spiritual discovery, something that would absolutely demonstrate the immortality of the soul, and that that would be the cause of a great counter renaissance . . . that the Renaissance with its skepticism and learning had destroyed the faith of the early Catholic centuries, and that the world has had, since the Reformation the results of skepticism and disbelief. . . .

In Quinn's language it all came out flat enough. But he and George Yeats took to each other at once and were quickly friends. Pound reported on March 17 that she had written back to say that she approved of Quinn and of American architecture, but of little else in the United States.

The Yeatses left shortly on their cross-country travels, with Yeats lecturing under the auspices of the J. B. Pond Lyceum Bureau. Yeats soon began to suspect that all was not well with Pond's affairs, and he asked Quinn to press for an accounting and prompt payment. On April 21 Quinn wired Yeats in Dallas: "Pond writes considers you great friend and that my pressing him your share proceeds does not improve that friendship. Rubbish." On investigation Quinn thought Yeats's intuition had been sound, and urged him to keep Pond up to the mark. Pond was bankrupt before the year was out.[9] The Yeatses returned to New York in late April, to spend most of a month as Quinn's house guests. On the day they arrived Jeanne Robert Foster was about to leave the apartment when they rang the doorbell; Quinn pushed her into a room across the hall from theirs, with orders to close the door and be silent—with the mischievous intention, apparently, of giving her a chance to overhear genius in its unbuttoned state. When the charade was over she met the Yeatses and became their friend thenceforward. The Sinn Fein chief Eamon De Valera happened also to be in the city; he asked to meet Yeats, and Quinn went round with him to De Valera's hotel. Quinn recorded his impressions for Standish O'Grady: ". . . though De Valera seems to be a narrow man, and outside of politics not a specially interesting man, I think him an absolutely honest man and a man who will not quit and will not know when he is beaten."[10] Yeats was generally tired and complained of rheumatic pains. Quinn hustled him through a round of thorough examinations by medical specialists and had his teeth X-rayed, but nothing more serious than bad tonsils could be discovered. Before boarding their return ship in Montreal on May 22, Yeats sent back Quinn's door key, which he had carried off with him. He also sent back high compliments on Quinn's hospitality: he "never intruded irrelevancies" upon his guests, and he had provided "less argument and more sympathy and understanding" than he had found anywhere else in America. He and his wife left Quinn's " 'happy and refreshed.' " [11] Ezra Pound commented without reverence upon the benefits of Yeats's American tour to his Irish tower: "Besides he'll have made enough to buy a few shingles for his phallic symbol on the Bogs. Ballyphallus or whatever he calls it with the river on the first floor." [12]

In Oxford on September 9 Yeats dictated to George a gay letter suggesting that Quinn rent Lady Ottoline Morrell's house in Garsington, on a hilltop six miles from Oxford. It was all ready to occupy with servants and gardeners in attendance, and he could have it for six months for £200; Quinn could invite his first house party by telegram from New York before starting over: "I would not have dared on my own responsibility to make you so masterly a suggestion but my wife is . . . a witch & sees into the future which makes me confident that if you don't do it, you will have missed your true destiny." George Yeats appended her own disclaimer: "Don't you believe this!" Yeats's gaiety persisted through the removal of his infected tonsils and a letter of October 30 describing the episode. Quinn had advised him to go to the best London specialist, but George Yeats had had a dream in which she and her husband disputed the merits of London and Dublin operators. Yeats in fact made an appointment with a surgeon in London, but when he went to the city he failed, through a general muddle, to find the man. He returned to Oxford and, "being a superstitious man, began to think the finger of providence was in it." When George "consulted the stars" they said that if he went to the London surgeon he would die of hemorrhage. A second figure on Dublin showed "the stars were as favourable as possible—Venus, with all her ribbons floating, poised upon the midheavens!" They crossed to Dublin, where Oliver St. John Gogarty, "with his usual exuberant gaiety," removed the tonsils. Gogarty talked literature as long as Yeats was conscious, and resumed when he came out of the ether. When Yeats hemorrhaged, Gogarty said reflectively: " 'I have been too thorough.' " Yeats considered his "possible end":

> I was looking, secretly, of course, for a dying speech. I rejected Christian resignation as too easy, seeing that I no longer cared whether I lived or died. I looked about for a good model (I have always contended that a model is necessary to style), but could think of nothing save a certain old statesman who, hearing a duck quack, murmured, "Those young ducks must be ready for the table," and added to that, "Ruling passion strong in death."
>
> Then I wondered if I could give the nurses a shock by plucking at the bedclothes.

Now, watching from the window his baby daughter Anne twisting about fretfully in her perambulator, he wondered: " 'Which is the greater bore, convalescence or infancy?' " He was beguiling his convalescence by arranging the portraits of his friends in his Oxford study. He recalled Swift's writing to Stella that he was bringing back from London to Dublin portraits of all his friends. Looking about at his own collection of "lithographs, photogravures, pencil drawings, and photographs from pictures and pencil drawings," Yeats reflected that "there is only one absent—John Quinn." He asked Quinn to send him a photograph of Augustus John's portrait drawing.

Jack Yeats was one of those upon whom Quinn was urging his praise of Joseph Conrad as "the greatest writer in English today." He sent Jack copies of Eliot's volume of poems from Knopf and Conrad's *The Rescue*. Jack Yeats found Eliot "amusing"; about Conrad he was unpersuaded. He had been busy lately "dividing everyone into amateurs and professionals." [13] He favored the amateurs and wished to be one of them always. He had "got a good way shovelling away the professional picture makers and novelists," and he suspected Conrad was one of the professionals. George Moore, in such a book as *Spring Days*, struck him as the one nearly true amateur among current novelists. Thinking back over *The Rescue* in the fall he concluded that it was not a great novel and that Conrad was now unlikely to write a great novel: "He has too much respect for the authority of convention and not enough for truth." [14] Conrad had shown his "slave" blood by "making up" his hero "by mixing the clothes of Deadwood Dick and Captain Kettle," rather than "going to life." *Spring Days* was drawn from living life, though it was only "a tale of people trundling along." Jack Yeats went on to develop his crucial distinction at a length unusual for him, and in terms of his best eloquent simplicity:

> The novelist, who respects his workshop more than life, can make breasts heave, and arms wave, and even eyes flash. But he cannot give his people pulses. To me man is only part of a splendour and a memory of it. And if he wants to express his memories well he must know that he is only a conduit. It is his work to keep that conduit free from old birds' nests and blowflies.
>
> Man cannot invent. When he thinks he is inventing he is only stirring with a wooden spoon. All of this is obvious to many people. But they forget it every now and then.
>
> There need be none of this stirring in painting, and that is why painting is greater than writing. Painting is direct vision and direct communication.

All of this spoke to something profoundly if confusedly important to Quinn. "With you, I am for the amateurs," he wrote on August 15. His understanding of the term was shallower and narrower than Jack Yeats's. The amateur in art he defined not as a conduit of racial awareness, rapt in "direct vision," but only as "the man who does not paint according to rule or formula"; the professional painter is the man who "develops a manner, repeats himself, becomes academic," and so is "done for." It was by this standard that Quinn continued to be interested in the art of Jack Yeats and even of Æ, who heard a different drum but still a drum, while he had lost interest in the art of Augustus John. But he was unwilling to disqualify Conrad, even on the grounds of his admitted professionalism. His defense was only iteration: "Conrad's books are rounded off and finished, but he is a very great writer, in my opinion the greatest writer in English today. . . ." Among his artist friends, Quinn said, he had long been speaking up for "the amateurs, the men who were constantly experimenting." (To be an experimenter is not the same as to be a conduit; Quinn had not really understood Jack Yeats.) He listed the pictures he would buy if he were "rich," by the painters who had escaped the taint of professionalism as he understood the term:

> I would first purchase, if I could get them: four or five of the best paintings by El Greco; about the same number of the best paintings by Goya; then five or six Daumiers; then five of six Courbets; then Cézanne—perhaps eight or ten of him if I were very rich; and then only the moderns—Picasso, Matisse, Derain, Braque, and some other modern Frenchmen, and J. B. Yeats.

It was the kind of "judgment," little more than fantasy on the face of it, that can drive one to despair about Quinn's art talk. Of course it expressed a homogeneous and defensible taste, and he was capable of deeper judgments. Taking off from a recent argument by Wyndham Lewis who, noting Quinn's "very great poussée towards Henri Matisse," charged that Matisse's use of oil paint was "too monotonously summary and thin," [15] Quinn expressed a general uneasiness in his own current feeling about the contemporary Frenchmen:

Much as I admire the work of modern French painters, they sometimes seem to me to carry their simplification, their abhorrence of
a story, of a complete scene, too far and to go in too much for
flowers and fruit and still-lifes and simplification of design that,
seen by themselves, are satisfying, but they would become mo-
notonous if seen in a large group of the same kind.[16]

What he was feeling, and fearing, was a new academicism, a "modern" professionalism among his idols, a negation of convention
becoming itself a convention, refusal of imitation becoming itself
iteration. Quinn's criteria, clearly, were more abstract, more aes-
thetical, less moral than those Jack Yeats was trying to explain and
apply. He was showing, too, in his diminished tolerance of the
moderns' evacuation of "content," an unconscious homesickness
for the "subject" pictures he thought he had renounced forever.

W. B. Yeats had failed in the event to persuade his father to
return to Dublin with him; and the old round started again, with
Quinn, afraid the old man would "die on his hands" far from his
brilliant and devoted family, begging them to get him away, they
begging their father to come, the father temporizing and offering
pretexts while continuing to live out his life stubbornly and beautifully on his own terms. There were various theories to explain his
reluctance. George Yeats felt that he dreaded above all things the
thought of helpless old age on the hands of his children. From one
remark of J. B. Yeats's Quinn had formed the impression that he
was willing to return if he could be sure of having a studio of his
own in Dublin, and he importuned the younger Yeatses to promise
him a studio. He put the case to Pound on September 24: "He is
81 years old, thin and with a cough, and his place is at home with
his family. He made a brave fight of it here. I admire him tremen-
dously. His youthfulness, his cheerfulness, his courage. He is a real
intellectual aristocrat. . . ." (The last phrase was Ernest Boyd's.)
Tall, thin, white-bearded, totteringly energetic, J. B. Yeats was still
an engaging and impressive figure. "He is a remarkable man in
every way and I am very fond of him," Quinn wrote Jack Yeats
on August 15. He had to admit that the old man looked well, but
he was afraid he might not survive another New York winter. To
W. B. Yeats his father again offered the fantastic excuse that he

could not leave New York until he had finished his self-portrait for Quinn, now nine years in process. On November 9 W. B. Yeats admitted defeat: he could do nothing with the old man. He thought of sending additional manuscripts that Quinn could sell for his father's keep; otherwise he did not know where the money was to come from, unless he undertook yet another lecture tour, as he was reluctant to do: "It is so much taken from life and work." [17]

So Mr. Yeats's life went on pretty much as usual. He still came often to Quinn's for Sunday dinner, traveling uptown from Petit-pas' about one in the afternoon and being sent home usually by taxi at four or five. He still frequently attempted pencil drawings of Quinn or of Mary Anderson, but these often turned into occasions of contention, with irritatingly long sittings and unsatisfactory results. Quinn had never liked any of J. B. Yeats's likenesses of him, and he told him so: ". . . your greatest failure has always been with me. In the painting that you did of me and in the drawings you have done of me you tend to paint or draw me as a soft-faced, gentle, mild-mannered, young, diffident, soft-spoken, shy, blushing, retiring student for the priesthood." [18] Mr. Yeats may have been overcompensating for his insight into the bullying side of Quinn's nature. He was not afraid to point that out to Quinn verbally, but he may have hesitated to set it down in the less transitory medium.

Meanwhile their intellectual dialogue continued, in meetings and letters. Early in January Quinn sent Mr. Yeats a copy of Æ's poem "Michael," which Æ had submitted to the *Dial* and the manuscript of which he had sent to Quinn. Mr. Yeats read the poem through repeatedly and wrote on January 19 in praise of it. As usual, he was moved to conceptual thought, to generalize in philosophical terms.

> I have an old prejudice against mystical poetry: it is of the fancy rather than of the imagination; as if the poet had foresworn human nature and for his own ease resolved to live in some celestial region away from the anxieties and warmth of our earthly needs— like those birds of paradise supposed to live always in the air because, though they had beautiful wings, they had no feet.

His terms were Coleridgean, Keatsian, and Yeatsian. Indeed they were family ideas; any Yeats might have said them, and the morality under the aesthetics was precisely that underlying Jack Yeats's separation of "amateur" and "professional." J. B. Yeats would not call Æ's poem "mystical," though it was full of "mystical vision"— "of the kind that rises of itself spontaneously to console us when we are face to face with the irremediable and the desolate; as natural as any cry of hope and desire and as incoherent and stammering." The poet had worked at a point too close to real affection and grief to be free for "the fictions of mystical reasoning"—for any kind of systematic mysticism: "He is too human to be so celestial, and is miles away from every kind of theology, heretical or orthodox." J. B. Yeats had returned once more, with a fresh vocabulary, to his old concept of the infinite rising in beauty and pain out of the finite. He quoted Æ's "magnificent farewell" lines (in "Michael") beginning,

> We choose this course or that, yet still
> The Everlasting works its will.
> The Slayer and the Slain may be
> Rivet in a secret harmony,

not recognizing, as Russell had forgotten, that they were a virtual quotation of Emerson's "Brahma."

In March Quinn showed J. B. Yeats two articles on his son by St. John Ervine.[19] Quinn thought they gave a distorted picture of the poet and, meditating a rejoinder, asked Mr. Yeats for his opinion, which came on March 24. J. B. Yeats thought the papers not only interesting but "sympathetic and friendly and quite sincere": Ervine had faithfully presented the side of W. B. Yeats he knew and should not be blamed for ignoring a side he had never seen. Yet the partial picture had set him thinking of his son as the amalgam of a marriage, the tense fusion of two bloods, Yeats and Pollexfen. His son was the "tongue," warm and fluent, that the Yeats blood had given to the Pollexfen "sea cliffs." * He recalled his dead wife's nature, still a dear enigma to him:

There is a good deal of his mother in Willie. I often said to her these words: "You know I have to take your affection for

---

* "Yet it was a Yeats [J. B. Yeats] who spoke the only eulogy that turns my head: 'We have ideas and no passions, but by marriage with a Pollexfen we have given a tongue to the sea cliffs.'" W. B. Yeats, *Autobiography*, p. 13.

granted," for I never saw the slightest sign of it, except once, and here was the manner of that "once": I had left the house and been gone a few moments when, remembering something, I returned and found her where I left her, and she showed so much pleasure that I was surprised and gratified—that was the "once." I knew and never doubted that, more than most wives, she was "wrapt up" in her unworthy husband. She was not sympathetic. The feelings of people about her did not concern her. She was not aware of them. She was always in an island of her own. Yet had you penetrated to her inner mind you would have found it all occupied with thoughts of other people and of how to help them. She was much liked by simple people—the poor and uneducated—for these people, knowing nothing of sympathetic discourse and its courteous ways, did not miss what others looked for and so were able to see her as she really was. *They* knew that she was not thinking of herself. . . . I used to tell her that if I had been lost for years and then suddenly presented myself she would have merely asked, "Have you had your dinner?" All this is very like Willie.

It was a valuable image of the mother of the poet, a person who has remained a shadow in the published annals of the Yeats family. In Willie, mixed with all this Pollexfen laconicism, were the Yeats traits of outgoing eagerness and chatty candor; and opposed to the Pollexfen self-confidence was the Yeats tendency to misgiving self-doubt. Ervine was to be forgiven for presenting less than the whole of a creature so mingled, genetically, as W. B. Yeats.

Quinn had been pressing J. B. Yeats to follow Joyce's *Ulysses* serially in the *Little Review*. Mr. Yeats had "admired it greatly" but with some of the same reservations he had felt at first toward *Dubliners* and *A Portrait of the Artist as a Young Man*: it "reeked of the cynicism of the slums" and was "critical and not creative." [20] But the news that *Ulysses* was again in trouble with the censors moved him to one of his great performances. "I must pester you with another letter on this most important subject," he began, on October 14 of his eighty-second year, "—for it is really a great issue—that, is, whether the books of Joyce and such as he are to go free or not"; and he went on, in an essay-letter that fills fifteen pages in a typewritten copy, to defend the moral function of such a work of art. In Joyce's novel he heard "the voice of each man's inner spirit," and he judged that "the gospel of individualism" was under frightened attack by "its enemy, collectivism." Joyce's influence, he thought, truly seen was strenuous and "bracing": "Self-discipline of the sternest kind is evident in every sentence he writes."

He then launched into an immense postscript in which he sought first to place Joyce within a moral spectrum ranging from "the beautiful" to "the filthy." He instanced two notable Irishmen, Oscar Wilde and Jonathan Swift, as devotees, each unhealthy in his extremity, of the two extremes:

> Wilde all relaxed and . . . made "rotten" by his absorption in the beautiful. . . .
>
> And then we have, on the other hand, Dean Swift, a man of great moral strength who did not know the meaning of fear; a singularly noble type of man, who put away from him every kind of self-indulgence, and all whose efforts went out to aid the wretched and the disinherited. And yet because he fought against himself and because he, though gifted with the highest capacity for enjoying what was beautiful (for was he not Pope's most intimate friend and literary counsellor?), he resolutely threw his eyes away from what was beautiful and gracious and gave all his study and all his thoughts to the ugly, he fell into madness and misery.

Beauty and ugliness, J. B. Yeats continued, are man's "two good friends to accompany him in life"; but he must "remain his own master, consulting first one and then the other." And he noted that Blake, the great madman of the middle way, who wrote: " 'The wild deer wandering here and there/ Are meant to keep the human heart from care,' " * wrote both Songs of Innocence and Songs of Experience. He recalled also that Rabelais, "the greatest master of the filthy" in the history of literature, was a "pious and most orthodox Catholic priest"; and told of Father Healy, who, when the ladies shrieked with fear when a skull was introduced in theatricals at a party in Dublin, "called out, in his piping voice: 'Put it in the scullery.' " But J. B. Yeats concluded that Joyce's true exemplar was Dante, the master of the hard:

---

* "The wild deer, wandering here and there,
  Keeps the Human soul from care."
      "Auguries of Innocence."

It is from Dante he gets that terrible hardness, that hardness of which Wilde had so little and Swift too much; for it is a Dantesque hardness and not a relaxed softness which inspires Joyce when he writes those so-called filthy passages to which people object. And the people who denounce him are really inspired not in the least by moral indignation. The whole movement against Joyce and his terrible veracity, naked and unashamed, has its origin in the desire of people to live comfortably, and, that they may live comfortably, to live superficially. It is impossible for any honest man who has given thought to the great issues of life to have any sympathy with this clamorous outcry. Joyce is a man of genius, inspired by an intense feeling for what is actual and true, and he sees the whole world, especially in his own native city, Dublin, living luxuriously in the lap of falsehood. He would awaken these people. He is a patriot, above all an Irish patriot. He is working for Irish regeneration. He would disperse the fog of false sentiment that has settled down on men's minds. He works with that strenuous purpose.

His analysis was interestingly close to Ezra Pound's conclusion that it was not the obscenity but the vitality of the moderns that got them into trouble with conventional opinion. Mr. Yeats took it as good news that Joyce was the most hated man in Dublin: "They are feeling their punishment and it is salutary." Being himself "of a luxurious and indolent turn of mind" and a lover of the beautiful, he found himself shrinking from the ugliness in Joyce and drawn to the great beauty there; but he could not, "like the Dublin people, take refuge in hating Joyce." He came back to Joyce as one of the artists of the great middle way, chief of whom was Shakespeare: "The great poets are men of great character who know too well the value of both the ugly and the beautiful to side with either in any such conflict." But the fundamental fact, morally and legally, was that such "hardness" and "ugliness" as Joyce's had nothing to do, in kind and in function, with the true "filthy." Joyce's books were enlighteners, and therefore they were fortifiers:

> I do not say that Joyce's books would make a man happy. I am not sure that Shakespeare makes a man happier. . . . Yet I am certain that a man is wiser, and therefore stronger, who has read deeply in such books as Joyce's.

On Christmas day Mr. Yeats thanked Quinn for a box of expensive cigars: "a compliment to my taste that my taste does not deserve." [21] He had composed a "Dialogue in Heaven" which the *Freeman* had accepted with pleasure, and he took a dry pleasure of his own at continuing to appear in print: "I think it may make some little stir and be a surprise to some of my friends; perhaps to Willie—and I am in my 82nd year." He devoted most of this Christmas letter to analyzing the difficulties he had been having with Quinn over his drawings. It was an old disagreement between them, Quinn impatient with his painstaking perfectionism, the old artist unwilling to give up a task until he felt it "finished." "The fact is, as I look at it, you crave for the implicit, and I am for the explicit," he wrote. "A sketch is the one; a finished portrait painted to the farthest is the other, or rather mostly so, like a portrait by Rembrandt." The conflict, perhaps, was the classic one between the studio and the academy. J. B. Yeats went on to develop it acutely and at some length:

> I am not sympathetic toward the sketch. It is, to me, merely a beginning and of no particular value in itself, even if it have attached to it the name Matisse. Of a sketch you are a better judge than I am, and you know what you want. I know it only as a good or bad beginning; a good sketch being a good beginning. I positively dislike a sketch if it is offered to me as a finished work of art. That is where I am at variance with all the modern artistic ideas. I have been a painter all my days, that is, a worker in the explicit, and never a sketcher. My sketches are not sketches. The sketch is a modern invention. A sketch is an affair of twenty minutes. A portrait is the result of many efforts, all of them tentative; its object the subtle truth of portraiture. *In its final form it becomes like a sketch.*

It was the most penetrating of J. B. Yeats's many insights into art and life, and he did well to italicize it: it was worth eighty-two years of work and thought. The sketch which was not a beginning but an end, the *sprezzatura* of careless absoluteness which is the finality of form—it was the vision of great art which his own art approached only at its rare best, but which was expressed by his whole beautiful personal presence, at once dense and fluent, tough and warm, coevally finite and infinite. What he was trying to describe, as he clearly saw, was the collision of two kinds of taste, traditional and experimental, classical and romantic, his own and Quinn's. In a sense his statement also dramatized the history of Quinn's taste. The work and the taste of J. B. Yeats were a taste of Quinn's comparatively recent "youth" as a connoisseur, some fifteen years before. They had been replaced by a taste for the "living," the questing, perhaps restless and irritable, essay into "vision" which Mr. Yeats could only see as sketching, not finished art. Quinn's letter to Jack Yeats had suggested some misgiving with the taste for the modern he considered fully confirmed. His continued patronage of J. B. Yeats was certainly an affair of loyalty and sentimentality, willingly given, but likely to show its shallow roots in a quibbling and fault-finding that was pointless exactly because it was fundamental.

Writing in March, George Russell made the general erroneous Dublin assumption that W. B. Yeats would bring his father home with him from America. He returned Quinn thanks for his check for the "Michael" manuscript and for his and J. B. Yeats's praise of the poem. Politics, the Troubles, were the heavy weight on Russell's mind; his detachment had not lasted. "The country here is in a devil of a state," he wrote.[22] Every newspaper told of new shootings and new arrests. Dublin was tense, with a midnight curfew in force. Irish politics had "fallen outside the circle of intellect and into the outer darkness of physical force," [23] and Æ saw no hopeful signs in the morass of violence and general mistrust. He still longed for a leader but saw none on the horizon. De Valera he found "personally pleasant and attractive" but too full of dangerous talk about " 'blasting Ulster out of the way.' " Continuing his dialogue with Quinn about the baneful influence of training upon the Germans, Æ cited as a comparable case his own experience as a boy in Ulster, where every Sunday School taught the iniquity of Catholics:

> The prizes given were all about the inquisition, thumb-screw, rack, burnings and such like mediaeval iniquities as if they were current Catholicism. I am not a Catholic nor do I like Catholicism but I see how the hatred of Nationalists and Catholics taught in Ulster from earliest years has made a people otherwise loveable enough insufferable politically and so blinded by prejudice that they cannot be argued with.

Van Gogh: Self-portrait

Derain: Window at Vers

Kuhn: Girl in White Chemise

Matisse: The Blue Nude

Rousseau: The Sleeping Gypsy [La Bohémienne Endormie]

Brancusi: Yellow Bird

Brancusi: Mlle. Pogany

Epstein: Mother and Child

Duchamp-Villon: Baudelaire

Picasso: Three Women at the Spring

Gris: Guitar, Glasses, and Bottle

Seurat: Les Poseuses

Gwen John: Mère Marie Poussepin

Matisse: Music (Sketch)

Maurice Prendergast: The Promenade

It was the other side of the coin from that which Rolleston had been showing Quinn, of the anti-Protestant indoctrination in Catholic southern Ireland.

In his sadness at the public condition Æ was being privately consoled by the ripening of his friendship with James Stephens, and by the ripening of Stephens's art before his eyes. Stephens had set out to tell again the whole of the Red Branch cycle of primitive Irish tales, and Æ considered his second volume, his version of the Deirdre, the best of all tellings of that classic Irish story. He described to Quinn his "enchantment" at hearing the author read from it, and went on to rich praise of the man:

> You have never I think met James Stephens. As a human being, a companion, he is the best I have met in Ireland since I was a boy. I rate him as an enchanting talker higher than Yeats, Moore or any other I have known. He is worth while paying a visit to Ireland to meet. He has abundance of that rare thing humanity, feeling, sympathy, kindness, humour, imagination all abundant and never failing. [*March 12, 1920.*]

Stephens and Quinn had not met, indeed never would meet, and it was only in 1920 that they exchanged photographs, but they had been corresponding for seven years and Quinn had been buying Stephens's manuscripts ever since his introduction by Æ in 1913. Stephens returned from a trip to Paris in the spring to find a typical package from Quinn: a copy of Eliot's Knopf volume of poems, Quinn's letter to the *Sun* on Poland, quoting Conrad, and his appreciation of the painting of Walt Kuhn, also from the *Sun*. Quinn's remarks on Kuhn, combined with his own response to what he had just seen of French painting and poetry, moved Stephens to an unwontedly full and philosophic statement on the condition of the modern arts—a denunciation of their basic heartlessness impelled by those motives in himself which Æ had just been praising:

> They all have, and particularly the poets, bags of technique and cartloads of ingenuity, and one wonders why, with such equipment, they seldom bring anything off which one wants to remember. . . . They suffer, every damned man of them, from lack of sensibility. That is, they are not sensitive, and, whether in poetry or painting, this lack nullifies every other good quality they have. They see everything but they don't feel anything, and conse-

quently almost the whole of contemporary art is half-baked and indigestible, and, for they mostly know there is something wrong which they try to remedy by tricks, it is hypocritical into the bargain. Fantastic as it may seem, I think that something of the masculinity of man has been submerged, and this "something" has rendered us all less sensitive and more touchy. I am inclined to call it feminism for want of a better definition. . . . They all try to make up by violence the power which the Greeks got by repose. . . . You would know how to describe its effect in the political sphere, but in poetry I describe it thus: the male sensitive power is dead.[24]

Potentially the statement offered the deadliest of the year's several shocks to Quinn's established taste—rendered, perhaps, partly dismissible for Quinn, though not easily, by its apparently casual inclusiveness, its failure to name names, its focus upon poetry rather than painting.

Lady Gregory wrote on November 9 to express thanks for the preceding day's "good postbag from John Quinn," which had included a long personal letter, his gift of the letters of Henry James, and a half-year's royalty of £25 from Putnams on sales of her *Kiltartan Poetry Book*. Having learned that she was doing a memoir of Hugh Lane, Quinn had written in Lane's praise. Like Russell, Quinn was "a good praiser" (in her phrase), and she was sorry his encomium had come too late for use. She had now been struggling for five and a half years for the recovery of Lane's pictures from London to Dublin, but she recalled that it had taken eight years to get the Irish gold ornaments back from the British Museum and she was not discouraged. Lane's statement to Quinn in New York before sailing on the fatal voyage of the *Lusitania*, that he designed his collection for Ireland, which Quinn had retailed to Lady Gregory, was hearsay and carried no legal value.[25]

Along with Pound's *Instigations* and *Poems by T. S. Eliot*, the two-volume Henry James letters were a standard gift item from Quinn in 1920. To Huneker and others he praised the letters for their evidence of supreme artistic and critical power and their "wonderful warmth of affection."[26] On November 9 Lady Gregory found the letters "already a delight"—many of them coming from the days when James was her friend in London and written to persons who were also her friends. Deeper into the letters on November 20, she was struck with the greater homeliness and naturalness of those to William James and Howells and Norton as compared to those to English friends, using the same language but a different tonality. She was searching in James's letters and in his autobiographical books, as also in Henry Adams, for a shape for her own autobiography, which had been laid aside again. And thinking of James in the context of Quinn's frenetic life, she had taken down *The American* and reread the account of his American man of business—no mean model for Quinn—"who suddenly feels as he sits in his cab (in which I feel sure some visionary must have sat before him) that he must have freedom for a while." She had had also a more direct vision of Quinn from H. W. Nevinson, who had seen him in New York, and who was now traveling about Ireland reporting on the Troubles for the *Daily Herald*—"this whirlwind of outrage and revenge that is about us," as she described the grim interval on December 8. Her letter of November 9 had been interrupted by a visit from a young farmer, a former tenant of hers, Malachi Quinn, whose wife had been shot by the infamous Black and Tans, the English special constabulary. The event may have provided Yeats with his brutal image in "Nineteen Hundred and Nineteen":

> Now days are dragon-ridden, the nightmare
> Rides upon sleep: a drunken soldiery
> Can leave the mother, murdered at her door,
> To crawl in her own blood, and go scot-free;
> The night can sweat with terror as before
> We pierced our thoughts into philosophy,
> And planned to bring the world under a rule,
> Who are but weasels fighting in a hole.

By January 25, 1920, T. S. Eliot could at last be sure that he would soon have an American book to show his mother and other interested parties. Knopf promised publication by March 15, and actually brought out *Poems by T. S. Eliot* on February 18.[27] Essentially the same small body of poems appeared in London a few days earlier, there called *Ara Vos Prec* and published by the Ovid Press in an edition of only 264 copies.[28] Of the London edition four copies were printed on Japan vellum and bound in morocco with the title in gold on the front; Eliot presented copy Number 1 of these four to John Quinn.[29] The prose pieces Quinn had held were now back in Eliot's hands, and he was planning a more systematic prose volume on "the criticism of poetry and the state of poetry at the present time." [30] In a touching and sometimes amusing way, Eliot and Pound kept laboring for each other's benefit, using Quinn as one of their major instruments. Eliot got at his suggestion by way of an analysis of the current state of literary journals and Pound's relation to them. The new magazine with the old name, the *Dial*, was now being edited in New York by Gilbert Seldes and Schofield Thayer, the latter a school and college friend of Eliot's. Eliot was bluntly unimpressed so far. "I don't see why the 'Atlantic Monthly' should have a competitor in dulness, and the 'Dial' is an exact copy of it," he wrote Quinn. "There is far too much in it, and it is all second-rate and exceedingly solemn." [31] He thought the magazine might be toned up by a London editor, "someone here empowered to receive and select." The London journals seemed to him equally bad, and Pound, along the way, had managed to alienate nearly all of them. It was getting to the point that Pound had nowhere to lay his head, and it was this that really troubled Eliot: ". . . I am worried as to what is to become of him." He asked Quinn for a "candid and confidential opinion about Pound and his future." All of which sounded like a fairly open invitation to Quinn to do something new for Pound, probably in connection with the *Dial*.

Quinn went promptly to work, for both men. He bought thirty-five copies of the Knopf Eliot volume and quickly became an enthusiast. He read it aloud on two evenings to friends "and made converts of both." [32] "They are great," he wrote of the poems to Pound: ". . . some of Eliot's things are like fugues, and others awfully witty. The Hippopotamus and Sweeny [*sic*]—hell, *all* of them, are great." [33] With his extraordinary verbal memory Quinn soon had most of Eliot's poems by heart, and he liked to recite them in company. He discussed Eliot's "rather long chatty letter" [34] about Pound's future with W. B. Yeats and his wife over dinner in his apartment. Yeats said that he did not care for the work of Eliot or Lewis, but of course he was devoted to Pound's interest. Quinn asked him to recommend Pound to the *Dial* editors as their representative abroad and Yeats agreed. Quinn then arranged a dinner at the St. Regis for Yeats, Seldes, Thayer, and himself; but when the time came Yeats was ill and could not appear, so Quinn put the proposition himself. Seldes and Thayer were agreeable, and Quinn wrote of the matter on March 6 to both Eliot and Pound. "I am glad you suggested Pound," Eliot replied blandly on March 26.

Pound stated his terms of acceptance, in a six-page letter to Thayer on March 24, with a copy to Quinn. It was an archetypal Poundian document, blunt, clear-headed, energetic. He would act as the *Dial*'s foreign editor, he said, if it appeared that they could understand each other at a level that satisfied him. He agreed to work energetically for the good of the magazine, and even to try to accommodate himself within the limits of recognized American philistinism, accepting such hard facts of life as that the United States Post Office was an archeological survival and that a work such as *Ulysses* was impossible to circulate. The American *Dial* editors, on the other hand, would have to convince him of their intellectual seriousness. He ran over a long list of English writers he might or might not be able to enroll, discussed his own theory of criticism, and put a test question: would they have printed Fenollosa's essay on The Chinese Written Character? He wanted to be sure that they meant to purvey serious mental fare not literary gossip. He offered a first complement of "Cantos," IV, V, VI, and VII, and estimated that he could be counted on for two a year in future. And he recommended that he be allowed to serve as direct paymaster to contributors, as he had done for the *Little Review*: if he saw his authors frequently he could come to know what they were working at, and the moment of "*thaw*" which occurred when cash was changing hands was the right moment to secure a promise of the next good thing to come.

Quinn approved Pound's arrangement with the *Dial*, and took the liberty of advising him to behave with "tact and discretion." He and Pound were special cases, Quinn considered, and could take liberties denied to less enlightened spirits: "You and I can swear in writing at each other, and talk and write straight from the shoulder, whereas some of these younger fellows don't understand it." [35] When Boni & Liveright brought out Pound's *Instiga-*

tions in April, dedicated to Pound's father and with a design by Horace Brodzky on the jacket, Quinn bought twenty-five copies.[36]

Pound had given his "chronique" to Thayer, starting on May 1, as "Paris, Milan, Venice, Trieste. . . ." He wrote Quinn on June 1 from Sirmione to thank him for negotiating his appointment on the *Dial*: it would be a convenient way to pay the rent, whether or not he could make "a decent woman" of the journal. He recommended his current regimen, fat and cheap, as something Quinn should try: "The present rates are 20 lire or one bone ($) Yankee per diem, & I overeat myself twice in the course of each.—With hot springs the other side of the moat to keep off apoplexy." After he had steeped for three days and felt fairly well within himself, Pound's anxiety turned to Eliot and he wrote Quinn again on June 4:

> I am momentarily at least & thanks largely to you, lapped in prospects of luxury.
> It is easier to lap me than Eliot.
> No use blinking the fact that it is a crime against literature to let him waste eight hours vitality per diem in that bank.
> Nor on the other hand that it will take £400 per year, with 3 or 5 years guarantee to get him out of it.
> (His wife hasn't a cent and is an invalid always cracking up, & needing doctors, & incapable of earning anything—though she has tried—poor little brute.)

What Pound proposed was an outright subvention, anonymously given, to rescue Eliot from the bank and restore him to literature full time: "Is there any bloody chance of raising this sum from four or five people who wd. keep their mouths shut?" As always he was ready to cut to the bone himself in order to help. If he got his *Athenæum* post again in the fall, he judged, he could contribute £50 in the first year and could continue that for two more years if both the *Dial* and the *Athenæum* kept him on; but Eliot would have to be kept in the dark as to the source of that portion of his subsidy. Once again Quinn offered generously to go along: he proposed to give £50 a year for three years of his own. But he was unwilling to ask anyone else for money; the *Little Review* had cured him of that for the time.[37] When Pound wrote on October 9, however, his summer euphoria had faded, he was again in need himself, and his "grandiose scheme" for rescuing Eliot had to be suspended. The *New Age* was "killing off 'B.H. Dias,'" Pound's dummy form as art columnist, and the *Athenæum* had given him "the *chuck*." He vowed to call upon Quinn's proffered £50 only if he could see a way to do some real good for Eliot with it.

In fact Pound had fallen into an uncharacteristic frame of deep depression, in which Europe at last seemed to him almost as bad as America. He had been in Europe, mainly in London, for "twelve years and a bit," with only one return to America for about eight months in 1910–11. Now he asked Quinn whether the time had come for him to return to America. He thought he could bring everyone he cared about in Europe along with him in a few second-class cabins. [38] He thought he might be able to keep himself going by lecturing or teaching at Columbia University or the College of the City of New York: "HAAvud" did not appeal to him. "I had in mind a descent into the inferno," he wrote on November 8, when the idea of a return had been set aside, but he was still gloomy and pessimistic. He sensed, and feared, a general slackening of his fibers: "Only question of whether living in hot house smelling orchids so exclusively, hearing only one's own divisions on the clavicord, etc. IS best for one's work. . . . I don't want to go soft, or get to producing merely 'objets d'art' instead of 'œuvres.'"

In the interval between Pound's two letters he had received Quinn's answer to the first, dictated on October 21. After saying that he did not have time to write fully, Quinn harangued for nearly seven pages, with all his biases blatantly audible. "You'd hate New York with its million Jews," he warned. "You would be thoroughly disheartened by the hostile atmosphere of this vulgar and sinister city." One soon suspects that Quinn is composing from a specific model, and then recognizes it as Henry James's pseudo-suicidal passage on the barbarism of America in his *Hawthorne*. Quinn's version ran: "You would find no Wyndham Lewises, no T. S. Eliots, no James Joyces, no W. B. Yeatses here. No art that would interest you except imported art. No first-rate men of letters. No pleasant coterie." Instead Pound would find much that would waste his spirit and tempt him to lash out; but that, Quinn advised, had better be left to "a swashbuckler like Mencken." He thought there was no hope at all of a university appointment, and that the prospect of public lecturing was both unpromising and

undignified. The great pre-war bear-leader, J. B. Pond, was as
mentioned a bankrupt. The whole platform process had come to
seem to Quinn a manifestation of the noise and emptiness of a
vulgar culture: ". . . and the fact that you are not an Englishman
but an American would not help, for two-thirds of this lecturing
stunt is snobbery and wanting to see and shake the paws of distinguished furriners, just as sentimental girls in country towns fall in
love with drummers in derby hats and loud ties and patent leather
shoes." If Pound insisted, Quinn would sound out Thayer as to
the prospect of a job for him on the *Dial* in New York; but he
could think of nothing else to propose, and he advised Pound once
more to stay where he was and count his blessings.

With a verbal grimace, Quinn flipped the coin over: "It's curious
that you should think of coming over here, when my thoughts
have been so often full of getting a place in France." Americans,
he said, were "mad . . . mad in their hurry. . . ." At last the Jamesian
model showed itself plainly: "Henry James couldn't live here. . . ."
Quinn returned to the polyglot formlessness of American culture,
which he estimated to need two hundred years before it could
hope to approach the "homogeneity" of European countries. In
New York Pound could expect to find "a million Jews who are
mere walking appetites, seven or eight hundred thousand dagos, a
couple of hundred thousand Slovaks, fifty or sixty thousand Croats,
and seven or eight hundred thousand Germans." Quinn did not
number the Irish. The nation as a whole was

> the most backward economically, the most provincial socially,
> the most reactionary, the most capitalistically controlled, the most
> influenced by money, has less freedom of the press, less of the
> sense of freedom, less real democracy than any civilized country
> in the world, with the possible exception of Germany.

Had it been possible to live without his work in the law, Quinn
said, he would already have removed to France. He was held in
America by his love for his sister in the convent in Ohio and his
sister in New York with her daughter, "and I work to live and
do some things for my friends and to buy things that I am interested in."

With its bigotry and self-pity, the letter was a peculiarly distressing document, one of Quinn's most unlovely performances. Especially offensive were its special-pleading vanity and its attempt to pander to Pound's prejudices as read by Quinn. In fact the letter was far more pseudo-Poundian than pseudo-Jamesian, crudely echoing Pound's biases and Pound's idiom, with none of his wit, bite, or shrewdness, none of his fire of earned and considered rage. The letter was a queer mingling of egotism and sycophancy, hard to forgive.

After years of rather guarded epistolary intimacy, Joyce and Pound met for the first time in person in Sirmione on June 8. Pound had supposed that Joyce's anonymous patron was Quinn; Joyce corrected that idea with some scorn: he had no exalted opinion of Quinn's generosity.[39] Pound now learned that Joyce's handsome windfall would bring him about £250 a year.[40] He summed up his impressions of the genius in a letter from Paris on June 19:

> Joyce—pleasing; after the first shell of cantankerous Irishman, I got the impression that the real man is the author of "Chamber Music," the sensitive. The rest is the genius; the delicate temperament of the early poems. A concentration and absorption passing Yeats'—Yeats has never taken on anything requiring the condensation of "Ulysses."
>
> Also gt. exhaustion, but more constitution than I had expected, and apparently good recovery from eye operation. . . .
>
> He is, of course, as stubborn as a mule or an Irishman, but I failed to find him at all *unreasonable*. Thank God, he has been stubborn enough to know his job and stick to it.

Quinn was slow to receive an answer to his cables offering Joyce advance payments on the manuscript of *Ulysses*, and he reported to Pound in mid-January that he had sent no money as yet.[41] But Joyce thanked him for drafts on March 11 and September 3, and on September 24 Quinn sent a further $100, with the resolution to pay no more until he saw the completed manuscript.[42] The total of $500 to date was about twice what Joyce had received for the serialization in the *Little Review*.[43] Quinn was receiving the manuscript piecemeal, and the text was still appearing in the *Little Review*, in a "mutilated" version, as Joyce bitterly noted.[44]

Joyce thought that at last he could see the end of his "six years' unbroken labour" [45] on the great manuscript. On March 11 he wrote Quinn that the "Nausikaa" episode had gone to the *Little Review* and he was at work revising "The Oxen of the Sun." He hoped to be finished in the late autumn, and hoped that Huebsch would undertake to publish the full volume. He was still adamant against any tampering with his text: "There must be no alterations whatsoever of my text, either that already consigned in typescript . . . or that added in proofs; and . . . I must have a first proof and a revise of the whole book." He was glumly unsurprised that Quinn had found no producer for *Exiles* in New York; * it was all a piece of representative Joycean history:

> Burnings, delays, deletions, translations which never appear (four people at different periods began translating my novel [*A Portrait*] into French, but whether they got beyond the title page or not I never heard), and abortive productions make the material side of my literary life extremely tiresome.[46]

In his letter of September 3 Joyce sketched out for Quinn the grand design of *Ulysses*, with its three main movements divided into eighteen episodes, three in the "Telemachia," twelve in the "Odyssey," three in the "Nestor." "I thank you for your kind words about *Ulysses*," he wrote, "and also for your material help, which I need." He was writing the sixth version of the "Circe" episode; "but I am satisfied that I have done what I set out to do," he quietly concluded. Joyce wrote twice in November from the *maison meublée* in Paris which Pound had found for the family. His children had begun their education in Italian, continued it in German, reverted to Italian, and were now faced with the need to learn French. His son was as tall as his father "and much hungrier." [47] His income from his patron was enough to permit them to "live, or rather not to starve" if the right situation could be found. "Ulysses causes a great deal of trouble to everybody, not excluding myself," Joyce mused. "He is one of the 'world-troubling seamen.' " [48] He had begun the novel in 1914 and now expected to finish it in 1921, after which he dreamed of a year's complete

---

* Jane Heap says that Quinn had turned down several offers by Ida Rauh to produce the play at the Provincetown Playhouse, apparently finding the facilities too inelegant, too "Washington Square": Margaret Anderson, *The Little Review Anthology*, p. 221.

rest. The notes for the novel filled a small suitcase. His new flat was the twentieth address at which he had worked on *Ulysses*, "and the coldest." [49]

Quinn had continued to warn Joyce, Pound, and the *Little Review* editors that sooner or later *Ulysses* would meet further suppression unless the text was radically "cleaned up." Pound did what he could with the adamantine author. When he tried to make some changes in the "Nausikaa" episode, which culminates in Leopold Bloom's involuntary orgasm at the sight of Gerty MacDowell's fringed drawers exposed in the swing, he got back from Joyce a "thoroughly insulting and abusive letter" [50]—in spite of which, he wrote, "I did myself dry Bloom's shirt" before sending on the text to the magazine.[51] Quinn was by now quite willing to see the *Little Review*'s fate come upon it. What he really feared was that suppression of the novel in the magazine might damn it forever for publication as a book in America; thus he was more anxious to see the novel withdrawn from the magazine than to see it edited. "The excuse for parts of *Ulysses* is the whole of *Ulysses*," as Pound put it.[52] For Joyce's sake and for the sake of the world-troubling seaman, Pound and Quinn sought to protect the possibility of the publication of the whole. B. W. Huebsch, Joyce's first American publisher, had been muttering inconclusively for some time about undertaking it, and Quinn thought he might be brought to the point. He was sure that suppression of the magazine would frighten Huebsch, with good reason, away from the book. Quinn and Huebsch had thought first of an ordinary trade edition of *Ulysses* at perhaps $2.50. But as he began to feel more and more certain that such an edition would run afoul of the censorship, Quinn began to urge to Huebsch, to Pound, and to Joyce a private edition of a thousand or twelve hundred copies at eight to twelve dollars, printed by Huebsch or someone else. He argued that such an edition would bring Joyce a better return than a trade edition, with far less danger of suppression. He put this case in detail to Joyce in a letter of August 15. On November 24 he cabled Joyce urging him to forbid further publication in the *Little Review* and to give the manuscript into his formal custody pending a conference with Huebsch "next week." On December 19, after a talk with Huebsch at his apartment, Quinn reported that Huebsch still seemed to be stalling, guarding his own interests, avoiding a definite answer. If he refused the novel Quinn thought they should try Boni & Liveright. And meanwhile, and above all, Joyce should get out of the *Little Review* and put all his energy into finishing the manuscript for some sort of book publication. Otherwise, "if he really wanted the martyrdom of suppression," as he phrased it to Walt Kuhn, "he would get it damn quickly." [53]

Quinn's impatience with Margaret Anderson and Jane Heap and all their visible editorial postures had long ago crossed the threshold of reason into sputtering exasperation. He could hardly think, speak, or write about them without foaming at the mouth. Miss Anderson in the flesh still stirred him to a sensual response,* and that combined with her official intolerableness probably explains some of the heat of his reactions to the whole question of *Ulysses* and the *Little Review*. In fairly temperate terms on September 24 he set down for Pound a vignette of a recent meeting:

> . . . Miss Anderson blew in to see me early in August without writing or telephoning; dressed in a becoming gray suit; looking a little thinner than before; and smiling and looking almost as embarrassed as a virgin in a law office, although all virgins are not embarrassed in a law office. . . . they were on the rocks. [Otto] Kahn had given her $200. She inquired whether I could help her with Max Pam who had given $400 at my suggestion a year or so ago when I made up that $1600. I finally gave her a check for $200. . . . That is the last contribution I shall make to the Little Review and I perhaps should not have made that.

The *Little Review* had already suffered four suppressions largely on account of *Ulysses*. What Quinn feared now was the real *quietus*, permanent exclusion of the magazine from the mails and automatic censorship of *Ulysses* in book form. There was no question in his mind that the text was technically censorable in the current state of the law and the current temper of the law's interpretation. Quinn refused to quarrel with the law, and there was enough of the Puritan in his makeup to render him sympathetic to its interpretation, especially as applied to the circulation of magazines, in

---

* ". . . I was extravagantly pretty in those days—extravagantly and disgustingly pretty." Margaret Anderson, *My Thirty Years' War*, New York, Covici, Friede, 1930, p. 15.

which "innocent" persons might be casually exposed to hard stuff. He made this point again and again, to everyone concerned, as in his powerful and unprintably gross letter of ten single-spaced pages to Ezra Pound on October 16: "There are things in 'Ulysses' published in number after number of 'The Little Review' that never should have appeared in a magazine asking privileges of the mails. In a book, yes. In a magazine, emphatically no." His advice was ruthlessly practical: lie low, get out of the magazine, avoid the eye of the law, bring out the privately printed book. Nobody obeyed, and the blow fell in late September when John Sumner, Secretary of the New York Society for the Prevention of Vice, swore out a warrant against the proprietors of the Washington Square Bookshop for selling copies of the July–August 1920 number of the *Little Review* featuring the Gerty MacDowell episode. As Pound put it to Joyce, " 'Nausikaa' has been pinched by the po-lice." [54]

For Quinn's mood in the matter the crisis arrived at a time about as unfortunate as possible. To his standard "driven" condition and his resentment of all such cases as gratuitous and of course unpaying intrusions upon his professional regimen, were added his accumulated rage at unheeded advice, and the coincidence that he had been at least marginally involved in two other comparable incidents within the year. James Huneker had asked him at the beginning of 1920 to read the manuscript of the novel he was then calling *Istar*, to give him an opinion of it, and to advise him on how to proceed in publishing it. Quinn enjoyed the reading, but he was sure the book was censorable yet difficult to expurgate successfully, for a trade edition.[55] He advised a private edition and by the end of the year *Painted Veils*, or "Painted Whores," as Quinn called it, had appeared unmolested in a Boni & Liveright edition of 1,200 signed copies.[56] In the spring Quinn had been called in to represent the publishers of James Branch Cabell's *Jurgen*, then under attack. He had the case removed from the Court of Special Sessions, where, as he wrote to Mitchell Kennerley whom he had represented in the *Hagar Revelly* case, "three judges would have convicted him in five minutes," [57] to the Court of General Sessions, where his motion was granted for a presentation of the case to the Grand Jury, followed by trial before a petty jury if an indictment was returned. The Grand Jury did indict, and thereupon Quinn abandoned the case, not liking the feel of it. Again he had refused to look at the matter save in the light of law and how the law could be contended with. He thought the book was dirty, and he would listen to no protestations of art or high-mindedness and no appeals to mount a chivalric crusade. "It is a book that ought to have been prosecuted and ought to be condemned," he wrote Arthur Symons on April 11. When Cabell and a representative of the publisher came to his office to present "all of the usual bosh and slush, . . . encomiums of the paradisical [*sic*] motives and intentions of the author," [58] Quinn checked them rudely and with considerable pleasure. "The book was more Aphrodisical [*sic*] than paradisical [*sic*]," he was certain. After his rebuff his visitors reminded him, he told Kennerley, "of the young mule who was kicked by the old mule. After it was kicked it wasn't as handsome as it was before but it knew more."

It was in this generally savage frame of mind that the old mule learned on Saturday, October 2, that the *Little Review* had been "pinched" again and would be up for hearings on Monday. Quinn was left with only one motive in the matter, but that a very positive one—to protect Joyce and what remained of the possibility of a book: "Careful plans have been formulating for a privately printed edition for $10,000, royalty to Joyce $1,500 or $2,000. Nice edition made. Prosecution avoided—all spoiled": so he reviewed the matter for Pound once more in the letter of October 16. That able, violent, ugly letter carried the heading:

> Re "The Little Review" (God damn it); the female rabbits who pose as the editors of it (God damn them); the warrant issued against them for the July-August number; their ignorance; the absurdity of their being editors of anything; their freshness; the wearisomeness of their poses—with certain recommendations.

When Watson, now reinstated as Quinn's clerk, received "their God damned piss written telegram" from Long Island in the office on Saturday morning and telephoned the message to Quinn, Quinn told him he "didn't give a curse for 'Little Review,' wished it back in the stockyards of Chicago where it came from." But he agreed to try to do what practical and unillusioned law could still do for Joyce and his novel. The persons he summoned to a conference on Monday morning in his chambers on the thirteenth floor of 31 Nassau Street should have had little illusion that they were mounting to a philosophical eyrie or a Round Table of knights of art. Certainly Quinn had no such notion of the place. He set down his blunt conception of the law and its appropriate furniture in a letter of this summer to Huneker:

> I have never wanted to make a law office comfortable. I have felt about law offices as what they really are—machines, rather harsh machines, for the grinding out of compromises for conflicting forces. I have never conned myself into the idea that the law was a fine thing by Brussels carpets or fine furniture. [*June 9, 1920.*]

Quinn's badgered guests included Miss Anderson and Miss Heap, the Washington Square Bookshop proprietors (who had been served with the actual warrant), and their "Jew lawyer." He described the beginning of the scene for Pound:

> Told them flatly didn't give a damn for "The Little Review," wouldn't waste two minutes on it, it would serve them damnably right if it were permanently excluded from the mails. They talked of broadening the public. I said, "You will be broadening the matron at Blackwell's Island one of these days, and serve you damn well right." [*October 16, 1920.*]

When the editors said that they had felt bound in conscience to follow the wishes of Pound and Joyce, who "wanted the thing printed without changes," Quinn replied, as he wrote Kuhn on the afternoon of the conference, October 4:

> that Pound and Joyce were in Europe and they were in New York; that Europe was old and New York was young; that Europe was civilized and N. Y. was not, and that it was all right for an artist such as Joyce to ask that, but the editor of a magazine ought to have knowledge of the conditions in the place where the magazine is published and exercise independent judgment, and not be a mere adding machine to register the punches or punctures of those who play it.

Quinn then telephoned to Sumner. "Tactful talk," as he described it to Pound. "Nothing got by spitting in public official's eye, even though it's a small eye." His first legal move was to have the case against the Bookshop people dismissed and the hearing before the magistrate put off for two weeks, until October 18. At the end of the day, recalling for Kuhn his warning to Joyce of "martyrdom" impending, he envisioned the scene to come:

> And lo! The shadow of approaching martyrdom seems to loom! Mr. Sumner of the Vice Society seems to loom, and will probably be cast for the part of Judas or Herod. Ezra Pound will be the Apostle John. Jane Heap might get away in man's togs with St. Peter, and in a pinch Miss Anderson might be cast for the part of the blessed virgin. Quite a cast that would be! As long as one's casting, we might as well cast good. You and Gregg would have to be the chorus and I suppose I would be expected to look out for the resurrection stunt.   [*October 4, 1920.*]

Quinn's next move, before a necessary trip to Washington for three days, was to ask Sumner, "as a favor," to lunch with him on October 15. He "talked Joyce to him . . . two hours. My interest in him personally. Didn't want magazine condemned. Frankly admitted there were parts in it should not have been published in a magazine." [59] He asked Sumner to drop the complaint in return for a virtual guarantee that no more of *Ulysses* would appear in the *Little Review*: he promised in effect to demand that Joyce withhold it—as of course he had virtually done already. Sumner revealed that he and his society had not really originated the complaint; the sequence had run as follows: the daughter of a leading New York lawyer received an unsolicited copy of the *Little Review* in the mail; she read the Joyce episode, was shocked by it, and demanded that her father take action against it; he complained to the District Attorney of New York County; the District Attorney "turned the case over to Sumner, and Sumner swore out the warrant." This story of the victimization of the innocent young was precisely the kind of thing that would appeal to Quinn's own sense of the proprieties and obligations of magazine publication and the dangers of their abuse. The case against the *Little Review* was only too good, as he saw it: he would be lucky to salvage anything for Joyce. Quinn was careful to point out to Pound that this was a case where an offended citizen had spoken out, not an instance of entrenched philistinism, "not a case where Sumner, or Comstockery, or the Society can be honestly knocked." [60] He wished to hear nothing, from Joyce or others, of a "persecution" of Joyce: Sumner had never even heard of Joyce before; nor would Quinn listen to cries of outraged principles or charges of American bigotry, as he warned Pound bluntly:

> Don't for God's sake write to me any more about the illiberality of the United States, or its laws. The statute is identical with the British Act, copied from it. Not so strong as the French Act. Not so strong as the Belgian Act. . . . So, don't blow off at your typewriter with the idea that this is a sign of provinciality, or anything peculiar to America. [*October 16, 1920.*]

Even tactically, he felt, the editors of the *Little Review* were standing on the wrong ground, if they hoped to work for the liberalization of the law by defying it:

> It can't even be pretended that such plain violations of the law are a good way to bring about its amendment. For such raw violations of the law, with subsequent convictions, are just the things that convince legislators that the law shouldn't be changed. . . .
> Law is changed by public opinion, discreetly organized and not by flagrant violations leading to convictions.[61]

For Quinn, then, the quesion was wholly empirical: how to retrieve something from a reasonable and irrefragable law which had the *Little Review*, and more importantly James Joyce, in its just grip.

Sumner agreed to do what he could to persuade the District Attorney to drop the charges in return for Joyce's promise by proxy of Quinn; but Sumner failed and the case proceeded to run its course. Quinn failed too to mend the behavior of Miss Anderson and Miss Heap, who, according to Sumner, when they were required only to appear in court to accept the service of the summons in place of the Bookshop people, took the opportunity to make " 'defiant' " speeches, refused to express any regret for their actions, " 'gloried' " in what they had done, vowed to do it again, and hoped the prosecution would continue: it "would be the making" of their magazine.[62] Quinn was horrified and incredulous: "Can you believe it? These women flopping into my office, being warned by me, hearing of my talk with Sumner of a friendly kind, being warned not to make speeches, and yet going up to the court and saying all these things." [63] In view of such behavior Quinn waived examination for them at the preliminary hearing on October 21 before City Magistrate J. E. Corrigan in the Jefferson Market Police Court. Before starting to Washington on the seventeenth Quinn dictated his long abusive recapitulation of events to date and left it to be sent to Pound with a copy for Pound to transmit to Joyce.

Magistrate Corrigan was a "liberal" man, a personal friend of Quinn's, and one who had had past disenchanting experiences with Sumner and his Society. There was hope of a dismissal at this early stage, and Quinn tried to exploit it. Corrigan refused to hold Miss Anderson and Miss Heap on Sumner's "mere affidavit" and retired to his legal chambers to read the passage under attack. ". . . chambers struck me as the right place to read the July–August number," Quinn remarked in his report to Pound at the end of the day. Fearing to give Miss Heap and Miss Anderson a chance to put on another dramatic and suicidal performance, as he looked at the matter, Quinn insisted that they waive examination, a technicality which meant that they would be held under bail for the Court of Special Sessions. He sent one of the juniors in his office to handle things until they reached a crucial stage, while he attended a big auction in the Bronx involving a corporation client, then returned to his office to take care of the ensuing dictation. When his time came in court he dashed uptown on the Sixth Avenue Elevated. Magistrate Corrigan was still busy at his chambering, and Quinn stood in the back of the court chatting with Sumner, looking over the audience. "It was an amusing scene," he wrote Pound:

There was Heep [*sic*] plus Anderson, and plus heaps of other Heeps and Andersons. Some goodlooking and some indifferent. The two rows of them looking as though a fashionable whorehouse had been pinched and all its inmates haled into court, with Heep in the part of the brazen madame. The stage was also filled with police officers in blue uniforms with glaring stars and buttons, women and men by tows [*sic*] and threes awaiting arraignment or sentence, niggers in the offing, chauffeurs awaiting hearings; pimps, prostitutes, hangers-on and reporters—also whores, on the theory of "Once a journalist, always a whore."
                                                      [*October 21, 1920.*]

When Quinn stood up to speak he found Miss Heap and Miss Anderson at his left shoulder, and he ordered them roughly back to their seats. He described his ensuing performance: "I hit out from the shoulder and I don't think that there has been quite the same kind of speech delivered in a New York court in my time. Part of the time Corrigan was shaking with laughter." Quinn identified Joyce and his writings and defended the seriousness and high quality of his art, then turned to the question of whether the "Nausikaa" passage was "filthy in the meaning of the law." Here he used some of the ammunition provided by J. B. Yeats's letter of October 14, though in a spirit which sounds narrow, tricky and repugnant, if his own account is accurate. He argued that it was "beauty that corrupted, filth that deterred." He spoke of the bracing filth of Swift and Rabelais and "contrasted the strong hard filth of a man like Joyce with the devotion to art of a soft flabby man like Wilde." But Quinn had clearly resolved upon a defense based not on principle but upon the practicality of the law and the situation, and so he proceeded. Filthy according to the statute, he argued, was "as filthy did. Not filthy in the abstract but filthy in its result, pragmatically filthy, and not filthy in the absolute." He tried to force Corrigan to accept "the syllogism that the average person reading the July–August number would either understand what it meant, or would not. If he understood what it meant, then it couldn't corrupt him, for it would either amuse or bore him. If he didn't understand what it meant, then it could [not] corrupt him." * In essence Quinn had argued that Joyce's story was not aphrodisiac because it was either incomprehensible, amusing, or tiresome, according to the reader. Magistrate Corrigan professed to be interested but unconvinced by the argument. He cited one passage, that " 'where the man went off in his pants,' " [64] as unmistakable in meaning and " 'smutty, filthy within the meaning of the statute.' " He would have to hold the editors under bond for Special Sessions. Quinn suggested that perhaps they could be paroled

---

* In the column "The Reader Critic" of the *Little Review* of June 1918, "S.S.G., Chicago" wrote: "I swear I've read his 'Ulysses' and haven't found out yet what it's about, who is who or where. Each month he's worse than the last. . . . Joyce will have to change his style if he wants to get on." In the copy of the issue of March 1918 which the author examined, a reader had penciled in the margin of the *Ulysses* selection: "silly, what I could understand & what wasn't repulsive."

to his custody—" 'technically only' ": " 'God forbid that I should want any woman in my custody, much less the two women who are at the bar in this case.' " Corrigan insisted on bail but set the figure at $25 for each. Neither Miss Heap nor Miss Anderson had the money, so Quinn's young associate gave his check for $50, to be repaid by Quinn. He assumed that he would be able to have the trial transferred next from the Court of Special Sessions, with its panel of three judges, to the Court of General Sessions, with its grand jury; but in the upshot the best he could achieve was a postponement to February 1921. Leaving the courtroom, Quinn profanely rebuffed a reporter's request for a statement.

Quinn again enclosed a copy for Joyce in his letter to Pound, to be sent on "with such recommendations or comments as you care to make." [65] He saw Joyce as left with three possible courses: to forbid further publishing of episodes of *Ulysses* in the *Little Review*; to "emasculate," or "castrate," or at least "circumcise" any "parts" he still insisted on publishing there; otherwise to expect certain suppression of the magazine and the probable death of any hope for printing the whole book in America. Quinn's own position was simple and unchanged: "I am interested in Joyce, and in having 'Ulysses' published, and in nothing else." [66] He was "bored with the thought" of the *Little Review*, and he wished he could believe Pound was one-tenth as sick of it. Pound evidently did forward copies of these letters to Joyce, with a covering letter seconding Quinn's opinion and advising Joyce to "turn the whole matter over to Quinn" and give him "an absolutely free hand," and reminding Joyce, ". . . I did, I think, explain to you that M.A. and jh had not spent any money on you. I got the original trifle that was sent you, and the printing deficits were paid by J.Q., and in general the editrices have merely messed and muddled, NEVER to their own loss." [67]

Quinn was writing to Joyce via Pound because he had no reliable address for Joyce, who was having trouble finding a habitable flat in Paris that he could afford. Joyce replied to Quinn, also via Pound, on November 17. After three pages of dry complaint about the hardness of his life, Joyce turned to the question of *Ulysses* and the *Little Review*. From Quinn's point of view Joyce's attitude was weasling and unsatisfactory; later he said that Joyce had "evaded" and "sidestepped" the issue.[68] So he had, though his tactics seem comprehensible enough in view of his distance from the scene and unfamiliarity with the principals, his long history of frustration in obtaining publication of any kind, and his misgivings about Huebsch and his proposed edition of *Ulysses* as a book. Joyce wrote as follows:

> Your suggestion that I withdraw Ulysses by cable from further serial publication leads to another consideration. You said that arrangements have been made with Mr. Huebsch to publish a private edition but that further prosecution may upset the scheme. I know nothing of this scheme and if it is organized by you and entrusted to him, I advise you to watch his movements very carefully.
>
> Several times during the two and one-half years Ulysses has been running, he wrote to me asking when it would be finished. When I decided to come here contracts were sent to Miss Weaver and to him. She signed. He refused to sign. Being penniless when I arrived (but for Pound's help), I cabled to him to send on something—royalties or an advance of royalties. He never answered. Three months afterwards he wrote to me from a Paris hotel asking me to call. He suggested that I delete passages and alter, etc., a question I did not discuss with him. He then asked me if I believed any one would publish. I told him there was a scheme for having it printed in Paris for European circulation, whereupon he said: "Oh, in that case I could print it off in New York from that edition and pay you nothing." He added: "That is something Mr. Quinn did not tell you." If I understand the meaning of words this means a threat to pirate an edition. To this Pound replies that Mr. Huebsch could not do so because the L.R. has established copyright for me by printing it there. If this is so, can that copyright exist if the publication is incomplete, or can there be any copyright in an immoral publication? Mr. [John] Rodker seems to think that the L.R. has suspended or will suspend publication as these continual seizures mean a dead loss of money. It would seem that no number has appeared since July-August, and we are now near December. The Mss of "Oxen of the Sun" (the episode after the sequestrated Nausikaa) was sent on by Pound [to the *Little Review*] in the first week in June. It has been in New York for the last five months. Mr. Huebsch has it in the type script he obtained in London [from Harriet Shaw Weaver], and you

have it in MS., but if a number subsequent to July-August has appeared, my intervention would be doubly useless. While I have no hesitation in entrusting the organization of a private edition to you, and have no objection to Mr. Huebsch as editor, provided there is somebody to watch his movements (for he is entitled to a refusal of the book on all grounds), I do not think that he would be slow to take advantage of any sign of weakness on my part, and as such he would interpret my withdrawal. If the book be withdrawn by the L.R., already, as seems the case, the matter is easier. If it be not, possibly the arrival of the Circe episode (a tasteful production on which I am now engaged) will decide the matter.

I do not know much about the L.R. I never had any letter from Miss Anderson. I had one, I believe, from Miss Heap. I received in all £50 for the serial rights, which Pound says is a trifle (as it is) from another source—yourself, I suppose [rightly]. I understood that it is or was a review of the better class to judge by its contributors. But if the truth must be told, I never read it (except for my own installments). So that I have a very hazy idea of its character. I scarcely think that Mr. Huebsch, as publisher-putative of a private edition, will be deterred by any public prosecution of the book as a serial, and that his edition is safe and lucrative. He gave me to understand that he made a sacrifice for art in publishing my novel [*A Portrait of the Artist as a Young Man*].*

It was a shrewd and wary letter, representative of Joyce's character and of his experience. He was suavely refusing to accept Quinn's alarmed (and accurate) interpretation of the probabilities of the situation, and had evidently resolved that letting matters run their own course was as good a policy as any. In writing to Pound he picked up Quinn's phrase that there was "one chance in nine" that the District Attorney might be persuaded to drop the prosecution to justify his feeling that "my intervention is useless." [69] And

---

* In granting permission to quote from Joyce's long letter the James Joyce Estate has asked the author to insert the following gloss: "Huebsch was not the man to pirate a book of Joyce or anyone else; he was not uttering a threat but pointing out to Joyce a real danger in publishing *Ulysses* in Europe. His warning was justified, since Samuel Roth in 1927 did exactly what Huebsch indicated could be done. The *Little Review* copyright was not as helpful as Pound expected." It needs to be remembered also that no commercial publisher in England or America was willing to publish *Ulysses* until long afterward.

to his close friend Frank Budgen he wrote: "Quinn and Pound want me to withdraw the book from the review so as to safeguard the private edition, but it is as broad as it is long." [70] Joyce's next letter to Quinn, on November 24, mentioned the *Little Review* only to say again that he assumed that it had ceased publication, and devoted itself almost entirely to Joyce's conditions for the proposed Huebsch edition of the novel, which he persisted in treating as a near-fact.

In moving for the shifting of the case to General Sessions and trial before a judge and jury, Quinn argued that large financial questions were at stake and that Joyce should not be made to run the risk of summary loss of his "American rights and possibly copyright." [71] Here he tripped over his own ingenuity, for the judge ruled that precisely because such large questions were at stake the case should be given an early trial in Special Sessions: transfer to General Sessions might mean a delay of a year or a year and a half. But the delay was exactly what Quinn had been angling for, as he explained to Shane Leslie in a letter of June 21, 1922: ". . . 'Ulysses' could be published and sold [privately] and then the trial would be largely academic." Quite clearly, Quinn was not concerned with the ethics or the psychology of censorship in general, nor with the fate of the *Little Review*, nor even with *Ulysses* in the context of the *Little Review*; he really meant what he said: he wished only to find a technically legal means to bring out the book and bring Joyce his money. Now he had lost his delay and his chance for a jury trial, and he had to face the panel of three judges. In December appeared a new issue of the *Little Review*, dated "September–December," containing what would be its last episode of *Ulysses*. Under the heading "An Obvious Statement (for the millionth time)" Margaret Anderson spoke editorially, after announcing the editors' "arrest" for printing *Ulysses*: "I know practically everything that will be said in court, both by the prosecution and the defense. I disagree with practically everything that will be said by both. *I do not admit that the issue is debatable.*"

Ideologically disappointing as Quinn's line of defense was, the development of the case made his pragmatic reading of the situation seem shrewd, even brilliant. By and large, he repeated his earlier arguments for *Ulysses* before the Solicitor of the Post Office

Department and before Magistrate Corrigan four months prior to the date of the present trial, February 14, 1921. When he tried to present the general case for Joyce's eminence and artistic seriousness the judges brought him up short: such matters were irrelevant to the question, which was whether certain specific passages in a work named *Ulysses* were obscene within the meaning of the statute. When one of Quinn's expert witnesses, Philip Moeller of the Theatre Guild, denied that the effect of the passage could be "aphrodisiac," one of the judges interrupted: " 'Here, here, you might as well talk Russian. Speak plain English if you want us to understand what you are saying.' " * Once more Quinn asserted that, being incomprehensible, *Ulysses* could not corrupt.† He compared the novel to cubistic painting: ". . . experimental, tentative, revolutionary, if you like, but certainly not depraving or corrupting." [72] The prosecution in the case was in the hands of an Assistant District Attorney, Joseph Forrester, whom Quinn identified for Shane Leslie as "an Irish Republican, formerly a Sinn Feiner, but now a revolutionary militant." Forrester proposed to read aloud the passages in question, but one of the judges protested that such disgusting matter should not be exposed before innocent young women—pointing at Margaret Anderson. Quinn informed him that she was one of the defendants in the case. Surely she could not have realized what she was printing, said the judge. The passages were at last read out in court, two of the judges pronounced them incomprehensible, and an adjournment of a week was taken for study of the text.

In the second installment on February 21 both sides continued their established tactics, Quinn arguing that only a Dubliner could understand the text, that other readers would be mystified, or, if comprehending, bored or disgusted; Forrester in a rage of denun-

---

* Month after month, the most aphrodisiac thing in the *Little Review* was a bust-cut of Mary Garden, very décolleté, decorating her testimonial to Crane's Chocolates.

† Margaret Anderson on Quinn's tactics: ". . . as a final bit of suave psychology (nauseating and diabolical), aimed at that dim stirring of human intelligence which for an instant lights up the features of the three judges— 'I myself do not understand "Ulysses"—I think Joyce has carried his method too far in this experiment. . . .' " "Ulysses in Court," *The Little Review*, January–March, 1921, pp. 22–5.

ciation of the book, the editors, and the rival attorney. Quinn then pointed to Forrester himself as the "chief exhibit" for the defense:

> 'Just look at him, still gasping for breath at the conclusion of his denunciation, his face distorted with rage, his whole aspect apoplectic. Is he filled with lewd desires? Not at all. He wants to murder somebody. He wants to send Joyce to jail. He wants to send these two women to prison. He would like to disbar me. He is full of hatred, venom, anger and uncharitableness. He is my chief exhibit as to the effect of "Ulysses." It may make people angry and make them feel as though they wanted to go out and tomahawk someone or put someone in jail, but it does not fill them with sexual desires.' [73]

In the same letter Quinn described his tactic, not unreasonably, as "a frank appeal to the three Judges' ignorance." He believed that he had persuaded two of the judges, but the third finally bent them to his view: "I got two of the Judges, who were *consciously ignorant*. I failed with the third Judge, who was *unconsciously ignorant*. . . ." [74] Miss Anderson and Miss Heap were each fined $50 and might have gone to jail as well if Quinn had not been willing to certify that there was nothing worse than "Nausikaa" in the novel. It was stipulated that no more of *Ulysses* could appear in the *Little Review*—a result in which Quinn may have found shreds of consolation.

Quinn's several defenses of *Ulysses* may have carried more dignity and more persuasion as delivered and in context. But his whole tone in recollecting the events suggests that he saw them as close to farce, with himself rather cynically keeping them at that level for his own purposes, and Joyce's purposes as interpreted by Quinn —toying with the persons and the issues so as to prevent their growing serious and articulate. It is easy to see why Joyce was unimpressed and Miss Heap and Miss Anderson hurt and angry. Quinn entered the case generally overburdened, and sickened at the fact that the case arose because his repeated plain advice had been stubbornly unheeded. He behaved, as he saw it, as a practical hodman of the law trying to save what he could of another man's bad cause. It is important to realize, too, that Quinn's apparently shoddy arguments, more elegantly phrased, formed much of the ground of decision twelve years later when *Ulysses* was cleared for

American publication—in a judgment which is generally taken as a model of enlightened jurisprudence.*

One may be both relieved and additionally offended to see that Quinn really did understand something of the majesty of the thing he had his hands on when he was carrying the fate of *Ulysses*. He proceeded not in ignorance or contempt of the book, but in the belief that its practical future would be served best by a calculatedly disingenuous defense. The best evidence of Quinn's feeling for the novel in isolation from the legal problem it presented is probably the exchange of letters with Shane Leslie in the spring of 1922, after Sylvia Beach had brought out her edition in Paris and copies were drifting into London and New York. Faced with the problem of reviewing the novel, Leslie wrote on May 24 to ask Quinn's views: "How about 'Ulysses'?" He made Quinn's own point: "It is an immensely powerful and fantastic book, largely incomprehensible to those who are not Dubliners, Irishmen or Jesuits." He was divided in his own mind, at once awed and frightened: "He fascinates, disgusts and bores, infuriates and astonishes on separate pages." But he had already resolved to emphasize the dangerous whimsicality of a brilliance he could not deny: "I look upon it as the suicide of the whole Irish literary movement." Leslie's letter elicited the ten-page response of June 21, 1922, already quoted. About half the letter is given over to recapitulating " 'The Three Trials of "Ulysses" ' "—as Quinn said he would have liked to entitle an essay he had no time to write. He goes on to refuse Leslie's judgment of the novel as "the suicide of the whole Irish literary movement," and counters by applauding, as strategy and as fact, Pound's praise of the book as a "European event":

> It is a great tour de force; a very great work, indeed. The works that it should be compared with are Swift's, at their best. Joyce is a great story-teller. He has done new things with the English language. His genius is Irish, his frankness in dealing with facts, his courage, his interest in all forms of life and his sense of similitude, are Irish. He is as Irish as Swift was, but no more related to the Irish literary movement than Swift was related to the Irish writers of his day.

* Mr. Jackson Bryer has pointed this out in an able essay, "Joyce, *Ulysses*, and the *Little Review*": *The South Atlantic Quarterly*, LXVI (Spring 1967), 148–64.

The patriots will claim that "Ulysses" is not a picture of Irish life and is incorrect and immoral. Let them say it! Joyce is not concerned with patriotic morality or immorality. Joyce has a great sense of reality, a magical gift in the telling of a story, and a style that is utterly his own.[75]

But it was, and still is, distressing that Quinn did not rise to mount a crusade for *Ulysses* on general principles as well as upon tricky manipulations of law and of prejudice. What hurts is the avoidance of the issue: the real quality of the work of art. The history of Joyce's novel, its trials and triumphs, was far from finished, and Quinn would have a good deal more to do with it. At the moment, the only benign result of the litigation he could foresee was the possible death of the *Little Review*. He wished it all possible ill. He believed that the magazine had been living, parasitically, on *Ulysses*, and he hoped it would perish now with the withdrawal of its host. He had grown nearly rabid on the subject of the magazine as a corrupting environment for genius, and again and again he advised Pound, Joyce, and others to turn their backs upon it. To Pound he wrote on October 28, a week after the hearing before Magistrate Corrigan: "The sooner you cut loose from the Little Review, finally and for good, the better it will be for you and your friends. It stinks." But the magazine was tougher than he supposed, and it was to outlive him by five years.

For a man such as Quinn all years were hard, but 1920 was perhaps especially so. One of the reasons for Quinn's warm personal feeling for Ezra Pound was that Pound was one of the few friends and beneficiaries among the artists who seemed to feel, and occasionally to show, some insight and sympathy for the continual tension of Quinn's professional life. Touched by Pound's concern, Quinn wrote him at the beginning of 1920, in a mood generally expansive and optimistic: "I have made money and lots of it, and spent it, lots of it, often like a drunken sailor. I have never loafed much in 28 years. The first ten at the bar here left no cash balance in the bank. During the last twelve I have made money and spent it." [76] He had recently taken on a new partner, William B. Crowell, and his new firm was known as Quinn and Crowell. Paul Kieffer, who had lasted longer than anyone else, was to be a junior partner. Quinn had got to the point now of thinking of a gradual letting go of responsibility and labor, and he planned to bring

Crowell forward as his heir in the practice of the office. But Crowell was a sad disappointment to him, and he was gone before the year was out. Kieffer had been with Quinn from 1909 to 1912, and again since 1918. Quinn thought him a competent general lawyer, but not quite the man to inherit his personal mantle. Furthermore, Kieffer was having spectacular troubles with his wife which made it hard for him to keep his mind on his work. Quinn showed a notable patience with the situation and a sympathy with the man married to a wife "one part insane and nine parts devil." [77] Crowell was succeeded by Sherman Woodward. Quinn was paying Kieffer in excess of $10,000 a year, Woodward $7,200, and his managing clerk, also a qualified lawyer, $6,000—"all good salaries," as he noted with satisfaction to Pound. He preferred in all his experiments to stick with men who were Harvard Law School graduates, like himself. He determined not to grieve about his failures but to keep experimenting until he was able to form an organization that suited him firmly: "Numbers I am going to have in now even though the payroll is enlarged for some months, and I will give them all a fair trial and keep the good ones. As Plato would say: Test them all and hold fast to those that are good." [78] Perhaps the major source of sanity and efficiency for Quinn and the work of his office was still Thomas J. Curtin, the chief stenographer. Quinn paid tribute to him in a letter to Conrad of February 5, calling him "my friend Curtin . . . who has been with me for over twenty years and who has the best head on him of any man I have ever been associated with." It was to Conrad too that Quinn tried to express his definition of his professional function and the satisfaction it carried for him. It is a statement that suggests that such a problem as the censorship of *Ulysses* was simply alien to his basic tastes in the practice of law: "The poetry of the practice of law for me is the clear analysis and correct statement of facts and the clear application of rules of law to the facts. I hate vagueness in law as much as I hate sloppiness in art." [79]

What Quinn identified as his "big constitutional law case" of this year was a better example of the kind of case and the kind of law he preferred to deal with. This case, perhaps the most important of his career, involved the question of the legality and constitutionality of the seizure and sale by the Alien Property Custodian of the federal government of about two-thirds of the capital stock of the Botany Worsted Mills, "a thirty million concern" [80] based in Passaic, New Jersey. Quinn had been interested in the legal problem of the Alien Property Act since its passage in October of 1917: much of the language of the Act came directly from his brief arguing for its adoption. In the Botany Mills case he was excited by the magnitude of the issue, of the sums involved, and of his potential fee, and by the chance to "do" a set of Germans. The case arose when Max W. Stoehr, a naturalized United States citizen, sued on behalf of family interests to protest the seizure in March 1918, and subsequent sale, of the Botany stock. The Stoehr interests contended that the stock in question was not alien-owned but American-owned, and that therefore the Alien Property Custodian had no right to take it over. Quinn was retained by the American company, and this meant that he worked in co-operation with the government attorneys against the attorneys of the German interests. Quinn and his staff put in months of solid work preparing their case in the winter of 1919–20, and he went to court in the first days of March with a printed brief of 179 pages with 51 pages of appendices. Mrs. Foster read the brief through to him twice before the trial, held before Judge Learned Hand in the United States District Court in New York, and Quinn then argued his case without further reference to the brief. He spoke for five hours one day and four hours the next. He was able to prove to Judge Hand's satisfaction that the transfer of the German-owned shares in the company to ostensible American ownership on February 15, 1915, had been a fabrication, a bit of dummy bookkeeping, "a rubber-stamp sham, a rubber-stamp trick, a rubber-stamp fraud," [81] contrived to forestall what had actually occurred, the seizure of the property of an enemy alien.

After the trial he sent marked copies of his brief to many of his friends. He had feared defeat in early stages, but after the hearing he was confident, writing to Pound on March 6 while awaiting Judge Hand's decision: "I have not the slightest doubt that the judge will dismiss the bill; in other words, that I will win." The victory would be his and no one else's: "I prepared the case, and I tried the case, and my brief is *the* brief in it." When Judge Hand's opinion in his favor was handed down on April 22, Quinn had that printed too and circulated it among his friends. He was disappointed that the opinion did not specifically assert the constitutionality of the Trading with the Enemy Act, though such was the practical effect of the decision. In reviewing the case to Frederick R. Coudert, he showed his satisfaction at a victory achieved by forceful application of the kind of law and the kind of evidence, big, tangible, and plain, that were his professional *métier:*

> . . . he made a sweeping decision in favor of the point I contended for, namely, that there never was any intention on the part of the German company to vest the stock in question in the New York company, that the whole thing was a fraud, and that it was not what on the face of the papers it purported to be. The facts overwhelmingly proved that contention, and, as you know, it is always better to win on the facts than on the law. The weakness in the argument of the counsel for the Government was that it centered and revolved around very little points of law, highly technical points of law, like the little ticking wheels of a little clock, actively ticking, very actively going around, very important little wheels, but not quite the kind of instruments on which to base a great decision. My facts, which I proved overwhelmingly, were like a big clock which didn't make much fuss and whose wheels seemed to go slowly around, whose pendulum seemed to take time in moving, but which had force behind them. [*April 26, 1920.*]

It was a satisfaction, too, to harvest a fee of $174,000 (Quinn's total fee for his work for the Alien Property Custodian).[82] In June Quinn contributed $1,000 to the preconvention campaign of A. Mitchell Palmer, formerly Alien Property Custodian and Attorney General, now a prominent candidate for the Democratic nomination for the presidency.

Immediately before the judgment in the Botany Mills case Quinn was drawn into another complex affair in which he performed equally to his own satisfaction. The ailing Woodrow Wilson forced out his Secretary of State, Robert Lansing, early in February and quickly replaced him, to the surprise and dismay of many persons, with Bainbridge Colby. It was felt that whereas Colby was decently qualified, Wilson had passed over other stronger and more logical candidates. Hostile critics and some loyal ones took his action as another sign of the President's illness and incompetence of judgment. Colby had been Quinn's first partner, and he had remained loyal to Colby, in spite of the fact that he referred to him in private as an "idiot." When there ensued a furor in the newspapers, in Cabinet and Congressional circles, and in the Senate Foreign Relations Committee, which threatened to withhold approval of Colby's appointment, Quinn offered his services on Colby's behalf and they were quickly accepted. He worked hard for six consecutive days on the matter and apparently turned it into another one-man show, and a successful one. He summed up the events in a letter to his great friend among the Catholic clergy in New York, Father John J. Wynne:

> I prepared the cross-examination of Parsons [Herbert Parsons, Republican National Committeeman from New York] and also Colby's case, with the result (a) nothing but grease left of Parsons' reputation, (b) the Republicans on the committee who had repeatedly announced that they were going to report the nomination without recommendation promptly reported it with a recommendation that it be confirmed, and then it was confirmed in the Senate without debate.   [*March 29, 1920.*]

Colby was painlessly instated on March 27. "Why?" Quinn asked rhetorically two days later: "Because the cross-examination of Parsons was prepared by a real lawyer, one John Quinn, and Colby's testimony and case were prepared by the same real lawyer, and so the Republicans on the committee in order to shield Parsons wanted no debate." [83]

Quinn's opinion of Woodrow Wilson did not improve. Ezra Pound wrote him on February 6, 1920, that he had just come from Jacob Epstein's new exhibition at the Leicester Galleries where he had been "damn hard hit" by three works, the busts of Margaret Epstein and Gabrielle Saonne and the *Christ*, an erect, full length, cerement-wrapped figure. He also liked the *American Soldier,* which he called "good, as Fisher was good," * but he especially recommended the other three works. The *Christ* Pound called "magnificent, absolute wipe off of Rodin and Mestrovic." But this figure affronted two of Quinn's standing prejudices, his con-

---

* Epstein's bust of Admiral Lord Fisher.

tempt for the bookish President and his old distaste for anything associated with death and its trappings. After he had seen photographs of the sculptures he wrote the Leicester Galleries refusing the *Christ*, because its face looked like Wilson's and because "I am not interested in mummies or any things that look like mummies, and the figure wrapped in grave clothes had too much of an appearance of a mummy lifted from a grave and braced up to interest me." [84] At least he did not have to invite such figures into his house. One month later he sent direct to Epstein his offer of £130 for *Gabrielle Saonne* and £80 for the *American Soldier*. Epstein accepted by cable on April 25. On April 11 Quinn sent Mrs. Epstein three more pages of advice on her husband's diet—still trying to deal transatlantically with his neuritis.

Now that he was not corresponding with Augustus John, Quinn's main link with the social side of artistic life in London was Arthur Symons. It was ironical that it should be Symons to whom Quinn wrote: "I would rather give a man money or lend him money than buy a work of art merely because he needed the money," [85] for he had been giving Symons money for years under the color of buying his works of art—his manuscripts. The process was costing him regularly five or six hundred dollars a year, and Quinn continued it not because he wanted the manuscripts but because he wanted to help "poor Symons." On May 17 Symons wrote him: "You are the most generous man I have ever met." At the beginning of the year he had asked Quinn's permission to dedicate his *Baudelaire: A Study* to him.[86] It was Quinn's systematic benefactions that allowed Symons to indulge the habit that was the breath of life to him, periodical binges in London with good hotels, good drink and food, and high talk in the cafés with artists and musicians and their attendant spirits. Symons wrote on January 9 of going with Augustus John to the New English Art Club to inspect his portrait of Iris Tree, whom Quinn knew and whose head by Epstein was in his collection. The portrait, Symons said, was " a reincarnation of Lucrezia Borgia—with that evil face Iris has; her orange-sunset hair; her eyes that follow you, never leave you alone. She's to me as evil as he makes her—but she's fascinating." Next month the painter and his subject were still on Symons's mind, in haunts well known to Quinn: ". . . . the vision of John at the Café, and Iris and her cosmetics! Decadence and obscenity, travels and sensations, luxuriousness— there's an epitome of the famous Café Royal!" [87] An epitome too, in the account, of the wishfully salacious nineties, lingering.

The thought of the place as an occasional haven for Symons was one of the reasons Quinn continued to correspond with Gwen John about the little castle of Vauxclair. It is clear from the tone of Quinn's letters that he stood in a divided frame of mind about the place, at once longing and dubious. That division may even be visible in the mixed tenses, past and present, of his detailed inquiry of February 14, which suggest an idea only half-successfully put down:

> Were the rooms comfortable? How many rooms were there in the chateau? Did it have any modern fittings in the way of hardwood floors or bathrooms? How was it heated? Was there a cellar under it? How far was it from any town? How does one get there from the town? Near what town is it? What neighbors are there, or how near are the nearest neighbors? What sort is the surrounding country? How much land is there around the place? And what is done with the land, whether used for grazing or farming? What sort are the roads? And where do the people get their produce from, like butter, eggs, milk, groceries, vegetables, chicken and meats, coffee and sugar? You spoke of their really not wanting it and of thinking that they would sell it to you and that it was not dear at all. Did they ever mention any price to you?

The Purchase Street syndrome was also still visible in that very American document. Gwen John's answer could only have been additionally tantalizing. The house had been bought by the present owners, largely as a speculation, for 20,000 francs, and now would certainly bring far more. Fifteen minutes' walk away, along a path lined with beech trees, was what amounted to a private bay, surrounded by cliffs bare of houses, running down to beaches along which one could walk for miles at low tide. The neighbors were said to be "savages" by the owners. But Gwen John discouraged the notion of a rural haven for the citified Symons and his actress wife, Rhoda: ". . . I don't think it is practical. I have heard it is his great pleasure to spend his time often with his literary and artist friends in London. He would be too lonely at Vauxclair, and his wife would not stay there three days, no, not one. I don't know her but my friend was her sister and so I know what she is like." [88] The simplicity of Gwen John's style did not prevent emphatic speech when the occasion justified it.

Jeanne Robert Foster had agreed to go abroad in the summer of 1920 as the companion and keeper of a wealthy and flighty young woman who had made a bad marriage, was suing for divorce with Quinn as counsel, and was believed by her parents to be in need of watching in the interval. Quinn wrote Gwen John that Mrs. Foster was sailing on June 28 and that he had asked her to look up Miss John when she reached Paris. He described Mrs. Foster as the author of two books of poems and a staff member of the *Review of Reviews,* "not at all 'literary' in her manner, but quite natural and unaffected." In his letter of introduction which she carried she was described as "a lady of culture and an admirer of your work." [89] The reclusive painter wrote back on July 10: "I feel excited about meeting Mrs. Foster. I have never met a poetess nor any woman writer. I am tortured by shyness with strangers but I am sure I shall like her." She reported as well that she had at last met Rhoda Symons, and liked her, rather to her own surprise: "& I am sure you would too." One of Mrs. Foster's commissions from Quinn was to instruct Gwen John in the use of the American camera he had sent her, if that ever arrived. Quinn mailed her a camera on February 9, and when it had not arrived after many weeks, he sent a second instrument. But Gwen John reported on July 18 that the first "Kodac" had finally made its way to her on July 10. When the second appeared it was taken over by Mrs. Foster.

Quinn continued to praise Gwen John's painting in letters to her, though he was still receiving far less of it than he wished. He wrote her that he considered her and Marie Laurencin "the two best woman painters living." [90] She had written him the preceding month:

> I don't know Mme. Laurencin's work, but I am going to see other work more now and be less shy if possible.
> I like being alone. But I don't pretend to know how to live, and sometimes I think everything I do is wrong.   [*July 18, 1920.*]

In his letter of August 14 Quinn proposed a new patronage arrangement whereby he would pay her $500 a year in exchange for two paintings, with any additional paintings to be paid for separately. He sent her at once $250 as his first half-yearly payment. Then a month later, on September 16, he raised his figure to $750 a year and promised to maintain it for at least three years. A week later he wrote Pound of this arrangement in confidence, and of Gwen John herself: "She is very shy, almost impossible to help, and lives in the greatest poverty." Quinn had heard that she lived for long periods on bread and water and often gave her money away.[91] In the same letter to Pound he repeated his offer of a £50 gift to Eliot whenever he should need it to get on with. On September 3, with Quinn's first $250 in hand, Gwen John wrote:

> I am very grateful to you. It takes my breath away and let me thank you for your manner of doing it.
>
> You may not want my work after this year, it may have changed, and not please you so much, so you must not consider it a contract after this year. . . . I know what girl I shall engage for a model, to-morrow.

But Quinn was sure of his judgment of Gwen John and of Marie Laurencin, and he began urging Marius de Zayas to offer a show in New York of "the two best woman painters living," probably early in 1921.

When Mrs. Foster and Gwen John got together in the fall they became friends at once. Mrs. Foster was able to lead the painter about the city more freely than had been her habit; they went to galleries together, called together on Henri-Pierre Roché with Quinn's introduction, and put the two "Kodacs" to use. Quinn at last had an image of the elusive Gwen, though he had still not met her. She took Mrs. Foster several times to see her friends the nuns in the nearby convent in Meudon, and she saw "the nuns' picture," Gwen John's portrait of "Mère Poussepin," which Quinn had coveted before and resolved to try for again after hearing it described by Mrs. Foster. But Mrs. Foster had gone to Prague when his first instruction about that arrived, and negotiations had to be postponed. Quinn wrote Gwen John on October 9: "I have become an enthusiastic convert of rubber-heeled shoes. . . . When walking with them on you feel that you are flying along the ground." He was trying to convert all his friends. Miss John had "India rubber heels" installed at once. He had also enthusiastically adopted light wool socks. But neither the rubber heels nor the wool socks prevented painful blisters on a week's walking trip in the Catskills in the last days of October and the first days of November.[92]

With Augustus John in limbo and Gwen John based in Paris, Wyndham Lewis remained the only London painter on Quinn's active list. And his letter to Lewis of February 5, 1920, carelessly patronizing and intensely irritating, amounted to a leave-taking of that painter too. Quinn mentioned that he had been brooding over the thought of making Lewis an offer in form of three or four hundred pounds a year in exchange for a certain minimum number of paintings, but had decided against it. Lewis just wasn't up to his standard, though he might reach it some day: "If you could paint as well as you can write you would be one of the great painters of our time. I feel that you will some time paint as well as you write, but you haven't yet, or at least so far as I have seen." [93] At about the same time, in a letter to Ambroise Vollard, Quinn spelled out his understanding of the limits and the governing energy of his personal function as a collector. He stipulated that whereas he immensely admired the genius of the older generation of pioneers among the French moderns, of Cézanne, Renoir, Degas, their prices were so high and their clientèle by now sufficiently established that they were not the right objects for his pursuit. He continued: ". . . . to me it is more interesting to buy the work of living artists, and besides there is a satisfaction in feeling that in buying the work of living men and in helping them to live and to create one is in a sense a co-creator or a participant in the work of creation, a feeling which does not exist in regard to the work of artists who have passed away." [94] Essentially it was Pound's 1915 definition of the patron as the sustainer of the active, needy creative spirit, now confirmed and programmatic in Quinn's sense of himself. Like his English list, his list of American enthusiasms, always short, had dwindled to a single name, Walt Kuhn. His whole field of vision as a collector was narrowing, and the focus within it sharpening and growing more intense. Only three sculptors interested him actively now, Epstein, Brancusi, Duchamp-

Villon, and the last of those, being recently, in effect, *mort pour la patrie*, would move into the status of a sentimental passion. So Quinn's essential field of search and possession had become the living painters of the School of Paris.

To Kuhn he was loyal both publicly and privately. He made only two important purchases from Kuhn in 1920, paying $625 for each of two of his Wild-West subjects of this period, *Entirely Surrounded by Indians* and *The Long-Horn Saloon*.[95] But he regularly advanced substantial sums to the painter, to be repaid in time by work of his choice. In the middle of September, for example, his credit with Kuhn stood at $1,000. To Horace Brodzky he sent lofty general praise of Kuhn: ". . . I think he is one of the most interesting artists living, and I admire his courage and disinterestedness and fidelity to his own high and austere ideals more than I can say." [96] In the midst of Kuhn's spring show at the De Zayas Gallery on Fifth Avenue, Quinn sent to F. J. Gregg on March 31, for publication in the *Sun*, an appreciation of about 500 words of "Walt Kuhn's Art," He enclosed a covering note to Gregg:

> When I think how much praise has been poured out upon the sentimental slush that goes for art on this side, and upon the work of men like John and Orpen in England, and when I see how the great, sincere art of Kuhn has been pecked at, I feel that what I have said about him, every word of which gives my deepest convictions, should be published.

The sentence was one of his unhappy anticlimactic structures, but it was honest enough, as was the article itself, when it appeared on April 4. Though marred by Quinn's "literary" habit of half-relevant decorative quotation—he quotes, Rossetti, Poe, Meredith, and Swinburne, and even Swinburne quoting Ecclesiastes in application to Blake—the little essay forms an able and enticing puff, as it was meant to do. Again it was the living art that he wished to see valued: ". . . and I thought we should not keep our praise only for 'our fathers who were before us' but should give it freely where it is deserved to the men of our own day, and in this case of our own city, who are achieving the miracle of imaginative and moving art." He went on to distinguish among the paintings themselves in an incisive and interesing way, and to sum up their general effect with a descriptive skill quite capable of leading one to 549 Fifth Avenue. Reading the item in the *Sun*, Walter Pach called it "an appreciation that any artist could feel proud to have drawn forth." [97]

Pach, Kuhn, and occasionally still Arthur B. Davies served as Quinn's friendly expert advisers when their opinions were needed in New York. It was Kuhn that Quinn called in for counsel when De Zayas sent word that a "superMatisse," a reclining nude woman, was available in Paris at $4,500. They looked at photographs together. Quinn liked it, but the price was high for him and Kuhn's reaction was tepid, and so for the time being he rejected the picture.[98] Pach had been helping out with French translations for Quinn for some time when Quinn determined in May that the arrangement should be regularized: it was time for some money to change hands. They agreed that Pach would translate letters in French from French artists and dealers, and Quinn's letters to them into French, for the modest fee of four dollars per thousand words. Pach calculated that he had done about ten thousand words to date, and Quinn duly sent his check for forty dollars.[99] Georgette Passedoit was also similarly employed with some regularity. It was partly out of loyalty to Pach that Quinn had regularly lent works from his collection to the annual exhibitions of the Society of Independent Artists, of which Pach had been treasurer for several years. It was Pach who persuaded Quinn to interest himself in a memorial volume for Raymond Duchamp-Villon, making the proposal in a letter of October 16, 1920: a volume opening with a biographical and critical essay by Pach, followed by excerpts from letters and reflective writings of the sculptor, followed by perhaps twenty-five photographs of his works. Quinn, naturally, was counted upon for money. Kuhn wrote him on September 26:

> I hope that you will find it possible to do something for the memory of Raymond Duchamp. He was the real stuff, and personally a fine chap. I liked him best of the three brothers. Let us hope that Pach, if he does the writing, gets some of Raymond's hardiness and not too much of his own "slippery elm." . . .

As an admirer of the sculptor's work since the Armory Show of 1913, Quinn was happy to oblige, and promised to underwrite the publication up to 3,500 francs. In the event, Pach finished his work in May 1922, his manuscript was corrected in New York by Marcel Duchamp, and the book was seen through the press, slowly, in Paris by Jacques Villon, to complete the family affair. Quinn bore all costs. He also showed his sentiment toward the sculptor in his manner of buying his *Head of Baudelaire*. Duchamp-Villon's widow had offered the work at 1,000 francs and Quinn had accepted it at once but insisted on paying an extra 500 francs. She then wrote that the price had been in error: the work should have been listed at 1,500 francs. Quinn again insisted on his extra 500 and sent his draft for 2,000 francs.[100]

In Henri-Pierre Roché, Quinn now also had his own man on the scene in Paris. Their relationship was as yet only loosely defined, but it was clarifying itself in practice, and in 1920 it began to produce results. Roché set down his sense of the matter at the end of the year: "I have the impression of acting like a dog trying to 'faire lever' some big birds in front of you, and you shoot them or not, as pleases you." [101] He was happy enough with his own pleasures in the chase. Not unnaturally, Quinn was coming to resent the patronizing references, which occasionally reached him, to himself as "the man who buys from photographs." Working hard for a living in New York, and faced with the need to make numerous quick decisions about works of art with no easy access to European showrooms, he rather frequently had to say yes or no to a photograph rather than an original. This meant that he made some mistakes that he regretted, but also that he came to possess a great many pictures he was delighted to own and which he would otherwise have had to pass by. His rule was to buy from photographs only works of artists whose style he already knew in the original, and to place a greater faith in photographs of sculpture than in photographs of paintings, where problems of color, modeling, and size were acute. With this problem Roché could be a great help: he could select works he thought would interest Quinn, could see that necessary photographs (usually made for Quinn by Man Ray) were faithful ones, and could interpret the work and the photograph in the light of his own judgment in an accompanying letter. Quinn's general cautiousness in the matter of photographs was indicated by his unwillingness to go in for the works of Modigliani or of Chirico, both of whom Roché had urged upon him: he had seen only photographs, no originals, and did not know either artist personally, and so he refused to take the plunge.[102] Meanwhile he believed he could trust Roché's statement that his collaboration was being sought by many Paris dealers, and that his own "petite collection personnelle" had increased in value at least a thousand per cent in ten years.[103]

At the Joseph Hessel sale in Paris in March Quinn pulled off a considerable coup in buying three paintings of Marie Laurencin, *Rêverie* at 8,000 francs, *La Guitariste* at 8,400, and *Femmes dans un parc* at 7,000, as well as two stunning works by Toulouse-Lautrec, *Femme retroussant sa chemise* at 11,200 francs and *Songeuse* at 21,900—all five pictures for just a little over $11,000. Then just five weeks later he was able to procure through Roché's good offices two other important Laurencins, her *Zebra* at 12,000 francs and her *Horsewoman* at 6,500 francs. Quinn expressed his approval of her work to Roché in the following terms: "One of the things that I like about Marie Laurencin is that she paints like a woman, whereas most women artists seem to want to paint like men and they only succeed in painting like hell." [104] On May 12 Quinn sent Roché an earnest of 750 francs, "not as a fee . . . but as a mark of my appreciation for the time and attention" he had given to the second Laurencin purchase. On October 9 Quinn proposed that they talk over in New York in the winter the basis of a more regular agreement. Roché wrote back contentedly on October 25: ". . . I shall stick to my own specialty: choosing the best pictures—and proposing them to your selection." Only a day later: "I often write you in a hurry, like today, and rather excited, or with the enthusiasm I have always when I see real first class works. (Comme un chasseur qui voit du beau gibier.)" * Roché's letters were sometimes in English, sometimes in French, sometimes in both. Quinn appreciated the value both of his selectiveness and his enthusiasm. It added up to just the kind of nervy cautiousness which seemed to him the right line to work along, and which is suggested by his signal to Roché on May 12: "I want some time to buy a couple of important Braques, but I want to be sure that they are very fine things and things that move me personally." In November, again through Roché, Quinn acquired through the Paris dealer Paul Rosenberg yet another im-

---

* "Like a hunter who sees fine game."

portant pair of Laurencins, *Femmes dans la Forêt* and *La Princesse (Ninon de l'Enclos)*, at 30,000 francs for the two.[105]

One of Roché's few failures with Quinn lay in his effort to interest him in Paul Klee, whom he presented (from Munich) in the following way—knowing Quinn's disgust with all things German:

> Sauf un, *Paul Klee*, de Munich, inconnu hier, aujourd'hui glorieux ici, sans doute demain gloire mondiale. C'est un génie individuel que je ne rattache pas spécialement à l'Allemagne; il est tout à fait international et adorable.*

A little later he described Klee as looking "like *a quiet Arab*." But Quinn was entirely unpersuaded: the man was a German, and he wanted nothing to do with him. Again Roché retreated amicably to his main line: "I join you without reserve in your patience and coolness and objectivity for making your collection: I may get hot hunting the best pictures, but the decisions must be cool." [106] He reminded Quinn that for the past two years he had been the only buyer of Marie Laurencin, and that it had been he who led Leo Stein to Picasso fifteen years before. He proposed now to extend his range of vision to the modern art of the whole of Europe, and he asked nothing better than to be allowed to put Quinn in touch with his discoveries—"car la direction actuelle de votre collection m'intéresse."† But Quinn would have preferred to see him spend all his energies on Paris and her artists.

Some of Quinn's most important transactions in art were now being carried out with the De Zayas brothers, Marius in New York and George in Paris. On April 21 he bought from them Gauguin's stark wood panel, *Caribbean Woman and Sunflowers*, for $2,600, and two works of Matisse, his sketch on wood for *Music* at $1,100 and his *Girl with Roses* at $600; at the same time he took three drawings of Constantin Guys, a lingering relatively conventional taste, at $750. With these dealers too he began taking deeper

---

* "Just one, Paul Klee, of Munich, yesterday unknown, doubtless famous everywhere tomorrow. His is a personal genius which I do not consider especially German; it is entirely international and adorable." To Quinn, September 13, 1920. [Klee was actually Swiss.]

† To Quinn, September 13, 1920. "For the real direction of your collection interests me."

plunges, from some of which he withdrew in time. On September 14 he agreed for a Matisse still life at $2,200. Then in the middle of December he nerved himself to spend $3,205 for a Renoir *Figure of a Woman*, $9,000 for Cézanne's *Portrait of a Woman in a White Cap*, and $4,500 for a Matisse *Nude*—probably the "superMatisse" he had rejected earlier in the year. But in about two months he backed off from part of this deep commitment, returning both the Matisse still life and the Cézanne portrait on February 21.

With another pair of dealer-brothers, Paul and Léonce Rosenberg in Paris, Quinn was now treating mainly for the work of Picasso and Marie Laurencin. Roché was the usual intermediary, scouting out the dealers' holdings, selecting, sending photographs and advice, judging price against quality. From Léonce Rosenberg in November Quinn took two Picasso still lifes for 45,000 francs. Of these works Picasso said, according to Rosenberg: " 'I may do more important—*larger*—but never *better*.' " [107] From Paul Rosenberg two weeks later Quinn bought Picasso's *Arlequin* at 35,000 francs and his *Fillette au Cerceau* at 25,000 francs. The Laurencin *Femmes dans la Forêt* and *La Princesse* had also come from Paul Rosenberg by way of Roché.

It was Roché also who put Quinn in touch with the Paris dealer Walter Halvorsen, who had two Matisses in which Quinn was interested, *Les Poissons Rouges* and *La Famille*. Roché presented Halvorsen as "a Swede, quiet, powerful." His prices were higher than Quinn felt able to pay, but Roché warned him that it was no use trying to beat him down.[108] Halvorsen sounded to Quinn like a potentially useful man, however, and Quinn took the trouble to send him an analysis of his own position as a collector which is in turn useful to the spectator trying to understand John Quinn:

> . . . I am a man of modest means and am neither a capitalist nor a man buying art generally. I am very limited, and must necessarily be limited, in the number of my purchases, and desire only the very best examples of an artist's work. I have done enough of "encouraging" artists, both American, English, and French, in years gone by. As I say to my friends, in buying art one does not go merely for numbers any more than in fishing one goes just for fish generally but one should look out for kingfish or brook trout or

other game fish. Buying art indiscriminately or the work of an artist indiscriminately is very much like catching fish in a net, only it is more expensive.   [*November 17, 1920.*]

His metaphor was of the same family as Roché's habitual metaphor of the chase. In spite of Quinn's bluster, and because of it, his statement helps one feel the pleasure he took in stalking a valuable and elusive prey with modest weapons, and bringing back prime specimens by the exercise of taste, skill, and nerve.

At about the same time, in a sentence of almost impenetrable awkwardness, Quinn sent to the sculptor Brancusi another estimate of his work for art: "But I am not a rich man and perhaps spend many times beyond my means and income what any other man that I know of, of my means and income, does for art . . . literally beyond any one I know of." [109] Both Brancusi and Raoul Dufy belonged in the category of special trust for Quinn, artists whose work he knew well enough to feel safe in buying himself direct from photographs without supplementary opinion. Dufy wrote on December 9 to offer *Bathers*, which he described as "a work a little didactic in character, but very strong and powerful in color." Of the general tenor of his career Dufy wrote touchingly: ". . . I pursue with my head and my heart my dream in plaster and paint, like a man who has nothing better to do here below." [110] Quinn bought the picture. Dufy's work was a marginal taste for Quinn, one of his milder affections. But Brancusi was one of the artists at the center of his passion as a collector. Choosing from photographs, and at an outlay of 50,000 francs, Quinn in November bought four important works of Brancusi's, two forms of each of two subjects: *Mlle. Pogany* in bronze and in colored marble, and the *Bird* in the same two materials. Brancusi sent them over with carefully mated pedestals and detailed instructions for mounting. And as emblems of gratitude and friendship he sent along three gifts: a drawing, *Study for Mlle. Pogany;* a wooden cup for the dining room; and a little hand in colored marble for Quinn to keep on his desk.[111] He also sent, on approval, along with the four works ordered, a little marble lower torso of a girl. Roché, who had talked with the sculptor before the shipment, recorded their conversation and his own estimate of the sculptor's habits:

I suggested Brancusi that we cable you first—he said no: he wanted to show it to you "like a flower," he would be glad if you enjoy it, even if you would not keep it. . . .

No man is more just and modest, I believe, in calculating his prices. He has terrific work. He goes on working at a thing for months when everyone declares that it is already perfect.

[*December 2, 1920.*]

In his avocations as in his vocation, 1920 had been a significant year for Quinn. Things had begun to come to larger, fewer points, and he felt more powerful and sure of himself, less dispersed in his tastes and energies. He had made money again, and spent it, again. Something of the scale of his ordinary expenses can be divined from a single item: $200 for a wedding present to Dorothy Dowling, the daughter of an old friend, Judge Victor J. Dowling. Mrs. Foster was abroad in the summer and fall, and he missed her keenly. That Dorothy Coates was at least culturally still in the picture is indicated by the fact that several prints which Quinn bought in the sale of the Goldstein collection in New York in March were earmarked "for Miss Coates." It was perhaps ominous that he had sold his horse at Durland's, 66th Street and Central Park West, in May. Against this could be set the ambitious walking tour in the Catskills in the late autumn, his regular strenuous weekend walks, and his occasional habit of picking up Mrs. Foster at her apartment on West 49th Street, when she was in the city, and walking with her all the way to his office at the southern tip of the island, perhaps with a call or two at galleries on the way. In September he had some trouble with his teeth, two of which proved abscessed. Three times the gum had to be lanced. The first two times were painful but the third painless, and Quinn suggested to Kuhn that perhaps the proud flesh about his teeth was "too proud to feel pain, or to acknowledge it." [112] The extraction of the bad teeth wrecked a "permanent" bridge in his mouth, and henceforth Quinn had to wear a plate.

His sister Julia Anderson had been lingeringly unwell, and Quinn was anxious to get her away from the city for a change of air and diet. For the three weeks after August 20 he took a cottage at Ogunquit for his domestic party: Julia, her nurse, her daughter Mary, his French couple Paul and Marie, Quinn himself. At the end of their holiday the whole party drove down, with a hired car and driver to whom Quinn gave a $12 tip, from Portsmouth to Boston, where they took the train in to New York. In Boston they happened to cross the path of the peripatetic De Valera, still campaigning on behalf of the Republican cause in Ireland. Quinn reviewed the scene for Kuhn, for transmission to Gregg:

> Boston was turned over to the Irish, who turned out, Gregg will be delighted to hear, one hundred thousand strong to greet deValera. I am told that seventy per cent. of the population of Boston is Irish. I saw no Jews on the street. In fact, the only Jews that I saw in Boston were a group of five or six at the station struggling to get ahead of all the Christians, principally Irish, and those Jews were on their way to New York. There are Jews there but they are submerged by the Irish. Gregg will be delighted to know that there is one spot on the earth where the Irish are on top of somebody else besides the English.
>
> [*September 13, 1920.*]

Back in the city, Quinn was sitting talking with Maurice Léon and Maître Legrand, a member of the French bar and a wounded veteran of Verdun, a few minutes after noon on September 16, when a great explosion shook Wall Street. He swiveled about in his chair and "saw a parachute-shaped cloud of smoke arise above the Wall Street front of the Assay Office." [113] It was the loudest and most ominous noise of the famous "Anarchist" Plot. To Jacob Epstein, who had written in concern for Quinn after reading of thirty-eight persons killed and many hurt among the lunch-time crowds, he replied in extraordinary terms. The anarchists, Quinn wrote on October 11, were "nearly all Russian Jews, I am sorry to say." Holding to the illusion of his own liberalism, he went on: "I am not speaking of socialists. I respect an honest socialist and admire many of them for their courage and disinterestedness in self-sacrifice. I am not an anti-Semite either. I haven't a bit of prejudice." Finally, inevitably: "Some of my best friends are Jews." So they were; but he seemed to learn nothing from them about the race as a whole.

In late November Quinn paid the visit which he tried to make at least once a year, usually shortly before Christmas, to his sister Clara, Sister St. Paul, in her convent in Tiffin, Ohio, and his old uncle, Father Jeremiah Quinlan, in his parish in El Paso, Illinois. He and Clara remained good friends, close and companionable, but he had little sympathy for her way of life, and he found the convent visit always a trial. The necessary narrowness of her life was a pain to him. On one of her rare visits to New York Quinn bought her a new pair of shoes, of the type required by her order. When she showed off the heavy black nun's brogans with delight later at the apartment, Quinn seemed to Mrs. Foster to be near tears. He would have liked to make queens of both his sisters. When he visited the convent he always brought his gifts to Clara in sufficient quantity so that all the nuns could share; and he regularly left a sum of money for the general work of the convent. The visits to Father Quinlan were a much purer pleasure, a genuine recreation to Quinn. The two would sit or stroll in a peaceful, leisurely way, talking of life and letters, and the cares of Quinn's career seemed farther away here than anywhere else. Of his uncle he wrote to John Butler Yeats after the 1920 visit: "At eighty he looks out upon life with the eyes of a Montaigne and the wit of a Rabelais, reading Virgil in the original and finding more beauties in it than the last time he read it thirty years ago," quoting the Bible with equal facility and pleasure from the Douay Latin, the King James, and modern Protestant versions.[114] Father Quinlan was not managerial or censorious, and one of his great virtues in Quinn's eyes was that he never said "Don't" to him.[115]

The leisure for reading afforded by the long train trip back and forth brought about a sort of comic comeuppance in 1920 to Quinn's habit of gratuitously "correcting" the writing of others. Almost the only pleasant feature of Quinn's bias-ridden letter to Ezra Pound of October 21, 1920, aside from his standard willingness to be of use, lay in his praise of Sherwood Anderson, whom he called the "one man here now writing who comes near to being an artist." Quinn considered *Winesburg, Ohio* "a good thing," but then went on to rephrase his warning to Pound to stay away from America: ". . . you would be happier on the edge of the desert of Sahara than you would living in the Winesburg, Ohio, country." Quinn knew the Ohio desert, and had fled from it to a more elaborate desert, which he professed to like little better. On the train to Ohio at this time Quinn read and "edited" a copy of

Anderson's new novel, *Poor White*. On December 9 he sent his marked copy of the novel to Anderson along with a letter explaining what he had done:

> In reading the book I annotated it, or did what I so often do with my own briefs in revising them before page-proofs: cut out the unnecessary words. I have never met you but you are manifestly a serious artist, and, because I take you to be a serious artist, I assume that you might be interested in seeing how an appreciative and interested reader amused himself as he went along by cutting out repetitions and so on.

Quinn had been particularly offended by the "eternally-recurring" phrase, "Bidwell, Ohio"—completely missing the purpose behind the drabness, the gridiron patterning of Anderson's style, as it labored to labor, to express eternal recurrence.

Actually Quinn's letter was a rather modest and attractive one. Unluckily it miscarried, going to a wrong address and reaching the novelist only on December 22. In the meantime the marked volume itself had arrived, of course with no accompanying explanation. Assuming that what was wanted was simply an autograph, Anderson, without turning the pages, signed his name on the flyleaf and returned the book to Quinn. When Quinn's letter at length arrived, Anderson wrote back and explained the muddle; he continued sweetly: "I am, indeed, sorry that you found these little irritations in my style. God knows it needs much improvement in many directions, and, I am afraid, always will. I am sorry to have been so stupid." [116]

1921

THE Virgilian idyll with Father Jeremiah Quinlan was no fit emblem of the actual state of Quinn's life. At about the time when he was traveling west in the late autumn of 1920 the financial panic of 1921 had broken out, the third and most severe of such general crises in his career. The panic of 1893 had meant little to him professionally, though it had cost him his savings of $1,800; the energy and general knowledgeableness he had shown in the panic of 1906 had given the first big leg up to his reputation as an able man of banking and corporation law; the panic of 1921 stretched to the utmost the powers of a man established in varied and important financial responsibilities. "The last six months have been a financial reign of terror," Quinn wrote Walter Pach on the fifth of May. The most demanding, as well as the most lucrative, of his clients was the National Bank of Commerce. He was legal adviser to the bank's officers, of whom there were more than thirty, each responsible for the affairs of perhaps a dozen companies, most of them now in deep trouble—banks in other parts of the country, companies "dealing in sugar, wool, cattle, hides, cotton, cloth, rubber, paper, and God knows what." [1] At the breaking point himself, he had to deal with men at the breaking point, "hysterical," or "bad-tempered," or "yellow." [2] For many weeks Quinn worked late into the evening of every day including Saturdays, Sundays, and holidays. He kept up with his work by doing nothing else, refusing all invitations, giving up smoking, the theatre, reading, and art. "I haven't had time to read a book in weeks or to see any art or read about art stuff," he wrote to Pound in an early stage of the crisis.[3] He hoped for a few hours some Sunday in which he could "play with art," but could not then foresee them. The whole staff of his office, the other lawyers, clerks, and stenographers, were working to capacity and beyond. Thomas Curtin, probably the most important person in the organization after Quinn himself, broke down early in January with a severe attack of diabetes and was out of action for most of the crucial interval. Quinn paid his bill at Roosevelt Hospital and then willingly underwrote the expense of weeks of convalescence at home and in the mountains.[4] Curtin had done more than any other man to keep Quinn's professional life possible for twenty-two years, and Quinn valued him as a personal friend. But it was a bad time to be sick.

Following the verdict against him in the United States District Court in April 1920, Max W. Stoehr of the Botany Mills had instituted a new case seeking an injunction to prevent the Alien Property Custodian from selling the seized stock in the Stoehr company. Quinn was again retained by the defendants and was involved for weeks in January and February of 1921 in preparing and presenting his case, which this time went all the way to the United States Supreme Court. He won his case in a judgment handed down on February 28, 1921, and he had at last what he had wanted, a validation from highest authority of the constitutionality of the Trading With the Enemy Act.

All this frantic professional activity meant of course no diminution in the usual flood of personal appeals; it meant only that they were harder to tolerate. Quinn exploded in several directions. He summed up his impression of his own public image in the wild figure of a letter to Walter Pach on May 5:

> . . . they seem to think of me as a sort of performing Buddhistic figure, an animated idol of some kind, with 7 heads, 14 eyes and ears, 7 tongues, 77 hands, and 47 feet, all bestirring themselves and acting in the interests—not of the idol—but of the self-seekers and of the "dear friends" whom I have befriended so often in the past. I may seem to them a sort of effigy, a sort of imaginary gold brick effigy, but if they only knew they would find that brass, or something of the hardness of brass, came nearer the mark. They know a damn sight better, as a matter of fact, but they choose to act otherwise, and in one breath they write hoping

that I am not overworking and in the next breath appeal to me
to do something for them.

In this context a one-page letter from Ezra Pound, asking Quinn to
pass on a message to the Japanese Noh actor Itow, was enough to
draw forth a nearly hysterical response—ten pages devoted to saying more or less profanely that he did not have time to write
letters. "I have tried to let you know how busy I am, how driven
I am, how harassed I am, but it does not seem to penetrate," he
wrote Pound on January 21, and went on to list a few of his
immediate unsought dilemmas:

> I have old man Yeats on my back. . . . I have Symons on my
> back with his recklessly extravagant wife. . . . His wife must have
> an apartment in London. She must have a motor car. She must go
> to Paris with him. And I am supposed to pay the bills. Well, I
> won't. T. W. Rolleston (just died, poor devil!) wanting to sell
> Greek vases to the Metropolitan Museum. . . .

The day before there had been a letter from Lady Gregory asking
him the names of magazines and agents who would list Coole Park
for rent, and asking him to send over some apples: a bad year in the
Irish orchards. Then Horace Plunkett wrote from Battle Creek
Sanatorium to beg the loan of "The Complete Grammar of Anarchy" out of which he wished to take some quotations " 'to
explain the true character of the conspiracy for the destruction of
the Irish people.' " "Plunkett writes," Quinn told Pound on January 21, "as though I had a special alcove in my library thoroughly digested and thoroughly classified and all arranged so that
all I needed to do would be to step up to it and tip the thing out
with one of my fingers and send it to him. I exist only to supply
Plunkett with pamphlets." Rather than search for it at home, Quinn
called Ernest Boyd, who did not have the pamphlet but recommended the Gaelic League Bookshop, who had sold their one copy
to a person who proved willing to lend it for two weeks. And so
on.

It was a hard life for a man who felt that he was also personally
conducting a national financial crisis. On the eighteenth had appeared a cablegram from James Joyce: " 'In financial difficulties.
Remit by telegraph as soon as possible two hundred dollars pending

completion of contract.' " [5] When Quinn's clerk Watson stuck the cablegram "under his nose" when he was "nearly distracted" he

cursed Watson for bringing that to my attention at that time. Good God Almighty, what do they take me for! . . . I am supposed to work on the contract, to advise about the contract, to negotiate it, to make the contract legally possible with this action, and yet at the same time to advance him money. And I suppose I will end by doing it. But, by God, there is an end of him too. I am not the father of his children. . . .[6]

On January 24 Quinn cabled Joyce: "Cabling money requested. Will endeavor write next three or four weeks. Do not cable me again any subject. Have endeavored make you and Pound understand am working limit my endurance." Perhaps the most infuriating thing about all these "thank-you" chores was the fact that it was actually simpler to do them than to refuse them—though he had no time either to do them or to refuse them. He put it to Pound: "Nine times out of ten these requests are so small that it seems easier to do the God damned infernal things than to refuse them and explain about it." [7] He had always detested "explanations." He knew his letter to Pound was a rant and did not apologize: "I suppose that a doctor would say, reading this letter up to this point, 'Why, that is neurasthenia; that man needs a rest; he needs somebody standing at his shoulder to tear up letters that have that effect on him.' And I suppose some such person would be right." [8] He invited Pound to take his letter "just as you damn please," and he commanded him not to answer it.

When Quinn wrote this letter on January 21 the most complex and exasperating of all his "thank-you" jobs was hanging in midflight. His motion for the transfer of the *Little Review* case from Special Sessions to General Sessions was under consideration, and much depended on the outcome. Moving the case to General Sessions might mean a delay of a year or more and a chance to hurry out an edition of *Ulysses:* "That will be a miraculous victory if I bring it about. If the court does not grant the motion, Joyce is gone." [9] It is important to remember that the whole of the *Little Review* case had to be conducted by Quinn in an interval of cruel tension, in which it was bound to seem the most unnecessary and infuriating of his strains. One feels this in his statement to Pound:

If you knew the feelings that were going through my mind in
court waiting to argue the damned motion, taking time and
strength on motion papers, affidavits and briefs and adjournments
and consents and stipulations that it was cruel to take from other
things, you would see how patient I felt about having things
dumped down indiscriminately upon me.   [*January 21, 1921.*]

As we have seen, Quinn failed in his motion for the transfer of
the case, and the final arguments were presented in the Court
of Special Sessions just a month after the date of his letter to Pound,
on February 21, with the consequences noted above. In the interval
Quinn had received George Russell's sardonic letter of January 7,
in which he said that if he were prosecuting, not defending, the
novel, he would attack Joyce on the ground that he was "breaking
up the Great Illusion which makes the world go round." Far from
making sex alluring, he was showing its native seaminess: "He
breaks up the illusion by which the human cavalcade is induced to
beget itself and send its progeny on further through the desert of
time." The real proponents of the Great Illusion, he thought, the
real fomentors of sexual sentiment, were such writers as R. W.
Chambers, with their "fascinating, lovely, dimpled girls, all curves
and allurements." As prosecutor, Æ said, he would "ask the witnesses, on their oath, would they not like to kiss and hug such
girls, and would they not vomit at the thought of kissing or hugging one of Joyce's girls." In point of fact Quinn actually incorporated a form of Russell's jeering "prosecution" argument in his
presentation of the defense.

It is not altogether clear whether Joyce considered the two
hundred dollars for which he asked on January 18 a further payment on the manuscript of *Ulysses* or an advance against his income
from the putative Huebsch edition of the novel—a project which
he preferred to believe was a good deal farther along than the facts
warranted. Quinn seemed to interpret the request as one for money
on the manuscript, and he grumpily summed up the matter in his
letter to Pound. During 1920 he had sent Joyce on the manuscript
$153.85 on February 5, $250 on August 16, and $100 on September
29—a total of $503.85. He did not believe any book dealer would
give that much for the manuscript even if it were complete, as it
was not. But he sent the additional $200. Joyce wrote, as it hap-

pened, on the same day as Russell, January 7—chiefly to insist that his royalty from the Huebsch "edition" must reach $3 or $3.50 per copy. His tone was lofty: "If Huebsch raises any objection, please withdraw the offer entirely and the typescript." As its members were being quarreled over in the courts, the great work was drawing slowly toward conclusion. The "Circe" episode was finished and in the process of being typed. Joyce suggested that when the episode reached New York the whole book down through that point be set up and proofs sent him. He promised to return proofs promptly, and probably accompanied by the "Eumeus" and "Ithaca" episodes, after which second proofs could be sent him. These he would return along with the final episode, "Penelope," Molly Bloom's great reverie, which he was willing to have checked by American proofreaders, whom he was inclined to trust now that the continent was "dry." "*Ulysses* can be published in May," he wrote confidently. He said that he was sending Quinn from Zurich (he was writing from Paris) a photograph of himself, and he asked Quinn to return the favor. On March 1 he wrote again in considerable depression. *Ulysses* was exhausting him, and he had again postponed the date of its probable completion: "I must live and live undisturbed, if possible, till June. After that *Ulysses* is finished and I shall go into a corner anywhere and lie down." He was struggling to subsist in Paris, with high rents and no teaching posts to be had. He had mortgaged his half-yearly income in advance, he said, on the assumption that the contract with Huebsch was signed, or virtually so.

In the afternoon of Monday, April 4, Quinn was called upon in his office by Dr. Joseph Collins, a medical man of literary pretensions who had met Joyce in Paris, and who brought with him a letter from Joyce instructing him to look into the state of Quinn's negotiations with Huebsch and try to discover whether or not anything tangible was to be forthcoming. In Dr. Collins's presence Quinn telephoned Huebsch and said again, as he had said many times, that Joyce "would not change a word" [10] of the text of *Ulysses*, and directed Huebsch to return the manuscript as he was interested only in an expurgated edition. Quinn then called Horace Liveright of Boni & Liveright and asked him whether he would wish to consider publishing *Ulysses* in spite of the fact that the *Little Re-*

view had just been convicted in the courts for printing portions of it. To Joyce Quinn presented Liveright's firm as one that had made a considerable success in publishing limited editions: they had done George Moore's *A Story-Teller's Holiday* and *Avowals* and Huneker's *Painted Veils* and were about to bring out Moore's *Héloïse and Abélard* and Gauguin's intimate journals. But none of those books, he warned Joyce, was "in the class" (he seems to have meant the "pornographic" class) of *Ulysses*. Liveright had agreed to give him a decision within the next week. Quinn warned Joyce too that his notion of a royalty rate on the proposed edition was much too grand. And he reminded him that the current stalemate on an American edition could have been avoided if he had withheld his novel from the *Little Review* when Quinn had first advised it, or perhaps even at the last minute when Sumner appeared willing to consider dropping his prosecution in exchange for a direct promise from Joyce to forbid further serialization: "I made that recommendation to you but you side-stepped it. You evaded it repeatedly in your letters. That is your affair and not mine, but your evasions made it impossible for me to get anywhere with Sumner." [11] Had he known of the financial storm approaching, he said, he would never have admitted the *Little Review* case to his office. He estimated that his attention to the case had cost him "thousands of dollars personally," for the time so spent had kept him from settling questions of fees due him for Government service. Now that March 4 had passed a new administration would pass upon his fees and there was a likelihood of their being reduced as much as 50 per cent.

Joyce was conventionally grateful to Huebsch for publishing *A Portrait of the Artist as a Young Man* and *Dubliners*, though drily irritated at Huebsch's manner of giving him to understand that he had "made a sacrifice for art" in doing so.[12] He agreed that by all reasonable standards Huebsch was entitled to the first refusal of American publishing rights to *Ulysses*. But he wanted the matter brought to a point, and he had no intention of altering a syllable of his text to ease things along. Huebsch was caught between art and practicality. As Quinn put it, he wanted *Ulysses* but not in the nude; he wanted him "slightly draped." [13] In a long letter of June 5 to Joyce, Quinn reviewed the course of his negotiations with

Huebsch and those, subsequent and concurrent, with Liveright, and sent along copies of his correspondence with the two publishers. "Huebsch wriggled and squirmed and did not want to let go," he wrote. "I told him repeatedly that it would have to be printed without a change, and then he would wriggle and wriggle." The Huebsch correspondence closed with a letter of April 15, "which bows him out of it after a good many wriggles." [14] When Huebsch was "wriggling his wriggliest" Liveright said he would publish the book.[15] When Quinn demanded a definite offer, Liveright wrote on April 21 agreeing to publish *Ulysses* but requiring an option on Joyce's " 'next three novels, not for limited editions, but for general publication where it would be possible. . . .' " [16] On the same day, however, Quinn received the manuscript of the "Circe" and "Eumeus" episodes. He set Watson of his office to reading them, and Watson advised him that those episodes "never could be published here without the certainty of prosecution and conviction." [17] Quinn then telephoned Liveright and told him that the terms of his letter of April 21 were impossible, but that in any case, having seen the new portions of the novel, he could not advise him to publish it unless he wished to risk "the certainty of prosecution and conviction." "He said he did not want to be convicted and so he dropped the matter. And that ends Liveright," Quinn wrote, also washing his hands of the matter.[18] Quinn had just discovered, on June 5, when he finally got to the bottom of his file of "Little Review, Joyce, Ulysses papers," Joyce's photograph which had reached his office on February 25. He promised to have it framed, and hoped Joyce would not be bored to receive a likeness of himself which he would soon have made. Apparently he had forgotten that Joyce had asked for a photograph in his letter of January 7. Quinn noted that he had not been photographed since 1914, when Arnold Genthe had taken him and W. B. Yeats together in New York.

In writing to Joyce Quinn had evinced a certain acrid pleasure in presiding over Huebsch's "wriggling" and in putting his "heel down on the head and body of the wriggler." [19] To Huebsch himself he wrote in a very different tone which perhaps fills out the range of his general feeling about Joyce, Joyce's hero, and their American fate:

. . . you may consider this letter as your complete and full "absolution." Absolvo te! I might almost add: Ite!—Go!—to or otherwise—the typescript goes to rejoice Joyce. So rejoice yourself and be glad that you escape the long arm of the criminal law and that you won't ever have to stand up in the stinking atmosphere of a New York criminal court and defend your fair name as a husband, if not father, and a publisher and a citizen from the heinous crime of publishing a book with the name of the far-wandering Ulysses. 'Twill be a unique book, but so was Ulysses. In it Joyce has drawn a long bow, a bow that no other writer living could draw. But don't regret the loss of this unique literary treasure from your list of publications. You will doubtless be able to console yourself with the thought that it is better to lose twenty Ulysses than spend thirty days in Blackwell's Island for one.

[*April 13, 1921.*]

The "manuscript" which Huebsch had held was a combination of *Egoist* galley proofs and typewritten pages which had been turned over to him by Harriet Shaw Weaver, the *Egoist* editor and Joyce's superbly generous patron. It had now been returned to Quinn and sent on to Joyce. In sending Quinn for the manuscript he was purchasing the "Circe" and "Eumeus" episodes, Joyce "threw in," "as a curiosity," the eighth draft of "Circe." Quinn estimated that "Circe" came to about eighty-five pages and "Eumeus," which he persisted in calling "Ecumeus," to about fifty-four pages. He wrote that he would not send any new money on account of these portions, or try to measure them against the $200 cabled in January, but would wait till he had the complete manuscript and then try to estimate a total figure.[20]

Meanwhile Joyce's good friend Sylvia Beach, the American bookdealer in Paris, had bravely and suddenly proposed to publish *Ulysses* herself, under the imprint of her shop, Shakespeare and Company. The whole thing, Joyce wrote in an undated letter received by Quinn on April 30, was "arranged here in a couple of days." Publication was promised for October, and Quinn would receive a prospectus in a few days. From the prospectus Quinn ordered ten copies of *Ulysses* in his letter of June 5 to Joyce: ". . . 5 out of the 100 copies on Dutch hand made paper at 350 francs each; 3 out of the 150 copies on paper D'Arches at 250 francs each, and 2 out of the 750 copies on hand made paper at

300 francs each." He hoped that this total of 2,800 francs would strike Joyce as "a fairly respectable order," and he asked Joyce to pass on his order to Miss Beach himself: Quinn had no time to write her. Meanwhile too Joyce's world-troubling seaman had met another tragicomic and Joycean misadventure in the amateurish process of Miss Beach's preparation of a complete typescript for the French printer. One of her volunteer typists, the wife of a British Embassy employee named Harrison, had left a portion of the manuscript on her table at home. Her husband saw it, read it, tore it up, and burned it in an offended rage. "Hysterical scenes followed, I believe, in the house and in the street," Joyce reported.[21] Perhaps recalling that he had himself burned much of the manuscript of *Stephen Hero*, the first form of *A Portrait*, years before, Joyce reacted temperately. But now the immolated pages existed only in the manuscript in Quinn's possession, and Joyce begged him to send them back for copying. He identified the passage in the "Circe" episode: "It begins about p. 60 or so, where Bloom leaves the brothel; there is a scene on the steps, and then a hue and cry in the street, and the beginning of the quarrel with the soldiers." He promised to return the pages by registered post, and he asked Quinn to entrust them to Miss Beach's mother, Mrs. S. W. Beach, who was sailing for Europe on May 4.

Quinn's response could hardly have endeared him to any of the principals save perhaps Mr. Harrison. He wrote Joyce:

> I rather admire that husband of one of your typists who found the typewritten copies of some of your MS on his wife's table, read it, tore it up and burned it. As to the "hysterical scenes which followed in the house and in the street" I should say that the wife, assuming she was still content with her husband, should have been much pleased at what he did. From his point of view he was playing the game right, shielding her, guarding her, and learning what she was doing and disapproving where disapproval was due. *[June 5, 1921.]*

When Mrs. Beach telephoned to arrange to receive the missing pages Quinn rebuffed her peremptorily. He refused to co-operate and said he would handle the matter in his own way and in his own time; he wrote to Joyce: "I didn't want to have the trouble of sending pages of the MS that you sent to me and getting them back.

I am tired of writing unnecessary letters. So I was in no mood to jump through a hoop to have the missing pages located and delivered to Mrs. Beach. When she called on the telephone I told her so. That particular week I was very much driven." [22] What he did do was to have the pages photographed and enlarged and sent direct to Joyce.

Quinn liked to have his generosity specified and acknowledged with some ceremony, and he got little of that from Joyce. Joyce's manner of accepting favors as the due of genius had by now worn very thin with Quinn. Ten days after his letter to Joyce he wrote to Pound: "I've had a hell of a time with Joyce and the Little Review. I'm up to date with Joyce and through with Joyce. If the measure of one's friendship is what people can get out of one, then God damn if I want to be a friend of people." [23] For Quinn the period was one in which the demands of friends seemed intolerable when coupled with the demands of his professional life. He put the case to Joyce on June 5: "It seems hard that one should go to almost the breaking point with a friend in order to get peace, but I will make a wilderness of friends if necessary in order to have peace." His reference at this point was to Pound, "the worst and most persistent one." In the same letter, however, Quinn was careful to let Joyce know that he expected to be in Paris in July "for a short *rest*," that he was taking Joyce's address along and would look him up. They had never met. From T. S. Eliot, who had met Joyce in Paris in the autumn of 1920, Quinn now received an impression of the man that was at once corroborative and palliatory:

> I found him quite charming, and liked him; though I can see that he is certainly a handful, with the true fanatic's conviction that everyone ought to forward the interests of his work. It is, however, the conviction of the fanatic, and not the artfulness or pertinacity of ordinary push; and the latter part of "Ulysses," which I have been reading in manuscript, is truly magnificent.
>
> [*May 9, 1921.*]

There, perhaps, were all the necessary points. Eliot was at that moment planning his own splendid praise of Joyce's book in rebuttal to Richard Aldington's deprecatory article in the April *English Review*. In "using the myth, in manipulating a continuous parallel between contemporaneity and antiquity," Eliot would write, Joyce had found a way of "controlling, of ordering, of giving a shape and a significance to the immense panorama of futility and anarchy which is contemporary history"; he had taken "a step toward making the modern world possible in art." [24] In a man of that accomplishment much, perhaps all, should be forgiven.

Since Pound had left England, Eliot wrote, his only contact with him had been two postcards without return address. His own work was going slowly forward against the practical obstacles of life. He condoled with John Quinn as one overworked financial man with another. At Lloyd's Bank he bore the sole responsibility for dealing with "all the debts and claims of the bank" arising out of the Peace Treaties. Quinn had tried his editorial hand on some of Eliot's poems, and Eliot replied mildly as follows:

> I see reason in your objection to my punctuation; but I hold that the line punctuates, and the addition of a comma, in many places, seems to me to overemphasize the arrest. That is because I always pause at the end of a line in reading verse, while perhaps you do not. [*May 9, 1921.*]

And he spoke again drably and anonymously of what would be another of the sacred texts of the modern movement in the arts: "I . . . have a long poem in mind and partly on paper which I am wishful to finish." *The Waste Land* was on its way.

To Joyce Quinn had cited three Irish friends who had made virtually no demands upon him in years of acquaintance: George Russell, "young Colum," and James Stephens.[25] Writing on the twenty-first of February Stephens did make a modest request which Quinn carried out cheerfully. Stephens asked him to retrieve from Huebsch, and to read, the manuscripts of *The Country of the Young* and *Deirdre*, the first two volumes of his proposed five-volume retelling of the Irish cycle of the *Tain Bo Cualnge*, the "Red Branch" cycle.* The manuscripts had been carried by Ernest Boyd to Huebsch, and had lain in his office, apparently somnolent, for five months. Most of Stephens's letter was given over to rich fooling on the publisher's difficult name. Stephens had met Huebsch and his new Scandinavian wife in Paris in October, and had asked

---

* Never carried beyond these two volumes. Macmillan published *Deirdre* in London in 1923 and *The Country of the Young* (as *In the Land of Youth*) in London and New York in 1924.

him "if he pronounced his name with a button-hook." Mrs. Huebsch "taught me to say Huebsch in two lessons, but I never was any good at the piccolo, and I always hung fire at the—bsch part. . . ." He went on:

> After all, I am only five feet three high* and cannot be expected to talk hard words like that, but you are a big fellow and I expect you can throw any word that ever was forged. Walk right into him and say it quick, and then, while he is astonished and dismayed, you pinch my MSS. and get home by a side street. That's that.

In any case, Stephens averred, he had just finished writing "the loveliest story that ever was written by mortal man." Quinn did collect the manuscripts and read them as instructed, and he wrote to Russell in high praise of the *Deirdre*. Earlier in the winter, learning that Stephens faced an operation, Quinn, who now considered himself so knowledgeable about bodily ailments and their right treatment that he meditated writing a "medical essay," sent him a letter of advice. Stephens wrote on January 14: "My operation is well over, and, except for superficial wounds, I am ten times the man I was two months ago." He was all right, "barring a certain stiffness in the centre of things," [26] and he thanked Quinn for sound counsel, which he had followed.

The Paris period of about three years upon which Ezra Pound was now embarked was a passage of relatively dead water in his career. Pound was incapable of dawdling or real inaction, but he was having trouble finding a center and a line. When his year's appointment as Foreign Editor of the *Dial* expired he bethought himself of the same post on the *Century*, and wrote Quinn on April 11 to ask him to make representations there on his behalf. Quinn did not answer or even read that letter and a much earlier one of February 7 until May 1. When he wrote it was in his most distracted and self-sorrowful mood, and he produced a bitter, antagonistic letter. He had been driven half-mad, he said, since November when the crisis began, and he had not had a single day's complete rest in all that time.[27] Of Pound's new proposal he wrote bluntly: "I am glad that I was able to land you with the Dial for a year, but because I got that idea and carried it out that is no

---

* Actually Stephens stood less than five feet high.

reason why you should expect me to be your literary agent with the Century." Writing to Wyndham Lewis three weeks later he made the affair sound even worse: "I got Pound the Dial job for a year, which paid him $750, and though he thanked me, at the end of the year he thought I could do the same trick with the Century. Then I rebelled and told him to go to hell." [28] Quinn now attacked Pound on an issue which had been galling him silently for some time: the feeling that he had lent himself gullibly to be an instrument of what now seemed to him Pound's bad taste in art. He wished, he said, that he could send back all the work of Wyndham Lewis's he had bought "as an example of your monumental folly re that sort of stuff and my monumental assinnity [*sic*] in falling for it and buying it." He said that he would be happy to sell all his Augustus Johns and most of his Epsteins for fifty cents on the dollar.[29] When Quinn wrote again a few days later it was in a somewhat penitential mood. He had had his periodic examination from Dr. Erdmann, with a good report, and he wrote a much more sweetly temperate letter. The examination involved a dosing with castor oil, an irrigation, and a scrutiny by proctoscope through the rectum. He was happy to hear, while still on his hands and knees, "that everything is satisfactory and all is well." [30] And after all his bluster six days before Quinn had put Pound's question to the *Century*—with a negative result.

He might rage at Pound and call him, to himself and others, the worst of his trials, but fundamentally he liked Pound and approved of him and could not stay angry at him. Pound was capable of decent if not demonstrative gratitude, and his sympathy for Quinn's harried existence and his basic good will had a genuine sound to it. Pound's requests might be numerous but they were usually modest and reasonable, and there was no escaping the fact that they were pointed at the welfare of others quite as often as at his own. To Pound as to Joyce Quinn gave notice of his coming abroad in the summer, though he said he was "not telling anyone" in England or Ireland or America. "I am not telling Douglas Hyde," he wrote, "for Hyde would tell Stephens and Stephens would tell Russell and Russell would tell Plunkett. . . ." [31] He foresaw a line running on to Symons, Rolleston, Shannon, Craig, Joyce, Eliot, Lewis, and so on, "and so to hell with them all. . . . I'm going for a vacation, by God," he warned Pound. Actually he wrote in a similar vein to Pound, Joyce, Roché, Brancusi, Rouault, and to a variety of art dealers in Paris.

When Quinn did visit Paris in the summer his concentration was upon the painters and painting, but he did also see Pound and Joyce, singly and together, several times during July. He invited Joyce to lunch or dine with him, but Joyce was unwell and asked Quinn to call upon him instead.[32] He found him at the apartment of his great French champion, Valery Larbaud, recovering from another spell with his eyes and reading proofs for Miss Beach's edition of *Ulysses*. Quinn handed Joyce a "gift" of 2,000 francs.[33] (Quinn subsequently included the sum in his payments on the *Ulysses* manuscript.) He found Pound rather on his uppers, spending most of his afternoons in the *pavillon* of the American expatriate Natalie Clifford Barney in the Rue Jacob, trying to compose the music for an opera based on the ballads of François Villon. Quinn offered him a discreet loan of $200 but Pound refused, thinking things must improve. Then on October 22, with Quinn back at home, Pound wrote to say he was ready to accept the loan, and signed himself "Yours ever, or for as long as you permit." Quinn sent $250 and a cordial message: "Don't think of paying it back and just forget it." [34]

By the end of the year Pound was feeling a bit more cheerful. He had moved into a new studio at 70 bis, Rue Notre Dame des Champs and had saved money by cleaning it himself and by building all his own furniture except a bed and a stove.[35] Quinn asked his opinion about a letter he had received from Sylvia Beach appealing for money for Joyce on the grounds that all men of good will should join in subsidizing him until *Ulysses* was out. "If Joyce is starving," he wrote Pound on November 29, "and you think I ought to send him 1,000 francs, I will do it, but I'll be damned if I'll do it because Miss Beach asks for it." Two weeks later he had raised his figure to "a couple of thousand" when he inquired again.[36] But Pound wrote that he did not think Joyce's state was so desperate as Miss Beach had suggested, and Quinn held onto his money. Quinn also regretted to Pound, aping his idiom, that the *Dial* prize of $2,000 had gone to Sherwood Anderson of "the Ammurrican skule of fiction." A prize for "services to letters of an American writer" should have gone to Pound: ". . . you more than Eliot or any other American writer." [37] Pound replied mildly and sadly: "I think the Dial wd. have done itself a good deal of harm, with the mid-western public, and I dare say mid-eastern, if they had given the 2000 dollars to me." [38] It was a forlorn thought for Christmas Eve.

In his harried letters of the spring of 1921 Quinn kept listing among his trials the lingering of John Butler Yeats in New York, the need to look after him, and bootless correspondence about him with his children in Ireland. Early in the spring the Petitpas sisters informed him that Mr. Yeats had paid nothing on his bed and board since Christmas and his bill stood at $339.50. When Quinn wrote W. B. Yeats about it Yeats replied that he had no cash and asked Quinn to pay the bill and take his repayment in manuscripts (as in the past): ". . . as though I was a MS sewer or a MS dealer," Quinn raged to Pound on May 1. Quinn's correspondence with W. B. Yeats continued otherwise warm, chatty, and interesting. On August 22 George Yeats had her second child, a son, Michael. Yeats wrote Quinn three days later to ask him to serve as the child's American godfather; Lennox Robinson would handle the Irish end of the duties. Their doctor had said the baby had a beautiful head; Yeats would only say that he was handsomer than a newborn canary, four of which had hatched out in his bedroom recently, "and nothing like as good looking as the same bird when it gets its first feathers."

John Butler Yeats was still arguing that he could not return to Ireland until he had finished his self portrait for Quinn. Quinn said he would be glad to take it as it was. The old painter objected that the painting was still " 'in a very embryonic condition.' " Quinn said it was a " 'venerable embryo . . . dangerously overdue.' " Mr. Yeats reminded him that the *Mona Lisa* was " 'in incubation four years.' " And that work, Quinn rebutted, was " 'one of the damndest monstrosities' " he had ever seen.[39] In an important passage in a letter of September 30, W. B. Yeats analyzed the psychic difficulty of his father's vacillation, indeed of his whole career, and then turned his insight toward self-scrutiny. His father was prevented from returning to Ireland by "sheer infirmity of will":

> It is this infirmity of will which has prevented him from finishing his pictures and ruined his career. He even hates the sign of will in others. It used to cause quarrels between me and him, for the qualities which I thought necessary to success in art or in life

seemed to him "egotism" or "selfishness" or "brutality." I had to
escape this family drifting, innocent and helpless, and the need
for that drew me to dominating men like Henley and Morris
and estranged me from his friends, even from sympathetic unique
York Powell. I find even from letters written in the last few
months that he has not quite forgiven me.

By his own standards, and in spite of the irritation whirling
around him, John Butler Yeats was having another good year, his
eighty-third. The flow of his wonderful letters was scarcely diminished, and they were among his own consolations in New York,
even if Quinn was too busy to savor them. "I hope this letter won't
bore you," he wrote Quinn at the beginning of the year. "When
the ideas come I like to write to you about them. . . . And please
don't suspect me of being self-opinionated or self-conceited. I have
what may be called '*an insulated mind.*' But for good luck I should
have been a John O'Dreams and a fool." [40] It was a view of himself
that both illustrated his son's judgment and declared it unworthy.
J. B. Yeats had been trying again to explain his distinction between
"the explicit and the implicit" in art. He tended to start such ideas
and leave them at a generalized point short of clarity, and Quinn
had found this one difficult. Two days later he was writing again,
having heard from Quinn after an unusually long interval: "After
so long a silence I was afraid. I trembled in the dark, being a man
of nerves."

Jeanne Robert Foster had given Mr. Yeats a copy of T. S. Eliot's
essays, *The Sacred Wood*, and the book had set him thinking again
on his own ideas of the function of poetry. "I think the end of
poetry is to make rich and significant with harmony the *passing
moment*," he wrote.[41] He was still coming back to "the finite and
the infinite," though he was not using those terms any longer. He
went on in a strain which again suggested a deep assimilation of the
thought and feeling of Keats and Matthew Arnold:

> I think it is, in part, at any rate, a condition of detachment
> which at the same time has an entire experience of every thing
> from which it is detached. Perhaps it is what is meant by con-
> templation. In this condition a man belongs neither to himself nor
> to the world. He is apart. And that aloofness is the effect of what
> is called Beauty; the curious thing that it is only by being of the

highest sensibility and, at most, profoundly moved that anyone can attain to this condition of sensibility.

Once more he turned his insight toward art in its sublime forms: "At great moments a man always turns away from life, from friends, even from himself, and gropes or soars into this condition of detachment. It is a law of human nature of which the writers of tragedy take full advantage." It was a part of what he had meant earlier when he had described the final effect of great art as being "like a sketch." Now in his postscript he gaily reduced the scale of his argument: lovers at night in a wood, hearing a nightingale, he suspected, "do, for a moment or two, forget their delirious selves— even they—and relax the hugging."

Mr. Yeats had been reading Turgenev and Chekhov, the latter over and over until he knew his stories almost by heart. Praising Quinn's "many-sided energy on behalf of friends," he compared him to the man of will in one of Turgenev's stories, the universal resort of persons of weaker force.* He made a charcteristic report on his notorious self portrait:

> I have been doing my very best. Some days I am on the pinnacle of hope and confidence, and then down in the valley of despond-ency. It fills my life. I have never an idle moment or idle thought. It is a long revel, just as satisfying to me as Gibbon's "Decline and Fall of the Roman Empire," and I think I have been at it almost as many years. This morning I scraped away all the paint, but now it looks very promising.

"Shall I tell you what I think of Matisse?" he gustily began his letter of September 7. He had seen Quinn's new Matisse, *L'Atelier*, or *The Painter and His Model*, one of the chief trophies of his summer trip abroad, and was at last willing, after years of carping, to concede that Matisse was "an honest man. . . . I regard him with an indulgent smile," he wrote. "I did think him an imposter." In the body of his letter he developed a theory of Matisse, in his effort to imitate "the *palpability* of flesh," as a small late follower of Michelangelo, and thus a paddler in one of the main streams of art. He identified the streams: "I think you will find that there

* To Quinn, May 4, 1921. The reference was probably to the nihilist Bazarov in *Fathers and Sons*.

have always been two streams of art—one from Michael Angelo, and the other from Raphael; and it is the story of the everlasting antagonism between energy and expression as a source of art, and on the other side a solicitude for form." In the dialectical mode so dear to his heart, Yeats was accepting, without naming, the Dionysian-Apollonian, or Classical-Romantic dichotomy. In any case, he admonished Quinn, it was his duty, "as a critic and connoisseur," to appreciate both grand tendencies. "I am glad that you are beginning to get a glimmer of what Matisse stands for," Quinn wrote back bluntly and loftily two days later. His own judgment, as usual, was vague, general, and superlative: Matisse was "one of the greatest artists living." [42]

The cruel demands of many kinds upon him in the winter and spring of 1921 sharply curtailed Quinn's dealings for art at that time. Harried as he was to the point of nervous collapse by the beginning of May, he had neither time nor spirit to think efficiently about art. Other factors reinforced this state of affairs: he had lost about $30,000 personally in the decline of securities; [43] he had been disappointed in some of the works he had bought on the evidence of photographs; and he was hoping to find a chance in the summer of 1921 to make his first direct reconnoiter of the Paris markets since 1912. These factors combined to put him into a surly or reluctant mood about life generally and art in particular. Virtually his only purchases of the spring were three pieces of sculpture, Raymond Duchamp-Villon's *The Horse* and his *Portrait of Dr. Gosset*, which he bought from the widow for 7,500 francs on May 11, and Brancusi's marble *Torso* at 12,000 francs on May 22. Such actions as Quinn took at this time tended to be uncharacteristically negative, or mere displays of adamancy. "I am through buying pictures from photographs," he wrote Walter Pach on May 5, very prematurely. "I have been too badly disappointed." His worst disappointment, as he made clear in a letter of May 1 to Roché, had been Marie Laurencin's *Zebra* and her *Horsewoman*. He liked these works so little that he said he was going to return them to Paul Rosenberg and ask that his investment in them be credited against future purchases. But in the event he kept the two pictures. On April 26 he authorized Martin Birnbaum of Scott & Fowles of 590 Fifth Avenue to sell Augustus John's huge *The Mumpers* at a price that would net him $10,000. He asked that the picture be offered with an accompanying explanation to the effect that " 'because of the sale of my country place the picture is too large for hanging in my apartment, and that that is the reason and the only reason for its sale.' " [44] But the picture was not sold at this time. It remained at the Metropolitan Museum, actually in storage, from May 1921 to January 1924, when it was rolled up and taken back to Quinn's apartment. John's *The Way Down to the Sea*, one of the popular successes of the Armory Show, much smaller than *The Mumpers* but still a big picture, was exhibited at the Metropolitan from 1915 to January 1923, when the Museum returned it to Quinn, pleading lack of space.

Though Quinn had for all practical purposes broken with John, he did not want their relationship talked of in those terms, hence the elaborate "explanation" to Birnbaum. He sniped at John in letters to Arthur Symons and others, commenting sourly, for example, on tales of John's carrying on with Iris Tree in London and wondering at the weakness of her husband, Curtis Moffatt, in allowing it. "The Café Royal and drink and women have utterly ruined John as an artist," he put the case to Symons in a letter dictated on a Sunday morning in the train between New York and Philadelphia. "He has lacked the will to make the great refusal. As an artist he is finished. He has been doing pot-boilers for some years. . . . I have no further interest in his work." [45] Quinn kept coming across things that added to his irritation with John. In the big loan exhibition of Modern French Painters which was on at the Metropolitan during most of 1921, to which he was one of the most important lenders, he saw the splendid Cézanne *Bather* which he blamed John's careless judgment for doing him out of, and wrote of the affair to Wyndham Lewis:

> The finest thing in the exhibition is a wonderful thing by Cézanne, in grey tone, of the nude boy with his hands at his hips and nothing but a breech cloth. Ten years ago or thereabouts, I was going to buy it of Vollard. But John happened along, shrugged his shoulders, and said: "It's an empty picture, and you (I) don't want that." That tipped the scale. I could have bought it then for 40,000 francs or about $8,000. It is worth $40,000 now.
>
> [*May 25, 1921.*]

In the same letter Quinn recalled with shame and anger the period of ten years before "when John was being a great man at my expense, a patron with my pocket-book," and mused bitterly: "What a damn fool I was in those days." He dismissed Lewis himself bluntly: "I shall buy no more of your work at the present time. I am through with buying tentative work." [46] Lewis, being contemporary with John in Quinn's experience, and occupying the same atmosphere, the London art world fouled, for Quinn, by John's presence, shared in his obloquy. So, unconsciously, did David Bomberg, one of the London artists whose work Quinn had bought on John's advice. Bomberg wrote in the spring, reminding Quinn that he already owned work of his and enclosing photographs of recent paintings. Quinn replied negatively and inclusively, though not unkindly:

> I hate to write this way, but patience has ceased to be a virtue and self defense has become a necessity. I should be obliged, therefore, if you would do the best you can to counteract the idea that seems to be common in England that I buy wholesale, or from photographs, or to help artists, or to encourage them, for I do none of these things.   [*May 26, 1921.*]

And in rebuffing Frank Harris who had tried to interest him in buying work of the sculptor William Zorach, Quinn described himself as "a man who, as the result of fifteen years of giving up to generous impulses, has developed into one of the most adamant resisters that I know of." [47]

Yet in spite of the general negativism of mood and action in this period Quinn was more or less constantly involved in what he called, comprehensively, "the art fight." To encourage Henri-Pierre Roché to pursue the *chasse* alertly in Paris, he sent him on the first of May another token payment of 1,000 francs with an additional 360 francs for expenses. For the Loan Exhibition of Impressionist and Post-Impressionist Paintings which ran at the Metropolitan Museum from May 3 to September 15, 1921, Quinn was the most generous and significant of the thirteen lenders named in the catalog. Bryson Burroughs, Curator of Paintings, came to his apartment to make a selection from his collection, and sat for hours in amazement as a vivid parade of capital paintings was carried past his eyes. Burroughs finally selected twenty-eight paintings: seven

Redons, six Matisses, four Derains, three Picassos, two Gauguins, and one each by Van Gogh, Cézanne, Toulouse-Lautrec, Dufy, Rouault, and Vlaminck. Then, when the paintings were going out, Quinn irresistibly included on his own motion the vibrant Matisse still life of apples. "The Apples will sing on the walls of that room," he told Burroughs.[48] Quinn traveled the exhibition itself as often as he could, not so often as he would have liked. He wrote Cornelius J. Sullivan, a Harvard classmate, of overhearing two ladies in town: " 'Well, I was up there and invariably the awfullest pictures belonged to John Quinn.' " He assured Sullivan, "I have got a lot more that are worse than those." [49]

"I have been very, very, very, very, dreadfully, dreadfully, horribly driven," Quinn wrote Arthur Symons at the end of May, and among other things "up to my neck in an art fight again. . . ." [50] The perennial problem of customs duty and taxation of works of art had again arisen, and Quinn, for whom the issue always sounded the charge, spent most of two weeks in the middle of May on attack and defense in Washington. In the House of Representatives his fight was against the restoration by the Ways and Means Committee of the customs duty on the importation of art; in the Senate the fight was aggressive, an attempt to persuade them to remove the current 10-per-cent sales tax on works of art. Quinn prepared two briefs, one for the House and the other, in part a repetition, for the Senate. Before the Sub-Committee of the Ways and Means Committee on May 10 he "talked nearly two hours and I think as brilliantly as a man ever talked before a Congressional Committee, if I do say it myself." [51] On the morning of May 18 he delivered an address on the subject in the opening session of the American Federation of Arts at the Corcoran Gallery in Washington, after which he carried their resolutions "hot from the griddle" to the Committee of the House.[52] As usual he sent copies of his printed briefs to many friends. At the end of the year he summed up for Roché the results he had achieved: "I won half of my fight on the art sales tax. Since 1918 there was a sales tax here of 10 per cent. I succeeded in reducing it to five per cent, and almost succeeded in having it taken off entirely. The House Tariff Bill kept art on the free list." [53] Quinn was more concerned personally with the import tariff, since most of his own buying was being done abroad.

Apologizing to George Russell for the fact that his letter of June 19 was the first in a long time, Quinn said that the preceding seven months had been the most exacting of his whole professional career, and he described the financial carnage out of which the country was just beginning to labor—"failures, fortunes wiped out, companies made bankrupt. . . ." [54] That he had survived the strain himself was a tribute to his restored health and the self-imposed simplification of his life outside the office: ". . . I have declined nearly all invitations and have scarcely gone anywhere, and have cut out smoking before dinner and have taken the best care of myself possible, consistent with working all the time." [55] "The excuses!" Æ wrote back on July 6. "My dear man you will be busy and overworked to the end of your life. Why?"

> Because you are in yourself a creature of immense vitality and you become a magnet attracting all kinds of forces to the centre where you sit. . . . I am not recommending you to change your soul for I think everybody gets the environment suited to them and which they really enjoy. With your temperament in a valley of the Golden Age you would change it to the Bronze Age in a week to get it lively and efficient.

As usual Russell's analysis was both sensitive and sensible, the line from Quinn's character to his destiny shrewdly drawn. He was both the driven and the driver. In any case he was dog-tired, and with the apparent upturn in business conditions in the summer he believed he could take a month's rest. "The Kid," Mary Anderson, now fourteen, had been suffering for some weeks with a low-grade throat infection, and his first scheme was to take her and her parents for a month to the Adirondacks or the coast of Maine. It was now nine years since his last trip to Europe. He had not returned in the interval for a variety of reasons: his disappointment in his 1912 visit, the intervention of the war, his illness and operation, his notion of the therapeutic virtues of the open-air life in the mountains or at the shore, his wish to spend as much time as he could with the little remnant of his family. But now a large credit insurance case which involved Lloyd's of London suddenly arose and gave him an excuse which he resolved to seize: he would spend his holiday abroad.

He sailed on the *Paris* of the French Line on June 25, with a plan to spend about a week in the capital attending to business and looking into art matters and then to go to the Brittany coast for an extended rest. In the upshot his plan was modified in ways which gave him great satisfaction. The visit turned into the richest cultural feast of his life. Held in the city by business cables and conferences, Quinn "sauntered, and saw what the galleries had of modern work." [56] He came away with two old convictions confirmed:

> . . . first, that good modern art is rare and requires great patience and time to discover; and secondly, that a collector should not purchase tentative work, or "to help the artist," or second or third-rate works, or what I call "scraps," or what enthusiasts call "beautiful" or "charming" little things.[57]

He renewed acquaintance with the great dealer Ambroise Vollard, and bought from him both a Seurat landscape and a late Cézanne landscape of Mont St. Victoire, which the master had left unfinished in several spots. Vollard told him that he had refused to sell the picture to other dealers, knowing they would have the unfinished bits painted in.

Both Jeanne Robert Foster and Henri-Pierre Roché were on the scene, and their wide acquaintance helped him to an entrée with a number of artists he was meeting for the first time, and gave some of those artists a chance to have a look at their first, in some cases their only, important American collector. With Roché and Mrs. Foster Quinn spent a day at Fontainebleau with Picasso and his wife, Olga. He bought three new Picassos, his large painting of two nude women (probably the *Deux Femmes Nues* for which he paid Paul Rosenberg 45,000 francs on November 26), to which Quinn gave the name of "The Two Bronze Women" and described to Lady Gregory as "almost as powerful and as strong as a picture of archaic sculpture"; a medium-sized abstraction; and a water color, *The Harvesters*, "a perfect gem." He saw André Derain and Mme. Derain several times, exchanging lunches and dinners with them, and from the painter he bought a three-quarter *Portrait of a Woman*, "a superb thing, one of Derain's best," [58] which he finished under Quinn's own eyes. That was art at its most contemporary: *wet* art. At a bargain, 13,000 francs, he secured from Georges

Bernheim the Matisse studio scene known as *L'Atelier* or *Matisse Peignant son Modèle*, showing the back of the painter at his easel, painting a nude model seated before a window in a studio full of flowers, "a typical Matisse, all light and colour." [59] The painter himself Quinn saw in his home in the suburbs of Paris, returned from a winter's painting in Nice, where he was known as the most industrious man in the city and where his neighbors were reluctant to believe he was a painter—he worked such long hours. But Quinn felt, he said: "like reminding him of Johnson's [*sic*] regret that Shakespeare had not 'blotted many more lines'—meaning that he sold too many small things." [60] Quinn had been overtaken by the fear that the modern French painters, and especially Matisse, were falling into facile and uncritical habits of work, doing too much too easily, without the thought and labor necessary to masterpieces. There were too many pictures to see.

At the home of Segonzac's father at Chaville, near Vincennes, Quinn visited the painter and carried away several drawings. Segonzac later wrote to apologize for the poverty of his entertainment, but Quinn had found the afternoon delightful. He heard again of Segonzac's habit of reading out Quinn's wartime letters to his comrades in the trenches: and they often " 'gave M. Quinn three cheers for his encouragement!' " Both Braque and Dufy he saw several times. Of Braque he bought two abstract still lifes and of Dufy a half-dozen water colors. Braque had been badly wounded in the war and had won both the *Croix de guerre* and the *Médaille militaire*. When they were motoring together and Quinn asked him about his wound, the painter invited him to lay his fingers in the runnel above his right temple, and Quinn did so. A *pneumatique* from Jules Pascin to Quinn at the Hôtel de Jena on July 16 suggests that they met amicably at this time in spite of the bitter tone of their last exchange of letters in April 1919.

When Georges Rouault met his American benefactor for the first time he bowed his head on Quinn's sleeve and wept.[61] They spent two afternoons together at the quaint Musée Gustave Moreau, housed in the atelier of Rouault's old master, where he served as curator. To Lady Gregory Quinn described Rouault as "a French Blake," [62] thinking of his gnomic work in paint and verse, his cranky spirituality. Rouault showed the illustrations he had in progress for Alfred Jarry's *Ubu Roi,* "very hard and striking—though at first glance crude—sketches, with a brush, in black and white." [63] To mark Quinn's second visit Rouault brought his three children in from Versailles, and Quinn thought the shy little boy and two girls so charming that he wished to embrace them.

Quinn called on Constantin Brancusi several times and fed twice on excellent meals cooked by the sculptor on the forge of his studio. The specialty of the house was *boeuf forgé.* And Quinn, Roché, and Mrs. Foster accompanied Brancusi down the Seine for a *déjeuner sur l'herbe* on a river island. Quinn was tempted to take along Erik Satie, the composer, whom he had met and who had charmed him, but thought the confrontation of Satie and Brancusi potentially too much for his nerves: ". . . I did not feel like refereeing a Carpentier-Dempsey verbal encounter." [64] He visited Jacques Villon and his wife outside Paris, and also saw Villon's brother Marcel Duchamp, already a good friend from New York, and the widow of the third brother, Raymond Duchamp-Villon, the sculptor. With them he discussed details of the book on Duchamp-Villon he had promised to subsidize, the text of which was being written by Walter Pach in New York. Aside from Joyce and Pound the only literary man with whom Quinn spent any time was Félix Fénéon, whom he remembered from Remy de Gourmont's account and revered as the loyal friend of Seurat. His apportioning of his time in Paris, heavily weighted toward art and artists, made graphic the diminished place that literature now occupied in his mind.

Still with Mrs. Foster and Roché, Quinn toured the French battlefields, motoring slowly and reflectively out from Paris to Verdun and back through the Argonne, Rheims, the Chemin des Dames, and Soissons. They traveled in early mornings and late afternoons and took a leisurely lunch and rested during the midday heat. Quinn was moved to awe and anger; ". . . an unforgettable sight!" he exclaimed to Lady Gregory:

I wish that Mr. President Harding and Mr. Secretary Hughes could see what the Germans did to the most prosperous part of France. And the cemeteries!—Miles of them. And the dugouts and the trenches and the ruin and desolation!—A new desert over one of the fairest parts of France. It made an ineffaceable impres-

sion upon me and made permanent my resolve never to forgive
the Germans or to forget what they did. I shall hate them and
despise them as long as I live. It would take a Dante, or greater
than Dante, to tell of the horror and desolation, the suffering and
the death that they brought to France; and only Dante's white
heat of hatred could do justice to the feeling that persons with a
sense of justice should have toward them. But I mustn't get on that
subject. . . .   [*May 11, 1922.*]

After a few days of absolute rest at Dinard Quinn was summoned back to Paris by telegrams about business affairs. Now at
long last he met Gwen John, who had evaded him since 1909.
He had nearly missed her again, for she happened to be absent
on a visit to Arthur and Rhoda Symons in Kent when Quinn first
reached Paris in early July. But now she was back in Meudon, and
Quinn and Mrs. Foster called on her several times in her reclusive
attic five flights up in a yellow plastered house looking out over
the Seine and the forest of Versailles. Seeing the work she had on
hand he was confirmed in his judgment of her as the finest living
woman painter, and again he admired the purity and dedication of
her life. "She is a very sincere, shy woman, but determined to live
her life and in her own way," he presented her to Lady Gregory.[65]
Gwen John had become a Catholic and was frequently in the company of the Dominican nuns in the nearby convent, where they
operated a school for orphan girls. Quinn was touched at the sight
of the crowds of little girls in their black costumes at play on the
dusty playground, and hurt to observe that they ate their bread
dry, without *confiture*. He gave the Mother Superior a check for
$500 to ensure that the pupils would never again have to eat dry
bread. Subsequently, when Mrs. Foster asked whether the gift had
been put to work, the Mother Superior tearfully confessed that
she had used Quinn's money to repair the leaking roof. She had
been praying for money for that purpose, and now word went
round the community that a miracle had occurred in answer to
her prayers. When Mrs. Foster wrote Quinn the story, he said
that he was glad at last to be a principal in a Catholic miracle but
he still wanted the children to have their jam: he sent a second
check.[66]

He also succeeded in buying from the convent Gwen John's

Mère Poussepin, for which he had been hankering at a distance for several years. When Mrs. Foster met Gwen John earlier in her own long visit abroad, she found "the nuns' picture" still incomplete, and she persuaded the painter to let her pose in a borrowed nun's habit so that she could finish the figure. It was painted in a palette as different as possible from Matisse's, in grey-blue tones of a hazy, chalky texture, "a beautiful, cool thing, a perfect gem," as Quinn described it.[67] Complexly drawn by art and sentiment, he bought it at once. His last full day in Paris, Sunday the fourteenth of August, was passed in graceful leisure with Miss John and Mrs. Foster, with a drive out of the city and a lunch in the woods, a walk about Versailles, then dinner back in the city at the Pavillon Bleu. Roché and Mrs. Foster saw him off on the boat train the following morning. "I never hated so much leaving anywhere or doing anything as I did leaving Paris," he wrote Gwen John from New York on August 24. Mrs. Foster had postponed her own sailing to October 1 and remained in Paris because she had commissioned Gwen John to do a portrait of her. "I am sure that you will make a beautiful, a very distinguished and noble thing of your painting of Mrs. Foster," Quinn wrote emotionally.[68] But for reasons which remain mysterious the work was never completed. In September for the first time Gwen John was discovering the pleasures and trials of a personal bank account.[69] Quinn had explained the mystery to her and provided the necessary element.

Writing to Symons he compared himself as he sailed for home to Shakespeare's reluctant schoolboy. He wished he were free to set off round the world: "I should have liked to go to the ocean for a month, and then, by slow journeys, have gone Eastward to Constantinople, to Suez, to India, Sumatra and China, and, around this time next year, across the Pacific to California. But, instead of that, I have had to return to the grind here." [70] It was the voice of a man still tired but one savoring rich satisfactions. He had moved about with people he liked, to see people he liked, and he had admired them and their work and their wives. He had steeped himself in Paris, too briefly, and had gone home with the contents of another small museum of the "living" art he craved, some of it barely dry. Now he could feel himself the friend of the artists, not merely their market. More than ever before or ever again, he felt an air of health about the whole occasion, in himself, in France, in the artists and their families. As he summed it up to Lady Gregory: "I was impressed by the strength and the vigour and the sanity and the urbanity of all these French artists." [71] His own life in New York was newly distasteful by contrast, and in writing to the London dealer Percy Moore Turner he set the life in art against the life in business:

> At the best, most artists live hardly and die poor. But they have had their dreams and have done what they wished to do. At least they have not had anything to do with business, which is oftentimes a combination of cunning, cowardice, trickery, and dirtiness, run by only mediocre minds, or by fools who wear themselves out in trying to get rich, and leave only a negligible amount of life to "enjoy" what they have gained.   [*October 1, 1921.*]

It seemed to him particularly infuriating when the world of business, wooed at great cost and apparently won, failed to provide him with the means to woo art. On November 17 he cabled Walter Halvorsen in Paris $2,396.35 for works of Seurat and Derain for which he had agreed in Paris, and wrote him on the same day that he would have taken Matisse's *The Interior* and *The Goldfish* at 93,000 francs had not his fee from the Alien Property Custodian been reduced by $19,000. But that was perhaps the fault of the world of art: if the *Little Review* had let him alone he might have been able to collect that fee when it was full.

"The art fight" had broken out on another front, a renewed irruption of the traditionalist attack on modernism in painting and sculpture, and Quinn was gaily involved. He was interviewed by reporters on September 6 and gave out a strong defense of modernism which appeared the following day in *The New York Times*, the *Herald*, and the *Tribune*. Then *The New York Times* of September 8 carried an attack by Joseph Pennell which Quinn reduced to two main charges: modern art was "dangerous" and it was "Bolshevist." He wrote to John Butler Yeats:

> The "danger" argument has been made against every advance in science or in art. It is a favorite argument with the Catholic Church. They used to think it was dangerous to read the Bible. The Bolshevist argument is a joke, for no one could be more

French than Derain, who was born in the city of Paris and is proud of it; Braque, who was born almost within the shadow of Notre Dame and is proud of it; Matisse, who is French of the French; and Cézanne, who was as French as Foch or Poincaré.

[*September 9, 1921.*]

Reverting to the robustness, the sanity of mind and spirit, the general good health of the moderns whom Pennell was calling "decadent," Quinn recast his impressions of the summer just past. Derain was a giant, Braque a great wrestler and boxer, and they and others like them had spent five years or more in uniform in the war: "If I were choosing a group of men to accompany me on an expedition to the North Pole, I do not know where I could get three better or stronger men than Matisse, Braque and Derain. And these are the men that old fossils like Pennell call decadents." [72] But he declined to conduct a newspaper controversy with Pennell, quietly interpreting their disagreement as one of honest and profound predilection, "not a matter to be argued about." He was showing, for the moment, a public mildness which was approved by Mr. Yeats, who liked to quote Keats's " 'Don't let us argue,' " and who again assured Quinn that he exempted him and his drawing room from his general dislike of the contentiousness of American conversation.

Quinn realized his own loneliness as a collector of the new art and was both proud and saddened at it. When Léonce Rosenberg wrote him in the late autumn to ask his advice about the wisdom of trying to dispose of a great bloc of about two hundred Cubist paintings at the Anderson Gallery, Quinn wrote back on November 26 warning him strongly away from the idea at this time: the pictures would not bring anything like full value in New York; they would be "slaughtered" and so large a carnage would have a bad general effect on the art market and the prices of single works. Rosenberg had assembled a list of Americans who were thought to be good prospects for his kind of paintings and he sent the list to Quinn and asked for comment. Quinn returned the following judgments on November 29:

Mrs. Harry Payne Bingham: "She is very rich, but she would not be interested in cubistic work. She has bought some Cézannes and Manets, but nothing later."

Mrs. Gano Dunn. "She would not, in my opinion, buy any cubistic work. She owns a Puvis and some other good things."

Mr. Hamilton Easter Field. "He is an artist and is the editor of a magazine called 'The Arts.' He is a man of some means but would not buy works in which you dealt, though it may be worth while to write him and send him some photographs of works."

Mr. Adolph Lewisohn. "He would not buy works in which you were interested. He has bought a good many paintings by Augustus John and one or two good Gauguins and has some good Renoirs."

Mrs. Eugene Meyer, Jr. "She might be interested. . . . She knows Mr. DeZayas and probably would not buy any modern French art except upon his advice."

Mr. William Church Osborn. "He is perfectly hopeless from your point of view. I know him well. He is a director of the Metropolitan Museum. His interest in art comes down no later than Manet, whose "Girl with a Parrot" he loaned to the Met. Museum. Perfectly useless to send him things."

Mrs. Charles H. Seuff. "Widow of a man who bought paintings by Manet and Puvis twenty years ago. Would not be interested in works that you have to sell."

Mr. Joseph Stransky. "He is the director of the Philharmonic Orchestra. Very cultivated man. He is a Hungarian Jew. I know him personally. Tells you the exact number of paintings he has. The last time I saw him he told me he had 157, and as I turned away I said to myself: "And you can have them and keep them." About forty-two per cent. of them are German and the rest come down no later than Manet. Useless from your point of view."

Mrs. George Vanderbilt. "She would not know art if she saw it outside of jewelry and dresses."

Miss Lizzie [*sic*] P. Bliss. "She has bought very heavily of the work of an American artist, Arthur B. Davies, and others. She has been a rather heavy purchaser of works by Cézanne lately. She would not be interested in cubistic work at all. I know her well."

Mr. Arthur B. Davies. "He is a cultivated American artist. I know him well. He might be interested in photographs of things dealt in by you. He has bought a good many cubistic paintings, Picasso, Braque, and one or two others."

Mr. Paul Daugherty. "He is an American landscape painter. Thinks his own work is great. He would throw photographs of things you might send him out of the window."

Mr. Harry Payne Whitney. "He is a great polo player, rich man, personal friend of mine. Splendid fellow. His wife is a sculptress. Buys many kinds of art but not cubistic work. Therefore it would be wasting a postage stamp to send him photographs. . . ."

Mr. Bryson Burroughs. "He is the curator of paintings at the Met. Mus. He is too poor to buy art. Besides, he paints his own feeble art, a pale reflection of Puvis. Useless to send him photographs. . . ."

Not, all in all, a cheering report. (A pale reflection of Puvis de Chavannes must have been nearly invisible.) Quinn did go on to volunteer the names of Arthur J. Eddy and Walter Arensberg as men who did buy current work. Quinn did not pretend to be quite alone.

It is interesting to see Quinn's and Rosenberg's easy habit of calling most of the advanced art of the young century "cubistic," as if it were all one in tendency. What Rosenberg meant by the term was made clear in a definition he supplied Quinn in a letter of December 21:

> Cubism between 1907 and 1920 was a strong reaction against "baroque," "sensual," "analytic," "anecdotic," "sentimental" art and the heroic effort for returning to high traditional art, the art of synthesis and construction.

The inclusion of the " 'analytic' " among the tendencies revolted against is puzzling, unless Rosenberg meant perhaps ethical, philosophical "analysis." But to have the modern movement called " 'high traditional' " is profoundly useful, for that helps one to see it as what it was in the ethos of these years, anti-romantic, austere, impersonal: classicist.

Something of Quinn's own self-sense, the yearning drive toward art and away from business, with its corollary urge toward Europe and away from America, came through audibly in his reaction to an evening with Charles ("Carlo") Loeser, an American of peculiar cultivation and elegance, of both mind and manner, cosmopolitan and connoisseur, back home after thirty-five years' residence in

Florence. Loeser had been brought by his friend and Quinn's, Walter Pach, for dinner and a tour of the collection, and afterward Quinn wrote to Pach of his reaction to the evening:

> I enjoyed having Mr. Loeser and you at my place the other night. It was a great pleasure to meet him and I hope I can have him over to my place again before he goes. A man of his urbanity and cultivation is a delightful contrast to the efficiency, insularity, banality, vulgarity and brutality that go to make up the average Amurrikan who tries to pretend that he is a gentleman but who doesn't know the meaning of the word. [*December 23, 1921.*]

Quinn's statement raises the question of his own gentlemanliness. It is a complex question, and perhaps not terribly important, except that it mattered so visibly to him. Nagging his subconscious mind all his life was the question of whether an Ohio Irishman in the hurly-burly of New York law could be a gentleman, a citizen of the cultivated cosmopolis, the world of light. Without doubt he persuaded himself that he had achieved it. He also persuaded others, in the flesh, and their valuation needs to be attended to. What is one to make of such a judgment as Lady Gregory's that Quinn was a greater "beauty" and a truer "intellectual" than W. B. Yeats—in a letter to Quinn himself? [73] It was flattery, and subconsciously Quinn must have known it as such. But perhaps only a gentleman would have known it as flattery. Quinn's whole life was a pursuit of gentlemanliness. Ford Madox Ford told Hemingway that John Quinn was almost the only American he could consider calling a gentleman.* Ford was a professional, a connoisseur of gentlemen, always on the watch for the breed. Quinn certainly looked the part, and looked the aristocrat, which is not the same thing. At fifty-one he was still an extremely good-looking man, with his

---

* " 'Is Ezra a gentleman?' I asked.
'Of course not,' Ford said. 'He's an American.'
'Can't an American be a gentleman?'
'Perhaps John Quinn,' Ford explained. 'Certain of your ambassadors.'
'Was Henry James a gentleman?'
'Very nearly.'
'Are you a gentleman?'
'Naturally. I have held His Majesty's commission.'
'It's very complicated,' I said, 'Am I a gentleman?'
'Absolutely not,' Ford said."
A Moveable Feast, London, Jonathan Cape, 1964, pp. 78–9.

Roman-emperor's face and head on the tall, strong, erect body housed in quiet, well-cut tweeds and worsteds. His was a powerful, elegant, often easy presence. He could be gracefully at home in any company. On the other hand it was not a constant presence, and perhaps not a natural one. It was too conscious, too fragile, too vulnerable to its company, to circumstance, and to small passions from within. It was not the presence of an achieved serenity of spirit. Quinn had the kind of egotism that is half confident, half frightened, never the modesty of deep self-trust. Quinn knew gentlemen and ladies: Judge Keogh, Walter Pach, Arthur B. Davies, Padraic Colum, Mrs. Foster, John Butler Yeats, Lady Gregory, George Russell, Standish O'Grady, Ezra Pound (three-quarters of him), Rouault, Brancusi, Braque, Roché, Gwen John. All of them tolerated him, all of them valued him in some way, most of them admired him, a few of them loved him. By and large what they valued in him was a genuine if inconstant charm, a generally trustworthy good will, an extraordinary efficient energy—a likeableness and a usefulness that generally successfully obscured certain traits at the heart of the man that needed a good deal of forgiving: vanity, bullying, rant, vulgarity of sentiment.

One of Quinn's gentleman friends, John Butler Yeats, set down for him in the spring of 1921 a few generalizations of his own on these subjects. Mr. Yeats had seen G. K. Chesterton, an old family friend, in New York in May and had drawn up for him a hierarchy of national types of conceit and complacency:

> I . . . told him that I had always supposed the most conceited and self-complacent man in the world was the Irish Protestant; and I did not refer to the men of Ulster, who have not the same serenity of conceit, but rather to the people who were Dowden's friends and even Mahaffy's friends. . . . The Irish Protestant does not consider it necessary that he should think or have ideas. He is exempt. He is built on such superb lines that he has only to go on living. [*May 4, 1921.*]

It was his own race of which he was speaking. Lately he had come to the conclusion that the Englishman and the American were even greater egotists and boors than the Irish Protestant. Again he specifically exempted Quinn, and he reacted charitably to one of Quinn's recent letters of complaint about manifold demands upon him: ". . . besides the interest of ideas and of comment it is refreshing as an account of such many-sided energy on behalf of friends. I don't believe anybody in any other country would have such things to tell." Quinn's position was similar to that of Turgenev's man of will, he thought: "Each of those wretches who rushed to you for help thought he was the only wretch. He did not know of the others. He did not know he was one of a rabble." [74]

The Irish psychology, and Irish affairs in general, were now looming larger in Quinn's mind than he had allowed them to do for some time. He had finally made his point in New York about his disgust with the Irish and his preoccupation with dearer motives, and he was no longer counted as one of the arch-patriot Irish. But his old loyalties were still quite capable of being stirred, and they were stirred again in 1921 by the crucial state of affairs in Ireland and the prospect once more of a possible settlement of the old bloody differences with England. His own position was unchanged, moderate or conservative: he wished to see a united Ireland, including Ulster, with full Dominion status under the mantle of Britain. The Sinn Fein demand for a free republic seemed to him extravagant and unwise, and he tended to suspect the Sinn Fein leaders of demagoguery, vulgarity, and exhibitionism. When Terence McSwiney, Lord Mayor of Cork, was carrying out his long hunger strike to the death, Quinn refused to believe he was not being fed in secret, and scoffed at the performance as a piece of "Chinn-Feign." And he had by no means forgiven the radical Irish faction for "going to bed with the Germans" during the war.

Quinn's heart and his pocketbook had been touched in the spring of 1920 by an appeal from Horace Plunkett, on behalf of the Dominion League, for funds to support "a first-class weekly journal and the conduct of a national propaganda" dedicated to shaping public opinion in Ireland, England, and America in favor of a permanent constitution for Ireland on Dominion lines. Plunkett's concern, he told Quinn, was to "rescue my unlucky country from the dreadful condition in which it now stands," and he summed up the dreadful condition:

Sinn Fein, being Separatist, is making the impossible an excuse for neglecting the possible, and amusing itself with romantic Ireland, which is, unfortunately, very far from being dead and gone, as our poet Yeats declared. It romances; and the Castle coerces. Both the romancing and coercing have now come down to an epidemic of shooting, which is settling into a hopeless and baleful routine of murders and reprisals, making all industrial development impossible. [*April 13, 1920.*]

It was an elegant and unselfish appeal for support for a position which Quinn already occupied in any case. Differently moving was James Stephens's story, peculiarly Irish and peculiarly exasperating, of the death of a young lad who was brought into the hospital ward when Stephens was convalescing from his operation. The boy had been shot in the stomach and he lived for thirty hours, in terrible pain, after an operation. He was given extreme unction by a priest who improvised an altar with two candles at the foot of his bed. After his death his father arrived, "an inarticulate man, bursting with his silent, difficult grief," and he paced up and down by his son's body saying, with "desperate, dumb iteration, 'Ah, you poor creature. . . . What would they shoot you for at all?'" The father went away at last, and "within three minutes" the crowd of patients in the ward "were all crowing and giggling and shouting again." [75]

Moved intellectually and emotionally, Quinn contributed generously to Plunkett's journal, which became the resurrected *Irish Statesman*, and he served on the Executive Committee of the American Committee for Relief in Ireland, which by 1922 had collected over a million pounds for distribution among those whose lives had been shattered in the Troubles. Much of the money was disbursed by the Irish White Cross, which, according to Quinn, was in danger of being discredited in America by "lying statements" from the British Embassy when he saved it by producing before the Executive Committee a letter in its praise from George Russell.[76] He also ordered thirty copies of Russell's essay, "The Inner and the Outer Ireland," which he called "one of the wisest and sanest things on the Irish question I have ever read," for distribution among friends whose opinions were likely to matter.[77]

Before he went abroad late in June Quinn wrote to most of his Irish friends. He spoke of the division of opinion in America, sympathy with the Irish demand for independence running up against the affection and admiration that had grown up in the country for

England as an ally during the war. He could see the logic of English reluctance to relinquish all control over an island so near, so unfriendly to herself, and potentially so friendly to Germany. Ireland was "such a damned convenient naval base," as Shane Leslie had pointed out.[78] "Personally, I do not care a rap by what name we go adventuring in time," James Stephens wrote. "Let it be kingdom or republic or colony, it is immaterial." [79] What was material, he thought, the one really crucial question, was whether Ireland was to have fiscal autonomy, control of her own money. Quinn held on to his hope for "genuine dominion home rule, and an undivided Ireland." In any case he thought he detected, and he wrote of to his friends, a new general spirit in Ireland, new seriousness and an air of capacity with which England must come to grips. He put it to Russell: "The days of whispering and backstairs-work, bickering and scheming and wire-pulling and working through women, have passed." [80]

Stephens's impression from close up supported Quinn's: "Ireland is as stiff as an iron bar and, short of absolute decimation, she will never give in. . . . There is nothing but the will to win and to outlast anything." [81] Feeling better about things by now, Plunkett also agreed, prematurely: "The new spirit you speak of has carried the young men to triumph against the trickery of Lloyd George, notwithstanding many acts of unwisdom due to their lack of experience." [82] But Russell was only cautiously hopeful and troubled with forebodings. He joined in the older generation's increasing respect for the new men: ". . . the rising generation is the best generation of young Irishmen I have known." But he too mistrusted Lloyd George and expected little to come of the current protracted negotiations between the Dail Eireann emissaries (first De Valera, then Robert Barton, Arthur Griffith, Michael Collins, G. Gavan Duffy, and Eamonn Duggan) and the English government. He hoped for the best, but had "nerved" himself for "a breakdown and more ferocious oppression and warfare." Having stated the case for reform in "The Inner and the Outer Ireland," and being cursed with a sense of justice, he had gone on in a second essay to state the Unionist case, equally real. He drily expected that the second paper would not be so popular as the first. And, being Russell, he was getting slowly on with a new book, "an original view of politics considered in relation to the Earth Spirit." [83]

From London where he was now re-established Shane Leslie wrote in the autumn, "There is no beginning or end to Irish crises here. . . ." [84] He himself wanted to see an Irish republic, but he judged it could not be Irish without a king, and not a republic with a king. In early December the negotiators in London reached agreement, and Lady Gregory wrote immediately and excitedly: "Today has come the definite news of the signing of the Peace Agreement, and I am so happy and excited I think I must have a little talk with you." [85] It seemed to her that there was suddenly "a new world to live in." Yet only a few days before they had had at Coole a more accurately premonitory experience. De Valera had addressed a large meeting outside Coole Park gates and reviewed a company of Volunteers. Lady Gregory's grandchildren, looking over the wall, reported that he had " 'a lovely voice and spoke in Irish.' " At the end there had been a brush with a military lorry and the arrest, by the Volunteers, of two strangers who were taking notes and photographs—evidently military officers ordered to follow De Valera's movements. The affair passed off without bloodshed, but there was good reason to dread "hearing the Black and Tans firing along the roads again and leaving charred ruins after them." [86] As the year wore away with the fearful hope of peace, she was arranging in an iridescent blue grass bowl from Tiffany's, given her years ago by John Quinn, periwinkle blossoms brought in from the woods by her grandchildren.

When Douglas Hyde wrote on December 16 the Dail was meeting for the third day, arguing in secret sessions whether to accept or reject the London agreement. He hoped for acceptance: ". . . we seem to have really hammered out a measure of real freedom. . . . So far as I can see, we have got almost everything we want under the new treaty. . . . I think we got the very most we could have got without war, and war is too awful to contemplate again." He informed Quinn in passing that he had dedicated to him his volume of rhymed proverbs, now printing. Shane Leslie wrote from London on December 15 with greater and more premature enthusiasm: "Well, the great Irish settlement has arrived in our lifetime. Ireland threw up a series of young men with fine mental equipment and the courage of bush-rangers." He had met Michael Collins and Arthur Griffith at the studio of Sir John Lavery, who was doing their portraits for presentation to Dublin, and had been impressed with both men. He expected that the Sinn Fein government, in such hands, would be "a very pleasant government to live under."

For the Abbey Theatre the tensions of 1918 to 1921 had been disastrous, with audiences dwindling and finally disappearing. In Dublin the curfew had been first set at midnight, then advanced to ten, nine, and eight. Men and women had no thought of an evening in the theatre, but wished only to "scuttle home," as Lennox Robinson put it,[87] from their day's work to avoid being caught up in one or another ambush. But prospects had turned upward again by June of 1921 with the coming of a truce with England. "Dublin was full of excitements every day," Lady Gregory wrote Quinn at the end of January in the new year:

> One evening as I came to the Theatre the streets were crowded, all looking at some passing lorries. I asked what was going on. "It's the Tans going!" And indeed they will leave a black name forever—but the crowd behaved very well, didn't cheer or boo, just kept up a sort of purr of delight!   [*January 29, 1922.*]

The treaty was accepted by a narrow margin in the Dail on the last day of 1921. Lennox Robinson telegraphed the news to Lady Gregory at Coole Park, and the little boy who bicycled out from Gort with the message shouted it out to the people along the roads, who cheered. At Coole Park gates he called out, " 'This is the first message I ever was sent, and I've brought the best message ever was brought!' "—and fell off his bicycle.[88] Visiting Bernard Shaw in England, Lady Gregory asked him if he would come back at last to a free Ireland, and he answered: "No, he would be looked on as the common enemy." When she suggested that he might "bring the two parties together," he said, " 'No, I find as I grow older I am a little fonder of England, just as Napoleon came to like France better than Corsica when he had conquered it; one always loves a conquered country!' "[89] But if Ireland had conquered England she had not conquered herself. The De Valera nationalists issued their manifesto repudiating the Treaty and shouted a new battle cry, "The Treaty or the Republic!" Now the Troubles took the form of civil war, "Free Staters" against "Republicans"; Irishmen turned their guns away from the English and upon each other.

In Quinn's local professional life, also, the year ended as it began, in a state of crisis. In the winter he lost one of the closest of his friends, James Huneker. Huneker died in the evening of February 9, 1921, and Quinn was informed by telephone an hour after the event. He wrote next day to Meredith Janvier of Baltimore, a friend of his and Huneker's:

> It was a tremendous shock. I loved him. We wrote to each other constantly and saw each other as much as we could. I am glad to think now that he knew that I loved him and that we wrote to each other in the most affectionate way. He is a victim of the machine, of devotion to his job. . . . I shall miss him more than I can say.

As always when death struck near him Quinn was not only saddened but offended and made angry by the approach of the specter. Losing Huneker was bad enough; almost worse were Quinn's cares with the widow. He did not mind having to settle the affairs of Huneker's rather pitiful estate, but he could not bear Mrs. Huneker's habit of coming to his office and sitting weeping in her widow's weeds, as she did through much of the winter and spring of 1921. From the point of vantage of that situation and the general trials among which it was set, and later of the mess he found in his office on his return from abroad, his six weeks in France seemed an impossible idyll. Now the autumn of 1921 turned into a time of "sleepless nights and days of worry" in a matter that tried Quinn's whole professional credit and that of his firm.[80] His organization was counsel to the big International Fur Exchange of St. Louis, one of the casualties of the financial panic of 1921. While Quinn was abroad one of his partners, without cabling him and without consulting the other two partners, sold out several millions of dollars' worth of furs without due advertisement.[91] The banks involved in the financing of the company, about fifteen of them, came back upon the company with suits for "conversion"—more than twenty-five separate suits aggregating over a million dollars, indisputably due to negligent legal advice and practice to which Quinn's good name had been lent in his absence. It was this situation to which he returned, and he was frightened and enraged. He described it to Pound, to whom he wrote regularly of his professional affairs in surprising detail, as "the worst experience I have ever had in my life." [92] In twenty-five years of practice, Quinn told him, no client of his had ever before lost "one dollar" by following his advice. That record had been accomplished by his

> knowing the facts, and not by assuming, by talking, instead of assuming, by inquiring and cross-examining, instead of assuming; by seeing that the other fellow or the officer of the Company actually did the thing, instead of contenting myself with a languid letter of advice to that officer that the Company should do something. [*April 28, 1922.*]

Now a good many dollars were about to be inevitably lost through the carelessness and failure in co-operation among his partners. Throughout the winter and the spring of 1922 Quinn struggled to keep the figure as low as possible and to restore the good name of his firm.

1922

THE state of Quinn's psyche always registered in the state of his soma, and his labors and their attendant anxieties culminated in January 1922 in a condition he described as nearly "complete nervous collapse, hypertension and blood-pressure and insomnia and nerves." [1] A "rheumatism" in his throat brought on the most frightening of his symptoms, an inability to swallow, and he took to his bed for a week of complete rest on a liquid diet. This brought him round, particularly by giving him time to think through the fur crisis, to climb down from his plane of tension, to resolve to do his best and let the chips fall. Learning of his illness and his harried state, Ezra Pound wrote him on February 21 that whereas most men desisted from labor when they were buried, Quinn would probably lift the lid of the coffin impatiently and carry on, or install a telephone before death so that he could continue dictation to his office. By late April the fur affair was pretty well wound up, and Quinn was feeling better. He had completed the reorganization of the company, and he had got them $582,007 in claims against Lloyd's underwriters after months of negotiation. He estimated that the suits for conversion, for which his own "employees" were to blame, might cost the company a half-million; but he had stopped worrying about that, having already more than offset the loss by the insurance claims, "to which they were not morally entitled, and if the other side knew the facts, legally entitled. . . ." [2] He assessed his achievement: "I have made up by my genius as a negotiator for the negligence of my employees." [3] But his disgust at his partners' performance meant another general reorganization of his staff. One of his partners was already "in 'Main Street' " and another was "about to walk," and Quinn was again "looking for a real lawyer." All these matters Quinn set down for Pound in a long letter of April 28, several pages of which he endorsed: "Tear up this page."

So Quinn survived the winter, but John Butler Yeats came to the end of his long noble way in the early morning of February 3, 1922. He had continued bright and vigorous and happy and apparently well, though he had been troubled by a racking cough for more than a year. He came occasionally for midweek evenings at Quinn's, and more often for Sunday dinner and the afternoon, after which he would walk home or be sent home in a taxi, depending on the weather and his own whim. Mme. Jais had succeeded the Petitpas sisters as proprietor of 317 West 29th Street, and Quinn found her less lively, blunter, but affectionate and kind and more truly considerate of the old man's wants. She promised Quinn to keep Mr. Yeats's room warm and faithfully did so, and she tried to see that he was warmly clothed when he slipped out for his early breakfasts around the corner on 28th Street at his "cabman's shelter," as he liked to describe the little café. He still took his dinners regularly at 317 and often sat up till midnight talking with friends who came in for dinner or the evening. Occasionally there was dancing to the music of the gramophone, and he took a gay part and picked up the new dances with ease.

About the twentieth of January Mrs. Foster, a frequent caller, wrapped him up and took him in a car to a dinner of the Poetry Society. A few days later at the MacDowell Club he was one of ten poets including Amy Lowell, "all of them quite as illustrious as myself," [4] who read from their own works. He read his poem "Autumn," beginning "Great lady of the dark'ning skies," but forgot to give the title, and he wondered what the company had made of his imagery. On January 24 Quinn telephoned Mrs. Foster to ask her to look in to make sure the old man was all right. She found him out but took the chance to go through his chest of drawers and ascertain that he needed socks, handkerchiefs, and underclothing. She and Quinn arranged to take him shopping on the twenty-seventh, combining with that errand a visit to the Kelekian Collection at the American Art Galleries where it was about to go

on sale. Having business at the galleries Quinn went on ahead and
sent Mrs. Foster for Mr. Yeats in the car. As was his habit on such
occasions Quinn rented a Packard touring car and driver from the
Bradley Packard agency at 210 West 43rd Street. It was a bright,
cold winter day, and Mrs. Foster was again careful to wrap Mr.
Yeats warmly. When they found Quinn dressed in a big fur coat
Mr. Yeats said he looked like a United States Senator. They inspected the Courbets, the Cézannes, the Corots, the Turners, and
other paintings. When Quinn admired a Lautrec self portrait J. B.
Yeats said it looked to him like the face of a man who should have
been guillotined. But he warmly praised, when his attention was
called to it, Seurat's formidable pouter-pigeon woman, *La Poudreuse*, which Quinn had determined to buy in the auction. They
joined in mocking a Degas pastel, a large female nude seen from
behind—" 'The washer-woman exposed,' " Mr. Yeats called it. He
seemed to be enjoying the pictures and the animation of the
crowded gallery, but Quinn noticed that he looked tired and
coughed distressingly. Divining that he enjoyed being alone with
Mrs. Foster, Quinn left them bundled in the big car for the drive
up Fifth Avenue. They shopped and had lunch and drove on to
Petitpas' (as the house was still called) for the balance of the afternoon. " 'It's such a pleasant thing to see the Avenue from the inside of a warm, comfortable car,' " he said to Mrs. Foster. " 'Quinn's
always so thoughtful.' " * Quinn did not learn until after his death
that he had kept silent about the fact that he had already seen the
Kelekian pictures, wishing not to spoil his host's pleasure in doing a
kindness. It had been, in fact, a day of general kindness that was
good to look back on a few days later when the old painter was
fatally ill.

At about eight in the evening of Wednesday, February 1, Mrs.
Foster telephoned to say that Mme. Jais had just called: Mr. Yeats
was very ill. Quinn summoned a car, picked up Mrs. Foster and
Dr. David Likely, and reached Petitpas' within the half-hour. There
they found Mr. Yeats sitting transfixed with pain on the side of his
bed, attended by Mme. Jais, her daughter and her daughter's

* Quinn, "Notes on John Butler Yeats," sent to W. B. Yeats, May 1922.
Most of my account of J. B. Yeats's final illness is based on this document of
51 pages.

friend, both student nurses, and another doctor. After injections of morphine and camphor he was sufficiently eased to lie back on his bed, propped up with pillows. Dr. Likely found edema of his lungs, caused by general weakness of the heart, and he feared that Mr. Yeats might last only a few hours. About midnight he fell into a short sleep and awoke free from pain. He said he "had gone to sleep in hell and waked up in heaven." When he saw Quinn he said: " 'Ah, Quinn, you are here? I'm glad to see you.' " He spoke of the unfinished self-portrait leaning against the wall. Mme. Jais resented the suggestion that he be "taken from her" to a hospital. Quinn succeeded in getting Mrs. Agda Lindstrand, the Swedish woman who had given him massages after his operation in 1918, to come for the night, and she and Mme. Jais sat up throughout the night. Quinn took his own party home at about one in the morning.

When he arrived the following morning, Thursday, he found Mrs. Foster already on hand. Mr. Yeats seemed comfortable and cheerful, drank tea, read the morning headlines, and asked whether he had had any letters from his family in Ireland. The portrait still leaned against the wall, and an unfinished drawing of himself occupied the easel in the middle of the room. If she would return tomorrow, he told Mrs. Foster, he would be able to "go on with her drawing." He expected to be up and about in a few days. During Quinn's visit of two hours Mr. Yeats talked with his usual wit and liveliness, chatted of art-student days with Samuel Butler in London, and remarked that seeing Laszlo's portraits on exhibition at Knoedler's had enabled him to return to his own portraiture with comparative satisfaction. From the morning paper Mrs. Foster read out the list of buyers and prices at the Kelekian sale at the Hotel Plaza. He was pleased that the big Cézanne still life had fetched $21,000 and that the Van Gogh self portrait had gone to the Detroit Museum, and amused that the fleshy Degas "Washerwoman" nude was going to the Brooklyn Museum " 'for the art education and enlightenment of high-school boys and girls.' " Mrs. Foster stayed on throughout the day, leaving only for dinner. Dr. Likely called twice in the morning and again in the evening. Quinn had cabled to the Yeats children in Ireland that their father was gravely ill before returning to the sickroom in the evening with

Mrs. Foster. They stayed on, chatting comfortably with the patient, and left him asleep, propped up on pillows, at eleven o'clock. Quinn described the final scene he saw:

> His room was very comfortable and there was no noise, not one jarring note, and only smiles on his face and on the faces of those who talked to him and listened to him. His complexion was clear, his eyes bright, and he was very cheerful and entirely without pain. One did not notice the dust on the books or the dingy wallpaper or the old and worn sofa. Cheerfulness and brightness and light seemed to fill the room and he was the center of it. He dominated the scene. He permeated the room. He was as brilliant as I ever saw him. I had seen him when he looked tired. But then he seemed very noble and a great person. The last words I heard from him . . . were in his high, musical voice: "Well, I'm glad you came. Come again and in a day or two I'll be up. Good-bye, Quinn! Good-bye!" And that was the last time I saw him or heard his voice. As we talked with him and smiled with him that last day I was struck by the fact that there was no decrepitude in him, that his body was fine and straight and slim, with none of the coarseness or feebleness or repulsiveness of old age.

Before breakfast on Friday morning Quinn's man Paul told him that Mrs. Foster had called from Petitpas' to say that Mr. Yeats had " 'taken a bad turn.' " As Quinn was about to telephone to inquire Paul amended his message: Mr. Yeats was dead; they had not wished to shock him with the blunt news. He had died quite easily just before seven in the morning. "He made a good exit," Quinn phrased the final event more succinctly. "Without any last or long good-bys to anyone he sank into his dream."

Quinn went at once to the house but remained downstairs all morning, keeping his distance from the body and the furniture of death: "I did not see him again, for I wanted to remember him and I do remember him as was in life." Dr. Albert Shaw, Mrs. Foster's superior editor on the *Review of Reviews*, sent white Killarney roses and lilies of the valley, and called on Saturday and asked permission to see Mr. Yeats's body. He had evidently come prepared, for when he returned downstairs he pronounced Browning's line from "A Grammarian's Funeral,": " 'Here lies our master, gracious, calm and dead.' " (So Shaw, or Quinn, misquoted the line: "This is our master, famous, calm and dead. . . .") Quinn, F. J. Gregg, and Mrs. Foster planned the details of the funeral and prepared the newspaper announcements. Many old friends of the painter and talker called on Friday and Saturday at the house to which he had given an identity. Mme. Jais and Mrs. Lindstrand sat up both nights with the body, and Mary Colum joined them on Saturday night. That night a death mask was taken by the sculptor Edmund J. Quinn. On the day of death, February 3, John Quinn sent a long cable to Lily and Lollie Yeats in Dundrum:

> Regret your father passed away this morning seven o'clock. He had good day yesterday, free from pain, and was cheerful. Talked last evening cheerfully. I left him sleeping at eleven o'clock last night, but felt end was near. He slept well during remainder of night, waking at intervals. The end came in sleep without pain or struggle. After conference please cable desires about burial. If resting place to be Ireland, temporary vault can be arranged here until spring. Everything was done for his comfort and peace of mind and he had best possible medical attention.

On the afternoon of Sunday, February 5, Mr. Yeats's friends gathered at Petitpas' and followed his body to the Episcopal Church of the Holy Apostles, just a block away at 28th Street and Ninth Avenue. After the service the body was carried to a temporary vault in Woodlawn Cemetery, followed by cars containing Mrs. Foster, Mme. Jais, John and Dolly Sloan, Padraic and Mary Colum, Ernest Boyd, Gregg, Quinn, and others. The vault was covered with flowers against "the dull red sun of a brilliant winter day." Quinn thought of the "vigorous, brilliant, manly man" that John Butler Yeats had been, and of the unfinished portrait that seemed to say: " 'Here I am. How do you do? Let us get on with our talk.' " His thought was all of the happiness, the energy, the usefulness of the life. All of this, and much more, he set down in a document of fifty-one pages he dictated and sent to the surviving Yeatses in May 1922.

The thing he had foreseen and dreaded for years, Mr. Yeats's death "on his hands" in New York, had at last arrived. His only consolation he phrased in a letter to Pound on February 7: "Thank God, there is no Mrs. Yeats to come down to the office in black." Now he and Mrs. Foster spent hours at Petitpas' sorting out the debris of the old man's busy loneliness there, throwing out the trash and sorting books, papers, and pictures for shipment back to Ireland. They found many letters from his children which he had carried about in his pocket until they were reduced to pulp. Most of the Pilgrim Father's papers were sent to his favorite Lily, the family's informal archivist. The much-mooted self portrait finally came to rest in W. B. Yeats's new house in Merrion Square in Dublin. Though it had been meant for himself, Quinn felt that it was more properly a family memorial. He put a peremptory stop to what he felt was a ghoulish plan to send on a bronze cast of Edmund Quinn's death mask.

From Ireland the surviving generation wrote their gratitude to Quinn and Mrs. Foster for their affectionate care of their father during fourteen years in New York. "In the end it happened as you feared," Jack Yeats wrote Quinn of his father's death "in exile." [5] He spoke of his father's regard for Quinn, repeatedly expressed in letters home, and went on to place his father in the spectrum of his own succinct aesthetics: "Like most fine talkers, I think he had a simple nature which flowed on. Talking is not such an usurpation as writing, which becomes mortised into a man's soul. Truthful painting does nothing but reveal." When Lollie Yeats wrote from Dublin on February 15 letters from her father were still appearing, though Quinn's cables and death itself had intervened. "We know that every possible thing was done for him that skill and devotion could do," she wrote. "We know this *because it was you* who took control." Lily had been ailing for months with what was wrongly diagnosed as tuberculosis, and she was unable to write until August 13. Then she spoke of the closeness and simplicity of her friendship with her father: "We could talk together for hours and could be silent together for hours." On the wall at the head of her bed she kept a framed and enlarged snapshot of her father standing with Quinn and his horse.

By this time J. B. Yeats's body had been removed to its permanent grave in Chestertown, New York, in the Adirondack foothills. Quinn sent photographs of the area, and Lily Yeats wrote: "Chestertown looks quiet and full of character and would have interested him in life." [6] She thanked Quinn for stopping the sending of the death mask, in doing which he had acted on the basis of his own feeling: ". . . a death mask is a thing that I should not want to have around." [7] It was Mrs. Foster who had proposed the burial in her family's plot in Chestertown Cemetery, and Mr. Yeats's children had acquiesced with thanks. In late July Quinn arranged for the body to be taken from the vault in Woodlawn and sent north by train. Mrs. Foster, who had been recuperating from illness at her home in Schenectady, joined the train at Saratoga, and she, the local undertaker, and two grave diggers formed the whole of the final burial party. Quinn quoted to W. B. Yeats from Mrs. Foster's letter of July 29 describing the scene: " 'When we reached the pine grove it was noon, a sunny day, with blue skies and white rolling clouds. Service was blurred by the wind in the needles and pierced with bird calls.' " [8] The grave was marked with a simple shaft of rough-hewn Adirondack granite.

In sending his first thanks in February W. B. Yeats had also written of a plan to publish at his sisters' Cuala Press a further small volume of his father's letters along with the fragment of autobiography that Quinn had elicited with such difficulty. Quinn would have liked to see a more massive and formal treatment of the letters, which he judged at least as worthy of respect as the letters of Henry James or Edward Dowden, and he urged that they be collected and carefully transcribed and a selection published in at least one large volume. When Yeats wrote on June 5 he and his wife and two children were fully instated in Thoor Ballylee for the first time, and he found it a piercing pleasure "to live in a place where George makes at every moment a fourteenth century picture." His thoughts and his letters were full of the writing of memoirs—his father's, his own, Lady Gregory's. He had just completed *The Trembling of the Veil*, the second volume of his *Autobiographies*, and had sent it off to be published by Werner Laurie, dedicated to John Quinn with the inscription "To John Quinn my friend and helper and friend and helper of certain people mentioned in this book." "If you violently object you must cable," he wrote Quinn on June 5, "for Laurie is in a devil of a hurry." Lady Gregory had been reading him what she had composed of her own memoirs, and had begun to pick up his criticisms and install them in her text "like a Greek chorus." [9] The objective manner of her book seemed to him the reverse of his own dream-crossed impressionism. He was pleased that the autobiographical record of the twentieth century in Ireland was thickening: "Hyde, Russell, Lady Gregory, my father, myself, will all be vivid to young Irish students a generation hence because of the memoirs we are writing now." Of his own part of the new generation he reported that "your godson" now had eight teeth and that Anne was all right aside from her "theology": in saying the Lord's Prayer she tended to interpolate such phrases as " 'Father not in heaven—father in the study,' " and to render "Kingdom," with which she had difficulty, as " 'Thine is the Kitten, the Power, and the Glorly' "; later, noting the advancing age of the animal, as " 'Thine is the Cat, the Power, and the Glorly.' " [10]

Quinn was pleased with the honor of Yeats's dedication, so handsomely phrased, as he had been pleased the year before with Douglas Hyde's dedication to him of his volume of rhymed proverbs, *Connacht Half-Ranns*. In company with Russell's dedication of *Imaginations and Reveries*, these meant that he had been gracefully saluted by three of the masters of the modern movement in Ireland. Yeats's first thought in fact had been to present the manuscript of his volume to Quinn. It was Lady Gregory who suggested the dedication instead: manuscripts were things that a man could buy. "You see," she exlpained to Quinn on July 2, "I am one of those you have helped, mentioned in the dedication, and so I think I had a right to say a word as to what I thought would do you most honour." When she wrote in January 1922 it had been in part to thank Quinn for his annual Christmas apples, which had reminded her of her old saying, " 'John Quinn encompasses.' " [11] Sending her greetings on December 10 for the new Christmas she looked back on another year of "horrors" in Ireland. But her own lonely work had gone on, and she had just read the first draft of her memoirs, 262,000 words, according to the typist's bill.

Partisan feelings in the internecine guerrilla warfare of the year were hot enough to cause a temporary estrangement between Jack Yeats, a De Valera "Republican" adherent, and W. B. Yeats, now a Free State Senator. Through newspaper reports and the letters of his friends Quinn followed the violent birth of the new Ireland with keen interest and with mixed exasperation and optimism. "I would not shed the blood of a single Irish wolf-hound for the difference between a republic and a free state," he wrote to Douglas Hyde on July 15. But there were many who were willing to shed human blood on the issue. Quinn still mistrusted De Valera as a vain demagogue, and he blamed the adoring Irish in America for turning his head. To Hyde he described the Republican leader as "a sinister and an evil figure and a bad man." [12] To Lady Gregory he wrote more equably: "I don't give up about Ireland. The Irish are great individualists, and vanity is at the bottom of much of their wildness and foolishness." [13] With the W. B. Yeatses at Thoor Ballylee and Lady Gregory at Coole Park, Quinn watched uneasily for news of fighting around Gort. Yeats reported that conditions were harmless if not wholly peaceful: "There was what seemed a raid at Coole; men came and shouted at night and demanded to be let in, and then went away either because the moon came out or because they only meant to threaten," he wrote on June 5. Yet when they left to occupy their new house at 82 Merrion Square in Dublin at the end of September, they left two feet of water in the ground-floor dining room in the tower; the Republicans had blown up the bridge carrying the road over the river at the base of the tower, damming the stream and causing the flood. Yeats was given time to remove the children to an upper room while the men laid the mine.[14]

George Russell was happy that Yeats was settling more or less firmly in Ireland again, after so many years spent mainly in London and Oxford. On August 18 he wrote Quinn in anticipation: "Dublin will be more interesting with him there. He has lived too much out of Ireland." He found the Yeats of recent years a bit formidable, "a very distinguished kind of person," and one whose friendliness had taken on a somewhat hortatory stance: "For years he talks when he meets me as if he were lecturing a public meeting about art or literature, and I am bored." But he had heard that George was "humanizing" her husband, and he hoped that he and his old friend might now be able to recover some of the easy intimacy of their youthful years.

Æ too had finished a new book, *The Interpreters,* and once again the manuscript went to Quinn. In his letter of August 18 Æ wrote at length on the troubled state of Irish politics, and again on October 19, asking Quinn to suggest an American financial expert accustomed to think in the large terms needed for the forthcoming discussions of money matters with Great Britain. He had been fearing that the near-anarchy in Ireland would force the closing of the *Irish Homestead,* which he had served as editor so long, so brilliantly and unselfishly. But a single appeal for funds to the paper's readers had brought in enough money to assure it continued life. The horrid alternative had been the lecture tour in America which Russell had fended off for years: ". . . but it seems people will pay large sums rather than let me go." [15]

   Russell's friend and helper Susan Mitchell, still counted the wittiest woman in Dublin, wrote gravely of the *Homestead's* straits in August: ". . . I cannot think that Æ's brilliant, faithful work cannot endure." [16] She thanked Quinn for a bit of free American legal work he had performed for her and her sister, and complimented him on the fullness and cogency of his letters: "No one writes to me so carefully except one woman correspondent, and she wants to save my soul." Then she went on stoutly to rebut some of Quinn's emphatic political dogmatizing. To his denunciation of De Valera as " 'politically and theologically illegitimate' " she replied that we all sprang originally from cross-breeding, and that she loved Jews and thought she would love Negroes, despite the "startling" contrast of teeth and complexion—although she had never met any to test her faith. Listening to the pointed, easy chat of such letters it is important to remember that Quinn could not have seen her or others like her for more than a dozen years, in his last quick trip to Dublin in 1909, or more probably in 1904, when he paid his last systematic visit. Such letters testify to a liking and trust established in a powerful early impression and sustained in correspondence and in public evidences of an earned reputation and regard.

   On February 3, 1922, James Joyce cabled from Paris with ultimate succinctness: "Ulysses published. Thanks." Quinn cabled back next day: "Congratulations publication Ulysses. Best wishes. Writing soon." Quinn did not miss the symmetry of the book's appearance on the day of John Butler Yeats's death in New York, and he commented on the phenomenon in the amiable portion of a letter to Joyce's brave fragile publisher, Sylvia Beach, on February 4:

And so the mystic symbol appears, for on the day that Mr. Yeats died, aged eighty-three, the old generation passing away, the birth of "Ulysses," the child of the new age, was announced by cable from Joyce. I am sure that the old man would have appreciated the far-wandering Ulysses if he had only lived to read it. How he would have enjoyed it! Chuckled over it! Read out from it and laughed over it!

Now Quinn was entertained by the consequences of the strategy, which he sometimes attributed to Pound and sometimes to himself, of booming *Ulysses* as "a European event," not an Irish event, denying its merely parochial provenance and denying the Irish patriots a chance to assail it, as they had assailed *The Playboy of the Western World*, as a "libel" upon Ireland. He noted that Ernest Boyd, Padraic Colum, and Shane Leslie were rushing into print to reclaim Joyce from Europe, for Ireland. He sought judgments of the novel from all his Irish friends.

Æ found *Ulysses* "an intellectual adventure" but not a wholly congenial one: "I see the ability and mastery while not liking the mood." [17] Joyce himself he thought unmistakably "very Irish." As usual he set the particular in the general context:

> The Irish genius is coming out of its seclusion and Yeats, Synge, Moore, Shaw, Joyce and others are forerunners. The Irish imagination is virgin soil and virgin soil is immensely productive when cultivated. We are devotees of convention in normal circumstances and when we break away we outrage convention.

"He is more than Huysmans was: an eye, an etcher with an eye," Quinn argued; [18] and he declared that Joyce had invented a style and "carried it, as Nietzsche would put it, beyond good and evil." [19] Lady Gregory recalled that she had last seen Joyce in Ireland when he had brought his little boy, now grown up, to call on her. She was noncommittal about *Ulysses*. She had thought *A Portrait of the Artist* "extraordinarily good"; but best of all she liked the lovely traditionary lyrics of *Chamber Music*. James Stephens had not read *Ulysses* and showed little inclination to do so: "It is too expensive to buy, and too difficult to borrow, and too long to read, and, from what I have heard about it, altogether too difficult to talk about." [20] From that innocent point of vantage, he saw Joyce as a case of arrested artistic development: ". . . incapable of any current impression . . . and the man that he is at forty-five or six is only and merely the boy that he was at nineteen and twenty-five." He too valued *Chamber Music* highest in Joyce's work. Quinn's dense ten-page letter about *Ulysses* and its "Three Trials" on June 21 failed to persuade Shane Leslie, who was reviewing the novel for the *Dublin Review*. Leslie wrote back on July 12: ". . . as long as I hold the Catholic symbols I wince at studied disrespect and perversion of sacred things. It is for that reason that I have gone for him furiously. . . ."

On the morning of February 4 while he was struggling with the details of Mr. Yeats's funeral Quinn received Sylvia Beach's letter inquiring about the state of the American copyright on *Ulysses*, and he sent off an angry reply at once. He had already told Joyce several times, he reminded her, that publication in the *Little Review* was sufficient to secure the copyright. The appearance of a detailed advertisement for the novel in the last issue of the magazine, he warned her, would assure that Sumner would have alerted customs officials to watch for shipments of the book; therefore she was to wrap his personal fourteen copies, the number to which he had increased his order, and hold them subject to his instructions. He enclosed his draft for $291.04 to cover the cost of five copies at 350 francs, three at 250, and six at 150; and he took leave bluntly: "If Joyce wants to write to me at any time it is open to him to do so and not through you. You will not misunderstand my wanting to write frankly and finally, especially finally, about this matter." [21] Miss Beach refused to be insulted. She wrote back on February 21: "I know that no matter how testy you like to seem, you are the kindest man alive." She had apparently accepted Pound's reading of his character. But at Quinn's complaints of his trials she flared up with a *mot* of her own: "While you were helping an old man to die, I was helping a young man to live." Quinn felt the force of that, but argued (mistakenly) that she was equally helping herself: [22] he had formed the impression that she was sharing equally in the profits of the book, in spite of the fact that she had written him that money had begun to come in and that after the printer was paid "Joyce will have the rest." *

* Sylvia Beach to Quinn, February 21, 1922. Ellmann says that Joyce's royalty was set at the "astonishing" rate of 66 per cent of the net profits. *James Joyce*, p. 520.

In any case Quinn still wished well to the book and to its author. On March 27 he wrote Miss Beach to report that copies of *Ulysses* were circulating in New York for as high as $50; he wanted her and Joyce to know this in setting their price on copies still unsold. He was still certain the book would be confiscated as soon as Sumner caught on to its presence. When he wrote to Joyce on April 4 he had just seen his first copy of *Ulysses* at Drake's, the book agent's, and thought it beautifully printed. Of Miss Beach's temerity he remarked: "She has tackled, with the audacity, if not the ignorance of amateurs, a really tough job. That is the job of beating the United States Federal and State laws." Drake had heard that an order had already been issued to stop importation of the novel. Now that the book was a book, complete, Quinn urged Joyce to send on to him what remained of the manuscript: "I will review then what I paid you on account of the MS., and write you whether or not I think there is anything further due you on account of the balance of the MS." [23]

With *Ulysses* a success of scandal and of esteem in Europe there was again talk of an American edition. Pound reported on February 21 that Horace Liveright had already offered in Paris to bring out the book in the United States "and hand over 1000 bones to J.J." He thought Liveright had the look of "a pearl among publishers"— one who actually paid.[24] In his letter of April 4 to Joyce Quinn said that he had recently had a letter from Liveright about the idea of an American edition. He promised to talk it over with him, but he was not optimistic. He reminded Joyce again that both Huebsch and Liveright had already refused to print an "undraped" *Ulysses*, that Joyce would not drape it, and that the undraped edition was no more publishable in America than before its European success— probably less so. He stated the case unequivocally once more on July 27 to Harriet Shaw Weaver, who was bringing out the Egoist Press edition (quickly suppressed) in England: "*Ulysses*, unexpurgated, unchanged, cannot be published in the United States without the certainty of prosecution and conviction, either by Huebsch or by Knopf or by Liveright or by Roth * or by any other publisher." In May Quinn advised Joyce against taking *A*

* Samuel Roth, who did in fact pirate much of *Ulysses* serially in the United States in his magazine *Two Worlds Monthly*.

Portrait of the Artist away from Huebsch and giving it to Liveright for a "Modern Library" edition, as had been proposed; he did not like the look of those cheap books and did not want to see Joyce's novel in that dress. At the same time he suggested to Joyce that he ought to do a "key" to *Ulysses,* clarifying structure and arcane references, and market that in a small edition.[25] In June he finally ordered Sylvia Beach to deliver his fourteen copies of the novel to Charles Pottier in Paris, who regularly attended to storage, packing, and shipment of works of art for him, and on August 25 they reached him in New York in good condition along with a consignment of paintings. On August 12 Mitchell Kennerley, just back from a trip abroad, wrote Quinn that he had received ten copies of *Ulysses* direct from Sylvia Beach in London, and that the last copy sold in London brought £20, with no more offered.

Alongside Joyce's masterpiece one of the age's poetic masterworks was accomplishing its birth. After studying and copiously revising the manuscript of *The Waste Land* Pound wrote to Eliot on Christmas Eve of 1921: "Complimenti, you bitch. I am wracked by the seven jealousies. . . ."[26] Then, characteristically, he conceived his touching "Bel Esprit" scheme to sell shares in the rival poet's future by collecting a fund to free him from his demanding duties in Lloyd's Bank. He sent a printed circular to likely friends in March and printed an appeal in the *New Age* for March 30, 1922. He was seeking thirty persons willing to invest ten pounds a year to guarantee Eliot a subsidy of £300 for long enough to establish himself as an artist. Of course the whole campaign had been organized without Eliot's knowledge. Pound wrote Jeanne Robert Foster on March 12 to express his confidence that the "ever resolute JQ" would commit himself to two shares. Quinn was game for a good deal more than that. The public appeal in the *New Age,* he wrote Pound on April 28: "took my breath away," and he wished the whole thing had been conducted privately. But he offered to take six shares, or seven on one condition: "I am perfectly willing to bind myself for $300 a year for five years"; and if Liveright were excluded he would make that $350. He also offered to try to sell the scheme to other donors in America, though he reminded Pound that the available evidence of Eliot's genius was a bit skimpy: he could only show the 1920 *Poems* and *The Sacred*

Wood. On June 20 Pound reported that he and Richard Aldington, both charter subscribers themselves along with May Sinclair, had promises for about half the first year's fund, though some of it was from "shaky sources." Quinn's first $300 was in, in cash. On July 4 Pound counted twenty-one of the requisite thirty donors. To Quinn's estimate that Eliot "ought to be self-supporting in five years" he responded with a bitter dithyramb on the life in art: "Its all bloody well saying *ought*." Eliot "ought" to be able to support himself in five years but it was highly unlikely that he would be. Pound remembered watching W. B. Yeats, aged forty-seven, taking out of the bank the last £5 of a sum he had got from Mrs. Pat Campbell for writing a play which he did not finish until five years later. Pound himself, he noted, a far more copious and easy producer than Eliot, had never earned £300 in a year. Such bare solvency as he himself had managed to achieve, he went on, was due in large part to the fact that his wife had an income of £50 a year, to which her family regularly added another £150. Pound cursed the publishers who "OUGHT to spot up" but never did. Horace Liveright, whom Quinn liked to scorn, was unique among them for innocently assuming that writers were worthy of their hire.

In the winter of 1921–2 Eliot had suffered a nervous collapse of such severity that he had been forced to take a leave of absence from the bank and enter a sanitarium in Lausanne. There, in the covert setting of the opening lines of *The Waste Land*, he had managed to complete the long poem that had been on his mind for more than a year, which he then submitted to Ezra Pound's hard critical gaze. Eliot explained the case to Quinn in a letter of June 25, 1922:

> I have written, mostly when I was at Lausanne for treatment last winter, a long poem of about 450 words [lines], which, with notes that I am adding, will make a book of 30 or 40 pages. I think it is the best I have ever done, and Pound thinks so too. Pound introduced me to Liveright in Paris, and Liveright made me the offer of 15% royalty and $150 in advance.

As he was honor-bound to do, he had offered Knopf the first refusal of the book, but Knopf said it came too late for inclusion in his autumn list. Liveright had agreed to use it in his own autumn list. But Eliot was displeased with the vagueness of the contract he had received from Liveright, and he asked Quinn to negotiate a contract such as that he had arranged with Knopf for the 1920 *Poems*. He gave Quinn full authority to settle all details. In view of the mysteries later to collect about manuscript versions of the poem it is interesting to note that Eliot now promised Quinn a preliminary copy: "I am sending you as quickly as possible a copy of the poem merely for your own interest, and I shall send you later the complete typescript with the notes, in the form to be handed to the publisher." [27]

From the correspondence it appears that Eliot did send one copy and perhaps two copies of the poem to Quinn in advance of the original Eliot-Pound manuscript which has become, even in its buried state (it has been lost to view ever since it entered Quinn's possession in 1922), a *locus classicus* of modern genius at work in composition and emendation. Eliot wrote on July 19:

> As it is now so late I am enclosing the typescript to hand to him [Liveright] when the contract is complete. . . . I had wished to type it out fair, but I did not wish to delay it any longer. This will do for him to get on with, and I shall rush forward the notes to go at the end. I only hope the printers are not allowed to bitch the punctuation and the spacing, as that is very important for the sense.

In the same letter Eliot proposed to make Quinn a gift of the manuscript in its crucial form: ". . . I should like to present you the MSS. of the Waste Land, if you would like to have it—when I say MSS. I mean that it is partly MSS. and partly typescript, with Ezra's and my alterations scrawled all over it." Whereas here it sounds at least possible that what Eliot "enclosed" with his letter of July 19 was the Ur-*Waste Land*, it comes clear in later letters that this was not the case: he now sent another, not-fair, copy. What is not clear is whether he had sent yet another preliminary copy between his letters of June 25 and July 19. For when Quinn wrote Eliot on July 28 he made it clear that he had received a typescript of the poem at least as early as the preceding day: he spoke of reading "the poems" at midnight of July 27 after a hard day, and of ordering "one of the careful stenographers" in his

office to make a copy of the poem for Liveright from the typescript. It is improbable, though not impossible, that a copy mailed
in London on July 19 would reach Quinn in New York on July
27; that improbability, along with Eliot's promise on June 25 to
send a copy "as quickly as possible," suggests that he had received
a copy prior to that sent on July 19. The point is worth laboring
because it affirms that Quinn possessed at least one copy of *The
Waste Land* aside from the famous Eliot-Pound original, and because it probably explains the mysterious typescript, differing in
interesting ways from published versions, which Quinn sent to Mrs.
Foster on July 31, 1922, and which she eventually, in 1961, gave to
the Houghton Library at Harvard. It seems probable that that
typescript was a copy made from the typescript or typescripts
sent forward by Eliot between June 25 and July 19 so that Quinn
could give Liveright something "to get on with."

In his letter of July 28 Quinn announced that the contract for
book publication of the poem with Boni & Liveright had been
completed. He admired the poem himself but took a dim view of
its public prospects:

> "Waste Land" is one of the best things you have done, though I
> imagine that Liveright may be a little disappointed at it, but I
> think he will go through with it. It is for the elect or the remnant
> or the select few or the superior guys, or any word that you may
> choose, for the small number of readers that it is certain to have.
> [*July 28, 1922.*]

He was afraid the text was too short, creating the same problem
as the *Prufrock* group had met with Knopf, and he wished Eliot
might go on and add "four or five more poems." His references to
the poem in the plural, as "the poems," suggest that he had not
grasped the unity of Eliot's text, the fact that it was one poem,
and complete, not capable of loose extensions. What he goes on to
say of the manuscript makes it clear that he had not yet seen the
original Eliot-Pound text:

> I shall be glad to have the MS. of "Waste Land" but I shan't let
> you "present it to me." When you finish the whole thing, poetry
> and prose [i.e. the poem and the accompanying notes], if you
> will send the MS. or the MSS. to me, I shall be glad to have it,

but you must agree to the condition that I send you a draft for what I think it is worth. I shall feel happier to do it that way.

Eliot's wish was to make a graceful return for Quinn's useful kindness, not to market a manuscript, and he wrote back on August 21:

... it will certainly not be any pleasure to me to sell it to you. I therefore hope you will accept it. But as I feel that you perhaps like some of my early poems best I should be glad, for example, to send you the manuscript of Prufrocks [sic] instead, and I hope you will let me do this.

He approved the Liveright contract warmly: "The contract seems to me as perfect as it is possible for a contract to be." He sent along the prospectus of "a quarterly review" he had been busy organizing: the majestic *Criterion* was about to see the light. Eliot also reported that he now had an offer from the *Dial* to print *The Waste Land*, and he was puzzled what to do about that, not wishing to ask Liveright to postpone his book publication.

During the month of August Quinn vacationed in the Adirondacks and "got the best month's rest that I have had in eight years." [28] Upon his return to the city he quickly collected to a head the various schemes to publish *The Waste Land* and reward its author, and he wrote of these matters to Eliot in an expansive mood on Thursday, September 7, in a letter of over eleven pages. His mood was so mellow that he even told Eliot that "You need never hesitate to write to me about a personal matter of this sort. I shall always try to squeeze in time for personal matters of that sort." On his return to the office on September 5 he had found a letter of August 31 from Gilbert Seldes, whom he identified as "a pleasant young chap," about the *Dial*'s wish, possibly conflicting with Liveright's, to publish the poem. Before Quinn got Seldes and Liveright together in his office on the seventh for discussions followed by luncheon with Quinn as host, the two men had met and already come to a loose agreement. The crux of the matter was not only the magazine's wish to publish the poem but also their wish to award to Eliot the annual *Dial* prize of $2,000 for service to letters in America; it was felt that the poem should appear in an American journal in advance of the award as one demonstrable validation of the award. Eliot's contract of July 29 with Liveright bound him to publish the book by November 1. Quinn and Seldes were able to persuade Liveright that publication of the poem in the *Dial*, followed by the announcement of the *Dial* prize award, would probably work to the advantage of his edition, with the date of that set a bit later. Details of an agreement were quickly settled. The *Dial* would publish the poem, without notes, as soon as possible; they would copyright the poem in Eliot's name, and would pay him for the poem at their standard rates for verse; they would announce that Boni & Liveright would soon publish the poem as a volume, with notes; they bound themselves to award the $2,000 prize to Eliot, and to announce it in advance of the book publication; they agreed also to buy 350 copies of the book when published; Liveright in turn agreed to delay his publication but to accomplish it by January 31, and to pay Eliot his $150 on publication and subsequent royalties as originally stipulated. The *Dial* purchase of 350 copies would virtually insure him against any possible loss.

All these conditions were set down in letters of agreement signed by Liveright and by Seldes as Managing Editor of the *Dial*, and Quinn sent copies on to Eliot. It seems an ingenious and admirable scheme, in which everybody got what he wanted and everybody profited, but particularly T. S. Eliot. Probably no poem of comparable length was ever more promptly, more variously, or more copiously rewarded. "So everything is all right," Quinn wrote with good reason, and "I think the matter is sewed up from all angles now." [29] He said that he would be writing to Pound shortly and would take the liberty of telling him in confidence of the *Dial* award, and he suggested that perhaps Eliot should do the same. *The Waste Land* in fact was first printed in the inaugural number of the *Criterion* in October 1922, which Eliot took care to withhold from America so as not to compete with its first publication there in the *Dial* in November 1922. The Boni & Liveright edition appeared on December 15, 1922. On September 21, after receiving Quinn's long letter of the seventh, Eliot wrote back in the terms of formal but feeling courtesy which made Quinn willing to serve him: "I am quite overwhelmed by your letter, by all that you have done for me, by the results that have been effected, and by your endless kindness. . . ." The keenest of all his pleasures in the affair, he said, lay in the pure sensation of disinterested kindness:

"the thought that there should be anybody in the world who would take such an immense amount of pains on my behalf." Grateful as he was for the honor and the cash of the *Dial* award, that part of the arrangement gave him his only misgiving. He felt that the prize should have gone to Pound, and that he himself should have been asked to wait until his friend's services to American letters had received the recognition they deserved.

After entering his name for three subscriptions to the *Criterion* Quinn again stated his position on the question of Eliot's manuscripts at some length:

> We won't quarrel about the MS. of The Waste Land, and the Notes. I'm sorry that you didn't agree to my suggestion. I'll accept it from you, not "for what I have lately done for you and in the past," but as a mark of friendship, but on this condition: That you will let me purchase of you the MS. of the Early Poems that you referred to. If you have the Prufrock only, then I'll purchase that. But if you have the MS. of the whole volume of your poems, including the Prufrock, I should *greatly value* that, and then I'll have two complete manuscripts of yours. If you leave to me the fixing of what the MS. of those poems would be worth, I would discuss the matter with one or two dealers in rare books and manuscripts and autograph letters and would be guided by their advice. If I had to choose between the MS. of The Waste Land and the Notes and the Prufrock MS. alone, I would choose The Waste Land MS. But I feel sure that you'll agree to my condition that I pay you for the MS. of the Early Poems. That meets your point and it gives me another MS. of yours, and each of us will have had his way and therefore to that extent will be happy.
>
> [*September 7, 1922.*]

In the midst of the general amiability it was growing clear that Quinn would receive an important dollop of manuscripts, and that the question of which were purchases and which were gifts was turning academic. In his answering letter of September 21 Eliot reaffirmed that as far as he was concerned the manuscript of *The Waste Land* would be a gift, and that the other group he was sending "must be valued at its actual market value and not at any value which it may (or may not) acquire in the course of time." The real value of the *Waste Land* manuscript, he judged, lay in its evidences of the work of Ezra Pound's expert obstetric hand—"worth preserving in its present form solely for the reason that it is the only evidence of the difference which his criticism has made to this poem." Pound had cut the poem severely and in Eliot's opinion immensely strengthened its impact. Among the passages excised was a long section in imitation of Pope; once a thing has been done perfectly, Pound said, imitators had better let it alone.[30] Quinn would be receiving the only copy of the suppressed portions, and Eliot trusted him to see to it that they never appeared in print. Eliot in fact was about to send Quinn everything of the kind he had: "I have gathered together all of the manuscript in existence."[31] He placed no great value upon the papers, especially as most of them were typescript "for which no manuscript, except scattered lines, ever existed." Included was a leather-bound notebook dating back to 1909 in which the poet had set down all his work of that period, and which contained drafts of poems subsequently published as well as of poems "unpublished and unpublishable."[32] Again he asked Quinn not to disturb their rest: "You will find a great many sets of verse which have never been printed and which I am sure you will agree never ought to be printed, and, in putting them in your hands, I beg you fervently to keep them to yourself and see that they never are printed."[33]

After he had seen the first issue of the *Criterion* Quinn wrote Eliot in praise of it on December 4: "It's a beautiful thing, beautifully printed and on good paper. That first number will be memorable. I hope you can keep it up." With a little further experience he found *The Waste Land* growing upon him. He had Mrs. Foster read it through to him a couple of mornings while he was shaving and thereafter he could, and on occasion did, recite it verbatim.[34] But he was full of scorn, expressed to both Yeats and Russell, of imitators of the new master, already appearing. "This country is full of imitators both in writing and in painting," he wrote Æ.[35] American painters had been aping Cézanne and Picasso, he said, and now the novelists were aping Joyce and the poets aping Eliot. "Eliotism is the fashion," he told Yeats,[36] grouping under that vague canopy even the poems of Wallace Stevens. He had dismissed Wallace Stevens's poems in the July *Dial* to Gilbert Seldes as "a joke," and assured Seldes that Stevens was "laughing in his sleeve" at them for publishing "such stuff."[37] In fact Stevens's group of six included some of the most striking and original short poems he would ever write: "Bantams in Pine-Woods," "The Ordinary Woman," "Frogs Eat Butterflies. Snakes Eat Frogs. Hogs Eat Snakes. Men Eat Hogs," "A High-Toned Old Christian Woman," "O, Florida, Venereal Soil," and "The Emperor of Ice-Cream."

Quinn's judgments were not always sound, but they were nearly always prompt and positive, the summary, overconfident pronouncements of a blunt man living in a terrible hurry. James Stephens wrote him at this time, "What with law, literature, painting and the criticizing of all these, you manage to get ten men's interest into and out of life, and one never knows at any moment in which of them you are to be sought." [38] In a year in which Quinn had stood near the birth-bed of two of the literary masterpieces of the half-century in English, it was hardly to be hoped that his collecting of art could show a like excellence; but in fact in 1922 Quinn sought and found a great deal of first-rate contemporary art, pretty certainly more than anyone else in America and perhaps as much as any private individual in the world. In proportion to available means he must have been the bravest and most energetic collector of his day. He knew his own temerity and valued himself upon it, though he was too good a business man to be wholly comfortable within it. Late in the winter of 1922 when Josephine Huneker was collecting her husband's letters for an edition she wished to bring out, Quinn gathered together for her 189 letters James Huneker had written him between 1903 and his death in 1921. When he sent them to her on March 3 he warned her that he would expect to review and possibly to edit any of those she chose to publish. By June she had selected twenty letters and Quinn took those back and scrutinized them. The only letter he altered significantly was one of ten years earlier in which Huneker had warned him against his extravagant hospitality to modern art. He struck out entirely Huneker's sentence: " 'You will unload some day with an appalling loss' "; and he altered the sentence: " 'You have 500 too many already,' " to read: "You have bought too many already with the purpose of helping artists." [39] Quinn did not wish to run the financial risk of the public appearance of such opinions, or to offer to Royal Cortissoz and other conservative critics such a handy stick to beat him with.

Lady Gregory, still laboring to recover Hugh Lane's pictures for

Ireland and dreaming of a future gallery of modern art with those as a nucleus, asked Quinn to list the artists who ideally should be represented there. It was an invitation to the kind of rather noisy fiats to which Quinn was too much given. He replied on July 17. Of the dead painters he preferred, in order, Cézanne, "the greatest painter of modern times"; Seurat, "the greatest draughtsman and colorist since Ingres"; and Henri Rousseau, "a naïve mind, a pure mind, an artistic saint, a man who has had an enormous influence upon the great living artists. . . ." Both Gauguin and Van Gogh he considered a cut below the other great dead. In the top rank of living artists he placed Picasso, Matisse, Derain, and Braque; in the second rank of the living, Rouault, "in his way a man of genius, a sort of French Blake," Dunoyer de Segonzac, Dufy, and Brancusi, "the Roumanian sculptor, half-god, half-faun, and a man of genius." In a letter of two weeks later to Æ Quinn went through the same stacking process with similar results, except that he included a third rank of living painters composed of Auguste Chabaud, Roger de la Fresnaye, Juan Gris, Jean Metzinger, Jacques Villon, and Marie Laurencin.[40]

Though one may be bored by the pseudo-critical terminology, and irritated by the whole bootless process of ordering genius hierarchically, one must see that he had shown an astonishingly interesting and accurate set of tastes for a preoccupied New York lawyer in 1922 with not much about him to afford standards of comparison. In the perspective of added time Quinn's judgments seem partly conventional, partly sophisticated, partly cranky, and generally sound. Doubtless he was already showing a certain amount of *post hoc* rationalization, some wishful justifications of decisions already made and money already invested. A great many objections, and compensations, spring to mind. The downgrading of Gauguin and Van Gogh seems gratuitous and wrong; but it is striking to have recognized the genius of Seurat and Rousseau. Derain and Segonzac may strike one as overvalued; but one is grateful and surprised to see Braque and Rouault justly valued. Is Seurat "a much greater artist than Renoir," as Quinn asserts to Russell? [41] One wants Renoir in the list of the great dead. What has happened in Quinn's lists to Redon, to Duchamp-Villon, to Toulouse-Lautrec, above all to Degas, the greatest of his blind spots? But of course in such letters as these to Russell and Lady Gregory he was not undertaking a systematic treatise on modern art, and it is wrong to hold him to any such standard.

Once again the most striking aspect of Quinn's pantheon is its virtual exclusion of everything not French. The English and Irish artists are all gone, and the Americans have not appeared. What is left is the School of Paris and its local ancestors. All the gods are French, or, as in the case of Picasso and Brancusi, essentially so. It is pretty certain, for example, that he omitted Gwen John from his lists because he could not consider her sufficiently French. Alongside his old sentimental affection for everything French, he had convinced himself that the central originality of modern art was a French creation, that the real "searching" and "exploration," since the time of Ingres, had been going on only in France. After fifteen years he was still angry at the Irish attack upon Synge as a "French decadent," and chronically sick of the standard American philistine view of the "decadence" of French artists. His own opposing rationale was rather weakly based on a burly assertion of the health and sanity of French art, demonstrable merely in the bodily vigor and good spirits of the artists themselves. With considerable wrenching of transitions, Quinn reverted to this idea in his letter to Russell on July 30. He came at the French, oddly, by way of himself, the Irish, the Americans, and the American Indians, in a line of thought set off by the death of John Butler Yeats, who stayed in his mind now as "a debonair man, buoyant and cheerful, with the sense of gaiety and love of life that the French have." This opened the way for his generalizations. "The French, it seems to me, often have a greater sense of happiness and a love of gaiety and amusement in small, simple things than we Irish have." Then he said a very queer and significant thing: "I say, 'we Irish,' for I have never felt that I was an American." But he developed the idea only farcically: there was no such thing as an American, "except the Indians, and they are being killed off fast." His French particulars were the roseate lingering impressions of his six weeks in Paris in the summer of 1921:

> Picasso, for example, struggles with his art, and is an art searcher and explorer, but he is most always happy. And Derain is a great giant of a man, a great painter, and is nearly always happy, except

when his wife beats him and breaks up a love affair with some other woman. His wife is a very beautiful woman, a real beauty. It must be interesting to have such a beautiful wife beat one up for an affair with another, presumably, beautiful woman. At any rate, Derain is a happy man. Braque, too, is always happy, though he works hard and almost seems to be cruel to himself at times in his art. Brancusi, the Roumanian sculptor, is always happy; a unique man. I never expect to see any man quite like him. Erik Satie, the musician, is always happy; and so is Matisse, with his abundant health, spending his winters at Nice and coming north to his home in the suburbs of Paris in the summertime—"following the sun," as he put it to me last summer.

In the late winter and early spring of 1922 the Sculptors' Gallery in New York put on three successive shows, of work by English, French, and American artists. For Quinn their effect was of course to confirm a judgment already rock-hard. In the midst of the third exhibition he wrote to Ezra Pound on April 28: ". . . the drop from the French Exhibition down to the level of the present American Exhibition is like going from marble to mud." Of his English possessions he wrote to Henri-Pierre Roché on March 5:

> Confidentially, I would be willing to part with all of them at about twenty-five cents on the dollar what I paid for them. . . . If I have been "easy" in some directions, as for example in buying the works of those Englishmen . . . that day has passed, and now I am hard and difficult.

His correspondence with the artists in France continued active and warm. Gwen John lamented her inability to make anything of the portrait of Mrs. Foster, which had never advanced beyond preliminary sketches and studies. She wrote charmingly in the spring of her work in the relative luxury of Quinn's new subsidy:

> I am quite in my work now & think of nothing else. I paint till it is dark, & the days are longer now & lighter, and then I have supper and then I read about an hour and think of my painting and then I go to bed. Every day is the same. I like this life very much.[42]

On May 9 she thanked him for a check and again promised to work hard to carry out her bargain with him. She recalled a visit to Pottier's shop in Paris with Mrs. Foster, where some of Quinn's treasures of the summer before had been collected for shipment, and where she was uncharacteristically "pleased and proud" at the showing of her own *Mère Poussepin* in the noble company: "I thought it the best picture there, but I liked the Seurat landscape." She was pleased too to learn that Quinn joined in her taste for plain, simple frames and her distaste for covering paintings with glass.

Georges Rouault sent back a bit of Quinn's own on August 1: "Like yourself, I have had a very hard winter and have been driven." He had been hard at work on four series of etchings and lithographs, *Ubu Roi, Ubu au Colonies, Guerre,* and *Miseréré.* He saw himself as moving slowly and humbly toward a style:

> . . . not in the direction of "the reincarnated tradition," as certain painter-gentlemen understood it, but I dream of "pure painting," not a style agreed upon, but one that shall be stripped cleaner and cleaner. However, I am not sufficiently naïve or sly to imagine that I can expect a *style;* one attains that when one deserves it and in the measure of one's sacrifice of his love and of his gifts.
>
> They make me smile, all those ninnies who are born "stylists by race."

Rouault continued to send Quinn lengthy excerpts from his gnomic notes on life and art, which he thought of as a "conversation" carried on with Gustave Moreau ever since the death of his and Matisse's master in 1898.

André Dunoyer de Segonzac reviewed his labors in the year since Quinn's visit—dozens of drawings and studies and, at last, two large completed paintings with which he felt "fairly satisfied." He sent Quinn photographs of the two big pictures and some of the studies, though he felt "a terror of photographs, my painting being falsified by them, especially the dark tones. . . ." [43] He had also been at work on illustrations for Flaubert's *Sentimental Education,* and for a book on boxing by Tristan Bernard for the *Nouvelle Revue Française.* Post-war Paris was still feeling dull and unreal: ". . . most of the places where one used to find amusement have rather the look of waiting-rooms. People have lost their sense of fantasy." But he divined in the French painters a general movement away from abstraction of which he approved. Men were talking of Corot and La Fontaine, and "perceiving that the plastic arts have their goals within themselves, outside of philosophy and of mathematics. . . ." Official art, on the other hand, was "as stupid as ever": "I saw the competition for the Prix de Rome: it was incredible and devastating." [44]

Raoul Dufy sent photographs of four landscapes, three new views of Sicilian scenes and one of Le Havre which Quinn had seen in Paris in 1921. Quinn bought the *Taormina*, a crowded view framed by broken white Roman columns. Dufy spoke of the nourishment he found in the rough island landscape and its Greek ruins: "Schools, formulas, methods, do not teach me. I must see the work of all time, varied like nature and life." [45] Agreeing and disagreeing, Quinn countered with a little lecture on the need for an artist to be "an *artist* and not a near-artist or a pseudo-artist or an art-artist or an amateur artist." Like Dufy, he did not believe in "schools or movements," but he did believe in the power of "influences," and in quality apart from schools and times as the only trustworthy ground of judgment in art. He cited his own pleasure in an ancient oriental bronze head of a woman, recently acquired, perhaps as much as a thousand years old, "one of the most beautiful things in the world": "I bought it, not because it was old, but because it was very beautiful, as beautiful as though it had been made by Brancusi today, and with the same sense of rhythm and beauty as is in his best work." [46] By the same token, he argued, one should buy new art not because it was new but because it was fine. The Brancusi *Mlle. Pogany*, for example, could be called as fine as the old bronze head, and that quality, not its modernity, was its validation.

Quinn was careful to make clear to Roché and the Paris dealers just what they and the artists owed him for his work in his one-man show before the congressional bodies controlling taxes and customs duties on art. He had made his final appearances before the Senate Finance Committee in the last two days of 1921. To Roché he wrote on January 27, 1922: "I had a walk-over, almost a reception, by the Senate Finance Committee . . . on Friday December 30th. They agreed with me in principle and even took my suggestions as to technical amendments in the present law about admitting original drawings and sketches." For Paul Rosenberg he reviewed his "art fights" in 1909 and 1913 as well as the one just completed, making clear that his drive throughout had been to reduce or remove the burden of levies upon art while it was fresh, near its source, before it turned into a commodity of exchange. He summed up his latest triumphs in a May 8 letter to Rosenberg:

> The Senate had dropped out the provision permitting etchings and lithographs to come in duty free and I had that restored. I also defeated the project of putting a 25 per cent. duty on art, except art one hundred years old. . . .
>
> I succeeded also in reducing the American sales tax on works of art from 10 to 5 per cent, and reserved the exception that such sales tax does not apply to sales by artists and sculptors, directly or indirectly, or through agents or galleries, of their own works, nor does it apply to transactions between dealers. . . .

Quinn continued touchy and uneasy about having to make a good many purchases on the sole evidence of photographs, and so he kept urging Roché on but at the same time urged him to proceed with caution. Modern work, with its tendency toward abstraction and away from naturalistic images, seemed to him particularly hard to photograph with a trustworthy result.[47] For this reason, as well as out of pure enjoyment, he grasped at every opportunity to see work that was on display in New York. He anticipated with some excitement, for example, the sale of the large collection of Dikran Kelekian at the Plaza on January 30 and 31, both because he wanted to see the pictures and possibly bid on them and because he wanted to see how such work would fare, in quantity, under competitive bidding in America. When he and Mrs. Foster and J. B. Yeats had a look at the collection in the preliminary view Quinn thought it on the whole rather timid and second-rate. He admitted there were three fine Cézannes and two good Picassos and some good early Corots—not the kind of late Corots that " 'make the leaves of the tree look like lace,' as the short-haired female art students put it; the Corots that are 'so full of poetry,' as the long-haired male art admirers put it; the Corots that are feeble and rotten, as I would put it." [48] Still, he agreed that the collection was good enough, big enough, and modern enough so that its sale would constitute a real test of the present commercial value of the kind of work into which he was sinking most of his own free cash. The results were anything but reassuring. Of the total ostensible sales of $254,879, only $91,000, he estimated, represented genuine purchases; all the rest were token bids entered by dealers who had been alerted to bid in works on which Kelekian was about to take a serious loss.[49] But for that stratagem, Quinn wrote Roché, "the sale would have been a slaughter, an Armenian massacre. . . ." [50] He resolved at once that if he ever reached the point of wishing to dispose of his own works in any quantity he would sell them in Paris and not in New York. He wrote to Ambroise Vollard to that effect just two days after the Kelekian sale. He went on to phrase his contempt of American motives in buying art:

> American taste has not reached the level of French taste. Americans still buy "for literary reasons." A very insignificant painting by Whistler brought $7000 . . . in dirty, muddy colors, of a young girl. I would not have given $50 for it and would not want it in my apartment. . . . Whistler has passed almost out of art and into literature, and people are buying him for literary reasons. . . .
>
> [*February 2, 1922.*]

What he was denouncing was his own first motive in buying art, long outgrown. What he himself bought from Kelekian was a Picasso landscape at $2,000, a price which he felt had been "bid up" on him because he had carelessly let it be known that he wished to buy it, and Seurat's handsome busty woman at her toilette, *La Poudreuse*, at $5,200. "I am very happy to have it," he wrote Roché of the latter.[51]

The three exhibitions, English, French, and American, at the Sculptors' Gallery early in the year were another chance to see modern work in quantity and in context—though many of the works shown were Quinn's already. Familiar as he was with those, it was a pleasure to view them in public and in a different company and air. Quinn wrote of the shows to Brancusi and described their setting, a well-lighted room twenty-five feet wide by sixty feet deep, with a painted brick floor, and walls hung with blue-gray drapery.[52] To the English show he lent twenty-two sculptures by Epstein and six by Gaudier-Brzeska, paintings by Augustus John and Gwen John and Innes, and drawings by Gaudier-Brzeska and Wyndham Lewis. To the French show in early April he lent fifteen

works of Brancusi and ten of Duchamp-Villon, along with paintings or drawings of Picasso, Rouault, Derain, Matisse, and Segonzac to serve as "background" to the sculpture. But after Brancusi
had seen photographs of the French exhibition Roché wrote that
he was "in despair, half ill" at the way his pieces had been disposed
in the room, against walls or in a clutter of irrelevant items: "He
was as sore and sensitive as a child weeping over his toys." [53] He
had taken Roché home to his white studio for dinner to air his
grief, but after four hours of talk he had cheered up and set to
work again.

Jeanne Robert Foster wrote an appreciative article on the sculptor in *Vanity Fair* for May 1922, and Quinn wrote of it to Brancusi
as "altogether charming." [54] The fey Roumanian was one of those
nearest to his heart as an artist and as a man. They had liked each
other in Paris in 1921, and they had written back and forth cordially now for years. He sent Roché a message for him in the
summer: "Please thank Brancusi for his patience and open-minded-
ness *and frankness*. I'm so glad we treat on [*sic*] such a frank and
friendly manner. Quite like him!" [55] With Brancusi's works, he
told Arthur B. Davies, he was never satisfied: " '. . . the more one
has the more one wants others.' " [56] But in fact his only significant
purchase from Brancusi at this time was his *Tall Column* in wood
and his wood carving of *Adam and Eve* with base, which he
accepted in August at 30,000 francs.[57] When Roché reported that
Brancusi was "often ill," "feverish and weak," Quinn's anxiety and
his lay medical urge stirred sharply. "Does he cough any?" he
wrote back. "Does he expectorate? Does he tell you that he has
night sweats? Or does he have any temperature in the afternoon?" [58] Quinn was thinking of his own more or less chronic
nervous tension and of the disease he dreaded most, tuberculosis.

Though he cared a great deal less about her as an artist, he followed accounts of the illness of Marie Laurencin with the same
eager sympathy. Paul Rosenberg wrote him on June 12 that she
was "going a little better, but I fear that she has an illness which
does not forgive. I believe she is struck by a cancer in the stomach. . . ." And he mourned, "Poor friend of mine, and how it is
sad to think: that at the time you get consideration, you have to
leave the earth!" A week later Roché wrote to Quinn: "She eats

now and speaks, and has again her maiden's soul and still the shadow of death in her forehead, so much more human humble and sympathetic than some weeks and months ago in her (rather selfish) glory." [59] And two days later he sent a new vignette of the sickroom that might have reminded Quinn of Yeats's cycle of lyrics on the dying Mabel Beardsley, "Upon a Dying Lady": "But she has all her friends around her, will be tyrannical again in her clever flattering way, and there will be competition among these friends to give or lend her money. . . . she has had a new operation with several things taken out of her, she can no more have children. . . ." [60] Quinn's advice on this occasion was lame enough: he suggested that Roché take her one of the books of the French self-help psychologist Emile Coué. His fascination with this quackery of the day was enough of a joke in the family so that his niece, Mary, named her chronically ailing mongrel puppy "Coué." And Marie Laurencin's illness forgave her after all; she lived on till 1956.

Quinn carried always in one corner of his mind the desire to provide his collection with historical depth by acquiring a few more good examples of the work of the fathers and grandfathers of the School of Paris. He knew that it was a potentially expensive idea and that he had to proceed warily: the same amount of money would buy a good deal more of contemporary art, and do more active good. But on February 2 he succumbed to the temptation of Cézanne's *Blue Mountain* at 60,000 francs from Vollard. In the summer he was tempted again but wary when De Zayas offered a putative Ingres portrait of Mme. de Staël, the authenticity of which had been questioned. Quinn wanted Derain to inspect the painting in Paris but permission was refused. De Zayas urged him on to buy and assured him the work was a true Ingres. Quinn then asked Charles Sheeler to interpret an equivocal statement about the painting by the French critic La Pauze. When Sheeler rendered a judgment in favor of authenticity Quinn wrote him an angry letter accusing him of overzealousness on behalf of De Zayas, for whom Sheeler was an agent. In the long run he was swayed crucially by the refusal of Derain's inspection, and he turned the picture down, writing De Zayas on June 1: "I did not want a bastard painting in my collection." But by this time Roché had located another Ingres, *Raphael et la Fornarina*, which the great Paris amateur Alphonse Kahn was willing to part with. He cabled Quinn on June 6: "Fornarina one hundred fifty." Quinn cabled back to suggest he try a bit of dickering: 150,000 francs was a lot of money for a picture less than a foot square. Roché cabled on June 11: "Kahn offended at my suggesting one forty." The original price had to be paid, and was paid. But in the autumn he resisted an irresistible picture, Daumier's bravura *Don Quixote*, which Paul Rosenberg offered him at the bargain price of 55,000 francs. Quinn refused point-blank, on the ground that he was already in very deep for the year and still had his eye on further big game.

Dealings for the work of Picasso, directly with the painter or with his principal dealer, Paul Rosenberg, and with Roché as intermediary in either case, went on throughout the first half of 1922. Roché knew that Picasso had a tantalizing heap of pictures in his studio which he had never shown to Rosenberg, and he suggested to the painter that he might sell some of these to Quinn direct. Picasso brooded it over. He was not sure he wanted to sell the pictures to anybody. On February 11 Roché wrote to recommend three Picassos at Rosenberg's: three draped women at 50,000 francs which he described as "giant women . . . the whole coloring has a sort of splendid and rich monotony"; a still life of a table with a jug and a loaf of bread at 25,000; and at 35,000, the great *Three Musicians*, Pierrot, Harlequin and Monk, one of the two versions of this culmination of synthetic cubism which Picasso had painted in the summer of 1921 in Fontainebleau, where Quinn, Roché, and Mrs. Foster had lunched with him *en famille*. On March 29 Roché wrote that Picasso that day "did attack the small hill of pictures in the corner of his studio." Roché commended particularly two works of the blue period, a Spanish landscape and a self portrait with a little red beard and also what he called the "small gigantic" or the "small giant women," [61] probably the *Four Classic Figures* in tempera on a tiny wood panel only four by six inches in size yet distinctly massive and classical in modeling and feeling.

It is very hard to tell from the correspondence or from published records just which of the paintings Quinn finally bought. He was willing to take almost any work of this master that he could find money for. It is clear that he did not buy the "two blues," for Picasso reneged on those: they were the last he had, and he decided he wanted to keep them himself. "He changes some times his mind like that, without seeming to know why—and remaining so friendly and sweet," Roché wrote on June 12. But he did buy the "small giant women" along with a group of others from Picasso and Rosenberg. Roché told of Picasso's refusal to accept Quinn's check from Pottier until he had actually delivered the picture, and cited this as an example of his ways of behaving where money was involved: "Picasso is at the same time very simple, very sweet, and very difficult with money—absolutely to be trusted as you know." [62] On June 1 Quinn committed himself to Paul Rosenberg for three Picassos, *Maternité, Fontaine à Fontainebleau,* and *Arlequin,* for the round sum of 93,000 francs. Three others from the painter himself were costing him 75,000 francs. The 60,000 francs to Vollard for the Cézanne landscape brought the total for major purchases of recent weeks to 228,000 francs, as he noted to Roché on June 7. In American cash it came to about $19,000.

Alongside the practical pursuit of pictures there were dealings with Picasso of a homelier kind. Roché wrote to Quinn in February of Picasso's dream of creating from the whole cloth a total domestic fabric, like Adam on the first day out of the Garden:

> Picasso would love to build a country home, with everything thought out anew by him, with new simplicity and new proportions, even the steps of the stairs, the windows—every piece of furniture: tables, seats, jugs, glasses, etc., created as for the first time, forgetting all what exists already. . . . He says it is the work he feels in his head, he would most love to do.
>
> [*February 19, 1922.*]

Then the painter volunteered to help Roché search about in Paris for old frames for his own pictures and others Quinn had bought, and the two spent July 2 traveling about in a taxi with the Cézanne landscape and what they called Picasso's "Pet Maternity," the one Quinn had just bought from Rosenberg, rummaging from shop to shop and ending up "in a forest of frames." [63] A month later, touched by Roché's account of Picasso's happiness with his little son, Paulo, Quinn wrote wistfully: "He is only about 41 or 42. I think if I were *that* age, I might be tempted to want to try my luck at a family." But at his own age, fifty-two, it seemed to him too great a risk; he could not be sure enough that he would survive to bring a son or a daughter to maturity.[64]

With Paul Rosenberg too Quinn enjoyed an epistolary conversation which was generally chatty and amicable but which suffered moments of stress, as in June when he suspected for a time that Rosenberg was shuffling pictures and prices on him, perhaps by changing titles. It seemed to him that perhaps *Arlequin* was becoming *Pierrot*, or vice versa, at an increase in price of several thousand francs. He wrote Roché angrily on June 7:

> I don't care how strenuous an artist or a dealer may be in handling his works, or how rigorously he plays the game, but I do expect honesty. If Rosenberg has been crooked in this matter I am through with him for good. Those who know me in this town know that that is my principle. De Zayas once tried it with me and he will never try it again [presumably the issue of the De Staël portrait]. Old Montross tried it with me once and I have quit him forever, which has cost him a good many thousands of dollars a year.

Roché and Rosenberg were able to reassure him quickly that no deception had been practiced or intended, and Quinn wrote Rosenberg on the twenty-seventh in a more peaceable spirit:

> I buy art for the love of art, for the pleasure of helping artists, to have important examples of the work of artists in whom I believe, and because of my interest in art generally. I enjoy what I call "the rigor of the game." I always like to be straightforward and I dislike very much all indirection.

For this testament he was rewarded with an anecdote from Rosenberg which suggested that even in Paris the way of the new art was beset with trials and perils:

> I had the visit of a very well known man who wrote books of very great painters and who has himself a splendid collection. He is of a very old and good family and is a rich man. But in art he is short sighted and stopped after the first impressionists. He saw at my exhibition paintings by Rousseau, Cézanne, Van Gogh, and he started to be so impolite, so rude, and used such bad terms against those artists and myself that I was obliged to have him put

outside, through two policemen! He wrote me after a very polite letter, with excuses, and saying that the sight of such paintings *makes him mad!*   [*July 11, 1922.*]

Quinn and Roché had still not settled upon any fixed rate or percentage as payment for the scout's services in pursuit of the living game. Quinn sent him every so often a sizable tip and Roché seemed well enough content. On January 13, along with a payment of 25,000 francs for work of Derain's, Quinn included an honorarium of 3,000 francs for Roché personally. On June 28 he sent another 4,000 francs, and Roché responded with thanks and an expression of his own pleasure in the hunt:

> Those new 4,000 francs you announce for me are very kind indeed. Certainly it is now a big work which takes some care and concentration and imagination and time: I feel often "comme un chien de chasse qui cherche la piste de lièvres"—but I enjoy it comme un chien de chasse too.*

On August 3 Quinn promised a further 2,000 francs, "making 10,000 in all for your work re art for me to date. . . . Is that enough?" he queried. "Be quite frank." He was also sending occasional unspecified sums to cover Roché's expenses—for travel about the city, photographs, postage and cables. He complimented Roché on both the liveliness and the usefulness of the letters which were coming very frequently now, almost daily in some periods, as in the spring and summer of 1922: "Your letters have been most interesting, and even exciting, pleasant excitement . . ." Quinn wrote on June 9; and three weeks later, ". . . what a satisfaction it has been for me to receive your disinterested, intelligent and enthusiastic, but at the same time balanced, reports and recommendations." [65] The two were hitting it off admirably; in their six weeks' association in Paris in the preceding summer acquaintance had ripened into friendship. In charmingly fractured English sprinkled with French phrases, Roché's letters were bringing Quinn exactly what he needed: prompt, clear, and knowledgeable advice from a man with an easy, ingratiating presence in all the circles that mattered to Quinn in Paris.

* To Quinn, July 11, 1922. " . . . like a hunting dog looking for signs of hares . . . ."

Quinn was not unaware that with the help of Roché, and given the rigor, the energy, and the nerve of their pursuit, he was accomplishing a work that would some day be recognized as capital: ". . . in a way our letters and cables are making a book of art history." [66] He heard with anger and envy of the carnage that Dr. Albert Barnes was wreaking among the Paris markets. Paraphrasing Swinburne (on criticism as "the noble art of praising"), he wrote Roché on the first of August: "If I had the money of that *brute* Barnes . . . what a time we would have had in the noble art of buying. . . ." Yet it was exactly the limitation of his means that made Quinn's collecting uniquely intense and impressive, made him, probably, the greatest American collector of the art of his day—as Mr. Alfred H. Barr, Jr., of the Museum of Modern Art, has judged him.[67] For it was not wealth but the lack of it that made the true "rigor of the game," put before him the exciting and exacting test of how much excellence he could acquire with modest means.

Feeling as always that "America has not got a real civilization," Quinn in an incautious moment in the summer of 1922 wrote Roché that he intended ultimately to leave his Picassos and his other French pictures to the French nation.[68] Roché's quick reply mingled pleasure, misgiving, prophecy, cautious advice, and a fine feeling for the delicacy and gravity of the question:

> Up to now I half-consciously believed we were working first for our pleasure and then for the Metropolitan or some other museums of the U.S.A.—Of course almost nobody in the U.S.A. cares for this new, living art. But when this art will have widely conquered the world and be known as much as Whistler, or Manet, or the Italians, it will be much and earnestly studied by some men in the U.S.A., students who will need it. It is impossible that some day the U.S.A. do not grow a civilization in art. (Already now the best articles published on Erik Satie have been written in Vogue by Rosenburg.) Will it not then be good for France that an explosive nucleus of her art, such as your collection, be in some great American museum, even if it has slept unknown for some time before? [*June 29, 1922.*]

He agreed, on the other hand, that it would be pleasant for himself and other lovers of French art if Quinn were to carry out the scheme of which he had spoken often in the past, of an elegant small estate near Paris, on the model of Alphonse Kahn's house in St. Germain, to house himself and his collection when he could break away for good from the killing American treadmill. By this time Quinn had realized that he had spoken carelessly, more sweepingly than he intended, and placed himself far out on a limb where he would be embarrassed to be discovered. He wrote on July 11 to correct the impression he had given Roché. He thought he would probably devise certain works to the French Government, "to be kept together, as it sees fit, in the Luxembourg or in the Louvre." He did not mean to give away his whole collection— "Most emphatically no"—or even his whole French collection. What he had in mind was "a certain selection of French works that are of museum rank and importance," a selection probably to be made by a committee of whom Arthur B. Davies would certainly be one if he should be living at the time. Everything else, the great bulk of his collection, would be sold with the proceeds going to his estate. No other group of persons could exert a claim on Quinn's affection or his loyalty approaching his feeling for his own family. He felt no leading whatever to leave his collection as a whole to any American institution, in existence or to be established. Again he spelled out his disgust with his native culture:

> I hate the primitivism of this country, its banality, its crudeness, the insanity of its ideas of speed, its lack of taste and the mechanization of life that is almost universal here. The damn country is too big.

It might have been a good thing, he thought, if the South had won the Civil War; then there could have been three republics—South, East, and West.

The pressure of Quinn's chase was intensifying as it narrowed, as he sought to bring his collection toward a finer and higher point, concentrating now not only on the French but also on the best of the French. Among the living Picasso was the man of the hour for him, accompanied at some distance by Brancusi and Matisse and Derain. Among the recent dead his passion went to Rousseau and Seurat. Outside this circle of excellence he hardly had time or patience to look. His interest in Oriental, African, and Polynesian art and artifacts continued, but mainly as a matter of quiet habit and as a rummaging among the ancestors of the modern. When Walter Pach was invited to give a course of lectures chiefly on modern art at the National University in Mexico City, Quinn asked him to look about for primitive sculpture for him. Pach wrote on September 20: "Mexico is a paradise for artists but hell for art collectors or business men. People here simply are not interested in doing business." He was finding it hard to get his hands on anything tangible that was worth having. In June Quinn sold a Chinese landscape for $1,600. At the same time he bought from Marius de Zayas an African primitive torso with stone base for $875; but accompanying this were Brancusi's marble *Head of an Infant* at $500, his wood carving *Chimera* at $700, and Seurat's enchanting, poetical *Les Poseuses*, his study of three slender nude models in the studio, at $5,500. From Bernheim Jeune on July 8 he acquired another capital Matisse, *The White Slave.* But the year's most intense excitement came in the pursuit of Rousseau and Seurat.

In the winter of 1922 Quinn heard that Walter Arensberg had suffered serious losses and was giving up his New York apartment and moving to California, some part at least of his collection to be sold privately by Charles Sheeler. Quinn knew Arensberg as "one of the few men here with money and courage to buy modern art," [69] and for the sake of the "art fight" in general he was sorry to hear of his reverses; but the situation let him acquire Rousseau's portrait of his own medical man from Sheeler at $1,500. In May he took Rousseau's *l'Enfant à la Poupée de Carton* from Georges Bernheim at 16,500 francs, and in June *Le Dirigéable* from the same dealer at 17,000. This gave him three good new examples of *le douanier*, but he yearned for at least one of the big capital extravagances of that knowing primitive. Roché had now learned that Robert Delaunay was trying to dispose of his Rousseaus, but one at a time and at high prices. He thought for a time that he might be able to get the big, handsome *La Charmeuse de Serpents* through Léonce Rosenberg for something like 80,000 francs. Quinn authorized Roché on June 28 to bid up to that figure for the painting, but by that time Roché had already tried and failed. The hunt for the big picture continued.

The pursuit of Seurat followed similar tracks, with better success. Again Quinn hoped for masterpieces, preferably big ones, but happily accepted smaller works of quality while waiting his chance. He missed out on one masterpiece in February, the gay and witty *Le Chahut*, the can-can dancers, when he failed to receive the catalog of the Goetz sale in Paris until after the sale was over. Roché had slipped up for once, in neglecting to cable, and Quinn was badly disappointed. The picture had passed to Mme. Kroller at the bargain price of 37,500 francs, when Quinn, as he had written Roché on March 5, would have been willing to go as high as 60,000 for it. Many of the best Seurats were in private hands, and negotiating for them required time and delicacy. In *La Poudreuse* from the Kelekian sale and *Les Poseuses* from De Zayas the year had already brought him two of the most seductive of the relatively small Seurat figure studies. In May Roché wrote of *Le Crotoy-amont*, a land-and-seascape, "It is a peach, a dream, a pure thing, so light and luminous. . . ." [70] Within the month Quinn had bought it from Félix Fénéon for 50,000 francs. [71] In May he had asked Roché to feel out Paul Signac, some of whose own paintings Quinn already owned, to see whether he felt any inclination to part with *Le Cirque*, the last-completed of Seurat's larger masterworks. Roché had also heard of yet another elderly private collector of Seurats, and he suggested to Quinn to hold off while he reconnoitered. On investigation the "old Seuratsman," as Roché had been calling him, turned out to be the husband of the painter's sister, now also dead. He did not want to think of selling his pictures because "his sister loved them so much." [72] The hunter and the pointer, Quinn and Roché, backed off at once, honoring the motive. But at this time, as Roché notified by cable on July 8, Signac invited an offer for *Le Cirque*. Félix Fénéon was asked to inspect the picture and render an opinion as to its quality and value, and Roché cabled on the eleventh that Fénéon had suggested a price of 250,000. Quinn cabled back on the same day: "Noninterested Circus price Feneons opinion." At that rate the picture would have come to something over $22,000. In a letter of July 19 Roché admitted that Fénéon's suggested price had "made me jump." But it turned out to have been based on a wrong measurement of the size of the canvas, and Signac had intimated that he thought his friend's ideas of price unnecessarily grand. On the twenty-fifth Roché wrote to suggest that Quinn try a bit of dickering: "Would you pay 150,000 for the Circus? We are entitled to make an offer to Signac after his (friendly) criticism of Fénéon's ultimatum." Signac had told Fénéon that he was holding onto *Le Cirque* as a *dot* for his daughter; Roché reflected, "but money is a 'dot' too. . . . I wonder if you should not make an offer." On the twenty-ninth Roché saw the picture himself for the first time and cabled to Quinn the same day: "Just seen Circus. Glorious thing. Perfectly preserved. Agree Fénéon saying probably best Seurat. . . ." Writing more at length later in the day he explained that he had got permission to view the painting while Signac was away in Brittany, and that he had "seated in an armchair in front of it—and looked quite close, and far, and close again. My cable explains itself." In conversations with Signac and Fénéon the figure of 150,000 francs had been mentioned more firmly. Quinn made the crucial move in a cable of August 2 to Roché: "Greatly interested yours and Feneon's opinion Circus probably best Seurat. Price satisfactory. Therefore very anxious secure if possible." In a letter of the same day he said that he had thought he was already "beyond temptation and beyond my means"; but he had succumbed to the splendor of the object and to Roché's persuasion: "But finally I gathered courage and assembled in my mind the forces of hope, and cabled as I did." Always on his mind now was the threat of the long purse and the large appetite of Dr. Barnes—a "brute," "a bully," "*such* a brute." [73] On August 11 he cabled Roché 3,000 francs to pay down on *Le Cirque* as an option to hold the picture until February 1, 1923, when full payment would come due, and Roché cabled, now from Berlin, that the arrangement was confirmed with Signac. [74] Now all Quinn had to do was find the money. He and Roché breathed deeply in relief and satisfaction; they had snared the queen of the whole collection to date. But Quinn felt he had to pull in his nets for a while; he warned Roché in the cable of August 11: "Have gone limit this purchase. Therefore no more purchases six months." He did not mean it absolutely; but it was the mood which probably explained his refusal of the Daumier *Don Quixote* in October. His investment for art in eight months of 1922, if the big Seurat is included, came to about $62,000 at least; undoubtedly there were other transactions of which no record has survived. It was a great deal of money out of a year's current earnings for a professional man, even a highly successful one. But what he got for his money was almost incredible: at least a dozen works "of museum rank and importance," and the three main Seurats, *La Poudreuse, Les Poseuses*, and *Le Cirque*, among the finest accomplishments of that master.

It was this feeling that he had gone in very deep, yet wanted to go deeper, coupled with an old and accumulating disgust, that now determined Quinn to make a housecleaning of his English collection, or much of it. Apparently the resolution began to come to a point during his trips to the English, French, and American shows at the Sculptors' Gallery in the winter and spring, when he was exposed to the three national arts in concentration and in juxtaposition. To Roché he wrote on May 20: "My second visit to the Sculptors' Gallery made me rather angry that I had bought so many Epsteins, about ten times too many; so many things by Lewis, twenty times too many; so many things by John, forty times too many." In writing to Pound he recalled sorely that between 1908 and 1915 he had paid out to Augustus John alone or to his dealer, the Chenil Gallery, more than $45,000. *The Mumpers* at £1,000, *The Way Down to the Sea* at £600, and the portrait of Arthur Symons at £400—nearly $10,000 for those three—particularly stuck in his craw.[75] He reduced his angry figurative selling rate another nickel: he would sell all his English works "tomorrow at twenty cents on the dollar." [76] He kept thinking how much French art he could buy now if he had that English money back. But the decision to sell was not an easy one to make. Quinn had always avoided the posture and the reputation of a trader or profiteer in art; he wanted to be, and to be known as, a collector, a possessor, one who bought and kept for love. In fact he had hardly ever sold a work that once entered his house, and it disturbed him to make a beginning in trading.

In the late summer he approached the London dealer Percy Moore Turner, whom he knew and trusted, with the idea of an auction or sale of a large selection of his English works in London. Before the end of the year it was agreed between them that Turner would show the works for sale in his gallery for a period of one month early in 1923, and that he would receive a commission of 10 per cent upon the original price to Quinn of the works sold and 20 per cent of any profit realized above the cost price.[77] The latter figure was raised to 25 per cent in Quinn's letter of January 9, 1923. He showed his general uneasiness about the proceedings in the conditions he laid down. He asked Turner not to exhibit or to advertise the works as Quinn's property, though he realized that his name would become quickly attached when people had seen the exhibit. He suggested a form for a "public" explanation when that was called for: ". . . I feel that these works belong in England. . . ."[78] If Turner were driven into a deeper corner he could say: " '. . . I am disposing of my English and certain American works and centering my purchases upon French works.' " It is clear too that Quinn's main anxiety was in regard to Augustus John's reaction to his move. He knew that he could not avoid appearing to betray an old intimacy that had once been warm and important to him. John's potential anger could cause a great deal of embarrassment even if it could work no practical difference. And John might find just cause for anger in having the most important collection of his work in existence dumped on the market in a heap. Quinn tried to put a bold face on the matter, but he was unquestionably fearful. In his letter of December 29 to Turner he resigned to him the decision as to whether or not to inform John or Knewstub of Chenil's in advance of the sale: ". . . I do not see the necessity of notifying them. That is a matter of personal art politics which I leave entirely to your discretion." Then he heard that John was coming over in late winter or early spring to serve on an art jury for a show in Pittsburgh, and he appended a postscript on December 30. He foresaw "a John boom" in the United States: "I think people will fall over themselves to be painted by him." He looked forward to the possibility of seeing John in the flesh, after the sale and after not having seen him for a dozen years, with obvious trepidation: "I do not expect to see him while here, though I will not avoid seeing him. I imagine he will be very angry when he hears of the sale of his things by me. To me it is the most matter of fact thing in the world." The last sentence was of course disingenuous and untrue. The works for the sale were

shipped on the *Olympic* on December 30: seventy-four paintings
in eight big boxes, seventy-two water colors and drawings, and
five sealed packages of etchings. In terms of shipping volume it all
came to 260 cubic feet or 6½ cubic tons. Quinn set the "total sale
price" to be asked at $62,855.[79]

Formal parting with Augustus John and his work would mean
the end of an era in Quinn's collecting of art. John had been the
first to teach Quinn to look at art as art: not an adjunct or decoration upon literature, but an independent discipline with its own
forms and its own integrity. In the dozen years since that primary
instruction the pupil had gone on, with the help of other tutors,
to develop a taste more sophisticated than the taste or the art of
his first master.

The year 1922 also saw a parting Quinn regretted a good deal
more sadly, and the end of an era in his patronage on the literary
side, though it was a finality unrecognized or unspecified. Apparently there had been no correspondence at all between Quinn and
Conrad in 1921. The latest letters had passed between them in the
summer of 1920, and those had spoken on both sides in terms of
rather guarded courtesy and embarrassed apology. Now early in
1922 Conrad sent Quinn a copy of his dramatization of *The Secret
Agent*, inscribed "with regards and best wishes." Quinn left the
gift unacknowledged for months, and when he wrote on July 17
attributed his delay to "months of anxiety and worry and, at
times, illness." He went on to express his own puzzled sense of
the decay of their friendship, on grounds which he found baffling
and unreal:

> Some cloud has seemed to come between you and me during
> this last year or two, but what caused it has been obscure—a
> minor mystery—to me. Whatever was in your mind, there was
> never anything, I hope, in any word of mine, and there was never
> any thought in my mind, that was either ungenerous or unfair
> to you.

He now ceremonially released Conrad from his promise to dedicate
to him his "Napoleonic novel":

> A long time ago you wrote of dedicating a book to me. Let
> me say in the fullest sincerity that I now do not want you to have

the slightest feeling that you are in any degree committed, by what you once wrote, to any such thing; nor do I expect it. You will, I feel sure, credit me with complete sincerity and utter lack of any feeling on that score. I cannot put it more strongly than that.

Most of the remainder of a fairly long letter was a review of his impressions of the French artists he saw on his Paris visit in the summer of 1921, a year earlier, emphasizing his wistful and admiring sense of their complex "health"—"all so sane and so strong and so honest." He explained that he had not crossed to England because he dreaded the "fatigue and strain" of London and of the Channel trip. He was sorry not to have seen their mutual friend "poor Symons" again. Had he gone to England, he said, he would still have avoided Ireland "for the sake of my own peace." He closed gracefully with good wishes for Conrad's work, for Mrs. Conrad's health, and for "a peaceful and happy summer" for them both. Writing to Conrad always brought out the best in Quinn, and this was a gentlemanly performance, though curiously elegiac and perhaps a bit paranoiac withal. He had good reason to be puzzled at the coolness he sensed in Conrad. Their grounds of mutual embarrassment—the abortive "dedication" of *The Arrow of Gold*, Conrad's sale of manuscripts to T. J. Wise, misunderstandings about the Doubleday collected edition—had ostensibly been all smoothed over. And yet, whereas his letter was a gracefully unstated invitation to Conrad to reply cordially and to take up their correspondence on the old basis of grave comradeship, it had the air of a man who has been hurt and expects to be hurt again.

Conrad appears to have accepted the matter in a so-be-it spirit. He did not reply for three months, and then he enclosed two pamphlets, the text of which had not appeared in book form, with a mere note of eight lines. He was afraid, he said, that "incorrigible sinfulness in the matter of correspondence" had given Quinn "a wrong impression" of his real feelings. He concluded: "Pray believe me they are as cordial and full of regard for you as ever. As I am too old to amend my horrible ways, I hope you will continue me your indulgence and think of me as kindly as you used to do." He signed his note, "Always faithfully yours"; but he had addressed Quinn, as he had not done since the first formal stages of their correspondence ten years before, as "Mr. Quinn." It was a suave little document, and the detached spectator might find appealing its air of sad kindliness and courtesy; but the mode of address, the brevity, the weary tone, even the elegance of phrase, added up to something chilling. Quinn would have been right to find the note not far from insulting. Clearly Conrad was not minded to specify grievances, if he felt grievances, or to excuse himself to Quinn, if he felt Quinn had grounds for displeasure, or formally to recognize the reality of disagreement in any way. He appeared to be courteously co-operating in the euthanasia of a relationship that had grown onerous to him.

Nineteen twenty-two had been a year of triumphs and trials. Quinn's physical and psychic tensions had accumulated to the point of crisis in the winter and again in the summer, in a pattern that had come to seem almost rhythmical. He was working too hard to quit, and too hard to continue. When Ezra Pound wrote in May to suggest a walking tour in Italy, mentioning "Padua, Siena, Verona, Venice and other places," Quinn felt he had to laugh off the idea. Roché too pressed him to come abroad again, and wrote of Jeanne Robert Foster on July 19: "All our friends like her so much and asks [sic] when you and she come again to France." When Quinn's old friend in Norwalk, Connecticut, Michael Monahan, Editor and Proprieter of the *Phoenix*, scraped together enough money for two months in Paris and England, Quinn staked him to an extra $150 that would allow him to make an excursion to Brittany as well.[80] But he felt that what vacation he could find time for himself this year must be domestic. Mrs. Foster was ill in the early summer with intestinal grippe, and Quinn thought she was close to a nervous breakdown as well. She refused to go to a hospital, though he urged it. Quinn's niece, Mary, had again been troubled with a chronic bad throat, and she also had to undergo an appendectomy at Roosevelt Hospital late in June. Quinn wanted a little free time with his family, the little of it that remained available to him. His doctors warned him that he needed a solid two months' rest, and he would have been delighted to take it. But Paul Kieffer, the only man in his office aside from Thomas Curtin whom he felt he could generally trust, was suing his wife for divorce and Quinn found him "utterly useless" much of the time.[81] Work held him in the city through July, while the Andersons went on ahead to a cottage Quinn had rented for two months at "Meadowmount," the Adirondack estate of the Milhollands, friends of Mrs. Foster's, near Lake Champlain and the towns of Elizabethtown and Westport. Reading of all this in a letter from Quinn, André Dunoyer de Segonzac was reminded of "the beautiful country of Lake Champlain, where I lived—in imagination—with 'The Last of the Mohicans' of Fenimore Cooper when I was twelve years old." [82] To Quinn it mattered more that the area had been a favorite retreat of William James. In early August he joined the Andersons. Paul and Marie were there to attend to the housekeeping. Mrs. Foster was nearby in the Milhollands' main house. The proprietors had named two low peaks in the neighborhood "Mt. Vida" and "Mt. Inez" in honor of their two daughters. Inez was a famous suffragette of the day. Quinn walked heroically, often with Mary and the rickety puppy Coué, knocked a golf ball about the improvised golf course, swam occasionally in the lake, and gave up smoking again.

He returned to the city much refreshed by "the best rest in eight years." Within a few weeks he was "driven" again and looked tense and thin and generally unwell, and Mrs. Foster feared he was genuinely ill. His doctors had told her after his operation in 1918 that he had a probability of six more years of life. She feared the worst. But he was working too hard, too successfully, to let go. A few figures suggest something of the scale of his life: he paid income tax for 1922 of $25,424 at the modest rates of those days; his rent for the year came to $5,196; the contents of his apartment were insured for $350,000. The running expenses of his modest appearing office were coming to about $100,000 a year.

As the year closed Léonce Rosenberg wrote of his evening at the Russian Ballet in Paris when *Pulcinella*, *Parade*, and *Le Tricorne* were performed with scenery, curtains, and costumes by Picasso. After *Parade*, "which is a *pure cubist work*, the whole House, composed of the greatest foreign and French personalities, stood up and cheared [*sic*] facing Picasso's box. It can be said that now he is consecrated great Master." [83] Roché wrote on December 19 that he had relaxed the chase as ordered. The pointer was dozing, but warily: "I just only keep my eyes open and ready."

1923

O N the second day of the new year Quinn sustained what he called a "shock," falling to the floor in his apartment and lying there helpless for nearly an hour before Paul found him, got him into bed, and summoned a doctor. In the preceding weeks he had had warnings in the form of extreme nervousness, sleeplessness, and "terrible beatings" in his head.[1] Lying in bed in the afternoon after his attack he felt as if he had a film over his left eye. After resting at home for a few days he was well enough to travel by train to Hot Springs in Virginia, and well enough to pause in Washington on the way to attend to a tax case. At the spa he rested, exercised mildly, and took the waters for two weeks, after which he felt largely restored. But his vitality was low and he noticed that whenever he was tired his left eyelid tended to droop. He attributed his attack to the clogging of his "system" with poisons due to overwork and anxiety. In the period of something over three months since the euphoric day after his Adirondack holiday when he settled the publications of *The Waste Land*, he had been involved in a series of twenty-three cases amounting to over half-a-million dollars for a Honolulu corporation, twenty-eight litigation cases in which he had negotiated claims for nearly a million dollars for $150,000, and litigation against one of the banks for which he was counsel in which he had settled a claim of $380,000 for $250,000.[2] He compared his age, fifty-three, uneasily to the sixty years of Arthur B. Davies, who had recently had a "shock" such as his own. Lady Gregory warned him that he must plan holidays in advance of his "symptons of overwork" and keep

566

to them. "Fifty-three seems very young to me," she wrote, "and you must keep yourself in 'the youth of middle age' by regular rests and change of scene." [3] Sound advice, of course, but difficult for Quinn to follow; he was back on the old hectic round within a few weeks of his attack.

To Conrad's polite note of October 27, 1922, Quinn replied on February 9: "I was glad to get your letter and to know that your feelings are as cordial and full of regard for me as ever, as mine are for you." The regular Christmas apples had gone forward from Quinn, and Jessie Conrad wrote to thank him for those on March 25. She also promised to send him a copy of the cookbook she had composed, due out the next week, and then she dropped a surprising comment: "You will be seeing Conrad when he is in New York." The thought astonished and delighted Quinn, who had in past years often tried, and once or twice apparently almost with success, to persuade Conrad to make an extended visit as his guest. He wrote back at once on April 5 to Mrs. Conrad: "I did not know Conrad was coming to New York. When is he coming? Whom is he going to visit here? I have not heard of his lecturing or doing anything else here. Perhaps he is just coming for a visit. It will be very pleasant to see him." On May 29 he thanked her for her gift of *A Handbook of Cookery for a Small House*, inscribed "To John Quinn Esq. with all good wishes from Jessie Conrad, 1923." He pointed out a misprint, "paper" for "pepper" on page 89, and wished she had left out all references to frying. Quinn's tone to Mrs. Conrad was polite and cordial, but by the date of his letter Conrad had come and almost gone, and Quinn was frustrated and angry at not having seen him. With no notice to Quinn Conrad had sailed from Glasgow on the *Tuscania* on April 20. It was only by local inquiry that Quinn learned that the novelist would be staying at the house of his American publisher F. N. Doubleday, in Oyster Bay on Long Island.

Several days after Conrad's installation at Doubleday's Quinn telephoned the publisher at home and proposed to motor down to Oyster Bay on the following day "to pay his respects to Conrad." Doubleday told him that the day was taken up with engagements. He waited a week and telephoned again, only to be told that Doubleday and Conrad were about to set off on a ten-day motor

tour of New England: " 'something might be arranged on his
return.' " [4] When they got back Quinn tried a third time and was
again rebuffed. Finally on the eve of Conrad's return to England
on June 2 on the *Majestic*, Quinn telephoned Doubleday to say he
was sorry he had not been able to see Conrad, and sent his regards
and best wishes for a pleasant voyage. Doubleday and his wife
sailed with Conrad. For Quinn it was an ugly and baffling episode.
He had behaved in a gentlemanly fashion and had been systematically and efficiently ignored—by whom, he was not quite sure. To
be so rudely snubbed in the effort to meet a man whom he valued
and whose regard he had earned was one of the most rankling
experiences of his life. He knew that Conrad was unwell and that
he was not officially "on view." But he also knew that he had seen
reporters in droves, had met many persons socially, and had made
two more or less public appearances, an informal talk to Doubleday employees and a reading from *Victory*, his most popular novel
in America, at a large soirée at the house of Mrs. Arthur Curtiss
James—to all of which Quinn had been denied access. He was still
seething in November when he wrote of the matter to Lady
Gregory:

> During the time Conrad was here he saw every second rate news-
> paper man and attended a reception arranged by Mrs. Doubleday
> and a tuft-hunter named Mrs. James, to which Jew dealers and
> publishers were invited but they did not invite me.
>
> [*November 15, 1923.*]

Quinn could make no sense of the episode. If Mrs. Conrad's
notice of his coming was any sign, Conrad had evidently not set
out with the thought of avoiding Quinn. Quinn could think of
nothing in their past relationship, or in the perhaps formal courtesy
of their recent letters, to preclude a meeting; and there was a great
deal to justify a meeting. If nothing else, Conrad must have been
curious to see all his old manuscripts *in situ* in their honored state
in Quinn's library. Quinn blamed first Doubleday, then Conrad,
then both. Trying to rationalize the affair to Lady Gregory, the
best he could do was to suppose some disgust of Conrad's in the
matter of the dedication of "the Napoleonic novel," now called
Suspense and promised for publication in December (actually left

unfinished at Conrad's death and published in 1926 with no dedication). But this seems lame and improbable. One would like to clear up the mystery of the unexplained disengagement of two men of honor. Richard Curle, Conrad's intimate friend, cannot account for it except by the general parlous state of Conrad's nerves at the time.[5] It is hard to avoid the suspicion that Conrad had been got at, probably over the preceding two years, and persuaded that Quinn was a trying and dangerous person, better avoided. Quinn was not at all placated by Doubleday's evasive account, in a letter in which he begged the loan of manuscript pages to be used as frontispieces for volumes in the "Concord Edition" of Conrad's works:

> Conrad was very frail when he was with me, and we found it necessary to take him home. I think the trip did him good, but how he ever had the nerve to leave England in his condition beats me. However, it didn't seem to do him any harm in the end, but I had many anxious moments during his visit. [*July 26, 1923.*]

The nearest approach to a solution of the mystery turns up in a not wholly trustworthy quarter, *It Was the Nightingale*, Ford Madox Ford's disheveled autobiographical volume, a book which often falsifies fact by careless handling of detail and by the kind of wrong emphases that follow from quirks of tone. Ford speaks at some length of his meetings with Quinn and Mrs. Foster in Paris in September 1923 when Quinn was arranging to rescue Ford and *the transatlantic review* from a financial impasse. According to the account, Mrs. Foster tried to prepare Ford for Quinn's probable overbearing ways and violent fits of temper, explaining that he was ill and in pain, and in a shattered state of nerves which she appeared to be tracing to the Conrad-Doubleday rebuff, treating that as a trauma that had altered the whole state of Quinn's psyche. She warned Ford not to bring up the matter: " 'It was a great misfortune that Conrad ever came to America. Mr. Quinn has never been the same again.' "[6] Ford gave Mrs. Foster the version of the case that he had received from Conrad: " 'Conrad was afraid to see him. . . . He was a sick man himself. . . . And he was told Mr. Quinn had a violent temper. . . The publishers told him not to see him. . . ."[7] Ford reviews his own last interview with Conrad:

... the last time I had seen Conrad he had told me he had refused to see Quinn. But he had felt bad about it. He acknowledged that Quinn had been a real benefactor to him. He had sold his later manuscripts to Mc —, I forget the name. He had imagined that Quinn would be enraged about it. He had really a right to be. But the war had been on. Conrad had been afraid of what the German submarines might do. He did not dare to send the mss. to Quinn in New York and he had been dreadfully pressed for money. Nobody could sell books. And Mr. — had pressed and pressed, offering very large sums. . . . He had had his family to think of. . . . And he had asked me, if I saw Quinn in Paris, to explain all this . . . about the submarines and the distance. And if necessary to apologise.[8]

But apparently Ford heeded Mrs. Foster's warning and never discussed Conrad with Quinn. And so Quinn was never to receive his "explanation" or his "apology" from Conrad—even from Conrad by agency of Ford. Ford's account has an air of probability and a ring of general truth: influenced by family need, wartime anxiety, and a chance for quick money on an advanced scale, Conrad had broken his bargain on the manuscripts with Quinn; he feared Quinn's just anger, even after Quinn had accepted the situation peaceably; in ill health in Doubleday's hands in America, he had been persuaded by Doubleday's picture of Quinn as a man of terrible rages and acceded to Doubleday's advice to avoid seeing him. In fact Quinn had wished only, humbly, to "pay his respects." He had had no intention of reproaching Conrad, or of creating a scene of any kind: Quinn's rages, by and large, were within his own control; he had them when he wanted them. In any case his good intentions made no difference in the situation as governed by Doubleday. And unquestionably it was this rebuff that determined Quinn to include all his Conrad material in his big housecleaning sale of his library that was to take place in the fall and winter of 1923–4.

That other housecleaning operation which was already under way, Quinn's attempt to dispose of his English pictures, went forward sporadically throughout the year and even into 1924. Primarily it was a housecleaning of the works of Augustus John, though Quinn also included in the sale certain other works he associated with John. Along with about sixty-five paintings by John he had sent to Percy Moore Turner in London about ten paintings by William Orpen, David Bomberg, Mark Gertler, Francis Dodd, Gordon Craig, and J. D. Innes. Turner had written on December 27, 1922, to say that he preferred to hold the sale in two main parts, paintings and drawings, and that he had hopes of disposing of the etchings *en bloc*. He explained his logic further in a letter of January 9. Separate sales would avoid overcrowding either show, would enable him to get the maximum amount out of the paintings, and give John buyers a chance to recoup and come back "with fresh cash" for the sale of drawings in the summer. On the same day, after he had studied Quinn's list of works and asking prices, he cabled: "John selling prices appear small. Can I augment at my discretion." All of this sounded sensible to Quinn and he gave Turner virtually a free hand. On the sixteenth Turner reported that the cases had arrived and the pictures were in good order in spite of a great deal of smashed glass. The show would open in the next week, as a show of Augustus John paintings, with the other paintings to be shown privately. Quinn had retained four John paintings toward which he felt the strongest sentimental obligation: the portrait of himself, though he had never liked it, the portrait of Arthur Symons, the big *The Way Down to the Sea*, which he had secured with such difficulty from Mme. Frida Strindberg, and the enormous *The Mumpers*.

William Marchant of the Goupil Gallery in London chided Quinn for not giving him a chance to treat for the Johns and other paintings, but Quinn said he had gone to the man who was handiest. Martin Birnbaum of Scott & Fowles in New York "wrung his hands" when he learned the paintings had gone to London for sale. Writing to Turner of these matters on February 5, Quinn also told of entertaining for dinner recently Captain R. Langton Douglas and his niece. Douglas, who had followed Sir Hugh Lane as director of the National Gallery of Ireland, had written him as early as August 31, 1920: "I shall consider it a great kindness if you will send me a list of rich Irishmen in America." Now he arrived, with a letter of introduction from W. B. Yeats, on the usual Irish "mission" of collecting money. Quinn found him "rather an amusing old boy." [9] He took the opportunity to unload on

Douglas and the National Gallery of Ireland a painting by Lambert Lombard, a minor painter of the sixteenth-century Flemish school, which he had bought in a careless moment in an auction at the Anderson Galleries for $310. The picture had been called *Rebecca at the Well,* but noticing a figure of Neptune in the painting Quinn took the liberty of renaming it "Penelope at the Well." He chose Penelope as "an appropriate Greek name," and argued that there could be no logical connection between a Jewish name and a Greek figure: ". . . art was a sin among the Jews" with their prohibition of images. He summed up: "Pen and Nep go together, but never Nep and Bec." [10]

Turner reported a brisk early trade. By January 23, three days before the formal opening, he had sold two Johns at £350 each, a painting and two water colors by Innes, while the National Art Collections Fund had reserved the big Innes *Arenig* at £400 and the Tate Gallery had reserved John's *Portrait of a Woman* at £500. Turner wrote: "This morning I had the visit of John himself, who took the matter very well, and liked the hanging of the pictures . . . and incidentally gave me permission to photograph what I wanted." [11] On the day of the opening, January 26, the *Morning Post* expressed itself. They identified the collection at once as "the property of Mr. John Quinn, a New York attorney," and reported the rumor that the sale had been arranged without the artist's knowledge. "For courtesy sake" the *Post* hoped that "this *on dit*" was false. So many paintings by one artist "suddenly thrown into the market must to some extent bring about a glut prejudicial to his personal interests, if not to his reputation as a painter." On scrutiny of the paintings themselves, however, the critic concluded that the quality of these earlier works in the mass was such as could only augment John's reputation. The early signs as to John's probable reaction seemed favorable, and Quinn breathed a bit easier.

On January 26 Turner wrote that he had sold the John *Head of a Boy* for 400 guineas; Quinn's suggested price had been £300. "Today" he had sold ten Johns for £2,000, which was £450 more than Quinn had asked. Turner figured that the cost to Quinn for the first £2,000 of sales had been £1,330. By January 30 the Tate Gallery had taken the *Portrait of a Woman* at £500 and *Washing Day* at £250. On February 15 Quinn totaled the sales reported to him thus far at £3,670 and thought that was "doing remarkably well." [12] Soon a nude had gone at £287.10, *Caspar and Pyramus*, a study of two of John's sons, at £350, *Conversation* at £325, *Girl with Red Kerchief* at £325, *Near Port-de-Bouc* at £90, and *Study in Red* at 350 guineas. In March, after the close of the show, *Woman Standing Against the Sky* was sold for £105. Turner now believed that he had exhausted just about all the possibilities of selling the oils in London. When he suggested that Quinn keep the remainder together and send it about as a "travelling" show in the United States, perhaps with Chicago as a base, Quinn quashed the idea at once in a letter of March 5. He said he had done all he ever intended to do in the way of "missionary work for art" in America. Such shows never sold anything, as far as he could see, and they resulted in a cheapening of the standards and the prices of artists who had to make their way in New York or not at all.

Turner had had no luck thus far with the etchings, and he thought Quinn had priced them too high. They had cost him just under £343 and he was asking £1,860. Turner thought they would bring no more than £800 to £900 at auction, and he suggested that he try for £1,500 now.[13] Quinn agreed to this. Turner was planning to bring the show of drawings on in the summer, probably in June. Quinn noted that press reports of the show of paintings had continued "rather good." He had certain instructions to give regarding the drawings. Whereas he realized that after the first years he had not had a chance at John's best paintings, he had had "the pick" of the drawings and he considered his collection "the finest John drawings in existence." [14] He asked Turner that his own name, usually in the form of "To Quinn" under John's signature, be carefully erased wherever it appeared on a drawing. He was aggrieved at his own designation as "a Tammany lawyer," which appeared to have become habitual in English accounts of the collection, and he tried to set Turner straight on the matter:

I have never been a Tammany lawyer nor have I ever been a member of Tammany Hall. I was rather prominent in politics for twelve or fifteen years, but always as an independent Democrat. While I went to National and State Conventions, I never was a member of Tammany Hall, never served on any of its committees, never held any office under it or affiliated with it and never was its lawyer in any sense . . . . If the statement were made in this town that I was a Tammany lawyer, I should have at once contradicted it and demanded and have secured its retraction.

[*March 26, 1923.*]

The tag evidently irritated him seriously, for a month later he again suggested to Turner that when the show of drawings came on he do his best to "disabuse the press" of the notion that he was a Tammany lawyer. ¹⁵

It is equally clear that his additionally awkward relationship with John himself was a good deal on Quinn's mind. Several of the newspaper accounts had made a point of the fact that Quinn had "dumped" his paintings on the London market without warning to John. To Turner he explained his action once more as follows:

> There was no point in my not advising John in advance of the sale, except two: That he might have arranged another exhibition ahead of ours in order to take the wind out of our sales [*sic*], and he would have done it, if he could, *thereby playing his own game*, and secondly, because I have not written to him for several years, and I had no intercourse for some years with him.
>
> [*March 26, 1923.*]

Only two days later he wrote again on the same subject. He had seen an announcement in the morning papers that John was sailing on the *Olympic*. He would serve on the judging committee of the Pittsburgh Art Institute, and he hoped as well to paint some American portraits and see some of the public and private collections that had " 'robbed Europe of its treasures.' " Quinn had no doubt that John would be happy to paint some rich Americans but otherwise he considered John's statement "what is vulgarly known as 'bull.' " ¹⁶ He vowed not to seek John out in America and he doubted that John would seek him out. The two had not met in over ten years, and in their last exchange of letters, five years before, both had agreed that Quinn had "ceased to care" for John's work.¹⁷

Quinn continued to worry the question in his letters to Turner. There had been talk that Scott & Fowles might be interested in taking over all the unsold pictures; Quinn thought this might be a good way out of an awkward impasse, and he gave Turner permission to shade prices if that would bring it about. But nothing came of the idea. By late April John was in New York, staying at the studio of Harrington Mann on West 67th Street, only a block away from Quinn's apartment, and being shown about the city by Martin Birnbaum. Quinn marveled that he could stand to see that much of Birnbaum. [18] Birnbaum told him John was getting $8,000 for a two-thirds figure (i.e., with hands) and Quinn thought that was fair to all parties. Birnbaum also told him that John had "growled" about him and complained of his selling his pictures without warning in advance, and there was the problem again. Quinn's feeling was at once fearful, defensive, and placatory:

> Personally, I should be very glad to show John courtesy or to have him dine with me or take him to the country occasionally, but as there would be between us that feeling that I have ceased to care for his work, and as he doubtless would not be interested in the work that I care for, there would be no common meeting ground.
>
> Therefore, I shan't make any overtures to him. In case he desires to see me I will treat him courteously and in a perfectly friendly way.[19]

Then Quinn heard reports that John was saying about New York that he had himself bought " 'two or three' " or " 'most' " of the paintings in the show at Turner's, and he wrote Turner for an opinion of that possibility on May 12. Turner replied on May 25 that he thought it quite possible that John had actually been buying several of his own oils when he came in the company of "a lady" who appeared to be buying the pictures, in cash. But Quinn had already made up his own mind that John was doubtless only advising the lady.[20]

Before the end of May John had made "a couple of overtures," and Quinn thought he would see him soon. By this time he had talked himself into a view of his sale as a "help" to John: ". . . I don't think he has any grievance against me at all." [21] Within the next few days they did meet and Quinn wrote blandly of the occasion to Turner:

> He was very pleasant and did not allude to the episode of my selling the paintings at all. I took him out riding with a lady and a

gentleman last Sunday afternoon. We motored to the Sleepy Hollow Country Club and had dinner and then we motored to my former country place [Purchase Street]. We got back about 12 o'clock. He was in good form and was as agreeable as ever.

[*June 15, 1923.*]

Meanwhile there had been developments in London. On April 6 Turner reported that John's dealer Knewstub had indeed organized a big rival John show at the Alpine Gallery. Turner had sold in the interval since the close of his show of paintings on February 24 only one John painting at £105 and three Innes drawings at £90.[22] He planned to open the show of drawings on June 28 or 29, though in fact the formal opening did not come till July 5. He asked permission to use Quinn's name frankly in the catalog of drawings; his name might be useful and in any case the pretence of anonymity had grown awkward and pointless: ". . . all London knows that the collection is yours."[23] But Quinn was still touchy about the direct use of his name and did not agree to it until July 2, three days before the opening, when he sent a cable.

But the situation had ripened in New York as well. In the first half of June Quinn and John met often and amicably. John dined at the apartment several times and made a drawing of his niece, Mary, in one evening and a drawing of Quinn in another evening. Jeanne Robert Foster remembers the second occasion, with John consuming a quart of whiskey in the course of the evening and apparently working and talking all the better for it.[24] He had a look at the results of ten years' growth in the collection and surprised Quinn by admiring much of it. John was to sail from Quebec on June 23, and on the night of the sixteenth Quinn saw him off on the train for Buffalo, where he was to paint a portrait. Apparently in all their meetings John never spoke directly of Quinn's current disposal of his works in London. But he had told a mutual friend that whereas he thought the sale of paintings had done him no harm, he feared the sale of drawings and etchings might damage his market severely, and he growled that " 'he had a family to support.' "[25] Brooding all this over, Quinn sent a confusingly double-minded cable on June 20 to Turner:

Been seeing John on old friendly basis. He fears sale of drawings may hurt his interests and would prefer private sales. If not too late would prefer not to have my name on catalogue. Please cable your judgment whether your sales will hurt Johns market. Do not wish to hurt his sales unnecessarily.

He sent after the cable letters of June 21 and 25 still bruiting the question indecisively. "I would not want John to feel that I was playing him a sharp trick," he wrote Turner on June 25. To avoid "hurting" John he was willing to take the risk of a financial loss that might follow from abandoning the public sale of drawings. "I like him personally very much," Quinn wrote on June 21. "The old friendly feeling was entirely restored. In fact, so far as I was concerned, it had never ended." (This was obviously untrue.) John's amiable behavior in New York had made it harder than ever for Quinn publicly to abandon his old commitment to John's work. On the other hand, he *had* abandoned it, and there was not much use in pretending. He knew, too, that John was not really hard up. He had painted several of his $8,000 portraits while in the United States, and was due to return in the autumn for a further harvest: ". . . in the John American market the clover would seem to be long." [26]

It was agreed between Quinn and Turner that the sale of drawings would proceed as scheduled. In the long run it did not matter much. Turner was already afraid that "the John market" was being "rather overworked" that season with three big sales—two of Quinn's and one of Knewstub's.[27] In advance of the opening he sold eight drawings for £35 to £100 each, but in the first week of the formal sale he was able to dispose of only one additional drawing. There had been a severe heat wave, and London was deserted. The show was to close on July 26, and Turner feared there would be a big remainder of Quinn's stock. He had had no luck whatever in finding a buyer for the etchings. Quinn accepted the situation without complaint. He thought Turner had handled the whole affair honorably and energetically and that their luck had been fair. He was disappointed about the drawings and etchings, which he considered finer of their kind than the paintings. Sales of the paintings had been satisfactory in quantity and price: he had made money on them over their original cost to him, but not enough money for anyone to accuse him of profiteering in Augustus John. Quinn arranged with Turner to keep on hand the unsold works and try to dispose of them piecemeal and privately. He was to continue seeking a buyer for the etchings as a group, and not be fussy about shading the price if necessary.[28] Quinn was not essentially shaken in his resolve to clear out his Johns and other English works and put the money into French paintings.

Partly because of his heavy investment in art in 1922, partly because he now had Roché on the scene in Paris to sort out the available works of genuine "museum rank and importance," Quinn's dealings for French art in 1923 were fewer, more discriminating, more crucial. Again he was trying to make his money go as far as possible, and do as much good as possible, by concentrating on work that was new, or nearly so. When Turner offered him Van Gogh's powerful *Asylum at St. Rémy* for £4,000 Quinn felt he had to refuse in spite of the majesty of the work: it was "rather a steep price." [29] In fact it was more than twice what he was paying for the big Seurat *Le Cirque*. Two months later he again refused when Turner, in need of cash for a house he wanted to build, offered him a "superb" Renoir landscape of 1875 from Turner's personal collection at £4,000. Quinn wrote: ". . . Renoir is beyond me, in price, and I must look forward in my collection and not backward." [30] The same set of motives made him look again and more critically at his Ingres *Raphael et la Fornarina* to which he had succumbed in 1922. He wrote to Roché on January 8, 1923: ". . . it is a beautiful thing, but it does not go with my other modern things." And he dropped a hint to Roché that he might be willing to dispose of the picture if a buyer appeared. In the same letter he made an offer of 20,000 francs for the smaller version of Rousseau's *La Carmagnole*, a gay country festival scene celebrating the Revolution. The picture actually fell to him in March at 23,000 francs. He was also strongly tempted by Roché's charming account of a big queer masterwork of another of the fathers of the School of Paris which Joseph Hessel was offering at 100,000 francs: Cézanne's portrait of his father, about four by five feet in size, a left profile view of the old man seated with his legs crossed in a straight chair, reading a newspaper, wearing a little cap and looking as if he were snatching a moment on his way to the mine or the potato field, done in a very dark heavy drawing, like a Rouault. Roché wrote on January 14 to say that Derain had seen the work and had

said: " 'Good—Cézanne was not yet influenced by impressionism.' "
Roché himself judged it "very cheap if compared with other Cézannes on the market—because it is rough, simple, direct, crude,
almost comical in the way the old man holds his newspaper, a little
"mad"—for me gigantic and genial." So it was, a picture with a
great deal of humanity. Roché asked Picasso to have a look at it,
and he too liked it. Quinn asked Roché to keep an eye on the
painting while he thought over the money problem.

On the ninth of January Quinn was finally forced to pay Marius
de Zayas the $1,200 he had owed him for months for two works of
Brancusi's. He had apparently delayed out of sheer willfulness and
a desire to cause as much trouble as he could for De Zayas and his
agent Charles Sheeler without actually losing the works. In the long
squabbling correspondence over the matter Quinn repeatedly addressed or referred to Sheeler as "Sheler," apparently with a design
to make the name sound as "German" or "Jewish" as possible. He
did not give in and pay his bill until De Zayas sent men to the
apartment with an order to pick up the Brancusis and return them
to his shop. The cases containing the last works he had bought
from Brancusi himself remained in the basement of his apartment
building from October until he got around to opening them early
in January 1923. But then he wrote of his pleasure to Roché:
"Please tell Brancusi how delighted I am with all of them. Each
one is more beautiful than the others . . . as beautiful as any Egyp-
tian or Hindu carvings or sculpture." [31] In the same letter he notified Roché that Mrs. Foster's new volume of poems, *Rock-Flower*,
was just out from Boni & Liveright, with a group of poems in the
middle inspired by and honoring Brancusi, "very beautifully and
exquisitely done." She was sending copies to both Roché and Brancusi, and Quinn suggested that it would be worth Brancusi's while
to learn enough English to read the poems in tribute to himself.
On February 20 as he sent 20,000 francs in payment for Segonzac's
Baigneuses Quinn enclosed an additional 3,000 for Roché personally.

By now *Le Cirque* was paid for and eagerly awaited in New
York, and Quinn again wrote Roché that if it lived up to its praise
he would plan to devise it eventually to France: "If it is, as you
wrote, the most important Seurat in existence, then it belongs in
the Louvre." [32] The painting came in on the *France* on March 10,

and Quinn allowed it to remain in its crate in the basement until the sixteenth, which would be the sixteenth birthday of his niece Mary Anderson: "So the day was celebrated doubly. . . ." [33] Mary and her mother, Julia Anderson, F. J. Gregg, and Quinn's attorney friend Maurice Léon joined him for dinner, after which the picture made its ascent with awkward ceremony. It proved too large to go into the elevator cage and had to be brought up on the elevator roof. Toasts were drunk to the two queens of the day. Quinn was well content: "It is very beautiful, exquisitely beautiful. . . ." [34] He approved the narrow gold frame which Paul Signac had designed to surround the main frame, painted by Seurat himself.

There was a lull now in the pursuit of art until the summer. Roché and the Paris dealers wrote that it was more than ever necessary to stay alert if one hoped for masterpieces: the Paris market was turning a bit mad, with many moneyed Germans as well as predatory Americans in the city. Roché warned Quinn on June 21: "Barnes is now ravaging Paris." Quinn turned some of his energy toward literary friends and their affairs. Art and literary interests came together for him in Mrs. Foster's poems, as they did when Quinn sent Roché one of the first copies of T. S. Eliot's *The Waste Land*, which Boni & Liveright had brought out on December 15, 1922. "It has new rhythm and sardonic humour," Quinn's note ran." [35] Eliot had written anxiously on December 27 to inquire whether Quinn had received "the manuscript of all my poems" which he had sent by registered post "some weeks ago" and which should have been in Quinn's hands by now. Quinn did not get around to acknowledging receipt of the famous packet until February 26, when he said that it had reached him about January 15. Of the Eliot-Pound original manuscript of *The Waste Land* he wrote as follows:

> I have read the manuscript of "The Waste Land" which you sent me with great interest. I have noted the evidence of Pound's criticisms on the poem. Personally I should not have cut out some of the parts that Pound advised you to cut out. Of course the portions which you have scrapped will never appear in print from the copies that I have.   [*February 26, 1923.*]

That manuscript and those of other poems Quinn would hold "largely in trust" for Eliot, he wrote, and he would undertake to supply copies whenever Eliot required them. He promised to have "the bound notebook and the other loose pages of the manuscript and the typewritten copies" placed in a solander case, as was his habit.

Quinn proceeded to the question of the "value" of the manuscript, making it clear that he was considering only the material apart from *The Waste Land,* the manuscript of which he was accepting as Eliot's gift:

> With the notebook and the loose sheets of paper, exclusive of "The Waste Land," there are some fifty-three pages of manuscript in the book and some five or six pages of loose manuscript, making roughly sixty pages. Then there are the typewritten drafts, which Drake [James F. Drake of 14 West 40th Street, Quinn's principal book dealer] did not rank as manuscript and disregarded in his valuation. He thought that a payment of $2 a page, which would be about $120, would be "about right." But I thought his figures were somewhat conservative and I am sending you London draft to your order for £29.14.10, the equivalent of $140, which I think is fair and reasonable. I trust you will agree with me. In fixing the price I am taking into consideration the condition stated in your letter, namely, that I "pay the present fair value of it, disregarding any prospective or future value."
>
> [*February 26, 1923.*]

Quinn noted with pleasure that as he was ordering additional copies of the Boni & Liveright book recently he had been told that the first printing of a thousand copies was sold out, along with 240 of the second thousand. Eliot's prompt reply on March 12 showed him well content with Quinn's arrangements: "I consider your payment for the manuscript very generous indeed, and feel that you have thwarted me in my attempt to repay you in some way for all that you have done." Whereas he was delighted to hear that 1,240 copies of his book had been sold, he wondered what had happened to the $150 that Liveright had promised him on publication and which had not appeared.

Eliot's account of his life in general showed a man at the breaking point. The labor and responsibility of the *Criterion* on top of his bank duties were driving him frantic, and he felt that he had to give up one or the other. He had been offered the post of literary editor of the *Nation*, but with a guarantee of only six months' tenure and at a salary which would mean a sacrifice of £200 a year as compared to his income from the job at the bank. "I have not even time to go to a dentist or to have my hair cut," he wrote. ". . . I am worn out. I cannot go on." [36]

Quinn had sympathy ready for a man who sounded as driven as himself, and he undertook to do something more for Eliot. He inquired of Liveright about the missing $150 and learned that it had gone forward on March 15. Then he set about his own private provincial form of Pound's "Bel Esprit" scheme for the rescue of T. S. Eliot. To Otto Kahn Quinn sent Eliot's 1920 *Poems*, *The Waste Land*, and *The Sacred Wood*, and asked if he would be willing to guarantee Eliot $200 a year for five years. Quinn himself guaranteed $400 a year for that period. Kahn agreed. Quinn made the same approach to Frank H. Munsey, a multimillionaire New York newspaper proprietor, who refused via his secretary, but kept the books. Quinn then sent his office boy with a letter to Munsey's secretary asking for the return of the books so that he could " 'send them to someone who was more interested in good literature.' " [37] He wrote also to Irene Lewisohn and to Archer Huntington but he had not heard from them when he wrote Eliot on March 27. Meanwhile Ezra Pound had approached Max Pam in Rome, but Pam would only promise to " 'talk the matter over' " with Quinn when he got back to New York—perhaps a year hence. So Quinn could write Eliot at the end of March that he had $600 a year sure for him and hopes of at least $1,000. Eliot cabled on April 2 to say that he had given up on the *Nation* proposal because their guarantee was inadequate and because they could not wait long enough for him to give the necessary notice to Lloyd's Bank. His cable continued: "Does extraordinarily generous offer hold if bad health forces leave bank without alternative position. Thank Kahn. Await letter." Quinn cabled back on the same day: "Offer holds for five years unconditional. Writing"; and followed this with a letter, also on the same day, in which he promised, "I will send you the first check in response to your letter, if that is satisfactory to you." The matter rested there until July, by which time it had developed that Otto Kahn's offer of $200 had been meant as conditional upon Eliot's leaving the bank. But in a letter to Eliot on July 23 Quinn pronounced his own offer as "unconditional, beginning now," and rendered up the cash in the form of a London draft for £89.19.1, or $400. He promised future similar payments in June of 1924, 1925, 1926, and 1927. (But by June 1924 Quinn was a dying man.) Eliot concluded a long letter of October 4: "I have not attempted to express my thanks. It is really beyond words. But you have been a greater support and encouragement to me than I can possibly say. It is unique."

In his letter of March 27 Quinn had excused himself from offering a larger personal subsidy to Eliot on the ground that he had recently got caught in Sir Horace Plunkett's drive to raise $150,000 to float the revived *Irish Statesman*. Quinn had put money in himself and had made one of an organizing committee of leading American Irishmen to promote the scheme for the paper, of which Æ had reluctantly consented to serve as editor.[38] Quinn was happy with the idea of W. B. Yeats as an Irish senator, but he thought it shocking that Hyde had not been similarly honored, and he wrote to Yeats, Russell, and Lady Gregory to press Hyde's claim. The state of affairs in Ireland generally seemed worse than ever. "Weasels fighting in a hole," Yeats had described Irish behavior in sorrow and disgust.[39] Shane Leslie wrote from London on March 22: "Friend after friend arrives with photographs of their smoking homes—Plunkett, Esmonds, Gogarty!" Æ estimated that fifty of his own paintings had been destroyed in the burning of collectors' houses, notably thirty-two of his best in the beautiful house of Sir Horace Plunkett.[40] People in Dublin, Susan Mitchell reported, were hanging on "from day to day, hoping the war will soon be over, and with the heart-sickness consequent on hope deferred." [41] Burning the house of Plunkett, who had given his whole life modestly and unselfishly for Ireland, struck her as a peculiarly "ugly manifestation of Irish character"—a cruel and wanton act. "Everything good and bad in Irish character has boiled up," she felt. "We are under no illusions now; our vanity is punctured; we have seen our ugly faces in the glass." On the other hand, she argued, the civil war was "the undoing of 700 years of idiotic government" under England, and it "could not fail to be terrifying." She joined in the stubborn hopefulness of her master, Æ: "But there is something sweet and loveable in Irish character still to be manifested and to build up life here." Æ predicted that in a dozen years Ireland would be ready to show herself "a brilliant country." For the moment, he remarked drily, she was "rather dull . . . from oversensation." [42] Characteristically, in "spare" time he was writing a new book "to keep my thoughts off passing sensations." [43]

With his Republican sentiments, Jack Yeats was still somewhat estranged from his brother in the Senate. Jack and his wife, Cottie, spent two weeks in the summer with Lady Gregory at Coole Park. She feared they would find it dull, much altered from the old days familiar to Quinn, when it was always full of guests. But the lively grandchildren helped out, and Lady Gregory commissioned Jack Yeats to make water color drawings of Anne's pony and Catherine's donkey, " 'owners up.' " [44] There was no more talk of buying pictures between Quinn and Jack Yeats. Quinn felt that Jack's price of £250 for a painting was too steep, and with his fixation on the French he turned his back on Ireland's one contemporary painter of genius.

Regularly now when she was in Dublin Lady Gregory stayed with W. B. Yeats and his wife in their eighteenth-century house in Merrion Square. In a September visit she found him taking time off from his "philosophy" to work on what was to be one of the great short poems of the century, his grand, harsh, irregular sonnet on Leda and the Swan. It had been promised for the *Empire Review*, but Yeats feared it was too improper for that journal. Lady Gregory had a major new work of her own to show, her Passion Play, *The Story Brought by Brigit*, which she read to Yeats and Lennox Robinson. "It is written with reverence of the Chief Figure, and no words given Him but His own," she assured Quinn. [45] "It is really a study of His enemies, of the rabble, and of the various interests that brought Him to His death." Both Yeats and Robinson were impressed and moved, as she herself was moved to hear Yeats praise her " 'great intellectual power' "—at seventy.

Yeats himself praised the play to Quinn as "a masterpiece." [46] In the same letter he again thanked Quinn for letting him have his father's self portrait, which he thought, even in its unfinished state, "marvelously like" and possessed of "a quality of light and air" the old painter had never achieved before. The portrait was one of the treasures of his new house at 82 Merrion Square, itself a treasure, with its study "that might be in a country house, mantelpieces and rooms magnificently made in 1740, and conversation good or bad every night." [47] Cuala Industries had now set up shop in the ground floor of the house, with George Yeats in charge of the embroidery in place of Lily, still ill in a nursing home near London. Yeats was hard at work on his "book of philosophy," his cranky, brilliant *A Vision,* and hoping to finish it by Christmas so that he could get back to writing verse. His work in the Senate he found undemanding and on the whole congenial, and he judged himself "quite a useful politician, having an inventive mind and no ambition." [48]

Before Christmas came round Yeats's work met a stunning and gratifying interruption and recognition when he was given the Nobel Prize for literature. Yeats's old schoolmate and Quinn's good friend F. J. Gregg heard the news in his post on the *Sun* on November 14, and he telephoned excitedly to Quinn, who immediately cabled his hearty congratulations. Quinn was pleased at the honor to his friend and to Ireland, and humanly glad that Yeats would now be, with luck and care, at last placed beyond material need. He reckoned that the money soundly invested would yield at least $3,000 a year. Jack Yeats was unsurprised at his brother's honor and wrote Quinn on December 18: "I think he should have had it some years ago." Shane Leslie, on the other hand, supposed that the honor had been given to Yeats rather than to Thomas Hardy because the selection committee had wished to pay a compliment to Ireland. No doubt, as Yeats was among the first to specify, the prize was a tribute to the Irish "renaissance" in general as well as to Yeats in particular. "It has struck a cheerful note in Dublin," Leslie wrote on November 30, "and done more to make the fine arts commendable and practicable to the Irish people than anything for a long time—since you set Hyde up with American money." Lady Gregory's fifteen-page letter of November 28 naturally gave much space to Yeats's honor, which made her "glad and proud"— for Yeats, for herself, and for the movement of which they had been captains. She was also amused at the new local respectability conferred upon both of them by the Nobel medal and accompanying cash:

> . . . in the years [Yeats] came here my friends and family in the neighbourhood never realized that he had genius, but knew or

thought he was a revolutionist, and lamented my folly and obstinacy in having him and other writers in the house instead of the ordinary "country house parties." Now some of them who remain are much impressed by the sudden descent of prosperity on him, and their respect for me has increased!

Nor could she forbear quoting T. P. ("Tay-Pay") O'Connor's specification of Yeats's and Ireland's debt to herself: " 'It is impossible to mention Mr. Yeats without adding something of what he and Ireland owe to the unselfish, devoted and unconquerable woman who has helped him and Ireland toward the great literary renaissance of modern days. I mean Lady Gergory. . . .' " But Yeats himself gave the idea its most elegant and adequate dress when he extended it to John Synge and included it in his official lecture to the Swedish Royal Academy as part of the prize ceremonies. He gives this account of the occasion in "The Bounty of Sweden" as included in his *Autobiography*:

> I am speaking without notes and the image of old fellow-workers comes upon me as if they were present, above all of the embittered life and death of one, and of another's laborious, solitary age, and I say, "When your King gave me a medal and diploma, two forms should have stood, one on either side of me, an old woman sinking into the infirmity of age and a young man's ghost. I think when Lady Gregory's name and John Synge's name are spoken of by future generations, my name, if remembered, will come up in the talk, and that if my name is spoken first their names will come in their turn because of the years we worked together. I think that both had been well pleased to have stood beside me at the great reception at your Palace, for their work and mine has delighted in history and tradition.[49]

W. B. Yeats figured largely in an exchange of letters between Quinn and Arthur Symons, the "rhymer" of Yeats's memoirs, in the summer of 1923 before Quinn went abroad. Symons wrote on June 12 of the pleasure he had found in that volume of the memoirs which Yeats had dedicated to Quinn: *"The Trembling of the Veil* of Yeats' is an absolute masterpiece—far and away the best thing he has ever done." Symons was writing his own "Confessions" and had carried his account through the "dramatic and tragic" time in Italy when he had gone out of his mind, and through "a minute

Lady Gregory in 1907. Drawing by John Butler Yeats.

relation of my awful sufferings in that nightmare of a place in London where I was cruelly kept for a year and a half." Symoms had still been officially in the care of a "keeper" when he and Augustus John and Agnes Tobin had kept gay company together in the summer of 1909. Now he wanted to know whether he might bring in "lightly and with but few details" an account of his meeting with Quinn at "the dancer's house . . . and the various adventures we and John and a few others had afterwards." [50] Quinn gave him *carte blanche*: "You can go as far as you like, so far as I am concerned." But he recalled their first meeting as earlier and very different: he remembered dining with Symons and W. B. Yeats in 1903 or 1904 in Woburn Buildings in London, leaving there about midnight, and walking about the city with Symons until two or three in the morning. Among other sights Symons had pointed out the church where the runaway Brownings were married.[51]

Æ had devoted most of his letter of April 5 to teasing Quinn "cynically" but systematically about the current condition of his taste for art, which he diagnosed as "art fever":

> I have seen it in others, and surmise it in you at a distance. A genuine love for painting, then an absorption in the pleasures it can give, then comes the stage when, somehow, the pleasure is lost and one wants the abnormal. The drugtaker is satisfied at first with a small dose, then he has to take bigger and bigger doses to give him his original sensations. So you have travelled from the normal to the abnormal in art.

Æ suspected that most of Quinn's French painters were merely offering "spiced art for jaded palates," and he advised Quinn to remember and apply the "so wise" counsel of Yeats's song, " 'She bade me take love easy.' " In pressing on for "impossible delights," constantly new sensations in his collecting, Quinn was forgetting, Æ feared, the quieter, deeper pleasures of art in its broad spectrum of times and forms, losing touch with its base in intellect and control and humane experience. He summed up his case with large tolerance: "The real thing which excites in art or literature is imagination and we don't tire of it." Quinn was undismayed and unpersuaded. He was sure he knew where he was going and how to get there. He knew now where he wanted to live as a collector, and how to concentrate and intensify his life there. He had no doubt that he had discovered the locus of excellence and of fascination: he wanted not literature but art; not all art but modern art; not all modern art but modern French art; not all modern French art but major works of a few masters. His ceasing to buy American art was a move toward concentration; so was his disposal of his English works.

Now in the spring of 1923 he made another major decision with the same end in view—to sell out the bulk of his huge personal library. The decision came with a peculiar wrench, for it meant denying the oldest of his cultural commitments. But he wanted space and he wanted money, and he set about the matter resolutely. His library numbered some 18,000 items of books and manuscripts, and there was a good deal of fat in it, particularly multiple copies of works he had bought out of one or another personal loyalty. He did not intend an absolute housecleaning, merely a reduction of his library to a reasonable civilized compass. As he worked on the matter it turned into something of a labor of love and of dismay. In the spring and summer before he went off to Nova Scotia for a month's rest in August, he made most of his selections of what to sacrifice. He found that the idea of his library's being reduced to a mere sale list was intolerable to him, and he set about making his catalog itself as much of a work of art as he could in the time to which he was limited. During most of June and July he worked from four to eight hours a day, much of it after hours and on weekends, arranging his list and composing and dictating notes to accompany favorite works. The notes were descriptive, or critical, or reminiscent, and they came from the information in his own head and in his books and his correspondence. He commissioned his scholarly friend Vincent O'Sullivan to write many similar notes for which he had no time himself. When he went off to Nova Scotia he left the material with the stenographers in his office and when he came back it was all "sliced up and arranged alphabetically and chronologically." [52] By the time he sailed for Europe in September the work was in fairly finished order.

Quinn had also been passionately involved since May in a case which was to prove one of the worst frustrations of his career as a lawyer and a lover of art, and it was this which took him abroad.

He had been retained by the New York art dealer George Joseph Demotte in a slander action against a formidable rival, the international dealer Sir Joseph Duveen. Demotte, who was perhaps the largest dealer in sculpture in the world, had bought from Prince Antoine d'Orleans an ostensible thirteenth-century Limoges *champlevé* enamel figure of the Virgin and had sold it to the Fifth Avenue jeweler Michael Dreicer for 350,000 francs. After making one payment of 50,000 francs, Dreicer had died, and his heirs, having called in Duveen for an expert opinion on the authenticity of the enamel, sued Demotte for liberation from the commitment to purchase and for the return of the money already paid. Duveen, whom Lady Gregory out of her own partisan passion identified as "the wretch who gained his knighthood by promising to build a London gallery to house the Lane pictures," [53] and whom Quinn denounced as "full of jealousy and meanness" and a habitual attacker of rival dealers,[54] was charged by Demotte, with Quinn as counsel, with having scattered "right and left" his opinion that the work was a modern forgery not more than five years old, and with having boasted that he would spend $100,000 to prove it false and would drive Demotte out of business in New York within the year. Demotte's slander suit in the New York Supreme Court for $500,000 in damages was "based upon five separate statements to five individuals made by Duveen" [55]—$100,000 per statement.

The case took one complex and sensational turn after another. Jean Vigouroux, the manager of Demotte's New York branch, was charged by Demotte with having pocketed money due the firm. Vigouroux countercharged that his employer had been marketing fake sculptures for years. In France it was alleged that a ring of sculpture thieves had been raiding French churches and public buildings and selling their trophies in England and America, and that Demotte had been a principal in a well-established trade in wholly false or heavily restored sculptures, selling to museums and moneyed individuals, especially in the United States. The widow of a Demotte workman claimed that her husband had been murdered—presumably to keep him from telling what he knew. Quinn wrote Roché on August 31 that he would be sailing on the *Paris* on September 12 to take depositions for the case in France. He expected to be there only a week or ten days, and he asked Roché to keep his coming secret: Duveen was in Paris, and Quinn felt quite sure the enemy would have him shadowed to see whom he was meeting. But on September 4 Quinn heard by cable from Mrs. Demotte that her husband had been killed the day before in a hunting accident. At the end of a day's hunting on his estate in the *département* of Loir-et-Cher, Demotte had died instantly when struck by a double charge from a shotgun dropped by a companion, Otto Wegener. Wegener was said to have attempted suicide when he saw what he had done, but been prevented by others in the party. In law Demotte's death automatically put an end to his slander suit. But Quinn resolved still to go abroad as scheduled to look after the affairs of the estate; and he was nursing the hope too that he might yet find some way to get back at Duveen. On September 7 in *The New York Times* Quinn issued a statement praising Demotte's connoisseurship and his business integrity, and vowing that he would soon have "triumphantly met" all the charges against him.

Quinn spent a hectic and frustrating three weeks in Paris trying to advance the cause, which he now looked on as his own as much as Demotte's, against what he soon concluded was the hopeless cowardice of his own clients. He had thought he might be able to clear the dead man's name by forcing Duveen to submit to arbitration by an international committee of experts the question of the authenticity of the disputed enamel. After Quinn had heard further rumors of Duveen's talk he wished to bring a new suit for criminal libel: he believed he could prove by the testimony of two bankers that Duveen had said that Demotte was lucky to have been killed because he would have lost his suit and been forced to commit suicide. Quinn tried again and again to persuade the widow, her two brothers, and their adviser Bienenfeld to fight their case, then he threw up his hands in rage and disgust. He was particularly incensed against Bienenfeld, whom he denounced as a Jew, a mere pearl merchant, a coward and a bully. He came to feel that he himself had been tricked and misused by a consortium of international Jewry composed of Duveen, Mrs. Demotte and her brothers, and Bienenfeld. He reviewed the experience in a letter of November 10 to Harriet Shaw Weaver:

> . . . I had three weeks of walking in slime and sewers and finally I got tired of it and chucked it. Mrs. Demotte, who is a Jewess, was advised by another Jew, a pearl merchant named Bienenfeld,

and she betrayed her husband, was false to his memory and allowed his name to rest under a stain which his son will inherit. I
have never met greater cowardice in my entire experience. When
I got out of the matter I took a spiritual bath as well as a physical
disinfectant. . . .

Not all his time in France was spent so unpleasantly. He was
able to get to Brittany for a few days' rest, and he found time in
Paris to visit galleries, studios, and cafés, and to see many of the
artists and writers he cared most about. Mrs. Foster had come with
him from America, and Roché came from Berlin to join him in
Paris, and one or both of them kept him company on most of his
calls. As in 1921, they had several burlesque rounds of golf at
Chantilly, Fontainebleau, and St. Cloud with Brancusi in his big
sombrero-style hat and Erik Satie in his bowler and carrying a
rolled umbrella. Quinn saw a good deal of Pound, Joyce, and
Ford Madox Ford, singly or together, and was photographed
with the three of them, Quinn looking tense and thin, against the
door of Pound's studio. Joyce and Brancusi came to dinner one
evening and afterwards Joyce and Quinn strolled and talked in
the city. Quinn warned him that he meant to include the manuscript of *Ulysses* in his library sale and promised him a share of
the profits if any. Joyce seemed to take the notion peacefully.
Quinn pleaded pressing engagements when Joyce offered to read
to him from his arcane "Work in Progress," *Finnegans Wake.*
Quinn was pleased to see him looking easier and more robust than
two years before, and he attributed Joyce's improved health to
the fact that he had followed Quinn's advice to have his teeth
looked after—losing seventeen teeth, seven abscesses, and one
cyst.[56]

Quinn had never met Ford before, but he had been impressed
by Pound's generous praise of him and his services as model and
monitor of Pound's generation of writers in English, and he
warmed quickly to Ford as he came to know him. He was further
induced by Mrs. Foster's affection for Ford * and by the fact
that she had now been named as New York editor of *the transatlantic review*, which Ford was struggling to get off the ground.

---

* Perhaps also by Ford's admiration for her. He called her a "ravishingly
beautiful lady" and "an admirable business woman." *It Was the Nightingale*,
p. 298.

Ford had put $2,000 of his own money into the magazine, and Quinn now staked him to $1,000 and promised as much again if it were really needed—as of course it would be. Ford, who grossly overestimated Quinn's wealth, later set down an amusing hyperbolical account of what it was like to move about Paris with Quinn in these days:

> Mr. Quinn was not the first very wealthy man I had met but he was the first I had gone about with for any time. It was impressive . . . to go about Paris with Quinn was to see the doors of palaces, banks, offices, fly open as if propelled by gunpowder. . . . And before him even the notaries departed from the routines of their lifetimes. It was as if he carried about with him the power to make you see fairy tales. . . .
>
> He appeared and at once the poor poets saw their one chance— if he would only glance at them—to realize then their material dreams. The rich refurbished their ideas of fantastic business operations that should make them as Emperors. . . .[57]

Usually with Roché and Mrs. Foster, Quinn visited Rouault at his little museum and Braque, Picasso, Brancusi, Segonzac, Derain at their studios. One evening they took dinner at La Péreuse, then adjourned with Segonzac to Brancusi's studio. From there they trouped to Derain's studio, up seven flights of stairs, he lighting their way with a match from above. After champagne with Derain they lighted their way down the seven flights with matches, crossed the courtyard to Segonzac's studio, where they repeated the ritual of the matches and the climb and descent of seven flights, before departing finally for their hotels at two-thirty in the morning. Quinn saw Gwen John several times, taking dinner with her once with the Mother Superior of the convent in Meudon and accompanying her again on a visit to her friends the Gervais. Quinn had commissioned a portrait of Mrs. Foster by Derain, but when he saw the first version he did not like it, thought it too sensual. " 'I know Quinn's trouble,' " Derain said. " 'He doesn't want a portrait; he wants "a Derain." ' " [58] He cheerfully began over.

On October 2 Quinn sent a note to Arthur B. Davies, who happened to be in Paris at the same time, inviting him to come to see three of his recent purchases—an El Greco, a Cézanne, a Matisse. The El Greco, from Paul Rosenberg, was *Christ Driving the*

Money-Changers from the Temple, a larger version of the subject in the National Gallery in London; the Cézanne was the big crude portrait of his father to which Roché had alerted him earlier, for which he now paid 99,475 francs, and which he described to Davies as "a very noble thing"; [59] the Matisse was a huge still-life interior, six by eight feet, costing 49,265 francs, which Quinn considered "the most gorgeous Matisse of the kind ever painted." [60] These were only the top of a notable list of purchases. He bought *The Jungle* of Rousseau which Ambroise Vollard called "le roi" of Rousseaus; of Picasso he took an early small nude, a cubist figure painting, *La Toilette* and *Les Baigneuses* of the rose period, and his cubist *Portrait of William Uhde,* "of a solemn, cathedral-like sombre beauty"; [61] of Braque he bought only a pencil and a sanguine drawing. In sculpture he concentrated entirely on Brancusi and took three pieces, a head in wood, the latest version of his marble bird, "almost shooting up into the heavens," [62] and a small highly finished fish, which he planned to use as a paper knife. By the time Brancusi had delivered the pieces to Pottier for shipment on December 10 a fourth work, a wooden "Torso" on a stone base, had been added. "They are all great things," Quinn wrote Lady Gregory of his Paris acquisitions, and though he expected the outlay would keep him poor for a year, he "could not resist them." [63]

The "spiritual bath" which Quinn felt he needed after the decay of the Demotte affair took the form of a hurried ten days in Italy. He and Mrs. Foster went by train to Venice for three days, thence by train to Bologna and Florence, then in a hired car to San Gimignano, Siena, Perugia, Cortona, Monte Olivieto, Assisi, Spoleto, and finally to Rome for three days. It was Quinn's first visit to the cradle of his culture, but he proved immune to its charms and splendors—irritable, preoccupied, bored, contemptuous. Even when he tried to lift his mood he was still obviously a man only miming his old energetic ways of behaving. Snapshots Mrs. Foster took at the time show a drawn, closed, stony face. Quinn was far from well. He was pale and thin and jumpy, and he slept very little. Mrs. Foster struggled to cheer him up and to smooth his way, rising early every morning, for example, to prepare the dish based on mashed prunes which seemed to be the only thing his digestion would tolerate. Both of them were glad to board the train for

Paris, where Quinn passed three days before setting off for Berlin for several days of conferences about patent rights in a motor fuel in which Roché was trying to interest him. Then he came back to Paris for a final two days before sailing for home on the *Berengaria* on October 27.

During his various periods in Paris Quinn had tried several times to secure an audience with Raymond Poincaré, President of the French Conseil des Ministres, but whereas a message granting an appointment had evidently been left at his hotel, Quinn for some reason did not receive it and had to leave without seeing Poincaré. On the day before he left for home Quinn dictated a letter of ten pages to Poincaré setting forth his views on the question of German reparations to France and on the attitudes to France and Germany likely to be taken by what he saw as perfidious Albion and pusillanimous Columbia. The industrial Ruhr basin, he said, was "the knot of the problem of the military fate of Europe in future." [64] In justice to herself for the wrongs of Germany, and for the sake of the future peace of Europe, France should demand that due reparations from Germany be paid to her and to Belgium and England by means of Germany's grant of at least 51 per cent of "the right of absolute property" in the "principal mines, factories, and railroad lines" in the Ruhr, to "a consortium" or a "Board of Trustees" who would manage the properties for the benefit of the Allies' war claims until those were satisfied. There would be no annexation of territory, and the owners of the properties would be indemnified by the German government. By this plan, Quinn argued, war claims would be paid equitably and fairly promptly, and Germany's power to make war would be sterilized for years to come. In his reply of November 14 Poincaré regretted that he and Quinn had not met, and expressed his and his government's agreement with Quinn's logic: ". . . it is necessary that Germany pay the reparations, not, as she has always claimed, by the additional profits of an ever-increasing wealth, but by her capital, for the reasons which you so justly mention."

Mrs. Foster remained behind when Quinn sailed, to sit for Derain's second attempt at a portrait. This time he painted her as a romantic beauty, and Quinn found that appropriate and satisfactory. She continued to see Gwen John and found to her dismay "many canvasses" rotting in the painter's Meudon attic, exposed to leaking rain. Gwen John said that all of them really belonged to Quinn but she had not been able to bring herself to send them. To Mrs. Foster a good number of the paintings seemed "excellent." [65] Gwen John was one of those who sent cordial messages to Quinn after his departure. She wrote on October 29: "Of all, the time I was most happy with you was at the Gervais'. You were a charming boy at my side." With her, apparently, Quinn had been able to dissemble the state of his nerves and his general health. His own letters to her were now beginning: "My dear Gwen." When Brancusi wrote on December 18 to report shipment of his four sculptures he went on to thank Quinn gaily for the gift of a little souvenir set of golf clubs in a white canvas bag which he had hung over his bedpost: ". . . I am beholding, from time to time, and with great pride, the nice clubs in the white case which you gave me, and I am making people believe that I won it as a champion—and if Satie had not been a witness, everybody would surely believe it!" Late in November Quinn made an offer of renewed patronage to Georges Rouault: 75,000 francs a year for "three or five years" in exchange for paintings of Rouault's own choice to that approximate value.[66] In a cable followed by three letters on the same day, December 18, Rouault happily acquiesced, and saluted Quinn in the third of the letters: "Goodbye or au revoir. I am happy today. On this dry land I am often sea-sick, more than you on the 'Berengaria.' " And James Joyce wrote in an amusingly similar vein on the fifteenth: "I am glad you liked your ocean trip. I prefer what a Dublin barrister once called *terra cotta.*"

On November 15, writing to Lady Gregory, Quinn reviewed his European trip and the feelings to which it had given rise in an appalling document of a dozen pages. The letter sounds like the work of a man sick in head and heart as well as body. The worst side of his nature, the bigotry and bullying and vindictiveness, rose up naked and ugly above their usual cover of energy and generous good will. He was still in a snarling rage at the collapse of the Demotte case. Their mere Jewishness was enough in Quinn's eyes to account for the "cowardice" of Bienenfeld and the surviving Demottes: it was a piece of representative "Jewish" behavior. Demotte himself, on the other hand, was "a gentleman and a great connoisseur and a Christian." [67] Meanwhile Duveen, by Quinn's account, had "fled from Paris to London and he is now over here [New York] repeating his libels." Lady Gregory's mere mention of her Passion Play was enough to set Quinn off on another anti-Jewish diatribe in his reply:

I have been reading a good deal of Christ this summer. I read Papini's Life of Christ. It puts the words of Christ as given in the Jew book literally and the other parts might have been taken from Lacordaire's sermons or Newman's sermons or any priest's sermons on the Bible. Of course I don't believe that Christ was divine or that anything good [*sic*] ever came out of the Jews or Jerusalem except filth and stench. We have two million seven hundred thousand Jews in New York City and they are awful. . . . When I was in Rome and saw the arch of Titus I almost cursed Titus for having destroyed Jerusalem. If Jerusalem had not been destroyed, the Jews might have stayed there, where they would have eaten and fed on each other. The dispersal of the Jews by Titus and the destruction of the temple in the city was one of the curses of the world.   [*November 15, 1923.*]

In her reply on November 28 Lady Gregory ignored the whole attack upon the Jews, and only remonstrated mildly against Quinn's professed skepticism: "How can you doubt the Divinity of Christ?"

On the subject of the Germans Quinn waxed no less scurrilous. On November 10 he told Harriet Shaw Weaver how on his trip to Berlin he had found the Germans "fat and bursting with energy and determination to get even with France." Now to Lady Gregory he expressed his indignation at seeing Germany, only five years after the war, "bursting with power, eight-track railroads, miles and miles of suburbs . . . tiled roofs and smoke-stacks multiplied a hundredfold on every hilltop. . . ." Considering the Armistice, as he did, "the mistake of the ages," Quinn said he would not be sorry to see Germany restore imperial government and scrap the Treaty of Versailles, thereby provoking France to "come in and clean up the Germans." [68]

Her first act would be to destroy the Cologne Cathedral, which is a whore among churches. Five hundred thousand Germans killed and cities destroyed would give Germany the object lesson which she sorely needs. In the old days when a person had a high fever they reduced the fever by bleeding him. Today, I believe, they are put in a bathtub with ice around them. The German temperature is rather high. They suffer from B-L-U-D-E pressure. The B-L-U-D-E pressure should be relieved. France should destroy the best part of Germany and break her up into three or four parts.

The *Berengaria* had returned Quinn to New York on November 2. On the following day he was back at his desk, and on the same day the first lot of the books and manuscripts of his library sale went on exhibition at Mitchell Kennerley's Anderson Galleries at 489 Park Avenue. A new circumstance had confirmed his determination to reduce his library drastically: 58 Central Park West, where his big apartment occupied most of the top, or ninth, floor, had been sold and Quinn had been given warning that he must vacate. The new owner wanted his apartment. Large as it was, his apartment had for long been too small to show adequately, or even to store adequately, his immense accumulation of books and works of art. Several rooms already resembled not a gallery but storerooms of a museum, with books, pictures, and sculptures in ranks and heaps. For some time he had been restless and dissatisfied with his library. It seemed "closed" to him—too big and too little used. Most of the books and manuscripts simply sat indefinitely, unvisited by himself or his friends. He determined to translate these possessions and the space they occupied into a more animated, variegated, and portable satisfaction—more pictures. Lady Gregory encouraged him in his intention to sell manuscripts as well as books: "I wanted you to sell them long ago. They are not like pictures that you can enjoy always; they have to be safely kept under lock and key and are a responsibility." [69] Now dispossession from his apartment put down any of his lingering doubts: if he held onto his library he would have to find a still larger apartment, or a house, or put his books in storage. Dispossession also supplied him with a neat public rationale for his sale; it was a handy thing to point to, in the midst of his own misgivings. At the last moment he was given a reprieve, a renewal of his lease for another year. But by the time that arrived the sale was under way.

He was by no means evacuating his library. He was reducing an enormous collection of nearly 18,000 items to a still imposing personal library of about a third that size. After he made his selection for the sale he wrote to Joyce, to Lady Gregory, and others to reassure them; as he described the situation to Lady Gregory: "I still have four or five thousand books left, all of yours and all of Yeats, those that I care most for, and duplicates." [70] Joyce's *Ulysses* manuscript, as he had warned the author in Paris, was due to go, and the fact involved Joyce and Quinn in their last interchanges of letters. Quinn wrote on November 15 to say again how glad he had been to find Joyce "in such good form, a new man with many years of health and vigor before you." Apparently because he could not penetrate the order of Joyce's arrangement of notebooks and sheets, Quinn had formed the notion that a portion of the manuscript of *Ulysses* had still not reached him. He now asked Joyce to send on the "missing" portion by registered post, first class, but to be sure not to mark the parcel "Ulysses": between five and six hundred copies of the first and second editions of the novel had been seized by the Post Office Department and burned in Washington. He reviewed the payments he had already made for the manuscript: $153 on February 5, 1920; $250 on August 6, 1920; $100 on September 29, 1920; $200 on January 24, 1921; $261 in August 1921 (by "gift" of 2,000 francs in Paris). To this accumulation of $964 he now sent Joyce an additional $236 to bring the total for the manuscript to a round $1,200. He proposed to include the manuscript in the third portion of his sale, and he promised to pay Joyce half of anything it brought over his own investment of $1,200: "I think you will agree that that is a very fair and even generous proposition." [71] Joyce cabled, "MS. complete," and wrote on December 15:

> Thanks for your draft. It is very kind of you to say you will divide the profits of sale of the *Ulysses* MS. with me. That being so, I can only hope that, as you have decided to dispose of it, your estimate of its probable selling price will prove to be a fraction, and not a large fraction, of the figure reached.

The exhibition and sale of the library were in the hands of Quinn's good friend Mitchell Kennerley, as master of the Anderson Galleries. The actual auctions took place in the afternoon and evening of three or four days in the middle of each of five successive months, beginning with November 12, 13, and 14 of 1923, and ending with March 17, 18, 19, and 20 of 1924. The 12,096 items (including a good many multiple copies) of the sale were cut into five alphabetical divisions (subdivided chronologically): "A–C," "D–H," "I–Morley," "Morris–Sterne," and "Stevenson–Zola." Kennerley treated Quinn and his buyers to five catalogs totaling 1,205 pages which were models of their kind: full, clear, systematic, elegantly printed and bound. To the notes prepared by Quinn and Vincent O'Sullivan were added expert thumbnail biographies which were the work of Charles Vale. On the back cover of each of the five volumes of the catalog Quinn had installed a quotation from the will of Edmond de Goncourt:

> "My wish is that my Drawings, my Prints, my Curiosities, my Books—in a word, these things of art which have been the joy of my life—shall not be consigned to the cold tomb of a museum, and subjected to the stupid glance of the careless passer-by; but I require that they shall all be dispersed under the hammer of the Auctioneer, so that the pleasure which the acquiring of each one of them has given me shall be given again, in each case, to some inheritor of my own tastes."

The volumes were animated by numerous illustrations: portrait photographs, facsimiles of manuscript pages, portrait drawings many of which were in the warm velvety pencil of John Butler Yeats. At the beginning of the first volume appeared "A Note by John Quinn," setting down his "reasons" for the sale and some of his feelings about it. He had determined to sell, he wrote, when faced with the "necessity of moving from my large old-fashioned apartment with large rooms and plenty of wall space." In contrast to Voltaire's description of Vauvenargues, Quinn said, his collecting had had exclusions as well as preferences, and "the hatreds and the bores were long ago cast out, or rather never secured a place on my shelves." The catalog would reflect "a widely interested intellectual life" and would serve as a partial record of "the admirations, the enthusiasms and affections of a lifetime": "Many of the books are records of friendships that have enriched my life." He protested his reluctance to speak at length of what his books and manuscripts had meant to him, "for they seem to me to be a part

of myself, even though I may smile a little at my own feeling."
Whereas Quinn's attitude to the sale was less soft and more brusque
than all this sounds, there is no reason to doubt the reality of a
sentiment which went back to his Ohio boyhood.

A sale so large, and including so many items of the first distinction, created a considerable stir in bookish circles in New York
and London. Shane Leslie wrote from London on November 30
to approve the de Goncourt sentiment: "Much better to watch
them flit instead of leaving them to be dumped after your death."
He reported excitement in London, especially over the Conrad
manuscripts. The catalog came in for particular praise on its own.
Christopher Morley wrote in the *New York Evening Post*, "Whoever catalogued the Quinn Library certainly surpassed himself: we
have never seen so fine a job of bibliographic annotation." *The
London Times Literary Supplement* spoke as follows:

> No more remarkable library of first editions of modern authors
> has ever been formed than that of Mr. John Quinn. The catalogue
> . . . will form a very valuable and permanent book of reference.
> The brief biographical details are unconventional and always in-
> teresting, often furnishing details and points of view to be found
> nowhere else. . . . One might go on quoting columns from these
> terse and often epigrammatic biographies.

But when his friend Bartholomew Moynahan wrote fulsomely to
say that his sale of his library would show that Quinn deserved
to be " 'classed with the immortals,' " Quinn pulled him up sharply
with an alternative definition of himself:

> I want to be classed with the alive, the living, the kicking, the
> fighting, the progressing; above all, the living. You will observe
> that I don't even use the word "mortal," because that has trooping
> right beside it the idea of termination. It's a bad word to play
> with and I always sidestep it and the idea. After a tour of Italy,
> from Venice to Rome and back, including Florence, Siena,
> Assisi and the rest, I have come back with increased love for
> modern living art, and am willing to let the dead art remain dead
> where it is buried.

The cultural case, pro and con, had perhaps never been put more
simplistically or with a more confident poverty of content. It

showed little else, but it showed Quinn's mind clear of doubt as to his own future courses.

The first volume of the catalog of the library presented as a frontispiece a photograph of Joseph Conrad with his handsome head turned full face, but the body in profile, hands in trousers pockets pulling back his coat to reveal an elegant checked waist-coat and a considerable corporation. The photograph was dated 1913 and inscribed: "In friendship to John Quinn." In a letter to Shane Leslie on November 14, the last day of the first unit of the sale, Quinn laid open the fact that it had been his treatment by Doubleday or Conrad, or both, in the spring that had determined him to make a clean sweep of his rich Conrad holdings: "If I had seen Conrad and had a talk with him I probably would not have sold *all* his manuscripts." The "A–C" catalog contained 236 pages listing 2,272 items, of which the Conrad items—books, pamphlets, manuscripts—numbered 230, or a tenth of the total. Included among them was the last pathetic evidence of Quinn's old friend-ship with the novelist and his wife, now lot Number 2,000:

A HANDBOOK OF COOKERY for a Small House. By Jessie Conrad. With a Preface by Joseph Conrad. 12mo, cloth.

London: Wm. Heinemann, [1923]

First Edition. Presentation copy from the author, inscribed on the flyleaf: "*To John Quinn, Esq. with all good wishes from Jessie Conrad, 1923.*" With the original addressed wrapper laid in.

It was well for Quinn that he did include his Conrad materials, for ultimately they were not only the stars but the salvation of the sale as a whole. Quinn's investment of about $10,000 in Conrad now returned just under $111,000. The New York dealer Gabriel Wells bought the autograph manuscript of *Under Western Eyes* at $6,900 and Jerome Kern got the manuscript of *Youth* for $2,300. Otherwise all the capital items were captured by the great Phila-delphia dealer, bibliophile, and terror of the auction rooms, Dr. A. S. W. Rosenbach: *Victory*, 1,139 pages in "two crushed brown levant morocco solander cases," at $8,100 (the highest price ever paid down to that time for the manuscript of a living author); *Chance* at $6,600; *Almayer's Folly* at $5,300; *Typhoon* at $5,100; *Nostromo* at $4,700; *The Nigger of the 'Narcissus'* at $4,500; *An*

Outcast of the Islands at $4,100; *Lord Jim* at $3,900; *The Secret Agent* at $3,900; *Falk* at $3,100; *The Secret Sharer* at $2,400; and *A Smile of Fortune* at $2,300. All told, Dr. Rosenbach was to spend some $72,000 in the five parts of Quinn's sale. But for him times would have been hard indeed.

In the excitement of the auction room after it was clear that Quinn had made a killing in Conrad, occurred an ugly double contretemps with Frank and Nelson Doubleday, father and son, which newly infuriated Quinn with that house. Mitchell Kennerley told him that Nelson Doubleday said to him while the auction was in progress: " 'Quinn is a bounder for selling the Conrad presentation copies.' " [72] At the close of the evening's sale F. N. Doubleday approached Quinn and the following dialogue ensued:

Doubleday: Now, Mr. Quinn, you ought to send a check to J. C.
Quinn: Why?
Doubleday: Because he needs the money.
Quinn: Why, you are his publisher and you recently told me that you had sent him $7500. Conrad must have been making forty to fifty thousand dollars a year and I don't see why I should send him a check. [73]

After the insulting treatment he had met during Conrad's spring visit, Quinn was in no mood to entertain these reprimands. He wrote furiously to Kennerley the following day:

I am not through with the sheeny assault upon me by his [Nelson Doubleday's] damned old father last night. That was one of the cheekiest things that ever was. I wanted to keep cool and I did, but I was boiling inside. You and I know the whole story and I am very much tempted to write to Doubleday and tell him that it was owing to the attitude of himself and Mrs. Doubleday that I first determined to sell the Conrad things and all of them.
[*November 14, 1923.*]

The same day, November 14, he began drafting a rejoinder to the younger Doubleday, quoting Kennerley's report of Doubleday's calling him "a bounder" and continuing: "You probably did not know that except for four or five *books* which Conrad presented to me I paid him *his own price* for every item I got from him." But then he received from F. N. Doubleday a letter that was sufficiently placatory to induce him to drop the whole quarrel. He did not send his letter to young Doubleday, but he did not cease to seethe in his own mind.

Quinn told strict truth when he said that he had paid Conrad's prices from the beginning for the manuscripts. Nor was he answerable for the fact that Conrad's popularity had advanced to the point where it returned Quinn 1,000 per cent on his investment. He had not held a "Conrad sale" as a profiteering or vindictive gesture. He had simply included the Conrad materials in a sale that was general and predetermined. The decision to include virtually all the Conrad papers was one partly based on a well-founded pique; but it was pure chance that the sale took place at the peak of Conrad's American popularity. Quinn awaited Conrad's own reaction to the sale with excitement and some trepidation, but he might have rested easy. To Quinn himself Conrad said nothing at all. To others he wrote in a tone which suggested some amusement and envy at Quinn's success with his genius, but no disgust or recrimination. In letters to Richard Curle, to Edward Garnett, and to F. N. Doubleday (whom he always addressed as "Effendi" —a play on Doubleday's initials) he showed chiefly a kind of sardonic amusement and contempt not at Quinn but at the course of events: the complex ironies of the rewards coming not to his art itself but to the manuscripts which he had tended to dismiss as the mere waste matter of the creative process; of his fame coming not from England but from America; of persons now finding him valuable for the first time because his manuscripts had made money. His favorite phrase in referring to the affair was "that idiotic sale." [74] The *Times* of London had published a list of the prices brought by his manuscripts, and Conrad wrote Doubleday immediately after seeing it, on November 20:

> All of you who went must have had a tense sort of evening at that sale. Was the atmosphere vibrating with excitement, or, on the contrary, still with awe? Did any of the bidders faint? Did the auctioneer's head swell visibly? Did Quinn enjoy his triumph lying low like Brer Rabbit, or did he enjoy his glory in public and give graciously his hand to kiss to the multitude of inferior collectors who never, never, never dreamt of such a coup? Well, it is a wonderful adventure to happen to a still-living (or at any rate half-alive) author.

The reverberation in the press here was very great indeed; and the result is that lots of people, who never heard of me before, now know my name, and thousands of others, who could not have read through a page of mine without falling into convulsions, are proclaiming me a very great author. And there are a good many also whom nothing will persuade that the whole thing was not a put-up job and that I haven't got my share of the plunder.[75]

Apparently the last sentence was as close as Conrad came to saying audibly that he felt entitled to some part of Quinn's profits. To Edward Garnett Conrad wrote very similarly on the following day, November 21. And here he did bring up the question of an understanding between himself and Quinn as to the handling of the manuscripts: "Yes, Quinn promised to keep the MSS. together —but the mood passes and the promise goes with it.[76] He sounded, surely, philosophical and forgiving. Conrad may have been recalling, though he did not mention, the fact that he himself had first broken the agreement with Quinn when he sold manuscripts to T. J. Wise.

In her own memoir, *Joseph Conrad and His Circle*, Jessie Conrad, who had been the real preserver of the manuscripts, made it quite clear that over the years she and Conrad had been satisfied with and grateful for the sums they had received from Quinn's purchases. In her only reference to the final sale she quoted Conrad's letter to Doubleday in this setting:

I had been teasing him because only the month before all the manuscripts I had been at such pains to preserve, and which later on we had sold to Mr. John Quinn, had been re-sold in New York for no less a sum than £24,000. We had received £2000, but Joseph Conrad was sportsman enough to be pleased at the sale "taking place during the lifetime of an author." . . .[77]

To Quinn himself Mrs. Conrad wrote promptly on November 18, immediately after seeing the announcement of the sale in the *Times*:

You must be feeling quite satisfied with the great success of your sale of Conrad's Manuscripts. Such prices are certainly a great compliment to an author and I believe nothing approaching it has ever happened during the life time of any writer before. The London dealers are now falling over themselves to sell things also.

She inquired with interest about the fragment of "The Sisters," which had not appeared in the list of items sold. She and Conrad had "argued" about it, she maintaining that Quinn had it, Conrad that he did not. In fact, in his one gesture of sentiment in the whole affair, Quinn had withdrawn from Kennerley on September 5 this fragment of an unfinished novel the copyright of which Conrad had given him in friendship and about which they had corresponded warmly. Mrs. Conrad closed her letter cordially: "We send you our very best wishes for Christmas and the New Year and earnestly hope that your health is better," and signed herself: "With kind regards." All this was surely friendly and pleasant to hear. But no sound came of the word Quinn really craved: some sign from Conrad that he recognized Quinn as an inhabitant of the same world as himself, the republic of letters.

In early stages of his library sale, when it was being generally and wrongly assumed that the huge success of the Conrad items had cut a die for the sale as a whole, Julian Messner, Vice-President of Boni & Liveright, approached Quinn with the suggestion that he now dictate a volume of his memoirs as a collector. Quinn, who still disliked Liveright and his firm, and frightened as always by the idea of mortality which he associated with talk of "immortality," rebuffed Messner rudely in a letter of November 16:

> I flatter myself that I have arrived at the head of my profession, and I have better uses for my time than dictating my memoirs. I am down here where the clover is long and where I can make more on one case in a week than I could out of a volume of memoirs. . . . Perhaps ten or fifteen years from now there may be something in the thought.

The clover in Quinn's library sale, in any case, grew shorter and shorter, and it soon became clear that the Conrad success had been a sport rather than one of a species. On the second day of the second sale, in a letter to his friend Roger Foster on December 11, Quinn noted with disgust that ninety-two volumes of *Charivari*, for which he had paid $560 because of their scores of Daumier plates, had brought only $110 at auction; and that the manuscripts of John Davidson's *Ballads and Songs*, "Ballad of a Nun," and "Ballad of a Poet," for which he had paid $260, $150, and $130 respectively, had brought $62.50, $40, and $30.

On the art front of Quinn's life, after the mild orgy in Paris in September and October, things rested generally quiet until the end of the year. Roché wrote from Paris on November 26 to say that the Germans were sinking their cash, of which they seemed to have a good deal, into paintings and pearls. "Dealers are selling mad," Roché wrote, and Georges Bernheim had told him: " 'We are grocers, we are no more art dealers.' " Early in December, still under the impression that he would have to vacate his apartment, Quinn wrote to Jacob Epstein to try to clear up the old matter of Epstein's *Mother and Child* which he had bought in 1916 in mistake for another work, and which had remained in the basement of 58 Central Park West ever since. Quinn had arranged with the sculptor's brother, Dr. Irving Epstein on Seventh Avenue, to take the carving into storage, but now he wished to balance up the financial side of the matter. He figured that the £300 he had paid Epstein for the work amounted to $1,437, that that sum at 6 per cent for the six years in which Epstein had possessed the money would have yielded interest of $516, making his essential payment to Epstein $1,953. He now proposed that Epstein send him two works the price of which came to roughly $2,000: the bronze bust, *Miriam*, at 300 guineas and the bronze head of Cunninghame-Graham at 150 guineas.[78] No record of Epstein's response has survived.

In June Quinn had given Walter Pach a further thousand francs in subvention of Pach's memorial volume on Raymond Duchamp-Villon, still in preparation. When Pach returned from Paris in the autumn he brought with him for sale certain Redon paintings which belonged to members of the Matisse family, and Quinn paid him 20,000 francs for two paintings, *The Death of Buddha* and *Mystic Heart*.[79] Certain discussions among Pach, Quinn, Joseph Brummer, the art dealer and connoisseur, and the Messieurs Bing, dealers in New York real estate and occasional patrons of the arts, on the notion of establishing a permanent museum of modern art in the city, matured quickly to an impasse. Pach, understanding the proposal in the terms that Quinn meant to "found an American Luxembourg," and apparently reading too much too soon into Quinn's intentions, tried to push the matter farther and faster than Quinn had any wish to go. Whereas Quinn was greatly interested in the idea of a museum of modern art, and was much attracted by Brummer's suggestion that he lend his collection to such a museum, probably for a minimum period of three years, he was not attracted in the least by Pach's assumption that he had in mind to *give* "pictures which perhaps cost me a half million dollars." [80] Quinn had thought, further, that Bing and Bing meant to donate a building to be used as a museum; that proving false diminished his own interest again. Pach concluded he could only let the whole question rest and wait for a more auspicious mood among the possible principals. As an index to the general mood around them Pach wrote Quinn on December 26 to describe his experience when he had gone to see Mrs. Henry Havemeyer to ask permission to print a photograph of one of her Manets in a book:

> . . . she said she would not like to let her Manet be made to sponsor the "modern art which certain people are trying to force down the public's throat." I thought I might tell you this since her collection was mentioned as one which might furnish some pictures for a modern museum.

Life was still remarkably lonely at the point where Quinn stood with modern art.

1924

AS time turned toward the last half year of John Quinn's life he was more genuinely ill than he or his friends had any means of knowing. Quinn was a hypochondriac so confirmed and so expert, so knowing, so vocal, and so detailed about his symptoms, that his friends and perhaps he himself had come to take his complaints less and less seriously, as signs of personality and of habit. He had been blessed with a big, strong frame and an animal economy fundamentally robust if tuned to an extraordinarily high pitch. Again and again over the years persons had seen his terrific energy and power of will pull him out of a seemingly dangerous malaise. His intestinal cancer of 1918 and his "shock" of January 1923 had been crises of undoubted gravity, but from both of those tests his recovery appeared to have been complete. Regular examinations of the intestinal tract had shown no recurrence of the cancer—everybody's major fear. In the spring of 1923, after Quinn had felt some intestinal soreness, Dr. Healy had found a slight enlargement of the liver but had advised him that it was nothing to worry about. Before Quinn went abroad in September 1923 Dr. Healy again examined him, again found the enlargement of the liver, and again gave no cause for alarm. In France Quinn suffered pain from "the tongue of the liver when I would lie on my left side, pressing down." [1] He had severe gas attacks and always had to take medicine for the gas before trying to sleep, on his right side. He slept badly and had trouble digesting the little he felt like eating. Mrs. Foster did what she could to comfort and cosset him, but he was constantly tired and irritable. Their headlong trip about Italy had been undergone with Quinn in that uncomfortable and inhospitable state. The trip home on the *Berengaria* was a rest and a restorative, as an ocean voyage always was for Quinn. But he still felt constantly tired in the autumn, low in vitality, and he had to labor to summon any warmth of interest even in those concerns which had been the breath of life for him: law contests, the society of his friends and his family, reading, talking, looking at art, the sale of his books which was supposed to intensify his pursuit of works of art. He was losing weight, and he pointed out the evidence to Dr. Healy in the shower after their occasional rounds of golf together in the autumn; but again Dr. Healy tried to reassure him, told him he was not seriously underweight. Quinn knew only that he felt wretched—low and in pain. But the very scarcity of his public complaints at the time probably indicated the depth of his concern and his fear. He tried as usual to tell himself that all he needed was a real rest.

The sale of the library continued, in its monthly installments, with Quinn in this frame of body and mind. The James Joyce manuscripts came under the hammer in the first evening, January 14, of the third unit of the sale, "I–Morley." After Joyce had cabled in December: "Manuscript complete," Quinn had finally straightened out the *Ulysses* papers, putting two manuscript notebooks where they belonged, after the loose sheets, and concluding that he could then offer "THE COMPLETE MANUSCRIPT of this remarkable work, one of the most extraordinary produced in modern times and hailed by critics as epoch-making in modern literature"—as his catalog described the manuscript which was offered "on over 1200 pages" in four blue morocco slip cases. Subsequently it developed that he still did not possess a portion of the printed text of the novel equivalent to about six pages of manuscript, and the lacuna was to create difficulty. As he had done with numerous items about which he cared particularly, being unwilling to let them go at an unworthy figure, Quinn in a letter to Mitchell Kennerley on January 10 set "reserve" or "bid-in" prices on his Joyce manuscripts—prices at which the auctioneer was to bid them in to be returned to Quinn's possession: $75 on the *Egoist* sheets and autograph corrections of *A Portrait of the Artist as a Young Man*, $200 on *Exiles*, $2,000 on *Ulysses*, $100 on

Joyce's translation of Hauptmann's "Before Sunrise," works for which he had paid, respectively, $100, $250, $1,200, and $100 (the last to the dealer Meredith Janvier of Baltimore).

Quinn wrote Joyce on January 21 to tell him the story of the bidding for *Ulysses* on Monday evening, January 14. Three bidders followed the treasure to $1,900, where one dropped out; A. S. W. Rosenbach bid $1,925, the remaining competitor, $1,950, then Rosenbach took it at $1,975. Quinn approved Kennerley's judgment in letting it go at just under the reserve price of $2,000. As an example of the way things were going in the general sales apart from the Conrad orgy, Quinn cited the fact that two long verse manuscripts of Meredith's, on which he had put reserve bids of $1,200 and $925, had come back on his hands at $750 and $650. Whereas he would not of course have to pay himself these sums, he would be obligated to pay Kennerley's gallery commission of 15 per cent on the "sale" price. After the gallery commission was deducted on the $1,975 for *Ulysses,* there remained a profit of $478.75 over Quinn's purchase price of $1,200. The half of the profits that Quinn had promised Joyce would come to $239.37, and Quinn said he would send that along as soon as he collected from Rosenbach, who had asked for six months' grace in which to pay up his bids, amounting in all to $72,000. To Joyce Quinn also felt moved to comment reminiscently on his sale and its long background.

> . . . this collection of books goes back to 1887, when I bought $237 worth of books with money that my Mother gave me, among them Walter Pater's first editions and a first edition of Hardy. She came into the room while I was on my hands and knees gloating over the treasures, and I can see her smile yet as she said: "Well, how long will they last you?"

They had lasted him, as he noted, thirty-six years.

When Joyce replied on February 5 he was in no mood for chat or sentiment. He wrote in what sounds like a cold rage, not so much at Quinn as at what seemed to him the coarse treatment and low valuation to which this record of his genius was being subjected.* He began: "Can you find out, directly or indirectly, for

* That Joyce was also angry at Quinn personally showed more plainly in his letters to Robert McAlmon and Harriet Shaw Weaver. He was especially

what figure Mr. (or Dr.) Rosenbach will relinquish his grip on his (or my) MS?" Inasmuch as Rosenbach had asked for six months "to fumble in other people's trousers to find the money," Joyce assumed that Rosenbach was open to an offer, and Joyce wished nothing so much as to recover his manuscript. A cable had been prepared urging Quinn "in the name of many persons" in Paris to withhold the manuscript from sale; but Joyce had "discountenanced" it on the ground that the manuscript was Quinn's absolute property. He could understand, too, he said, that in selling a large library one was pretty sure to take a loss, and that a few successes would be quickly offset by other failures. In view of the "general feeling of stupor and indignation here at the result" in the sale of the *Ulysses* manuscript, Joyce wanted Rosenbach approached, even if he had to buy back his own manuscript. He reminded Quinn, doubtless in order to hold before his eyes an example of *real* generosity, that Harriet Shaw Weaver had quietly made him a present of £22,000—"and if Mr. (or Dr.) Rosenbach is inclined to resell the MS. at a reasonable profit I think his inclination should be indulged, though I should not like to give him all the £22,000." Loftily, but not unkindly, Joyce now rejected Quinn's offer of the poor half of the profits on the sale of the manuscript to Rosenbach:

> . . . please cancel the amount you kindly promised me out of the proceeds of the sale. You have had outlay enough already on account of me—cables, correspondence, defence of the *Little Review,* binding, etc.

---

offended at Quinn's implied valuation of *Ulysses* in taking back the two Meredith manuscripts for $1,400 as he was letting Joyce's manuscript go for $1,975. The Meredith works were two long odes, "Alsace-Lorraine" (50 pages) and "Napoleon" (57 pages). To McAlmon Joyce wrote: "On the same day he bought back two poems by George Meredith (about 70 pp. of MS) for $1400 or 1500. He offered to send me half of the net proceeds less fees, etc in six months. I wrote declining to accept it. I do not think he will put my letter up for auction." ([N.D. early 1924]. *Letters of James Joyce,* I, 208.) To Miss Weaver he wrote: ". . . I consider such a sale now and by a wealthy man (who had made me part owner of the MS before the sale) a grossly stupid act which is an alienation of valuable property. It is a pity that I was obliged to write such a letter [as that of February 5 to Quinn] but what is one to do when a MS of 500,000 words is sold by an admirer who on the same day buys back a few pages of not very meritorious verse by a prose writer for almost the same sum?" (February 8, 1924. *Letters,* I, 211.)

On February 15, apparently before he received Joyce's letter of February 5, Quinn wrote again to ask Joyce to write out and send to him a copy of the last six pages of *Ulysses*, missing from the manuscript, so that Rosenbach could have an absolutely complete copy. Rosenbach had happened to be absent from the auction room when the announcement was made of the pages lacking. Quinn had found Rosenbach a likable man, and he presented him to Joyce now as "rather an amusing cuss, sardonic and witty." But Joyce had already taken a stand on the "missing" pages on February 5: "It must be understood . . . that I will not write in any pages on the MS. to 'complete' it. The additions were made by me on printed proofs." By February 29, when he wrote Joyce again, Quinn had learned from Rosenbach that he had bought the manuscript because he valued it personally and wished to possess it and to use it—" 'because I am interested in the book and the author and for my own personal library.' " Quinn doubted that he would be open to an offer, even from the author, but he asked Kennerley to speak on Joyce's behalf to Rosenbach, who was to sail for Europe on the next day, March 1. Quinn warned Joyce not to intimate to Rosenbach that he meant to hold the manuscript against a future sale at a profit, if he hoped to get anywhere with him.[2] When approached by Joyce Rosenbach did refuse to sell, and he came back with an offer to buy the corrected page proofs of the novel. Joyce was forced to retreat into silence and into sardonic comment to his friends: " 'When he receives a reply from me all the rosy brooks will have run dry.' "[3]

The library sale continued, on an inclined plane running downward, the returns upon Quinn's original investment growing poorer and poorer. The stir created by the prices realized on the Conrad manuscripts continued to raise excitement, unwarrantably extended to the sale as a whole, and Quinn was forced to read in the press and hear from his friends comment upon the immense success of an undertaking which seemed to him a lamentable failure. On February 23 he wrote Walter Pach: "I am getting sick and tired of all the blabber about the 'great' sale of my books. It was not a sale. It was a slaughter, the slaughter of each part being worse than the preceding part. . . ." He noted that the books and manuscripts in the fourth unit of the sale on February 11 to 13, which had cost him more than $32,000, had gone for just half that sum. When Quinn summed up his income from the sale as a whole after the close of the final installment on March 20, he estimated that he had realized about $170,000 for items that had cost him about $250,000. The total yield would have seemed less disgraceful but for the fact that the Conrad materials had brought in nearly two thirds of the whole: $111,000. They had been not only the stars but also the salvation of his sale; without them the showing would have been pitiful indeed. "But I have no regrets," Quinn wrote Gwen John on March 13. To Joyce he wrote: "While I made on the Conrads I have lost on hundreds of others. But I am damned glad to get rid of the mountain of books that covered my apartment, on the walls and shelves and in the halls and closets, till they were like an incubus." [4] His feeling was more trustworthy than his figure of speech. He had a bit more space in which to breathe and move now, and he had translated a possession which had come to seem "dead," "finished," into the means of adding to a possession which was "alive," "kicking": $170,000 would buy a great deal of art at 1924 prices, if one were not trying to deal in works sanctified by time and established reputation—and if one could summon the energy for a systematic pursuit.

By January Quinn felt his energy reduced to "just enough to crawl down to the office and get through a day's work and come back." [5] During the month he was examined several times by Dr. Healy when he continued to lose weight and to feel soreness and pain in his stomach and abdomen. On January 18 Dr. Healy had the area completely X-rayed and saw evidence of the enlarged liver but no trouble in the intestines, and he still seemed disposed to take Quinn's complaints lightly. Quinn now called in Dr. Henry C. Fleming, who at once diagnosed cirrhosis, or hardening, of the liver. Quinn had been abstemious all his life and he felt the irony of being afflicted with the drunkard's disease; but it was a relief of sorts to have a name put to his ailment and to be recognized as officially ill. He explained the anatomy of the matter to Roché: ". . . when it first began to enlarge and harden the pain was almost unendurable. The liver is in a tough muscular sac, and it is like putting a man in a tight coat that is too small for him. In order to breathe he has to burst the coat." [6] He had begun to be tortured as well with racking fits of coughing, and he feared that such spasms might burst the sac about the liver; but Dr. Fleming assured him that there was no such danger. Quinn still told himself that when he could get some rest and slow the tempo of his life he would come round again as usual.

With Joyce, Pound, and Eliot off his hands for the time being, Quinn's active beneficence to current literature was now confined to his limited subsidy of Ford Madox Ford and *the transatlantic review*. He had given Ford $1,000 in Paris in the autumn of 1923 and, drawn by his own and Mrs. Foster's respect and liking for Ford, had promised to go that high again, but no further, if it was needed. "He is an honest man and an able man and I hope he will succeed," he wrote Roché of Ford on February 15. On January 11 he sent Ford another $500, promised one more like sum if required, and agreed to see what he could do for Ford with his favorite fellow-benefactor, Otto Kahn.[7] In the same letter he turned down flatly Ford's offer of a copy of the life mask of Ezra Pound which had recently been made in Paris: "under no circumstances" did he want a life mask of Pound or anyone else. The only thing worse was a death mask. On January 27 he cabled Ford a final $500 and wrote to Maitre Albert L. Legrand of the French bar on the same day: "I think it is lost money. But I said I would stand by Ford to that extent and I have kept my word." James Joyce had made brief and ominous mention of Ford and his review in his letters of December 15 and February 5. On the latter date he wrote:

> He has been pressing me to give him something, but I am not eager for publication at present. I could, perhaps, detach one passage for him, but he fears prosecution and seizure on the charge of blasphemy. The second number of his review came out on Saturday. . . . Between lack of funds, printers' errors, absconding secretaries and general misunderstandings, it appears to be shortening peoples' lives.

The work of his own to which Joyce was referring was his second, far more arcane, masterpiece which appeared *seriatim* for many years in *transition* as *Work in Progress* before collecting itself in 1939 as *Finnegans Wake*. Joyce had civilly offered to read parts of it aloud to Quinn in Paris in October, but Quinn had pleaded pressing engagements. Quinn's pessimistic estimate of Ford's situation proved accurate: *the transatlantic review* lasted barely a year.

Quinn continued to correspond with Major Percy Moore Turner, who was still trying quietly to dispose of Quinn's English paintings, drawings, and etchings, chiefly works of Augustus John. John had postponed his planned return to the United States in the autumn of 1923 because he was busy "painting a princess." It was John who reported to Quinn that Turner was going in with John's old dealer Knewstub in a new gallery in London. When Quinn inquired Turner explained that he would be a director in Knewstub's reorganized Chenil Gallery, but would also continue his old private business at the Independent Gallery.[8] It was to Turner only in London that Quinn confided his decision to take a further radical step toward reducing his general collection in order to point all his resources with greater concentration in the direction of the School of Paris. He had resolved to put on sale at Scott & Fowles in New York virtually his entire collection of the works of Jacob Epstein: "25 or 26" examples, certainly the most important single collection of that master's work in existence at the time.[9] The sale would be stunning news to the sculptor and to the London art world generally, but, as he had with the sale of his Johns, he consulted neither the artist nor anyone else but treated the affair as exclusively his own concern. On April 1 Quinn wrote to Stevenson Scott, one of the proprietors of the gallery at 667 Fifth Avenue: ". . . I will fix my prices at not only reasonable figures but at figures making losses to me after deducting your commission. It is my desire to sell or I should not have the exhibition." Clearly it was not his intention to make money but, by simplifying his collection, to find the means to intensify his collection. On April 8 he delivered to Scott & Fowles a group of twenty-three works of Epstein with quoted prices as indicated: 1. *Nude Woman Seated*, $350; 2. *Euphemia Lamb*, $1,000; 3. *Romilly John*, $600; 4. *Birds*, $1,000; 5. *Lillian Shelley*, $600; 6. *Carving in Flenite*, $750; 7. *Iris Tree*, $1,000; 8. *Mother and Child*, $500; 9. *Old Italian Woman*, $600; 10. *Head of an Irish Girl*, $600; 11. *Augustus John*, $750; 12. *The Tin Hat*, $650; 13. *Meum I*, $1,000; 14. *Meum II*, $750;

15. *Admiral Fisher*, $750; 16. *Bernard van Dieren*, $500; 17. *The Countess of Drogheda*, $700; 18. *The Duchess of Hamilton*, $1,000; 19. *Lieutenant T. E. Hulme*, $500; 20. *Muirhead Bone*, $500; 21. *Mrs. Epstein*, $550; 22. *Gabrielle Saonne*, $800; 23. *An American Soldier*, $600. Along with his list of "asking" prices Quinn supplied a list of minimum "selling" prices, and these ran from one hundred to four hundred dollars less per item. Within a month, for reasons which are not clear, Quinn had asked for the return of six works which were then unsold: *Birds, Carving in Flenite, Mother and Child, Meum I, The Countess of Drogheda, The Duchess of Hamilton.* By the end of 1924 nine of the remaining seventeen works had been sold: *Euphemia Lamb* at $800; *Romilly John* at $540; *Lillian Shelley* at $540; *Old Italian Woman* at $550; *Augustus John* at $600; *The Tin Hat* at $650; *Admiral Fisher* at $600; *Muirhead Bone* at $500; *An American Soldier* at $500.

Augustus John was back in New York in the flesh in April, but by that time Quinn was feeling so low and ill that he hardly ever left his apartment except to go down to his office, and he saw very little of John. He promised to try to persuade Thomas Fortune Ryan, who had remained Quinn's important client since he set up for himself in 1906, to commission John to paint his portrait. But on June 9 he wrote John, confessing failure: Ryan had begged off on the score of rheumatism which would make the sittings too painful. Quinn was trying hard to hide from Ryan how wretched he felt himself; he was convinced that "the old pirate," as he called Ryan in private, would fire him at once and take on another lawyer. At about the same time there came one final flurry in Turner's sale of Quinn's English works in London. No buyer had yet offered for the 115 Augustus John etchings, which Turner was still holding for sale as a group. But on May 3 Turner wrote that he had an offer of £400 for a group of five paintings and one drawing of Augustus John's—works for which Quinn had paid £645.15 and for which he had been asking £970 in the London sale. On June 24 he cabled Turner to let them go for the price offered. This last bargain deal would make a total of twenty-seven paintings and ten drawings sold for $24,743.22. Quinn's profit on the whole enterprize came to a mere $4,471.02, and Turner realized about £1,000 in commissions. The results showed no marked appreciation in the value of John's works, and Quinn could certainly be spared the embarrassment of making a "killing" in Augustus John—a crumb of comfort.

Since the beginning of 1924 Quinn's dealings for art, with one stunning exception, had been small and retrospective. The Epstein sale, the John sale, and the library sale were neither small nor in intention retrospective; but they were negative in being a disposal rather than an acquisition, and they were regretful in being the denial of preferences once close and warm. Fundamentally Quinn saw them as moves to clear space, to convert to cash, and to rest energy for a big new indulgence of a taste that at last knew fully and finally where it was going. But though Quinn could not know it, or confess it, his work as a collector, indeed his work of any kind, was just about done.

On the first day of 1924 Henri-Pierre Roché wrote from Paris to say that he had just seen in its finished state the second portrait of Jeanne Robert Foster by Derain: "It is to me more like the "atmosphere" of Mrs. F. than herself, I like it." On January 7 Roché cabled news of Pottier's shipment of the Derain and of other works which were parts of the late harvest from Quinn's Paris visit in the autumn of 1923: "Three Gwens, Derain portrait, four Brancusis sailing Paris." On January 10 Quinn sent 41,000 francs in payment for three of the Brancusis, his marble bird, the head in wood, and the little marble fish. On February 20 he sent Paul Rosenberg 6,500 francs for Picasso's cubist portrait of Uhde. On March 24 he sent off Gwen John's check for 10,753 francs. The franc had declined in value in the winter of 1924, and in making all his payments to French artists and dealers at this time Quinn was either sending dollars or figuring francs at the old higher rate—so as to avoid profiting by a financial accident at the expense of the artists.

It now seems almost symptomatic that it should be at this stage that Quinn met his first complete defeat in his long running fight to prevent or reduce tax and tariff levies upon original works of art. In the last previous skirmish, that of 1921, he had managed to halve the sales tax in the Revenue Act, securing a reduction from 10 to 5 per cent. In the winter and spring of 1924 he tried once more to persuade Congressmen to remove the tax entirely. He thought he had carried his point before the Senate Finance Committee, but then Senator Smoot "pleaded for revenue and talked the whole committee around. . . ." [10] Quinn pursued his fight to the floor of the Senate, with Senator Walsh of Massachusetts making his motion. In the long run the 5 per cent tax was restored to the 1924 bill by the Conference Committee of both houses. Quinn blamed the result, and the psychology of opposing argument, upon the passage of the Veterans' Bonus Bill.[11]

One final triumph, perhaps his greatest, was to be granted Quinn in his career as a collector of art. As in the case of Seurat's *Le Cirque*, the triumph was equally Roché's. On the first day of February Roché cabled: "Kahnweiler just received huge Rousseau beating even Charmeuse [*La Charmeuse de Serpents*]. Mailing photo next week." On the same day he sent off a letter whose broken form and hurry of phrase expressed his urgency and excitement:

I have seen yesterday a Rousseau which has quite upset me to me, it beats even the Charmeuse

Kahnweiler has just received it   Picasso saw it there and told me to go at once, thinking of you

I went it is still in his cellar   almost nobody has seen it yet

I have dreamt of it all the night

It is one of the *absolute* paintings I ever saw

To me it puts in the shadow the Daumier I have sent you a photo of and the Signac's Cézanne

It has not been photoed yet—it is going to be

I have strongly impressed Kahnweiler that you must have the first photo, that he ought to have your opinion before he exhibits the picture to the public

If it is exhibited, it is sold. It will make a noise. All Rousseau lovers will be at it. It will go to Tcheko Slovaquia.

To me it is *the* Rousseau. I would gladly give the two next best Rousseaux I know for it—including the Charmeuse.

Kahnweiler has said 175,000. I was ready to hear 200,000. I am afraid the price goes up when he has the picture in full light upstairs and when the sensation is created.——Perhaps we may secure it before that.

I do not describe it fully to you: the photo will do it.

There is the desert, a distant range of mountains, the night sky, a mighty strange stately lion against it, he quietly smells a big sleeping woman, lying at the foreground, she is dreaming ["of love" crossed out], her face is "inouïe," the lion is probably going to eat her, but perhaps he will walk away.

I have never been more thrilled by a painting in my life.

[He quotes his cable of the same day.] The colours are equal to the composition. That is they beat for me any other of Rousseau. They are a poem strange simple. Perfect state of conservation.

In case of danger I'll do all possible to buy an option. I would even suggest you buy before having the photo. If you miss it you would be more inconsolable than for the Charmeuse. I risk gladly all my worth and all your confidence to back this picture

always yours

H P Roché

During the two weeks and a few days which were needed to complete the transaction for *La Bohémienne Endormie* Roché sent forward almost daily some new bit of information or urgency, by letter or cable.

On February 2, the day following his first letter and cable announcing the discovery, Roché wrote: "It beats anything I know of Rousseau in sweet ghostly splendour. It has a dark soul like the Charmeuse, happens at moonlight." On the fifth he cabled again, the first formal proposition from Kahnweiler:

Kahnweiler offering following option Rousseau ten thousand francs if refused from photo. One hundred seventy-five if bought. Picasso says most wonderful Rousseau. German dealers now Paris buying heavily. Roche never saw more convincing picture. Photo leaving tomorrow. Dimensions two meters [by] one thirty-five.

His cable on the following day came through as a stammer: "Rousseau now publicity exhibited creatin unanimous sensation. Price moderate for unic quality. Would risk option." His cable of the next day, February 7, adduced weighty testimony:

Quotation Brancusis own words fascinated originalest Rousseau something for friend Quinn. Delaunay thinks price low. Roche thinks necessary gem of your collection. Begs you buying option before Friday noon. Please cable anyway.

Quinn had maintained an unbroken silence during this week of bombardment, but he now yielded to Roché's plea for an answer and sent a bargaining and temporizing cable on February 8:

Cables give no statement subject. Cannot decide till see photograph. Unwilling pay ten thousand option. Too high. Would be willing pay four thousand two hundred fifty francs option till decide photograph.

Evidently Roché's first rapturous letter of February 1 had not yet reached Quinn, and so his series of notes and cables had been making excited commentary upon a thing still fundamentally mysterious to Quinn. On the ninth Roché cabled again: "Doucet confesses picture more important than his Charmeuse. Kahnweiler accepts your price for option." Roché could now draw a deeper breath: he and Quinn had the prize under at least temporary control. On the eleventh he wrote: "I hope and believe it will be, if you take it, one of your greatest joys as a collector—and one of the best gems of your collection." His cable on the fifteenth added further expert testimony: "Villard whose Rousseaux collection we saw proclaims this picture greatest miracle. Is despairing not possessing it."

On February 15, two weeks after Roché's first assault, Quinn capitulated, in a rather skeptical and reluctant cable:

From photograph Friday would not have purchased but reliance opinions others your recommendations cabled you today one hundred seventy-five thousand francs payment Kahnweiler tomorrow. He may continue exhibition picture reasonable time if desired provided insured. Greatly overworked. Writing fully very soon. Thanks. Regards.

On the same day (which was two days after the completion of the fourth installment of his library sale) Quinn explained further in a letter to Roché: "It was your great enthusiasm, never so great about any other work of art, that really bowled me over and prompted me to buy." He could hardly have resisted, as long as he had money in his pocket, without repudiating Roché as an adviser. Roché cabled his satisfaction on February 18:

Hourra. Picture bought insured delivered Pottier twenty-seventh. Hesitation would have been fatal. Public subscription was being prepared for offering Louvre. Unanimous compliments all friend. Please take rest when possible.

By letter on February 21 Roché reported that Kahnweiler had had *The Sleeping Gypsy* on exhibition at the Galerie Simon for a week and that "hundreds of people" had been in to see it.

The treasure reached New York on the *Paris* on Saturday, March 8, and was delivered to Quinn's apartment on the following Wednesday, March 12. Quinn was horrified to find that it had been damaged in three places as a consequence of what seemed to him inexcusably careless packing by Pottier. The canvas on its stretcher had been only lightly nailed into the frame, and in traveling it had slipped out of the frame, leaving the bare nails exposed and ready to cut the canvas to bits. Quinn was so relieved that the damage had been minor, and so pleased with the picture itself when he saw it, that he made no complaint of Pottier's work until his last letter to Roché late in June. To welcome *The Sleeping Gypsy* Quinn had invited a dinner party composed of F. J. Gregg, Joseph Brummer (whose portrait had been delightfully painted by Rousseau in 1909), Arthur B. Davies, and Jeanne Robert Foster. After coffee Quinn took his guests into his drawing room for the unveiling of the painting, and they all drank a champagne toast " 'to its beauty.' " [12] In the general glow of the evening, Quinn got off a cable to Roché to tell his pleasure: "Wondrous color and composition. Beautiful, moving, stupendous. Davies and others think wonderful. Most grateful your efforts. Best wishes. Writing." [13] In the promised letter next day Quinn described the reception he and his guests had given Rousseau's work, and the impression it gave now by daylight in its situation on a table against a wall between two windows facing east out over Central Park: ". . . as the sun comes into the two windows it sort of fills the picture with light until it looks wonderful." He tried to sum up his judgment of his and Roché's coup:

> It is indeed one of the most beautiful paintings that I have ever seen, far finer than Charmeuse. Rousseau was perhaps at the height of his power when that picture was painted in 1897, perhaps forty-six or forty-seven years of age. Later on, when he became surer of himself and when his touch was more certain, he did not paint over what he had previously painted and hence his paint is thinner. This painting has a wonderful depth of color that even the later ones lack. . . . it was, as they say in the old English ballade [*sic*], "a glorious victory." It is, as you say, "the gem of my collection."

Roché replied on March 28: "No letter has ever given me so much pleasure, since I am busy with pictures. . . ." He tried again to express the first stunning effect of *The Sleeping Gypsy* when he saw it in Kahnweiler's cellar: "J'eus le coup de foudre." *

After reading Roché's account of having seen old Ambroise Vollard slipping out of his limousine to buy *pâté de foie gras* in the best shop in Paris, then climbing back into the car where a beautiful girl awaited him, Quinn wrote on March 20: "But why shouldn't he, as he has such an eye for art. More power to him—with the ladies, and less power to him when I come to deal with him the next time I buy art." It was a prevision all too optimistic. The securing of *The Sleeping Gypsy* was essentially the end, the hearteningly splendid last movement, of Quinn's collector's life. He knew he was ill, though he hardly dared guess how ill. He was keeping his condition fairly well hidden, aside from his grievous thinness of body, from his family and friends; but he was behaving in a consciously wary and conservative way in spending money. He made a few more gestures, but they were negative, or tentative, or trivial. He refused the chance to buy certain notable pictures: Lautrec's *l'Assommoir* and *A Clowness*; a Daumier and four Rouaults; Van Gogh's *l'Hôpital d'Arles*. He sounded nearly ready to abandon another of his oldest and warmest affections when he wrote Roché on February 28: "I don't think I shall bother with Gwen John very much now. She intimated to Mrs. Foster that she would have no paintings to sell for some little time. She wants to give her next three or four paintings to me and then we will be even." He asked Roché to keep an eye on a painting that Georges Braque had in progress; if it turned out well he thought he might be tempted by that one. He was gratified to hear that Derain had refused to take any pay for the second portrait of Mrs. Foster, after the first had failed to please Quinn, and he felt like buying "something important" of Derain's in compensation, if Roché and Derain would make a choice and send him a photograph.[14] Art and literature came together in the last of Quinn's benevolent gestures: the memorial volume for Raymond Duchamp-Villon, which he had underwritten, was ready for printing in March, as its composer Walter Pach reported.[15] It would appear in a little edition of 300 ordinary and twenty de luxe copies.

It was to Gwen John that Quinn succeeded best in evoking the *ambiance* of his last treasure, *The Sleeping Gypsy:*

* "It was love at first sight," or "I was struck by lightning."

It is a night scene, full moonlight, a grave, beautiful scene in the desert . . . a great lion in the middle, sort of sniffing at the arm of the woman, who is facing away from the lion. One does not know whether the lion is going to devour her or go away and leave her alone. But he has a wicked eye. The painting sings, every part of it, and the whole of it is perfect. . . . I think it is not only the greatest painting Rousseau ever did . . . but one of the greatest paintings of modern times.   [*March 13, 1924.*]

By now Quinn had undoubtedly forgotten that Gwen John had been the first to pronounce to him the name of *le douanier* Rousseau, in her letter of August 22, 1911, when she described Rousseau's work at the recent *Independants'*, and identified him as the queer genius who at fifty "felt he must paint and so he painted, not knowing at all how to paint." It is homely and interesting, too, to see that it is the *subject* as much as the treatment which grips Quinn after all the years in which he had persuaded himself that his taste had grown too sophisticated for that emphasis.

When Mrs. Foster returned from France on December 18 of 1923, and Quinn met her at the dock, she had been shocked to see how much more thin and tired he looked than when they had parted in Paris six weeks before. All during the winter he was nervous and weak, and he seemed to want her with him constantly. Almost every Sunday when the ground was not covered with snow they tramped, often with F. J. Gregg, on the New Jersey Palisades, or over the grounds of the Sleepy Hollow Club, or in the hills around White Plains. They continued walking into the spring, but Mrs. Foster noticed that the distance was growing less and that each outing seemed more exhausting to Quinn than the last. But he kept doggedly at it, feeling that it was "good for him," that he "needed exercise." When his old friend Eddie Robinson notified Quinn that he was coming up from Washington for a visit, and proposed a long hike, Quinn agreed for an eight or ten mile tramp, and described their customary ration: one sandwich of rare roast beef, one of hashed chicken, and coffee to be made in a pail over an open fire. "I haven't been up to the mark lately but I will tell you about it when I see you," he wrote his friend dully.[16] As in the sale of his books and the narrowing of his art collection, Quinn was pulling in his life around him. He drank nothing, not even wine at dinner, and had abjured even his after-dinner cigar; he gave up coffee and tried milk. Nothing helped, and he was in constant pain.

On January 1 of 1924 came the last formal reorganization of his office, with Quinn, Paul Kieffer, Sherman Woodward, and Robert P. Stewart as partners. Quinn blamed his partners for making it impossible for him to get the rest he believed would set him right. They insisted on their own vacation times, or on being ill themselves, and kept the office understaffed so that he felt he could not leave. A month before his death he described the situation of the winter and spring to Roché:

> Nobody in my office said: "Mr. Quinn, why don't you go away? Why don't you leave this work? Why don't you let those men do it?" I had no one around me to say that. But when the break came it came quickly. The pain became intolerable. . . . For the last six weeks I have had hell. For the last four weeks more hell. I won't bore you with it. I don't know whether I have made the turn or not.   [*June 25, 1924.*]

He carried on during these months by doing virtually nothing but the day's work. Julia and Mary Anderson or Mrs. Foster came almost every evening to take dinner and sit with him, reading or talking. Quinn found it impossible to sit in any position for long at a time. He ate and slept badly. The fifth and last unit of the library sale ended on March 20. Early in May, Quinn went out to a dinner where Edna Ferber was to speak; he sat through the dinner but got up and walked out, in pain and pique, when Edna Ferber rose to talk. The very vagueness and reticence with which he spoke of his condition to friends show how baffled and ill and frightened he was. To Michael Monahan he wrote on May 8: "I haven't been very well the last couple of months—liver. And it's a damn troublesome and annoying thing. But I don't want to write about it." Two days later he wrote to Lady Gregory: "I haven't been very well for the last two months, and the doctors don't seem to be able to do much for me although they know perfectly well what the cause is. It is not malignant but it is very uncomfortable."

"The break" came in the fourth week in May, when Quinn determined that he could not go on any longer in the office, that he had to get away for "a rest." On May 24, his last day in the office, he took time to dictate a strong protest to the telephone company against the installation of a dial telephone in his apartment: "... they are a nuisance and a vexation"; and to cable Roché: "Unwell three months. Enlargement hardening liver. Not fatal but very painful. Leaving today for country, back ten days. ...." Quinn ate a gloomy lunch with Jeanne Robert Foster at the Brevoort, then left with Eddie Robinson for what was proposed as a week's rest at the Mayflower Inn in Washington, Connecticut. But he disliked the place and remained only one day, moving on to the San Soter Sanatorium in Newburgh, New York, which he liked better but where he found no more comfort in body. On May 27 came the last pathetic flutter of an earlier *beau geste:* Quinn took over from Macmillan's at fifteen cents each the remaining twenty copies of the little blue Quinn-Russell-Plunkett *Irish Home-Rule Convention* of 1917. Mrs. Foster went off for ten days in Maine with her sister who was ill. When she returned she found Quinn at home: he had decided that since the pain was equally bad wherever he was he might as well suffer with the things he loved around him. He now had a full-time night nurse, and Julia Anderson or Mrs. Foster came in during afternoons and evenings to help Paul and Marie look after him until the nurse came on duty. In the middle of June, Paul and Marie went off to France, ostensibly summoned by a cable saying that Paul's father was dangerously ill. Quinn then had to have nurses around the clock.

Exacerbating Quinn's last days was the knowledge that the French couple who had served him for five years had been systematically robbing him for some time. A little investigation of the supplies in the apartment showed why they had left when they divined Quinn's condition, and why they would not return. Quinn's cellar of wines and whiskies, which he valued at about $3,000, proved to be virtually empty, and inquiry revealed that Paul had been carrying out and selling a few bottles at a time for many weeks. Also missing were quantities of clothing, luggage, and linens worth hundreds of dollars. Thinking over his bills for food and household supplies, Quinn estimated that he had been robbed of sixty to seventy dollars a month on that side for years. "Besides that he was a traitor to me," he wrote Roché on June 25. "He took a thousand francs from a bitch abroad [perhaps Dorothy

Coates] to spy on me and to write her who I was seeing and who was here." After the thieves had left Quinn engaged an English couple, of whom he found the wife intelligent and a good cook but the husband "a perfect bone-head—not bone-head, an ivory-head. Bones are a little porous. His is pure ivory." Furthermore, he was convinced the man had tuberculosis, and he resolved to send him away if Dr. Fleming confirmed his diagnosis.

The worries of the office were of course being kept from him. The Andersons, Mrs. Foster, Thomas Curtin and the men in the office could no longer hide from themselves the fact that Quinn was dying—of a metastasizing cancer radiating out from the liver. On Saturday, June 21, Dr. Healy found a hardened and swollen gland in Quinn's thorax, and terrified and angered him by telling him, for the first time, that he was gravely ill and that the chances were against his recovery. Dr. Fleming had gone off to Canada for the month of June with a wealthy patient. Quinn called in a throat specialist, who told him that the swollen gland was probably due to a minor infection. He was troubled with persistent constipation and with violent and protracted spasms of coughing which lasted sometimes for an hour or more and forced him to walk the floor in search of relief. After he "finally took enough stuff to blow up a citadel" [17] he had a massive evacuation and found some relief from the coughing. What sleep he got was induced by morphine, and he suffered his old trouble of night sweats, so severe that the nurse sometimes had to bathe him with alcohol and change his bedding and pajamas several times in a night.

Such was the posture of things when Quinn called in Thomas Curtin and dictated the last letter in a life of letter writing, that of twelve pages to Henri-Pierre Roché on June 25. Four days after Dr. Healy's examination, he was trying to dismiss the report as "a brainstorm on his part resulting in a vicious assault upon me and upon my confidence in my ability to go through this thing." [18] He was full of fearful hope, and full of his customary *expertise* about his organs and their condition, the liver in its "tough muscular sac" and the "direct portal circulation." He had discovered something called "compensatory circulation" which he believed was going to help save his life: "Already some little veins on the right side are showing under the skin with their enlargement. That

is a good sign. . . ." He still believed that his ailment was cirrhosis
of the liver, nothing worse, but that he was so generally "run-
down" that something else might carry him off: "I may get a bad
cold or pneumonia or jaundice may set in and poison the blood
stream." Quinn described the estate on the Great South Bay of
Long Island—"about fourteen acres, beautiful shade, beautiful
lawns, gardens and flower gardens"—which he had engaged for the
summer, which Dr. Healy had ordered him to give up, and which
he hoped Dr. Fleming would restore to him when he returned
from Canada at the end of June. Most of the remainder of the
long letter was given over to art matters, with Quinn taking a
negative view of everything except the current work of Braque,
which he thought he would buy "if it comes off well and is a real
masterpiece." For Roché personally he enclosed a draft for $300
which he said he would have made $500 but for recent terrific
expenses: "I hope you will be satisfied with that merely as a slight
appreciation of my indebtedness to you in getting me the Rousseau." After characteristically minute calculations of Roché's expenses for cables, Quinn included a supplementary sum of $32.55.
He warned Roché that it might be a long time before he could
write again. He asked him not to speak to anyone of his condition,
"not even to Brancusi." He said he had been "thrilled" to read of
Roché's week in a pine forest in the south of France, and he hoped
that some day they might go there together. On receipt of the
letter Roché cabled on July 8: "Thankful for good long letter and
enclosure. From what you say I have instinctive confidence in Doctor Fleming. Heartiest wishes from yours, Roche." When the cable
was brought to him next day Quinn scribbled directions on it for
an answer: "Quinn very week [sic] sees nobody no attention
office matters May be two months before crisis passed because
mistake did not go away rest early January. But holding own—
has will to go through it, etc. Reply by letter under Curtin's name
—add anything that is discreet JQ."

Mrs. Foster had been keeping in touch privately with Roché
since Quinn's condition began to look unmistakably grave about
the beginning of June. When she wrote that she and Quinn would
apparently have to abandon their thought of a trip to Brittany,
Roché wrote back on June 16 to lament the sacrifice: he had

thought of taking a house near them in Brittany, along with Mme. Hessel, who was the real-life original of Kathe, the woman in the queer and beautiful quadrilateral love story Roché was to write many years later as *Jules et Jim*, when in 1953 at the age of seventy-five he suddenly declared himself a novelist. Reading between the lines of her letter he had divined the gravity of Quinn's illness. "I cannot yet imagine him giving up, even temporarily, his proud way of walking," he wrote now on June 16, and "Is golf for ever finished for him?" He wished Quinn would be leaving a son behind "having his face." In her diary entry for July 5 Mrs. Foster wrote of sitting with Quinn: "He was weaker his color ghostly. The water fluttering his poor chest and abdomen, but his eyes were glorious, his face noble and beautiful." Quinn talked of their going to Italy, taking a small house there in the autumn. She held his hands and he noted how white they were. The room was full of flowers—daisies, peonies, country roses—which were her gift and others'. Quinn pronounced the Jamesian sentences: " 'My girl, when I get out of this I'm going to live. I've never lived.' " When she recounted the scene to Roché he spoke his sympathy with the feeling of the unlived life, and with her lament that Quinn lay at the point of death without ever having learned to love: "Yes John had & has to learn still about love. He has known late the right woman. I see your yellow dress and hat, and the flowers in the room." Roché was due to come to New York in the middle of October with Firmin Gemier and the French Theatre, and he hoped to have two months then in which to see a bit of Quinn and Mrs. Foster. But he offered to come now, at any time, when summoned—only hoping that it might be possible to bring Mme. Hessel with him. They could be together only in the summer. After receiving Quinn's long letter Roché wrote Mrs. Foster on July 14: "I have received a wonderful letter from John—but which makes me tremble. When I have finished translating to Germaine [his wife] the parts of it concerning his health, both she and I had tears rolling down our cheeks."

By July 21 Quinn seemed barely alive, his body skeletal but swollen with fluid, his color yellowed from the involvement of the liver. He was hardly able to move or even to speak, and he redictated his will, making sure that was in order, with what seemed his last strength of will and voice. In her diary Mrs. Foster described him as she saw him that day: "John is still alive. His head is a skull with yellow skin drawn over it—his face a mask of pain—his eyes faded to a light blue—but filled with light and un- earthly. His arms are flails of bone—his poor body a skin swelled with water. . . ." She took him roses and larkspur, and read to him from the lives of St. Augustine, St. Ambrose, and St. John Chrysostom. On the twenty-third a quantity of fluid was drawn off Quinn's abdomen. The following morning Mrs. Foster met Julia Anderson and Mary, who of course were haunting the apart- ment as she was. Mary, now seventeen, was on vacation from her schooling at the Convent of the Sacred Heart in Manhattan. Mrs. Foster was called into the sickroom to help with an enema. Quinn spoke to her: " 'Where have you been so long?' " When she left the room he called feebly: " 'Goodbye, dearest.' " She treasured the fact that his last words to her were a commitment. In the after- noon of the twenty-seventh she put her arms around him; his eyes followed her, and he tried to speak but could not. Clara Quinn, Sister St. Paul, arrived from her Ursuline convent in Tiffin. The following morning, July 28, John Quinn died at six-thirty.

Mrs. Foster, who considered herself and Roché, with reason, as the persons aside from Quinn's family who had lived closest to the heart of his affections and his values, sent Roché a long heart- broken account of the end on August 2. He wrote back on the fourteenth: "I do not realize yet that I shall see John no more, on this earth. I still subconsciously think that we shall have a trip in Spain in the fall." He told of receiving letters of sympathy from Paul Signac and Georges Braque. From the little Mediterranean town of St. Raphaël, Constantin Brancusi had written Roché in his impressionistic French on August 4:

Cher ami
J'aurai volu vous voir avent mon depart mais je ne pas pu vous trouver La mort de Quinn m'a profondement touché et je voulé vous demander s'il n'a pas quelqu'un de trés prés pour que je un mot ecrire. . . .*

---

* Papers of Henri-Pierre Roché. "Dear friend I would have wished to see you before I left but I could not find you. The death of Quinn has touched me deeply and I wanted to ask you whether there was not someone close to him so that I could write a word. . . ."

About this time too Roché sent Mrs. Foster a copy, largely in French, of the grieving recollections of Quinn he was setting down for his own son:

> You have lost there, my son, a great, good and noble friend. . . .
> He would have been able to do so many more beautiful and use-
> ful things, so much good! Now that he is gone, I regret more
> and more to have seen so little of him. . . . Mrs. Foster and I sat
> on the couch and he opposite us on the blue chair turned back-
> ward. And we talked . . . not long enough, alas! He had, like
> all superior spirits, qualities that were profound, serious, solid;
> sometimes there was something seductively childlike about him,
> and he would laugh like a child. And then suddenly his face
> would recover its serenity, which was nevertheless always a bit
> troubled. . . . It is atrocious to leave life this way, in full maturity,
> in full happiness, for he seemed happy, in full activity! I loved
> the look of him, very gentlemanlike; his slimness, his distinction,
> his silences, his eye of an observer, even of a scrutinizer, which
> saw and penetrated things. I would have had complete confidence
> in him, in any matter. He had, too, though high-keyed and sen-
> sitive, great lucidity and great calm. What a loss, my son, and
> how I understand your grief! . . . I wish I could have seen more
> of him, to have come to know him better. . . . I did not quite un-
> derstand how gravely ill he was. But I shall stop talking of him;
> I only make you more sad. . . . [19]

In his letter to Mrs. Foster on July 21 Roché had suggested that a death mask be taken if Quinn died: "I ask it solemnly to his fam-ily." Knowing Quinn's view of such gestures as morbidities, Mrs. Foster apparently did not even pass on Roché's thought, for he accepted her "decision" in the matter in his letter of August 14.

Mrs. Foster and Roché continued writing back and forth, mourn-ing together and comforting each other. "Yes, I want to go with you to the place where he lies, and talk of him there," Roché wrote.[20] They made plans to spend time together, probably in France, to compose a joint memoir of Quinn as they had known him. Bitterly comforting Mrs. Foster, as well as multiplying her frustration and grief, was the knowledge that she and Quinn had loved each other, but that there could never be, in life or death, a marriage, a possession, a public or private union. Roché wrote: "I so much not only wish but need to talk with you about John's things—and Miss C[oates] and Miss S[mith]. I want to understand. Yes you always were to me too John's fiancée." [21] In Quinn's death as in his life, Mrs. Foster was left with a love that was a terrible reality but that could act only "in vision and in veto."

On July 14, two weeks before Quinn's death, Isabella Stewart Gardner, "Mrs. Jack," another of those whom Aline Saarinen has called, along with John Quinn, "The Proud Possessors," died in her false Venetian gem of a house on the Fenway in Boston. Late at night on August 1, four days after the death of Quinn, Joseph Conrad talked comfortably with Richard Curle in his bedroom at "Oswalds," his house in Kent. They spoke of the death of "Mr. John Quinn, the American lawyer, whose great collection of Conrad manuscripts had shortly before been dispersed in New York." [22] According to Curle, Quinn's death "did not come home" to Conrad "with a reminder of his own mortality." " 'They get such strange diseases,' " Conrad said, "speaking at large." "He had never met Mr. Quinn," Curle explains: "it was not like the death of a dear friend." [23] Within thirty-six hours Conrad was dead of heart failure.

One of the last letters Quinn saw was that of July 3 from Jacques Villon which told how the copies of Walter Pach's memorial volume on Raymond Duchamp-Villon had been dispersed. A copy of the regular edition and one of the de luxe edition had been sent to Quinn the day before. Quinn had supplied a list of thirty-four friends chiefly in France and England who were to receive copies of the regular edition. Pach was to receive a de luxe copy. Villon asked permission to keep seven rather than the six copies of the de luxe edition that had been stipulated for the family of the sculptor "as we are five brothers and sisters and there is my father and my sister-in-law, the wife of Duchamp Villon." Roché was to take charge of a large bloc of the regular edition, and Villon would distribute about a hundred copies among friends and art critics in France, a few copies would be held in reserve, and the few that remained would be put on sale at forty francs per copy. Villon concluded with thanks for Quinn's final piece of *largesse*: "... I ... thank you in my name and in the name of my family for having made possible, by your generosity, the erection of this lasting monument to the memory of my brother." Quinn's gift copies of this volume brought forth letters of thanks which drifted into his office after his death, among them one of July 27 from "poor Symons," just back from six weeks in France, who babbled of seeing

> Iris [Tree], Nancy [Cunard], Count Primoli, Donna Maria Galese, the Duchesse de Clermont-Tonnerre, André Gide, Lady Rothermere, Natalie Clifford Barney—l'Amazone de Remy de Gourmont—and Romaine Brooke. . . . Jean Cocteau, Edmond Jaloux, André Germain, the de Myers, Yvette Guilbert, La Casati, and I know not how many others.

Sylvia Beach—who would have heard of it from Joyce or Pound—had told Symons that Quinn was "unwell." Quinn probably saw, though he would have been almost beyond caring, Lady Gregory's thank-you letter of July 11: "Today I have had a beautiful book, 'Printed for John Quinn and his friends', and with my name written in it, tho' not by you." Lady Gregory was just back at Coole after a fortnight in London, where she thought she saw the first sign of an approaching triumph in her nine-year fight to recover the Lane pictures for Ireland—coming, ironically, through the intervention of her and Quinn's old *bête noire,* Sir Edward Carson, now Lord Carson. She had visited her two granddaughters in school at Folkestone and filled them with strawberries and cream, and visited her grandson Richard on Speech Day at Harrow, where she found him "in his first little tail coat." In London, Bernard Shaw had given her a copy of *Saint Joan* and tickets for the performance of the play, and she was charmed to find in the text and on the stage a certain bit of business which had been her invention:

> . . . I had been staying with them when he was writing that act 'On the Loire,' and when the wind changed and the little boy called out, I said, 'If I were writing that for Kiltartan I should make him sneeze,' and I found he had put that in.* I was quite proud.

---

* Dunois: . . . I have business for you there.
Joan. What business?
Dunois. To pray for a west wind. I have prayed; and I have given two silver candlesticks; but my prayers are not answered. Yours may be: you are young and innocent.
Joan. Oh yes: you are right. I will pray: I will tell St. Catherine: she will make God give me a west wind. Quick: shew me the way to the church.
The Page [*sneezes violently*]. At-cha!!!

For Quinn it was too late for anecdotes, even good ones.

In the twenty-eighth volume of the diary she had been keeping for many years, Lady Gregory in Ireland noted on July 30: "A great blow yesterday—a cable from N.Y. 'John Quinn died this morning' [from Curtin]. . . . America will seem very distant now without that warm sympathy & interest & the children will miss his Christmas apples—So my day and night have been sad & I am heavy hearted. . . ." She cabled on the same day to Quinn's small surviving family: "Deeply grieved for dear kindest friend."

In his cable of August 5 from St. Malo James Joyce showed more feeling than he commonly expressed: "Deeply shocked to hear of death of John Quinn. Please accept my sympathy in grateful remembrance of his friendship and kindness." * On the second of August Walter Pach wrote from the little town of St. Raphaël in France to Thomas Curtin:

> . . . I chanced to see from the window Mr. Brancusi, the sculptor, who was spending the day in the same small town here where I am working. I ran out to meet him and almost the first thing he told me was that Mr. Quinn had died. . . . To say that I am stunned by the news is almost less than true, for I can hardly believe it now. However, Brancusi was so certain of it that I suppose there is no use fighting against the fact,—and it is a deep loss and grief to me. You know what it means to the artists—both those whose friend Mr. Quinn was in a personal way and those who simply had the encouragement of knowing that there was such an art lover in the world. . . . I cannot get it through my mind that Mr. Quinn is gone. It will be very long before any of us realizes what it means.

Joan. God bless you, child! Coom, Bastard.
They go out. The page rises to follow. He picks up the shield, and is taking the spear as well when he notices the pennon, which is now streaming eastward.
(*St. Joan*, Scene III)

* In spite of his rankling grievance about the sale of the *Ulysses* manuscript, Joyce showed his concern and sorrow to be real in two letters to Harriet Shaw Weaver. On July 30 he wrote: "There is very bad news current about Mr. Quinn's health. I hope it is not true." And on August 16: "I did not wish to be the sender of bad news but a few days after my last letter to you the Paris papers announced the death of John Quinn. . . . If his judgment had grown weak I hope it was due to business worries rather than to suffering. He was a man who would have hidden both. . . . I was greatly shocked to hear of his death as he had many good qualities." *Letters*, I, 219–20.

Calling cards and letters of tribute and sympathy accumulated in the hundreds at Quinn's apartment. Though Quinn had not attended Mass for many years, and though a recitation of the Latin Mass was one of his standard parlor performances, he had willingly accepted the last rites of the Church. A couple of years earlier he had persuaded Mrs. Foster to join the Catholic Church, arguing that if there was any chance of their meeting after death he wanted her fully qualified. John Quinn's funeral was held on Wednesday, July 30, at the Church of the Paulist Fathers at 59th Street and Columbus Avenue. Quinn had wished to lie down with his parents and his dead brother and sisters, and so his living sisters, Julia Anderson and Sister St. Paul, his dear niece, Mary, and a few of his oldest friends attended his body on the long train trip to Fostoria, Ohio, and saw it placed in the family plot. As an ensign of the family's permanent Irishry, Quinn had directed in his will that a Celtic cross be placed over the graves of his father and his mother. An old friend in the law in New York, Judge Richard Campbell, spoke the feeling of men like himself who had known Quinn in his ordinary personal and professional life, as a human being and a man of affairs; Campbell wrote to Mrs. Anderson on August 26:

> I saw poor Michael Monahan at the funeral and he told me he was feeling particularly lonely and unfriended. There was a strong bond between Michael and John and myself and one other: poor Mitchell McDonald, who at seventy-two lost his life in the Tokio earthquake. Mitchell would write to me from Japan and would inquire grandly for "Prince John" with the pride we all felt in him as a tremendous Irishman, proud, masterful, and everlastingly capable.*

* Quinn and Mrs. Foster had occasionally discussed the idea of reincarnation, and he told her he thought it quite possible that he would come back from the grave. When she asked him what form he would take he answered. " 'Oh, Cuchulain, of course!' " He said he felt, in fact, that he had already in his way reincarnated Cuchulain, that he had *been* Cuchulain. After his death, with Quinn and the greatest of the Irish legendary heroes in mind, Mrs. Foster set down the following verses:

> From what barrow shall I arise
> With memories of what rath,
> I, who wander in a strange land
> In exile, remembering?
> When must I stir in shadow

That would have warmed Quinn—more comprehensively but no more poignantly than Ezra Pound's brief sentence in a letter to Thomas Curtin on August 28: ". . . J.Q. had his right to: 'artifex pereo.' " *

> Upon the ancient tumuli
> A thin wraith wavering in the wind
> Less than a forgotten sigh?
> I remember the mighty men
> And the lips of my Beloved
> And the tall bards chanting
> To raise up the battle-slain.
> From what barrow shall I arise
> When Niamh returns
> And the Grey of Macha rouses Cuchulain
> From his long sleep?

* *Qualis artifex pereo:* said by Suetonius (*Nero*, XLIX, 1) to have been Nero's last exclamation before he died; in the Loeb translation: " 'What an artist the world is losing!' " Pound had to take liberties with the context in order to apply the phrase.

Endings

BIG men die in New York every day, and John Quinn's death created no great public stir. It was his work as an art collector that drew the heaviest attention in the typically drab newspaper notices of his death. *The New York Times* on July 30 did speak of personal qualities: "His keen mind enabled him to penetrate immediately to the heart of a question—or a man—and his ready wit made him a delightful companion but a formidable opponent." The *World* on July 29 called him "one of the world's leading collectors of modern art," and identified him as "the leading spirit" behind the 1921 post-impressionist exhibition at the Metropolitan Museum. The fullest and warmest of the obituary notices appeared in the *Sun* for July 29, under the heading, "A Courageous Connoisseur." It was almost certainly written by "El Greggo," Frederick James Gregg, and it put the emphasis where it belonged, on Quinn's bravery as a collector, his readiness to engage with the new and unsanctified in art. An Irishman himself, Gregg very properly reminded readers of Quinn's lifelong lover's quarrel with Irish affairs; and he seized this first opportunity to urge that Quinn's art collection be preserved and used as the whole he had made it:

> John Quinn . . . was probably the most courageous patron of the arts of his time. It was not his way to wait until men's reputations were made before buying their work. He bought the pictures, sculpture and manuscripts of men whose names, when he made the venture, were known to but few but whose eminence is now undisputed. What was caviare to the general was sure to please John Quinn, provided it had in it the substance of genius.

He did not buy manuscripts or works of art in order to make a profit on them, but because he loved good work and wanted to help those who created it.

. . . it will be a pity if these works are sold separately, or at all. Quinn was an individualist of taste, broad, enlightened, receptive of new ideas. His collection ought to find a home somewhere in its integrity. He himself never seemed to bother much how he hung his treasures in his unassuming home. He was always ready to lend them to exhibitions where he believed they would be viewed intelligently. No better service could be rendered to modern art than to keep them together.

. . . He was a dependable friend of Irish freedom and a wise and moderate counselor of its advocates. Altogether a man who had added to the distinction of this city and who had enriched its cultural spheres passed away when John Quinn died.

The only thing like a considered and extended memorial to Quinn appeared in a nine-page article in the *Catholic World* for November 1924 under the title, "John Quinn: Lawyer, Book-Lover, Art Amateur." It was written by James J. Walsh, "M.D., Ph.D., Sc.D.," an Irish-American medical man who had known Quinn, not intimately, for twenty years in New York. Walsh traced Quinn's rise from humble origins to eminence in his profession, and spoke of the striking energy and variousness of his career, his busy and serviceable concurrent lives as lawyer, Irish politician, and patron and appreciator of arts. Quinn's death, Walsh thought,

> was the passing of a man who had exemplified better than it is given to most men, how it is possible to have life and have it more abundantly, because he had not used it merely for the making of money, though he had plenty of opportunities to do so, but for that broadening of the spirit of man in this time of its probation that, humanly speaking, represents the only satisfying explanation of the meaning of life.

It was a partial reading of Quinn, a bit too soft and sentimental. In fact Quinn's shade had to wait thirty-four years for more accurate justice, both fuller and tougher, when Mrs. Saarinen, in a chapter in *The Proud Possessors*, gave him his first and only satisfactory treatment in print. Less-formal tributes to Quinn appeared as letters to the editors of the papers, as for example an "Appreciation of John Quinn" by a friend of many years, George F. Parker, in *The New York Times* for August 6; and "John Quinn a Fighter" by M. Frederic McAlpin in *The New York Times* for August 9. McAlpin recalled living in the same quarters in Cambridge with Quinn in 1895 when McAlpin was a freshman in Harvard College and Quinn a senior in the Law School. McAlpin recounted an incident in which Quinn knocked down a Boston policeman who laid a hand on him without sufficient reason—as a dramatization of American independence, to force an arrest which would give him a chance to demonstrate in court the inviolability of the individual. McAlpin saw the affair as a *beau geste* of Americanism: "John Quinn was a character for Americans to admire: he was a product of the best of American institutions. He could have been produced by no other country in the world." But the aristocratic Irishman Sir Shane Leslie, recollecting John Quinn recently in his own old age, thought not of Quinn's Americanism but of his Irishness and his cosmopolitanism, and called him "the fairest, most cultured Irishman I ever met." [1]

It would have been asking too much to expect John Quinn to die without a quarrel. His death, and his testamentary provisions, created two obvious grounds of contention: his mistresses and his art collection. Quinn's will made it very plain that he looked upon his own success as a thing accomplished for the benefit of his immediate family and no one else. His basic estate was devised to his sister Julia Anderson and thence to the line of her issue, which was to say to her daughter, Quinn's niece, Mary. Of the specific bequests of money in the will, the first and most touching was a gift of $500 to Dr. U. H. Squires, Quinn's high-school principal in Fostoria, now living in elderly retirement in Hebron, Nebraska. Thomas Curtin, the longest established and perhaps the most valuable contributor to the success of Quinn's office, identified in the will simply as "my friend," was left $15,000 and named an executor of the estate. (But Curtin himself was dead within the year.) To his sister Clara, the nun, in absolute faith that she would be looked after by Julia, Quinn left only an outright $2,500, plus the income from a trust fund of $10,000 to be administered by Julia, in addition to a provision of $25,000 should she elect to "leave the

Convent" within two years of Quinn's death. Ada Smith, Quinn's first regular mistress and still a family friend, was given $25,000 "as a token of my regard and esteem for her and of her kindness, and as a mark of appreciation of her kindness to me and to my family." "As a token of regard" the larger sum of $40,000 was left to the more recent incumbent, Dorothy Coates. Quinn's executors were also ordered to "account to her for an investment which I made for her some years ago, on which she has been receiving six per cent," and to "pay her at the rate of three thousand dollars ($3,000) per year pending the settlement and adjustment of my estate. . . ." Everything else, including the art collection, the still immense personal library, and the furnishings of the big apartment, was left to Julia Anderson and her descendants.

Thomas Curtin was given "full power" to destroy "any or all personal letters or papers of a personal and a nonliterary character . . . either letters to me or copies of letters from me." Jeanne Robert Foster was asked to scrutinize "all my autograph letters of writers or persons of note" and to decide which were to be kept and which cataloged and sold. Quinn further ordered that copies be made of "all autograph letters to me which may have a literary or artistic or historical interest," asked that Mrs. Foster make a selection of the best of these, that they be, at the discretion of the executors, sealed up and put away for "ten or twenty years," after which time they should be deposited in the New York Public Library "for the use of such writers or students of literature or persons interested in Irish writers as may care to consult the same." (Mrs. Foster took it as a sign of Quinn's weakness of body and confusion of mind that he had said nothing to her in his last weeks of the responsibility he intended to lay upon her for the winnowing of his immense and valuable collection of letters, numbering in the thousands.) Quinn referred in his will to his earlier instructions to executors in regard to the disposition of his letters, including the suggestion that a selection of the letters might, with the consent of the writers, be published "as a possibly interesting record of literary and artistic history of the last fifteen years." Quinn understated the possibility as a publication in "one or two volumes."

Quinn's directions in his will for the disposition of his art collection were lamentably vague and potentially confusing. Only three pictures were specifically named and disposed. "I direct that the painting called "The Circus" by Seurat be given and donated to the Louvre Museum of Paris, France," he ordered. Quinn had not forgotten that old promise to Roché and Paul Signac. The oil portraits of himself by Augustus John and John Butler Yeats were devised to Julia Anderson, as were the oil and water color-paintings by their dead sister Jessie Quinn which had helped to keep Quinn's bedroom at 58 Central Park West a primitive Fostorial enclave in the midst of the general cosmopolitanism of his house. Julia was also invited to select what she wished among the paintings of George Russell and Nathaniel Hone or among the general supply of drawings and lithographs, and she was specifically bequeathed all the pencil drawings of members of the family, which would have been mainly executed by John Butler Yeats and Augustus John. Aside from *Le Cirque*, all this was to say nothing of the great body or the dominant character of Quinn's collection. Of this essential collection the will spoke only as follows:

> I have given written directions as to the sale or other disposition of my paintings, sculpture and statuary. I include with the paintings, sculpture and statuary all other objects of art and glassware, which shall be duly catalogued and sold at public auction after being properly advertised.
>
> I give my executors and trustees power to sell any particular object or objects of art, paintings, statuary, sculpture or antiques at private sale that in their judgment and discretion may be sold to better advantage than at public auction.

Thomas Curtin was again named as the man who knew most about the cost and the value of items in the collection, and the one to be chiefly consulted in the preparation of an inventory and a catalog.

The separate "instructions" to his executors to which Quinn referred several times in his will were a semi-formal document of seven pages which he dictated on January 31, 1918—on the eve of his major operation for intestinal cancer. In that document, which he saw as not essentially outmoded by the six and a half years and the growth and shifts in emphasis of his collections, he gave very general directions for the treatment of his books, letters, and art in the event of what he carefully euphemized as "an accident" to himself. He envisioned that the bulk of his art collection would be disposed of at auction, but he stipulated that his executors should have the right to sell privately, if they thought best, his "advanced art work." He thought that most of his early purchases could go perfectly well at auction: ". . . the Russell things, the Jack B. Yeats things, the Nathaniel Hone things, the Mr. Yeats things, the Lawsons, the early Kuhns, and so on, are quite sane. . . ."; likewise the three main works of Puvis de Chavannes, *The Way Down to the Sea* by John, and *Doña Ana* by Charles Shannon, all at the Metropolitan, John's *The Mumpers* in Thomas Fortune Ryan's art gallery, and the other Shannons in Quinn's apartment; he thought too that "the Gauguin, the Van Gogh, all the Derains, the Cézannes, the two [in 1918] Matisses, all the John paintings and drawings" might bring good results at auction. What troubled him in anticipation of a sale was "the advanced work, the cubistic work and the Brancusi carvings." Buyers of such work, he wrote in 1918, were "comparatively few"; he instanced "Miss [Lily] Bliss, Mr. Arthur B. Davies, Mrs. Eugene Meyer, the Modern Gallery, Mr. [Walter] Arensberg, and a few others." Quinn recommended that Davies be asked to make the discrimination, deciding which works should go at once to auction, which should first be tried out at private sale. And he offered the name of Walter Pach as a good man to handle the cataloging of his French works.

So far as the art was concerned, the will and the "instructions" boiled down to a directive to the executors to sell, more or less promptly and by means of their own choice, all the art works except *Le Cirque* for the Louvre and the few personal and conventional pictures devised to Mrs. Anderson. Quite obviously, Quinn had no intention but to liquidate his collection and convert it into cash for the benefit of his heirs, his immediate family. There was apparently no thought of leaving the collection as a whole to his family, or to anyone else: no suggestion of leaving all or part to the Metropolitan Museum or to any other existing museum; or of establishing a "John Quinn Museum" or any other form of "American Luxembourg." Equally, Quinn's old tentative promise to Henri-Pierre Roché to give back to France a selection of his most important French works had gone by the board—reduced to the single, admittedly stunning, work of Seurat's to the Louvre. One wishes that the final gesture of Quinn's career as a collector might not have been so wary and unimaginative. In the light of the courage and animation that had gone into the making of the collection, one must be disappointed that his daring did not survive his illness, that the Quinn collection must go out, in the words of one of his beneficiaries, with a whimper. One respects Quinn's human, Yankee, and Irish motive in wishing to pass on to his direct heirs the fruits of his labors: so to affirm that it was they for whom he had been working all his life. Still, the spectator must regret that his action had to be so absolute and to take a form so crass. It was as if at the end he trusted nothing but money. Had the Museum of Modern Art existed when Quinn was ready to die the case might have been different—though I doubt it: he seems to me to have behaved in character. The establishment of the Museum of Modern Art five years later, in any case probably owed something to the forceful warning given by the negative example of the disappearance, as it were, of Quinn's big, brave, vivid accumulation into thin air—as it seems in retrospect.

Quinn's decision to liquidate his collection was bound to make trouble among those close to him who had admired the progress and the fruits of his pursuit of modern art. His pursuit of females, discreet and conventional as it had been in its main courses, also left one embarrassing legacy. Dorothy Coates showed herself quite unwilling to accept Quinn's provision for her in his will. She pronounced herself his official relict, and quite unsatisfied by the will's suggestion that she was no more than a cast mistress. Quinn had never really stopped seeing her, but in recent years he had found her more and more a trial, his visits less and less a pleasure. When he found her a particular strain on his nerves he was forced to extravagant devices to secure his peace. At one point he even sent her to Europe, where she wrote from the Bay of Naples: " 'I am looking at Vesuvius. Vesuvius is looking at me. Both of us are burning.' " [2] One of Jeanne Robert Foster's unofficial functions during the last two years of Quinn's life was to try to fend off Dorothy Coates's calls by telephone and in person and thereby reduce her inroads upon his energy. Quinn's family were not entirely ignorant of the existence of such persons in Quinn's life, in a vague and unspecific way, but they had hardly heard the name of this person who manifested herself noisily after his death. In assaults upon the family and the executors, she declared herself Quinn's "wife" and "widow" and demanded a wife's share of his leavings. They rebuffed her and advised her to be well content with the $40,000 and the mysterious "investment" Quinn had left her, but she persisted in her demands. Thomas Curtin soon began to feel that she was dangerous and mad, especially after he heard she had threatened injury to Mary Anderson, Quinn's niece. Private detectives were hired to watch over Mary's comings and goings for a time.

Trouble with Miss Coates boiled up intermittently during the two years in which Quinn's complex estate was pending settlement in the Surrogates' Court. On January 8, 1926, Jerome Hart, a sixty-five-year-old writer who lived, like Miss Coates, at the Hotel Majestic, wrote to Maurice Léon, one of Quinn's executors, and threatened to "ventilate" certain facts (apparently indiscreet letters from Quinn to Dorothy Coates) unless she were given her just deserts. Miss Coates herself repudiated Hart's action, said she had had no part in it, and described herself as "embarrassed" and "indignant." [3] She took the opportunity, however, to reassert her intimacy with Quinn and his collection: "John Quinn I knew for twenty-five years—long before he had money to buy pictures. I know every picture that he bought and its history." Hart was held on bail of $1,000 on the charge of sending the threatening letter, called before the Court of Special Sessions, and discharged there on February 26. Miss Coates had by now reduced her demands upon the estate and rested her case upon the mysterious clause in Quinn's will which ordered his executors to "account" to Miss Coates for "an investment which I made for her some years ago, on which she has been receiving six per cent." The executors could find record of only one investment by Quinn in the name of Dorothy Coates: $2,455 worth of railroad stock which he had sold for her and on which he had paid her interest for several years. When the matter finally came up for a hearing in Surrogates' Court on June 15, 1926, Miss Coates offered in evidence check stubs showing average payments of $3,861 "for a period of years," and she argued that that income was an earnest of an investment of at least $50,000 in her name. She now claimed that sum in addition to the $40,000 the will had allotted her. Her brother and sister testified that Quinn had promised them that Dorothy Coates would be "taken care of" if anything happened to him. Surrogate O'Brien disallowed Miss Coates's claim, holding that the mere fact of the annual income was not proof of any specific investment to which she was entitled. The general assumption was that Quinn's payments to her were for services rendered.

In *The New York Times* account of the hearing Dorothy Coates was described as having been "for some time a protegé [sic] of John Quinn." [4] Next day she announced, through her attorney, Milton Ives Livy, that she intended to appeal the decision, and that she had been "misquoted and misrepresented" in the newspapers. She had never been John Quinn's "protegée," she protested, but she had been and was Quinn's "legal wife in the eyes of man and God," in a relationship that went back twenty-five years. Quinn had asked her not to make the union public because she was a Protestant and he a prominent lay Catholic, she said; she had honored his wish and had always trusted to his probity and worldly wisdom to provide for her ultimate rights as a wife and widow. Livy refused to answer when asked when and where the marriage had taken place. [5] Quinn's surviving partners, as attorneys for the executors of the estate, at once denied Miss Coates's story. Livy reaffirmed it and specified circumstances, still sufficiently vague: the marriage had occurred "between twenty and twenty-five years ago" "somewhere in New York State." [6] At this point Dorothy Coates abandoned her cause, and the public book of John Quinn's love life was closed.

When Quinn died, the dream of those friends who had lived closest to him and to his art was to keep his collection together and to make it somehow public. They desired this in the cause of modern art itself and of Quinn's honor as one of its boldest champions. F. J. Gregg, in his *New York Sun* paragraph on the day after Quinn's death, had seized the first possible opportunity to urge the preservation of the collection as the vivid whole that Quinn's nerve and taste had made it:

. . . it will be a pity if these works are sold separately, or at all. . . . His collection ought to find a home somewhere in its integrity. . . .

When Ezra Pound wrote to Thomas Curtin on August 28, 1924, to accord Quinn the laureate phrase *artifex pereo* (and to volunteer his services to the estate), he urged that Quinn's collection be allowed to remain in the United States, intact if possible, public if possible. That was the vehement desire as well of Gregg, of Walter Pach, of Henry McBride, of Arthur B. Davies, and of course of Roché and Mrs. Foster in their letters to each other and in pleas to the executors. Running counter to this common dream of Quinn's friends in art, quite apart from the problem that Quinn himself had ordered his collection sold, was the general inhospitality of the executors to art, and their natural wish and that of the family to simplify the estate and to convert it promptly into the most negotiable and portable form. Mrs. Anderson was by no means ignorant of art or immune to its appeal; but her tastes in art were conservative, and she had no wish to live with the burden of several thousand art objects of any kind. She had seen the way a large collection could take command of a life. Quinn's executors were Thomas Curtin, Maurice Léon, an old friend in the law, and the National Bank of Commerce, represented chiefly by C. Allison Scully, a vice-president. None of them was particularly knowledgeable about art or sympathetic to Quinn's "wild" kind of art, though of course Curtin knew more than anyone else of the practical history of the collection, the provenance and cost of specific items. Roché wrote guardedly of Léon to Mrs. Foster on August 14, after he had heard Léon was to be an executor: "I have kept souvenir of Maurice Léon as a cold man. But I have seen him superficially in his office, not as a John's friend." The National Bank of Commerce felt itself embarrassed as the custodian of a mass of Quinn's kind of art, and their impulse was to dispose of it all as quickly as possible. An official of the bank said to Walter Pach, " 'Say, Pach, we don't want Wall Street laughing at us as the Cubist Bank. We've got to be careful.' " [7]

The dream of keeping the collection together in America, as a tribute to its own quality and a perpetual memorial to John Quinn, died hard. "Yes, if we could keep the essential of the collection together!" Roché wrote to Mrs. Foster.[8] What the situation cried out for was an American Maecenas, a single person or public body who would come forward with the requisite courage and cash to buy the collection in its integrity at a fair figure. The sad fact that no American Maecenas appeared was a sign of the daring of Quinn's taste. What Roché had called earlier the "explosive nucleus" of a museum of modern art lay waiting, and no American came forward to claim it. Those who had the nerve lacked the cash, and those who had the cash lacked the nerve. One of Quinn's modest suggestions to his executors was that perhaps Arthur B. Davies might be able to collect a fund of about $250,000 to buy in the cream of his French collection—that which he himself most hoped to preserve. But even the gentlemanly Davies, who had a long history of success in "finding" money in the purses of wealthy ladies, failed this time. Unless the collection were to be held indefinitely in limbo, then, waiting a purchaser, the only course that appeared to be open to the executors was to disperse the collection, relying on their own best lights and on the letter and spirit of Quinn's instructions. As businessmen with a complex and unfamiliar commodity, they feared that the value of the works might plummet if they kept them long on their hands—as Quinn himself had seemed to fear in advising that the collection be liquidated within two years. No one involved had any means of knowing that Quinn's pictures and sculpture would multiply many times in "value" within a generation, and that they could now be sold for a good many millions of dollars.

Within the limits of their situation, it must be said that Quinn's executors behaved well: they proceeded slowly, they sought advice, they resisted panic urging to dispose of the whole mass by a quick public auction in New York, they observed Quinn's stated wishes. The only thing that moved swiftly was the single unequivocal case: *Le Cirque* which had been devised to the Louvre. The gift of that masterpiece was announced in newspapers on August 19, 1924, though the formal presentation did not take place until January 30, 1925, a Saturday afternoon, when a ceremony was held at the Art Center on East 56th Street in New York, with the French Ambassador as honored guest. *Le Cirque* was the first gift by an American to the Louvre, and officials of the museum had needed some time to decide to accept it at all. Quinn's taste in French art was more advanced than official French taste: neither the Louvre nor the Luxembourg at that time held a single work by

Seurat. When Jacques Doucet heard of Quinn's gift he presented to the nation Seurat's main study for *Le Cirque*, which had been in Doucet's personal collection. *Le Cirque* now hangs in the Jeu de Paume, with a plate identifying the donor only anonymously, as the gift of "an American." Many voices, but particularly Gregg's and McBride's, were raised in New York, asking that the Quinn collection be put on show and sale as a whole and at once; but other voices, and Quinn's own instructions, demanded less haste. Roché had been asked to advise and to help with the valuing and cataloging, and he did not reach New York until the middle of October, and then with only limited time free. Walter Pach, just back from France, was queried as to what was said to him in Paris about selling the collection. In a letter to Thomas Curtin he wrote that the Paris dealers had all warned that a sale in New York would bring very low prices, perhaps one-quarter of the cost of the works to Quinn, whereas a sale in Paris would show a profit over his costs. Pach and the French dealers pointed to the disastrous results of sales in America by Kelekian, De Zayas, and Léonce Rosenberg.[9] On January 12, 1925, Roché sent the executors from his hotel in New York a list of eighteen suggestions for handling the sale of the collection—generally advising caution, discrimination, careful selection of markets and times of sale according to the particular kinds of works involved.

By that time the executors had in hand the most impassioned of the attempts to preserve the honor and the unity of Quinn's collection, Jeanne Robert Foster's eight-page letter of October 18, 1924, to Thomas Curtin as executor. In the three months since Quinn's death she had exhausted her hope of keeping the works together as a memorial to his name, but she gave in with great bitterness:

> Since we do not love art sufficiently in this country to preserve the collection intact as a memorial to him, let us not go down in art history as eternally disgraced by our method of its disposal. It will be a hundred years or more (or perhaps never) until we see a man of Mr. Quinn's nature again.

Mrs. Foster told of a conversation with Quinn two weeks before he died in which he spoke in one of his standard veins of gloomy hyperbole: " 'If anything happened to me and there was a sale of my paintings, there would be a slaughter.' " He predicted that his. Irish paintings would " 'go for nothing,' " that the Rouaults would only return cents upon his dollars, that such things as the large Picasso nudes " 'could hardly be given away.' " Mrs. Foster spoke from the point of view of one long acquainted with art and its markets and of one who had shared directly in Quinn's recent expenditures of nearly $100,000 on art in Paris. She cited opinions she had collected of experts as to the proposed general auction of the collection in this first winter: Joseph Brummer, for example, had predicted " 'an unparalleled catastrophe.' " In Mrs. Foster's own opinion, ". . . it would result in such a slaughter of valuable works of art that it would not only be a catastrophe but a blot on the memory of the man who sacrificed much to bring this magnificent collection together." She foresaw few American buyers—Dr. Barnes, Miss Bliss, Mrs. Havemeyer—and warned: "This means the buying in for hundreds of dollars by cunning dealers of precious things that they can hold for a time and re-sell for many thousands." Since the works must be sold, she pleaded that the disagreeable business be carried out with dignity, caution, and art. Her advice was that the collection should be divided into lots and sold, slowly and not by auction, "in the three great capitals of the world, Paris, London and New York," by agents working at the usual dealer's commission. She described the art she had in mind:

> Selling paintings is an art and depends on a skilful whetting of the buyer's appetite, a certain amount of withholding, an intensive publicity, the element of surprise, the element of rivalry and of rarity and a certain psychological something called personality.

She was talking about that process in which Quinn had found the keenest pleasure and which he had called "the rigor of the game." Finally Mrs. Foster cited the consummate example of Ambroise Vollard, whom she had seen bring out from one or another dusty reservoir, every time Quinn called, only one or two hitherto undisclosed paintings: " 'Just another gem.' " Mrs. Foster's hope was that Quinn's treasures might be dispersed with that kind of loving and lingering art.

First at 31 Nassau Street and later at 58 Central Park West, where the lease on Quinn's apartment had been renewed, Mrs.

Foster would be busy for more than a year at her own labor of love. With Quinn's favorite secretary, Florence Thompson, she worked at the big task of reading, selecting, editing, transcribing, and re-collecting the thousands of letters to and from John Quinn which Thomas Curtin brought in a box at a time, and which finally took the dense reduced form of the thirteen volumes of transcripts to be deposited in the New York Public Library.

The truth was that nobody had ever seen, and nobody would ever see, the Quinn collection in anything like its integrity. Henry McBride, the art critic of the *Sun*, told what it was like in general terms to pay a casual visit to the collection *in situ*:

> Mr. Quinn himself was none too accessible, and even I, to whom he was invariably kind, had but the vaguest notion of his purchases. To visit his rooms was but little help, for the canvases were stored back to back against the walls, and piled high upon each other, like goods in a warehouse.[10]

In an article in *The New York Times Magazine* of January 3, 1926, Sheldon Cheney described the full treatment of a serious student of the modern movement in art accorded a "showing" of the collection:

> It was an evening some three years ago that I first went to see some of the treasures that were piled apparently without rhyme or reason against the walls, under the beds and in unexpected nooks and corners. . . . There was little of art to be seen immediately as one entered the dim rooms; rather an impression of a theatrical prop room, with strange-shaped objects peeping out from under dustcaps—the bulgy Brancusi sculptures, no doubt— and only here or there a painting hung openly on a wall. And the works so hung seemed little likely to justify the reports that had excited me, of vast treasures of Cézanne and Derain and Matisse, of Picasso, Redon and Rousseau.
>
> After dinner talk drifted . . . to the latest "period" of Picasso, to the misfortune of the world in losing the youthful Gaudier-Brzeska in the war (his finest sculptures were here in these rooms), to the growing recognition of Cézanne's mastery as a water colorist. I quickly learned that I would find here no sympathy for certain modernistic gods recently set up in Teutonic countries— particularly Kokoschka and Lehmbruck—to whom I had done some worship. But there was not a side of contemporary French

art that Mr. Quinn could not illuminate for me more clearly than any one had been able to do before.

. . . What would I like to see most? Well, the one-man Matisse show in Paris had been a bit of a disappointment, and I would like to see some of his earlier work. Right then and there my faith in Matisse was fully restored, for the whole pageant of his accomplishment was set before my eyes.

Picasso I had seen only in snatches. So we adjourned to what had been a bedroom, through corridors choked with canvases and sculptures, and from a most unlikely looking corner were drawn a dozen paintings that simply swept me off my feet. Here was Picasso of the Harlequins, Picasso of the "blue period," Picasso the Cubist (and all Cubism rose in my estimation), Picasso painting great structural women almost without color, and Picasso compressing the bigness of those earlier periods into almost gem-like little canvases. All this, shown to the accompaniment of John Quinn's quiet enthusiasm, made up an experience which is perhaps my most vivid memory out of all my encounters with art.

Cheney went on to speak of the revelation, in quantity, of Seurat, "these opalescent things"; of Redon, "such caressing, lovable colored things"; of Derain; of "Vlaminck at his best, and Marie Laurencin with her grace and cool coloring and feminine sophistication"; of Braque, Dufy, Segonzac. Cheney mentioned the Vorticists, "who had recently been very noisy in London," and was immediately offered a private Vorticist exhibition: but "the hour was already disgracefully late, and my senses swimming with gorgeous memories." Next day he went back to see the Vorticist work. Aside from the quantity and the quality of the collection, what dominated Cheney's impression was the feeling that here was a body of art that kept alive because it was lived with, built into the passion and the structure of its owner's life: "From John Quinn's collection the smell of the museum, of the embalmer, was absent. There was living beauty in generous measure where he stacked his canvases." In his closing definition of Quinn as a collector Cheney put his emphasis upon the bravery and independence of a man who staked his modest means upon art not as a commodity but as an object of affection: ". . . John Quinn, taking no comfort in authority, was our most courageous and far-sighted collector—America's greatest adventurer in the field of the arts."

It was not quantity that gave the Quinn collection its peculiar power, though it was big enough in all conscience. His collection was never fully cataloged. The only formal catalog, "The John Quinn Collection of Paintings, Water Colors, Drawings & Sculpture," published in 1926 by the Pidgeon Hill Press of Huntington, New York, lists about 1,300 paintings and drawings and about 75 works of sculpture. These figures probably represent about half the total of Quinn's possessions when the collection was intact and at its fullest. Aside from his Oriental, African, and Polynesian art and artifacts, which numbered in the hundreds, his collection probably reached a total of about 2,500 items, of which about 600 were paintings in oil. By the gigantesque standards of the typical American mass collector, the animal that Berenson liked to call a "squillionaire," that would only make a good amateur showing. Quinn's was an incredibly rich shirt-sleeve collection, formed by a man working out of his own current earned income, loving the process as well as the product of art, working as near as he could to the point of creation. Henri-Pierre Roché found the right word for Quinn's collection, writing thirty years after his death—it was "intense": "la plus intense qui fut or qui sera" (the most intense that was or will be).[11]

What one felt in his collection, can still feel in it, was intensity, energy, dynamism: it was an animated thing. Even as the record of the history of a taste it was interesting: moving from the first basically literary impulse in the portraits of the writers, to the genetic and parochial affection for Irish painters and subjects, to Augustus John and the English, to the first tentative braveries of the Armory Show pictures, and then the swift settling upon the real love of Quinn's life, the School of Paris, along with the effort to secure representative examples of the ancestors of that school. The intensity of Quinn's collecting showed even in his mistakes; the collection was full of trial and error. He did not own 2,500 works "of museum rank and importance"—far from it. There were hundreds of mistakes, measuring rigorously; but even those had their intensity as instances of risks willingly run: they were homely children, but not unloved. It must be remembered, too, that Quinn's essential career as a collector, the period in which he was pursuing the new when it was new, lasted only a little over ten years. In those ten years he put together probably the finest body of work in private hands of the following major artists: Derain, Matisse, Picasso, Redon, Rouault, Rousseau, Segonzac, Seurat; Augustus John, Gwen John, Jack Yeats; Kuhn, Lawson, Maurice Prendergast; Brancusi, Duchamp-Villon, Epstein, Gaudier-Brzeska. This is to say nothing of many interesting artists of the second rank, or the few stunning examples of the Old Masters of French modernism such as Cézanne, Gauguin, and Van Gogh. There was remarkably little in Quinn's hands that could be called trash, or even third-rate.

I think it was really this sense of the enclosed energy of Quinn's collection, hidden away in Quinn's apartment, never having been allowed to emit its full charge, that made critics like Henry McBride and F. J. Gregg wish for an auction of his whole collection: for that would be the only way one would ever see and feel the force of the thing as a whole. That intensity was what Sheldon Cheney had in mind when he wrote: "It should, of course, all be made available to the world." Equally obviously it was the peculiar dynamism and high incidence of excellence in the collection that made Pound and Roché and Mrs. Foster and other friends so desolate when it proved impossible to preserve it as an integrity and a memorial to Quinn. In the circumstances, with both a Quinn Gallery and a public auction ruled out by the absence of a Maecenas and the terms of Quinn's will, the disposal of the collection could satisfy no one.

The first movement in the liquidation of the works met with a natural but not altogether deserved derision. Again following Quinn's own advice, the executors had put Joseph Brummer in charge of the liquidation, and Brummer had been quietly selling off single works and small lots as opportunity offered for some months. The entire Picasso collection, for example, numbering more than sixty works, had already been sold to Paul Rosenberg, the painter's main dealer in Paris. Brummer's first public move was to arrange a so-called "memorial exhibition" of selected works from the Quinn collection at the beginning of January 1926. The *Art News*, which reacted from the beginning in a critical tone to the handling of Quinn's works, carried an announcement in its issue of December 19, 1925: "After eighteen months of delay, a part of the Quinn Collection is at last to be shown, prior to dispersal at some future date, not specified." The journal went on to promise a show of "more than 150 paintings, drawings, and works of sculpture" at the Art Center on East 56th Street, from January 8 to January 30, with a private view on Thursday, January 7. In their issue of two weeks later, January 2, the *Art News* gave up the whole first page, with two articles and a photograph of *La Bohémienne Endormie*, as well as the lead article on the editorial page, to generally sardonic commentary upon the exhibition. It was announced that the number of works to be shown had been reduced by more than half, and that the "memorial" exhibition was really a sale—the first and only public sale. After the show the whole collection would be for sale at Brummer's private gallery, the American Art Association Galleries on East 57th Street. The feature article, "Art World Amazed at the Contents of Quinn Memorial," recorded "considerable surprise" about town at the poor quality of the show, and pointed out that "the fifty-odd works chosen give an utterly false impression, not only of the collection, but also of the mentality of John Quinn." The writer quoted "a prominent critic who knows the collection thoroughly" (probably McBride or Gregg; Dorothy Coates took pains to point out that *she* was not the prominent critic) who tried to define the sides of Quinn that would not be memorialized in the show as projected:

> "John Quinn was not merely a collector, in the sense that one could name a dozen such in this town alone. His strength did not lie in the acquisition of isolated masterpieces, nor can it be claimed that his collection gives a complete historical survey of his time. . . .
>
> "No. It was not Quinn's judgment, it was his enthusiasm and exuberant vitality that made him the greatest force in modern art. While others were hesitating, waiting for something that looked like a safe buy, Quinn dashed in and bought with both hands. . . . When he was right, he was magnificently right. When he was wrong, his confidence and courage were so tremendous that he almost convinces one. Had the collection been put up at auction immediately after his death, he would have swept America off its feet."

The editorial reverted to the same points with comparable extravagance, calling Quinn's collection "the most famous collection of modern times" and his name one that "had already become an international legend," and assuring the reader that the executors had been "bombarded" after Quinn's death by "letters and telegrams from all over the world" pleading for a chance to see or buy his works: "That was eighteen months ago. In eighteen months, by delays, hesitancy, shilly-shallying, this immense legacy of good will has been all but dissipated, until now, when the sale is announced, barely a newspaper troubles to notice it."

All this commentary, of course, was written a full week or more before the actual opening of the exhibition; when the time came most of the New York newspapers, and even the *Art News* itself, noticed the show handsomely and intelligently. The *Art News* of January 9 carried an interview with one of the Brummer brothers, taking exception to the view of the "prominent critic," and protesting that the exhibition was in fact "representative" of Quinn's tendencies. The works shown had swelled in number again since the last count made by the *Art News*, and the journal was now willing to concede that one of the four rooms in which the show was presented offered works that were "worthy in every respect of the great collector [they were] intended to commemorate." Brummer had tried to solve the problem of "representing" Quinn's taste by giving two rooms to French works, one to American, and one to English. It was an unimaginative scheme and it did not work, either mathematically or aesthetically. It did offer one superb room of French masterpieces, bringing together the big Matisse still life, *Le Cirque*, Picasso's *Maternité* and *The Sad Mother*, *La Bohémienne Endormie*, Segonzac's *Two Bathers*, Gauguin's *Promenade au Bord de la Mer*, Marie Laurencin's *Femmes dans un Parc*, Redon's *Pandora* and *L'Initiation à l'Étude*, Cézanne's *Portrait of Mme. Cézanne*, the Van Gogh self portrait, and Toulouse-Lautrec's *Woman Seated in a Garden*. Nobody could quarrel with any of that, or deny that this main gallery showed Quinn's taste at something like its most intense. Still, the group did not "represent" the show as a whole, nor did the whole "represent" John Quinn. The selection of eighty-four paintings and drawings and eight sculptures was simply too small and too uncritical to give off the force of the collection as a whole: its vitality, its range, or its passion. Alongside the real thing, the selection feels like a toy, and one oddly skewed. Quinn's holdings in sculpture, for example, could only be farcically mimed by a group that included three Brancusis, three Duchamp-Villons, one Manuel Manolo, and a single Epstein. And Quinn's painting collection was not "represented" by setting five works of Arthur B. Davies, five of Innes, two Derwent Lees, and two Severinis against only four Picassos, three Matisses, and a single Rouault. Brummer and the executors seem to have been aiming at a history of Quinn's taste, rather than a definition of its central emphasis and energy. And, consulting their own taste rather than his, they included far too much that was merely safe and pleasant.

But there was enough at the Art Center that was sufficiently bold, French, and excellent to express Quinn if one focused on that, and enough to reanimate the critics who were being given their only chance to see a fair mass of Quinn's acquisitions in one place at one time. Sheldon Cheney's *New York Times Magazine* article of January 3, 1926, anticipating the actual showing of the pictures, was the first of the major responses to the Quinn "memorial." Cheney spoke again of the intimate interweaving of Quinn's possessions and his life, and pointed out the *phenomenal* character of Quinn and his collection—the "something arresting" to be found in "the spectacle of a distinguished American lawyer—counsel for eminent banking interests and big business—taking up with the 'wild men' of modern art, with the painters and sculptors whom the academicians berate as Bolsheviki and irresponsible 'Reds' intent on driving beauty and order out of the world." Cheney estimated Quinn's works as "the finest collection of modern art in America," and he pointed out the radicalism of Quinn's position: "How extraordinary his personal judgment was, how far his taste ran ahead of the times, is only now becoming apparent. . . ." Feature articles, generously illustrated by photographs of works in the exhibition, appeared in most of the major dailies immediately after the opening. In its Sunday supplement of January 10 the *World* gave the show a full-page spread of photographs in the execrable color of those days, as well as a separate article, generally patronizing in tone. In the *Sun* for January 9 Henry McBride expressed "surprise" that the collection kept the quality of his first impressions of it: ". . . nothing has staled . . . everything is alive and pertinent." For McBride the show convicted the museums that were still neglecting such work "with sin," and proved that Quinn "as a collector, had genius." Both Gregg and McBride got off final parting shots at the methods that were being used to show and sell the pictures. McBride wrote in the *Dial*:

> . . . the procedure resolves the Quinn Collection into money and nothing else. It leaves the modern art situation in America precisely where it was and Mr. Quinn might just as well have dabbled in stocks or drygoods as in art. A public auction, on the other hand, would have been a magnificent gesture, compelling professional attention, and awakening the public conscience as nothing else that can be thought of.[12]

And Gregg delivered himself darkly in the *Independent*:

> . . . the so-called "John Quinn Memorial Exhibition" at the Art Center . . . has served only to give the public a peep behind the scenes, to lift a corner of the curtain behind which some not-disinterested persons had succeeded in concealing the most important collection of modern art anywhere in the world.[13]

Motivated not only by the high quality of certain masterpieces but, probably, by the prevailingly quiet tone of the selections offered in the "memorial" exhibition, the *New York Times Magazine* writer on January 10 was one of the several who felt an already "classical" quality in the Quinn collection:

> John Quinn's collection, part of which is now on view at the Art Centre, hardly could be expected to lift the hair on the conservative head today. Although most of the art shown still answers to the name modernist, the almost classic quality prevailing throws over the whole a harmonizing garment of style. It becomes clear that we have in this stirring group of paintings the great men of the new movement, those who broke ground for the future without breaking faith with the past, and Mr. Quinn's choice of representative examples was made with acumen.

Forbes Watson, who was perhaps the most generally knowledgeable and civilized American art critic of the day, also felt something classical in Quinn's accumulation. While calling Quinn "the most advanced American collector of his day" and the one considered by the artists themselves "the most intrepid American collector," Watson also felt that his death marked the *closing* of "one of the most vivid and exciting epochs in the history of art in America." [14] Perhaps so—though one has grown accustomed to thinking of Quinn as the first significant American patron of modernism in art, the father of a new American impulse. From another point of view, holding on to the fact of Quinn's pioneer function, his career as appreciator and patron of the new can be seen as the close of a rhythmical movement in the tide of taste, the end of the primitive moment in American modernism, which began to stir after the turn of the century, spoke out emphatically in the Armory Show of 1913, offering to a few men such as Quinn a new artistic vision, and was about ready when he died to find itself canonized and as it were conservative. With Quinn died the dangerous youth of modernism in American taste in art. Watson returned to this view in two articles based on the Quinn collection in successive issues of *The Arts* in January and February of 1926: the collection was a triumph of personal taste working amid the confusions of "the excitable period in which he fought for modern art," a period which was "one of the most enthusiastically uncritical through which American art and artists have passed." [15] As Watson saw the grounds of confusion,

> On one side were the conservatives deploring the fact that the young artists had gone mad, and on the other side were the young artists determined to be different at any cost, and condemning all art that was not different, while at the same time they praised a great deal of painting and sculpture that had nothing to recommend it except its obviously "modern" mannerisms.[16]

The generally approving or sympathetic tenor of the opinions quoted above did not mean that the battle for modernism had been won in America. Even to the small minority of Americans who cared seriously about art of any kind, John Quinn seemed a lonely figure, and to most of them a ridiculous figure. Nor was the battle won even among the critics of art, most of whom still floated in the general bath of conservative taste. So enlightened a critic as

Forbes Watson, for example, still found the "naïveté" of *La Bohémienne Endormie* "excessive." [17] Royal Cortissoz of *The New
York Herald Tribune* spoke for the great mass of those helplessly
and hopelessly immune to art that was not photographic, or sentimental, or literary, or sanctified by time, and who had to see such
a taste as Quinn's as cranky and queer if not downright perverse.
Cortissoz wrote on January 17, 1926, after the memorial exhibition
had been running for ten days:

> . . . it is hard to see how an intellect as lucidly efficient in its
> operation as Quinn's could have reasoned out any sort of valida-
> tion for the curious paintings which dominate this exhibition. It
> is, we surmise, only by giving the imagination free rein that the
> Modernist draws certain works here into the cosmos of art at
> all. . . . [Quinn] was brilliant in argument. But we remain puzzled
> as to what he could possibly have said in justification of the bulk
> of these pictures. They are crude, ugly, uninteresting produc-
> tions, and they throw us back wearied.

Of course professional modernism may have its bigotries too, and
Quinn had at least his full share of them—as in his undiscriminat-
ing scorn for those who "kept their optics on the Coptics," or in
his striding through the Uffizi Gallery in 1923, eyes straight ahead
in a corridor of his own prejudice, with the statement: " 'Now
there are just two things I want to see here.' " Those are vulgari-
ties, softened, by no means completely, by broader more heartening hospitalities such as his affection for primitive sculptures and
for Oriental art, his ability to see that his Sumatran head was as
fine as his Brancusi *Mlle. Pogany* (and no finer). That Quinn
showed a general contempt for the old in art cannot be denied—
though, in the good old American way, he probably showed more
than he actually felt. His sweeping dismissals were partly a pose,
partly a necessity. In the general terrible hurry of his life, to practice affections at all he had to focus them, to intensify within a
narrow range of choice. That meant that both his loves and his
scorns took intensified forms, and got verbalized in vulgar terms.
He habitually gave in to the national disease of pretentious and
extravagant statement.

When the "memorial" exhibition closed at the end of January
Le Cirque went off to its home in the Louvre, and the process of

turning the Quinn collection back into cash continued and hastened. By private sale and by auction, a work or a few works at a
time, within little more than a year, by February 1927, the insub-
stantial pageant of his collection had faded. Joseph Brummer announced that by January 23, 1926, he had disposed of more than
200 pieces: 32 paintings of Picasso and 30 of his works in other
media; 4 paintings and 23 drawings and lithographs of Matisse;
a painting and 27 drawings of Segonzac; 9 paintings of Derain;
8 of Redon; 8 of Guys; 5 of Davies; 5 of Maurice Prendergast;
and so on—from one to four works by more than a score of other
artists. The major public sale in Paris was an auction held at the
Hôtel des Ventes on October 28, 1926. That the "art fight" was
far from won at this date even in the cradle of modernism was
suggested by such gestures as *L'Œuvre's* asking in front-page articles for three days before the sale: "What Idiot Will Pay the Big
Price for The Sleeping Gypsy?" The shrewd idiot who did so
was the dealer Bing, who carried off Rousseau's *naif* masterpiece
for 520,000 francs after only thirty seconds of brisk bidding. The
price was considered sensationally high. That picture, Cézanne's
portrait of his father at 280,000 francs, and the great Matisse *Blue
Nude* at 101,000 francs made up most of the total sales of 1,650,000
francs. Other works went for from 5,000 to 50,000 francs.

By the time of the final general clean-up auction at the American
Art Galleries in New York, held in four sessions from February 9
to February 12, 1927, the collection was reduced to a bit over 800
items—a figure which included much sculpture, the main body of
Quinn's American work, his primitive and Oriental pieces, a few
items of manuscript and autograph letters, and a good deal that
was only high bric-a-brac. On the first day of the sale Matisse's
Still Life with Apples went to F. V. Dudensing for $1,225 and
Charles Shannon's portrait of W. B. Yeats sold for $625. In subse-
quent sessions Durand-Ruel paid the highest price for a single item,
$8,000 for Puvis de Chavannes's *The Beheading of St. John the
Baptist*, which they had sold to Quinn for $12,000 in 1911; Scott &
Fowles bought Ingres's *Raphael et la Fornarina* for $4,100;
René Gimpel took "Mr. Quinn's huge John," *The Mumpers*, at
$1,900 and Maurice Prendergast's *Promenade* at $1,400 for the
Detroit Museum; Dudensing gave $1,600 for Derain's early *Le*

Joueur de Cornemuse; John's portrait of Arthur Symons went to Scott & Fowles for $800 (it had cost Quinn nearly $2,000); Shannon's *Summer* went for $400 and his portrait of *Lilah McCarthy as Doña Ana*, which Quinn had kept for long on loan to the Metropolitan, at $350. The works of Maurice Prendergast and Ernest Lawson sold steadily and at a respectable level: $400 to $800 each—a little less in most cases than they had cost Quinn. "Buyers evidenced little enthusiasm for the more radical examples of modern art," *The New York Times* commented on February 11 after the second session of the sale. Some "geometrical abstractions" and "vorticist studies" brought as little as $7.50 each. On the last night a Matisse bronze head of a boy sold for $350 to Kraushaar, Epstein's *Bernard Van Dieren* and *Iris Tree* to Scott & Fowles for $360 and $350 respectively, and his *Mother and Child* for $350 to W. C. Findlay. Joseph Brummer himself bid in an African head for $300.

All in all, it was a fine time to buy good art cheap. In the final New York auction the remnant of what Quinn himself would have considered the second and third ranks of his collection fetched a respectable figure of $91,570. For Quinn too had bought cheap—by present standards fantastically cheap. His collection as a whole, in its essential form only a little over ten years in the making, in which he had invested about a half-million dollars, sold altogether at a loss of about one hundred thousand dollars. By "squillionaire" standards, Duveen-Frick-Mellon standards, such figures were small potatoes. There were men in America who occasionally paid half a million dollars for a single picture. But again, that was another order of experience, safer as well as larger. Quinn's dangerous quarry had been the New Masters.

Quinn's art collecting was the handsomest and probably the healthiest thing he did. The heart of his collection, the French work, was simply superb, dazzling in its range and force. What Quinn collected was excellent in itself, and his purpose was respectable, potentially admirable. His collection was more to him than a demonstration of power or a setting for the ego. For Quinn loved his pictures and wanted to share them. I am impressed by the number of persons who speak of Quinn's *quiet* enthusiasm for his pictures. When he got really close to art there was something in it that centered him down toward what was purest and best in his own nature. It did not matter that most of his collection spent most of its time in unvisited heaps. To Quinn that was a temporary situation, one he would set right when he got more time and money. My supposition is that had he been granted the further twenty years of life that he might have expected, and had he been able to add to his fortune enough to satisfy him as a legacy to the family he loved above all, he would have seen to it that his collection passed intact into one or another kind of public possession. But he was interrupted, and what he expressed at his hurried end was the loyalty that had dominated his entire contest with time: that to his family. When Alfred Barr called Quinn the greatest American collector of the art of his day, he was not thinking of massive accumulation but of a man who, in proportion to his means, garnered the greatest amount of excellence, in such a way and at such a time as would do the most good to artists and to art. Quinn had taste but above all he had nerve and susceptibility, bravery ready for the bravery around him while it was still brave.

Notes

BEGINNINGS: 1870–1904

[1] Quoted in Joseph Hone, *W. B. Yeats*, London, Macmillan, 1962, p. 183.
[2] *J. B. Yeats: Letters to His Son W. B. Yeats and Others, 1889–1922.* London, Faber and Faber, 1944, p. 73.
[3] To Martin J. Keogh, June 15, 1916.
[4] To C. C. Burlingham, August 1, 1918.
[5] August 25, 1917.
[6] To George Moore, March 14, 1917.
[7] Quinn to W. B. Yeats, September 27, 1902.
[8] August 16, 1902.
[9] To W. B. Yeats, September 27, 1902.
[10] November 25, 1902.
[11] To W. B. Yeats, June 6, 1903.
[12] To R. C. Gaige, March 4, 1903.
[13] June 28, 1903.
[14] To Quinn, April 28, 1903.
[15] April 28, 1903.
[16] To James G. Huneker, December 23, 1903.
[17] December 16, 1903.
[18] To Quinn, March 18, 1904.
[19] Ibid.
[20] Interview with Mrs. W. B. Yeats, April 1964.
[21] January 7, 1904.
[22] To Quinn, January 20, 1904.
[23] To Quinn, May 17, 1903.
[24] To Quinn, September 11, 1903.
[25] To George W. Russell, January 7, 1904.
[26] To Quinn, January 20, 1904.
[27] To Quinn, May 1904.
[28] "In Memory of Eva Gore-Booth and Con Markievicz."
[29] July 28, 1905.

1905–1907

[1] To Quinn, January 13, 1905.
[2] To Quinn, July 28, 1906.
[3] To Quinn, May 30, 1905.
[4] *The Autobiography of William Butler Yeats*, Garden City, N.Y., Double-day Anchor Books, 1958, p. 17.
[5] To J. B. Yeats, July 15, 1905.
[6] To Quinn, September 27, 1905.
[7] April 4, 1906.
[8] December 8, 1905.
[9] November 28, 1906.
[10] To Quinn, June 21, 1906.
[11] July 13, 1906.
[12] To Quinn, November 25, 1906.
[13] To Quinn, September 7, 1906.
[14] To Quinn, December 11, 1906.
[15] To W. B. Yeats, July 13, 1906.
[16] To Quinn, September 5, 1907.
[17] W. B. Yeats to Quinn, February 18, 1907.
[18] To W. B. Yeats, August 23, 1907.
[19] July 3, 1907.
[20] To Quinn, July 19, 1907.
[21] To Quinn, October 4, 1907.
[22] Ibid.
[23] To W. B. Yeats, January 22, 1908.

1908–1909

[1] Hone, *W. B. Yeats*, p. 243.
[2] Quinn to Florence Farr Emery, July 1, 1908.
[3] To Lily Yeats, December 20, 1908.
[4] To Quinn, January 4, 1908.
[5] To W. B. Yeats, May 23, 1908.
[6] To W. B. Yeats, December 20, 1908.
[7] To Quinn, January 7, 1908.
[8] Ibid.
[9] W. B. Yeats to Quinn, November 15, 1908.
[10] Ibid.
[11] June 5, 1908.
[12] To Quinn, July 19, 1907.
[13] To Quinn, April 27, 1908.
[14] To Quinn, June 20, 1908.
[15] To Quinn, July 26, 1908.
[16] July 1, 1908.
[17] To Florence Farr Emery, June 5, 1908.
[18] June 25, 1908.
[19] April 15, 1909. In Borrow the full passage runs, " 'There's night and day, brother, both sweet things; sun, moon, and stars, brother, all sweet things;

there's likewise the wind on the heath. Life is very sweet, brother; who would wish to die?' " *Lavengro*, Ch. xxv.

[20] To Quinn, April 27, 1909.
[21] January 12, 1909.
[22] To Quinn, April 27, 1909.
[23] January 3, 1909.
[24] To Townsend Walsh, September 3, 1909.
[25] Ibid.
[26] Quinn to W. B. Yeats, June 5, 1921.
[27] To Townsend Walsh, September 3, 1909.
[28] July 15, 1909.
[29] To Ezra Pound, March 17, 1920.
[30] Ibid.
[31] Augustus John to Quinn, December 18, 1909.
[32] January 31, 1910.

1910

[1] To Quinn, January 31, 1910.
[2] To Quinn, May 25, 1910.
[3] *Autobiography*, p. 95.
[4] To May Morris, July 15, 1910.
[5] Interview with Paul Kieffer, December 1962.
[6] To Quinn, November 24, 1910.
[7] January 6, 1910.
[8] July 14, 1910.
[9] March 8, 1915.
[10] To Quinn, July 15, 1910.
[11] October 26, 1910.

1911

[1] January 5, 1911.
[2] To Quinn, February 13, 1911.
[3] To Quinn, December 7, 1910.
[4] To Quinn, February 20, 1911.
[5] To Quinn, February 13, 1911.
[6] Ibid.
[7] New York, Pellegrini & Cudahy, 1952.
[8] P. 103.
[9] Quinn's 1911 diary.
[10] *Chiaroscuro*, p. 121.
[11] Ibid.
[12] November 15, 1911.
[13] *Chiaroscuro*, p. 122.
[14] March 7, 1912.
[15] To Quinn, September 25, 1911.
[16] March 8, 1912.

1912

¹ March 8, 1912.
² To W. B. Yeats, March 16, 1913. *Letters*, p. 159.
³ To Quinn, September 1, 1912.
⁴ To J. B. Yeats, August 24, 1912.
⁵ May 24, 1912.
⁶ To George W. Russell, May 15, 1912.
⁷ To Conrad, February 11, 1912.
⁸ To Quinn, March 27, 1912.
⁹ To Quinn, March 15, 1912.
¹⁰ To Quinn, May 10, 1912.
¹¹ To Quinn, December 8, 1912.
¹² May 24, 1912.
¹³ To Conrad, February 11, 1912.
¹⁴ To Augustus John, July 8, 1912.
¹⁵ To Conrad, August 10, 1912.
¹⁶ To Augustus John, July 8, 1912.
¹⁷ Ibid.
¹⁸ August 29, 1912.
¹⁹ July 20, 1912.
²⁰ October 22, 1912.
²¹ To Quinn, September 1, 1912.
²² To Quinn, November 1, 1912.
²³ Ibid.
²⁴ Ibid.
²⁵ Letter to the author, March 28, 1964.
²⁶ *John Sloan: A Painter's Life*, New York, E. P. Dutton & Co., 1955, p. 104.
²⁷ July 1, 1908. *Letters*, p. 108.
²⁸ Quoted in Milton W. Brown, *The Story of the Armory Show*, New York, The Joseph H. Hirshhorn Foundation, 1963, p. 31.
²⁹ May 24, 1912.
³⁰ Brown, op. cit. p. 56.

1913

¹ *Letters*, p. 158.
² Interview with the author.
³ *Letters*, pp. 158–9.
⁴ Brown, op. cit. p. 95.
⁵ Ibid. p. 97.
⁶ Ibid. p. 99.
⁷ April 30, 1913.
⁸ Walter Pach, *Queer Thing, Painting*, New York, Harper & Brothers, 1938, p. 203.
⁹ To Russell, July 30, 1913.
¹⁰ Brown, op. cit. p. 170.
¹¹ To Russell, January 15, 1913.

[12] Ibid.
[13] To Quinn, July 3, 1913.
[14] To Quinn, December 29, 1913.
[15] December 23, 1913.
[16] To Quinn, August 12, 1913.
[17] To May Morris, December 16, 1913.
[18] August 17, 1913.
[19] To Quinn, March 16, 1913.
[20] To Quinn, February 9, 1913.
[21] To Quinn, April 12, 1913.
[22] To Quinn, July 18, 1913.

1914

[1] To Jessie Conrad, January 9, 1914.
[2] January 20, 1914.
[3] To Conrad, February 28, 1914.
[4] To Quinn, July 22, 1914.
[5] Garden City, New York, Doubleday & Co., 1947, p. 215.
[6] To George Russell, June 2, 1914.
[7] March 25, 1914.
[8] To J. G. Huneker, April 30, 1914.
[9] May 4, 1915.
[10] To Quinn, July 12, 1914.
[11] Ibid.
[12] To Quinn, March 14, 1914.
[13] Ibid.
[14] Ibid.
[15] Ibid.
[16] Ibid.
[17] To Quinn, September 25, 1914.
[18] Ibid.
[19] W. B. Yeats to J. B. Yeats, February 23, 1910, *The Letters of W. B. Yeats*, ed. by Allan Wade, New York, Macmillan, 1955, p. 549.
[20] To Quinn, September 6, 1914.
[21] To Quinn, September 25, 1914.
[22] To Quinn, October 31, 1914.
[23] To Quinn, March 14, 1914.
[24] To Quinn, July 8, 1914.
[25] To Quinn, December 10, 1914.
[26] November 9, 1914.
[27] To Douglas Hyde, December 31, 1914.
[28] Ibid.
[29] To Quinn, August 24, 1914.
[30] To Quinn, September 18, 1914.
[31] To Quinn, December 10, 1914.
[32] January 9, 1914.
[33] Quinn to Jacob Epstein, February 26, 1914.
[34] To Quinn, February 19, 1914.
[35] To Ambroise Vollard, October 5, 1914.

[36] To Martin J. Keogh, November 25, 1914.
[37] To James G. Huneker, July 9, 1914.
[38] To James G. Huneker, November 5, 1914.

1915

[1] To Quinn, January 12, 1909.
[2] To Quinn, September 9, 1915.
[3] To Quinn, April 10–14, 1915.
[4] April 16, 1915.
[5] To Quinn, May 5, 1915.
[6] April 12, 1914.
[7] To Quinn, March 8, 1915.
[8] To Quinn, April 28, 1915.
[9] April 3, 1915.
[10] To Quinn, July 8, 1914.
[11] To Quinn, November 24, 1915.
[12] January 8, 1916.
[13] To Quinn, April 3, 1915.
[14] To Quinn, October 24, 1915.
[15] To Quinn, October 9, 1915.
[16] To Quinn, August 13, 1915.
[17] Augustus John to Quinn, April 3, 1915.
[18] To Quinn, August 13, 1915.
[19] Ibid.
[20] To Quinn, March 5, 1915.
[21] "In Memory of Major Robert Gregory."
[22] Henri-Pierre Roché to Quinn, July 11, 1922.
[23] To Walter Pach, October 8, 1915.
[24] Walter Pach to Quinn, October 10, 1915.
[25] To Quinn, October 21, 1915.
[26] To Quinn, August 10, 1915.
[27] March 8, 1914.
[28] January 14, 1915.
[29] To W. B. Yeats, April 24, 1915.
[30] To George and Thomas Keats, December 21, 1817.
[31] To W. B. Yeats, April 24, 1915.
[32] To Quinn, April 30, 1915.
[33] To Quinn, June 24, 1915.
[34] Ibid.
[35] Ibid.
[36] To Quinn, December 19, 1915.
[37] Ibid.
[38] To Quinn, June 24, 1915.
[39] December 24, 1915.
[40] Maud Gonne to Quinn, July 15, 1915.
[41] To Quinn, May 4, 1915.
[42] W. B. Yeats to Lady Gregory [? September 26, 1902], *Letters*, p. 379.
[43] To Quinn, July 4, 1915.
[44] To Russell, September 23, 1915.

45 October 11, 1915.
46 January 13, 1915.
47 To Quinn, July 4, 1915.
48 Ibid.
49 To Russell, June 8, 1915.
50 To Quinn, July 13, 1915.
51 To Quinn, August 12, 1915.
52 Ibid.
53 Ibid.
54 Ibid.
55 Ibid.
56 To Quinn, September 7, 1915.
57 To Quinn, September 9, 1915.
58 Ibid.
59 Ibid.
60 To Quinn, April 3, 1915.
61 To Quinn, May 19, 1915.
62 To Quinn, March 20, 1915.
63 June 8, 1915.

1916

1 *Scholars and Gypsies*, London, John Murray, 1963, p. 139.
2 To Quinn, August 18, 1916.
3 To Quinn, May 8, 1916.
4 Starkie, op. cit. p. 151.
5 May 23, 1916.
6 "In Memory of Eva Gore-Booth and Con Markiewicz."
7 To Joseph Conrad, May 1, 1916.
8 To James G. Huneker, May 1, 1916.
9 *Life and the Dream*, pp. 176–7.
10 To Joseph Conrad, June 29, 1916.
11 To Quinn, May 24, 1916.
12 Quoted to Joseph Conrad, August 2, 1916.
13 To Ezra Pound, July 29, 1916.
14 Quinn to Pound, August 12, 1916.
15 Ibid.
16 August 13, 1916.
17 To Quinn, August 24, 1916.
18 To Quinn, August 21, 1916.
19 To Quinn, August 13, 1916.
20 To Quinn, August 14, 1916.
21 To Quinn, September 1, 1916.
22 Ibid.
23 To Quinn, September 28, 1916.
24 To Quinn, September 1, 1916.
25 Ibid.
26 To George Russell, January 13, 1916.
27 To Quinn, October 12, 1916.
28 To Quinn, December 29, 1916.

[29] To Quinn, February 4, 1916.
[30] Ibid.
[31] Ezra Pound to Quinn, February 26, 1916.
[32] Ibid.
[33] Christopher Hassall, *Edward Marsh: Patron of the Arts*, London, 1959, pp. 383-4.
[34] To Quinn, August 15, 1916.
[35] To Joseph Conrad, February 28, 1916.
[36] To Quinn, April 12, 1916.
[37] "Henry James: An Appreciation," *The North American Review*, CLXXX (January 1905), pp. 102-8.
[38] To Quinn, May 24, 1916.
[39] To Quinn, February 27, 1916.
[40] To Conrad, June 29, 1916.
[41] To Quinn, August 10, 1916.
[42] Ibid.
[43] Ibid.
[44] To Conrad, April 1, 1916.
[45] To Quinn, February 27, 1916.
[46] To Jacob Epstein, May 19, 1916.
[47] To Quinn, January 5, 1916.
[48] Ibid.
[49] To Pound, March 15, 1916.
[50] November 24, 1916.
[51] *Gaudier-Brzeska: A Memoir*, London, John Lane, 1916.
[52] To Quinn, March 12, 1916.
[53] To Jacob Epstein, September 8, 1916.
[54] To Quinn, March 16, 1916.
[55] To Quinn, March 18, 1916.
[56] Quinn to Pound, July 1, 1916.
[57] To Pound, July 29, 1916.
[58] To Pound, May 16, 1916.
[59] To Conrad, April 12, 1916.
[60] May 19, 1916.
[61] To Quinn, July 10, 1916.
[62] Ibid.
[63] Ibid.
[64] Ibid.
[65] May 13, 1916.
[66] To Jacob Epstein, May 19, 1916.
[67] May 26, 1916.
[68] February 4, 1916.
[69] To Gwen John, December 18, 1916.
[70] April 23, 1916.
[71] To Marcel Duchamp, July 27, 1916.
[72] To Georges Rouault, July 28, 1917.
[73] April 27, 1916.
[74] To Quinn, February 18, 1916.
[75] December 18, 1916.

[76] June 19, 1916.
[77] To Quinn, February 4, 1916.
[78] August 25, 1916.
[79] Ibid.
[80] To Jules Pascin, December 14, 1916.
[81] To James Huneker, August 18, 1916.
[82] July 7, 1917.

1917

[1] October 10, 1917.
[2] To Jacob Epstein, March 4, 1917.
[3] To Quinn, October 26, 1917.
[4] To Quinn, August 27, 1917.
[5] May 18, 1917.
[6] November 22, 1917. See below, p. 314.
[7] To Quinn, June 1, 1917.
[8] Pound to Quinn, January 24, 1917.
[9] Ibid.
[10] To Pound, March 15, 1917.
[11] Quinn to Ezra Pound, January 12, 1917.
[12] Ibid.
[13] To Quinn, January 24, 1917.
[14] Joyce to Pound, April 9, 1917. *Letters of James Joyce*, Vol. I, ed. by Stuart Gilbert, New York, Viking Press, 1966, p. 102.
[15] To James Joyce, April 11, 1917.
[16] Quinn to Arthur Symons, September 23, 1917.
[17] Ibid. The article appeared in May 1917.
[18] Quinn to B. W. Huebsch, March 23, 1917.
[19] Quoted by Nora Joyce to Quinn, April 30, 1917.
[20] To Quinn, May 13, 1917.
[21] Ibid.
[22] To Quinn, May 29, 1917.
[23] Joyce to Pound, April 9, 1917.
[24] May 5, 1917.
[25] To Quinn, July 10, 1917.
[26] June 4, 1917.
[27] To Quinn, April 11, 1917.
[28] Ibid.
[29] March 15, 1917.
[30] Quinn to Ezra Pound, April 3, 1917.
[31] To Quinn, April 11, 1917.
[32] June 4, 1917.
[33] December 29, 1917.
[34] To Quinn, May 22, 1917.
[35] To Quinn, July 4, 1917.
[36] Ibid.
[37] To Quinn, September 4, 1917.
[38] To Alfred A. Knopf, September 26, 1917.
[39] Ibid.

[40] To Alfred A. Knopf, October 4, 1917.
[41] To Quinn, September 21, 1917.
[42] To Quinn, November 14, 1917.
[43] To Quinn, October 4, 1917.
[44] *See* Donald Gallup, *A Bibliography of Ezra Pound*, London, Rupert Hart-Davis, 1963, pp. 41–3.
[45] To Quinn, January 24, 1917.
[46] May 15, 1917.
[47] To Quinn, March 26, 1917.
[48] To Quinn, May 18, 1917.
[49] To Quinn, April 18, 1917.
[50] To Quinn, May 17, 1917.
[51] Ibid.
[52] To Quinn, June 30, 1917.
[53] June 2, 1917.
[54] To Ezra Pound, October 31, 1917.
[55] [? May 1917]. *The Letters of Ezra Pound*, ed. D. D. Paige, New York, Harcourt, Brace, 1950, p. 111.
[56] Letter to the author, March 28, 1964.
[57] To Pound, November 1, 1917.
[58] To Quinn, December 24, 1917.
[59] December 14, 1917.
[60] Quoted in Richard Ellmann, *James Joyce*, New York, Oxford University Press, 1959, p. 433.
[61] Margaret Anderson, *My Thirty Years' War*, New York, Covici, Friede, 1930, pp. 174–5.
[62] To Quinn, December 30, 1917.
[63] To Quinn, May 5, 1917.
[64] To Quinn, May 17, 1917.
[65] To Quinn, June 30, 1917.
[66] To Ezra Pound, January 12, 1917.
[67] To Ezra Pound, April 29, 1917.
[68] To Quinn, December 4, 1917.
[69] July 28, 1917.
[70] To Ambroise Vollard, March 4, 1917.
[71] To Quinn, April 4, 1917.
[72] August 22, 1917.
[73] To Quinn, N.D., received December 20, 1917, from New Orleans.

1917 CONTINUED

[1] January 1, 1917.
[2] To Jacob Epstein, March 28, 1917.
[3] Ibid.
[4] Ibid.
[5] January 1, 1917.
[6] Quinn to Margaret Dunlop Epstein, September 4, 1917.
[7] To Quinn, July 20, 1917.
[8] To Quinn, September 8, 1917.
[9] To C. C. Burlingham, October 4, 1917.
[10] To Quinn, December 29, 1917.

[11] To Quinn, July 30, 1917.

[12] To Quinn, September 20, 1917.

[13] November 7, 1917.

[14] To Quinn, November 22, 1917.

[15] To Quinn, November 3, 1917.

[16] Ibid.

[17] Ibid.

[18] Ibid.

[19] October 10, 1917.

[20] December 1, 1917.

[21] Ibid.

[22] To Quinn, November 29, 1917.

[23] Ezra Pound to Quinn, June 4, 1918.

[24] To Quinn, December 10, 1917.

[25] Lily Yeats to Quinn, March 11, 1918.

[26] To Quinn, May 12, 1917.

[27] *The Charwoman's Daughter*, London, Macmillan, 1912.

[28] To Quinn, June 1, 1917.

[29] Ibid.

[30] September 15, 1918.

[31] To Quinn, January 18, 1917.

[32] To Quinn, March 21, 1917.

[33] To Quinn, March 26, 1917.

[34] To Quinn, June 15, 1917.

[35] Ibid.

[36] Ibid.

[37] To Quinn, November 19, 1917.

[38] Ibid.

[39] Ibid.

[40] To Quinn, May 23, 1917.

[41] Ibid.

[42] To Quinn, July 28, 1917.

[43] To Quinn, May 23, 1917.

[44] To Quinn, August 8, 1917.

[45] Ibid.

[46] *Joseph Conrad: A Short Study of His Intellectual and Emotional Attitude Toward His Work and of the Chief Characteristics of His Novels.* Garden City, N.Y., Doubleday, Page & Co., 1915.

[47] To Quinn, April 12, 1916.

[48] July 18, 1917.

[49] To Quinn, May 6, 1917.

[50] To Quinn, received February 12, 1917.

[51] To Quinn, May 6, 1917.

[52] To Quinn, October 10, 1917.

[53] August 25, 1917.

[54] Ibid.

[55] To Quinn, October 17, 1917.

[56] London, T. Fisher Unwin, 1919.

[57] To Quinn, July 9, 1917.

[58] *Irish Issue*, p. 3.

59 To Quinn, October 16, 1917.
60 October 4, 1917.
61 To Quinn, October 16, 1917.

1918

1 To James G. Huneker, April 18, 1917.
2 January 23, 1917.
3 To Joseph Conrad, February 18, 1918.
4 Ibid.
5 To Ezra Pound, June 10, 1918.
6 September 15, 1918.
7 To Lady Gregory, September 15, 1918.
8 Ibid.
9 Ibid.
10 September 8, 1918.
11 September 3, 1918.
12 February 19, 1918.
13 To Quinn, February 10, 1918.
14 Ibid.
15 Ibid.
16 To Quinn, February 22, 1918.
17 To Quinn, March 3, 1918.
18 To Quinn, December 7, 1918.
19 To Quinn, February 6, 1918.
20 To Pound, January 17, 1918; Knopf to Quinn, February 2, 1918.
21 To Quinn, April 27, 1918.
22 To Quinn, June 21, 1918.
23 To Quinn, May 27, 1918.
24 Ibid.
25 To Ezra Pound, January 17, 1918; February 2, 1918.
26 Pound to Margaret Anderson, [? January 1918], *Letters*, p. 129.
27 To Ezra Pound, February 2, 1918.
28 To Ezra Pound, December 3, 1918.
29 To Quinn, February 19, 1918.
30 To Quinn, April 30, 1918.
31 To Quinn, February 19, 1918.
32 Ezra Pound to Quinn, June 21, 1918.
33 Ibid.
34 To Ezra Pound, February 26, 1918.
35 Pound to Quinn, February 18, 1918.
36 The *Little Review*, IV, 11 (March 1918), p. 33.
37 To Quinn, April 3, 1918.
38 Ibid.
39 To Ezra Pound, March 14, 1918.
40 Ibid.
41 Ibid.
42 To Quinn, July 23, 1918.
43 September 15, 1918.
44 To Quinn, October 10, 1918.

45 March 4, 1918.
46 To Quinn, May 28, 1918.
47 Ibid.
48 To Quinn, November 20, 1918.
49 To Quinn, October 10, 1918.
50 Pound to Quinn, November 15, 1918.
51 Ibid.
52 Ibid.
53 To Quinn, November 20, 1918.
54 To Pound, December 5, 1918.
55 To Quinn, November 15, 1918.
56 Ibid.
57 Ibid.
58 To Quinn, February 8, 1918.
59 To Quinn, July 23, 1918.
60 Ibid.
61 Ibid.
62 Ibid.
63 To Quinn, September 4, 1918.
64 Interview with the author.
65 "Blood and the Moon."
66 February 11, 1918.
67 September 4, 1918.
68 July 23, 1918.
69 *See* Ellmann, *James Joyce*, pp. 104-8.
70 "The Evening Star."
71 To Quinn, February 21, 1918.
72 Ibid.
73 To Quinn, August 8, 1918.
74 To Quinn, March 28, 1918.
75 To Quinn, August 29, 1918.
76 Ibid.
77 Ibid.
78 To Quinn, August 8, 1918.
79 April 13, 1918.
80 To Quinn, August 29, 1918.
81 Quinn to George Russell, October 3, 1918.
82 Ibid.
83 To Quinn, October 6, 1918.
84 Ibid.
85 October 17, 1918.
86 To W. B. Yeats, September 15, 1918.
87 To Quinn, March 11, 1918.
88 To Quinn, October 14, 1918.
89 Ibid.
90 To Quinn, September 12, 1918.
91 August 13, 1918.
92 Ibid.
93 Ibid.

[94] To the author, January 6, 1964.
[95] Ibid.
[96] To Ezra Pound, March 14, 1918.
[97] To Raoul Dufy, February 2, 1918.
[98] To Georges Rouault, March 4, 1918.
[99] Walter Pach to Quinn, May 23, 1918.
[100] To Quinn, March 21, 1918.
[101] To Quinn, December 29, 1918.
[102] Walter Pach to Quinn, October 29, 1918.
[103] To Quinn, June 5, 1918.
[104] To Quinn, March 22, 1918.
[105] To Quinn, June 10, 1918.
[106] Augustus John to Quinn, November 22, 1918.
[107] To John Knewstub, January 9, 1919.
[108] To Jacob Epstein, January 21, 1918.
[109] Ibid.
[110] Ibid.
[111] Postmarked August 2, 1918.
[112] October 2, 1918.
[113] September 15, 1918.
[114] To Russell, November 26, 1918.
[115] Ibid.
[116] To Quinn, November 9, 1918.
[117] October 3, 1918.
[118] October 26, 1918.
[119] To Jack B. Yeats, December 20, 1918.
[120] December 8, 1918.
[121] November 9, 1918.

1919

[1] April 10, 1919.
[2] To Quinn, July 31, 1919.
[3] To Joseph Conrad, June 19, 1919.
[4] September 29, 1919.
[5] November 22, 1919.
[6] April 3, 1919.
[7] To Quinn, July 10, 1919.
[8] Ibid.
[9] To W. B. Yeats, January 13, 1919.
[10] To Quinn, June 14, 1919.
[11] Ibid.
[12] To Quinn, July 11, 1919.
[13] Ibid.
[14] Ibid.
[15] To Quinn, December 13, 1919.
[16] John Sloan to Quinn, December 20, 1919.
[17] January 13, 1919.
[18] To J. B. Yeats, May 23, 1919.
[19] Walter Pach to Quinn, January 13, 1919.

20 To Walter Pach, January 14, 1919.
21 To Percy Moore Turner, May 28, 1919.
22 To R. J. Coady, September 4, 1919.
23 To Walter Pach, April 28, 1919.
24 To Walt Kuhn, June 28, 1919.
25 To Walt Kuhn, November 18, 1919.
26 To John Knewstub, April 26, 1919.
27 May 10, 1919.
28 To Arthur Symons, December 27, 1919.
29 Ibid.
30 April 4, 1920.
31 Ezra Pound to Quinn, January 27, 1919.
32 June 16, 1919.
33 June 16, 1919.
34 May 3, 1919.
35 To Jacob Epstein, June 27, 1919.
36 January 27, 1919.
37 To Mme. Raymond Duchamp-Villon, August 26, 1919.
38 To Quinn, September 20, 1919.
39 No date, received October 28, 1919.
40 September 12, 1919.
41 To Quinn, August 9, 1919.
42 Ibid.
43 September 22, 1919.
44 To Quinn, July 27, 1919.
45 Ibid.
46 September 29, 1919.
47 To James G. Huneker, April 8, 1919.
48 Interview with Jeanne Robert Foster.
49 January 8, 1919.
50 To Quinn, January 26, 1919.
51 Quinn to T. S. Eliot, April 29, 1919.
52 To T. S. Eliot, June 30, 1919.
53 To T. S. Eliot, August 26, 1919.
54 To Quinn, July 6, 1919.
55 Ibid.
56 November 9, 1919.
57 October 10, 1919.
58 To Quinn, December 13, 1919.
59 Ibid.
60 To Lady Gregory, April 26, 1919.
61 To Quinn, January 12, 1919.
62 To Quinn, September 29, 1919.
63 To Quinn, March 19, 1919.
64 October 8, 1919.

1920

1 September 13, 1920.
2 June 30, 1920.

[3] To Walter Pach, January 16, 1920.
[4] April 15, 1920.
[5] July 17, 1920.
[6] To Walt Kuhn, September 21, 1920.
[7] January 15, 1920.
[8] February 14, 1920.
[9] To Ezra Pound, October 21, 1920.
[10] August 15, 1920.
[11] Quinn to J. B. Yeats, June 4, 1920.
[12] To Quinn, June 1, 1920.
[13] To Quinn, June 29, 1920.
[14] To Quinn, November 17, 1920.
[15] Wyndham Lewis to Quinn, June 14, 1920.
[16] To Jack B. Yeats, August 15, 1920.
[17] To Quinn, November 9, 1920.
[18] June 4, 1920.
[19] "Some Impressions of My Elders," I and II, *North American Review*, February and March 1920.
[20] To Quinn, March 24, 1920.
[21] December 25, 1920.
[22] To Quinn, March 12, 1920.
[23] Ibid.
[24] James Stephens to Quinn, May 12, 1920.
[25] Quinn to R. J. Kelly, December 18, 1917.
[26] To James G. Huneker, June 4, 1920.
[27] Donald Gallup, *T. S. Eliot: A Bibliography*, New York, Harcourt, Brace, 1947, p. 5.
[28] Ibid. p. 4.
[29] Ibid. p. 5.
[30] To Quinn, January 25, 1920.
[31] Ibid.
[32] To T. S. Eliot, March 6, 1920.
[33] March 6, 1920.
[34] Ibid.
[35] April 23, 1920.
[36] To Ezra Pound, May 1, 1920.
[37] To Ezra Pound, September 24, 1920.
[38] To Quinn, September 24, 1920.
[39] Richard Ellmann, *James Joyce*, p. 494.
[40] To Quinn, June 4, 1920.
[41] January 15, 1920.
[42] To Ezra Pound, September 24, 1920.
[43] James Joyce to Quinn, November 17, 1920.
[44] To Quinn, March 11, 1920.
[45] Ibid.
[46] Ibid.
[47] November 17, 1920.
[48] Ibid.
[49] To Quinn, November 24, 1920.

[50] Ezra Pound to Quinn, October 31, 1920.

[51] Ezra Pound to Quinn, November 8, 1920.

[52] Ezra Pound to James Joyce, *Letters*, p. 151.

[53] October 4, 1920.

[54] Ezra Pound to James Joyce, circa October 1920, *Letters*, p. 150 (wrongly placed in 1919).

[55] To James G. Huneker, January 5, 1920.

[56] To James G. Huneker, November 4, 1920.

[57] March 11, 1920.

[58] Ibid.

[59] To Ezra Pound, October 16, 1920.

[60] Ibid.

[61] Ibid.

[62] Ibid.

[63] Ibid.

[64] Quinn to Pound, October 21, 1920.

[65] Ibid.

[66] To Ezra Pound, October 16, 1920.

[67] Ezra Pound to James Joyce, circa October 30, 1920; see *Letters*, pp. 150–51.

[68] To James Joyce, April 13, 1921.

[69] Joyce to Ezra Pound, November 5, 1920. *Letters*, III, ed. Richard Ellmann, p. 28.

[70] [? November 1920.] *Letters*, III, 30.

[71] To Shane Leslie, June 21, 1922.

[72] Ibid.

[73] Ibid.

[74] Ibid.

[75] Ibid.

[76] January 25, 1920.

[77] To Ezra Pound, September 24, 1920.

[78] Ibid.

[79] February 5, 1920.

[80] To Ezra Pound, March 6, 1920.

[81] *Brief*, p. 23.

[82] Stanley Coben, *A. Mitchell Palmer: Politician*, New York, Columbia University Press, 1963, p. 134.

[83] Quinn to Father John J. Wynne, March 29, 1920.

[84] To the Leicester Galleries, March 6, 1920.

[85] April 11, 1920.

[86] January 27, 1920.

[87] To Quinn, February 10–21, 1920.

[88] To Quinn, April 4, 1920.

[89] June 26, 1920.

[90] August 14, 1920.

[91] To Ezra Pound, September 24, 1920.

[92] To Gwen John, November 20, 1920.

[93] February 5, 1920.

[94] March 2, 1920.

95 To Walt Kuhn, May 29, 1920.
96 April 19, 1920.
97 To Quinn, April 5, 1920.
98 To Walt Kuhn, July 3, 1920.
99 Walter Pach to Quinn, May 19, 1920.
100 Quinn to Mme. Raymond Duchamp-Villon, May 1, 1920.
101 December 2, 1920.
102 Quinn to Henri-Pierre Roché, September 24, 1920.
103 Henri-Pierre Roché to Quinn, September 13, 1920.
104 September 24, 1920.
105 Cable to Henri-Pierre Roché, November 5, 1920.
106 To Quinn, September 13, 1920.
107 To Quinn, November 22, 1922.
108 October 26, 1920.
109 November 5, 1920.
110 December 9, 1920.
111 Constantin Brancusi to Quinn, December 7, 1920.
112 September 29, 1920.
113 To Walt Kuhn, September 17, 1920.
114 Quinn to J. B. Yeats, December 1, 1920.
115 Ibid.
116 December 22, 1920.

1921

1 To James Joyce, April 13, 1921.
2 Ibid.
3 January 21, 1921.
4 To W. B. Yeats, June 5, 1921.
5 Quinn to Ezra Pound, January 21, 1921.
6 Ibid.
7 Ibid.
8 Ibid.
9 Ibid.
10 To James Joyce, April 13, 1921.
11 Ibid.
12 James Joyce to Quinn, November 17, 1920.
13 To Horace Liveright, May 11, 1922.
14 To James Joyce, June 5, 1921.
15 Ibid.
16 Ibid.
17 Ibid.
18 Ibid.
19 Ibid.
20 Ibid.
21 To Quinn, circa April 19, 1921.
22 June 5, 1921.
23 June 15, 1921.

[24] "*Ulysses*, Order and Myth," *The Dial*, LXXV, No. 5 (November 1923), p. 483.

[25] June 5, 1921.

[26] James Stephens to Quinn, February 15, 1921.

[27] May 1, 1921.

[28] May 25, 1921.

[29] To Ezra Pound, May 1, 1921.

[30] To Ezra Pound, May 7, 1921.

[31] To Ezra Pound, June 15, 1921.

[32] James Joyce to Quinn, July 12, 1921.

[33] To Ezra Pound, November 29, 1921.

[34] Ibid.

[35] Ezra Pound to Quinn, December 19, 1921.

[36] To Ezra Pound, December 12, 1921.

[37] Ibid.

[38] December 24, 1921.

[39] To W. B. Yeats, June 24, 1921.

[40] February 19, 1921.

[41] To Quinn, February 21, 1921.

[42] September 9, 1921.

[43] To Henri-Pierre Roché, May 1, 1921.

[44] To Martin Birnbaum, April 26, 1921.

[45] June 12, 1921.

[46] May 25, 1921.

[47] To Frank Harris, April 22, 1921.

[48] April 7, 1921.

[49] May 24, 1921.

[50] May 31, 1921.

[51] To Walter Pach, May 11, 1921.

[52] To Walter Pach, May 14, 1921.

[53] December 29, 1921.

[54] Quinn to Russell, June 19, 1921.

[55] Ibid.

[56] To Lady Gregory, May 11, 1922.

[57] Ibid.

[58] Ibid.

[59] Ibid.

[60] Ibid.

[61] Interview with Jeanne Robert Foster.

[62] May 11, 1922.

[63] Ibid.

[64] Ibid.

[65] Ibid.

[66] Interview with Jeanne Robert Foster.

[67] Ibid.

[68] To Gwen John, August 29, 1921.

[69] Gwen John to Quinn, September 9, 1921.

[70] August 29, 1921.

[71] May 11, 1922.

[72] Quinn to J. B. Yeats, September 9, 1921.

[73] July 12, 1914.

[74] To Quinn, May 4, 1921.

[75] James Stephens to Quinn, February 15, 1921.

[76] To George Russell, June 19, 1921.

[77] Ibid.

[78] To Quinn, May 15, 1916.

[79] To Quinn, June 22, 1921.

[80] June 19, 1921.

[81] To Quinn, June 22, 1921.

[82] To Quinn, July 8, 1921.

[83] To Quinn, July 6, 1921.

[84] To Quinn, October 22, 1921.

[85] To Quinn, December 7, 1921.

[86] Ibid.

[87] *Ireland's Abbey Theatre*, London, Sidgwick and Jackson, Ltd., 1951, p. 120.

[88] Lady Gregory to Quinn, January 29, 1922.

[89] Ibid.

[90] To Ezra Pound, November 29, 1921.

[91] To Ezra Pound, December 29, 1921.

[92] Ibid.

1922

[1] To George Russell, July 13, 1922.

[2] To Ezra Pound, April 28, 1922.

[3] Ibid.

[4] J. B. Yeats to Quinn, January 26, 1922.

[5] To Quinn, February 21, 1922.

[6] To Quinn, August 13, 1922.

[7] To W. B. Yeats, April 4, 1922.

[8] To W. B. Yeats, July 30, 1922.

[9] W. B. Yeats to Quinn, June 5, 1922.

[10] Ibid.

[11] Lady Gregory to Quinn, January 29, 1922.

[12] July 15, 1922.

[13] July 30, 1922.

[14] Hone, *W. B. Yeats*, p. 349.

[15] George Russell to Quinn, October 19, 1922.

[16] To Quinn, August 2, 1922.

[17] To Quinn, August 18, 1922.

[18] To George Russell, June 19, 1921.

[19] To George Russell, July 30, 1922.

[20] To Quinn, August 16, 1922.

[21] To Sylvia Beach, February 4, 1922.

[22] To Ezra Pound, April 28, 1922.

[23] April 4, 1922.

[24] Ezra Pound to Quinn, February 21, 1922.

[25] To James Joyce, May 11, 1922.

[26] *Letters,* p. 169.
[27] June 25, 1922.
[28] To T. S. Eliot, September 7, 1922.
[29] Ibid.
[30] T. S. Eliot, interview with the author, April 1964.
[31] To Quinn, September 21, 1922.
[32] T. S. Eliot to the author, July 23, 1963.
[33] September 21, 1922.
[34] Jeanne Robert Foster, interview with the author.
[35] July 30, 1922.
[36] To W. B. Yeats, July 30, 1922.
[37] Ibid.
[38] August 16, 1922.
[39] To Josephine Huneker, July 12, 1922.
[40] July 30, 1922.
[41] Ibid.
[42] To Quinn, March 27, 1922.
[43] To Quinn, August 6, 1922.
[44] Ibid.
[45] To Quinn, June 6, 1922.
[46] To Raoul Dufy, June 27, 1922.
[47] To Henri-Pierre Roché, January 27, 1922.
[48] To Paul Rosenberg, January 24, 1922.
[49] To Henri-Pierre Roché, February 19, 1922.
[50] Ibid.
[51] Ibid.
[52] March 10, 1922.
[53] To Quinn, May 14, 1922.
[54] June 28, 1922.
[55] To Henri-Pierre Roché, August 1, 1922.
[56] Ibid.
[57] To Constantin Brancusi, August 5, 1922.
[58] June 9, 1922.
[59] June 19, 1922.
[60] To Quinn, June 21, 1922.
[61] Henri-Pierre Roché to Quinn, July 11, 1922.
[62] To Quinn, July 11, 1922.
[63] Henri-Pierre Roché to Quinn, July 2, 1922.
[64] To Henri-Pierre Roché, August 3, 1922.
[65] June 28, 1922.
[66] To Henri-Pierre Roché, June 9, 1922.
[67] Interview with the author, September 1966.
[68] June 17, 1922.
[69] To Henri-Pierre Roché, February 19, 1922.
[70] To Quinn, May 25, 1922.
[71] Cable to Henri-Pierre Roché, June 23, 1922.
[72] Henri-Pierre Roché to Quinn, July 10, 1922.
[73] To Henri-Pierre Roché, August 3, 1922.
[74] To Quinn, September 9, 1922.

[75] To Ezra Pound, April 28, 1922.
[76] To Henri-Pierre Roché, May 20, 1922.
[77] To Percy Moore Turner, December 29, 1922.
[78] Ibid.
[79] Ibid.
[80] To Ezra Pound, July 12, 1922.
[81] To Douglas Hyde, July 13, 1922.
[82] To Quinn, August 6, 1922.
[83] To Quinn, December 22, 1922.

1923

[1] To Henri-Pierre Roché, January 8, 1923.
[2] Ibid.
[3] November 28, 1923.
[4] To Lady Gregory, November 15, 1923.
[5] Letter to the author, March 28, 1964.
[6] *It Was the Nightingale*, Philadelphia, J. B. Lippincott, 1933, p. 311.
[7] Ibid., p. 309. Ellipses in original.
[8] Ibid., p. 310.
[9] To Percy Moore Turner, February 5, 1923.
[10] To R. Langton Douglas, February 21, 1923.
[11] To Quinn, January 23, 1923.
[12] To Percy Moore Turner, February 15, 1923.
[13] To Quinn, February 23, 1923.
[14] To Percy Moore Turner, March 26, 1923.
[15] To Percy Moore Turner, April 27, 1923.
[16] To Percy Moore Turner, March 28, 1923.
[17] Ibid.
[18] To Percy Moore Turner, April 25, 1923.
[19] Ibid.
[20] To Percy Moore Turner, June 4, 1923.
[21] To Percy Moore Turner, May 31, 1923.
[22] Percy Moore Turner to Quinn, April 12, 1923.
[23] May 25, 1923.
[24] Interview with the author.
[25] To Percy Moore Turner, June 21, 1923.
[26] To Percy Moore Turner, June 25, 1923.
[27] To Quinn, June 13, 1923.
[28] To Percy Moore Turner, July 23, 1923.
[29] To Percy Moore Turner, January 4, 1923.
[30] March 24, 1923.
[31] January 8, 1923.
[32] Ibid.
[33] To Henri-Pierre Roché, March 17, 1923.
[34] Ibid.
[35] To Henri-Pierre Roché, January 8, 1923.
[36] To Quinn, March 12, 1923.
[37] To T. S. Eliot, March 27, 1923.

[38] *Letters from Æ*, ed. Alan Denson, London, Abelard-Schuman, 1961, p. 236.

[39] "Nineteen Hundred and Nineteen."

[40] George Russell to Quinn, April 5, 1923.

[41] To Quinn, February 22, 1923.

[42] To Quinn, April 5, 1923.

[43] Ibid.

[44] Lady Gregory to Quinn, October 5, 1923.

[45] Ibid.

[46] November 3, 1923.

[47] Ibid.

[48] Ibid.

[49] W. B. Yeats, *Autobiography*, pp. 373-4.

[50] To Quinn, June 12, 1923.

[51] To Arthur Symons, July 21, 1923.

[52] To George F. Parker, November 16, 1923.

[53] To Quinn, October 5, 1923.

[54] To Henri-Pierre Roché, July 13, 1923.

[55] Ibid.

[56] To Harriet Shaw Weaver, November 10, 1923.

[57] *It Was the Nightingale*, pp. 312-13.

[58] Jeanne Robert Foster, interview with the author.

[59] October 2, 1923.

[60] To Lady Gregory, November 15, 1923.

[61] Ibid.

[62] Ibid.

[63] Ibid.

[64] October 26, 1923.

[65] Henri-Pierre Roché to Quinn, November 11, 1923.

[66] To Georges Rouault, November 28, 1923.

[67] To Lady Gregory, November 15, 1923.

[68] Ibid.

[69] October 5, 1923.

[70] November 15, 1923.

[71] November 15, 1923.

[72] Unsent letter, Quinn to Nelson Doubleday, November 14, 1923.

[73] To Lady Gregory, November 15, 1923.

[74] E.g. in a letter to Richard Curle in "Nov. 1923": *Conrad to a Friend*, edited by Richard Curle, Doubleday, Doran & Co., Garden City, N.Y., 1923, p. 175.

[75] G. Jean-Aubry, *Joseph Conrad: Life and Letters, Garden City*, Doubleday, Page & Co., 1927, II, p. 324.

[76] *Letters from Joseph Conrad, 1895-1924*, edited by Edward Garnett, Indianapolis, Bobbs-Merrill, 1923, p. 295.

[77] New York, E. P. Dutton & Co., 1935, p. 262.

[78] To Jacob Epstein, December 5, 1923.

[79] To Walter Pach, December 3, 1923.

[80] To Walter Pach, December 4, 1923.

1924

[1] To Henri-Pierre Roché, June 25, 1924.
[2] To James Joyce, February 29, 1924.
[3] Ellmann, *James Joyce*, p. 570.
[4] January 21, 1924.
[5] To Henri-Pierre Roché, June 25, 1924.
[6] Ibid.
[7] To Ford Madox Ford, January 11, 1924.
[8] Quinn to Percy Moore Turner, December 6, 1923.
[9] To Percy Moore Turner, March 13, 1924.
[10] To A. Lawrence Lowell, May 12, 1924.
[11] To Bessie C. Lemley, June 2, 1924.
[12] To Henri-Pierre Roché, March 14, 1924.
[13] March 13, 1924.
[14] To Henri-Pierre Roché, February 28, 1924.
[15] To Quinn, March 12, 1924.
[16] To Edward Robinson, April 24, 1924.
[17] To Henri-Pierre Roché, June 25, 1924.
[18] Ibid.
[19] Undated; translated by the author.
[20] Undated letter, evidently early September 1924.
[21] Ibid.
[22] Richard Curle, *The Last Twelve Years of Joseph Conrad*, Garden City, New York, Doubleday, Doran & Company, 1928, p. 201.
[23] Ibid.

ENDINGS

[1] *Long Shadows*, Wilkes-Barre, Pa., Dimension Books, 1967, p. 187.
[2] Aline Saarinen interview with Ezra Pound, May 1957.
[3] *The Art News*, January 16, 1926, p. 2.
[4] June 16, 1926.
[5] *The New York Times*, June 17, 1926.
[6] *The New York Times*, June 18, 1926.
[7] Aline Saarinen interview with Walter Pach, February 1956.
[8] Circa September 1, 1924.
[9] Walter Pach to Thomas Curtin, October 15, 1924.
[10] "Art World Has Its Busiest Week," *The New York Sun*, January 9, 1926, p. 11.
[11] Henri-Pierre Roché, "Hommage à John Quinn, Collectionneur," *La Parisienne*, August–September 1954, p. 12.
[12] "Modern Art," *The Dial*, LXXX, No. 3 (March 1926), p. 260.
[13] "Europe Raids the John Quinn Collection," *The Independent*, CXVI, No. 395 (February 27, 1962), p. 240.
[14] Foreword to *The John Quinn Collection of Paintings, Water Colors, Drawings & Sculpture*, Huntington, N.Y., Pidgeon Hill Press, 1926.
[15] "The John Quinn Collection," *The Arts*, January 1926, p. 6.
[16] Ibid. pp. 6, 8.
[17] Ibid. p. 13.

A Selected Bibliography

Anderson, Margaret. *My Thirty Years' War*. New York, 1930.
The Art Center. *Memorial Exhibition of Representative Works Selected from the John Quinn Collection*. New York, 1926.
Association of American Painters and Sculptors. *Catalogue of International Exhibition of Modern Art . . . at the Armory*. New York, 1913.
Baines, Jocelyn. *Joseph Conrad: A Critical Biography*. New York, 1960.
Barr, Alfred H., Jr. *Matisse: His Art and His Public*. New York, 1951.
———. *Picasso: Fifty Years of His Art*. New York, 1946.
———. *What Is Modern Painting?* New York, 1943.
Beach, Sylvia. *Shakespeare and Company*. New York, 1959.
Behrman, S[amuel] N[athaniel]. *Duveen*. New York, 1952.
Bodkin, Thomas. *Hugh Lane and His Pictures*. Dublin, 1956.
Brooks, Van Wyck. *Days of the Phoenix: The Nineteen-Twenties I Remember*. New York, 1957.
———. *John Sloan: A Painter's Life*. New York, 1955.
———. *Scenes and Portraits: Memories of Childhood and Youth*. New York, 1954.
Brown, Milton W[olf]. *American Painting from the Armory Show to the Depression*. Princeton, 1955.
———. *The Story of the Armory Show*. New York, 1963.
Bryer, Jackson R. "Joyce, *Ulysses*, and the *Little Review*," *The South Atlantic Quarterly*, LXVI, No. 2 (Spring 1967), 148–164.
Bulfin, William. *Rambles in Eirinn*. Dublin, 1907.
Cheney, Sheldon. "An Adventurer Among Art Collectors," *The New York Times Magazine*, January 3, 1926, 10, 23.
Coben, Stanley. *A. Mitchell Palmer: Politician*. New York, 1963.
Colum, Mary. *Life and the Dream*. Garden City, N.Y., 1947.
Conrad, Jessie. *Joseph Conrad and His Circle*. New York, 1935.
Conrad, Joseph. *Conrad to a Friend: 150 Selected Letters from Joseph Conrad to Richard Curle*. Ed. Richard Curle. Garden City, N.Y., 1928.
———. "Henry James: An Appreciation," *North American Review*, CLXXX (1905), 102–8.
———. *Last Essays*. Ed. Richard Curle. London, 1926.
———. *Letters from Joseph Conrad, 1895–1924*. Ed. Edward Garnett. Indianapolis, 1928.
———. *Notes on Life and Letters*. Garden City, N.Y., 1922.

———. *A Personal Record*. New York, 1912.

Coxhead, Elizabeth. *Lady Gregory: A Literary Portrait*. London, 1961.

Craven, Thomas. *Modern Art*. New York, 1934.

Curle, Richard. *Joseph Conrad: A Study*. Garden City, N.Y., 1914.

———. *The Last Twelve Years of Joseph Conrad*. Garden City, N.Y., 1928.

Curtis, Edmund. *A History of Ireland*. London, 1957.

Elgar, Frank, and Robert Maillard. *Picasso*. Trans. Francis Scarfe. New York, 1960.

Eliot, T[homas] S[tearns]. *The Complete Poems and Plays*. New York, 1958.

———. *Selected Essays, 1917–1932*.

———. "*Ulysses*, Order, and Myth," *Dial*, LXXV (1923), 483.

Ellmann, Richard. *James Joyce*. New York, 1959.

Epstein, Jacob. *Epstein: An Autobiography*. London, 1963.

Faulkner, Peter. *William Morris and W. B. Yeats*. Dublin, 1962.

Follett, Wilson. *Joseph Conrad: A Short Study of His Intellectual and Emotional Attitude Toward His Work and of the Chief Characteristics of His Novels*. Garden City, N.Y., 1915.

Ford, Ford Madox. *It Was the Nightingale*. Philadelphia, 1933.

———. *Joseph Conrad: A Personal Remembrance*. Boston, 1924.

———. *Parade's End*. New York, 1962.

[Foster, Jeanne Robert]. "Art Revolutionists on Exhibition in America," *Review of Reviews*, XLII (1913), 441–8.

Foster, Jeanne Robert. *Neighbors of Yesterday*. Boston, 1916.

———. "New Sculptures by Constantin Brancusi," *Vanity Fair*, XVIII (May 1922), 68, 124.

———. *Rock-Flower*. New York, 1923.

———. *Wild Apples*. Boston, 1916.

Gallup, Donald Clifford. *A Bibliography of Ezra Pound*. London, 1963.

———. *T. S. Eliot: A Bibliography*. New York, 1953.

Gaunt, William. *The Pre-Raphaelite Dream*. New York, 1966.

Giedion, Siegfried. *Space, Time and Architecture*. Cambridge, Mass., 1941.

Gilot, Françoise, and Carlton Lake. *Life with Picasso*. New York, 1964.

Gimpel, Rene. *Diary of an Art Dealer*. Trans. John Rosenberg. New York, 1966.

Gogarty, Oliver St. John. *William Butler Yeats: A Memoir*. Dublin, 1963.

Greene, David. H., and Edward M. Stephens. *J. M. Synge, 1871–1909*. New York, 1959.

Gregg, Frederick James. "Europe Raids the John Quinn Collection," *Independent*, CXVI (1926), 240–41.

Gregory, Isabella Augusta. *Irish Folk-History Plays*, second series. New York, 1912.

———. *Lady Gregory's Journals, 1916–1930*. Ed. Lennox Robinson. New York, 1947.

———. *Our Irish Theatre: A Chapter of Autobiography*. New York, 1913.

Guggenheim, Peggy. *Confessions of an Art Addict*. New York, 1960.

Hassall, Christopher. *Edward Marsh: Patron of the Arts*. London, 1959.

Hemingway, Ernest. *A Moveable Feast*. London, 1964.

Hendy, Philip. *The National Gallery London*. London, 1960.

Hone, Joseph. *The Life of George Moore.* New York, 1936.
———. *W. B. Yeats, 1865–1939.* London, 1962.
Huneker, James Gibbons. *Ivory Apes and Peacocks.* New York, 1915.
———. *Letters of James Gibbons Huneker.* Ed. Josephine Huneker. London, [1922].
———. *Painted Veils.* New York, 1964.
———. *Steeplejack.* New York, 1920.
Hyde, Douglas. Diary, 1904–1905.
Hyde, H. Montgomery. *Famous Trials 9: Roger Casement.* London, 1964.
Inglis, Brian. *The Story of Ireland.* London, [1956].
James, Henry. *The Letters of Henry James.* Ed. Percy Lubbock. 2 vols. New York, 1920.
Jean-Aubry, Gérard. *Joseph Conrad: Life and Letters.* 2 vols. Garden City, N.Y., 1927.
John, Augustus. *Chiaroscuro: Fragments of Autobiography.* New York, 1952.
The John Quinn Collection of Letters. Transcripts, ed. Jeanne Robert Foster. 13 vols.
John Quinn 1870–1925 [i.e. 1924] *Collection of Paintings, Water Colors, Drawings & Sculpture.* Huntington, N.Y., 1926.
Joyce, James. *Dubliners.* New York, 1916.
———. *Letters.* 3 vols. Vol. I ed. (1957) by Stuart Gilbert; reissued (1966) with corrections by Richard Ellmann; Vols. II and III ed. by Richard Ellmann. New York, 1966.
———. *Finnegans Wake.* New York, 1939.
———. *A Portrait of the Artist as a Young Man.* New York, 1928.
———. *Ulysses.* New York, 1934.
Kain, Richard M. *Dublin in the Age of William Butler Yeats and James Joyce.* Norman, Okla., 1962.
Kazin, Alfred. *On Native Grounds: An Interpretation of Modern American Prose Literature.* New York, 1942.
Keats, John. *The Letters of John Keats, 1814–1821.* Ed. Hyder Edward Rollins. 2 vols. Cambridge, Mass., 1958.
Leslie, Shane. *The Irish Issue in Its American Aspect: A Contribution to the Settlement of Anglo-American Relations During and After the Great War.* London, 1919.
———. *Long Shadows.* Wilkes-Barre, Pa., 1967.
The Library of John Quinn. 5 vols. Anderson Galleries Catalogues nos. 1768, 1783, 1794, 1806, 1820. New York, 1923–4.
The Little Review, III–XI (1916–24).
The Little Review Anthology. Ed. Margaret Anderson. New York, 1953.
Lewis, Wyndham. *Letters.* Ed. W. K. Rose, London, 1963.
McBride, Henry. "Art World Has Its Busiest Week," *New York Sun,* January 9, 1926, p. 11.
———. "Modern Art," *Dial,* LXXX (1926), 260–62.
MacBride, Maud Gonne. *A Servant of the Queen.* London, 1938.
Masters of Modern Art. Ed. Alfred H. Barr, Jr. New York, 1954.
Meredith, George. *Letters of George Meredith.* Ed. William Maxse Meredith. 2 vols. London, 1912.
Moore, George. *Hail and Farewell.* 3 vols. London, 1947.

1913 Armory Show 50th Anniversary Exhibition 1963. New York, 1963.

Norman, Charles. *Ezra Pound.* New York, 1960.

O'Connor, Ulick. *Oliver St. John Gogarty: A Poet and His Times.* London, 1964.

O'Faolain, Sean. *The Irish: A Character Study.* New York, 1949.

Pach, Walter. *Queer Thing, Painting: Forty Years in the World of Art.* New York, 1938.

Picasso: 75th Anniversary Exhibition. Ed. Alfred H. Barr, Jr. New York, 1957.

Pound, Ezra. *The Cantos of Ezra Pound.* London, 1954.

——. *Gaudier-Brzeska: A Memoir.* London, 1916.

——. *The Letters of Ezra Pound, 1907–1941.* Ed. D. D. Paige. New York, 1950.

——. *Literary Essays.* Ed. T. S. Eliot. London, 1954.

——. *Lustra of Ezra Pound, with Earlier Poems.* New York, 1917.

——. *Pavannes and Divisions.* New York, 1918.

Pyle, Hilary. *James Stephens: His Work and an Account of His Life.* London, 1965.

Quinn, John. Diaries, 1904, 1911.

——. "Jacob Epstein, Sculptor." *Vanity Fair,* IX (1917), 76, 114.

——. "James Joyce, A New Irish Novelist," *Vanity Fair,* VIII (1917), 49, 128.

——. *Max W. Stoehr, Suing in His Own Behalf as a Stockholder in Stoehr & Sons, Inc., and in Behalf of All Others Similarly Situated. . . .* Brief. New York, 1920.

——. *Memorandum Against the Imposition of Any Duty on Original Works of Art.* Brief. New York, 1921.

——. *Memorandum Against Taxing Sales of Works of Art.* Brief. New York, 1921.

——. "Roger Casement, Martyr: Some Notes for a Chapter of History by a Friend Whose Guest He Was When the War Broke Out," *The New York Times,* August 13, 1916, V, 1–4.

——. *Senate of the United States, Committee on Finance, In the Matter of the Protest of Munition Makers Against the 8 Per Cent Excess Profit Tax. . . .* Brief. New York, 1917.

——. "Walt Kuhn's Art," *New York Sun.* April 4, 1920.

Ray, Man. *Self Portrait.* Boston, 1963.

Read, Herbert. *Art Now.* London, 1948.

Reports of the American Committee for Relief in Ireland and the Irish White Cross. New York, [1922].

Robinson, Lennox. *Ireland's Abbey Theatre: A History, 1899–1951.* London, 1951.

Roché, Henri-Pierre. "Adieu, Brave Petite Collection," *L'Oeil,* No. 51 (March 1959), 34–41.

——. *Jules et Jim.* Paris, 1953.

Rosenbach, A[braham] S[imon] W[olf]. *Books and Bidders: The Adventures of a Bibliophile.* Boston, 1927.

Rosenberg, James N. *Painter's Self Portrait.* New York, 1958.

Rothenstein, John. *The Tate Gallery.* London, 1963.

A.E. [George William Russell]. *Collected Poems.* London, 1920.

Russell, George William, Horace Plunkett, and John Quinn. *The Irish Home-Rule Convention.* New York, 1917.

[Russell, George William]. *Letters from Æ.* Ed. Alan Denson. London, 1961.

Saarinen, Aline B. *The Proud Possessors: The Lives, Times, and Tastes of Some Adventurous American Art Collectors.* New York, 1958.

Schwab, Arnold T. *James Gibbons Huneker: Critic of the Seven Arts.* Stanford, 1963.

Shattuck, Roger. *The Banquet Years: The Arts in France, 1885–1918.* Garden City, N.Y., 1961.

Shearman, Hugh. *Anglo-Irish Relations.* London, 1948.

Sheehan, Daniel D. *Ireland Since Parnell.* London, 1921.

Slocum, John J., and Herbert Cahoon. *A Bibliography of James Joyce.* New Haven, 1953.

Starkie, Walter. *Scholars and Gypsies: An Autobiography.* London, 1963.

Stein, Gertrude. *The Autobiography of Alice B. Toklas.* New York, 1933.

——. *Picasso.* New York, 1939.

Stein, Leo. *Appreciation: Painting, Poetry, and Prose.* New York, 1947.

——. *Journey Into the Self.* Ed. Edmund Fuller. New York, 1950.

Stephens, James. *The Charwoman's Daughter.* London, 1912.

——. *Collected Poems.* New York, 1926.

——. *Deirdre.* London, 1923.

——. *In the Land of Youth.* London, 1924.

——. *The Insurrection in Dublin.* New York, 1916.

Synge, John Millington. *The Aran Islands.* Boston, 1911.

——. *Plays.* London, [1932].

Tharp, Louise Hall. *Mrs. Jack: A Biography of Isabella Stewart Gardner.* Boston, 1965.

Ussher, Arland. *The Face and Mind of Ireland.* New York, 1950.

Van Dieren, Bernard. *Epstein.* London, 1920.

Vollard, Ambroise. *Recollections of a Picture Dealer.* Boston, 1936.

Walsh, James J. "John Quinn: Lawyer, Book-Lover, Art Amateur," *Catholic World,* November 1924, 176–84.

Walsh, Townsend. *The Career of Dion Boucicault.* New York, 1915.

Watson, Forbes. "The John Quinn Collection," *The Arts,* IX (1926), 3–22, 77–92.

Wilenski, Reginald Howard. *Modern French Painters.* New York, [1940].

Wolf, Edwin 2nd with John Fleming. *Rosenbach: A Biography.* Cleveland, 1960.

Woodward, Daniel H. "Notes on the Publishing History and Text of *The Waste Land*," *Papers of the Bibliographical Society of America,* LVIII (1964), 252–69.

Yeats, John Butler. *Essays, Irish and American.* Dublin, 1918.

——. *J. B. Yeats: Letters to His Son W. B. Yeats and Others, 1869–1922.* Ed. Joseph Hone. London, 1944.

Yeats, William Butler. *The Autobiography of William Butler Yeats.* Garden City, N.Y., 1958.

——. *Collected Plays.* New York, 1952.

——. *The Collected Poems of W. B. Yeats.* New York, 1951.

——. *The Letters of W. B. Yeats.* Ed. Allan Wade. New York, 1955.

——. *A Vision.* New York, 1938.

Index